AF831243

SECOND EDITION

# MANAGEMENT CONTROL SYSTEMS

SECOND EDITION

# MANAGEMENT CONTROL SYSTEMS

FRANK G. H. HARTMANN, KALLE KRAUS AND GÖRAN NILSSON,
ROBERT N. ANTHONY, VIJAY GOVINDARAJAN

McGraw Hill

London Boston Burr Ridge, IL Dubuque, IA Madison, WI New York San Francisco
St. Louis Bangkok Bogotá Caracas Kuala Lumpur Lisbon Madrid Mexico City Milan
Montreal New Delhi Santiago Seoul Singapore Sydney Taipei Toronto

*Management Control Systems,* Second European Edition
Frank G.H. Hartmann, Kalle Kraus and Göran Nilsson, Robert N. Anthony, Vijay Govindarajan
ISBN-13 9781526848314
ISBN-10 0077133269

Published by McGraw-Hill Education
338 Euston Road
London,
NW1 3BH
Telephone: +44 (0) 203 429 3400
Website: www.mheducation.co.uk

**British Library Cataloguing in Publication Data**
A catalogue record for this book is available from the British Library

**Library of Congress Cataloguing in Publication Data**
The Library of Congress data for this book has been applied for from the Library of Congress

Portfolio Manager: Sabrina Farrugia
Content Developer: Maggie du Randt
Content Product Manager: Ali Davis

Text Design by Kamae Design
Cover design by Adam Renvoize



ISBN-13 9781526848314
ISBN-10 1526848317
eISBN-10 1526848325


Printed in Great Britain by Bell and Bain Ltd, Glasgow

# Brief Table of Contents

# Detailed Table of Contents

# Case Grid

| Chapter | Case number | Case title and authors | Key concepts covered |
|---|---|---|---|
| 1 | 1.1 | Maybach. *Frank Hartmann, Radbound University* | strategy, management control system design |
| 1 | 1.2 | Abrams Company. *J. G. San Miguel* | responsibility centres, financial performance measurement |
| 1 | 1.3 | Enron. *Frank Hartmann, Radboud University* | management control system design, scandals |
| 1 | 1.4 | Wal-Mart Stores, Inc. *Vijay Govindarajan and Julie B. Lang, Tuck School of Business at Dartmouth* | strategy, cost reduction, management control system design |
| 1 | 1.5 | Southwest Airlines Corporation. *Vijay Govindarajan, Julie B. Lang and Suraj Prabhu, Tuck School of Business at Dartmouth College* | strategy, HR, management control system design |
| 2 | 2.1 | Gyros. *Göran Nilsson, Uppsala University* | corporate governance, stakeholders, management attention |
| 2 | 2.2 | Northern Light: Growing Pains. *Göran Nilsson Uppsala University* | contingencies; volatility and uncertainty, adjusting the MC |
| 2 | 2.3 | Scania: A case of differentiation and low cost. *Göran Nilsson, Uppsala University* | strategy, differentiation, low-cost |
| 2 | 2.4 | Biotool. *Torkel Strömsten, Stockholm School of Economics* | corporate governance, performance measurement, short-termism |
| 2 | 2.5 | Tesla: Climate change and the future of the electric vehicle. *Emma Sjöström, Misum, Stockholm School of Economics* | CSR, greenwashing, implementation |
| 3 | 3.1 | A matter of ethics?, *Frank Hartmann, Radboud University* | ethics, types of ethical reasoning |
| 3 | 3.2 | Do not fool yourself!, *Frank Hartmann, Radboud University* | people's cognitive limitations and the potential of data to mislead us |
| 3 | 3.3 | Decision-support systems and ethics. *Ted Welten, Erasmus University* | when our quantitative analyses suggest decisions that are against ethical standards |
| 3 | 3.4 | Cultural issues: Netflix Culture. *Ted Welten, Erasmus University* | international differences in culture relevant to control |
| 3 | 3.5 | 'In Control' at FBS Executive Education. *Frank Hartmann, Radboud University* | turn-around management at Executive Education (real life case) |
| 4 | 4.1 | BookWorm. *Ebba Sjögren, Stockholm School of Economics* | responsibility centres, discretionary expense centres, profit centres |
| 4 | 4.2 | MoreSki. *Malin Lund, Stockholm School of Economics* | responsibility centres, discretionary expense centres, engineered expense centres, revenue centres, decentralization |

| Chapter | Case number | Case title and authors | Key concepts covered |
|---|---|---|---|
| 4 | 4.3 | BreathEZ. *Ebba Sjögren, Stockholm School of Economics* | responsibility centres, discretionary expense centres, profit centres |
| 4 | 4.4 | Responsibility centres. *Johan Åkesson and Mikael Cäker, Gothenburg University* | responsibility centres, profit centres, investment centres, expense centres, non-financial measurement |
| 4 | 4.5 | Grand Jean Company. *Joseph G. San Miguel* | responsibility centres, revenue centres, expense centres |
| 5 | 5.1 | SLA contracting. *Ted Welten, Erasmus University* | service level agreement: how to negotiate between two partners, role of control |
| 5 | 5.2 | SLA control and reinforcement. *Ted Welten, Erasmus University* | service level agreement: how to control a running contract, issues that may arise |
| 5 | 5.3 | Transfer pricing in multi-unit firm, *Frank Hartmann, Radboud University* | transfer pricing and suboptimization |
| 5 | 5.4 | North Country Auto, Inc. *Mark C. Rooney* | transfer pricing |
| 5 | 5.5 | Transfer pricing in international firm: Interaction of control and tax. *Ted Welten, Erasmus University* | interaction of control and tax |
| 6 | 6.1 | Miracles on Ice. *Göran Nilsson, Uppsala University* | differentiation and integration |
| 6 | 6.2 | The Washer. *Göran Nilsson, Uppsala University* | cross-functional integration, the silo problem |
| 6 | 6.3 | The Motorway-PPE. *Salman Ahmad, Aston Business School, Ciaran Connolly, Queen's University Belfast and Istemi Demirag, Tallinn University of Technology* | project control |
| 6 | 6.4 | The cross-functional management project. *Göran Nilsson, Uppsala University* | cross-functional integration, product development, speed |
| 6 | 6.5 | New product development at Big Fish. *Angela Liew and Julie Harrison, University of Auckland* | product development, cross-functional integration |
| 7 | 7.1 | Ramirent. *Kalle Kraus, Stockholm School of Economics* | inter-organisational management control system design |
| 7 | 7.2 | Working Capital Management. *Kalle Kraus, Stockholm School of Economics* | inter-organizational management control systems, working capital management |
| 7 | 7.3 | Outsourcing Unilever. *Frank Hartmann, Radboud University* | inter-organizational management control systems, outsourcing |
| 7 | 7.4 | The Supply Chain of the Clothing Industry. *Nandita Farhad and Andrea Fried, Linköping University* | inter-organizational management control systems, strategy, supply chain management, industry analysis |
| 7 | 7.5 | J.L Apparel Limited. *Nandita Farhad and Andrea Fried, Linköping University* | inter-organizational management control systems, outsourcing, supply chain management, supplier evaluation, rank-based rewards |

| Chapter | Case number | Case title and authors | Key concepts covered |
|---|---|---|---|
| 8 | 8.1 | Tight budgetary control. *Frank Hartmann, Radboud University* | budgetary control, tight and loos budgetary control |
| 8 | 8.2 | Rolling forecasts or budgets? New wine in old wineskins? *Paul Thambar, Monash University* | budgeting, rolling forecasts |
| 8 | 8.3 | Budgeting at FHP Motors. *Göran Nilsson, Uppsala University* | budgeting, micro-management |
| 8 | 8.4 | Beyond Budgeting/Rolling Forecasts. *Knut Fahlén, Ekan Management* | beyond budgeting, rolling forecasts |
| 8 | 8.5 | Svenska Handelsbanken: Sustaining growth in a decentralized organization. *Hamish Scott, Ashridge and North Network Ltd* | decentralisation, non-budgetary control |
| 9 | 9.1 | MedalRain. *Ebba Sjögren, Stockholm School of Economics* | investment centres, return on investment (ROI), economic value added (EVA) |
| 9 | 9.2 | TurnAround. *Malin Lund, Stockholm School of Economics* | investment centres, return on investment (ROI), residual income (RI), economic value added (EVA) |
| 9 | 9.3 | Setting an appropriate target: continuous improvement or benchmarking? *Kalle Kraus, Stockholm School of Economics* | target setting, benchmarking, continuous improvement |
| 9 | 9.4 | Performance measurement in a cooperative using a BSC. *Paul Thambar, Sarah Adams, Matthew Hall, Yolande McNicoll, Yuval Millo and Ms Wen Shi He* | balanced scorecard, non-for-profit, cooperatives |
| 9 | 9.5 | Frescent: sustainability and the balanced scorecard. *Emilia Cederberg, Stockholm School of Economics.* | balanced scorecard, sustainability, reward systems |
| 10 | 10.1 | The Triathlon Guy and the Golf Girl. *Göran Nilsson, Uppsala University* | extrinsic and intrinsic motivation, motivation crowding |
| 10 | 10.2 | Rome-work. *George Kominis and Alvise Favotto, Adam Smith Business School, University of Glasgow* | budgeting, bonus systems, motivation |
| 10 | 10.3 | Eaglet plc: the phone call. *George Kominis and Alvise Favotto, Adam Smith Business School, University of Glasgow* | renumeration, balanced scorecard, motivation |
| 10 | 10.4 | What is CEO talent worth? *David F. Larcker, Usman Liaqat and Brian Tayan* | Incentives, dysfunctional effects |
| 10 | 10.5 | The pitfalls of achieving cost-efficiency in the creative organization. *Jan Pfister, University of Turku* | intrinsic motivation, creativity, company culture |

| Chapter | Case number | Case title and authors | Key concepts covered |
|---|---|---|---|
| 11 | 11.1 | Future gains and future pains. *Ted Welten, Erasmus University* | behavioral economics, asymmetric utility |
| 11 | 11.2 | Profit warning. *Ted Welten, Erasmus University* | real profit warning, with causes and consequences |
| 11 | 11.3 | Risks or challenges? Tiffany's and Quest Diagnostics. *Ted Welten, Erasmus University* | differences in risk appetite between line managers and controllers |
| 11 | 11.4 | Unilever. Professor *Frank Hartmann,* Radboud University | replacement of CEO after disappointing results |
| 11 | 11.5 | Risks or challenges? Toshiba. *Ted Welten, Erasmus University* | differences between management control and risk management, including the roles of CEO and CFO |
| 12 | 12.1 | Controller involvement. *Frank Hartmann,* Radboud University | fiduciary role of controllers, and how it can be put at risk. |
| 12 | 12.2 | Crisis management: strategic or tactical responses? *Frank Hartmann, Radboud University* | companies responses to the COVID crises and the role of risk management |
| 12 | 12.3 | Ethical dilemmas in a controller job. *Frank Hartmann, Radboud University* | ethical dilemmas, earnings management and controller responsibilities. |
| 12 | 12.4 | Nucor Corporation (A). *Vijay Govindarajan, Tuck School of Business at Dartmouth* | responsibility centres, budgeting, expense centres, profit centres |
| 12 | 12.5 | Aluminum Container Corporation. *Vijay Govindarajan, Tuck School of Business at Dartmouth* | investment centres, strategy, residual income, return on investment, non-current asset valuation problems, incentive systems |
| Case end of the book | A1 | Quality Metal service Center. *Vijay Govindarajan, Tuck School of Business at Dartmouth* | investment centres, return on investment (ROI), residual income (RI) |
| Case end of the book | A2 | Pirelli. *Paolo Perego, Free University of Bolzano-Bozen* | Information overload, consistency, judgment |
| Case end of the book | A3 | Johansen's: The New Scorecard system. *Luann Lynch, Jennifer Forman and Graham Gillham, Darden case nr. UV-7131* | Balanced scorecard, leading and lagging indicators, performance evaluation |
| Appendix | Appendix | Case: Variance Analysis Problems. *John Dearden.* | Variance analysis |

# Preface

All types of organization are essentially groups of people interacting with one another. These people typically work at various levels and functions within the organization, perform various tasks and apply their various skills. A central question for all organizations is how to align managers' and employees' behaviour with the organization's mission, goals and strategies. Here *management control systems,* the focus of this book, play a key role. We define a management control system as comprising a combination of control practices designed and implemented by top managers to increase the probability that lower-level managers and employees will behave in ways consistent with the organization's mission, goals and strategies. These control practices can take many forms, such as budgets, mission statements, transfer pricing arrangements, codes of conduct, performance measures and reward systems. In the book we systematize the various control practices into three types: *input controls, throughput controls* and *output controls.* This follows an intuitive logic that lower-level managers and employees provide important cognitive abilities, skills and personal values to the organization (which top management can try to influence via input controls), which is transformed via the execution of effort, i.e., the actual work and organization of lower-level managers and employees (which top management can try to influence via throughput controls) into some sort of performance, or 'results' (which top management can try to influence via output controls). The actual combination of input, throughput and output controls will differ between organizations, depending on the differences in their missions, goals and strategies, which are influenced by, for instance, the markets they serve and the nature of their value creation processes.

Our definition of management control systems expresses that we focus our attention on systematic processes in organizations that are deliberately designed to facilitate cooperation and goal achievement. Thus we are primarily interested in systematic and continuous, rather than ad hoc and incidental, control efforts. The distinction between input, throughput and output controls has been proven to 'stand the test of time'. In the new era we live in, with digitalization and climate change, the need for, and use of, information changes quickly, but the distinction between input, throughput and output controls remains relevant. The three types of control practices also highlight the important message of this book, that management control systems are about so much more than performance measurement and incentives. We intend to send a powerful message about the need to use a broad conception of what a management control system is. We provide a wider presentation of the organizational systems, structures and processes that enable managers and employees to take decisions, perform actions and influence the behaviour of other organizational members. It is this holistic and systematic view on creating organizational performance that distinguishes this book from others. It also helps us highlight that management control systems have an important 'enabling' role; top managers need to design control practices that help maintain or enhance the skill set, job motivation and organizational commitment that lower-level managers and employees aim to contribute to the organization. They need to perceive control practices as something that supports them, that they can use to identify problems, prioritize issues and develop ideas for improvements. This supportive and empowering side of management control systems is very important to take into account when deciding on a management control system.

Frank G.H. Hartmann, Kalle Kraus, Göran Nilsson

# About the Authors

**Frank G.H. Hartmann** is a Professor of Accounting at the Nijmegen School of Management, Radboud University in the Netherlands. He has a wide experience in researching issues in Management Control and controllership. His teaching spans undergraduate, MBA, executive and professional controller programmes as well as PhD programmes across the globe. Frank holds several editorial board positions, is co-author of a Dutch series on accounting and control, and is widely published in journals such as *Accounting, Organizations and Society, Management Accounting Research and Behavioral Research in Accounting.*

**Kalle Kraus** is a Professor of Accounting at the Stockholm School of Economics, Sweden. He has broad experience in teaching Management Control to students and management teams in Bachelor, Master, MBA and executive programmes. He has been awarded Best Teacher awards from Masters as well as MBA students. Kalle is involved in a number of research projects, such as inter-organizational management control and control in non-for profit organizations. He holds several editorial board positions and is widely published in journals such as *Accounting, Organizations and Society, European Accounting Review* and *Management Accounting Research.*

**Göran Nilsson** is a Senior Lecturer of Management Control at Uppsala University, Sweden. After having worked as a controller in two Electrolux companies for several years, he wrote his doctoral thesis about Lean Management at the Stockhom School of Economics. His main interest is management control under dynamic and uncertain circumstances and he has published a book about the agile company with Lennart Francke, former CFO of Handelsbanken. He is also leading a knowledge sharing group of senior controllers and participates actively in the public debate through debate articles and popular scientific articles, as well as through lectures and seminars for practitioners.

**Robert N. Anthony** was the Ross Graham Walker Professor Emeritus of Management Control at Harvard Business School. Robert has been a director of Carborundum Company and Warnaco, Inc., both Fortune 500 companies. He has consulted for many companies and government agencies. Among Robert's awards are the Distinguished Accounting Educator of the Year Award from AAA, Comptroller General's Award of the U.S. General Accounting Office and Distinguished Service Award of the Harvard Business School Association. Robert is widely seen as the founding father of the discipline of management control as a fundamental topic in business education.

**Vijay Govindarajan** is the Earl C. Daum 1924 Professor of International Business at the Amos Tuck School of Business Administration at Dartmouth College. Professional credits include Outstanding Teacher of the Year, voted by MBA students during several academic years, and Outstanding Business School Faculty, named by Business Week. Vijay is widely published in journals such as *Harvard Business Review, Academy of Management Review* and *Strategic Management Journal* and books as *Strategic Cost Accounting.*

# Acknowledgements

Our thanks go to the following reviewers for their comments at various stages in the text's development:

The selection of cases is always vital to a successful management control systems course. In this context, our sincere appreciation goes to the authors and supervisors who are responsible for case development. Each has been recognized in the citations to the cases. We are particularly indebted to the companies whose cooperation made the cases possible. Requests to reproduce cases should be directed to the copyright holder.

Associate Professor Torkel Strömsten, *Stockholm School of Economics*
*Visiting Professor KTH Royal Institute of Technology*
Dr. Emma Sjöström, *Research Fellow, Stockholm School of Economics*
Assistant Professor Ted Welten, *Senior lecturer, Erasmus University Rotterdam*
Associate Professor Paolo Perego, *Free University of Bolzano-Bozen*
Johan Åkesson, *Senior Lecturer, School of Business, Economics and Law at the University of Gothenburg*
Dr. Salman Ahmad, *Lecturer in Accounting, Aston University, Birmingham.*
Dr. Ciaran Connolly, *Professor of Accounting, Queen's University Belfast*
Professor Istemi Demirag, *Professor of Accounting, Tallinn University of Technology*
Dr. Angela Liew, *Senior Lecturer, University of Auckland*
Dr. Julie Harrison, *Associate Professor, University of Auckland*
Associate Professor Andrea Fried, *Linköping University*
Dr. Paul Thambar, *Senior Lecturer, Monash Business School, Monash University*
Dr. Knut Fahlén, *Management Consultant, Ekan Management, Sweden*
Dr. Emilia Cederberg, *Assistant Professor Stockholm School of Economics*
Dr. Alvise Favotto, *Lecturer in Accounting, University of Glasgow*
Dr. Georgios Kominis, *Lecturer in Accounting, University of Glasgow*
Dr. Jan Pfister, *Senior Lecturer, University of Turku*
Richard Rensen, *External Lecturer Nyenrode Business Universiteit.*
Associate Professor Mikael Cäker, *Senior Lecturer, University of Gothenburg*
Dr. Li-cheng Chang, *Senior lecturer, University of Kent*
Dr. Carl-Johan Petri, *Senior Lecturer, Linköping University*
Lorraine Morris, Senior Lecturer, *University of Wolverhampton*

In writing this text, we hope that you will share our enthusiasm both for the rich subject of management control and for the learning approach that we have taken. As always, we value your recommendations and thoughts about the book. Your comments regarding coverage and content will be most welcome, as will your calling our attention to any specific errors. Frank Hartmann, Professor of Accounting at the Nijmegen School of Management, Radboud University, Postbus 9108, 6500 HK Nijmegen or frank.hartmann@ru.nl.

Every effort has been made to trace and acknowledge ownership of copyright and to clear permission for material reproduced in this book. The publishers will be pleased to make suitable arrangements to clear permission with any copyright holders whom it has not been possible to contact.

# Guided Tour

## Learning Objectives

Each chapter opens with a set of learning objectives, summarizing what you will learn from each chapter.

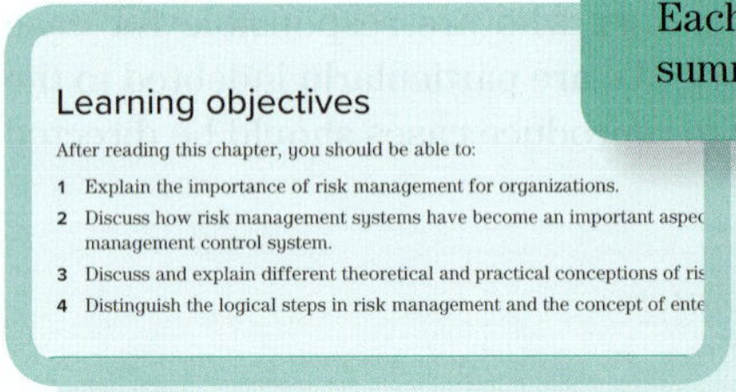
Learning objectives

After reading this chapter, you should be able to:

1 Explain the importance of risk management for organizations.
2 Discuss how risk management systems have become an important aspec
management control system.
3 Discuss and explain different theoretical and practical conceptions of ris
4 Distinguish the logical steps in risk management and the concept of ente

## Real world vignettes

Real world vignettes ensure a strong link to the real world from the outset of each chapter. They provide an insight into real-life situations and companies that embody important management control topics that will be covered in the chapter.

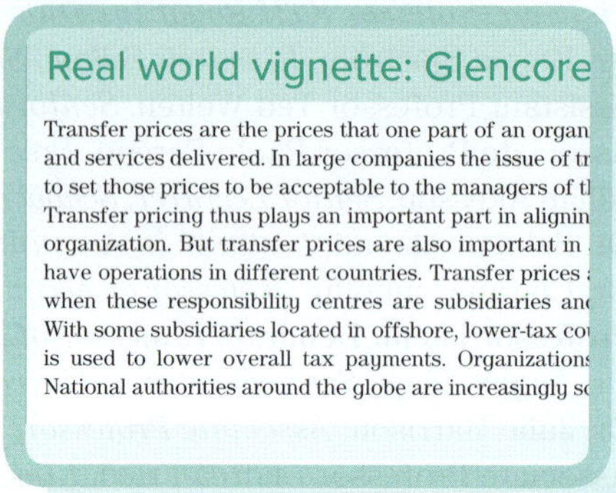
Real world vignette: Glencore

Transfer prices are the prices that one part of an organ
and services delivered. In large companies the issue of tr
to set those prices to be acceptable to the managers of t
Transfer pricing thus plays an important part in alignin
organization. But transfer prices are also important in
have operations in different countries. Transfer prices
when these responsibility centres are subsidiaries an
With some subsidiaries located in offshore, lower-tax co
is used to lower overall tax payments. Organizations
National authorities around the globe are increasingly s

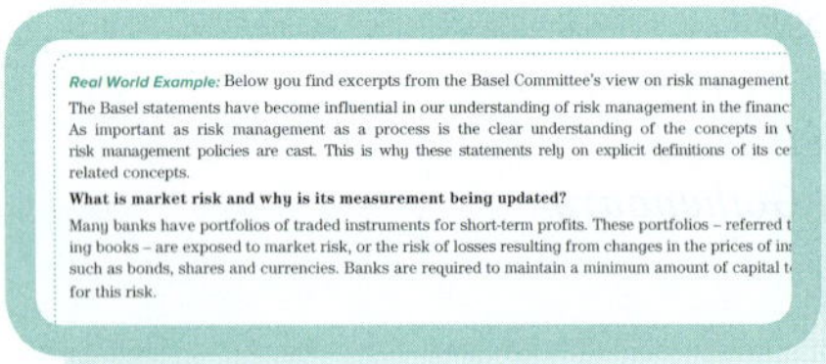
*Real World Example:* Below you find excerpts from the Basel Committee's view on risk management
The Basel statements have become influential in our understanding of risk management in the financ
As important as risk management as a process is the clear understanding of the concepts in
risk management policies are cast. This is why these statements rely on explicit definitions of its ce
related concepts.

**What is market risk and why is its measurement being updated?**

Many banks have portfolios of traded instruments for short-term profits. These portfolios – referred t
ing books – are exposed to market risk, or the risk of losses resulting from changes in the prices of in
such as bonds, shares and currencies. Banks are required to maintain a minimum amount of capital t
for this risk.

## Real world examples

Examples are extensively integrated into the chapters. These examples reinforce the relevance of the chapter contents to real life and show how management control affects real companies.

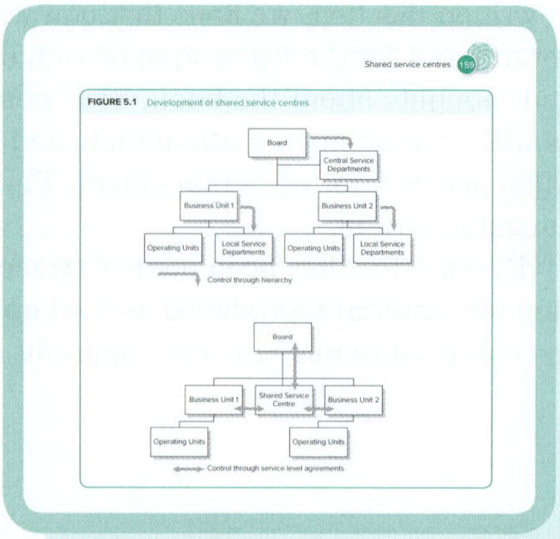


## Figures and Tables

Each chapter provides a number of figures, tables and exhibits to help you to visualize the various models, and to illustrate and summarize important concepts.

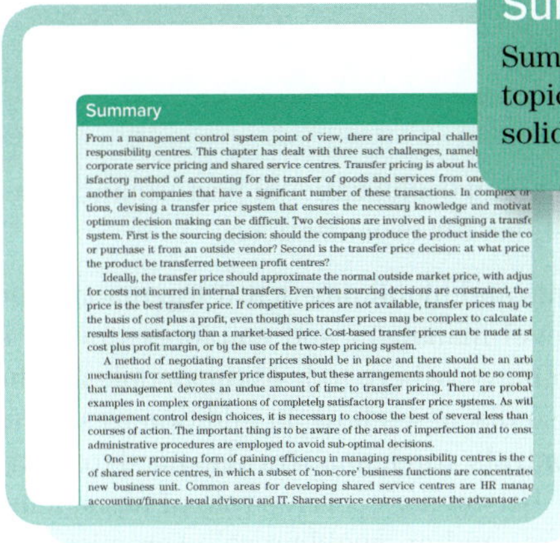

Summary

From a management control system point of view, there are principal challe[...]
responsibility centres. This chapter has dealt with three such challenges, namel[...]
corporate service pricing and shared service centres. Transfer pricing is about h[...]
isfactory method of accounting for the transfer of goods and services from on[...]
another in companies that have a significant number of these transactions. In complex or[...]
tions, devising a transfer price system that ensures the necessary knowledge and motivat[...]
optimum decision making can be difficult. Two decisions are involved in designing a transf[...]
system. First is the sourcing decision: should the company produce the product inside the co[...]
or purchase it from an outside vendor? Second is the transfer price decision: at what price[...]
the product be transferred between profit centres?

Ideally, the transfer price should approximate the normal outside market price, with adjus[...]
for costs not incurred in internal transfers. Even when sourcing decisions are constrained, the[...]
price is the best transfer price. If competitive prices are not available, transfer prices may b[...]
the basis of cost plus a profit, even though such transfer prices may be complex to calculate[...]
results less satisfactory than a market-based price. Cost-based transfer prices can be made at st[...]
cost plus profit margin, or by the use of the two-step pricing system.

A method of negotiating transfer prices should be in place and there should be an arbi[...]
mechanism for settling transfer price disputes, but these arrangements should not be so comp[...]
that management devotes an undue amount of time to transfer pricing. There are proba[...]
examples in complex organizations of completely satisfactory transfer price systems. As wit[...]
management control design choices, it is necessary to choose the best of several less than[...]
courses of action. The important thing is to be aware of the areas of imperfection and to ens[...]
administrative procedures are employed to avoid sub-optimal decisions.

One new promising form of gaining efficiency in managing responsibility centres is the c[...]
of shared service centres, in which a subset of 'non-core' business functions are concentrate[...]
new business unit. Common areas for developing shared service centres are HR manag[...]
accounting/finance, legal advisory and IT. Shared service centres generate the advantage [...]

## Summaries

Summaries provide an opportunity to recap and review the main topics presented in each chapter to ensure you have acquired a solid understanding as you work through the book

## Suggested additional reading

Each chapter features a list of comprehensive readings and references, comprising the latest research and practitioner-oriented literature to broaden your knowledge and understanding of the chapter topics.

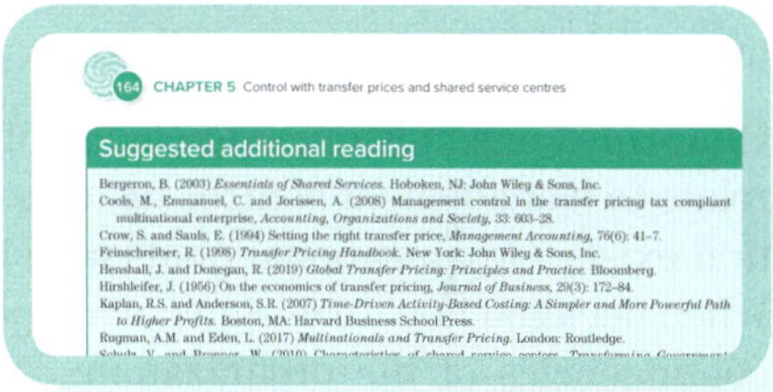

164 CHAPTER 5 Control with transfer prices and shared service centres

Suggested additional reading

Bergeron, B. (2003) *Essentials of Shared Services*. Hoboken, NJ: John Wiley & Sons, Inc.
Cools, M., Emmanuel, C. and Jorissen, A. (2008) Management control in the transfer pricing tax compliant multinational enterprise, *Accounting, Organizations and Society*, 33: 603–28.
Crow, S. and Sauls, E. (1994) Setting the right transfer price, *Management Accounting*, 76(6): 41–7.
Feinschreiber, R. (1998) *Transfer Pricing Handbook*. New York: John Wiley & Sons, Inc.
Henshall, J. and Donegan, R. (2019) *Global Transfer Pricing: Principles and Practice*. Bloomberg.
Hirshleifer, J. (1956) On the economics of transfer pricing, *Journal of Business*, 29(3): 172–84.
Kaplan, R.S. and Anderson, S.R. (2007) *Time-Driven Activity-Based Costing: A Simpler and More Powerful Path to Higher Profits*. Boston, MA: Harvard Business School Press.
Rugman, A.M. and Eden, L. (2017) *Multinationals and Transfer Pricing*. London: Routledge.

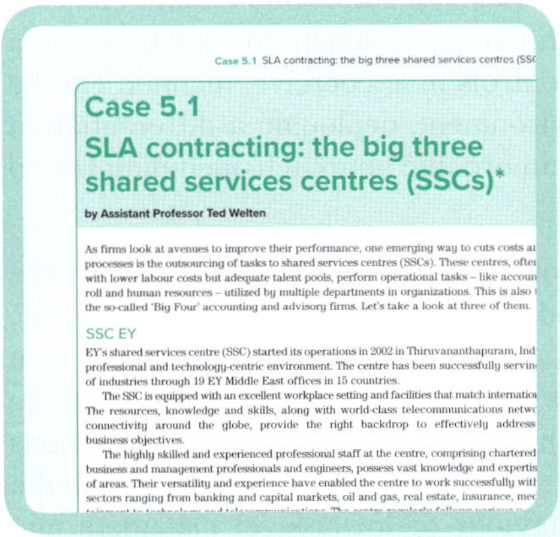

Case 5.1 SLA contracting: the big three shared services centres (SS[...]

Case 5.1
SLA contracting: the big three shared services centres (SSCs)*

**by Assistant Professor Ted Welten**

As firms look at avenues to improve their performance, one emerging way to cuts costs a[...]
processes is the outsourcing of tasks to shared services centres (SSCs). These centres, ofte[...]
with lower labour costs but adequate talent pools, perform operational tasks – like accoun[...]
roll and human resources – utilized by multiple departments in organizations. This is also [...]
the so-called 'Big Four' accounting and advisory firms. Let's take a look at three of them.

SSC EY

EY's shared services centre (SSC) started its operations in 2002 in Thiruvananthapuram, Ind[...]
professional and technology-centric environment. The centre has been successfully servin[...]
of industries through 19 EY Middle East offices in 15 countries.

The SSC is equipped with an excellent workplace setting and facilities that match internatio[...]
The resources, knowledge and skills, along with world-class telecommunications netw[...]
connectivity around the globe, provide the right backdrop to effectively address[...]
business objectives.

The highly skilled and experienced professional staff at the centre, comprising chartered[...]
business and management professionals and engineers, possess vast knowledge and expertis[...]
of areas. Their versatility and experience have enabled the centre to work successfully wit[...]
sectors ranging from banking and capital markets, oil and gas, real estate, insurance, me[...]

## Cases

Each chapter features a selection of cases that emphasize actual practice. The cases not only require you to analyse situations, but also give you a feel for what actually happens in companies

# Road map

**Part 1** of the book, entitled 'Management control systems: managing organizational performance', deals with the meaning and significance of management control systems for organizations.

**Chapter 1** discusses the nature of management control systems and highlights that if top management fails to implement the appropriate control practices, lower-level managers and employees might not have a clear sense of what decisions to take, what results to achieve, where to lead the people and how to use the resources under their responsibility. The chapter also discusses how, in addition to selecting an appropriate combination of input, throughput and output controls, top managers also need to systematically think through how to achieve an appropriate 'balance' between a coercive role of management control systems (i.e., a control device for use by top managers) and an enabling role (premised on a need to enhance the lower-level managers and employees' capabilities, and to capitalize on their intelligence by giving them the freedom to innovate and engineer solutions to concrete problems).

**Chapter 2** expands our knowledge of what mission, goals and strategies actually mean and how they relate to management control systems. An organization's mission concerns the reason why the organization exists. Organizational goals may be of many different kinds, such as financial and strategic goals. When deciding how to design a management control system, top management also needs to consider the contingencies of the organization. The contingencies include, among other things, the environment, strategies and technology. All these factors are shown to influence the selection of an appropriate combination of input, throughput and output controls. An organization facing a stable and certain environment, deploying a low-cost strategy and a manufacturing technology, is likely to benefit from a mechanistic approach, including heavy reliance on throughput controls in a 'coercive' manner. On the other hand, an organization facing a dynamic and uncertain environment, deploying a differentiation strategy and a service technology, is more likely to benefit from an organic approach, including heavy reliance on input controls in an 'enabling' manner.

**Chapter 3** discusses human behaviour. It details how the economic model of human behaviour, the psychological model of human behaviour and the sociological model of human behaviour each point to, and focus on, different characteristics of such behaviour. Often a particular management control system design is based on a specific view of what humans are, as laid down in these models. Understanding the similarities and differences between these theoretical models of human behaviour, and the limitations of management control system design and use, is important, since we are not interested in guiding the behaviour of some ideal type of individual, but rather the behaviour of lower-level managers and employees, who are real human beings.

**Part 2** of the book, entitled 'Management control systems: applying organizational architecture', deals primarily with throughput controls – i.e., how top managers direct lower-level manager and employee behaviour through formal delegation of decision-making responsibility and by specifying how behaviours are to be performed or not performed.

**Chapter 4** expands our knowledge of how top managers can direct the behaviours of lower-level managers and employees by designing appropriate responsibility centres. Should the various organizational units be responsible for only revenues (revenue centres) or only costs (expense centres) or both revenues and costs (profit centres) or also assets employed (investment centres)? As such, the assignment of responsibility to the different organizational units is an important and vital step to ensure the effectiveness of the management control system in large organizations. This tends to be forgotten by many top managers, who want to start directly with budgeting and the design of performance measurement systems and incentives.

**Chapter 5** notes that the structural design is not intended to create responsibility centres that are free to do what they want. Rather, the challenge is to orchestrate the actions of such centres to achieve the mission, goals and strategies by joint effort. One critical challenge here is how to account for goods and services that are delivered from one unit to another. But such internal transfers cannot happen for free, which is why management control systems should provide practices which ensure that consumers of such goods and services pay the producers appropriately. This chapter deals with three such control practices, namely transfer pricing, corporate service pricing and shared service centres.

**Chapter 6** reflects on the 'silo'-based organization created through the responsiblity centre arrangements by highlighting a number of additional structural choices that need to be made. An organization can be organized according to a functional structure, a business unit structure or as a matrix. Or it can primarily rely on a 'project' type of organization. This chapter deals with these additional structural choices, and discusses, for instance, lean management, a traditional way to plan projects (the waterfall method) and a more flexible way to manage projects (agile project management).

**Chapter 7** continues the reflection on the 'silo'-based organization by highlighting that, so far in the book, there has been a clear hierarchical authority structure between top managers, managers of the various responsibility centres and the rest of the employees in the company. But, considering the significance of inter-organizational relationships, it is necessary for managers to extend the notion of organizational architecture beyond the company's borders. Inter-organizational management control systems are conceptually different from traditional (internal) management control systems. Compared with coordinating activities within an organization in which hierarchical authority is one important basis for control, inter-organizational coordination takes place between legally independent organizations where there is no clear formal hierarchical authority in place.

**Part 3** of the book, entitled 'Management control systems: the performance management process', deals primarily with output controls – i.e., making managers and employees accountable for certain 'results', or output, through planning, measuring and following up on important performance targets. It discusses the most commonly used output controls: budgets, financial and non-financial performance measures, reward systems and risk management systems.

**Chapter 8** deals with one of the most common output controls, namely budgeting and forecasting. Budgeting is the heart of many management control systems and may fulfill a number of different roles, such as planning, monitoring, creating motivation, as well as reinforcing reflection and communication. We discuss the pros and cons of budgeting and how the budgeting process can be executed in a top-down, bottom-up or iterative manner. The chapter also deals with the beyond budgeting movement, which has suggested that budgeting should be abandoned and replaced with rolling forecasts. Another suggestion is to separate the budgeting process into three different processes, namely target setting, forecasting and resource allocation.

**Chapter 9** deals with the central question, 'How well are the organization as a whole and the various responsibility centres performing?' Performance measurement systems form the basis for such an analysis. By comparing the outcome of the chosen performance measures with appropriate performance targets, managers can assess the performance of the company. The chapter discusses general considerations when designing and using financial and non-financial measures. It also describes one widely adopted performance measurement system, namely the balanced scorecard, which systematizes the performance measures into a number of perspectives: financial, customer, internal business processes, and learning and innovation.

**Chapter 10** expands our understanding of compensation and incentives, often considered a cornerstone of output controls. The most influential theories on incentives and motivation, namely agency theory and self-determination theory, are reviewed in terms of their implications for designing incentive systems. It is shown that the two theories are fundamentally different in how they view motivation and consequently the proper design of an incentive system.

**Chapter 11** emphasizes that as all organizations face uncertainty, one key challenge for top managers is to determine how much risk to accept when developing the business. Risk management tools and techniques, such as risk maps and scenario analysis, and the creation of special roles, such as risk officers and risk managers, are designed to help top management to deal effectively with uncertainty and associated risk and opportunity. This chapter deals with this important aspect of management control systems, namely risk management.

**Part 4** of the book, entitled 'Management control systems: summary and outlook', consists, as its name suggests, of a summary and outlook discussion.

**Chapter 12** summarizes the main messages of the book. It also expands the discussions in Chapter 3 about the role of human behaviour in management control system design and use, by paying attention to the function and role of the controller. We detail the responsibilities of this function, and describe some developments in the role of the controller, in terms of both opportunities and challenges. The chapter ends by discussing some recent trends within the area of management control systems research and practice, and their implications for controller roles.

# Transform learning with Connect®

Boost grades, stimulate engagement and deliver an amazing course

**Connect®** is an online platform that integrates the science of learning with award-winning adaptive technology, to offer students and teachers a more effective teaching and learning experience.

> "Connect increases my students' knowledge and has made my teaching more effective."
>
> **University of Birmingham Business School, UK**

## The Three Pillars of Connect®

**Flexible and high quality content tailored to your course**

Use a combination of your content with McGraw-Hill and OER resources to customise your course with the support of our dedicated academic and implementation consultants.

**Detailed reporting and analytics**

Monitor progress and improve efficiency with detailed Connect® reports. Students and teachers can use real-time performance measurement tools to monitor learning and focus on the gaps that require more attention.

**Ease of set-up and continuous support**

McGraw-Hill offers comprehensive service, support and training - face-to-face, online or over the phone, throughout every phase of working with us to ensure easy set-up and access to the platform.

## Bring theory to life **within Connect®**

Students can **test and apply their knowledge** with our engaging excercises and activities within Connect®

Discover the features on offer for your discipline on the next page!

# Connect® for Accounting

We have a wide selection of resources on hand to help students gain valuable practice during their course. By applying what they have learned to real world scenarios and consistently testing their knowledge of the subject matter, these tools help prepare them for the real world of accounting.

## Assignable Case Studies

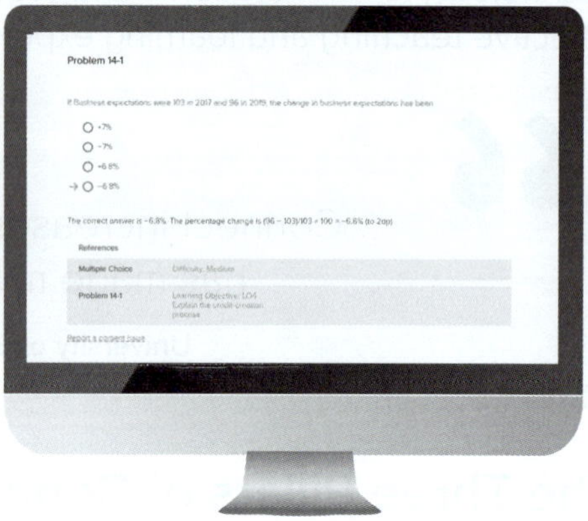


Students will develop strong analytical skills studying a series of case studies from innovative companies. Each case study is accompanied by questions which test the students application on theory and concept.

Assignable within Connect, these case studies keep the subject matter current and allow for students to obtain real-world practice during their study.

## PowerPoints

Engage students with the textbook content during lectures with the powerpoint versions of each chapter, complete with learning objectives, figures and exercises.

## Test Bank

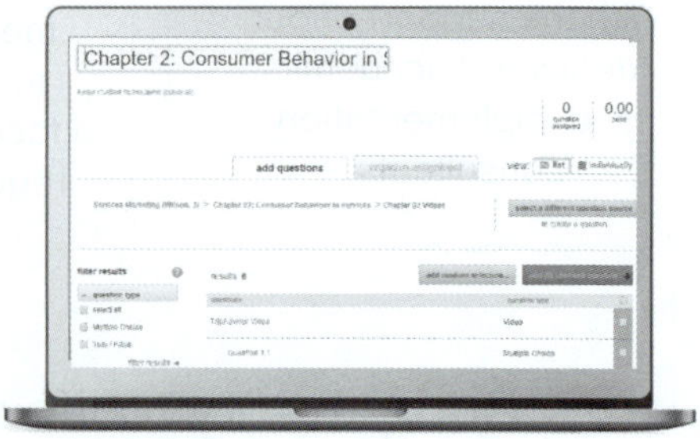


Build your own question banks relating to end-of-chapter material and featuring video case content to both test student knowledge and ability, and ensure engagement with existing real world cases.

## Instructor Manual

Equip yourself with your very own instructor manual of solutions, broken down chapter by chapter, to provide quick support and ease when navigating end of chapter questions.

Part 1

# Management control systems: managing organizational performance

Part 1 of the book, entitled 'Management control systems: managing organizational performance', deals with the meaning and significance of management control systems for organizations.

Chapter 1 discusses the nature of management control systems and highlights that if top management fails to implement the appropriate control practices, lower-level managers and employees might not have a clear sense of what decisions to take, what results to achieve, where to lead the people and how to use the resources under their responsibility. The chapter also discusses how, in addition to selecting an appropriate combination of input, throughput and output controls, top managers also need to systematically think through how to achieve an appropriate 'balance' between a coercive role of management control systems (i.e., a control device for use by top managers) and an enabling role (premised on a need to enhance the lower-level managers and employees' capabilities, and to capitalize on their intelligence by giving them the freedom to innovate and engineer solutions to concrete problems).

Chapter 2 expands our knowledge of what mission, goals and strategies actually mean and how they relate to management control systems. An organization's mission concerns the reason why the organization exists. Organizational goals may be of many different kinds, such as financial and strategic goals. When deciding how to design a management control system, top management also needs to consider the contingencies of the organization. The contingencies include, among other things, the environment, strategies and technology. All these factors are shown to influence the selection of an appropriate combination of input, throughput and output controls. An organization facing a stable and certain environment, deploying a low-cost strategy and a manufacturing technology, is likely to benefit from a mechanistic approach, including heavy reliance on throughput controls in a 'coercive' manner. On the other hand, an organization facing a dynamic and uncertain environment, deploying a differentiation strategy and a service technology, is more likely to benefit from an organic approach, including heavy reliance on input controls in an 'enabling' manner.

Chapter 3 discusses human behaviour. It details how the economic model of human behaviour, the psychological model of human behaviour and the sociological model of human behaviour each point to, and focus on, different characteristics of such behaviour. Often a particular management control system design is based on a specific view of what humans are, as laid down in these models. Understanding the similarities and differences between these theoretical models of human behaviour, and the limitations of management control system design and use, is important, since we are not interested in guiding the behaviour of some ideal type of individual, but rather the behaviour of lower-level managers and employees, who are real human beings.

# Chapter 1

# Introduction to management control systems

## Learning objectives

After reading this chapter, you should be able to:

1. Explain why organizations have a need for management control systems to attain their mission, goals and strategies.
2. Discuss the reasons why lower-level managers and employees do not automatically behave in line with the organizational mission, goals and strategies.
3. Explain the differences between the top-down and bottom-up functions of management control systems.
4. Discuss the various types of control practices – input, throughput and output controls – available to top managers when they design the organization's management control system.
5. Discuss the enabling and coercive role of a management control system.

## Real world vignette: The enabling role of management control systems

A recent CIMA report took data from 78 UK-based innovation companies and found that they used management control systems to enable their innovative activities. Input controls, such as job-specific recruitment and orientation programmes for new employees, were widely used and highly effective for innovation. In addition, output controls, such as routine analysis of performance against budget, were associated with better overall performance in innovation companies.[1] Therefore, when reading this book you will find strong arguments to 'kill the myth' that management control systems are simply a way for top managers to ensure the obedience of lower-level managers and other employees. When designing an appropriate combination of input, throughput and output controls top managers also need to find ways to profit from the skills, motivation and commitment of their lower-level managers and employees. As such, management control systems have an important 'enabling' role – that is, top managers need to design control practices that help maintain or enhance the skill set, job motivation and organizational commitment that lower-level managers and employees aim to contribute to the organization. The lower-level managers need to perceive control practices as something that supports them, which they can use to identify problems, prioritize issues and develop innovative ideas. This supportive and empowering side of management control systems is very important to take into account when deciding on how to design an appropriate management control system. It has been found that truly groundbreaking innovation companies, such as Netflix and Spotify, realized the benefits of designing enabling management control systems from the start.[2]

## Introduction

A central question for all organizations is how to align managers and employees' behaviour with the organization's mission, goals and strategies. Take the Red Cross, for example. Its mission is to prevent and alleviate human suffering in the face of emergencies. Or Scania, a world-leading provider of transport solutions, including trucks and buses. One of Scania's goals is to drive the shift towards a sustainable transport system, creating a world of mobility that is better for business, society and the environment. Or Inditex, one of the world's largest fashion retailers with, for instance, the Zara brand. Inditex's strategy is for its brands to work together closely as a single company, globally focused on the key elements of fashion production – design, manufacture, distribution and retail – thereby bringing the customers closer than ever to the products they want at affordable prices. The Red Cross, Scania and Inditex all have numerous managers and employees, and they all need to put considerable efforts into designing appropriate management control systems. Why? Because a well-designed management control system is one of the key factors to help ensure that the behaviour of Red Cross, Scania and Inditex managers and employees is aligned with the organization's mission, goals and strategies. In this book we define a management control system as *comprising a combination of control practices designed and implemented by top managers to increase the probability that lower-level managers and employees will behave in ways consistent with the organization's mission, goals and strategies.* This definition

[1] Luther, R., Haustein, E. and Ebber, G. (2018) Management control in UK innnovation companies. CIMA Report, July.

[2] Mankins, M. and Garton, E. (2017) How Spotify balances employee autonomy and accountability. *Harvard Business Review*, February; Nimdzi Insights (2017) How Netflix does it. https://www.nimdzi.com/how-netflix-does-it/

expresses that we focus our attention on formal control practices that are deliberately designed by top managers. Examples of control practices are budgets, mission statements, transfer pricing arrangements, performance measures and reward systems.

When presenting management control systems as an issue of top managers and lower-level managers and employees, we emphasize that understanding management control systems is about understanding organizations of a considerable size. Most small organizations, consisting of only a few people, have little need for the systematic, complex and costly design of management control systems that we present and discuss in this book. Smaller firms, by definition, employ fewer people, such that communication between top managers and the rest of the organization is more direct than in big firms, and will remain more informal. The distinction between top and lower levels of managers within an organization is therefore crucial to our understanding of the organization's need for management control systems. The essence of such organisations is that not all the power to make decisions that affect the future of the organization resides at the highest levels in the organization. Some of this power is shared with lower-level managers and employees. As, in larger organizations, lower-level managers have the authority to take decisions on their own, such organizations specifically need formal control practices, such as performance measures and value statements, that facilitate motivation and cooperation between the organization's managers and employees. Without them, organizations may go astray and fail in achieving their mission, goals and strategies.

In many cases companies' failures can be directly attributed to the lack of appropriate management control systems. This means that these failures could have been avoided by the proper design and use of such systems. Understanding the nature of these failures, therefore, helps us to better understand where management control systems fail, and what potential weak spots they have. Recently, companies such as Volkswagen and Wells Fargo have become well known for lapses in control practices to keep managerial and employee behaviour on track. And, some years back, Ahold, a Dutch multinational company operating chains of supermarkets, was near collapse following a strong growth strategy involving many international takeovers in Sweden, the USA and elsewhere.[3] The attention these organizations paid to pleasing the stakeholders by achieving pre-set performance targets resulted in behaviour that eventually went against stakeholder interests. Performance pressure may influence people to commit fraud in reporting performance levels that have no economic substance. If it is coupled with an organizational culture of improving reported performance by every means possible, failure is likely to happen some day.

## Top-down and bottom-up roles of management control systems

We have now established that organizations cannot do without formal management control systems. If the top managers fail to implement the appropriate control practices, lower-level managers and employees will often not have a clear sense of what decisions to take, what results to achieve, and where to lead the people and how to use the resources under their responsibility. We call this the top-down role of management control systems.

And, without appropriate control practices, top managers will not have a clear sense of what lower-level managers have done (i.e., the decisions they are taking, what results they are achieving, where they are leading the people and using the resources under their responsibility) and what lower-level managers think (i.e., what local contingencies might attract unsatisfactory attention due to the current strategies and management control system design). We call this the bottom-up role of management control systems.

When we define a management control system as comprising 'a combination of control practices designed and implemented by higher-level managers to increase the probability that lower-level

[3] Jong, A., DeJong, D.V., Mertens, G. and Roosenboom, P. (2007) Investor relations, reputational bonding, and corporate governance: the case of Royal Ahold, *Journal of Accounting and Public Policy*, 26(3): 328–75.

managers and employees will behave in ways consistent with the organization's mission, goals and strategies', we assume that lower managers in the organization do not automatically perform such actions. Indeed, there are a number of reasons why lower-level managers and employees may not automatically perform in line with the organization's mission, goals and strategies. Hence the need for both top-down and bottom-up roles of management control systems.

1 *Lower-level managers and employees may not automatically understand the mission, goals and strategies of the organization, nor how they can contribute to these.*

An important first reason for the need for management control systems is that lower-level managers and employees need to become aware of how they can contribute to the achievement of the organizational mission, goals and strategies. This is not a trivial issue, because these are typically defined centrally and, therefore, are not immediately meaningful to lower-level managers and employees. For example, common goals for many organizations include to have a certain amount of revenue, to earn a certain amount of profit and to achieve a certain profit margin. But when the organization aims to achieve a certain amount of yearly profit, this does not mean that individual managers and employees automatically understand how this profit should be achieved. Take the example of a sales manager. Should a sales manager increase the selling price and, therefore, try to earn more contribution margin? Or should the selling price be lowered, such that the sales volume goes up, resulting in a higher profit? And should profit only be high this year, or should the sales manager also pay attention to next year's profit levels? If so, this probably means that the manager should think just as hard about keeping customers as about maximizing profit this year. This relatively simple example shows that even if an organizational goal is relatively easy to measure, as is the case with organizational profit, top managers need to design control practices that help operationalize the goal and thereby inform lower-level managers and employees about the required direction of their efforts and decisions. In reality, however, many organizations often have goals that are even less easily measurable than profit. For such goals, the need for operationalization is even bigger. Not-for-profit organizations typically have goals defined in terms of delivering maximum quality services to a variety of external stakeholders, subject to the available funding. In such cases, the need to provide lower-level managers with a clear direction for their efforts and decisions is even greater.

An important first function of a management control system is therefore its top-down function to provide lower-level managers and employees with a clear sense of direction that helps them take actions, make decisions and achieve results that help the organization to achieve its mission, goals and strategies. Bottom-up, a management control system should inform top managers about the progress of the efforts of lower-level managers.

2 *Lower-level managers and employees may not automatically agree with the organizational mission, goals and strategies.*

A second reason for the need for management control systems is that lower-level managers and employees may not automatically be motivated to achieve the organization's mission, goals and strategies. This can be the case even if such organizational goals are operationalized and clearly communicated. Such motivation may be lacking because managers and employees have private goals that are incompatible with the goals of the organization. Private goals include goals that managers try to achieve out of self-interest, and that lead to the consumption of organizational resources for private reasons. Examples of such dysfunctional consumption are managers' inclination to increase holiday and leisure time, or simply the overconsumption of the organization's internal goods and services. More importantly, however, managers may have private goals that they try to achieve out of a genuine interest in the organization's well-being. Such managers may even disagree with the ways in which top managers formulate the mission, goals and strategies. Such disagreement is likely to occur because lower-level managers often have better information about the local conditions of the organization. For example, a sales manager is often better informed about local market conditions than top managers in the organization. Lower-level managers also often have more specialized skills than top managers. Sales managers typically have more commercial skills than higher-level general management. Note that benefiting from local information and from specialized managerial skills are two important reasons why organizations decide to rely on lower-level managers in the first place.

An important second function of a management control system is therefore its top-down function to motivate lower-level managers and employees to take actions, make decisions and achieve results that help the organization achieve its overall mission, goals and strategies. Bottom-up, management control systems should facilitate information sharing and communication so top managers can benefit from the specialized skills and knowledge of lower-level managers and employees.

3 *Lower-level managers and employees may not automatically have the resources needed to act according to the organizational mission, goals and strategies.*

A third reason for the need for a management control system is that lower-level managers and employees are not automatically able to achieve the organization's mission, goals and strategies. This can be the case even if such organizational goals are operationalized and clearly communicated, and if lower-level managers feel motivated to achieve them. To act in line with the organizational mission, goals and strategies, lower-level managers and employees need both personal skills and monetary and physical organizational resources. While obvious, the lack of personal skills is sometimes hard to detect, as lower-level managers may often find excuses for their poor performance. They may do so by pointing at others or by using external circumstances to explain their failure to make an organizational contribution. Sales managers may, for example, blame the general economic situation for disappointing sales levels, rather than their lack of commercial skills. They may also blame the production managers for a lack of product quality that reflects in dissatisfied customers. The provision of sufficient monetary and physical organizational resources to lower-level managers is also a challenge for most organizations. It is clear that such resources are necessary conditions for the managers to take purposeful actions. However, as resources are costly, it is crucial that the provision of resources results in a sufficient return. This is, of course, not easily established a priori.

An important third function of a management control system is therefore its top-down function to ensure that lower-level managers and employees have the skills and the organizational resources they need to perform in line with the organizational mission, goals and strategies. Bottom-up, management control systems should enable lower-level managers and employees to acquire the support to develop their skills as well as the organizational resources to execute their responsibilities. Table 1.1 summarizes the discussion.

**TABLE 1.1** Top-down and bottom-up roles of management control systems

| Origin of the need for management control systems | Top-down role of management control systems | Bottom-up role of management control systems |
|---|---|---|
| 1. Lower-level managers and employees may not automatically understand the mission, goals and strategies of the organization, nor how they can contribute to them | Explain mission, goals and strategies in as operational a way as possible. Support coordination across business functions at decentralized level | Report on goal achievement; provide input when goals are unrealistic. Enable coordination and cooperation with other decentralized units |
| 2. Lower-level managers and employees may not automatically agree with the organizational mission, goals and strategies | Motivate lower-level managers and employees to strive for the organizational mission, goals and strategies | Facilitate top managers to benefit from the specialized skills and knowledge of lower-level managers and employees |
| 3. Lower-level managers and employees may not automatically have the resources needed to act according to the organizational mission, goals and strategies | Resource allocation, develop personal skills of lower-level managers and employees | Enable lower-level managers to acquire the support and resources to execute their responsibilities |

In order to reap the benefits of the top-down and bottom-up roles of a management control system, its design and use has to be well thought through. Top managers have a variety of control practices to choose from, which is what we turn to next.

## A management control system 'package' – input, throughput and output controls

We have now established the need for a management control system and its top-down and bottom-up roles. The question for top managers then becomes: What are the various types of control practices they can use to form an appropriate management control system for the organization? When we ask top managers this question, the majority of them (too) quickly answer: budgeting, performance measures and incentive schemes. The idea of 'what gets measured gets done' is strongly rooted in many managers' mindsets. These are undoubtedly very important control practices in many organizations (and thoroughly discussed in Part 3), but an important message in this book is that the range of control practices is much wider. In fact, control practices can usefully be divided into three types; we label these *input controls, throughput controls* and *output controls*. This division is broadly meant to provide a way in which we can systematically discuss and design control practices. It follows an intuitive logic (see Figure 1.1) that lower-level managers and employees provide important cognitive abilities, skills and personal values to the organization (which top management can try to influence via input controls), which are transformed via the execution of effort – i.e., the actual work and organization of lower-level managers and employees (which top management can try to influence via throughput controls) – into some sort of performance, or 'results' (which top management can try to influence via output controls). From this it follows that top managers need to carefully think through how to design and use input, throughput and output controls to help the organization achieve its mission, goals and strategies.

In most organizations, the way in which lower-level managers and employees are controlled is always through a combination of these three types of control practice. Designing a management control system is therefore about choosing the relative emphasis that is put on 'cognitive abilities, skills and personal values', 'work and organization', and 'results'. This 'conceptual typology' has proven very

**FIGURE 1.1** Three types of control practices: input, throughput, output

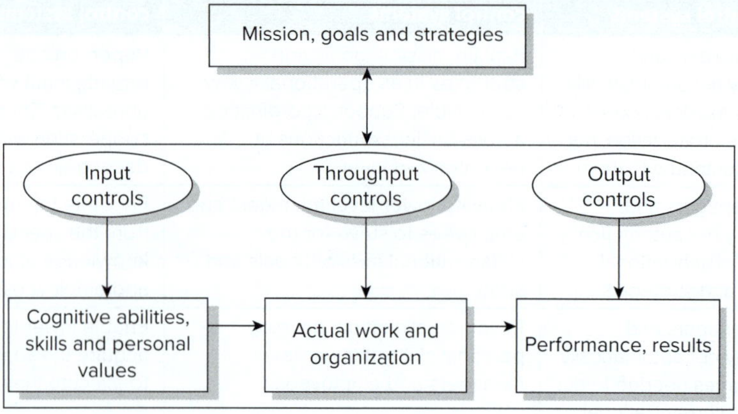

useful for making top managers aware of the broad array of control practices available to them when designing a management control system for their organization.

## Input controls

Input controls have to do with the people in the organization, and the capabilities, characteristics, knowledge and intentions they bring to their function. Top managers can systematically design control practices that help to ensure that these capabilities, characteristics, knowledge and intentions increase the chance that the lower-level managers and employees will engage in such behaviours as can be deemed consistent with the organization's mission, goals and strategies. The most commonly used input controls are as follows.

- *Employee selection processes:* In many organizations, top managers put considerable efforts in designing systematic screening processes for job candidates. The idea is to try to ensure that only people who embrace the organization's mission, goals and strategies are recruited and promoted. The main idea with systematic employee selection processes is that if an organization simply hires the 'right' people, the probability that manager and employee behaviour will be in line with organizational mission, goals and strategies increases. This requires a thorough understanding of how managers will behave, which is considered in more detail in Chapter 3.

**Real World Example:** The consulting company McKinsey is well known for its systematic selection process. On the homepage of its website, it states: 'While there's no exact template for success at McKinsey, our people share some qualities that help make us successful-and that make working more fun.'[3] These qualities, according to the homepage, are personal impact, entrepreneurial drive, problem-solving skills and leadership abilities. The employee selection process focuses specifically on identifying individuals who score 'high' on these qualities.

- *Value statements:* Many top managers we talk to emphasize the importance of formally communicating and systematically reinforcing organization-wide values and beliefs through mission statements and credos. The main idea with designing value statements is to inspire lower-level managers and employees, and guide their search for new opportunities.

**Real World Example:** The international company Beiersdorf, with brands such as Nivea and Eucerin, emphasizes in its Annual Report[4] that an important key to success is its employees' united understanding of shared values, and their strong identification with the company and its brands. These values are formally communicated through a value statement comprising four core values: 'Care, Simplicity, Courage, Trust'. The company describes these in its values statement as follows.

- Care: we act responsibly towards our colleagues, consumers, brands, our society, and our environment.
- Simplicity: we strive for clarity and consistency, making decisions quickly and pragmatically, and focusing on what is essential.
- Courage: we are committed to bold objectives, take initiative, learn from our mistakes, and see change as an opportunity.
- Trust: we say what we mean, keep our promises, and treat others with respect.

---

[3] McKinsey & Co (n.d.) Interviewing: we want you to succeed. Available at: https://www.mckinsey.com/careers/interviewing (accessed 7 May 2020).

[4] Beiersdorf (2018) Annual Report. Available at: Beiersdorf-Annual-Report-2018.pdf (accessed 7 May 2020).

***Real World Example:*** Another example is Netflix, whose corporate vision is 'to continue being one of the leading firms of the internet era'.[5] One way to formally communicate and reinforce this vision is through a value statement that contains the following key values: Continuing leadership; Internet; Entertainment.

- *Employee socialization processes:* In many organizations, employee socialization processes are vital to ensure basic conditions that enable lower-level managers and employees to be informed about organizational mission, goals and strategies. These should not simply be ad hoc activities but systematically designed processes that include introduction programmes for new managers, organizing training programmes to enhance competencies, and influencing collegiality, citizenship and culture. As with value statements, the main idea with designing systematic employee socialization processes is to inspire lower-level managers and employees, and guide their search for new opportunities.

***Real World Example:*** The Swedish fashion company H&M, for instance, has well-known trainee programmes with the purpose of enhancing the competencies of its future leaders. H&M describes these programmes as offering a unique, broad introduction to H&M, and deep knowledge about different areas and departments within the company.[6]

In addition to designing appropriate input controls, it is important for top managers to be aware of the importance of management style. Usually, lower-level managers' attitudes towards the organization's mission, goals and strategies reflect what they perceive their superiors' attitudes to be, and their superiors' attitudes ultimately stem from the CEO and other members of the organizational highest ranks. Managers come in all shapes and sizes. Some are charismatic and outgoing; others less so. Some spend a lot of time talking to people ('management by walking around'); others rely more heavily on written reports. When evaluating the effect of top management style on lower-level managerial behaviour we often discuss this in terms of 'tone at the top'; that is, top managers set the example for lower-level managers in the way they act, the opinions they proclaim and the norms they seem to adhere to. Audit professionals and advisory agencies on corporate governance have traditionally stressed the importance of 'tone at the top' as a powerful way to make lower-levels managers behave in line with the organizational mission, goals and strategies. 'Tone at the top' often affects behaviour because many lower-level managers, willingly and consciously, as well as unwillingly and unconsciously, often reciprocate the behaviour they see displayed. We want to emphasize, however, that management style is not a control practice. As we have discussed, control practices are designed (by top managers), i.e., they design a process for employee selection, they design value statements and they design processes for employee socialization.

More in-depth discussions of input controls are often found in books on human resource management (HRM). It is important to stress, however, that designing appropriate input controls (especially value statements) is ultimately the responsibility of top managers, even if they often delegate some of this responsibility (for instance, regarding employee selection and socialization processes) to the human resource department. In this book, Chapters 3 and 10 provide thorough discussions about 'people' and how they are motivated. Such understanding is vital when designing appropriate input controls.

---

5 Rancord Society (2019) Netflix's Mission Statement & Vision Statement: a Strategic Analysis. Available at: https://www.rancord.org/netflix-corporate-vision-statement-mission-statement-strategic-analysis (accessed 7 May 2020).

6 H&M careers (n.d.) Available at: https://career.hm.com/content/hmcareer/en_se/student/education/hm-trainee-programs.html (accessed 7 May 2020).

## Throughput controls

Managerial effort is a generic term that applies to all the observable actions and choices managers make as part of their managerial responsibilities. The actions and choices are made by managers in the context of their managerial role, and because managers and employees often do not automatically act and choose in line with organizational mission, goals and strategies, top managers also need to implement throughput controls. These control practices direct lower-level manager and employee behaviour through formal delegation of decision-making responsibility to lower-level managers, and by specifying how behaviours are to be performed or not performed. The most commonly used throughput controls are as follows.

- *The organization's set of rules:* When top managers are asked about throughput controls, the first example they give is always the prescription of certain behaviours of managers in some specific situations through policies, guidelines or codes of conduct – what we label the organization's set of rules. These throughput control practices describe crucial 'dos and don'ts' of lower-level managers and employees concerning, for example, the way they report their accounting performance, the way they do business in foreign countries, and the way they deal with HR-related, ethical or environmental issues. We use the word 'rules' as shorthand for all types of formal instructions, including standing instructions, job descriptions, standard operating procedures, manuals and ethical guidelines. Rules range from the most trivial (e.g., paper clips will be issued only on the basis of a signed requisition) to the most important (e.g., the organization is not allowed to expand its operations into country X, or capital expenditures of more than €1 million must be approved by the board of directors). Many rules are in force indefinitely – that is, they exist until they are modified, which happens infrequently. Some rules are guides – that is, organization members are permitted, and, indeed, expected, to depart from them, either under specified circumstances or when their own best judgement indicates that a departure would be in the best interests of the organization. For example, even though a rule specifies the criteria for extending credit to customers, the credit manager may approve credit for a customer who does not currently meet these criteria, but who has been valuable to the company in the past and is likely to become so again. Such departures may require the approval of higher authority, however. Some rules are positive requirements that certain actions must be taken (e.g., fire drills at prescribed intervals). Others are prohibitions against unethical, illegal or other undesirable actions – for instance, requiring signatures and other evidence that a transaction has been authorized and separating duties. One important function of these control practices is to establish limits to the opportunity-seeking behaviour that all organizations try to encourage (for instance, through value statements). These codes of conduct are sometimes explicitly communicated to the outside world, to signal their importance to the organization.

**Real World Example:** The Australian sports equipment producer Quiksilver, for instance, communicates that it is committed to conducting business in an ethical manner and expects its manufacturing partners to share this same commitment. Accordingly, it has established a code of conduct, titled QUEST (Quiksilver Ethical Standards of Trade), to prevent abusive or illegal conditions in the workplace, and prevent human trafficking and slavery. QUEST includes a Supplier Workplace Code of Conduct, and all agents, vendors and factories are required to participate in the QUEST programme as a condition of doing business with Quiksilver.[7]

- *The organizational architecture:* One important way to control the behaviours of lower-level managers and employees is by systematically designing appropriate structural arrangements for the

[7] Quiksilver (n.d.) Modern Slavery Act Statement. Available at: https://www.quiksilver.co.uk/customer-modern-slavery-act-statement.html (accessed 7 May 2020).

organization's mission, goals and strategies. In this book we use the expression 'organizational architecture' to denote these various structural arrangements that are designed by top managers. Should they employ a functional structure for the organization, in which each manager is responsible for a specified function such as production or marketing? Or a business unit structure in which managers are responsible for most of the activities of their particular unit, and the business unit functions as a semi-independent part of the organization? Or a matrix structure in which functional units have dual responsibilities – i.e., a mix between a functional and a business unit structure? Or a project structure, where the responsibilities mostly are related to ongoing projects? Or should the organization engage systematically in formal cooperations with other organizations, and form joint ventures and outsourcing arrangements? The organizational architecture also concerns designing appropriate responsibility centres. Should the various organizational units be responsible for only revenues (revenue centres) or only costs (expense centres) or both revenues and costs (profit centres) or also investments (investment centres)? It also concerns how transfer pricing and cost allocation systems should be designed if the different organizational units are interdependent. Finally, it encompasses designing job descriptions and roles for employees.

***Real World Example:*** Starbucks Coffee works diligently with its organizational architecture to maintain its competitive advantage. As the largest coffee house chain in the world, it continuously ensures that its organizational structure matches current business needs. Starbucks has a matrix organizational structure (see more on this type of structure in Chapter 6),[8] which involves intersections among various components of the business. There are four main features of the matrix structure: functional hierarchy, geographical divisions, product-based divisions, and teams. For instance, the company's product-based divisions intersect with functional groups and geographical divisions, which in turn intersect with other parts of the organization.

When we emphasize that the design choices regarding the organizational structure are important throughput controls and therefore a key part of an organization's management control system, many top managers we talk to admit that they often forget this. They tend to focus on rules, such as policies and codes of conduct. Such throughput control practices are important but a key message in this book is that the organizational architecture is a very powerful (but often forgotten) way to direct lower-level manager and employee behaviour. We therefore devote Part 2 of this book to these throughput control practices.

## Output controls

A third way to direct lower-level manager and employee behaviour is by making managers accountable for certain 'results', or output. As previously discussed, these are the control practices commonly emphasized when top managers are asked to describe their management control systems. 'What gets measured (and rewarded) gets done' is a quote commonly referred to by top managers when they discuss their control philosophy. Output controls work through planning, measuring and following up on important performance targets. They direct lower-level manager and employee behaviour through expressing expectations of what is a 'good enough' performance. The most commonly used output controls are as follows.

- *Budgets:* Budget preparation is one of the most important processes in a majority of organizations. An operating budget is the organization's yearly plan, and is often decided in negotiations between top managers and lower-level managers. The end product of such negotiations is an agreed-upon budget of the anticipated revenues and/or expenses and/or investments for the coming year. In Chapter 8, budgets will be thoroughly discussed.

---

[8] Panmore Institute (2019) Starbucks Coffee's organizational structure & its characteristics. Available at: http://panmore.com/starbucks-coffee-company-organizational-structure (accessed 7 May 2020).

**Real World Example:** Danske Bank, for instance, launched 'Danske Bank's Budget Guide 2019', intended as a quick reference guide to help facilitate the 2019 budget planning of companies. The guide sought to answer the following questions with 2019 budgeting in mind: What is the outlook for the global economy and selected countries/regions? What is the outlook for sales to a particular country/region with a focus on consumer spending and investment? What should a company with production or sales in a particular country/region expect in terms of wage and price growth?[9]

- *Financial and non-financial performance measures (often combined with reward systems):* Most organizations put an enormous effort into selecting performance measures that 'best' reflect the organization's mission, goals and strategies. Often they use a combination of financial measures (for instance, sales, profit, return on capital employed, operating cashflow) and non-financial measures (for instance, customer satisfaction, quality, productivity, employee satisfaction). By comparing the outcome of the chosen performance measures against appropriate standards, top managers can assess the performance of lower-level managers and employees. In addition, making managers accountable for results is often emphasized even further through linking managerial compensation to the achievement of certain performance targets. Performance measurement and incentive systems are discussed in Chapters 9 and 10.

**Real World Example:** Fiat Chrysler Automotive, for instance, stressed in its 2018 Annual Report[10] the importance of product quality and customer satisfaction to its ability to produce vehicles to meet product quality standards, gain market acceptance and satisfy customer expectations. It therefore monitors such measures at Group Executive Council and Product Committees meetings.

- *Risk management:* All organizations face uncertainty, and thus one key challenge for top managers is to determine how much risk to accept when developing the business. Risk management tools and techniques, such as risk maps and scenario analysis, and the creation of special roles, such as risk officers and risk managers, are designed to help top management to deal effectively with uncertainty and associated risk and opportunity, enhancing the capacity to build value.

**Real World Example:** The Norwegian oil company Equinor (formerly Statoil) works diligently with climate-related business risk. Equinor's business is subject to strict climate regulations and the company uses internal carbon pricing, scenario analysis and sensitivity analysis to assess and manage climate-related risk. Climate-related risk factors are identified by considering main sources of change, such as market, policy and regulatory, technology, physical and reputation.[11]

Reflecting the importance of output controls, Part 3 of the book is devoted to the use of budgeting, performance measurement systems, reward systems and risk management.

---

[9] Danske Bank (2018) Danske Bank budget guide 2019, 12 September. Available at: https://research.danskebank.com/link/BudgetGuide120918/$file/Budget%20Guide_120918.pdf (accessed 7 May 2020).

[10] Fiat Chrysler Automobiles (2018) Annual Report. Available at: https://www.fcagroup.com/en-US/investors/financial_regulatory/financial_reports/files/FCA_NV_2018_Annual_Report.pdf (accessed 7 May 2020).

[11] Equinor (2019) Climate-related business risk and our strategic response. Available at: https://www.equinor.com/en/how-and-why/sustainability/climate-related-business-risk-and-our-strategic-response.html (accessed 7 May 2020).

## Enabling and coercive management control systems

So far, a main message in this chapter is that top managers have a wide variety of control practices to choose from when they design their organization's management control system. The distinction between input, throughput and output controls is a powerful way to demonstrate this variety, and it is a distinction that 'stands the test of time'. In the 'new era' we live in, with digitalization and climate change, the need for, and use of, information changes quickly (from 'small' data to 'big' data, more focus on sustainability measures, etc.), but the distinction between input, throughput and output controls remains relevant. The three types of control practices also highlight the important message of this book, that management control systems are about so much more than performance measurement and incentives. The fact that Part 2 of the book is entirely devoted to throughput controls – which make up the organizational architecture within which output controls are designed – sends a powerful message about the need to use a broad conception of what a management control system is.

This also means that this book has a rather comprehensive view of what it means for an organization to be 'in control' or 'out of control'. These terms are increasingly used in the business press and beyond about whether the organization is on the right track towards reaching its mission, goals and strategies. It is clear by now that although these terms are fashionable statements, the actual design and use of management control systems is more dynamic than these terms suggest. Understanding this dynamic is probably the best way to create a feeling of being 'in control'.

The too narrow focus on performance measurement and incentives among many managers has also contributed to a commonly shared view that management control systems are simply a way for top managers to ensure the obedience of lower-level managers and other employees. When we talk to lower-level managers and employees, many of them view certain control practices as structural devices for use by top managers to 'check' what they are doing, to coerce them into cooperation, or to force them to do things they would never do of their own free will. We acknowledge that such a 'coercive' role of management control systems might indeed be appropriate when designing some of the organization's control practices. For instance, there are certain rules (i.e., throughput controls) that should never be broken under any circumstances: a rule prohibiting the payment of bribes, for example, or a rule that airline pilots must never take off without permission from the air traffic controller. It can also be appropriate that top managers simply decide on a certain organizational architecture and/or specify rules for the range of geographical regions the organization can expand into.

However, when designing an appropriate combination of input, throughput and output controls, top managers also need to find ways to profit from the skills, motivation and commitment of their lower-level managers and employees. This was emphasized in the Real World Vignette at the start of this chapter, with the examples of Netflix and Spotify. Management control systems have an important 'enabling' role as well – that is, top managers need to design control practices that help maintain or enhance the skill set, job motivation and organizational commitment that lower-level managers and employees aim to contribute to the organization. They need to perceive control practices as something that supports them, that they can use to identify problems, prioritize issues and develop ideas for improvements. As illustrated in the Real World Vignette, research has shown that many innovative organizations have an extensive use of control practices. This supportive and empowering side of management control systems, which we denote the enabling role, is very important to take into account when deciding on a management control system.

Some control practices are more enabling in nature, such as input controls in the form of, for instance, a value statement. However, research has shown that for throughput and output controls, certain features of the development process for designing and implementing these controls can help to foster a perception among lower-level managers and employees that these controls are enabling. *Lower-level manager and employee involvement during the implementation process* is one such feature. For instance, designing the 'right' performance measures or rules should be seen as a process of periodically reviewing, revising and refining the rules and measures. Here top managers need to involve lower-level managers and employees as they have the local knowledge and hands-on experience of how certain measures 'work' or 'do not work' for performance evaluation. *Lower-level manager and employee understanding* is another feature – that is, they should be able to understand the underlying logic of a specific control practice. If top managers invest time in discussing with lower-level managers and employees about the working of local processes, how they fit into the organization as a whole, and the underlying rationale for why the control practice is in place, the enabling role is strengthened. Finally, research has shown that *communication and visualization* is an important feature for creating enabling control practices. If top managers systematically communicate with lower-level managers and employees about the purpose as well as achievements of the various control practices, the motivation and acceptance of those practices are likely to increase. Providing a graphical representation of a number of performance metrics so that managers and employees understand how they are connected to one another and to the organization's mission, goals and strategies are also likely to increase motivation and acceptance. In the remaining chapters, these principles will be applied in order to systematically reinforce the need to design and use management control systems in an enabling way.

## Summary

A management control system comprises a combination of control practices designed and implemented by top managers to increase the probability that lower-level managers and employees will behave in ways consistent with the organization's mission, goals and strategies. Organizations cannot do without formal management control systems. If top management fails to implement the appropriate control practices, lower-level managers and employees will often not have a clear sense of what decisions to take, what results to achieve and where to lead the people, and how to use the resources under their responsibility. Control practices can usefully be divided into three types: input controls, throughput controls and output controls. In addition to selecting an appropriate combination of these three types of control, top managers also need to systematically think through how to achieve an appropriate 'balance' between a coercive role of management control systems (i.e., a control device for use by top managers) and an enabling role (premised on a need to enhance the lower-level managers and employees' capabilities, and to capitalize on their intelligence by giving them the freedom to innovate and engineer solutions to concrete problems).

## Suggested additional reading

Bisbe, J., Kruis, A.M. and Madini, P. (2019) Coercive, enabling, diagnostic, and interactive control: untangling the threads of their connections, *Journal of Accounting Literature*, 43: 124–44.

Chenhall, R.H. and Moers, F. (2015) The role of innovation in the evolution of management accounting and its integration into management control, *Accounting, Organizations and Society*, 47: 1–13.

Grabner, I., Posch, A. and Wabnegg, M. (2018) Materializing innovation capability: a management control perspective, *Journal of Management Accounting Research*, 30: 163–85.

Jordan, S. and Messner, M. (2012) Enabling control and the problem of incomplete performance indicators, *Accounting, Organizations and Society*, 37: 544–64.

Luther, R., Haustein, E. and Webber, G. (2018) Management control in UK innovation companies. CIMA Report.

# Case 1.1
# Maybach*

**by Frank G.H. Hartmann**

Please read the following news item concerning Maybach-Manufaktur GMBH:[1]

> *Daimler – the parent company of Mercedes-Benz – will make a decision whether to continue with its ultra-luxury Maybach brand within the next two years, a new report finds. Daimler revived the Maybach brand to compete with the likes of Rolls-Royce, but slow sales have the German company reconsidering Maybach's future. Maybach sales have been slow since the brand's re-launch and Daimler only managed to sell 146 Maybach vehicles in a particular year, about a tenth of the sales originally predicted for the marque. 40 per cent of Maybach dealers have already shut their doors. According to the CarConnection, Daimler CEO Dr Dieter Zetsche has admitted that there are no future Maybach models in the works. The Maybach 63 and 57 – which are largely based on the last-generation Mercedes S-Class – have continued relatively unchanged since their launch and the limited-edition Landaulet isn't expected to bolster sales. Zetsche admits that Daimler has 'not decided yet' if Maybach will be the recipient of a new model and says the decision to design a new model or kill the brand entirely will be made within the next two years.*

## Questions

1 What are the choices that managers of Maybach are faced with, according to this analysis?

2 What kind of behaviours should be elicited by an appropriate management control system?

3 What happened to Maybach? Which decisions were taken and how were these decisions motivated?

---

* This case was written by Professor Frank G.H. Hartmann, Radbound University

[1] Johnson, D. (2008) Daimler considering ending Maybach production. Available at: http://www.leftlanenews.com/daimler-considering-ending-maybach-production.html (accessed 14 June 2013.)

# Case 1.2
# Abrams company*

**by J. G. San Miguel**

Abrams Company manufactured a wide variety of parts for use in automobiles, trucks, buses and farm equipment. There were three major groups of parts: ignition parts, transmission parts and engine parts. Abrams' parts were sold both to original equipment manufacturers (OEMs) and to wholesalers. The wholesalers, in turn, resold the parts to retailers, who sold them as replacement parts to consumers. The latter market was called the 'aftermarket' (AM).

## Product and marketing divisions

As shown in the partial organization chart in Exhibit 1, Abrams had a 'product division' for each of its three part groups. Each of these product divisions was managed by a vice president and general manager, and was expected to earn a target return on investment (ROI). Each product division manufactured parts in several plants and sold a major portion of its manufactured parts to OEMs. Each product division had its separate OEM sales department (see Exhibit 1) that worked closely with OEMs to

**EXHIBIT 1** Partial organization chart

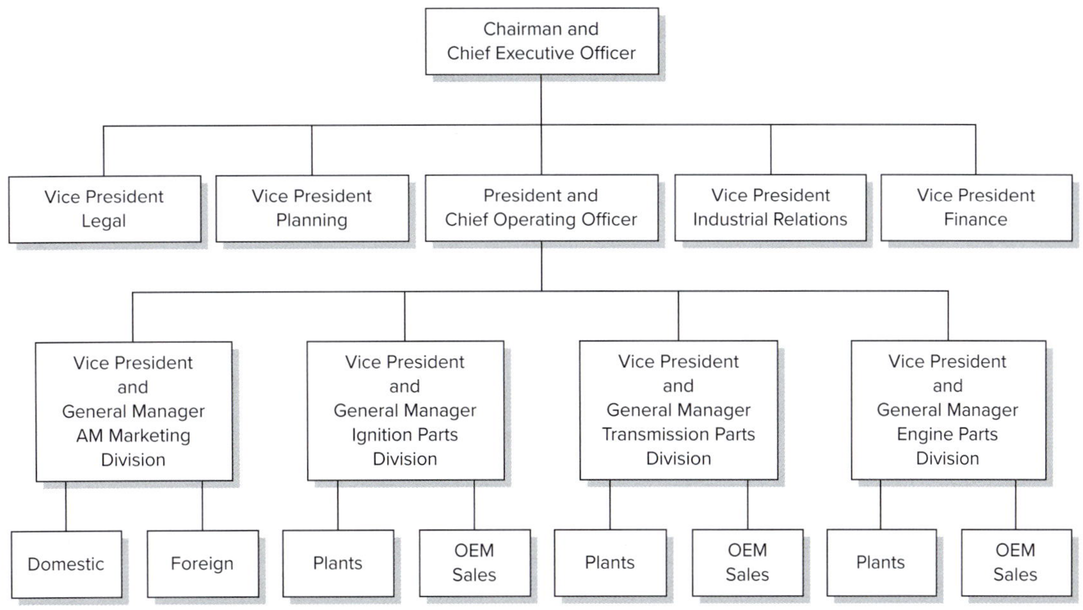


* This case was adapted (with permission) by Professor J. G. San Miguel Naval Postgraduate School, from a case written by Professor J. S. Reece, University of Michigan. 

develop new products or change existing products. The remaining manufactured parts were sold by the product division to Abrams' fourth division, called the AM marketing division (see Exhibit 1) or 'AM division', as it was known to managers. This division was also managed by a vice president and general manager, and was solely responsible for marketing Abrams' entire line of parts to AM wholesalers. The AM division operated several company-owned parts distribution warehouses in the US and foreign markets. The AM division was also expected to earn an annual return on investment target.

## Inside and outside sales

In 1992, the four divisions' sales totalled $500 million, which included 'inside' sales of $100 million from the three product divisions to the AM division. The $500 million sales were recorded as approximately $130 million for the ignition parts division, $100 million for the transmission parts division, $90 million for the engine parts division and $180 million for the AM division. After elimination of inside sales, Abrams' outside sales totalled about $400 million. Because of anticipated growth in the parts aftermarket due to the increase in the number of vehicles being driven and their ages, one of top management's goals for the AM division was for its sales to reach 50 per cent of Abrams' total outside sales.

## ROI for the manufacturing plants

Continuing the company's ROI strategy, each manufacturing plant within the three product divisions had an annual ROI target to meet. Each product division's OEM sales were traced to the plants that made the parts. The plants maintained finished goods inventories and shipped parts directly to OEM customers. A plant's ROI target was based on budgeted profit (including allocations of division and corporate overhead expenses and an imputed income tax expense) divided by actual beginning-of-the-year net assets (defined as total assets less current liabilities). Exhibit 2 contains an example of the Rochester plant's

**EXHIBIT 2** Actual 1992 ROI computation – Rochester Plant

| ABRAMS COMPANY – TRANSMISSION PARTS DIVISION<br>Rochester Plant Profit and ROI statement, 31 December 1992 | |
|---|---|
| Sales revenue | $124,866 |
| Cost of goods sold | 73,230 |
| Gross margin | 51,636 |
| Operating expenses | 20,792 |
| Division expenses assigned | 11,340 |
| Corporate expenses assigned | 3,420 |
| Profit before taxes | 16,084 |
| Taxes imputed | 4,825 |
| Profit | $ 11,259 |
| **Net assets assigned as of 1 January 1992** | |
| Total assets: | |
| Cash and receivables | $ 25,000 |
| Inventories | 12,875 |
| Property, plant & equipment at book value | 86,560 |
| Total assets | 124,435 |
| Less current liabilities | 26,135 |
| Net assets | $ 98,300 |
| Return on investment | 11.5% |

actual 1992 ROI computation. Actual ROI was actual profit divided by actual beginning-of-the-year net assets.

Top management's stated reason for including allocated overhead expenses and taxes in determining profit was to have the plant profit figure resemble the profit calculation for external financial reports to shareholders. The CEO felt this gave a plant manager a clearer perspective of the costs of doing business and the plant's contribution to the corporate bottom line, and added more realism to the plant's results.

The beginning-of-the-year net assets amount was used in the ROI measurement because, in management's view, investment added during a given year resulted in little, if any, incremental profit in that year. The investment was likely to increase future profits. Top management felt that such investments might not be proposed if managers were penalized (in the form of higher net assets and lower ROI) in the first year of the new investment. Because the investment base for the year was 'frozen' at the beginning-of-the-year level, maximizing profit during the year was equivalent to maximizing ROI. For beginning-of-the-year net assets, cash and receivables were allocated to plants on the basis of sales revenue, while inventories, property, plant, equipment and current liabilities were traced specifically to each plant. Historical cost less accumulated depreciation (book value) was used to value property, plant and equipment. The AM division's ROI was measured in the same manner as the plants' ROIs.

## Marketing strategies

The OEM sales department within each of the three product divisions worked with the OEM's engineers to develop innovative and cost-effective new parts to meet the customers' requirements, and serviced customer accounts for parts already being supplied to the OEMs. Each of these OEM sales departments was expected to meet an annual sales revenue target. Because the product divisions' customers (OEMs) were different from the AM division's customers, top management did not feel that the OEM and aftermarket sales organizations should be combined. Even the three product divisions' OEM marketing efforts were not consolidated in one sales organization because each division's OEM marketers tended to work with different people within a given OEM's organization (i.e., ignition, transmission and engines). Moreover, two of the three product divisions were independent companies before being acquired by Abrams. Thus, there was a long tradition of doing their own OEM marketing.

According to Abrams' executives, the factors critical to success in the OEM market were: the ability to design innovative and dependable parts that met the customer's quality, performance and weight specifications; meeting delivery schedule requirements so that the OEM could minimize its own parts inventories; and controlling costs. Cost control was important because the market was very price competitive. In the aftermarket business, availability of parts was by far the most important factor to the wholesaler, followed by quality and price.

## Incentive compensation plan

Approximately 50 Abrams line and staff managers participated in an incentive bonus plan. The dollar amount of the corporate-wide bonus pool was established by a fixed formula linked to corporate earnings per share. Each participant in the bonus plan received a number of standard bonus points. The higher the participant was in the organizational hierarchy, the more standard points he or she received. The total of these points for all participants was divided into the total bonus pool amount to arrive at a standard dollar award per point. Then, this standard rate was multiplied by the participant's number of standard points to arrive at the participant's standard bonus dollars. However, the actual bonus could vary (upwards or downwards) by as much as 25 per cent at the discretion of the participant's superiors.

In the case of a plant manager, the standard award also was adjusted by a formula that related percentage of standard award to the plant's profit variance (budget versus actual profit). For example, if the plant's actual profit for the year exceeded its budgeted profit by 4 per cent, the plant manager's bonus was raised from 100 per cent of standard to 110 per cent of standard. In making this bonus adjustment, the plant's actual profit was adjusted for any favourable or unfavourable gross margin variance caused by sales volume to the AM division being higher or lower than budgeted. For example, if a plant's favourable profit variance was attributable to a favourable gross margin volume variance on sales to the AM division, the plant manager's bonus would not be raised above 100 per cent of standard. Similarly, the plant manager would not be penalized if the AM division actually purchased less from the plant than the amount that was agreed to by AM division when the plant's annual profit budget was approved by top management.

## Management comments

In general, top management was satisfied with the present management systems and performance measurement scheme. In discussions with the case writer, however, they mentioned three areas of concern.

First, there always seemed to be a few disputes over transfer prices of parts sold by the product divisions to the AM division. Whenever possible, by corporate policy, internal sales of parts were made at outside OEM market prices. If a part had been sold as an OEM part several years earlier, the original OEM market price was adjusted upwards for inflation to arrive at the sales price to the AM division. This procedure caused virtually no disputes. Problems occurred when the part being transferred was strictly an AM division part. That is, it was a part never sold by Abrams in the OEM market and for which there was neither a current OEM outside market price nor a former OEM market price that could be adjusted for inflation. Usually, such transfer price issues were resolved by the two divisions involved, but occasionally the vice president of finance was asked to arbitrate a dispute.

Second, top management felt that the product divisions too often tended to treat the AM division as a captive customer. For example, when the AM division and an outside OEM customer were placing competing demands on a specific manufacturing plant, it appeared that the plant often favoured the OEM customer because the OEM customer could take its business elsewhere, whereas the AM division could not purchase parts outside. Top management was not willing to let the AM division sell a competitor's product, feeling this would reflect adversely on the overall image of the company. The AM division was expected to convince the appropriate plant manager to undertake the manufacture of its parts needs.

Third, top management felt that both the AM division and the three product divisions carried excessive inventories most of the year. The vice president of planning said, 'Thank goodness we have a generous Christmas vacation policy here. At least the inventories get down to a reasonable level at year-end when our production volume is low because of a large number of employee holiday vacations.'

## Questions

1. Evaluate each of the concerns expressed by top management, and if necessary, make recommendations appropriate to the circumstances described in the case.
2. What is your overall evaluation of Abrams' management control system? Describe any strengths or weaknesses that you identified but did not include in answering the previous question. What changes, if any, would you recommend to top management?

# Case 1.3

# Enron *

**by Frank G.H. Hartmann**

One of the most striking examples of the role of management control systems in good and bad times is found in the Enron case. When this case unfolded, it shocked the world of accounting, control and governance. How could things have gone so wrong? Perhaps the most striking aspect of the Enron case is the speed with which things can go wrong after the systems have proved to be failing, as the following extract shows.[1]

## Enron formed after merger

*Enron was formed in 1985 following a merger between Houston Natural Gas and Omaha-based InterNorth. Kenneth Lay, who had been the chief executive officer (CEO) of Houston Natural Gas, became Enron's CEO and chairman, and quickly rebranded Enron into an energy trader and supplier. Deregulation of the energy markets allowed companies to place bets on future prices, and Enron was poised to take advantage.*

## Enron named America's most innovative company

*By 1993, Enron had set up a number of limited liability special purpose entities that allowed Enron to hide its liabilities, growing its stock price. Analysts were already criticizing Enron for 'swimming in debt', but the company continued to grow, developing a large network of natural gas pipelines, and eventually moving into the pulp and paper and water sectors. Enron was named 'America's Most Innovative Company' by Fortune for six consecutive years between 1996 and 2001.*

## Misleading financial accounts

*Creative accounting allowed Enron to appear more powerful on paper than it really was. Special purpose entities – subsidiaries that have a single purpose and that did not need to be included in Enron's balance sheet – were used to hide risky investment activities and financial losses. Forensic accounting later determined that many of Enron's recorded assets and profits were inflated, and in some cases, completely fraudulent and non-existent. Some of the company's debts and losses were recorded in offshore entities, remaining absent from Enron's financial statements.*

*During the late 1990s and into the early 2000s, more and more special purpose vehicles were created that allowed the company to keep debts off the books and inflate assets. These entities, along with other accounting loopholes and poor financial reporting, let Enron ultimately hide billions in debt from special deals and projects.*

---

* This case was written by Professor Frank G.H. Hartmann, Radboud University.

[1] Folger, J. (2011) The Enron collapse: a look back, 1 December. Available at: http://www.investopedia.com/financial-edge/1211/the-enron-collapse-a-look-back.aspx (accessed 14 June 2013).

## Sell-off

*In August 2001, shortly after the company achieved $100 billion in revenues, then-CEO Jeff Skilling unexpectedly resigned, prompting Wall Street to question the health of the company. Kenneth Lay once again took the helm, and both Lay and Skilling, in addition to other Enron executives, began selling large amounts of Enron stock as prices continued to drop – from a high of about $90.00 per share earlier in the year, to less than a dollar. The US Securities and Exchange Commission (SEC) opened an investigation.*

## 2 December 2001

*Less than a week after a white knight takeover bid from Dynegy was called off, Enron filed for bankruptcy protection. The company had more than $38 billion in outstanding debts. In the following months, the US Justice Department initiated a criminal investigation into Enron's bankruptcy. Several Enron executives and Enron's auditor firm, Arthur Andersen, have since been indicted for a variety of charges, including obstruction of justice for shredding documents and conspiracy to commit wire and securities fraud, and some have been sentenced to prison.*

## Questions

1. Identify the ways in which Enron was not on the right track towards reaching its mission, goals and strategies.
2. What are the most important factors of this control problem?
3. Could an appropriate management control system have avoided this problem?

# Case 1.4

# Wal-Mart Stores, Inc.*

### by Vijay Govindarajan, Julie B. Lang and Suraj Prabhu

Founded by Sam Walton, the first Wal-Mart store opened in Rogers, Arkansas, in 1962. Seventeen years later, annual sales topped $1 billion. By the end of January 2005, Wal-Mart Stores, Inc. (Wal-Mart) was the world's largest retailer, with $288 billion in sales. (See Exhibit 1 for comparative financial data.) In 1995, Wal-Mart sold no grocery; by 2005, the company was market leader among supermarkets in the United States. Wal-Mart was the largest private-sector employer in the world. The information technology that powered Wal-Mart's supply chain and logistics was the most powerful, next only to the computer capability of the Pentagon. The company owned more than 20 aircraft, which were used by managers to travel to its stores in far-flung locations. The number of miles flown by Wal-Mart managers

---

* This case was written by Professor Vijay Govindarajan, Professor Julie B. Lang (T'93) and Suraj Prabhu (T'06) of the Tuck School of Business at Dartmouth. 

**EXHIBIT 1** Comparative financial data on selected companies

| | Five-year average: 1999–2004 | | | | |
|---|---|---|---|---|---|
| | Wal-Mart | Home Depot | Kroger | Costco | Target |
| Return on equity (percentage) | 21.2 | 19.7 | 20.1 | 13.4 | 17.3 |
| Sales growth (percentage) | 11.6 | 13.7 | 4.5 | 11.9 | 6.8 |
| Operating income growth (percentage) | 11.1 | 15.9 | (13.8) | 10.0 | 13.3 |
| | 2004 data | | | | |
| Sales ($bn) | 288.2 | 73.1 | 56.4 | 48.1 | 46.8 |
| As percentage of sales: | | | | | |
| Cost of goods sold | 76.3 | 66.6 | 74.7 | 87.5 | 68.7 |
| Gross margin | 22.7 | 33.4 | 25.3 | 12.5 | 31.3 |
| Selling and administration | 17.8 | 22.6 | 20.0 | 9.6 | 20.9 |
| Operating income | 5.9 | 10.8 | 1.5 | 2.9 | 7.7 |
| Net income | 3.6 | 6.8 | (0.2) | 1.8 | 6.8 |
| Inventory turnover | 7.5 | 4.8 | 9.8 | 11.3 | 5.9 |
| Return on equity (percentage) | 23.2 | 22.1 | (2.5) | 12.8 | 15.6 |

in the company-owned aircraft would place Wal-Mart on a par with a medium-sized commercial airline. Wal-Mart had the largest privately owned satellite communication network in the United States and broadcast more television than any network TV.[1]

Wal-Mart's winning strategy in the US was based on selling branded products at low cost. Each week, about 138 million customers visited a Wal-Mart store somewhere in the world. The company employed more than 1.6 million associates (Wal-Mart's term for employees) worldwide through more than 3,700 stores in the United States and more than 1,600 units in Mexico, Puerto Rico, Canada, Argentina, Brazil, China, Korea, Germany and the United Kingdom. (The first international store opened in Mexico City in 1991.) Wal-Mart also obtained a 38 per cent controlling share in the Japanese retail chain Seiyu in order to capture a slice of the world's second largest market, estimated at $1.3 trillion.

In 2002, Wal-Mart was presented with the Ron Brown Award for Corporate Leadership, a presidential award that recognizes companies for outstanding achievement in employee and community relations. In 2004, *Fortune* magazine placed Wal-Mart in top spot on its Most Admired Companies list for the second year in a row.

By 2005, Wal-Mart held an 8.9 per cent retail store market share in the United States. Put simply, of every $100 that Americans spent in retail stores, $8.9 was spent in Wal-Mart. Procter & Gamble, Clorox and Johnson & Johnson were among its nearly 3,000 suppliers. Though Wal-Mart may have been the top customer for consumer product manufacturers, it deliberately ensured it did not become too dependent on any one supplier; no single vendor constituted more than 4 per cent of its overall purchase volume. In order to drive up supply chain efficiencies, Wal-Mart had also persuaded its suppliers to have electronic 'hook-ups' with its stores and adapt to the latest supply chain technologies, like RFID, which could increase monitoring and management of inventory.

Wal-Mart used a 'saturation' strategy for store expansion. The standard was to be able to drive from a distribution centre to a store within a day. A distribution centre was strategically placed so that it

[1] Wal around the world, *The Economist*, 6 December 2001; Can Wal-Mart conquer markets outside the US?, *Financial Times*, 7 January 2003.

could eventually serve 150–200 Wal-Mart stores within a day. Stores were built as far away as possible but still within a day's drive of the distribution centre; the area then was filled back (or saturated back) to the distribution centre. Each distribution centre operated 24 hours a day using laser-guided conveyer belts and cross-docking techniques that received goods on one side while simultaneously filling orders on the other. Wal-Mart's distribution system was so efficient that it incurred only 1.3 per cent of sales as distribution costs compared to 3.5 per cent for its nearest competitor.

The company owned a fleet of more than 6,100 trailer trucks and employed 7,600-plus truck drivers, making it one of the largest trucking companies in the United States. (Most competitors outsourced trucking.) Wal-Mart had implemented a satellite network system that allowed information to be shared between the company's wide network of stores, distribution centres and suppliers. The system consolidated orders for goods, enabling the company to buy full truckload quantities without incurring the inventory costs.

In its early years, Wal-Mart's strategy was to build large discount stores in small rural towns. By contrast, competitors such as Kmart focused on large towns with populations greater than 50,000. Wal-Mart's marketing strategy was to guarantee 'everyday low prices' as a way to pull in customers. Traditional discount retailers relied on advertised 'sales'.

## Management control system

Each store constituted an investment centre and was evaluated on its profits relative to its inventory investments. Data from more than 5,300 individual stores on items such as sales, expenses, and profit and loss were collected, analysed and transmitted electronically on a real-time basis, rapidly revealing how a particular region, district, store, department within a store or item within a department was performing. The information enabled the company to reduce the likelihood of stock-outs and the need for markdowns on slow-moving stock, and to maximize inventory turnover. The data from 'outstanding' performers among 5,300 stores were used to improve operations in 'problem' stores.

One of the significant costs for retailers was shoplifting, or pilferage. Wal-Mart addressed this issue by instituting a policy that shared 50 per cent of the savings from decreases in a store's pilferage in a particular store, as compared to the industry standard, among that store's employees through store incentive plans.

Early in Wal-Mart's history, Sam Walton implemented a process requiring store managers to fill out 'Best Yesterday' ledgers. These relatively straightforward forms tracked daily sales performance against the numbers from one year before. Recalled Walton, 'We were really trying to become the very best operators – the most professional managers – that we could. . . . I have always had the soul of an operator, someone who wants to make things work well, then better, then the best they possibly can.'[2] His organization was really a 'store within a store', encouraging department managers to be accountable and giving them an incentive to be creative. Successful experiments were recognized and applied to other stores. One example was the 'people greeter', an associate who welcomed shoppers as they entered the store. These greeters not only provided a personal service, their presence served to reduce pilferage. The '10-Foot Attitude' was another customer service approach Walton encouraged. When the founder visited his stores, he asked associates to make a pledge, telling them, 'I want you to promise that whenever you come within 10 feet of a customer, you will look him in the eye, greet him, and ask him if you can help him.'[3]

In return for employees' loyalty and dedication, Walton began offering profit sharing in 1971. 'Every associate that had been with us for at least one year, and who worked at least 1,000 hours a year, was eligible for it,' he explained. 'Using a formula based on profit growth, we contribute a percentage

[2] Joan, M. (2002) *What Management Is: How it Works and Why it's Everyone's Business.* New York: Free Press, p. 189.

[3] http://www.walmart.com

of every eligible associate's wages to his or her plan, which the associate can take when they leave the company, either in cash or in Wal-Mart stock.'[4] In fiscal 2005, Wal-Mart's annual company contribution totalled $756 million.

Wal-Mart also instituted several other policies and programmes for its associates: incentive bonuses, a discount stock purchase plan, promotion from within, pay rises based on performance not seniority, and an open-door policy.

Sam Walton, the founder of Wal-Mart, believed in being frugal. He drove an old beat-up truck and flew economy class, despite being a billionaire. He instilled frugality as part of Wal-Mart's DNA.

## Questions

1 What is Wal-Mart's strategy? What is the basis on which Wal-Mart builds its competitive advantage?

2 How does Wal-Mart's management control system help execute the firm's strategy?

*Sources: The Quest for Global Dominance: Transforming Global Presence into Global Competitive Advantage* by Vijay Govindarajan and Anil K. Gupta, © 2001 by John Wiley & Sons, Inc. Chapter 4. *What Management Is: How it works and Why it's Everyone's Business* by Joan Magretta, © 2002 The Free Press. *Sam Walton: Made in America, My Story* by Sam Walton, © 1992 Doubleday. http://www.walmart.com.

---

[4] Walton, S. (1992) *Sam Walton: Made in America, My Story.* New York: Doubleday, p. 132.

# Case 1.5

# Southwest Airlines Corporation*

**by Vijay Govindarajan, Julie B. Lang and Suraj Prabhu**

By January 2005, Southwest Airlines Corporation's (Southwest) year-end results marked 32 consecutive years of profitability, a record unmatched in the airline industry. Southwest, which was incorporated in Texas, commenced customer service on 18 June 1971, with three Boeing 737 aircraft serving three Texas cities: Dallas, Houston and San Antonio. In 2004, it boasted a fleet of 417 Boeing 737 jets and provided service to 60 airports in 31 states throughout the United States. Southwest was well entrenched as the nation's low-fare, high-customer-satisfaction airline. (Refer to Exhibit 1 for five-year financial highlights.)

Southwest had the lowest operating-cost structure in the domestic airline industry, and consistently offered the lowest and simplest fares. In 2004, the airline had 31,000 employees and generated total operating revenues of $6.5 billion from a passenger load factor of 69.5 per cent. Its stock exchange symbol was LUV, representing Southwest's home at Dallas Love Field, as well as the theme of its employee and customer relationships.

---

* This case was written by Professor Vijay Govindarajan, Julie B. Lang (T'93) and Suraj Prabhu (T'06) of the Tuck School of Business at Dartmouth. 

**EXHIBIT 1** Comparative financial data on selected companies

| | Five-year average: 1999–2004 | | | | |
|---|---|---|---|---|---|
| | Southwest | United | American | Delta | JetBlue |
| Return on equity (percentage) | 10.91 | NA | NA | −85.33 | NA |
| Sales growth (percentage) | 6.64 | −1.88 | −1.14 | 1.01 | NA |
| | 2004 data | | | | |
| Sales ($bn) | 6.5 | 16.4 | 14.3 | 18.6 | 1.3 |
| *As percentage of sales:* | | | | | |
| Cost of goods sold | 68.8 | 77.3 | 98.1 | 81.1 | 63.3 |
| Gross margin | 29.2 | 22.7 | 1.9 | 18.9 | 33.5 |
| Operating income | 8.5 | −5.2 | −23.3 | −0.8 | 9.0 |
| Net income | 4.8 | −10.5 | −36.4 | −4.1 | 3.8 |
| Return on equity (percentage) | 6.6 | NA | NA | NA | 5.3 |

In 2005, for the ninth year in a row, *Fortune* magazine recognized Southwest Airlines as the most admired airline in the world and, among all industries, listed Southwest Airlines as number five among America's Top Ten Most Admired Corporations. Since 2002, *Business Ethics* magazine has listed Southwest Airlines in its '100 Best Corporate Citizens', a list that ranks public companies based on their corporate service to various stakeholder groups. In 2005, the American Customer Satisfaction Index (ACSI) recognized Southwest Airlines as leading the industry in customer satisfaction, and *InsideFlyer* magazine awarded Southwest for best Customer Service, best bonus promotion and best award redemptions in 2004.

## The Southwest difference

Southwest did not employ the 'hub-and-spoke' approach used by other major airlines, such as United, American and Delta. Instead, its approach was short haul and medium haul and point-to-point (e.g., Dallas to Houston, Los Angeles to Phoenix). As a result, about 80 per cent of its passengers flew non-stop, the overall average passenger trip length was 758 miles and the average airfare $91.15. Southwest had no assigned seats, paid its crews by trip, and used less congested airports (e.g., Baltimore instead of Washington's Dulles or Reagan; Manchester, NH, instead of Boston, MA). About 60 per cent of Southwest's passenger revenue was generated by online bookings via southwest.com. PhoCusWright reported that southwest.com was the number-one airline website by revenue and Nielsen/Net Rating identified it as the largest airline site in terms of unique visitors. In 2005, Southwest continued to push its online presence and launched several automation services, including Ding!, a desktop application that provided exclusive deals.

Southwest consistently sought out ways to improve its efficiencies and pass on the cost savings to its passengers. In 2004, Southwest had reduced the headcount per aircraft to 74 from 85 in 2003. It hedged about 85 per cent of its fuel and oil needs, and as a result saved about $455 million. It entered new airports after a process of diligence and with a sense of commitment to the people it served (in its entire history, Southwest has pulled out of only five airports).

---

1 Joan, M. (2002) *What Management Is: How it Works and Why it's Everyone's Business.* New York: Free Press, p. 199.

2 Freiberg, K. and Freiberg, J. (1996) *NUTS! Southwest Airlines' Crazy Recipe for Business and Personal Success.* Austin: Bard Press, Inc., p. 65.

Southwest pilots were among the only pilots of major US airlines who did not belong to a national union. National union rules limited the number of hours pilots could fly. But Southwest's pilots were unionized independently, allowing them to fly far more hours than pilots at other airlines.

Other workers at Southwest were nationally unionized (total workforce unionization was at 81 per cent in 2005), but their contracts were flexible enough to allow them to jump in and help out, regardless of the task at hand. From the time a plane landed until it was ready for takeoff took approximately 20–25 minutes at Southwest, and required a ground crew of four plus two people at the gate. By comparison, turnaround time at United Airlines was closer to 35 minutes and required a ground crew of 12 plus three gate agents.

CEO Herb Kelleher, who founded Southwest, was deeply committed to a philosophy of putting employees first. 'If they're happy, satisfied, dedicated, and energetic, they'll take real good care of the customers. When the customers are happy, they come back. And that makes the shareholders happy.'[1] Southwest's walls were filled with photographs of its employees. More than 1,000 married couples (2,000 employees) worked for the airline. Southwest employees were among the highest paid in the industry and the company enjoyed low employee turnover relative to the airline industry as a whole.

Southwest's culture of hard work, high energy, fun, local autonomy and creativity was reinforced through training at its University of People, encouragement of in-flight contests, and recognition of personal initiative.

Being in the people business meant a rigorous approach to hiring new employees. In 2004, Southwest reviewed 225,895 resumes and hired 1,706 new employees. The company's hiring process was somewhat unique: peers screened candidates and conducted interviews, pilots hired pilots, and gate agents hired gate agents. To better understand what the company sought in candidates, Southwest interviewed its top employees in each job function (e.g., pilots, gate agents, baggage handlers, ground crew) and identified their common strengths, then used these profiles to identify top candidates during the interview process. Southwest hired for attitude as much as aptitude. Noted CEO Kelleher, 'We want people who do things well, with laughter and grace.'[2]

Southwest initiated the first profit-sharing plan in the US airline industry in 1974 and offered profit sharing to its employees every year since then. Through this plan, employees owned about 10 per cent of the company stock. For fiscal 2003, Southwest offered its employees $126 million in profit sharing.

## Questions

1 What is Southwest's strategy? What is the basis on which Southwest builds its competitive advantage?

2 How does Southwest's management control system help execute the firm's strategy?

*Sources:* www.southwest.com; *What Management Is: How it Works and Why it's Everyone's Business,* by Joan Magretta, © 2002 The Free Press. *NUTS! Southwest Airlines' Crazy Recipe for Business and Personal Success,* by Kevin Freiberg and Jackie Freiberg, © 1996 Bard Press, Inc. Southwest aims east (condensed), case study written by Steven Sullivan under the supervision of Paul W. Harris, University of Virginia Darden School, Case no. UVA-M-0464. The talent myth, *New Yorker,* 22 July 2002.

# Chapter 2

# Mission, goals and strategies

## Learning objectives

After reading this chapter, you should be able to:

1. Explain the difference between the stakeholder and the shareholder views.
2. Define corporate governance and discuss how it might influence the management control system of an organization.
3. Define corporate social responsibility, and discuss if and why you think organizations should work with it, or not.
4. Discuss what types of goal an organization might have and how they are related.
5. Describe different forms of strategies.
6. Describe the logic behind contingency theory, and exemplify how factors such as the environment, strategy and technology might influence management control system design in the organization.

## Real world vignette: Boeing 737 MAX

In October 2018 a flight from Jakarta crashed in the Java Sea soon after takeoff, leaving 189 passengers and crew dead. Only a few months later the same thing happened to a plane from Addis Ababa, which also crashed just a few minutes after takeoff. This time 157 people died. Both planes were of the same model, the Boeing 737 MAX. Both accidents are also believed to have been linked to automated commands from a malfunctioning manoeuvring system.

Because of the accidents, and the problems with the manoeuvring system, all Boeing 737 MAX planes were grounded and not allowed to fly as of March 2019. $240 billion has been mentioned as an estimation of the total cost for Boeing, which includes a huge loss of goodwill for the company due to these tragic events.

It is difficult to determine how this could happen, but we are going to have a look at the arguments of Stan Sorscher.[1] He is a former Boeing engineer and a union representative; an engineer with an interest in management control systems. Sorscher blames what he calls the cost-cutting culture that was introduced in the Boeing organization in the late 1990s; a culture that favours cost-cutting initiatives from top managers, creating shareholder value for the owners and where engineers identifying problems are seen as making trouble, according to Sorscher. He also claims that it is the opposite of a culture built on productivity, innovation, safety and quality, and compares it with the culture Boeing had in the mid-1990s.

The old 'quality' culture focused, according to Sorscher, on increased productivity through the employees' engagement and initiative, strong integration between teams, as well as between employees and managers, and a strong customer focus. The new culture, on the other hand, focuses on top managers and shareholders instead of employees and customers. Sorscher also claims that the cost-cutting culture very well may be suited to suppliers of commodities like Wal-Mart and Amazon, but not to a high-end manufacturer of airplanes.

## Introduction

In Chapter 1, we defined a management control system as comprising a combination of control practices designed and implemented by top managers to increase the probability that lower-level managers and employees will behave in ways consistent with the organization's mission, goals and strategies. But in order to properly analyse if a certain behaviour is consistent with mission, goals and strategies, we need to understand how these come about. Any mission, goal or strategy needs to be related to what the purpose of the organizations is and for whom it exists. Not surprisingly, this depends on whom you ask, but in a market economy there are basically two major views on this topic: the *shareholder view* and the *stakeholder view*. According to the shareholder (or owner) view, organizations exist to satisfy the goals of their owners, or as Milton Friedman expressed it:

> *. . . there is one and only one social responsibility of business [. . .] to use its resources and engage in activities designed to increase profits so long as it stays within the rules of the game, which is to say, engages in open and free competition without deception and fraud.*[2]

---

[1] Adolph, C. (2019)SPEEA engineer breaks silence on Boeing's MAX 737. Read this letter. Available at: https://www.kuow.org/stories/boeing-engineers-break-silence-on-max-737-read-this-letter (accessed 25 September 2019).

[2] Friedman, M. and Friedman, R.D. (1962) *Capitalism and Freedom*. Chicago, IL: University of Chicago Press.

However, advocates of the stakeholder view claim that organizations exist to satisfy the goals of a broader set of groups, including employees, customers, suppliers, lenders and society.

The sometimes rather intense debate between shareholder and stakeholder proponents has been going on for a very long time; for instance, the quote above from Milton Friedman is from 1962! But even though the debate has been intense – Milton Friedman at one point accused his opponents of 'preaching pure and unadulterated socialism'[3] – it is not necessarily a dichotomy where you need to fully adhere to one of the views.

For example, it is not at all unusual that long-term owners realize how important different stakeholder groups are for the survival and long-term success of the company. So even if the owners are considered the ultimate stakeholder, top managers may still act in a way that takes the needs of several stakeholders into account. Still, the difference between a short-term shareholder view and a stakeholder view is often significant, and so is its impact on the design and use of management control systems in companies.

To some extent the shareholder and stakeholder views tend to be linked to ownership structures, and the shareholder view in particular is often linked to the stock market. For companies on the stock market, keeping the share price up is usually a top priority for top management. One possible explanation for this is that a low share price creates a higher risk for a hostile takeover, something that top managers want to avoid. A hostile takeover means that an owner that is not wanted by top management or the major present owners – it may even be a competitor who wants to close down the company – buys shares in the company with the purpose to gain control of it.

The shareholder view has dominated over the stakeholder view for most of this century. One expression of this is the above described change from a customer and employee focus to a shareholder focus in Boeing, a change that we have seen in many other organizations. But there are also indications that this may be changing again, not least with regard to the increasing focus on climate change and sustainability. Another strong indication pointing in this direction was a Statement on the Purpose of a Corporation released by the Business Roundtable in America. In August 2019 this Roundtable, consisting of CEOs from many leading American companies, from Apple to Wal-Mart, issued this Statement, which was signed by 181 CEOs. It ended as follows:

> *Each of our stakeholders is essential. We commit to deliver value to all of them, for the future success of our companies, our communities and our country.*[4]

## The shareholder view

The shareholder view implies that organizations exist to fulfil the demands of the owners, which often include a high return on the owners' investment at as low a risk as possible. This view provides the owners with a special status compared to the other stakeholders and the arguments for this include those listed below.

- The original owners founded the organization and only the owners have the legal power to close it down as long it obeys the laws where it operates. The owners also have the formal power to impose their will on the organization, for instance regarding strategic direction. Legally the owners thus have a special status in most countries.
- The owners take a higher risk than the other stakeholders since the owners can claim only the residual. This means that the owners will get any money from the company only when everybody else – employees, suppliers, lenders, tax authorities – have had their 'share'.

[3] Friedman, M. (1970) The social responsibility of business is to increase its profits, *New York Times Magazine*, 13 September.

[4] https://www.businessroundtable.org/business-roundtable-redefines-the-purpose-of-a-corporation-to-promote-an-economy-that-serves-all-americans (accessed 25 September 2019).

**FIGURE 2.1** The shareholder view

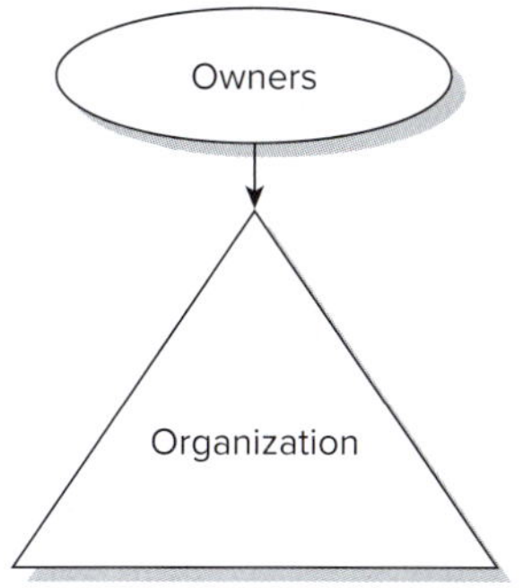


- The company cannot survive in the long run if the owners get no return on their investment. This means that all the other stakeholders are also dependent on the owners getting a fair return.

If we go back a hundred years or more, the situation concerning ownership was very different to what we often see in today's organizations. In those days, the owner was normally also the manager, which meant that the owner was in direct control over the organization. However, in the early twentieth century this started to change with a development that is often referred to as the separation of ownership and control.[5] The owners, especially in the United States, started to invest in companies through the stock market while the managers of the same companies often were people hired to do the job.

In agency theory[6] this relationship between the owners and the manager is referred to as the principal–agent relationship, where the owners are the principals and the managers the agents. The principal delegates the authority to manage the company to the agent. This was a very practical solution for companies with a dispersed ownership, as well as for owners with interests in several companies. However, it did also pose a problem since the owners (principals) could no longer be sure that the managers (agents) worked in their best interest. Were the managers not more likely to make decisions that were in their own best interest, rather than in the owner's best interest? This problem is commonly referred to as the principal–agent problem.

Today the principal–agent situation is common in most larger organizations, especially if they are listed on the stock exchange. This means that it is in the interest of the owners to address this problem in one way or another. This may be done in many different ways, and these may be more or less successful, but regardless of how this is being done it is usually referred to as being about 'corporate governance'.

## Corporate governance

Corporate governance relates to the shareholder view; it deals with how owners and owner representatives of different kinds act to influence the organization to work in the best interest of the owners. Corporate governance may include a wide range of activities, from extensive communication between the owners and the managers, to owners just selling off their shares when they no longer believe in the company. The concept of corporate governance began to attract attention in the 1980s, grew stronger in the 1990s and became a major force in the 2000s.

One important reason why corporate governance and the owners in general have received increased attention in recent decades is probably that owners look different now compared with how they looked

---

[5] Berle, A.A. and Means, G.C. (1932) *The Modern Corporation and Private Property*. New York, Macmillan.

[6] Agency theory will be discussed more thoroughly in Chapter 3 as well as Chapter 10.

a few decades ago. Perhaps the most important owner type in many countries today is pension and mutual funds, whose fund managers and analysts constantly seek to get the best return for their clients. A focus on daily indexes of value development, with incentive programmes linked to the index, does quite often create a rather short-term focus among these analysts. And even if many fund managers communicate with the top management in the companies they invest in, they probably do not have as good insight into the organizations as do traditional owner types, such as families and investment companies.

Some even claim[7] that we have seen a change from industrial capitalism to financial capitalism, implying that corporate governance shaped by financial actors and financial markets has established a dominating financial logic. At the most extreme, the organization becomes just a black box in the eyes of the owners, where the owners' only concern is that the organization delivers a return on their investment. The contrast with more traditional owner types is strong, where owner families develop a very good understanding of their organization and its business over decades.

The current logic of the financial markets places high demands on the organizations, their reporting and internal control. These demands have, in fact, increased significantly in the aftermath of the accounting scandals of the early 1990s, particularly those involving Enron and WorldCom. Because these scandals mainly appeared in the United States, that is also where this development originated. The major feature in the development is the federal law called the Sarbanes–Oxley Act, commonly known as SOX, passed in 2002. The purpose of the act is to give better protection to stock owners by strengthening the corporate governance, financial reporting, auditor independence and internal control in companies.

While SOX certainly has many supporters, it has also been the subject of heavy criticism because of the considerable costs this regulatory framework imposes on companies. The act is not only of interest for US companies but, indeed, also for many other companies, because all companies listed on the New York Stock Exchange must follow it. Moreover, this development has also reached Europe directly as many European countries have issued similar laws or codes. Some companies have even decided to leave the stock exchange because they want to avoid these frameworks and all the work they involve.

Corporate governance involves a large number of different means that can be used by the owners, or by others in the interest of the owners, in order to govern the company. Some of the more common ones are described below.

- *The board of directors:* The board is appointed by the owners and is the formal channel for the owners to govern the organization. Boards function differently in different countries, but usually a main task for the board is to hire and fire the CEO. The board usually also makes important strategic decisions and has an ongoing dialogue with the CEO.
- *Financial reports*: A stock listed company must supply quarterly financial reports, usually according to the accounting standard IFRS. The reports present the profitability and financial situation of the organization. These reports are usually highly anticipated by the financial markets and have a major impact on selling and buying decisions among actors in the market.
- *Auditing and internal control*: Practically all organizations of a certain size must engage auditing firms to audit their financial reporting. Stock listed companies also often have to follow a framework for internal control, depending on where they are listed. The purpose of auditing and internal control is mainly to secure the quality of the financial reporting, and the demand for this has increased significantly in the past decade following the aforementioned accounting scandals.
- *Incentive programmes*: different forms of incentive and bonus programmes are frequently used to align the goals of the owners with those of managers. The idea is basically that if managers make more money by making the owners happy, they will do so. However, how effective incentives are is heavily under debate and we return to this topic in Chapter 10.

---

[7] Davis, G. F. (2009). The rise and fall of finance and the end of the society of organizations, *Academy of Management Perspectives*, 23(3): 27–44.

- *Investor meetings*: Just like privately held firms, stock listed companies often arrange meetings with representatives from important investors, including fund managers and analysts. The purpose of these meetings is for the top managers to be able to explain better the organization's situation to the investors and for the investors to explain better their expectations of the organization. One important function of these meetings can be to serve as a powerful reminder of the interest of the owners and for the investors to gain a permanent presence in the minds of the managers.
- *Media*: The expansion of business journalism is one important part of the rise of financial capitalism, as it enables shareholders to be better informed about the company they have invested in. What the media report about an organization is, therefore, extremely important for both the organization and its investors. A problem is, of course, that the quality of the media's reporting varies and sometimes is perhaps formulated to sell papers rather than to better inform investors.

A very interesting question is how the corporate governance discussed here influences the management control systems and internal affairs of organizations. There is also an extremely lively debate on this and, while some claim that corporate governance and a focus on the owners make organizations more effective, others claim that this instead makes them so short term in focus that it actually destroys value in the long run – which may be the case at Boeing as described in the Real World Vignette. Unfortunately, research does not have much to offer here to clarify the situation, because we know far too little about the topic. But something we do know is that managers in countries where the stock exchange dominates, such as the UK and the US, do seem to be more short term in outlook, and that financial incentives seem to encourage earnings management and manipulation of accounting numbers. However, we know less about whether or not these effects, in turn, will hurt the long-term performance of the organization.

What we can see in Figure 2.2 is that Europe's largest stock exchange, the London Stock Exchange, enjoyed remarkable development from 1985 to 2000 (in fact, it was good from the mid-1970s). The index increased steadily during this period. However, since 2000 the development has been a much rockier road. Given the number of factors that influence value creation this cannot be considered evidence of how corporate governance influences shareholder value. However, it is certainly not an indicator that corporate governance increases shareholder value, since the index development has been very weak during the time when corporate governance has been most pronounced.

**FIGURE 2.2** London Stock Exchange development 1985–2019

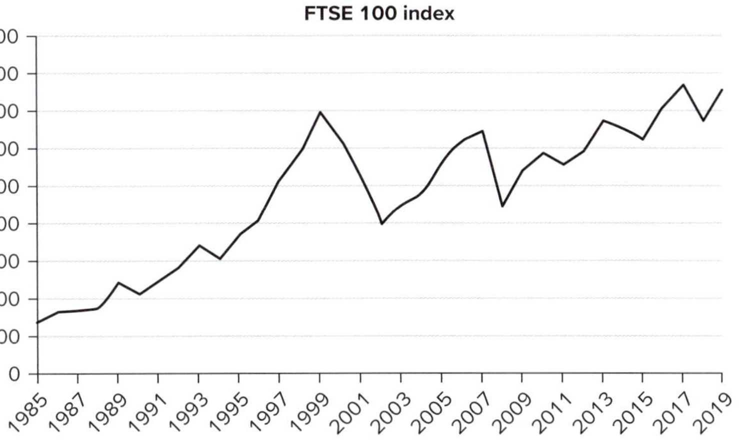

## The stakeholder view

The stakeholder view implies that organizations exist to fulfil the demands not just of the owners, but of several stakeholder groups. This means that no stakeholder permanently holds a special status as more important than the others. However, this does not exclude the possibility that some stakeholders, at least for the moment, are more important for the organization than others.

Some of the arguments for the stakeholder view are listed below.

- The organization is not just dependent on the owners for its survival and success, but on all the different stakeholder groups. Even if the owners are the only ones that have the legal right to close down the organization, if the customers stop buying from the organization, if no one wants to work for it or if no one will lend money to it, the result is very likely to be the same.
- It is ethically questionable to systematically favour one group over the others.
- Ensuring that stakeholder groups such as customers and employees are happy will also lead to higher profitability, since happy customers come back, and happy employees are more motivated.
- Considering all stakeholders is a more long-term view and thus more sustainable, especially if society is considered a stakeholder.

An organization's stakeholders are individuals and organizations who, in one way or another, contribute to and benefit from the organization in question. These groups of individuals or organizations have often been defined as follows.

- *Owners:* Among other things, owners invest capital in the organization and expect to get a return on their investment.
- *Customers:* Pay the organization in order to get products or services in return.
- *Employees:* Devote their time and competency, and in return they get paid and, hopefully, have a stimulating job.
- *Suppliers:* Provide the organization with products, material and services in return for payment.
- *Lenders:* Like the owners, the lenders supply the organization with capital, although in the form of loans, and in return they receive interest.
- *Society:* Society supplies the organization with infrastructure, education for future employees, protection from crime etc., and in return expects the organization to follow laws and regulations, pay tax, provide jobs, and so on.

**FIGURE 2.3** The stakeholder view

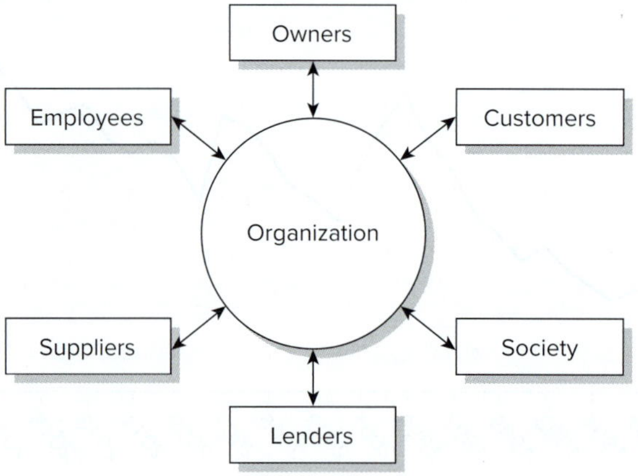

This group of stakeholders has tended to expand over time, and some also include what they call secondary stakeholders, such as the media and special interest groups. These groups do not necessarily interact directly with the organization, but rather through the primary stakeholders such as actual or potential owners, customers or employees. This does not mean that the secondary stakeholders are less important. A secondary stakeholder such as the media might very well be of major importance if it has substantial influence over the primary stakeholders.

## Corporate social responsibility

Just like corporate governance, CSR is an old phenomenon that has gained a lot of attention this century. It could be seen as a reaction to the strong shareholder and corporate governance trends, but may also be explained by changes in society. One such change is globalization, which has had positive effects such as increased communication and decreased poverty, but also has had negative effects. One such is that global companies are less influenced by governmental actions – for instance, concerning working conditions or environmental effects – since they can move their operations if they wish to avoid these.

The other change is that the pressure from stakeholders and society has increased in this respect. Some primary and secondary stakeholders that have put an increased pressure on companies in this way include consumers, business partners, national governments and NGOs. NGOs are non-governmental and non-profit organizations that strive for a certain goal such as, in the case of Greenpeace, protecting the environment. NGOs became key drivers in the development of CSR, often acting like a type of auditor evaluating companies' behaviour in this respect.

Even the United Nations has played a role in increasing the pressure on companies to work with CSR. One example was when the former secretary general of the UN, Kofi Annan, in 1999 launched the Global Compact initiative with the following statement:

> *We have to choose between a global market driven only by calculations of short-term profit, and one which has a human face. Between a world which condemns a quarter of the human race to starvation and squalor, and one which offers everyone at least a chance of prosperity, in a healthy environment. Between a selfish free-for-all in which we ignore the fate of the losers, and a future in which the strong and successful accept their responsibilities, showing global vision and leadership.*[8]

The purpose of the initiative was to make companies more aware of their social responsibilities regarding issues on human rights, labour standards, environment and corruption.

The pressure also increased the media's attention on companies' role in society, and triggered greater examination of multinational and global companies' impact in less developed countries. CSR also soon became a lucrative business, seeing a large number of consultants and experts emerge. This group also became vital for the development, not least in the way they formulated the rhetoric around and arguments for working with CSR. Basically, there are three types of arguments for working with CSR:

1 *Ethical:* It is fair to other stakeholder groups besides the owners, and it is more sustainable.
2 *Business:* It is good business to have happy employees, and to offer the customers sustainable products and services.
3 *Fashion:* Everybody else seems to do it, so we must not be left behind.

Early on, CSR was often motivated by ethical concerns, and it was also often seen as being in conflict with profitability and the owners' interest in the way Milton Friedman described. But when the consultants became more involved, the rhetoric started to change in the direction that CSR was good for the business and a prerequisite for making a good profit. With this purpose it is often referred to as strategic CSR or creating shared value (CSV), but it has also become a fashion as almost every company of a certain size discuss CSR or corresponding concepts on their web pages.

[8] UN Secretary General, Kofi Annan, proposes Global Compact in address to World Economic Forum in Davos, 1 February 1999.

However, what CSR really is about is far from clear, although one common definition is that it is about organizations' voluntary concern about social and environmental issues. It is about taking more action than the organization has to in order not to harm its own or suppliers' employees, people whose environment is affected by the organization or other groups affected by the organization in some way.

In practice the CSR work in organizations often includes a number of formal and informal tools such as those listed below.

- *Code of conduct*: A document that clarifies the corporate view on what is appropriate conduct in different situations. This is often used not only with employees, but also towards suppliers.
- *Sustainability reporting*: Public reporting, often following the global reporting initiative, on performance in social and environmental aspects.
- *Internal reporting channels*: Whistleblowing or ethical hotlines whereby employees can report on behaviour not in line with corporate policy.
- *Culture and values*: The prevailing values among managers and employees often have a greater impact on their behaviour than written rules.
- *Personal example*: How top managers behave often has a major impact on values and behaviour among employees.
- *Storytelling*: One important tool in shaping values is often the telling of stories in an organization. The stories often refer to how a certain individual – a top manager or perhaps the founder of the organization – behaved in a certain situation.
- *Training*: Often compulsory training programmes are used to inform managers and employees.
- *Intranet*: The intranet is often used in order to inform and influence employees.

Equally important is how the organization communicates to stakeholders, the media and the public what it does. In fact, sometimes CSR is accused of being more about communicating a positive image of the organization's CSR activities and less about the actual activities. This highlights the similarity with financial reporting, and the tension between what is reported externally and the internal control, in the sense that reporting a good financial performance does not necessarily imply a good performance in reality. There is always a great risk of window dressing in reporting, regardless of whether it is financial reporting, CSR reporting or something else.

**Real World Example:** The Volkswagen emissions scandal, Dieselgate, is one of the best-known examples of when a company tries to look much better than it actually is. In order to understand how this could happen, we may have to go back to 2007, when Martin Winterkorn became CEO of the Volkswagen Group. He put up the very ambitious goal to make VW the biggest car producer in the world. This meant, among other things, that VW had to grow in the US market where it was quite small, since the US market was the largest in the world.

The plan to expand on the US market met with two problems. The first was that Americans preferred petrol, whereas VW competed mainly with diesel cars. The second was that emissions requirements in the United States were much tougher than in Europe. The solution to this problem was to launch a campaign together with other diesel car producers, called Clean Diesel. The idea was to make the emissions from diesel cars so low that they would appear as a better alternative than petrol cars.

One idea considered by VW was to use the BlueTEC technology used by Mercedes, in order to make the cleanest diesel possible. However, Winterkorn was strongly against this as he thought that VW should develop its own technique, which it tried to do. This meant that Winterkorn had invested a lot of prestige in this technique.

Allegedly, Winterkorn also had a hot temper, a very low acceptance for failure and the VW culture was known to put a lot of pressure on employees.[9] All this probably made the engineers working with the new

[9] Cremer,A. and Bergin, T. (2015)Fear and respect: VW's culture under Winterkorn, *Reuters*, 10 October. Available at: https://www.reuters.com/article/us-volkswagen-emissions-culture-idUSKCN0S40MT20151010 (accessed 29 April 2020).

emissions technology less eager to tell Winterkorn that they had failed to develop the technique required by the clean diesel campaign. If we allow ourselves to speculate a little bit, the engineers may even have seen it as a better alternative to manipulate the software so that the emissions appeared much lower than they actually were, than to tell Winterkorn they had failed.

But regardless as to who made the decision to manipulate the software, it was manipulated so that the emissions technique worked only in a laboratory context. The emissions were very low in the laboratory tests, while the emissions during normal use of the car were actually were very high.

The board of directors and top management need to think their position through when it comes to the shareholder view vs. the stakeholder view. This position will have a major impact on how *mission, goals* and *strategies* are formulated. But what do these three terms really mean? We turn to this next.

## Mission

An organization's mission (or purpose, as some managers call it) is about the reason why the organization exists. As we can see in the examples below, the mission may address how to improve the lives of customers, but also how to improve environmental and social aspects of society.

**Real World Example:** IKEA's mission is described as follows:
*At IKEA our vision is to create a better everyday life for the many people. Our business idea supports this vision by offering a wide range of well-designed, functional home furnishing products at prices so low that as many people as possible will be able to afford them.*

The world's leading pet food producer, Mars Petcare, has the following mission:

*A better world for pets*

And Neste, a Finnish oil company that recently turned to renewable energy, has a mission that reflects this change:

*Creating responsible choices every day*

Unsurprisingly, Tesla has the following mission:

*Tesla's mission is to accelerate the world's transition to sustainable energy.*

The argument that organizations should focus more on the mission or purpose of the company is often linked to stakeholder thinking. But it is often also pragmatic, because most lower-level managers and employees do not find financial measures very motivating. They may very well accept them and find them perfectly reasonable, but they seldom become engaged in the daily job because of a goal to achieve a ROE (return on equity) of 12 per cent or a profit of €10 billion. This is usually far too abstract to inspire people.

A mission or purpose, on the other hand, can often be perceived as more tangible and thus is more motivating. Not only may the purpose be inspiring for the individual person working in the organization, it may also be something that managers and employees can gather around, thereby strengthening team spirit. Moreover, an inspiring mission may also attract people to the organization – people that sympathize with the mission. In this way the organization can attract more competent people and at the same time strengthen team spirit even further by employing people that care for the same purpose. As discussed in Chapter 1, the mission also forms the basis for an important input control, the value statement.

## Different types of organizational goal

Organizational goals are important since they tend to be more concrete than the mission. There are financial goals and strategic goals, as described below. While the financial goals often, but not always, are linked to the owners, the strategic goals often relate to both missions – how we are going to contribute to society – and financial goals – how we are going to be profitable.

### Financial goals

Regardless of whether you acknowledge the shareholder view, the stakeholder view or something in between, the financial goals are very important for the organization. In financial theory, the goals of the owners are usually expressed as high *profitability* and low *risk*. This means that the owners want to get good money back on their investment and they want to be reasonably certain that they are going to get it regularly.

However, in so-called non-profit organizations, profit is not a goal at all. This is for instance the case in many public service organizations, sports clubs, churches and political organizations. Such organizations may, however, still have financially related goals such as amount of money raised or different types of cost measure.

#### *Profitability (for-profit organizations)*

Profitability is usually expressed as the *return on investment* – that is, profit (revenues minus costs) divided by invested capital. In the basic form of this equation, 'invested capital' refers to the shareholders' investment, which consists of proceeds from the issuance of stock, plus retained earnings. The shareholders' investment (i.e., equity) is the amount of financing that was not obtained by debt (i.e., by borrowing). This measure is also referred to as *return on equity* (ROE), defined as net profit/equity. For many purposes, the source of financing is not relevant; 'invested capital', therefore, means the total assets. This is the case in *return on assets* (ROA), defined as operating profit/total assets.

ROE and ROA are both ratios expressed as a percentage and there are some problems related to these that we will return to in Chapter 9. Other commonly used profitability measures are different types of absolute profits (such as operating profit and net profit) and profit margins (profit/sales; for instance operating margin and net margin).

Profitability is of course a very important measure in a profit-driven organization. It is a measure of to what extent the owners are getting a good return on the capital that they have put into the company. Owners normally want a return that is in line with the interest they for instance may get at the bank, plus an extra premium for the risk the owners are taking. The owners take a risk when they invest in the company since they may lose some or all of their investment. The higher this risk, the higher risk premium they usually want.

Profitability is, however, also important for other reasons. Since good profitability is a sign of a sound company, it is also very important for banks and others who consider lending money to the company. A profitable company is more likely to be able to pay interest and to pay back a loan. For similar reasons, profitability may be of interest to suppliers who consider selling to the company, potential employees who consider taking a job in the company and even customers who wish to have a long-term relationship with the company.

Moreover, profitability is also important for the financing of further investments in the company. So, if top management wants the company to grow this can be financed, fully or partly, through the profit the company is making every year. This means that top management does not have to go to the bank or issue more stocks every time they want to make investments. In some extreme cases, such as IKEA and H&M, strong profitability has made it possible for the companies to expand massively without borrowing money from the bank.

***Real World Example:*** The Volvo Group recently updated its financial goals.[10] The aim is now that the Group's operating margin shall exceed 10 per cent measured over a business cycle. In addition, the Financial Services Unit's financial goal is to earn a return on equity of 12–15 per cent.

### *Cost effectiveness (non-profit organizations)*

If you are a for-profit organization, cost and cost effectiveness will be captured through the profitability calculations, but they can also be important goals in themselves. This is especially so in non-profit organizations where the profit cannot be calculated. In these organizations one important goal is not to spend more money than their allowance from the state or municipality. On the other hand, the organization should perhaps not spend considerably less money either, since that might imply it is not doing its job. Often the goal is to achieve as much as possible given the amount of money that is being spent or to put how much is achieved in relation to what is spent, sometimes popularly referred to as 'bang for the buck'. It could for instance be cured diseases put in relation to the cost of the hospital. But even if this does imply a sound ambition, it is often rather difficult to find good measures of this effectiveness.

## Strategic goals

Strategic goals complement the financial goals and can be of many kinds. They often describe how the organization is going to build or sustain a competitive advantage. Companies can compete with higher customer satisfaction – for instance, through higher quality, better design, higher service level or by being more innovative than competitors. They can also compete with lower prices than those of competitors, for instance if they have a more efficient manufacturing strategy, a better network of suppliers or a more efficient distribution system.

***Real World Example:*** The fulfilment of IKEA's mission (mentioned above) calls for appropriate financial and strategic goals. IKEA combines the following goals: functionality, low prices and high volumes. In order to reach these goals the following aspects of the strategy are important:

- *Worldwide network of cheap but good suppliers:* The fact that IKEA often buys very large volumes makes it easier for its suppliers to charge a low price.
- *Efficient global logistics system:* This is partly made possible by the famous flat-pack system, which makes the transport of the products much cheaper.
- *Customers doing part of the work themselves:* The flat-pack system usually requires that customers assemble the products themselves. Although somewhat inconvenient (and sometimes very irritating!), this makes lower prices possible.

In some rare cases, companies have developed a strategy that makes it possible to reach both the goal of high customer satisfaction and the goal of lower cost compared to competitors. Case 2.3 offers one example of such a company.

# Strategy

So far, we have concluded that organizations have strategic goals and that these goals are supported by different strategies. However, we are now going to dig a little deeper into what a strategy really is. First, we are going to have a discussion on how the strategies are formed and then we are going to take a look at different types of strategy.

[10] Volvo Group, Financial Targets. Available at: https://www.volvogroup.com/en-en/investors/financial-targets.html (accessed 29 April 2020).

## Forming of strategies

### Deliberate strategies

According to one very established perspective, referred to as the *design perspective*, strategy should be designed to *fit* the organization's environment and capabilities. A firm develops its strategies by matching its core competencies with industry opportunities, often by the use of a SWOT analysis, where SWOT stands for Strengths, Weaknesses, Opportunities and Threats. Strategy formulation is a process that senior executives use to evaluate a company's strengths and weaknesses in light of the opportunities and threats present in the environment and then decide on strategies that fit the company's core competencies with environmental opportunities. This perspective is in line with contingency theory, and suggests that strategy should be based on both external and internal contingencies.

The *positioning perspective* is not so very far from the design perspective, but here the focus is more on choosing a more generic strategy than to carefully plan and design a very specific strategy suited to the specific organization. In a way this also moved the focus away from the technique to the actual strategy, but it also led to a simplification in at least two respects. The first was the aforementioned move from highly individual and unique strategies to more generic ones. The second was the relevant contingencies to consider when choosing the strategy. Instead of considering a number of external and internal contingencies as well as the organization's goals when designing strategy, the main focus was now moved to the structure of the industry.

So far we have discussed two traditional and well-known perspectives on strategy and they have some common features. One is that the design or choice of strategy is the result of a systematic analysis; it is about a *deliberate*, rational process where a number of well-based choices and decisions are made by top management or experts. It is also a forward-looking process where the strategy is first designed or chosen and then implemented, and there is not much concern in these perspectives about difficulties in implementing the strategy.

### Emerging strategies

Another perspective that we will take a closer look at is the *emerging strategy* perspective.[11] The background to the theory is that strategies, no matter how cleverly designed or chosen they are, might not be successfully implemented and, even if they are, might not work very well in practice. It is often argued that strategy implementation often fails, perhaps as often as in 90 per cent of cases, and this could be for a number of reasons, including insufficient communication, employee resistance, unadjusted management control system including incentive system, lack of competency, underestimation of the extent of the change, and so on. Moreover, what might look like an absolutely brilliant idea when sitting behind a desk or in a meeting room does surprisingly often not work so well when put into use. It is a very difficult task to take into account all factors and circumstances in reality, when designing a new strategy. This is the reason why political initiatives, even with the best of intentions, often fail.

These arguments above have led the proponents of this perspective to separate *deliberate* strategies from *emerging* ones. The deliberate strategies are formulated by top management in the way we have already discussed, while the emerging ones gradually emerge out of how problems are dealt with in practice.

When managers or employees face small problems in their daily work they try to think of ways to overcome them and if they do find a way and it works, they will probably make it part of their ordinary routines. Together with other solutions found by other employees, these small changes might actually change the direction of the organization and, therefore, change its strategy. This could be purchasers who discover that when they buy from old and established suppliers they always get the deliveries of the goods on time, whereas from new and perhaps cheaper suppliers they often do not. Therefore, the

[11] For example, Mintzberg, H. (1994) *The Rise and Fall of Strategic Planning: Reconceiving Roles for Planning, Plans, Planners.* New York: Free Press.

purchasers might stop looking for cheaper suppliers and stick to the ones they know can deliver, and by that they change the strategy to select suppliers to experience-based instead of price-based. If salespeople discover that it is easier to sell the products or services to another type of customer than they traditionally have sold to, they are very likely to continue to do so and, by doing that, they have developed a new strategy regarding which customer groups to target.

The emerging strategy perspective has replaced designing, planning and choosing with *learning*. Organizations learn through experimenting how to handle different tasks and which direction to take. It is not about being exceptionally clever when sitting behind your desk; it is about trying out different methods in practice to see what actually works, as illustrated in Gordon Siu's story in the Real World Example below, about bees and flies trapped in a bottle.

**Real World Example:** 'If you place in a bottle half a dozen bees and the same number of flies, and lay the bottle horizontally, with its base to the window, you will find that the bees persist, till they die of exhaustion or hunger, in their endeavour to discover an opening through [the base] while the flies, in less than two minutes, will all have sallied forth through the neck on the opposite side . . . It is the bees' . . . intelligence that is their undoing in this experiment. They evidently imagine that the issue from every prison must be where the light shines clearest; and they act in accordance, and persist in too-logical action . . . and the greater their intelligence, the more inadmissible, more incomprehensible, will the strange obstacle appear.

'Whereas the featherbrained flies, careless of logic . . . flutter wildly hither and thither, and meeting here with the good fortune that often waits on the simple . . . end up by discovering the friendly opening that restores their liberty . . .' .[12]

## Types of strategy

*Corporate strategy* is about being in the right mix of businesses. Thus, corporate strategy is concerned more with the question of *where* to compete than with *how* to compete in a particular industry; the latter is a *business unit strategy*.

### Corporate strategy

At the corporate level, one of the most significant dimensions along which strategic contexts differ is the extent and type of diversification undertaken by different firms. In terms of their corporate-level strategy, companies can be classified into one of three categories.

A *single industry* firm operates in one line of business. A single industry firm uses its core competencies to pursue growth within that industry.

**Real World Example:** Microsoft is a company devoted to one industry, namely software. Unlike Apple the company is not interested in making hardware, even if it has made some attempts in that direction. This means that Microsoft does not have control over the hardware development and cannot be certain that the software and hardware is always 100 per cent compatible. But this strategy still makes sense given that Microsoft wants to be the market leader. If it made its own hardware, it would probably have to be the market leader in hardware too in order to become the market leader in software, and not even Apple has managed to achieve that. Microsoft now develops software that is compatible with all PCs, and by becoming the dominating player it has made the hardware producers adjust their products to Microsoft's software. This also means that Microsoft can concentrate on what it does best, which is software, and leave the hardware to others who are better at it.

Another group consists of firms that operate in a number of industries, and their businesses are connected to each other through operating synergies. We refer to these firms as *related diversified firms*.

[12] Gordon Sui, quoted in Peters, T.J. and Waterman, R.H. (1982) *In Search of Excellence: Lessons from America's Best-Run Companies*. New York: Harper & Row.

Operating synergies consist of two types of linkage across business units: (1) ability to share common resources; and (2) ability to share common core competencies. One way related diversified firms create operating synergies is by having two or more business units share resources such as a common sales force, common manufacturing facilities and a common procurement function. Such a sharing of resources helps the firm reap the benefits of economies of scale and economies of scope.

An *unrelated business* firm operates in businesses that are not related to one another; the connection between business units is purely financial. In such an organization, except for financial transactions, its business units have little in common. There are few operating synergies across business units. The headquarters functions like a holding company, lending money to business units that are expected to generate high financial returns. We refer to such firms as *unrelated diversified firms* or *conglomerates.*

**Real World Example:** A well-known British conglomerate is Virgin,[13] which operates in a large number of industries, including airlines, the media, financial services, health clubs, travel agencies and radio. Virgin started out on a modest scale in the 1970s with a record shop followed by a small mail-order record company. However, everything changed when the very first album released by the record company, Mike Oldfield's *Tubular Bells,* became a huge hit, eventually selling an estimated 15 million copies. This turned the shop/record company into a major record company and became the start of the Virgin Group. Sir Richard Branson and Virgin have since sold Virgin Records and founded companies in a vast number of industries, which employ around 70,000 people with an estimated revenue of almost £13 billion.

According to Virgin's website (www.virgin.com) there are a number of factors that help the Virgin companies to be successful, including the brand, Branson's reputation and network, the management style and empowerment of the staff. Accounts of the management style and empowerment can be found in a number of public statements made by Sir Richard, such as: 'you can't be a good leader unless you generally like people', 'employees think for themselves' and 'I have to be willing to step back'. Virgin has also tried to avoid the traps of a huge corporation, and has very little hierarchy and a minimum amount of corporate bureaucracy. In order for the Virgin Group to start a new company, it has to have the potential to meet four out of five criteria: it must be innovative, challenge authority, be better than the competitors, offer good quality, and exist in a growing market.

These criteria do not include anything regarding synergies, but the companies, which are supposed to be part of a big family, are expected to actively help one another. This opens up the very interesting possibility of learning by doing different things, rather than doing the same thing, and that solutions from one specific industry can inspire solutions in other industries. This is a potential opportunity in conglomerates that is not present to the same extent in single industry or related diversified companies.

## Business unit strategy

When we discuss business unit strategy we are going to focus on Porter's generic strategies. Not necessarily because this is the only or even best description of business unit strategy, but rather because it is pedagogical and easy to understand. According to Porter,[14] the structure of an industry should be analysed in terms of the collective strength of five competitive forces (see Figure 2.4).

1 *The intensity of rivalry among existing competitors:* Factors affecting direct rivalry are industry growth, product differentiability, number and diversity of competitors, level of fixed costs, intermittent overcapacity and exit barriers.

2 *The bargaining power of customers:* Factors affecting buyer power are number of buyers, buyers' switching costs, buyers' ability to integrate backwards, impact of the business unit's product on buyers' total costs, impact of the business unit's product on buyers' product quality/performance and significance of the business unit's volume to buyers.

---

[13] This Real World Example is based on various sources, in particular this one: www.esecourses.com/cfincase.pdf (accessed 19 December 2012).

[14] Porter, M.E. (1980) *Competitive Strategy: Techniques for Analyzing Industries and Competitors.* New York: Free Press.

**FIGURE 2.4** Industry structure analysis: Porter's five forces model

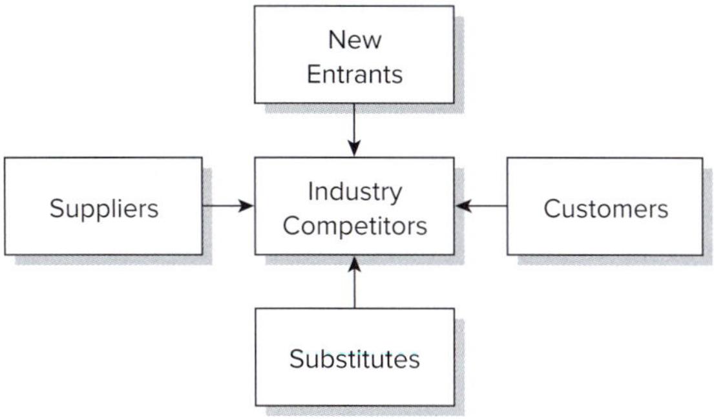


*Source:* Adapted from Porter, M.E. (1980) *Competitive Strategy: Techniques for Analyzing Industries and Competitors.* New York: Free Press.

3 *The bargaining power of suppliers:* Factors affecting supplier power are number of suppliers, suppliers' ability to integrate forwards, presence of substitute inputs and importance of the business unit's volume to suppliers.

4 *Threat from substitutes:* Factors affecting substitute threat are relative price/performance of substitutes, buyers' switching costs and buyers' propensity to substitute.

5 *The threat of new entry:* Factors affecting entry barriers are capital requirements, access to distribution channels, economies of scale, product differentiation, technological complexity of product or process, expected retaliation from existing firms, and government policy.

The five-force analysis is the starting point for developing a competitive advantage as it helps to identify the opportunities and threats in the external environment. With this understanding, Porter claims that the business unit has two generic ways of responding to the opportunities in the external environment and developing a sustainable competitive advantage: low cost and differentiation.

*Cost leadership* can be achieved through such approaches as economies of scale in production, experience curve effects, tight cost control and cost minimization (in such areas as R&D, service, sales force or advertising).

The primary focus of the *differentiation* strategy is to differentiate the product offering of the business unit, creating something that is perceived by customers as being unique. Approaches to product differentiation include brand loyalty, superior customer service, dealer network, product design and product features, and technology.

Porter is very convincing when he argues that an organization should not try to satisfy everyone if it wants to be competitive. It has to make a choice between these two strategies and should least of all 'be stuck in the middle', which means that it has neither a competitive advantage in cost leadership nor differentiation. However, as Case 2.3 illustrates, some organizations actually manage to find a strategy that will give them both a differentiation and cost advantage.

We will return to these two strategies when we discuss contingencies next.

## Contingencies

For an organization to deliver on its mission and reach its goals it is important to consider what situation it is in – or, as it is often expressed in the literature, what the contingencies are. The contingencies of an organization include for instance the business environment, the strategy (which was discussed above), the technology, its size and national culture. All of these contingencies may be very important to consider when the management control system of the organization is designed and used, but we are going to focus on three of them, namely the environment the organization is working in, the strategy of the organization and what technology the organization deploys.

## The environment

A fashionable expression today is that 'We live in a VUCA world!' Even though the abbreviation VUCA was coined in the 1980s[15] and has been used for a long time in the United States Armed Forces, it now seems to have spread to the field of business. VUCA stands for:

- *Volatility*: The world is changing very fast, perhaps faster than ever.
- *Uncertainty*: It is very difficult to foresee how the world is going to change.
- *Complexity*: Change is driven by several, contradictory forces.
- *Ambiguity*: Reality is blurred, and cause–effect chains are unclear.

It can be discussed to what extent this is a reasonable description of the environment that most organizations are facing or not. But it is probably fair to say that more organizations are facing this environment today compared to some decades ago. However, let us go back to a time when the situation was quite different from today . . .

***Real World Example:*** When Henry Ford started to produce cars on an industrial scale about a century ago, he faced a situation that probably many car producers today envy. He had, at least for quite some time, no or very little competition. He had a reliable level of demand so that he could always sell everything he produced and the demand increased at a steady pace every year. Moreover, he produced only one car model, the Model T, with no variances at all. Or, as he so famously put it, 'The customers can have any colour they like as long as it is black!' The production planning was not complicated at all because Ford produced only one type of car that looked exactly the same year after year, and the company knew exactly how many cars to produce. In an extremely stable situation like this, staff on the shop floor did not need to think very much, nor did they need to communicate with one another. They performed only the same standardized task day in and day out, year in and year out. They could not even talk to each other and they probably did not understand one another, because the workforce spoke 50 different languages. They usually stayed in the company since they knew that they made twice as much money at Ford compared to any alternative employer. Decisions can very well be centralized in an organization like this as they are rather infrequent, and Henry Ford also insisted on making all important decisions himself. So, it was an extremely hierarchical and centralized organization where decisions were made at the top and executed on the shop floor. The work tasks were very much standardized, repetitive, and called for very little thinking or communication on the part of the workforce, and important performance measures probably focused on aspects such as productivity and cost.

The management control system design, especially with regards to throughput control, in the above example worked very well, at least until General Motors started to introduce, among other things, different colours. But would it work in a business today? Many would answer 'no' to that question. The situation for most organizations today is often said to be totally different. Competition is fiercer, customers make greater demands on variety among other things and their preferences change much faster. Take the smartphone industry as an example where technology changes all the time along with customers' preferences, and nobody knows which smartphone producer will be the winner tomorrow.

In this situation, lower-level managers and employees need to be more customer focused and decisions need to be decentralized down the hierarchy. Making all the important decisions at the top would not be possible because that would make the organization too slow. People in operations need to work in teams and cooperate well in order to be flexible and able to meet changing demands in the market. Productivity and costs are still measured but so are quality, lead times, technical innovation, customer satisfaction, market share and many other things.

[15] By the two leadership scholars Warren Bennis and Burt Nanus.

***Real World Example:*** Spotify[16] is a modern company with a very special system for throughput control. The employees are organized in small teams called squads. A squad does not have a budget, but what it does have is a long-term mission that is set by management, such as: 'Make the car a better place to listen to music.' The mission and how many people there are in a squad is basically all that the teams do not decide for themselves.

The squads set their own goals and priorities, and decide for themselves how they are going to conduct their work. A performance measure might be 'How much more music people are listening to in the car.' Empowerment and trust are at the heart of the system, which means that the employees are allowed a very high degree of autonomy. The squads are then organized in a structure similar to that of a matrix organization in order to increase the communication in different dimensions.

There are two main reasons for all this. The first is that Spotify believes that the squads make better decisions, but above all they make faster decisions and the whole organization thus becomes more flexible. The other reason is that employees like working in an environment like this and Spotify wants to attract the best people to the organization.

The management control systems in the two organizations described in our Real World Examples are of course extremely different, almost like the opposite poles on a continuum. The Ford system to a very large extent relied on throughput controls that followed a 'coercive' logic, whereas Spotify focuses on throughput and input controls that follow an 'enabling' logic. The two systems are also very similar to the mechanistic and organic systems, as described in Table 2.1.

**TABLE 2.1** Mechanistic and organic management control systems

| Mechanistic MCS | Organic MCS |
|---|---|
| Motivation through pay | Motivation through contributing to goals |
| Specialized, defined responsibilities | Cooperation, teamwork and interaction |
| Hierarchic communication | Horizontal communication |
| Formal and tight | Informal and loose |
| Supervision | Encouragement |
| Internal focus | External focus |
| Narrow cost and productivity measures for evaluation | Broader and mainly non-financial measures for learning |
| Planning and budgeting | Flexibility and creativeness |
| Technology and routines | People and culture |

*Source:* Based on Burns, T. and Stalker, G.M. (1961) *The Management of Innovation.* London: Tavistock.

According to the creators of this framework, it is the need for innovation in the organization that determines what framework is the best fit for the organization. In an organization with a great need for innovation the organic system is the best fit, while a mechanistic system works very well in an organization with very little need for innovation. Of course, the need for innovation is to a large degree dependent on the environment of the organization. If the environment resembles that of a VUCA world – and Spotify would probably argue that it does – the need for innovation is very likely to be significant.

But if the organization's environment is better described as stable, certain, simple and clear – as in the case of Ford – a mechanistic system may very well make a better fit, since cost-efficiency is probably more important than innovation and creativeness. It could be argued that McDonald's is such a company, with stable demand and very little change in its offerings – a Big Mac looks more or less the same today as it did 40 years ago. Accordingly, the management control system of McDonald's also has many similarities with the mechanistic system.

[16] The Agile Warrior (2017) The Spotify playbook. Available at: https://agilewarrior.wordpress.com/2017/11/21/the-spotify-playbook/ (accessed 25 September 2019).

## Strategy

We discussed strategic goals and strategy above, and the strategy of the company is also a contingency that often has a significant influence on what type of management control system is best fitted to an organization. We are going to illustrate this with two Real World Examples of Porter's strategies.

***Real World Example:*** When Ryanair restructured in 1992 it was with the clear strategy of becoming a low-cost alternative in the airline industry. This was going to be achieved through a strategy that included a number of features. Quick turnaround times in order to keep the planes in the air and an increase in the utilization of assets were important features. Another was working with smaller regional airports, because regional airports charge less for takeoffs and landings. Operating one single aircraft model was also an aspect of the strategy, as this reduces costs and increases flexibility for both maintenance and staff, since everybody is trained on the same type of plane. But perhaps the best-known feature is the 'no frills' strategy. By charging extra for whatever additional service the passenger wants, the basic price can be kept down. Later Ryanair also added online ordering and check-in, and even closed its check-in desks at airports to drive costs down further. Recently, Ryanair has received negative publicity since it refuses to give compensation to customers whose flights have been cancelled.

***Real World Example:*** Linn Products is a Scottish audio equipment company involved in several technologies, ranging from vinyl to digital streaming. The company supplies Aston Martin cars as well as the royal household in the UK with sound systems. Linn is extremely devoted to product development and often comes up with original technical solutions. However, product development does not stop once the product is finished, as Linn continually develops the product after it is put on the market. This means that if you happen to be the owner of a Linn Sondek LP 12 turntable from 1973, you can upgrade it with the latest technology and make it sound as good as a new one.

Another aspect that Linn focuses on is the dealer, and certain demands are placed on the 'real' Linn dealers. One of the most important demands is that they have a separate listening room in the shop, decorated like a living room, which must contain only one set of loudspeakers at a time. At a conventional audio dealer the dealer has only to push a button if you want to compare different speakers, but at a Linn dealer the dealer will have to take out the two (or five if you are listening to a surround system) speakers in the listening room, carry in the others that you would like to listen to and plug them in.

This will, of course, cause much more work for the dealer, especially if you listen to many sets of loudspeakers! But the reason for this, according to Linn, is that if you are going to really hear what a set of speakers sounds like, you cannot have other, passive speakers in the room as they will interfere with the sound. However, Linn dealers claim that they make more money selling Linn, and this is because the customers value the extra quality in Linn's products and are willing to pay more for them. Linn customers are, in fact, extremely loyal and there is a joke in the industry claiming that Linn is not so much about technology as it is a religion!

What Ryanair needs is low costs, including cheap employees, in order to succeed with its strategy. Ryanair's management control system to a large degree resembles the mechanistic system, which according to contingency theory constitutes a good fit with this strategy. Linn, on the other hand, needs innovative and passionate product developers as well as equally passionate or 'religious' retailers to succeed. With this strategy a mechanistic management control system would probably have been a catastrophe, since it might have killed everybody's passion. An organic system, on the other hand, seems much more appropriate, even if it probably leads to higher costs.

We can also compare this discussion with the arguments put forward by Stan Sorscher in the Real World Vignette at the start of this chapter. The cost-cutting culture in Boeing that Sorscher talks about resembles the mechanistic system, whereas the quality culture Boeing had before resembles more the organic system. And when Sorscher claims that the cost-cutting culture may fit a commodity dealer such as Wal-Mart but not a high-end airplane producer such as Boeing, his arguments are perfectly in line with contingency theory!

However, it should be pointed out that not all examples are as clear-cut as these. At the beginning of the chapter and in the section titled 'Different types of organizational goal', we discussed IKEA, which just like Ryanair, has a low-cost strategy. Does this mean that the management control system in IKEA resembles the mechanistic system? Even if parts of it might do that, corporate culture and loyalty from the workforce are some very important elements in IKEA and in these respects it definitely resembles more an organic system.

## Technology

Technology – that is, how the goods or services are produced – is also very important for the design of a management control system. Technology is important for many reasons, not least because management control system theory has predominantly been developed for manufacturing organizations. By manufacturing organizations, we mean organizations whose main activity is to produce and market tangible goods, and which carry those goods in inventory before selling them on markets to earn a monetary return.

In contrast, we talk of service organizations where service delivery is the main activity an organization performs. Such organizations typically differ from manufacturing organizations in that they produce and market intangible services, are highly reliant on the expertise and creativity of professional employees, and are less able to rely on standardization of operations and procedures. Even if this is something of a generalization as manufacturing can be very complicated and service highly standardized, let us for the sake of argument accept this generalization for the moment. These characteristics, then, have several consequences for the nature of the control problems in such organizations and the way in which management control systems can be designed and used to help handle those problems. Let us take a closer look at some of the common differences between manufacturing and service industries.

Goods can be held in an inventory, which is a buffer that dampens the impact on production activity of fluctuations in sales volume. Services cannot be stored. The airplane seat, hotel room, hospital operating room, or the hours of lawyers, physicians, scientists and other professionals that are not used today are gone for ever. Thus, although a manufacturing company can earn revenue in the future from products that are on hand today, a service company cannot do so. It must try to minimize its unused capacity.

Moreover, the costs of many service organizations are essentially fixed in the short run. In the short run, a hotel cannot reduce its costs substantially by closing off some of its rooms. Accounting firms, law firms and other professional organizations are reluctant to lay off professional personnel during periods of low sales volume because of the effect on morale and the costs of rehiring and training.

A key variable in most service organizations, therefore, is the extent to which current capacity is matched with demand. Service organizations attempt this matching in two ways. First, they try to stimulate demand in off-peak periods by marketing efforts and price concessions. Cruise lines and resort hotels offer low rates in the off season; airlines and hotels offer low rates at weekends; and public utilities offer low rates on slack periods during the day. Second, if feasible, service organizations adjust the size of the workforce to the anticipated demand by such measures as scheduling training activities in slack periods and compensating for long hours in busy periods with time off later. The loss from unsold services is so important that occupancy rates, 'sold hours', load factors, student enrolment, hospital admissions and similar indications of success in selling available services are normally key variables in service organizations.

Another difference is that a manufacturing company can inspect its products before they are shipped to the consumer, and their quality can be measured visually or with instruments (tolerances, purity, weight, colour, and so on). A service company cannot judge product quality until the moment the service is rendered, and even then the judgements are often subjective. Restaurant management can examine the food in the kitchen, but customer satisfaction depends to a considerable extent on the way it is served. The quality of education is so difficult to measure that few educational organizations have a formal quality control system.

A major difference is that manufacturing companies add equipment and automate production lines, thereby replacing labour and reducing costs. Most service companies are labour intensive and cannot do this. Hospitals do add expensive equipment, but mostly to provide better treatment, and this increases costs. A law firm expands by adding partners and new support personnel.

Some service organizations operate many units in various locations; each unit is relatively small. These organizations include banks, fast-food restaurant chains, car rental companies, petrol service stations and many others. Some of the units are owned; others operate under a franchise. The similarity of the separate units provides a common basis for benchmarking and evaluating performance not available to most manufacturing companies. The information for each unit can be compared with systemwide or regional averages, and high performers and low performers can be identified. However, because units differ in the mix of services they provide, in the resources they use and in other ways, care must be taken in making such comparisons.

For many service organizations, comparison between goal and output is complicated, impossible or even misleading. For example, in the financial services industry, the 2008 financial crisis showed that performance in the short run was inconsistent with performance in the long run. Selling subprime mortgage loans to people who would not be able to repay them in the future is a good example of the resulting problem. Selling loans may, indeed, contribute to the organizational goal of turnover in the short run, but loans not repaid clearly work against goal attainment in terms of value maximization in the long run. Such timing differences are especially frequent in service delivery, because of the lack of hard and timely measurements of actual outputs with many services.

The problematic measurement of actual outputs is also dominant in service organizations that are part of the semi-governmental sector. For example, the actual outputs of hospitals are also notoriously hard to describe in real time, as some cures and treatments deliver their true effects many years down the road. Some of these effects can best be described in terms of preventing certain illnesses or further health deterioration, which again does not lend itself to immediate and objective measurement. Organizations with a not-for-profit goal face comparable difficulties, with outputs sometimes best described in terms of their societal impact, and in other cases by the amount of funds collected.

This discussion seems to imply that while manufacturing organizations often benefit from management control systems with a focus on throughput and output controls, service organizations more often benefit from systems with a focus on throughput and input controls. While manufacturing organizations often benefit from a mechanistic system, service organizations rather benefit from an organic system. That services often are produced in cooperation with the customer while goods are not, that service production often requires highly skilled professionals while manufacturing does not, and that service organizations often can rely less on standardization, all point in that direction.

However, even if this quite often is the case, it is as stated above also something of a generalization. We have already mentioned that McDonald's has a rather mechanistic management control system, while audio system manufacturer Linn has a much more organic one. But if we consider that the service process of McDonald's, serving hamburgers, is rather simple, standardized and that the company wants to keep costs down, it still makes sense. Likewise, if we consider that Linn produces complicated, high-end products and competes on quality rather than price, it also makes sense. This is a good illustration that different contingencies actually may, and often do, point in different directions and that reality is often more complicated than we think!

## Summary

There are two main views on why and for whom organizations exist. According to the shareholder view, the purpose of organizations is to fulfil the goals of their owners. When we discuss the goals of the owners we usually think about high profitability and low risk, but they can have other or additional goals depending on the owners and what type of organizations we are referring to. According to the stakeholder view, organizations do not exist just to satisfy the owners' goals, but to satisfy the demands of a number of different groups, including the owners. Stakeholders are groups that both contribute to and benefit from the organization, and groups commonly referred to as stakeholders include, apart from owners, customers, employees, suppliers, lenders and society. All these groups must be adequately satisfied to continue to contribute to the organization in order for the organization to survive.

There are two strong movements that relate to this discussion. These are corporate governance, which relates to the shareholder view, and CSR, which relates to the stakeholder view. There are at least two important drivers behind the increased focus on corporate governance. One is the expansion of new owner categories such as pension funds and mutual funds. Another is the increased legislation, such as SOX in the United States, following a number of accounting scandals there. Corporate governance can be executed in a number of different ways, including the appointment of board members, meetings between owner representatives and managers, auditing or, quite simply, the owners selling their shares if they are not satisfied.

CSR is about an organization's voluntary concern about social and environmental issues. The drivers behind the increased interest in these issues during this millennium include globalization and increased pressure from stakeholders including the media. In order to protect themselves from bad publicity most organizations have started to work systematically with CSR. Just like corporate governance there are many methods to use when working with CSR, including formulation of a code of conduct, sustainability reporting, and nurturing of organizational values and culture in line with good ethics.

The board of directors and top management need to think through their position when it comes to the shareholder view vs. the stakeholder view. This position will have a major impact on how mission, goals and strategies are formulated. An organization's mission (or purpose, as some managers call it) concerns the reason why the organization exists. Organizational goals may be of many different kinds, such as financial and strategic goals. Financial goals are related, for instance, to how fruitful the owner's investment is. Strategic goals often describe how the organization is going to gain or sustain its competitive advantage.

When deciding how to design a management control system, top management also needs to consider the contingencies of the organization. The contingencies include, among other things, the environment, the strategy and the technology. An organization facing a stable and certain environment, deploying a low-cost strategy and a manufacturing technology, is likely to benefit from a mechanistic approach, including a focus on throughput controls in a 'coercive' manner. On the other hand, an organization facing a dynamic and uncertain environment, deploying a differentiation strategy and a service technology, is more likely to benefit from an organic approach, including a focus on input controls in an 'enabling' manner.

## Suggested additional reading

Burns, T. and Stalker, G.M. (1961) *The Management of Innovation*. London: Tavistock.

Friedman, M. and Friedman, R.D. (1962) *Capitalism and Freedom*. Chicago, IL: University of Chicago Press.

Harrison, J.S., Barney, J.B., Freeman, R.E. and Phillips, R.A. (eds) (2019) *The Cambridge Handbook of Stakeholder Theory*. Cambridge: Cambridge University Press.

Mallin, C.A. (2010) *Corporate Governance*. Oxford: Oxford University Press.

Porter, M.E. (1980) *Competitive Strategy: Techniques for Analyzing Industries and Competitors*. New York: Free Press.

Rahbek, E. and Pedersen, G. (eds) (2015) *Corporate Social Responsibility*. London: SAGE Publications Ltd.

Steiber, A. and Alänge, S. (2016) *The Silicon Valley Model: Management for Entrepreneurship*. Cham: Springer.

# Case 2.1

# Gyros: a drama in three acts*

**by Göran Nilsson**

## Act I: Euphoria

The biotechnology company Gyros is based in Uppsala, Sweden, and supplies a technology for analysis of liquid through micro-channels in what looks like a CD. It was founded as a spin-off from the major life science company Pharmacia around the turn of the century. Around this time there was great optimism in society in general, and among investors in particular, concerning high-tech companies in industries such as IT, telecoms and biotech. These kinds of enterprises received substantial coverage in the media and were generally valued very highly on the stock market. Accordingly, access to capital was very good for those who wanted to start new ventures. The same was also true of human capital, since Pharmacia moved out and left literally hundreds of highly competent researchers in the Uppsala region for other employers like Gyros to hire.

The generosity among the investors continued during the whole first act, which lasted for a couple of years. Whenever there was a need for more capital it was usually only a matter of asking somebody in top management, who would pick up the phone, call one of the owners/board representatives and get a positive confirmation on the request.

The enthusiasm in society and among investors was very much shared by the CEO and his management team. Since the CEO was very charismatic he also spread his enthusiasm down through the organization. The willingness of the owners to put in more capital whenever it was needed also sent a signal that supported this process. Management also invested in a great many social activities and parties for employees. The impact of this on the organization was also positive since the employees became very enthusiastic, worked hard and had lots of fun. Spirits in the organization were thus very high and Gyros was a pleasant company to work for.

The main task during this period was product development and this was also where the attention was directed. When prioritizing between speed, cost and quality it appears as if speed came first. Gyros also managed to create a product that it tried to establish on the market during this act, but the quality was not very good nor was the product sufficiently adjusted to specific customer groups' needs. In hindsight, top management think that the organization was far too focused on technology and not sufficiently focused on customer needs during this act.

## Act II: Turmoil

The environment characterized by great optimism turned to pessimism during Act II, which lasted for more than half a decade. This was partly due to factors like 9/11 and the global recession, but it was also due to the fact that the investor market now began to think that many companies similar to Gyros were probably significantly overvalued. One possible reason contributing to this was that many companies like Gyros failed to live up to the very optimistic and possibly unrealistic expectations of the market. This drastically decreased investors' willingness to invest. The situation changed from one where the investors were more or less throwing money at projects like this, to one where they were extremely cautious.

The owners of Gyros had by now become rather fragmented, which resulted in a complicated situation where the nervous owners were not only edgy towards Gyros and its management, but also to some

* This case is based on a research study conducted by Associate Professors Göran Nilsson and Jaan Grünberg, both from Uppsala University.

extent in conflict with one another. The board meetings also became much more frequent and often rather stormy. The situation, according to top management, also resulted in a lot of demands on them to produce (preferably) optimistic plans and forecasts, followed by extensive evaluations, analyses and explanations as to why the goals in these forecasts were not met.

This situation put three tough demands on Gyros, in particular on its top management, which now also included a new CEO. The first demand was to supply the board with all the information it requested. The second demand was to secure enough financing to keep the ship afloat. The demands were both urgent. If they did not meet the demands concerning information to the board the board members would surely come back to them until they did, and if they still refused the managers could probably start looking for other jobs. The financing issue was equally urgent since Gyros could not survive without infusions of capital as long as they did not have any sales revenues worth mentioning. This brings us to the third and more long-term demand, which is to get a product out on the market and start selling.

Perhaps due to the very urgent nature of the first two demands, these took up virtually all of the managers' attention. For most of this act the managers were all occupied with serving the board as well as looking for additional sources of capital. But that did not mean that the managers were not aware of the third and more long-term demand. They were very much aware of it. The board reminded them of it constantly, they made several forecasts about how they would get a product out on the market and, perhaps most importantly, they were also very much aware of how important this was for the survival and success of the company. But there was simply no time to act on this demand since all of their time was devoted to fulfilling the other two more urgent demands.

This meant that top management had very limited time to manage and control the organization, which was left more or less to take care of itself. However, this does not mean that the organization was totally unaffected by the situation. Far from it. The most obvious impact was that it had to cut down significantly on employees, another was that the high spirits and optimism had evaporated. But when it concerned their daily work the employees had to conduct it more or less as they saw fit with very little direction or interference from top management. The employees thus continued their work and did not have to concern themselves much with top management's problems. This was seen as a much bigger problem by management than by the employees. According to top management this prevented them from managing the organization in a more customer- and market-oriented direction, and therefore delayed the time it took to get a product out on the market.

## Act III: ?

Your task is to put yourself in the situation of the top-management team in Gyros, during Act II. The members of the team are fully occupied with serving the existing and potential new owners with information. At the same time they understand that they cannot go on like this for ever. They have been in this frustrating situation for several years now and they increasingly realize that it is not going to change unless they do something radical about it.

As members of the top-management team in Gyros you need to answer the following questions.

### Questions

1. Which are the most important problems that management is facing and how do these problems relate to one another? Which problems are at the root of the problems and which problems are more a consequence of the root problems?
2. What can management do about the situation? Can they do anything? Discuss one or more possible routes of action. Also discuss why you think or why you do not think that management would be successful if they choose this route (or these routes).

# Case 2.2

# Northern Light: growing pains*

**by Göran Nilsson**

Joanna is the business development manager at a small but growing smart TV producer called Northern Light. The company has managed to compete with the elephants in the business through high quality, technological development and exclusive design, even though its prices generally are much higher than its competitors'. Even if the company is still very small compared to its competitors, it is growing steadily and has very good profitability. But what worries Joanna is that everything seems to be so unstructured and ad hoc at the company. People do not seem to have a plan or processes to follow, and just keep chasing whatever ball that they happen to put their eyes on.

The people in marketing come with new ideas to R&D all the time, and R&D seem to hear about or invent new technologies and functions all the time, especially since smart TVs took over. 'We have to be in the front line!', they keep saying. This also means that there are lots of last-minute changes when a new product is set into production and many of the changes are not very well prepared from a production perspective. If we then add the large number of varieties that are being produced and the fact that marketing always wants products a week ago, the situation gets very hectic. It may have worked well when there were only a few dozen people in the company, but now there are more than a hundred, and increasing.

Joanna got a degree in business administration a few years ago, but unlike most of her friends at the university she did not want to become a management consultant. She preferred to work for one organization and follow its development, rather than to move around all the time. When she meets her old friends she often says, 'I am a management consultant too, but I am faithful to one company!' The reason she ended up at a high-tech, male-dominated company like this is probably because of her father who is an engineer and used to be the manager of an ABB company. All of his stories about these kinds of organization have probably left a mark on her.

. . . but let's get back to her problems. The trouble is that there is no stability in the organization; everything seems to be changing all the time. The technology changes, customer demands change, the products change, and production orders and priorities also change all the time. Everything changes except the employees, that is. They seem to stay on, even if the company has to employ more people all the time. The employees are to a large extent technology buffs, who want everything to be as high-tech and sophisticated as possible. Joanna can't help thinking that the employees have a lot of freedom and that it is a bit of a kindergarten sometimes, especially in R&D.

A very popular trend is agile project management, but Joanna is not really sure what it is actually about. She has also been thinking about some other management and control models that have been discussed a lot. Lean management is of course something that has been discussed a great deal. Joanna is particularly interested in 5S and the standardizing of processes, and how this can create some structure in the organization. She has also been thinking about the balanced scorecard model and how it could help to measure things like costs, lead time and quality. She thinks that one problem is that they do not know how well they perform since they do not do much follow-up at all. She also wonders what other management and/or control models might help them. Neither lean management nor the balanced scorecard seem to be as fashionable as they once were.

Speaking of the balanced scorecard leads Joanna back to some of her father's stories about ABB and how it worked with what it called T50, autonomous teams and EVITA, the latter of which was balanced

* This case is based on a research study conducted by Associate Professors Göran Nilsson and Jaan Grünberg, both from Uppsala University.

scorecards designed by the teams themselves. But somehow it does not sound very much like the twenty-first century, just like his old Pink Floyd records that he loves to play, she thinks and smiles.

### Task

Your task is to help Joanna with her problem. Your discussion should address the following points.

- An analysis of the contingencies and problems that Northern Light is facing. Also discuss the important strategic considerations it must bear in mind and the choices it may have to make.
- An analysis and discussion of what you think will help Northern Light in its current situation. The discussion may be more general and/or could include more specific management concepts that you would recommend (or perhaps advise against). The discussion should result in a recommendation to Joanna.



# Case 2.3

# Scania: a case of differentiation and low cost*

**by Göran Nilsson**

Scania is a truck manufacturer owned by Volkswagen; it is interesting for several reasons. One is that it has for decades been very successful and profitable. It even managed to handle the financial crisis around 2009 without showing a loss in any year, in an industry that is extremely dependent on the ups and downs in the economy. Another reason is that it, through the use of a number of interesting strategies and solutions, manages to produce high-class trucks and at the same time be most cost effective. Selling trucks is a risky business because demand is very unstable and, as we have just mentioned, highly dependent on the state of the economy. During a boom, customers buy many trucks in order to both replace old ones and increase capacity, but during a recession customers buy fewer trucks. The up- and downturns in the economy are also hard to predict, especially in developing countries, where Scania has many customers.

Scania is extremely focused on the truck industry. It does sell related products, such as buses and engines for boats, but these are only spin-offs from the main product. Its strategy is to offer customized trucks of high quality, which look good, are easy to drive and offer a strong brand image. This, in turn, allows Scania to charge a relatively high price for the trucks and rumour has it that it never gives any discounts on the price. At the same time Scania claims to have very low production costs compared to those of its competitors. Deploying a strategy that combines high quality and customization with low cost is not a very easy task, but one reason why Scania has managed to do so is its so-called module system.

---

* This case was written Dr Göran Nilsson, Uppsala University.

Every truck built by Scania comprises a number of modules put together so that they will meet the specific need of the customer. This means that if a customer has a special request, all Scania has to do is change one small part of the truck, a module, whereas a competitor may have to design a whole new truck. The module system also makes it possible to combine different features in a more flexible way. Some of the modules are, of course, the same in many trucks and can, therefore, be produced in large numbers, which tends to keep the costs down. But the entire trucks – that is, the modules put together – are produced in very small batches, as they are made to meet the specific needs of every customer. The module system, therefore, makes Scania very flexible, as well as cost efficient.

Managers in Scania are mainly recruited internally, and have a sound knowledge of both operations and customers. They often have cross-functional meetings where they meet managers from other departments and discuss issues of mutual concern. Scania also has a production control system that it calls the Scania Production System (SPS); this has many similarities to the renowned Toyota Production System (TPS).[2] In fact, the two companies were brought together by a US professor, Thomas Johnson, as he thought that they were both exceptionally skilled and could benefit from learning from each other. SPS is based on the three basic values: customer first, respect for the individual and elimination of waste. Customer first implies that the customer is always the most important stakeholder. Respect for the individual deals with how people in the organization act towards one another. Elimination of waste is about removing everything that does not add value to the customer, thereby improving the working processes. The SPS also consists of four main principles that deal with standardized working procedures, quality, order-based production and continuous improvement. Every employee is expected to participate in the improvement work.

Scania has abandoned the old budget process in favour of rolling forecasts. The rolling forecasts are made four times a year for the following four quarters of a year and aim to increase Scania's flexibility.[3] Besides, it is not only the financial numbers that count. Scania has a number of key performance indicators (KPIs) divided into four areas: personnel, quality, delivery and costs. Apart from costs, its KPIs are mainly non-financial, and focused on the needs of customers and employees. The non-financial figures are believed to be more accurate and easier for employees to understand. The management control system in Scania is designed to support the strategy, including aspects such as flexibility, customization and high-quality products, but also low cost.

### Questions

1. How would you describe the external contingencies that Scania is facing?
   - a How do you think that the strategy fits with the external contingencies?
   - b How well do you think that the management control system of Scania fits with its strategy?
2. Scania's strategy, including its module system, which it has held on to since the 1950s, has proved very successful.
   - a Why do you think that Scania has managed to hold on to this strategy for so long?
   - b Given Scania's success, why do you think that its competitors have not copied its strategy?
3. Can you name other companies with a similar strategy and similar competitive advantages to Scania?

---

[2] There is more about TPS and lean management in Chapter 6.

[3] Budgets versus rolling forecasts is a topic that we discuss in more detail in Chapter 8.

# Case 2.4
# BioTool: a biotech company's innovation journey*

by Torkel Strömsten

## The invention

In 1953 Crick and Watson discovered the 'secret of life' when they built a model of the human genome at the University of Cambridge. Fredrick Sanger, also from Cambridge, in the 1970s invented a method that made it possible to 'read' or sequence human DNA, which also saw him awarded the Nobel Prize in Medicine in 1977. The development of the company BioTool is a story clearly linked with the two discoveries mentioned above, which also has its starting point in a laboratory in Cambridge.

One of the founders of BioTool, Patric Anderson, finished his PhD in chemistry at Stockholm University in 1986. Having decided to continue within academia he applied for a grant that would take him to Cambridge and England. The postdoctoral period at the Laboratory for Molecular Biology (LMB), Cambridge University, was challenging in many ways. Anderson's aim during that period in Cambridge was to sequence the gene for bovine mitochondrial phosphate-carrier protein and then learn how to sequence DNA according to the Sanger method – the dominant method then and still today. At this time, the Sanger method was very labour intensive and involved several tedious operational steps. For example, it involved the use of gel slabs, which also made it expensive. Anderson then started to think about different ways to improve the method, or rather simplify the handling of it. The idea was to follow 'the activity of DNA polymerase during nucleotide incorporation into a DNA strand by analysing the pyrophosphate during the process', as Anderson explained it. With a background within the research of photosynthesis, it was natural for Anderson to think about how enzymes could be used in the sequencing process, using pyrophosphates that in turn made it possible to achieve a light-driven pyrophosphate synthesis.

Anderson's idea was aligned with the Watson and Crick discovery that the nucleotides adenine, guanine, thymine and cytosine bind together two DNA strings only in certain combinations (adenine with thymine and guanine with cytosine, and vice versa). Anderson's idea was, when a test was going to be done, to add the nucleotides one at the time, together with a set of enzymes with different functions. With Anderson's background in enzyme research, he saw the possibility to use enzymes in order to decide the order of the nucleotides. If there is a hit (guanine are paired with cytosine) a chain reaction will start with the help of the enzymes polymerase, sulfurylas and luciferas, which will create a light flash that can be registered by a camera. One important piece of the puzzle was the idea to use apyrase, another enzyme. With this enzyme the surplus of the nucleotides is broken down and also takes out the light (ATP). The next nucleotide is automatically put in place and the whole process would then start over again until the whole sequence is mapped.

However, finding funding for the project proved very difficult. Back in Sweden, Anderson applied for funding in order to develop the method further, without any luck. However, he decided to use resources from other projects in developing his method and a first publication was accepted. Despite this,

* This case was prepared by Torkel Strömsten PhD at the Stockholm School of Economics, as the basis for class discussion rather than to illustrate effective or ineffective handling of an administrative situation. The case is based on a longitudinal research project comprising more than 40 interviews. The case is complemented with a variety of secondary data. Names and figures have been disguised in order to maintain confidentiality.

Anderson was not able to attract research funds for developing his method. He thought that 'one reason might be that this was not basic research. I was developing a method of DNA sequencing, a general method, and this seems generally to be harder to get money for. Sanger did for example study the mitochondria and in this process he developed his sequencing method.'

In 1990 Anderson moved to Uppsala University and became a full professor. He then started to cooperate with Donald McFarland, Professor in Biotechnology and some of his doctoral students around DNA sequencing. The contact with Donald McFarland was important in finding ways to commercialize the method. McFarland was well connected in both academia as well in Swedish business life. He had earlier started new ventures based upon his research. The next step was to make the method automated. A new set of people were then engaged, both professors and some new PhD students.

With funding from McFarland's research group, up to eight PhD candidates worked on the project. Anderson had an idea that the washing step could be eliminated by utilizing a nucleotide-degrading enzyme. Soon after having worked on this, he managed to obtain data that could verify his theory. After some setbacks regarding how the sequencing showed false signals (solved by identifying and lowering the content of ATP sulfuylase), Anderson and his research group then used a new source of ATP sulfuylase, yeast.

Soon, they started to see results that could be commercially interesting. Anderson's discovery in sequencing short strands of the human DNA was taking place when the Human Genome (HUGO) project was initiated. The HUGO project was given considerable attention in the media, and Anderson and McFarland discussed how their invention could be linked to what the HUGO project did.

The initial idea was to start with the sequence of short and middle short DNA strands and then develop the instrument into a full-scale whole genome sequencing method. With the HUGO project behind them, the inventors saw that there would be an increased need for drug discovery to know more about the human genome on a more specific level. The HUGO project had sequenced the total human genome. What Anderson and his research group could do with their method was to sequence short and middle short DNA strands, but also single bases, so-called single nucleotide polyphosphates (SNPs). SNPs would give researchers viable information about missing things in the human genome and in the development of new drugs.

A first idea was to find a large company that could license the method and take it out to a market. One choice of partner in Sweden for this type of method at this time was Biopharma, a division within a local pharmaceutical company. Anderson had earlier established a cooperative agreement with Biopharma's exploratory research group. However, around 1996, Biopharma was in transition to merge with the American pharmaceutical company Upjohn, and was about to sell its biotech division to Britain's Azra Medical. The new company had no interest in Biopharma's exploratory research group and would not invest in the technology. As Biopharma showed no interest in the invention, the manager at the exploratory research group, Charles Labbé, decided to join Anderson and his team, and to create a company around the method: BioTool.

A patent was acquired based on the sequencing-by-synthesis. According to Anderson it was not a strong patent but 'controlling it would make the discussion with the venture capitalists easier. It could create worries and that was not considered good of course.'

As it turned out, McFarland with his expanding network in the Swedish life science cluster, had become a scientific adviser to a newly formed venture capital firm, SLS Cap. As a consequence, Anderson, McFarland and Labbé started to discuss with SLS about a partnership and a potential seed investment in BioTool.

SLS Cap describes the situation like this: 'Our reason to invest in the firm was at the time the technology's possibilities to perform short and middle short DNA sequencing for clinical diagnostics. We were very excited about the development, when Anderson managed to develop the protein to increase the read length' (King, founder, Scandinavian Life Science Capital).

Having invested in just two firms before, SLS Cap invested SEK20 million into the new company in 1997. It was decided that BioTool was to be located in Uppsala, a city with a long tradition in developing biotech tools for the pharmaceutical industry.

SLS Cap was a young venture capital firm, founded in 1995 by two investment bankers, one with a background within life science academia. SLS Cap could benefit from knowledge from one of the most prominent venture capital firms in the world, namely Lingfield Venture Partner. Through its network, one of the founders of the Boston-based venture capital firm assisted SLS Cap and was also used on its advisory board: 'He has been very generous with sharing his knowledge and experience. This has made it possible for us to act in ways that we would not have been able to do otherwise. So, we have benefited greatly from his knowledge about how to run a venture capital firm.'

However, the technology to develop the read length of the DNA strands proved to be hard to develop and make robust enough. In the end, the plans and sales budget were estimated based on the future SNP market. To split the firm into two application areas was not seen as a positive thing and the efforts to develop the technology made by Anderson and his research associates at Uppsala University were not further developed by the engineers at BioTool. Instead, the SNP market became the focus for the firm and, as a consequence, the technology was geared towards this user group. 'We thought that all laboratories should have a BioTool instrument, just like the PCR machines. And based on that we could figure out how much money we would sell for. Even if we only would reach 10 per cent, it would still be a lot of money' (Patric Anderson, inventor).

The view of the market was rosy. The value of the SNP market was recognized to be about SEK1 billon in 1999. The growth of the SNP market was thought to be 35 per cent annually and, in 2004, the market would be worth SEK6 billion. The firm planned to reach break-even in 2002 and, in 2004, the turnover would have reached some SEK1.5 billion, thus a market share of around 25 per cent. Then it would, according to the plan, be a profitable company, employing about 300–500 people.

## Building the company

Since the bulk of the people engaged in transforming the BioTool technology into a product had their background in one of the world's largest biotech tool companies, Biopharma, with decades of experience in developing tools for drug development and testing in the later phases of clinical tests, it was in this area that they were most able to identify applications.

In order to get the firm up and running, a 'serial CEO' was hired. This CEO of a so-called venture partner of SLS Cap had worked as CEO and general manager at several start-up firms, and brought with him a 'starter kit' to get BioTool up and running quickly. To save time, the CEO brought in the same accountants he had used before and the same business reporting system was put into use. One decision that in hindsight would prove to be important was that he used the same software company that previously had been used for other companies. Overall, the CEO chosen by the venture capital firm had a strong influence on the development of the firm's administrative routines.

Product development was concerned with 'productifying' the research of Anderson and McFarland. These activities took place in parallel with the organizational development activities. Milestones related to developing prototypes of the instrument were decided upon.

It was decided that the product would be part of a 'system' that would consist of three parts: an instrument (where the DNA analysis was conducted); a reagent kit (which was needed in order to conduct the analysis); and a software program (where the analysis could be visualized and analysed together with results from databases). The idea was to use a 'razor blade' business model, selling hardware and software systems that in turn would consume reagents. It was by selling reagents that the actual profit was going to be made. The instrument, TJW348, could read 348 tests simultaneously and manage about 15,000 tests a day. Capacity-wise this would surpass alternative technologies. The software program should be able to foresee theoretical results for the analysis, create a database for the SNP sequences and enable a qualitative assessment of the data collected.

*Even if it is difficult for the R&D people to asses how much money will be used, they know the most important milestones and are able to say how long it will take to develop the product. Then it is easy to determine whether we are behind or ahead time-wise according to the development plan. It was about developing P0, P1, P2 and so on . . . that is, different generations of prototypes, how long it should take and how much it would cost. We revised development costs every month.*

After the first phase of setting organizational routines, the CEO was replaced with John Sanders in 1998. Sanders had a long background within the biotech industry and had worked for both Biopharma, ABI and Optipharma, another Uppsala-based biotech supply company.

Thus, the venture capital firm and the management started the process of developing 'milestones' to be reached within certain time frames. These milestones involved, as mentioned above, first the development of prototypes. Second, there was a need for a certain number of employees in order to reach the different prototype milestones. Third, in order to launch the product, the firm would have opened up a subsidiary in the United States. Further, the commercial market for the BioTool technology was defined. John Sanders put it like this in the annual report from 1999: 'This [the market] is not the DNA sequencing market as such, but rather the segment of applied genomics that studies genetic variability between individuals.'

Sanders and his management team, as well as the board of directors, decided that the company was going to approach firms and academic institutions that were involved in the early processes of drug discovery, where SNPs were assumed to become a major tool in the identification of target molecules. This meant that the potential users were decided to be researchers in academia, pharmaceutical companies, and companies active in drug discovery or similar activities. For the users, the benefits in relation to the traditional DNA sequencing methods, electrophoresis and hybridization would, according to the firm, be a technology that was more reliable, user friendly, faster, more cost effective and flexible.

The process of translating the new technology to a product was also permeated by the formulation of milestones to be reached in a certain time. One of those involved in the development of the instrument put it like this: 'Everything was designed to shorten the time to achieve different milestones. Time objectives were of great importance. The quality as well was certainly important, but cost was never an issue. We never compromised on time and quality.'

The majority of the R&D staff came from Biopharma. Having been part of a large multinational company they were not used to the routines of working within a small start-up. They were more used to competing for resources, and had experienced that delays or running over costs might be harmful in the next allocation phase. Working for BioTool was a different experience, as is illustrated in the following quote:

*The R&D staff were very worried about costs running over budget by some SEK10 million. Once they came to me and said: "We need more money, because TechCo [a supplier] wants 10 million more than we had estimated." In a few hours I phoned the board members and secured the money. This was totally new for these people and very encouraging, and it increased their loyalty to the company.*

For the venture capital firm, the logic is well described by the venture partner: 'For the venture capitalist, it means so much that a company is successful, and so very little that a firm does not perform well. So, in a fund, if there are just a few companies that perform well, it is those companies that make the fund successful. Therefore the venture capitalist invests more and more in those companies. It is very seldom that a venture capitalist invests more money or time in a firm when it is underperforming. Often they know early on what firms will do well.'

BioTool was growing at a very fast pace from its start in 1997, in terms of numbers of employees. The company was far from profitable however; break-even was moved forward and was now planned to happen in 2005. The company's head office and production facility were located in Uppsala, Sweden, and a US sales office was soon opened located in San Francisco, California. In Japan and some other countries BioTool was represented by independent distributors and agents. Early on, the BioTool management also became involved as shareholders through stock options in the company.

The board of directors was filled with owners and other representatives that could give the firm legitimacy. Among others, a Nobel Prize winner was elected to the board, as were well-known industrialists with backgrounds in some of the best-known Swedish firms. SLS Cap was of course also represented on the board as the major owner of the firm.

The early route outlined for rapid development and launch of an instrument dedicated to a certain, well-defined production step in DNA analysis also left imprints on the development of BioTool's production facility. Considerations of how the BioTool System was going to be combined with other instruments or production facilities on the customer side (in which producer–user interfaces were going to be activated) had to be decided in advance. Since a rapid launching of the instrument was such an important issue for the management, to set up its own production unit for the hardware was not a possibility. While the Stockholm-based Radical Tech was the first supplier used for prototype development, JointInc in northern Sweden later became the main supplier. JointInc provided the whole physical production process and stock-keeping for BioTool.

Considering the interaction around the BioTool System from the users' perspective, a system consisting of a large number of activities was outlined, where the DNA analysis was the last in a chain of more or less closely related items. Before being used in the BioTool System instrument, a choice of which SNPs to analyse had to be made. This choice was dependent on the application area and the numbers of SNPs in focus. These could vary from one single SNP to hundreds of SNPs. Second, the customer had to design and develop an assay for each one of the SNPs. This central activity was time consuming and also labour intensive. How labour intensive depended on the analysis system used. The third step involved so-called PCR amplification and preparation of the tests. The number of tests per SNP can vary between one and hundreds, and the scope of this step also varies among different suppliers' systems. The fourth and last step concerns the DNA analysis (which BioTool supplied), post treatment and evaluation of data.

When deciding on what activity to develop in this cycle of activities, BioTool chose to go only for the DNA analysis, partly because this was the activity that was in general seen as the bottleneck in the process, but also because this made it possible to focus on something manageable. Having tried to cover or integrate BioTool in the other activities would not have been a viable strategy since it would involve more resource and extend the development phase further. This was also a strategic choice that fitted into the logic to reduce the time from prototype to a ready-to-sell instrument.

Many, if not all, of the milestones developed around the product were also met. In fact, BioTool seemed to be able to fulfil most of the goals created by the venture capital firm. John Sanders put it like this in the annual report for 1999: 'We met every key milestone set for 1999, culminating in the commercial introduction and first sales of BioTool System . . .'.

After this statement the key milestones are described: Alpha and beta site testing completed, serial production started, commercial availability, sales and support office opened in San Fransisco, USA, sales force established, first orders from USA and Europe received, patent portfolio strengthened, private placement raises SEK120 million . . . along with developing relationships with renowned opinion leaders who, through their publications in prominent research journals, could contribute to the verification of the new method (of utmost importance to any supplier of research instruments).

## Finishing the product development and IPO

After three years as a company, BioTool launched its first product, the BioTool System, in late 1999. The tough time schedule meant that the product (or system) was developed rather close to the original idea of how the technology could be used. In order to keep to the tight time schedule the firm continued to hire people. The instrument was developed, prototypes were out for test usage at potential customers. BioTool's supplier, JointInc, started to produce the BioTool System and in November that same year the company got its first customer when a large US pharmaceutical company purchased a BioTool System. The price of the instrument was decided to be in the range of SEK750,000. In this price, the software program was included but not the reagent kit necessary to conduct the DNA analysis.

The results from the first installations revealed that the users found the system easy to use, fast and reliable. Once the customers were educated on the instrument, they did not demand a lot of support to interpret the result of the DNA analysis. The first customer put it like this: 'It is an important system for us. It is indeed reliable as it has a built-in control, which makes the instrument very fascinating. I think everybody in industry engaged in drug discovery finds it fascinating actually.'

The competitive landscape consisted of both small start-ups like BioTools as well as established life science companies. However, no competitor could match the easiness and precision in the analysis that BioTool could provide.

In fact, soon the US pharma giant had purchased another system, and within a year had invested in five systems all in all and had become a prime reference customer for BioTool. More companies and academic institutions followed as customers. For example, Harvard Medical School purchased a system, as did other leading academic institutions.

Only three years after investing in the company, SLS Cap could provide its investors with an 'exit'. The firm was a success story of great magnitude. BioTool received some SEK875 million in the IPO. The company's shares were offered at a price of SEK100 in 2000. The IPO was a great success, was heavily oversubscribed and created massive interest nationally as well as in the international press. Soon the stock price went up to SEK200, just a few months later the same year. The valuation of the firm went from SEK3 billion to SEK5 billion in just a few months. SLS Cap stayed as a major owner after the IPO, together with two of the founders, Patric Anderson and Donald McFarland.

### Questions

1. The management control system is implicitly described in the case, but what can you say about it? Does it seem to work well? What type of control practices are used, and why?
2. In what way do you think the owners influenced the 'innovation journey' of BioTool?
3. What does the future of the company look like? Justify your answer? In what dimensions does it look good? In what dimensions can you see problems arise?

# Case 2.5

# Tesla: climate change and the future of the electric vehicle

**by Emma Sjöström**

On 29 June 2010, Tesla Motors' CEO Elon Musk rang the bell at the NASDAQ opening ceremony, accompanied by his colleagues, his wife and his young twin sons. Tesla Motors was the first American carmaker to go public since Ford's launch in 1956.

The stock market embraced Tesla; in fact, the company's share value increased 41 per cent on its first day of trading alone. This was two years after the all-electric sports car, the Tesla Roadster, first started roaming the streets: the company's only model so far. The media reported that a 'potent mixture of star power and eco chic' fuelled the strong debut at the stock exchange.

A new model was introduced to the market every two or three years. The stock price kept rising. In September 2012, the stock traded at US$29.35. A year later, it traded at US$190.90; in September 2014 it reached US$279.20. There was big debate, however, as to whether or not Tesla was a sound investment. While its stock surged, some critics warned of a 'Tesla bubble'. In April 2017, Tesla was worth more than Ford, in spite of Ford having sold more than 58 times the amount of vehicles as Tesla in 2016 (see Exhibit 1 for the Tesla stock chart). Tesla's market gap to auto manufacturer General Motors was about US$3 billion. Only once, in October 2016, had Tesla posted a profit.

As Elon Musk arrived in the office on a December day in 2017, he was thinking about the questions he had received at a recent press event: Would he be able to deliver enough batteries? What were his thoughts on the reports of child labour in the supply chain? How was the company going to reduce $CO_2$ emissions in production? These were all valid questions.

Musk turned on his computer and started writing a document titled: *Macro-Environmental Factors: What Will Influence the General EV Market – Particularly Tesla – Over the Next Five to Ten Years?* What should he put on the list?

**EXHIBIT 1** Tesla, Inc. stock price through 31 December 2017

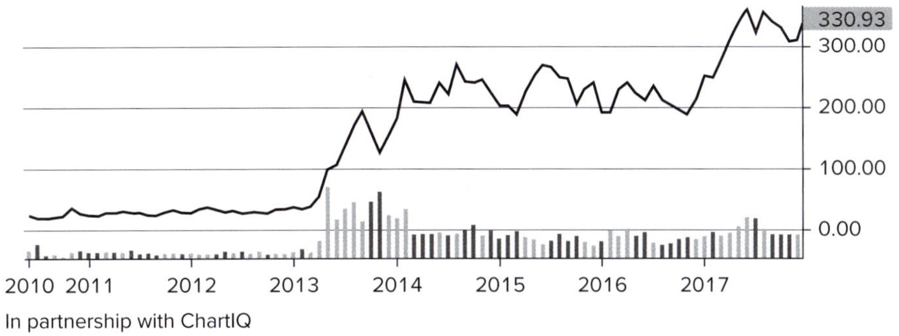


*Source:* Yahoo Finance.

This case was written by Dr Emma Sjöström, Misum, Stockholm School of Economics.

## Climate change: a game-changer for business

The Paris Agreement was adopted to the sounds of enthusiastic whistles and resounding applause on 12 December 2015. A major victory was the legally binding goal to hold global temperatures 'well below 2 °C above pre-industrial levels and to pursue efforts to limit the temperature increase even further to 1.5 degrees Celsius'. The Paris Agreement, which was ratified by 174 countries of the 197 parties to the United Nations Framework Convention on Climate Change, set out a global action plan to put the world on track by avoiding dangerous climate change.

France's foreign minister, Laurent Fabius, led the Paris conference and said that this 'ambitious and balanced' plan was a 'historic turning point' in the quest to reduce global warming.

Governments were committed to fulfilling the Paris Agreement, and the business sector was expected to contribute as well. In actual fact, the business sector did not have much of a choice. Climate change had also become a competitive issue, implying severe business risks, such as disrupted supply chains, and presenting opportunities for innovation of products, services and business models. In 2015, Unilever's CEO said natural disasters linked to climate change cost his company about €400 million a year. Meanwhile, thanks to energy efficiency programmes in the manufacturing process, companies such as GM and Ford had reduced $CO_2$ emissions as a means to improve their bottom lines, by offering fuel efficiency in the user phase.

In order to thrive – or even survive – companies and investors needed to understand how climate change would impact markets, regulation and operations and, thereby, take corresponding action.

### Electric vehicles

Electric vehicles (EVs) were marketed as a more climate-friendly option to internal combustion-engine (ICE) cars. EVs used electric propulsion, which was energy efficient and did not cause local emissions (see Exhibit 2 for definitions of the different kinds of automotive engines).

**EXHIBIT 2** Different types of engine

***ICE – internal combustion engine***

ICEs are traditional engines, powered by gasoline, diesel, biofuels or even natural gas. While today's ICEs are significantly more efficient and have lower emissions than those from decades ago, the fundamental technology – burning fuel to create power – remains the same.

***HEV – hybrid electric vehicle***

The HEV – such as the Toyota Prius – is powered by a combination of an ICE and an electric motor (hybrid vehicle drivetrain). The batteries can be charged in a few ways, either by spinning an electric generator when the ICE is operating or, in some cases, by converting the vehicle's kinetic energy into electric energy through systems like regenerative brakes.

***PHEV – plug-in hybrid electric vehicle***

PHEVs are in many ways very similar to HEVs in that they have a hybrid vehicle drivetrain and use both an ICE and electric power. Their rechargeable battery can be charged by plugging in to a power source. When the battery is depleted, the plug-in hybrid starts acting as a regular hybrid, with the combustion engine taking the role of primary power source.

***BEV – battery electric vehicle***

The BEV has no ICE or fuel tank at all, and runs on a fully electric drivetrain powered by rechargeable batteries. These vehicles need to be plugged in to a power source to charge, and depending on the vehicle, they have varying charging times and driving ranges.

*Source:* Canadian Fuels Association.

Electric cars relied on regular charging from the local electricity network, so the extent to which they were an environmentally superior alternative to ICE vehicles in the user phase depended largely on the local energy mix. A Norwegian report stated that, from a life-cycle perspective, EVs caused fewer $CO_2$ emissions than cars with internal combustion engines – that is, conventional vehicles. This calculation was valid when using the average European electricity mix, and including the energy consumption for extracting, preparing and distributing energy, as well as emissions from production. However, it may not hold true for a country such as China, where 60 per cent of the country's energy consumption in 2017 came from coal.

A Swedish study, however, which also adopted a life-cycle perspective, stated that an electric vehicle emitted more $CO_2$ than a moderately consuming diesel vehicle. This would largely be due to the carbon footprint of producing the lithium-ion battery packs that powered all-electric vehicles. The study estimated that manufacturing an EV battery could produce the same $CO_2$ emissions as driving a diesel car up to 250,000 km. Industry representatives pointed out that the study looked in the rear (view) mirror: the calculations were based on what battery production had looked like until today, yet did not account for potentially less emission-intense manufacturing in the future.

Electric cars were no longer purely an environmental statement; they were also a symbol of technological status. The enthusiasm for EVs was mirrored in worldwide sales, which continued to rise. Global plug-in vehicle deliveries reached 1,223,600 units in 2017, 58 per cent higher than for 2016. These included all battery electric vehicles (BEVs) and plug-in hybrid electric vehicle (PHEV) passenger car sales, light trucks in the USA/Canada and light commercial vehicle in Europe; 66 per cent of sales were pure electric and 34 per cent were plug-in hybrids (see Exhibit 3).

**EXHIBIT 3** Global electric vehicle sales

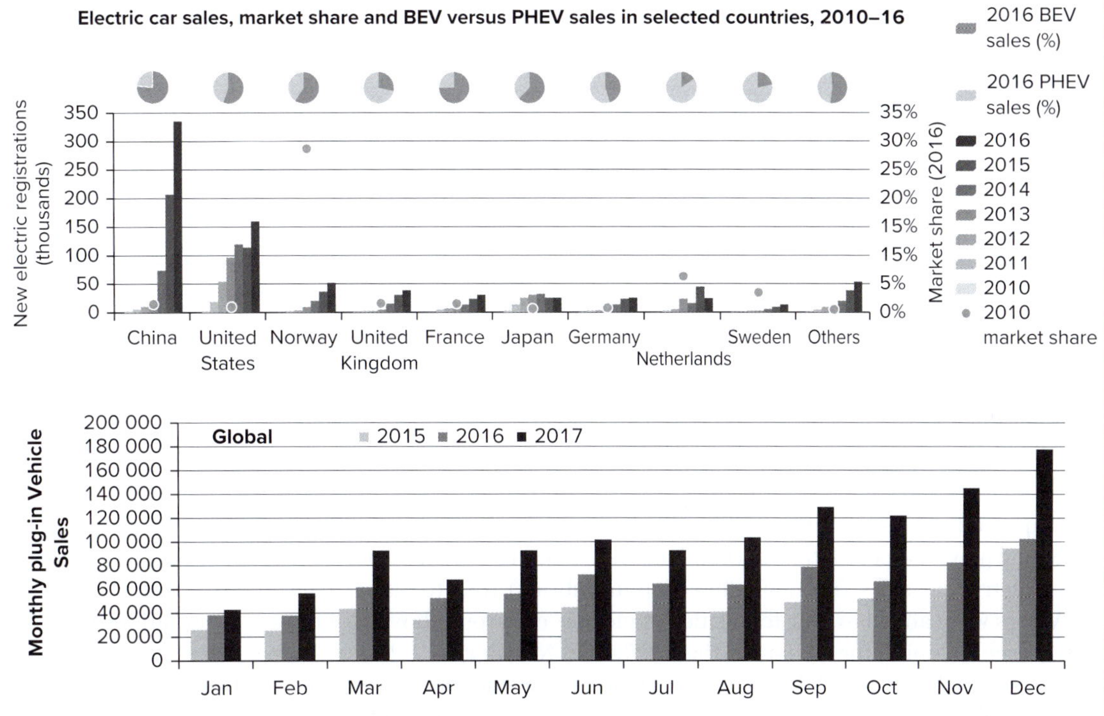


*Source:* International Energy Agency (2017) and EV-volumes.com (2017).

China had increased its significance as a market and as a manufacturing base for electrically chargeable vehicles, accounting for roughly half of the 1.2 million plug-in electric vehicles sold worldwide in 2017. Chinese carmakers made 47 per cent of all plug-in electric vehicles sold in 2017.

Plug-in vehicles captured a world market share of just 1.3 per cent. In 2017, several established carmakers, from Jaguar Land Rover to Volvo Cars, announced plans to bring electric versions of their vehicles to market in the next few years. According to forecasts, electric vehicles were expected to be 30 per cent of new car sales by 2040.

The battery industry's success was closely tied to the EV industry's success. Batteries accounted for up to half an EV's cost of production. Japanese Panasonic was the world's largest supplier of EV batteries globally (see Exhibit 4). It was also building the so-called Gigafactory in Nevada, USA, with Tesla. The construction of Northvolt, Europe's largest battery factory, was scheduled to begin in 2018. The full factory would be completed in 2023 and would produce 32 GWh per year in Sweden in 2018, with a focus on green battery technology.

**EXHIBIT 4** Top EV battery manufacturers, MWh per year (2015)

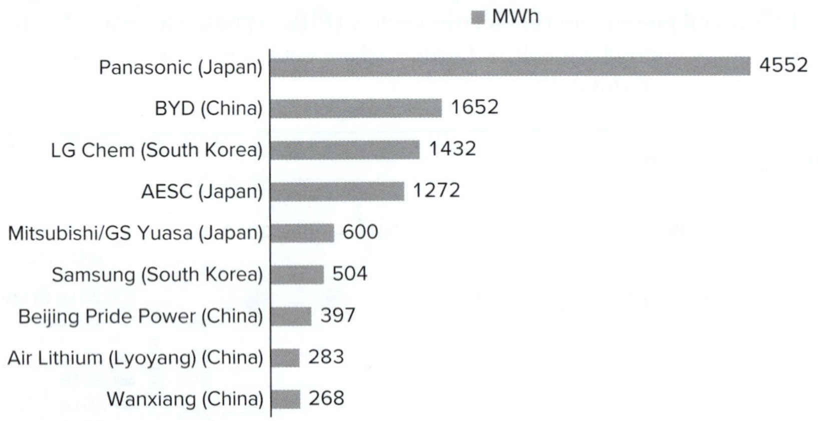


*Source:* CleanTechnica (2016).

Cobalt was a critical raw material in lithium-ion battery production. It had been reported that dangerous working conditions, risks to people's health and child labour were huge problems in the cobalt mines of the Democratic Republic of the Congo (DRC). Two-thirds of the world's cobalt was found in the DRC, which was one of the world's poorest and least developed countries.

## Norway: EVs hit record levels

Norway stood out as a country where electric vehicles had penetrated the market exceptionally well. The country, with a population of only 5 million, had more than 10 per cent of the global all-electric car fleet. Electric car sales (not including plug-in hybrids) rose to 39 per cent in 2017 from 29 in 2016. If PHEV cars were added to this, total sales of electric cars rose above half of new registrations in Norway in 2017 (see Exhibit 5 for a chart of the EV fleet in Norway).

The country had the goal that 100 per cent of new car sales by 2025 would come from zero-emission vehicles. According to analysts, the achievements were mostly limited by the supply and not the demand, even considering that, more than in almost all markets, 15 different all-electric models were offered in Norway.

**EXHIBIT 5** Electric vehicle fleet in Norway

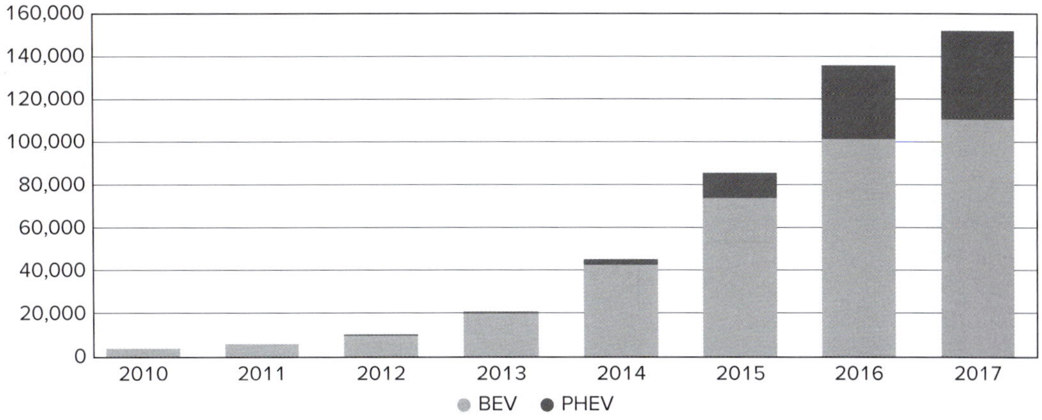


*Source:* Elbil.no (2017).

The history of electric vehicles in Norway began in 1970. Climate policy was the main driver behind the development. Norwegian greenhouse gas emissions totalled 53.9 million tons of $CO_2$ equivalents in 2015, of which those coming from domestic road traffic accounted for approximately 19 per cent. While road traffic emissions had been stable the last few years leading up to 2015, they had increased 30 per cent since 1990. Considering that 98 per cent of Norwegian energy came from hydroelectric power plants, and since EVs in Norway used domestically produced energy, driving an EV as opposed to a conventional vehicle was considered to reduce $CO_2$ emissions by 100 per cent.

### Government interaction

The Norwegian government had played a central role in establishing the Norwegian EV market.

According to the EV Norway website: 'Norway has what is probably the world's best incentives for zero emission vehicles and correspondingly the world's highest number of electric cars per capita by a wide margin.'

The first EV incentives were introduced in the early 1990s, starting with exemptions on all road toll charges, registration taxes and annual licence fees. Municipalities then began offering EVs free parking in municipality-owned parking lots, and company EV cars received a tax reduction.

Over time, additional benefits were put in place: the 25 per cent Norwegian VAT (Value Added Tax) was removed from the sale of all EVs in 2001; after an initial trial period, permanent access to bus lanes was introduced nationwide in 2005; and, starting in 2009, EV owners could use main road coastal ferries at a discount.

In order to reduce climate gas emissions from the transport sector, the Norwegian government started Transnova in 2001. The organization aimed to support the testing of new technologies to expand their reach. Thanks to Transnova funding, charging stations were established on a larger scale. In order to promote EVs in municipalities, the association Grønn bil ('green car'), received financial help, with the goal of facilitating adaption to the EV technology.

By 2013, no other country in the world had more incentives for buying and using electric vehicles than did Norway (see Exhibit 6 for incentives across countries).

**EXHIBIT 6** Financial incentives and EV market share by country in 2014

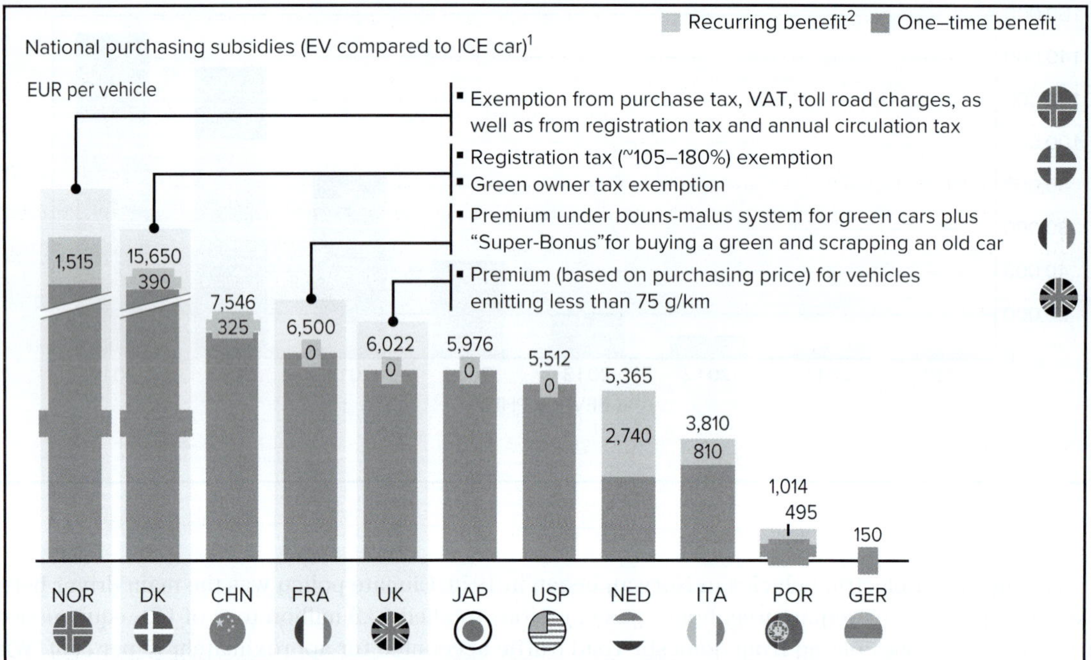


1. Calculations (annual benefits) based on compact class car vs. xEV (sub sidies are usually created in a way that also new/fuel efficient cars receive benefits, e.g taxes based on CO2 emissions): only national subsidies counted–additional local subsidies/incentives might exist

2. Cumulated recurring benefit assuming a 5 year holding period

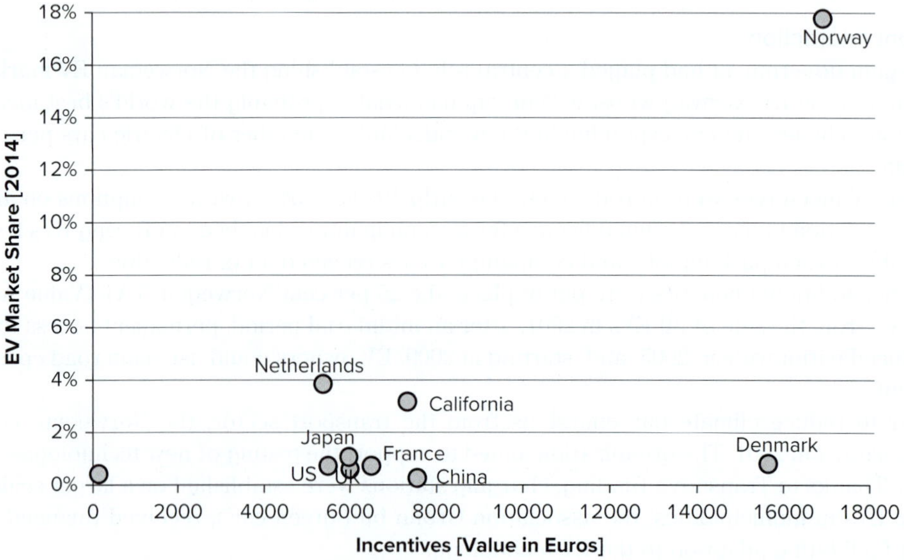


*Source:* Amsterdam Roundtables Foundation & McKinsey (2014).`

### Infrastructure

In order to extend EVs' range, EV sales were closely linked to the development of new infrastructure since EVs were dependent on charging stations. One study from 2015 concluded that 'charging point infrastructure has a positive impact on households' EV ownership in developing EV markets'.

As mentioned earlier, Transnova initiated a support programme for charging stations in 2009 – the only government incentive initiated at a national level during this time. The cities of Oslo and Akershus initiated their own infrastructure support programmes; most charging stations offered free charging during the initial period. By 2013, however, most demanded payment.

As of 2010, most EVs were equipped with Li-ion batteries that, according to manufacturers, had a 10-year service life. The first public fast-charging stations were launched in 2011. Fast chargers could recharge theabattery up to 80 per cent in 20–30 minutes. However, fast charging was a lot more time consuming at sub-zero temperatures, which led to EVs having a shorter range in the winter. Transnova, as well as some Norwegian counties, gave financial support for fast chargers.

### Users

The Norwegian Electric Vehicle Association was founded in 1995 as an Oslo Energy and Municipality of Oslo initiative. The organization became an important player for market development due to activities such as mapping the charging stations, and recruiting new drivers by offering test drives and connecting EV users through internet platforms. The association had a consumer benefit focus as well since it was in close contact with the EV industry and could provide politicians with information.

In 2013, the yearly member survey concluded the following:

> *The typical Norwegian EV user is a middle-aged family father with higher education and income, and he owns a Nissan LEAF as one of two cars. He uses his electric car on a daily basis instead of a traditional petrol or diesel car. He uses the electric car for commuting, after work activities, and not for longer holiday trips. He agrees on that his electric car saves him money and time and he is very satisfied as an EV owner. His next car will also be electric. [. . .] The broad package of incentives convinced him to buy his electric car. Although, it was the zero purchase tax and VAT that made the electric car competitive for him to consider in the first place. Low fuel cost, free toll roads and access to bus lanes are also important incentives.*

EVs would be expensive in Norway if it were not for the removal of VAT and the elimination of the vehicle registration tax, which depended on the value of the car. Government incentives such as these substantially lowered the price of electric cars. Studies of the perception of EV advantages revealed that economic benefits were the main drivers behind purchasing an EV.

## Tesla, Inc.

Tesla, Inc. (originally Tesla Motors) was an EV car manufacturer headquartered in Palo Alto, California. Tesla was incorporated in 2003 by engineers Marc Tarpenning and Martin Eberhard. The initial aim was to 'prove that electric cars could be better than gasoline cars', and Tesla's mission was 'to accelerate the world's transition to sustainable transport'.

Tesla engineers first designed a drivetrain for a sports car built around an asynchronous motor. Nikola Tesla took a patent on such an engine in 1888, thus it has been the inspiration for the company name. Over time, the Tesla brand had become synonymous with Elon Musk, the young billionaire who made his fortune on PayPal, an online financial services company. Musk was known for his big visions and entrepreneurial spirit, including his ambitions to explore and colonize the planet Mars through his SpaceX venture (a company that developed and launched space craft). He invested heavily in Tesla, becoming chairman of the board in 2004 and CEO in 2008.

Tesla was not only an automaker, it was also a technology and design company focusing on innovation within the field of energy. This was also reflected in how the company had taken full ownership of its value chain. For example, through the company SolarCity (co-founded by Elon Musk), Tesla could offer energy storage services, including a turn-key residential battery back-up service. The Tesla Gigafactory 1 was a solar-powered lithium-ion battery factory, built primarily for Tesla, Inc. It was capable of matching the current world lithium-ion battery capacity production. Tesla had also launched its own Supercharger stations – a network of free charging stations that could charge Tesla batteries in a matter of minutes instead of hours.

Following much hype, the Tesla Roadster was launched in 2008; it was the first car model conceived by the Tesla team. The two-seater all-electric sports car would provide the value of a high-end sports car at a lower cost to the customer and a lower resource cost to the planet. With an acceleration of 0 to 100 kmh in 3.9 seconds (which is faster than many gasoline-propelled sports cars) and a range of 394 km per charge of its lithium-ion battery, the Roadster set new standards for electrical transport.

The Tesla Model S was launched in 2012 as the world's first electric premium sedan. With a compact battery that was integrated into the chassis under the occupant cabin, the vehicle had room for up to seven passengers. As EVs do not have an ICE, there was even room for storage. In 2015, and again in 2016, it was ranked as the world's best-selling plug-in electric car. The Tesla Model X was a crossover utility vehicle introduced in the USA in 2015, and internationally the following year (Exhibit 7 displays a picture of the Tesla Model X). The four-door sedan Tesla Model 3 was launched in 2017. When Tesla opened for pre-orders of the Model 3, it took almost US$10 billion in just two days.

**EXHIBIT 7** The Tesla Model X

*Source:* Grzegorz Czapski/Shutterstock

Tesla cars were not for everyone, at least not from the start. Elon Musk was quoted as saying that 'The strategy of Tesla is to enter at the high end of the market, where customers are prepared to pay a premium, and then drive down market as fast as possible to higher unit volume and lower prices with each successive model.' The Tesla Roadster base price was US$109,000. Tesla Model 3 prices started at US$35,000.

## Tesla in Norway and Sweden

Tesla entered the Norwegian market in autumn 2013, during a time in which a number of Norwegian manufacturers went out of business. The Tesla Model S was the first luxury EV to be launched on the Norwegian market. It had a range of up to 480 km, which was a jump from 160 km, or 90 km during winter conditions, which was the average range of existing models on the Norwegian market in mid-2013.

Tesla was well received. In March 2014, the Tesla Model S became the highest-selling car in a single month in Norway's history, ahead of the Volkswagen Golf, and Norway was the second-largest market in the world for the Model S, the largest marketing being the USA.

Tesla sold 8,460 cars in Norway in 2017, which amounted to 5.3 per cent of total car sales. Operating a total of 12 stores in the country, Tesla was Norway's seventh best-selling car brand.

**EXHIBIT 8** Tesla Model S registrations in Norway and Sweden respectively

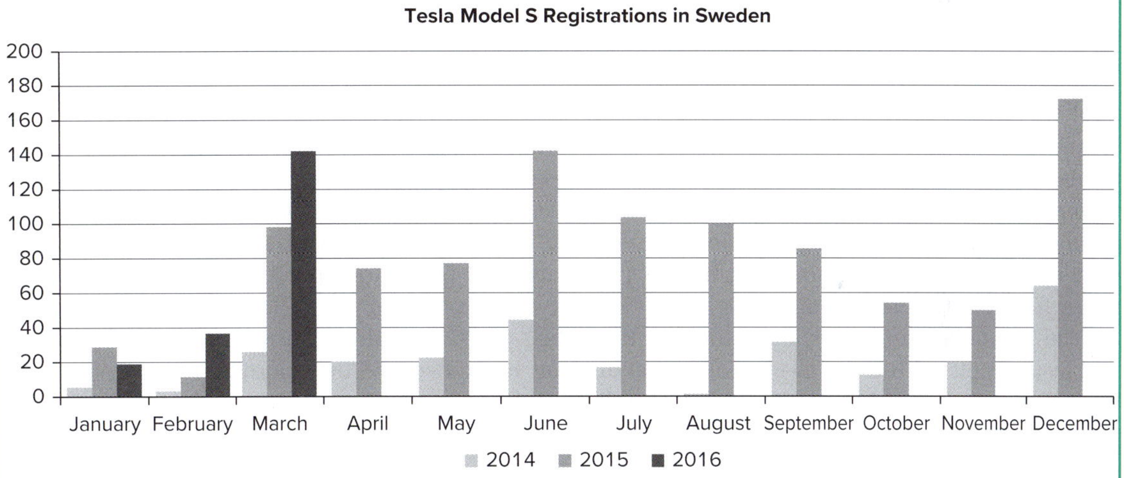


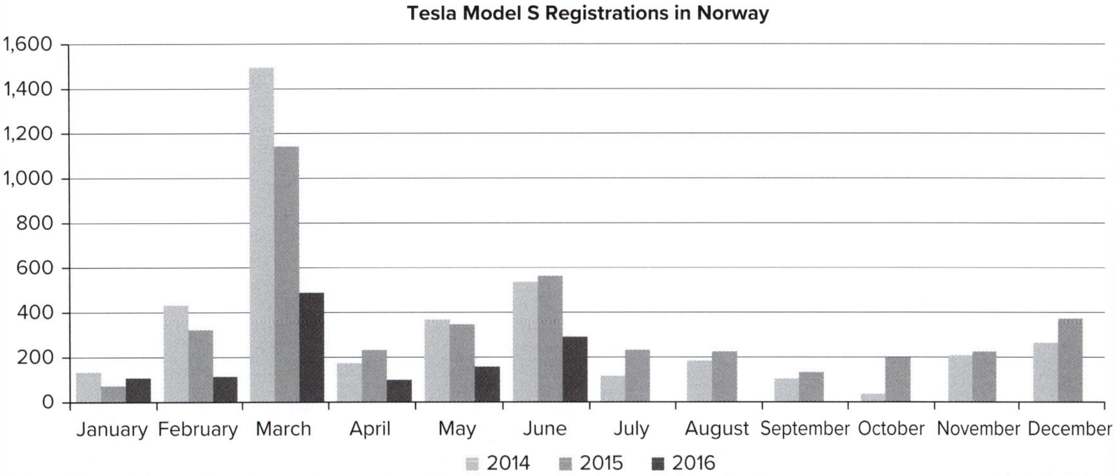


*Source:* Electrec.co (2016).

Meanwhile, in neighbouring Sweden, the total amount of Tesla cars registered amounted to 3,709 by the end of 2017. Tesla had a market share of 0.3 per cent based on the number of newly registered cars. (Exhibit 8 depicts Tesla Model S registrations in Norway and Sweden.)

A study from 2016 revealed that 42 per cent of car owners in Sweden were willing to buy an EV as their next car purchase (45 per cent of them men and 39 per cent women). A total of 83 per cent of respondents said their main motivating factor was for the sake of the environment. For the 37 per cent of respondents who said they would not consider buying an EV, the main reason was the limited mileage before having to charge the car's battery again.

The Swedish government offered exemptions from vehicle tax for five years for all biogas, ethanol, electric hybrid or low-consuming energy-efficient cars. Since 2012, cars that emit no more than 50 grams of carbon dioxide per kilometre ('super environmental cars') have also been eligible for a premium of SEK40,000 (€4,200). This was not at the point of sale, however; it was only after the buyer sent in the proper paperwork to the authorities. Tesla had 6.6 per cent of market share in the super environmental cars segment. The programme was originally designed to cover 5,000 low-carbon vehicles; Sweden reached this threshold in mid-2014 and extended the programme on a year-to-year basis, which left car buyers uncertain as to whether the programme would continue.

The new Tesla Model 3 had encountered delivery delays due to production bottlenecks, and was expected to reach Europe by the end of 2018. Tesla had four stores in Sweden (two in Stockholm, one in Gothenburg and one in Malmö) and two service points.

### Looking ahead

Meanwhile, in California, Tesla CEO Elon Musk continued his efforts to accelerate the world's transition to sustainable transport. Plans for the future included more affordable electric cars produced in a higher volume, solar-powered roofs, mid-size vehicles, SUVs and pick-up trucks, as well as the refinement of autonomous vehicles and the creation of a sharing economy, in which cars could be requested and driven while the owner is not using them. Or, as Musk had put it, to expand Tesla's line to 'cover the major forms of terrestrial transport'.

The December sun was shining through Elon Musk's office window. It was now lunchtime, and he had just completed the macro-environmental analysis he had started that morning. He pondered what his next message should be to his 18 million followers on Twitter . . .

### Questions

1 In what ways is climate change a game-changer for business?

2 Which macro-economic factors will influence the EV market? Conduct a PESTLE[1] analysis.

3 If you were head of sales and marketing in the Nordic region, and Elon Musk had asked you to present your thoughts on how to expand sales in Sweden, what would be your main points?

4 If you were head of investment at a pension fund, based on what arguments would your firm choose to invest or not invest in Tesla?

[1] PESTLE stands for Political, Economic, Social, Technological, Legal and Environmental factors. By understanding these external environments, organizations can maximize the opportunities and minimize the threats to the organization.

# Chapter 3

# Managers, human behaviour and organizations

## Learning objectives

After reading this chapter, you should be able to:

1 Explain the importance of understanding human behaviour for management control system design and use.

2 Describe how different models of human behaviour in economics, psychology and sociology inform management control system design and use.

3 Describe how the management control system model of human behavior provides an integrated perspective on human behaviour that informs management control system design and use.

4 Describe the importance of culture, social values and ethics for the design and use of management control systems.

## Real world vignette: Banking in London

One of the major financial centres in the world can be found in London. In the City of London, where some 300.000 people work, one can find many extremes in the way people live and work. This means that during the working week, the City is a vibrant community of well-dressed and well-behaved financial experts, with their very special ways of going about. The weekends show a different picture: the City is strangely empty, with little sign of the enormous number of people working there and the enormous amounts of capital being traded.

This contrast stimulated the curiosity of Dutch journalist Joris Luyendijk, who spent three years interviewing employees in the City. He lived with bankers, as sociological researchers often do; with the aim to discover what is 'really going on', they aim to melt into the crowd, understand the world from within, and try to think like the bankers do. Obviously, Luyendijk was researching the City with a specific quest. He wanted to understand how bankers behave, how they think and act, and whether bankers are different to any other employee. With the 2007-2008 financial crisis having finally resolved itself, the question was whether something was learned, and whether the practices in the industry had changed. The crisis began with banks trading in many bad products, without much consideration of the risks involved. The end came when heaps of taxpayers' money was used to 'bail out' those banks and traders that were responsible for the damage. Luyendijk expected to hear the bankers defend themselves, tell us that their lives had changed after the crisis.

Overall Luyendijk conducted some 200 interviews during his three-year stay in the City. He felt like he had entered another universe, in terms of the size of the industry, the prices people paid for rent and private schools for their children. He was stunned by the hours worked, and the salaries and bonuses earned. Had much changed since the crisis? Luyendijk did not get this impression. Oversight on trading had not much improved, he concluded, and he does not sketch a very comforting picture. Bankers are not at all motivated to commit fraud, yet the complexity of their work, and the fierce competition between banks, and between bankers, governance and control are extremely difficult.

Between the front office, which is engaged in trade, and the back office, which is responsible for organizing the logistics, sits the middle office. This office is responsible for setting the direction for traders and ensuring that they act within the law and the strategic goals of the bank. In the old days, long before the crisis, this middle office almost ran the bank, and consisted of people having an interest in long-term stability. But now, as one of the interviewees suggested, the only role of the middle office was to keep the files that the bank would need to push through the paper shredder when the next crisis called for an external investigation.[1]

## Introduction

Now more than a decade after the start of the financial crisis (also called the *credit* crisis) of 2007–2008, the question is whether we can say that the firms operating in the world of international business and finance are back 'in control'. This crisis started with the defaulting of very risky mortgage loans in the USA, was followed by bankruptcy and privatization of banks in many countries and sent shocks to the financial system around the world. Many well-known (investment) banks were involved, such as Goldman Sachs, Lehman Brothers, Merrill Lynch and Morgan Stanley. Several hundred banks in the USA alone were somehow affected or failed. Given the strong financial relationships between financial institutions in today's economic reality, problems in one company easily shift to another. This is why we speak of a crisis in the financial world, rather than of management control system problems in individual firms. Such a wording could easily mislead us into thinking that we could not sensibly speak of management control system problems at the level of individual companies. But we can, and we need to if we are sincerely interested in how things went out of control and how we can keep it from happening again. After more than a decade of commentaries, analysis and reviews, the questions about what went wrong and how we can avoid another crisis are not fully resolved. The description of the ways of working in the financial sector points to a multitude of factors and circumstances that hinder clear answers to these questions. At the core of such descriptions lies the fact that it is the complexity of human behaviour that seems to puzzle us most. For the well functioning of *input controls* in particular, some basic understanding of the drivers of human behaviour is vital.

---

1 *Telegraph* (2015) Swimming with sharks: my journey into the world of the bankers by Joris Luyendijk, review: 'prophet of doom'. Available at: https://www.telegraph.co.uk/books/what-to-read/swimming-with-sharks-bankers-joris-luyendijk-review/  (accessed 15 September 2019).

If we go back to the definition of a management control system provided in Chapter 1, 'a combination of control practices designed and implemented by top managers to increase the probability that lower-level managers and employees will *behave* in ways consistent with the organization's mission, goals and strategies', it is clear that we need to make an attempt to understand human behaviour in some depth. Human behaviour, even when considered individually, is hard to predict. But when humans work together in organizations and interact to achieve the organization's mission, goals and strategies, predictability sometimes becomes even nearly impossible.

The banking sector is clearly one where a lot of changes have been taking place over the past few decades, enhancing competition and global presence. Once, banks were seen as relatively stable and uninteresting from a management control system perspective. They thrived on throughput controls, a culture of risk aversion and a preference for simple financial operations, focusing on saving, borrowing and lending. Growth, enhanced competition and globalization of financial institutions went hand in hand with a shift towards taking on more risky activities, by dealing in complex financial services. The 2007–2008 crisis was the proof of how such changes challenge the management control systems in place. On top of the complexity associated with human behaviour in general came the complexity and unpredictability of the forces at work in the international economy. It is in this context that we need to design and use management control systems. The financial crisis, like the crisis in the dotcom sector at the start of the millennium, makes us focus on the need to understand how humans are inclined to behave amid the complexity of firms operating in today's societies. This complexity is enhanced by the multitude of parallel demands from investors, consumers and the general public, as already discussed in Chapter 2. In the case of dotcom firms like Enron and WorldCom the problem appeared to lie in a human's inability to assess whether these firms were truly creating value, or rather just looking like they created value (see the Real World Example of Enron).

**Real World Example:** The biggest casualty of the dotcom crisis was the Enron Corporation. Having won *Fortune* magazine's praise for being 'America's Most Innovative Company' for six years in a row, it filed for bankruptcy in 2001. Shareholders lost tens of billions of dollars and employees lost their jobs. Enron was managed according to a business model in which large debts were hidden from the balance sheet. While arguing that it was creating shareholder value, its true financial results were bad. The old and new CEOs, Kenneth Lay and Jeff Skilling, as well as CFO Andrew Fastow, were seen as the main perpetrators and were sentenced to imprisonment. The company's auditor, Arthur Andersen, was found guilty of allowing the accounting manipulation that Enron concocted.

In 2000, Enron designed throughput controls in the form of a code of conduct for all its employees; the introduction is presented below. Clearly, this code of conduct was an unreliable signal of the true values within the company.

**Enron code of conduct**

*As officers and employees of Enron Corp, its subsidiaries, and its affiliated companies ('Enron' or collectively the 'Company'), we are responsible for conducting the business affairs of the Company in accordance with all applicable laws and in a moral and honest manner. To make certain that we understand what is expected of us, Enron has adopted certain policies, with the approval of the board of directors, all of which are set forth in the enclosed booklet, revised July 2000. Please note that Enron has added the principles of human rights; provided further description of our business ethics policy with respect to our legal contracts, the selection of outside counsel, and the making of disparaging remarks, oral or written, about Enron by employees; provided further clarification of Enron's policy with respect to confidential information and trade secrets; decreased the number of days passwords are valid under Enron's communication services and equipment policy; provided additional information with respect to the criminal penalties and civil fines assessed by the US government under the Foreign Corrupt Practices Act; and clarified Enron's policy with respect to conflicts of interests, investments and outside business interests of employees.*

*The Code of Ethics contains commonsense rules of conduct with which the great majority of Enron employees routinely conform. However, I ask that you read them carefully and completely and that, as you do, you reflect on your past actions to make certain that you have complied with the policies. It is absolutely essential that you fully comply with these policies in the future. If you have any questions, talk them over with your supervisor, manager or Enron legal counsel.*

*Source:* Enron Code of Conduct (2000, p. 1).

Enron in particular is still showcased to demonstrate a development from a relatively old-fashioned energy company, creating value by trading in physical energy products, towards one in which value was created by smart – but not really smart – speculations on energy prices. In such situations it appeared that the company's management control system failed, and we need to understand why. We also need to understand how management control systems, which aim to guide human behaviour in line with the organizational mission, goals and strategies, sometimes need to include elaborate risk management systems. This increased attention to risk management is certainly a result of the various crises and is the topic of Chapter 11 in this book. In the current chapter, we will focus on human behaviour in general, guided by a basic question: What do we need to know about human behaviour to make it 'controllable'? We need to go beyond the observation that human behaviour is complex and unpredictable to provide basic understanding of how we should look at human behaviour. We need to understand why people do the things they do, and especially why people behave the way they do in an organizational context. To reduce the complexity and unpredictability of human behaviour we need to pay attention to several explicit views on humans as managers. To provide such views we need to make use of the insights that the social sciences provide us. Space constraints do not permit full overviews of these sciences, but will point out some key characteristics of the way in which human behaviour is explained in economics, psychology and sociology. Each of these sciences points to some structural characteristics of human behaviour, and they do so differently. To make such differences visible, we will refer to them as constituting different models of human behaviour. Economics, psychology and sociology thus use different models of human behaviour, which is important to recognize since they, therefore, also have different implications for the design and use of management control systems. The way we understand, and are able to predict, the relationships between management control practices and human behaviour depends on what model we use in our analysis. This may sound rather theoretical, but when evaluating the pros and cons of different management control practices, it appears that we often have an implicit understanding of human behaviour, and that disagreements about the appropriateness of such practices are rooted in different implicit models. Explicating this understanding is therefore of direct practical significance. Different models of human behaviour have different practical implications for management control system design.[2]

The remainder of this chapter is structured as follows. In the next section we will introduce our conceptual model of human behaviour in a more detailed way. In particular, we will show how the economic model of human behaviour, the psychological model of human behaviour and the sociological model of human behaviour each points to, and focuses on, different characteristics of human behaviour, and also how each raises and answers important questions. We will see that a particular management control system design is often based on a specific view of what humans are, as laid down in these models. We will see how the economic model of human behaviour emphasizes human preference for value and money, how the psychological model of human behaviour points to humans being

[2] Lindenberg, S. (1990). Homo socio-oeconomicus: the emergence of a general model of man in the social sciences. *Journal of Institutional and Theoretical Economics*, 146(4): 727–48.

social and cognitive creatures that have many material and immaterial needs, and how the sociological model of human behaviour enables us to see such behaviour as resulting from their membership of groups, which creates such things as informal culture and power structures. After that we continue with an attempt to take from these models those elements that are directly important for the design and use of management control systems. We will call this the management control model of managers. This model mixes the insights from the theoretical model, focusing on human motivation, human learning, and human social and ethical needs and interaction. The model also points us to the importance of human cognition, and of the role of ethics in management control system design and use. For each of these aspects of human behaviour we will illustrate how they may influence the design and use of management control systems. At the end of this chapter we will, however, also point to some consequences of using this model for what management control systems cannot do. There are, in other words, boundaries to the kinds of behavioural intervention that management control systems can provide. Understanding these limitations of management control system design and use is also important, since we are not interested in guiding the behaviour of some ideal type of manager, but rather the behaviour of lower-level managers and employees that are real human beings.

## Models of human behaviour

Our current practical understanding of management control systems is sometimes based on a partial and simplified view of what humans are and how humans behave. For example, if we are to believe the many managerial handbooks of the kind that you typically find in airport shops, telling you about the 'seven habits' you need to display for success, or the 'six coloured hats' that people should wear to achieve group cooperation, or the 'big five' personality factors that drive human behaviour (see the Real World Example), management is a matter of applying checklists. They also seem to suggest that humans can do whatever they want to do as long as they learn certain behaviours or perform certain simple tricks. According to such a view, management is simply the application of some principles, and failure in management is due simply to the fact that those principles have wrongfully not been applied. Disappointing as it may sound, the truth is far more complex. Surely there are tricks and principles that can help you to avoid bad things? Moral principles like 'do not lie' and 'be nice to others', and functional principles like 'do not make calculative errors in your performance report' and 'finish your work on time', are certainly correct, at least most of the time. But when it comes to a more active and positive influence on human behaviour, these simple principles of good behaviour are not sufficient to guide such behaviour. Moreover, these principles often lack straightforward applicability in complex situations, in which they are most needed. What if telling the truth means you are rude to others? What if finishing your work on time means that you are likely to make more calculative errors? This goes for general principles of human behaviour, but it also goes for some of the slogan-type wisdoms that we observe in the area of management control system design. One well-known slogan states that 'what you measure is what you get', or that 'what gets measured gets improved'. Both these slogans provide a strong endorsement of controlling people's behaviour by constant and meticulous measurement of what they do and what they achieve. It suggests that the only thing you need to do to influence people towards the activities and goals that are good for the organization, requires measurement, coupled perhaps with appropriate financial rewards. However, more than a century of serious social research is now available that tries to find out what the drivers of human behaviour really are. Especially in the fields of economics, psychology and sociology this is the main question, and the answers can hardly be called straightforward.

***Real World Example:*** Here we display some popular views on management that have inspired managers over past decades. It is important to note that although these typologies often have a great deal of inspirational value due to their attractive simplicity they also lack the analytical precision to guide a more fundamental analysis of managerial challenges.

**The seven habits of highly effective people**

Steven Covey's model of the 'seven habits of highly effective people' stylizes much of what we believe is good and pragmatic behaviour of people in organizations. It is an example of an attempt to reduce enormous amounts of wisdom into a limited category of behavioural styles. Obviously, the analytical rigour of these styles is limited, since many people will interpret the same behaviour differently. Still such typologies are popular and therefore must be considered useful.

**TABLE 3.1** The seven habits of highly effective people

| |
|---|
| Be Proactive |
| Begin with the End in Mind |
| Put First Things First |
| Think Win–Win |
| Seek First to Understand, Then to Be Understood |
| Synergize |
| Sharpen the Saw |

*Source:* Covey, S.R. (2015) *The Stephen R. Covey Interactive Reader – 4 Books in 1: The 7 Habits of Highly Effective People, First Things First, and the Best of the Most Renowned Leadership Teacher of Our Time.* Mango Media, Inc..

**The six coloured hats**

Edward de Bono's 'six coloured hats' is a good example of the many models and representations of the way people think. The colours represent different thinking styles; they can be used in group processes to enable different arguments for and against a certain proposal, and to stimulate creativity. Their value lies in their playful use rather than analytical rigour.

**TABLE 3.2** The six coloured hats

| Colour of hat | Interpretation |
|---|---|
| Red | Symbolizes our way to think based on intuition, emotion and gut feeling |
| Yellow | Symbolizes optimism and a focus on all the positive outcomes of the choice |
| Blue | Symbolizes control and procedural rigour in the decision process |
| Black | Symbolizes pessimism and a focus on all the negative outcomes of the choice |
| White | Symbolizes the need to know the facts and to look at available information |
| Green | Symbolizes creativity and letting your fantasy go, or engage in brainstorming |

*Source:* de Bono, E. (2017) *Six Thinking Hats.* Penguin.

**The big five personality factor model**

One branch of psychology focuses on personality. Personality refers to individual characteristics in terms of how people think, feel, act and behave. Personality psychologists focus on these individual characteristics as well as on how they make up a person. The current, most popular personality model is based on five factors.

**TABLE 3.3** The big five personality factor model

| Personality factor | Potential impact on performance |
| --- | --- |
| Openness to experience | Relevant to jobs requiring independence and focusing on innovation |
| Conscientiousness | Relevant to jobs requiring independence and strong attention to detail |
| Extraversion | Relevant to jobs requiring strong social skills, with strong levels of competition and when dealing with unpleasant people |
| Agreeableness | Relevant to jobs requiring strong social skills and when dealing with unpleasant people; less positive with strong levels of competition |
| Emotional stability | Relevant to jobs requiring strong social skills and when dealing with unpleasant people |

*Source:* Judge, T.A. and Zapata, C.P. (2015) The person–situation debate revisited: effect of situation strength and trait activation on the validity of the big five personality traits in predicting job performance, *Academy of Management Journal*, 58(4): 1149–79.

We will look briefly into the ways in which these social sciences provide us with a model of human behaviour. It is, of course, not the intention to explain these models in the highest level of detail, nor to provide an overview of developments in the social sciences. Rather, our direct interest lies in their different views as to what makes a 'good' management control system. As economics, psychology and sociology differ in focus, and perspective, they also differ in their advice on the way management control systems may affect human behaviour. In this sense, these three ways of looking at human behaviour enable us to discuss and explain why opinions about appropriate management control systems have not yet converged into simple principles. It also explains why the simple slogan-type admonitions fail. One other interesting illustration of such failure can be found in discussions around the old slogan, attributed to the founding father of the communist Soviet Union, Lenin, who taught us that 'trust is good but control is better'. Indeed, nowadays many commentators argue for the reverse. They argue that the fall of Soviet communism and indeed the 2008/9 financial crisis point to the importance of trust, and the fallibility of the control-by-measurement philosophy (i.e., too much focus on output control). As we will see, psychology points us to the importance of trust in interpersonal relationships, and also that it is a balance between (informal) trust and (formal) management control systems that we should strive for. An understanding of the complexity of human behaviour is needed if we wish to master it. This requires a good understanding of the various dynamics in which human behaviour takes place, as well as reliable prediction of how lower-level managers and employees will react to management control systems. Making a good and informed judgement about management control system design, based on our explicit understanding of human behaviour, will increase the chance for successful interventions to change and improve lower-level manager and employee behaviour.

## The economic model of human behaviour

The first model of human behaviour is based on economics. Economics is the social science that investigates how people make rational and deliberate choices and decisions in their quest to maximize utility. Utility is a formal term in economics, which means many things to many people. In most economic analysis, utility is expressed in monetary terms. This does not mean that in the economic model of human behaviour people are only interested in money, nor that they should be interested only in money. It does assume, however, that people are interested and motivated to obtain the kinds of things that money can buy. It also assumes that one of the main motivators humans have to give their time and efforts to an organization is to get monetary payments in return. This assumption seems reasonable in general, although, as we will see, people are motivated by much more than money. The economic model also assumes that people are very calculative in deciding how much effort to put in, in return for the money they can earn, and this is sometimes outright unrealistic.

In any case, the economic model of human behaviour has become very influential. Looking back at the Real World Vignette presented at the outset of this chapter, many would argue that the behaviour displayed by managers and employees in the financial sector is best understood by these people's preference for maximizing the pay-off from their work, with little regard for the damage done to others. It almost looks as if they take the economic model as a normative guide for how they should behave, rather than as just a theoretical explanation of how they behave.

Within this general economic view, the most important and influential model of human behaviour has been provided by *agency theory*. As already briefly mentioned in Chapter 2, this theory considers organizations to be no more than performance contracts between a principal (the owner) and an agent (the managers). Agency theory describes how an organization in principle is no more than a (collection of) principals and agents that engage in contracting, in which an agent commits themselves to work for a principal.[3] The principal thus employs the agent, and the question that agency theory asks and answers is what the contract should specify to make the agent work in the best interest of themselves and of the principal. In other words, what contract reduces the *agency problem* caused by the agent potentially working only for themselves. The focus in the analysis lies with designing the so-called, payment function in the contract. This payment function specifies the relationship between how the agents perform and what they receive in terms of monetary rewards. Agency theory sees such performance contracts as optimal, although the exact form of the payment function depends on various contextual factors. For example, when there is no external uncertainty, and payment is based purely on how the agent performs, then a simple pay-for-performance contract may work well. However, if external uncertainty is high, and the agent is risk averse, the optimal contract may include a higher proportion of fixed pay. The principal in that case carries more risk, but may not mind that since that fits their entrepreneurial profile.

Agency theoretic ideas about management control system design and use are very popular. Proponents of management control systems that are primarily based on performance metrics coupled with monetary rewards (i.e., output controls) almost always base their views on agency models like the one sketched. Agency theory is, as it were, a theory based on the use of performance indicators and a reward structure that rewards outcomes. It pays very little attention to input and throughput controls. However, such direct application of agency theoretic advice in management control system design and use is often too short-sighted. It forgets that agency theory is an explanatory theory and not a normative ideal. It also forgets that monetary incentives are just one of the many ways in which human motivation is activated. Money cannot buy everything, and therefore is not the only way in which humans can strive for utility. Still, agency theory has had a substantial influence on the design of reward systems in organizations, and we will therefore discuss it further with regard to incentives in Chapter 10. As the examples below clearly illustrate, the discussion on the appropriateness of paying bonuses is not yet settled.

***Real World Example:*** This bank CEO thinks bonuses are baloney.

Wait, what's this? The head of one of the world's biggest banks thinks bonuses are a waste of time?

Deutsche Bank AG's (DB) new CEO John Cryan has already broken a few taboos since he took over at Germany's biggest and most prestigious bank, suspending dividends and slashing thousands of jobs in an effort to undo the damage done by generations of ill-advised empire-building. But at a speech in Frankfurt on Tuesday, he went one further, attacking one of finance's most cherished concepts – the bonus.

[3] Jensen, M. and Meckling, W. (1976) Theory of the firm: managerial behavior, agency costs and ownership structure, *Journal of Financial Economics*, 3(4): 305–60.

'I have no idea why I was offered a contract with a bonus in it because I promise you I will not work any harder or any less hard in any year, in any day because someone is going to pay me more or less, . . .'

For years, decades even, it's been an article of faith on Wall Street that a big component of variable, performance-related pay has been essential to get the best out of employees. Before the 2008 crash, it wasn't uncommon for the fixed component of senior bankers' packages to be only 10 per cent of their total remuneration. But the crash, and the ensuing revelations of mis-selling, insider trading and market-rigging have created a powerful body of evidence to suggest that the bonus culture had created a monster, encouraging reckless risk-taking and downright criminality among a few and jeopardizing the global financial system in the process.

*Source:* Smith, G. (2015) This bank CEO thinks bonuses are baloney, *Fortune*, 25 November. Available at: https://fortune.com/2015/11/25/this-bank-ceo-thinks-bonuses-are-baloney/ (accessed 30 April 2020).

***Real World Example:*** Deutsche Bank AG is set to post its fourth annual loss in five years, but that doesn't mean nobody will get a bonus.

'We are aware that this is a sensitive topic, but obviously we will compensate our people according to their operating performance,' chief executive officer Christian Sewing said on a conference call. 'Deutsche Bank will remain a global bank, an international bank, and that means that if the performance is there, we pay in a competitive way.'

Deutsche Bank has sought to strike a balance between cutting costs and rewarding its best employees to keep them from joining competitors. Sewing's comments came after he suspended the lender's dividend for two years to help pay for a 7.4 billion-euro ($8.3 billion) overhaul that will see it renounce the ambition of competing toe-to-toe with Wall Street firms

[. . .]

For his part, Sewing said he will tie his personal wealth closer to the bank's fortunes by investing a 'substantial amount of my fixed salary' over the next years. While he didn't get more specific, a person familiar with the matter said Sewing plans to start investing 25 per cent of his salary in Deutsche Bank shares. Reuters reported the figure earlier.

*Source:* Comfort, N. (2019) Deutsche Bank to pay bonuses to deserving staff, Sewing says, *Bloomberg Business*, 9 July. Available at: https://www.bloomberg.com/news/articles/2019-07-09/deutsche-bank-to-pay-bonuses-if-staff-deserve-them-sewing-says (accessed 30 April 2020).

Despite the continuing influence of the economic model of human behaviour, recent developments in economics have amended this model substantially, under the label of *behavioural economics*. Although the classical rational human actor, who makes deliberate choices in a quest for maximum utility, remains valid in most circumstances, behavioural economists emphasize that there are specific circumstances in which even rational people make irrational decisions. People do not merely show random irrational behaviour but, more interestingly, such irrational behaviour can even be predicted. There are systematic deviations from rationality that can be predicted and modelled in ways that economists prefer. Among the findings in behavioural economics is that people change their behaviour based on the way a choice is presented. For example, people seem to prefer a game in which they can 'win' a certain amount of money by gambling, than a game in which they first receive an amount of money and may lose it in a gamble. People also overestimate the likelihood of events with a very small objective probability, and seem also very bad at estimating the value of events in the future. They discount future monetary gains, for example, far too strongly in comparison to the real interest rates in the financial market. In even simple experiments, people are shown to judge the value of an object they possess as higher than its objective value in the market, leading to asymmetry in value judgements when buying or selling that object. Humans are simply not as rational as traditional economic models assume, and this is important also to those who believe that the economic model of human behaviour is in itself the right model to inform management control system design. It means that such design and use should take into account that people react strongly to the way a bonus system is designed, and that people may in fact be distracted or biased by elements that should not matter.

**Real World Example:** Do investors get too attached to the stocks they own and overvalue their worth?

Behavioural economists have long known that when you own things – your house, your car, your possessions in general – you're more likely to become attached to them and to overvalue their worth. Does the 'endowment effect' also affect investors? Do we get too attached to the stocks we own?

It sounds silly, but hundreds of experiments show that we become overly attached to all kinds of meaningless possessions – even coffee cups. In one classic experiment conducted by Nobel laureate Daniel Kahneman and behavioural economist Richard Thaler, participants were given a mug to keep and then offered the chance to sell it to potential buyers.

The new owners were immediately reluctant to part with their new possession, demanding roughly twice as much money as the potential buyers were prepared to pay.

The endowment effect, sometimes known as status quo bias, is also found in the animal kingdom. In one study, chimpanzees were offered a choice – peanut butter or frozen fruit juice sticks? Just over half – 58 per cent – chose the peanut butter. Others were endowed with the peanut butter and given the choice of exchanging it for juice; at that point, 79 per cent elected to keep the peanut butter. Similarly, a majority of those assigned the juice refused to part with it.

*Source:* O'Mahony, P. (2017) The endowment effect: falling in love with stocks and coffee cups, *Irish Times*, 18 July. Available at: https://www.irishtimes.com/business/personal-finance/the-endowment-effect-falling-in-love-with-stocks-and-coffee-cups-1.3153812 (accessed 30 April 2020).

Behavioural economics, for example, explains the well-known phenomenon of continuing with projects that do not create value because of large investments in the past. This negligence towards sunk costs is a systematic emotional bias. Yet, being aware of people's biases and systematic deviations from rationality and utility maximization is not sufficient for remedying them. In fact, behavioural economics shows how persistent and strong those biases are. Even if people realize that they are biased, they may still pursue their 'wrong' behaviour.[4]

## The sociological model of human behaviour

The second model of human behaviour is provided by sociological science. According to the sociological view, people are considered to be members of groups in which certain rules and patterns of behaviour exist. Sociology emphasizes that when it is time to explain and predict human behaviour we should pay attention not so much to the individuals and their considerations, but rather to the collective set of individuals the individual belongs to. Groups have certain internal rituals, certain conventions, that make the group really a group. For example, certain groups of friends have certain ways of greeting one another, certain groups of a certain age dress in similar ways according to what they feel is the fashion, and certain groups of colleagues at work celebrate the organization's successes in distinct ways. Larger groups of individuals form communities, activity groups, and also countries and nations. A typical way of talking about such group conventions and norms is by reference to the term 'culture' (we will come back to this term in the next section). For now, it is important to bring home the point that many behaviours that we observe in reality can only be explained by what the whole group is doing. According to a sociologist, it is quite senseless to ask an individual why we would dress up in a suit and tie when we attend a management meeting, since there is no real individual 'why' question that we ask. There is no immediate economic or psychological benefit to wearing a suit and tie, other than that everybody does it, and by doing so we signal that we want to belong to the group. But much behaviour is not even based on any such

[4] Weedon, C. (2004) *Identity and Culture: Narratives of Difference and Belonging.* UK: McGraw-Hill Education.

conscious deliberation. Much behaviour is imitative, and this certainly goes for many personal routines. The music we enjoy, the books we read, may seem the outcome of a deliberate choice, but also a function of the kinds of music and kinds of books that our social environment presents to us. Fashion goes beyond these trivial examples, however, as we often observe that certain organizations start to adopt certain ways of working, and, deliberately or not, imitate what their competitors are doing. Even many management control practices that we discuss in this book are adopted by top management, not because it was clear that they would bring economic or psychological benefit, but 'because everybody else does'.[5] Looking back at the Real World Vignette at the start of this chapter provides an example of a sociological analysis of bankers' behaviours in the City of London. While it may be true that these people do everything to earn as much money as they can, that is not the whole, nor the only, story. The way these people behave in their banking environment is just the way people behave in the banking environment. When you are educated to become a banker you are not just learning about the techniques of the job but you are also informed about how these people behave, that they sometimes wear pinstripe suits, and that they wear Rolex watches. Another important focal point of sociology that is of direct relevance directed to management control system design and use is the role of power in and between groups. Sociology wants us to pay attention to not so much only the formal power, like that of top managers in the firm, but also to informal sources of power. These do not simply originate from formal organizational structures but are also embedded in the knowledge and practices of people. For example, when looking at the way hospitals are organized, we often observe that the board of the hospital does not set the strategic agenda, but rather the professional doctors do. In a certain way, the professional group of doctors have the medical knowledge that drives the key processes in the organization. Their ability to organize themselves strongly as professionals makes them the implicit source of power in hospitals. This is important to understand, sociologists argue, because if we conceive management control systems as always following the formal hierarchy of the organization we may wrongly forget a strong reason why these systems may be ineffective.[6]

***Real World Example:*** Will diversity training always change behaviour? Let's look at a specific case . . .

In 2018, two black men were arrested in a Starbucks shop in Philadelphia. They had entered the shop and had asked to use the bathroom. After they had declined the request to place an order, since they were waiting for a friend, Starbucks called the police and an arrest was made. Starbucks responded to this incident by announcing that all of its shops would be closed for half a day, during which employees would be given diversity training. Based on this incident and the response by Starbucks, many firms recognized the need to prevent their employees from exhibiting gender or racial bias. But the question is whether such short courses help? And do such courses change both attitudes and behaviours?

A team of researchers decided to investigate the effectiveness of these types of training. They designed a study in which three groups of participants engaged in different forms of training. An online training course was followed by the employees of one large company. One group of employees received gender-bias training, the second group engaged in training that focused on gender, race and sexual orientation, while the third group was trained in inclusive leadership. This training did not mention bias or stereotyping but focused instead on psychological safety and active listening rather than on stereotypical biases.

The researchers tested how the attitudes and behaviours of the participants changed during a series of emails sent after the training, which introduced new company initiatives and asked employees to participate. These initiatives concerned the nomination of colleagues to engage in a mentoring programme, to recognize a colleague's performance and to engage in a telephone talk with a new hire on a new project. The findings suggested that

---

[5] Modell, S. (2009) Bundling management control innovations, *Accounting, Auditing & Accountability Journal*, 22(1): 59–90.

[6] Sloof, R. and von Siemens, F.A. (2019) Effective leadership and the allocation and exercise of power in organizations, *Leadership Quarterly*.

training had very little effect on attitudes and almost no effect on behaviour. The findings also showed, however, that the effect sizes differed across men and women and across US and foreign employees. Overall, the researchers concluded that stronger interventions may be needed to change employee behaviour. This may be done by longer and more intense training, or by showing rather than telling what good behaviour is. Changing hiring and promotion policies to benefit women and underrepresented minorities may have stronger and more lasting effects.

*Source:* Chang, E.H., Milkman, K.L., Gromet, D.M., Rebele, R.W., Massey, C., Duckworth, A.L. and Grant, A.M. (2019) The mixed effects of online diversity training, *Proceedings of the National Academy of Sciences*, 116(16): 7778–83.

## The psychological model of human behaviour

The psychological model of human behaviour is the third model to which we will devote explicit attention here. It is the model of human behaviour that, in a certain way, seems best known to us. It is the model of humans whose behaviours are driven by a multitude of beliefs and desires, much like the way we talk about our motives, goals and intentions in everyday life. Within the psychological model of human behaviour that is developed in the social sciences, however, the focus lies on two generic drivers of behaviour: beliefs and desires. Beliefs constitute our knowledge about the world. Desires constitute the way we want the world to be. In scientific psychology, there is a multitude of theories about how we come to have certain beliefs, how we obtain knowledge about the world, and how we learn. There is also a multitude of theories about how people formulate and pursue their desires. Important theories for management control system design focus on what motivates humans to engage in certain behaviours. These theories help us understand why people become motivated to direct their efforts towards achieving organizational missions, goals and strategies. The better these theories become, the more knowledge we have on how to design and use a management control system.

Motivation is a central concept within the psychological model of human behaviour. Motivation is defined as the direction of effort, the amount of effort and the persistence of effort that people exert towards certain personal or professional objectives. Motivation is not just a drive or the amount of work done. Direction, level and persistence are what counts. This means that management control system design and use should pay attention to these three elements. Theories on human motivation inform us that some motivation is, more or less, automatic, but that motivation can also be activated and stimulated.

Regarding the latter, a theory that has gained great popularity is the so-called goal-setting theory.[7] This theory states that people are motivated by clear and challenging goals that they either state for themselves or that they are asked to achieve by their superiors. Goal theory emphasizes that goals should be clear in the sense that they should provide people with a clear target to reach. People should also have sufficient personal and organizational resources to reach the goals. Goal-setting theory is seen as a relatively successful theory in organizational psychology. It certainly is inspirational to management control system designers that believe in target setting and measuring target achievement as the most important technical feature of a management control system. Goal theory seems, therefore, in line with economic theory, even if goal theory pays more attention to the psychological process that underlies motivation. The theory points, for example, to the importance of *self-efficacy* of people, which is people's belief that they are able and enabled to reach the goals.[8] Goal theory, however, does not have all the answers to control problems. For example, when there are multiple goals and when goals are uncertain or constantly changing, goal setting has little motivational power. Also, when goals are difficult to achieve due to external hindrances, goal setting may fail. Some theorists have argued that goal setting may not be

[7] Locke, E.A. and Latham, G.P. (2006) New directions in goal-setting theory. *Current Directions in Psychological Science*, 15(5): 265–8.

[8] Bandura, A. (1997) *Self-Efficacy: The Exercise of Control.* New York: Freeman.

powerful if not coupled to some, monetary or other, reward. Such economic arguments are advanced by those adhering to the so-called expectancy theory of motivation. According to this view, people will act even more economically than goal theory presupposes, as they are motivated to do only those things with the highest expected reward.[9]

Regarding the automatic drivers of motivation, many theories have been developed, tested and rejected over the many decades in which motivation has been studied. However, the belief that humans are motivated to fill the needs they have remains one quite robust view. Originally, this view was developed into the well-known Maslow's pyramid of five human needs. Maslow showed that higher-order needs (such as self-actualization, or self-realization) were driving motivation only after lower-order needs (food, shelter, safety) had been fulfilled, suggesting that motivational forces have a logical order.[10] The reality appeared more complex, but modern versions of this theory suggest that humans have a strong urge to direct and control their own lives.

*Self-determination theory* is the modern representation of that idea. It tries to cover a full range, from motivational drivers, which range from motivators located outside the individual (which traditionally were called extrinsic motivators) to intrinsic motivators that drive people to learn and develop. Underneath this classification lies the idea that intrinsic sources of motivation do not just create compliance and obedience, but result in true satisfaction and happiness (this is elaborated further in Chapter 10). This intrinsic motivation plays an important role in the workplace, because managers may intrinsically like the projects they are working on and may be intrinsically motivated to engage with other people in striving for certain goals and objectives. The Latin saying *labor ipse voluptas* (labour itself is the reward) is a strong and relatively cheap way to get desirable behaviour. Self-determination theory thereby provides a strong voice against the role of management control systems as focusing only on extrinsically obtained compliance and obedience. Work quality may benefit from intrinsic drivers. This may stem from factors outside the management control system, but there are also ways in which the management control system and process may stimulate such intrinsic drivers.[11]

There is an important potential role here for bottom-up control processes and enabling control systems, as discussed in Chapter 1. Self-determination theory, and its implications for motivation and incentives, is frequently discussed in the general debate today and we can see an increasing influence from the theory on practice. Therefore, we will discuss the theory and its implications for reward systems further in Chapter 10.

Besides this focus on motivation, which is a crucial element of psychological theory, at least two other parts of contemporary psychology theory are of importance. We will mention them briefly.

The first of these developments is the clear interest contemporary psychology has in the way people know and learn about the world. The questions that psychologists who focus on human *cognition* try to answer is how people digest information, how people learn by changing their beliefs, how people make sense of complex situations, and so on. Cognition is about the way people observe the world and understand the world. Human cognition is a factor that is often overlooked both in the whole managerial process and in management control system design. It is now well understood that people may not have a full understanding of the context in which they work and, when thinking in terms of management control systems, may see performance reports they do not understand. This interest in cognition is not only aiming at scientific understanding of how people see, hear and think, but also to help practice to improve and simplify the ways in which we communicate. We wrongly assume that everybody sees the

---

[9] Lawler III, E.E. and Suttle, J.L. (1973) Expectancy theory and job behavior, *Organizational Behavior and Human Performance*, *9*(3): 482–503.

[10] Maslow, A.H. (1943) A theory of human motivation, *Psychological Review*, *50*(4): 370.

[11] Deci, E.L. and Ryan, R.M. (2012) Self-determination theory, in P.A.M. Van Lange, A.W. Kruglanski and E.T. Higgins (eds) *Handbook of Theories of Social Psychology* (pp. 416–36). Thousand Oaks, CA: Sage Publications Ltd.

world in the same way, or that everybody understands performance reports in the same way. But some people may be able to see a structure in reports, whereas others may be overwhelmed by an overload of information. Accountants, and other financial professionals, often overestimate the readability and transparency of their reports. But different people may read the same report in different ways, focusing on different details and drawing different conclusions from them. On the other hand, understanding how people see, hear and think also helps us to be careful about the ways opinions are formulated. With the rise of social media, we are bombarded with potentially relevant information, but we also know that a lot of information is 'fake news'. How can we select the right information and disregard unreliable news facts? The focus on cognition is also something that connects psychologists with behavioural economists. Together they join forces with neuroscientists to look into the human brain for evidence of right and wrong information processing.[12]

The second important development in psychology comes from the recognition that people, even if we are considering them as individuals, do not work in a social desert, but rather that social contacts are an explicit part of what makes humans function well. This has long been recognized in the field of social and organizational psychology, but the importance to us is that such social structures also help individuals to perform well, to behave in line with others and to adapt their behaviours. Sociology points, as we have seen, to the general importance of the group to explain individual behaviour, but in psychology the effects on the individual of such social factors are explored. In particular, this has led to an increased interest in the potential role of all kinds of social factors for management control system design and use. Among these factors, interpersonal trust has received much attention. When people trust one another, they are more open and honest with one another, collaborate better and are more motivated to help one another. Interpersonal trust thus seems a perfect way to steer behaviour, despite what Lenin may have said. Research, however, also shows that it can be abused, and that interpersonal trust may disappear with the introduction of certain control practices, since the introduction of additional controls may signal to lower-level managers and employees that they are not trustworthy, especially if the control practices are perceived as coercive rather than enabling. However, when certain control practices are implemented to help people perform better, and to give people fairer performance evaluations, they are also shown to enhance trust.[13]

Another important area of interest for management control system design and use is related to the way such systems support equity and justice. Although in economic theory the idea is that people are mainly interested in maximizing their own utility, and sociology may point to the importance of similarities rather than differences in groups, psychologists have convincingly demonstrated the importance of social comparison. There is much to indicate that people care about how others are treated, and constantly compare themselves to others. People do care, for example, about *distributive justice*, which means that everybody gets a fair share of the value that the organization creates. This inclination explains why sometimes people feel ashamed when they get more money than somebody else, especially if they believe they did not deserve this, since they did not work harder or excel in any way. Also *procedural justice* seems important, which means that people cherish the idea that the management control system is fair to everybody, and does not favour one over another. When a performance measurement system is considered to be fair and objective, the performance verdict it gives may be acceptable, even if it is unfavourable. This is not the case when such systems are deemed subjective or fallible. When the procedural justice of the system is high, it has also been shown that the top managers responsible for the system are trusted. This shows that psychology informs us about many interactions between

[12] Helfat, C.E. and Peteraf, M.A. (2015) Managerial cognitive capabilities and the microfoundations of dynamic capabilities, *Strategic Management Journal*, 36(6): 831–50.

[13] Libby, T. and Lindsay, R.M. (2018) The effects of superior trust and budget-based controls on budgetary gaming and budget value, *Journal of Management Accounting Research*, 31(3): 153–84.

so-called soft (psychological) factors and hard (design) factors, and suggests that their complex interactions determine the effectiveness of the management control system.[14]

It may also be clear that these and other psychological insights are the outcome of, sometimes quite complex, academic studies. This is also true for studies on personality that try to combine the various insights about human behaviour into categories of people. Currently, many psychologists agree that the so-called 'big five' theory on personality is a neat and concise description of varieties and similarities in people's attitudes and behaviours that have a predictive effect on job performance. Whereas such studies are not often used by top managers directly, the insights they provide have a lot to offer to continue to improve our understanding of management control systems and the way they intend to enhance performance. To this we devote more attention in the next section. Table 3.4 summarizes the three models of human behaviour presented thus far in the text, and their implications for management control system design and use.

**TABLE 3.4** Models of human behaviour in summary

| | Economic model | Psychological model | Sociological model |
|---|---|---|---|
| *Control is about:* | Agency problems | Behaviour | Behaviour of groups |
| *Control serves:* | Contracting | Motivation | The structures that create power, identity and culture |
| *Key control issue:* | Indicators to measure value creation | System to motivate managers | Optimal distribution of power such that individuals are enabled |
| *Model of man:* | Self-interested utility maximizer | Social creature with various 'needs' | Culturally raised an educated group member |
| *Focus lies with:* | The superior's problem of control | Managers' behavioural patterns | Managers' identity, values and norms |
| *Good control practice:* | Measure and reward value creation | Everything to motivate managers | Support managers' identity, values and norms |
| *Motivation:* | Implied in utility function | A complex issue | Drives are determined by background and group needs |

## The management control systems model of human behaviour

The question that management control system designers and users need to answer is of course not what kind of theories exist about human behaviour, but rather what these theories tell us about the potential effects of different control practices on human behaviour. Somehow we need to combine and integrate the theoretical insights from these three models to create a model of human behaviour that can be used in the design of a management control system that enables us to, as well as possible, predict its behavioural effects. Unfortunately, we cannot avoid some complexity when conducting such an analysis, because that is inherent to human nature. Even the best theories still predict a range of possible behaviours that different people will exhibit in similar circumstances. The contrast between what we think we know about human behaviour in a specific situation and what we are actually able to cast in social scientific laws is significant. However, despite the fact that we do not have one overall theory of management control systems, we are able to formulate some principles that should guide the design and use

[14] Rupp, D.E., Shapiro, D.L., Folger, R., Skarlicki, D.P. and Shao, R. (2017) A critical analysis of the conceptualization and measurement of organizational justice: is it time for reassessment? *Academy of Management Annals*, 11(2): 919–59.

of such systems. We could think of these principles as a management control system model of human behaviour. These three elements are derived from the social sciences, and can therefore be regarded as evidence based. The first principle states that management control systems should motivate managers and employees. The second principle states that management control systems should take into account managerial and employee abilities and inabilities. The third principle states that management control systems should support a healthy, social and ethical climate. We will now turn to each of these principles in more detail.

## Principle 1: Management control systems should motivate managers and employees

Trying to understand human motivation in full is not an easy task, as we have seen in the previous sections. A multitude of existing theories on human motivation illustrate this. However, it is important that management control system design is based on principles of human motivation that appear to be generally valid, and to point to motivational pitfalls that should be avoided when designing such systems. To this aim, the social sciences point out some rather clear dos and don'ts. There are two principles of human motivation that deserve to be followed when designing and using management control systems in organizations. We will introduce each principle, explain its validity, and will point to circumstances under which the motivational principle loses its validity and applicability. This latter set of insights is also important, since organizations' failures that can be attributed to defective management control systems can often be traced back to either a poor understanding of what makes managers and employees prefer certain courses of action over others, or to a lack of understanding of the conditional nature of human motivation.

### *Managers and employees should be motivated by the goals that they are asked to achieve*

One of the most effective ways in which managers and employees can be motivated is by providing them with goals to be achieved. As we have argued, motivation is a combination of the effort, direction and persistence of human efforts, and having clear goals has a positive effect on these three elements. Effort is the amount of time and energy that humans spend in performing a certain activity. This energy can be physical or cognitive, but in all cases reflects the value that people are willing to invest in a certain course of action. Generally, effort levels increase when humans are confronted with a goal that is clear, not too distant and the achievement of which is considered an accomplishment. Direction of effort is almost as important as level of effort, since spending effort in the wrong direction is at best equal to not spending effort, but may in fact work against the organization's mission, goals and strategies. When traders in the City of London were aiming for high returns on their portfolios, they were spending effort, but in the wrong direction since they were not considering the riskiness of the overall portfolio. Clearly, our analyses now should recognize that the management control system was stressing the wrong goals, which were motivational *in the wrong way*, as it were.

*Persistence* relates to duration of effort and is an important condition for effort to be spent until the organizational mission, goals and strategies are reached. Organizations do not need short-term explosions of managerial and employee motivation, but rather longer-term devotion to a certain course of action. They also need managers and employees not to give up at the first signs of potential failure, but to push on. Giving people goals that are set in time helps them to spend their effort over longer periods of time. Here we need to take into account the insights provided by behavioural economics. Distant goals may not be motivational in themselves, since managers and employees may discount their importance. Helping them set a time frame and sticking to that helps to keep them motivated. In Part 3 of this book, on the performance management process, this consideration is crucial.

Important limitations to the motivational effects of goals exist, which are mostly related to failure to meet the conditions under which goals are seen as a way to reach a valuable result. Sometimes, goals can be seen as a threat, and not meeting the goal as a failure, even if the performance level was still sufficient. This is a factor stressed in the *psychological model* of human behaviour but easily forgotten by those emphasizing an *economic model*. The *behavioural economics model* emphasizes that managers and employees may react very strongly to not meeting a goal, which they may perceive as incurring a loss. Goals may also lack the clarity to provide a sense of direction, especially when multiple goals should be achieved at the same time, or a goal that is clear by itself needs to be achieved in a turbulent environment. Giving people a specific profit target may seem like a clear goal, but when the economic tide is adverse, such clarity does not translate into motivation. Also, perception and communication affect the working of goal setting, and we need to be aware of how managers and employees get informed about organizational goals and the ways to achieve them. Typically, managers receive information about goals through various channels, both formal (e.g., budgets and other official documents) and informal (e.g., conversations). Despite this range of channels, it is not always easy to specify clearly what top management wants done. An organization is a complicated entity, and the actions that should be taken by any one part to further the common goals cannot be stated with absolute clarity even in the best of circumstances. Moreover, the messages received from different sources may conflict with one another, or be subject to differing interpretations. For example, the budget mechanism may convey the impression that managers and employees are supposed to aim for the highest profits possible in a given year, whereas top management does not actually want them to skimp on maintenance or employee training since such actions, although increasing current profits, might reduce future profitability.

Overall, therefore, while goal setting is an important tool in management control system design, it should be used with care.

### *Managers and employees should be motivated by the rewards they may get from their efforts*

Although, according to some, money is the root of all evil, in reality money plays a crucial instrumental role in our society in getting things done. This is most obvious in market transactions, in which goods are transferred between transacting partners in exchange for money, and in the delivery of services. A crucial characteristic of market transactions is that the amount of money paid for a good or service holds a more or less direct relationship with the quantity or quality of the good or service provided.

In firms and other types of organization, the relationship between the services provided by employees and the monetary reward that these employees get in return is less clear, and in fact subject to various rules and regulations. Such relationships may theoretically range from fixed pay arrangements, in which employees get paid a fixed amount of money regardless of the actual goods and services they provide, to arrangements in which pay varies with goods and services delivered. Such arrangements are typically known as performance-related reward systems.

After reading the previous sections, it must be clear that, from an economic point of view, this is all that a labour contract should encompass. In reality, most organizations have pay systems that fall somewhere in the middle. This depends on various institutional settings, as labour laws, trade unions and professional organizations have various levels of influence on the types of contracts between organizations and their employees in different countries. These differences, which are clearly present between the United States, Europe and Asia, determine the possibilities to arrange for optimal reward structures for employees. Top managers are normally less protected by labour laws that put restrictions on labour contracts. For top management levels, we therefore observe higher variation in reward structures between organizations and managerial functions, and top managers are thus generally eligible for more pay-related reward policies. Also, top managers may be less risk averse.

Despite the omnipresence of pay-for-performance schemes, there is no generally satisfactory answer yet to the question of whether variable pay 'works'.[15] Whether it is the bonus arrangements in the financial industry that brought serious trouble for Lehman Brothers, Société Générale, and many other banks

[15] See also Chapter 10, which deals more thoroughly with compensation, incentives and motivation.

during the financial crisis of 2008, often pay-for-performance schemes are criticized for having led to the wrong decisions and actions by managers. One reason is that variable rewards have the tendency to lose their attraction over time, as they are regarded by the manager as part of the fixed salary. Another reason is that when rewards are linked to goal achievement, they may lead to internal competition within the organization, which destroys cooperation and overall performance. A third reason is that, since good performance often shows much later than the decision that causes this good performance, it is very difficult to design reward structures that motivate managers and employees to make good decisions. Because of this, such reward structures in fact motivate managers and employees to enhance only short-term performance, which may run against the longer-term strategies of the firm. The big question, therefore, is what kinds of behaviours we want to stimulate and what kind of culture we want to create. The role of financial rewards in answering these questions cannot be underestimated.

Note that this principle emphasizes the role of *financial* rewards but that is not the only type of reward that managers and employees can get from their jobs and their achievements. In the longer term, promotions that are based on good performance are an important motivational force, as are the kinds of non-financial and even immaterial rewards by receiving praise and compliments. In any particular case it is important to realize that it is always the different types of rewards that *together* motivate managers. In addition, we should point to the advantage of variable reward schemes in that they allow organizations to control their labour costs, as these costs go up and down with the organization's overall performance. This, however, is not an advantage in terms of the *motivation function* that such systems may have. In Chapter 10, we continue this important discussion of the relationship between performance measurement, motivation and reward systems. As will be discussed there in much more detail, some widely diverging views exist with regard to the importance of financial rewards for management control.

## Principle 2: Management control systems should consider managerial and employee abilities and inabilities

A singular focus on motivation could easily lead to the misconception that management control systems should be designed based on managerial and employee characteristics and behaviours that are static. Especially when we focus on those control practices that claim to measure organizational and unit performance, we may be wrongly inclined to think of those practices as static, i.e., that measure performance *as is*. Indeed, the whole notion of control has, to many outside the management control system field and practice, strong connotations of stability, rigidity and fixation. Clearly, our earlier focus on managerial and employee motivation does too little to amend that view. If we are not careful, management control systems are seen as a tool to curb managerial and employee freedom, learning and creativity under the flag of enhanced motivation. Therefore, we need to pay explicit attention to the dynamics of managerial behaviours and the role of dynamic factors such as freedom, learning and creativity. As discussed in Chapter 1, we need to emphasize also the *enabling role* of management control systems. Both the traditional economic model of human behaviour and some motivational theories give only limited attention to these factors, but some more innovative research in psychology does recognize the importance of freedom and creativity. The role of management control systems in managerial and organizational learning is sometimes underemphasized.

### *Managers and employees should be encouraged to learn and innovate*

A static and coercive view on management control systems endorses the assumption that top managers, other managers and employees are always aware of the best direction forward and that the control systems are simply there to make them move into that direction. This is most explicit in agency theory, but also in expectancy theory and, to some extent, goal theory. However, we should not forget that everybody learns from day to day, and should be more ambitious to design and use management control systems to help people learn. Obviously, learning involves building up experience, getting appropriate feedback on efforts and results, and being enabled to try again. Much professional learning is indeed by trial and error, and the educational and enabling role of management control systems therefore also lies in elucidating the relationships between what individuals do and what kinds of results they get. It is not enough to simply reward or punish results, but to establish the connection with actions. It is not the right place here to discuss all potential learning effects of the various control practices. Throughout each of the remaining chapters in this book, those practices are discussed, and the aspect of learning can be discerned. As a general rule, this means that we should not only be focused on the immediate effect of control practices on managerial and employee behaviour, but also on longer-term effects. A critical question to ask is what longer-term effects this particular control practice has. Learning itself has the obvious positive effect that people become better in their jobs, that they better understand what actions they will have to take to achieve the goals. However, learning also has indirect effects on self-efficacy – the feeling that you can do your task well – and thus also on motivation.

### *Managers and employees' tacit knowledge should be cherished*

Extending the theme of human learning and creativity, we need to be aware of how humans really take decisions. Both economics and a large part of traditional psychology emphasize the conscious decisions that people make. Whether described as rational utility maximization or goal- and reward-seeking motivation, they point to a dominant role of the human conscious mind. Humans first think and then act. Already the sociological view provides some amendment, since it emphasizes that much of human behaviour is group and culture based, which suggests that it is somewhat automatic, and not subject to much pre-thought. But, especially with the rise and popularity of behavioural economics, came the reflection that to understand human action we need to make a distinction between actions that are deliberately chosen and those that are not. Deliberate choice means that they are chosen in a conscious way, that managers and employees fully understand what they are doing, and that they are able to explain their motives for taking an action. Automatic actions are the actions that managers and employees take on impulse, or without too much reflection. The meaning and significance of these types of automatic action are still not fully understood. One the one hand, there are those who emphasize that such automatic actions may lead to biases. This is typically the view within behavioural economics, which aims to show that humans deviate from rationality considerations by systematically using their automatic decision system rather than their conscious decision system. These systems are sometimes labelled System 1 and System 2, respectively. System 1 is seen as the emotional system, which strongly activates when confronting new, unexpected and risky situations, and in case of outright stress and fear. Here it is often clear that a more deliberate reaction would be better for the organization, but this requires that the management control system is able to regulate managerial and employee responses in such situations. If we look at the social process in the financial sector, which we described in the Real World Vignette at the outset of this chapter, many of the impulsive behaviours can be explained by people mimicking one another's behaviours or overreacting to risks, losing their overview of what is really going on. Some people believe that in such behaviours humans really show their animal spirits.[16] As we will argue more fully and more comprehensively in Chapter 11, one of the main reasons that organizations engage in formal risk management systems these days is that they want to make sure that risks are not constantly perceived as fearful events, but rather as part of everyday normal organizational life. Such normalization of managerial and employee responses to new and risky events is also why organizational budgeting systems (see Chapter 8) are designed in such a solid and bureaucratic

[16] Akerlof, G.A. and Shiller, R.J. (2010)*Animal Spirits: How Human Psychology Drives the Economy, and Why it Matters for Global Capitalism.* Princeton, NJ: Princeton University Press.

way. They help people realize how time and organizational results go together, and how short-term negatives may be repaired by longer-term positives. Many control practices can therefore be explained by their secondary and longer-term function in keeping managers and employees' conscious attention along the way. But, of course, the power of emotions can also be positive. Much joy in work comes in the form of being excited about new investment opportunities, new markets and new clients. The associated optimism may be irrational, but at the same time very functional. And, more importantly, much managerial and employee expertise is tacit, and does not express itself in conscious deliberation. Expertise – whether it is playing the piano, seeing a performance pattern in a complex set of financial statements, or seeing market developments that the organization needs to respond to in a creative way – is also part of managers and employees' unconscious action repertoire. Perhaps these unconscious, 'gut feeling'-type behaviours are what makes innovative companies outlive their conservative competitors. The danger is that stressing only conscious deliberation – by, for example, forcing managers and employees to fully account for the reasons for their decisions – has been shown to hamper such expertise.

### *Managers and employees should be helped to overcome natural cognitive limitations*

Certainly, the attention to the presence and working of management control systems, and their effects on managers and employees' conscious and unconscious decisions, is important, but should not suggest that unconscious decisions are always good. The more we are aware of the fact that many of the decisions we take, and judgements we form, are not based on careful consideration of objective information, the more we are able to decide whether this is the outcome of tacit expertise, or rather constitutes an undesirable bias. Acting on gut feeling and motivating choices by saying that 'it feels good' may have to be put aside as a reference to, and example of, poor judgement. The fields of financial management and management accounting emphasize that we should always be aware of the objective, quantified information that is available, and that we should take the time to digest that information and use it to form our decisions and judgements. Clearly, verbal and qualitative management reports cannot do all of the work. Is this a paradox? Two remarks are in order. First, we gain better understanding of how we perceive the world around us. Now that it is obvious that the world becomes more complex, or at least that the amount of informational streams makes the world appear more complex, we need to be aware of our ways of processing this. At the organizational level, we need to integrate the financial performance of the organization with its environmental performance and social performance. The question is how we should deal with the information overload. When invoking different response systems, the advice could be to simply try to control emotional reactions, for example by simplifying and aggregating information. Typically, organizations produce performance reports, using traffic-light colours to give quick and clear cues on performance. While an understandable strategy, to make green signify 'good', yellow 'average', and red 'bad' performance, using these markers may have a negative effect of its own. Colour summaries may stimulate emotional reactions and turn attention away from underlying material information. There is also increasing evidence on how people might deal with information that comes in loads. Psychology researchers have studied the old adage 'sleep on it' and have evidence that taking in a lot of information, and letting it rest for some time, may result in better decisions.[17] It is doubtful whether this works for all decisions and types of information, but it at least suggests that managers and employees may not need only good information, but also the time to overcome the cognitive boundaries they would face when having to digest it too quickly. Interestingly, standards for internal (management) reporting are being developed and offered by commercial firms.[18]

---

[17] Bos, M.W., Dijksterhuis, A. and van Baaren, R.B. (2011) The benefits of 'sleeping on things': unconscious thought leads to automatic weighting, *Journal of Consumer Psychology*, 21(1): 4–8.

[18] For example, the IBCS Institute, https://www.ibcs.com/ (accessed 21 September 2019).

## Principle 3: Management control systems should support a healthy, social and ethical environment

It is important for the designers of formal management control systems to take into account the effects such systems have on informal processes, such as (work) ethics, social values and culture. These factors have direct and indirect consequences on performance. It is quite evident that few organizations can successfully implement their organizational mission, goals and strategies without appropriate informal processes. Such processes, in totality, create the social context in which managers and employees take actions and make decisions. They consist of both external norms and internal norms.

External norms are norms of desirable behaviour that exist in the society of which the organization is a part. These norms include a set of attitudes, often collectively referred to as the work ethic, which is manifested in managers and employees' loyalty to the organization, their diligence, their spirit and their pride in doing a good job (rather than just putting in time). Some of these attitudes are local – that is, specific to the city or region in which the organization does its work. In encouraging companies to locate in their city or state, chambers of commerce and other promotional organizations often claim that their locality has a loyal, diligent workforce. Other attitudes and norms are industry-specific. The railroad industry, for example, has norms different from those of the airline industry.

In today's electronics industry, the eye often is on zones of remarkable industrial renewal, for example on Silicon Valley or the Chinese Hangzhou region. Silicon Valley is a stretch of northern California that measures about 800 square kilometres. For the past several decades, it has been the major source of new business creation and wealth in the American economy. Silicon Valley attracts people with certain common characteristics: an entrepreneurial spirit, a zest for hard work, high ambition and a preference for informal work settings. Over the past 60 years, Silicon Valley has created companies such as Hewlett-Packard, Microsoft, Apple, Sun Microsystems, Oracle, Cisco Systems and Intel. Even after the most recent boom-and-bust cycle, the old-line companies and the dotcom survivors have kept up Silicon Valley's reputation as the centre of technology innovation. Hangzhou in China's Zehijang Province is a city region that calls itself the Silicon Valley of China. It covers an area of about 105 square kilometres and hosts the headquarters of such innovative new Chinese companies as Alibaba, Hikvison and Dahua Technology, as well as the research and development centres of older companies like Motorola, Nokia and Siemens.

### *Culture matters (a lot) for management control system design and use*

The famous German sociologist Max Weber explained the capitalist working spirit in the Western world, pointing at the values within traditional Protestant theology. Still other cultural values are national; some countries, such as India and China, have a reputation for an excellent work ethic. In Europe and the USA, a positive work ethic is sometimes considered to stem from the puritan values of Protestantism.[19] Other studies have defined culture as the collective mental programming of the human mind, which distinguishes one group of people from another.[20] They suggest a major impact of culture on various business processes, as well as the shape of national institutions such as labour unions and trade unions. Such organizations that act in the interest of employees have a big, even if declining, influence on an organization's policies and the relative power of top management and lower-level managers and

---

[19] Hofstede, G. (2001) *Culture's Consequences: Comparing Values, Behaviors, Institutions, and Organizations across Nations*, 2nd edn. Thousand Oaks, CA: SAGE Publications.

[20] Weber, M., Baehr, P.R. and Wells, G.C. (2002) *The Protestant Ethic and the 'Spirit' of Capitalism and Other Writings*. Penguin. Zhang, S.C, Liu, W.Q. and Liu, X.L. (2012) Investigating the relationship between protestant work ethic and Confucian dynamism: an empirical test in mainland China, *Journal of Business Ethics*, 106(2): 243–52.

employees.[21] Interesting in this respect is also the existence of large cultural differences between organizations' institutional and political environments, such as measured by the Corruption Perceptions Index (CPI).[22] This index ranks the perceived corruption of a country's public sector, and is based on a combination of surveys and assessments of corruption among the public.

***Real World Example:*** The importance of organizational culture to the functioning of individuals and their organizations cannot be underestimated. But the same can be said about the complexity of this concept, and it is easy to underestimate this complexity of the concept of culture and use it in all kinds of contexts to 'explain' what is happening. Academic researchers try to be more exact about it. Culture has therefore become a concept that is heavily studied in the fields of sociology and anthropology, in which it is usually associated with the dynamic and evolving characteristics of groups of people. Cultures manifest themselves through shared language, rituals and symbols. Hofstede's dimensions of culture have been influential in management thinking, as culture is seen as a powerful way to make people work together.[23]

**TABLE 3.5** Hofstede's and Minkov's model of culture

| Cultural dimension | Meaning |
|---|---|
| Individualism–collectivism | Extent to which people feel independent or rather a member of a group |
| Uncertainty avoidance | Extent to which uncertainty and ambiguity are appreciated and accepted |
| Masculinity–femininity | Masculinity (femininity) is the extent to which outings of explicit power and competition are positively (negatively) valued |
| Power distance | The extent to which less powerful members accept that power is distributed unequally |
| Long-term orientation | The extent to which the future and past are seen as dynamic or static |
| Indulgence | The extent to which people prefer to be free in what they do and prefer to follow their impulses |

*Sources:* Minkov, M. (2018) A revision of Hofstede's model of national culture: old evidence and new data from 56 countries, *Cross Cultural & Strategic Management*, 25(2): 231–56. Hofstede, G., www.geerthofdstede.nl (accessed 21 September 2019).

Inside the organization, these sources of cultural norms blend to form norms of acceptable, desirable and sometimes laudable behaviour among managers and employees. They are often addressed with such general labels as organizational culture, management style or tone-at-the-top. Cultural norms are extremely important for at least three reasons. First, they may explain why two organizations, with identical management control systems, may vary in how the managers and employees perceive the control practices. Second, culture can explain why organizations are hard to change. Attempts to change control practices almost always meet with resistance, and the larger and more mature the organization, the greater is the resistance. Part of this is due to the fact that organizations have informal lines of communication that do not correspond with the lines on an organization chart. Such charts depict the formal relationships – that is, the official authority and responsibilities – of each manager. A chart may show,

[21] Blanchflower, D. and Freeman, R.B. (1990) Going different ways: unionism in the US and other advanced OECD countries. National Bureau of Economic Research, working paper number 3342: 6, 42.

[22] Researched, calculated and published annually by Transparency International, www.transparency.org.

[23] Hofstede, G., Hofstede, G.J. and Minkov, M. (2010) *Cultures and Organizations: Software of the Mind* (revised and expanded 3rd edn). New York: McGraw-Hill USA.

for example, that the production manager of Division A reports to the general manager of Division A, but in the course of fulfilling her responsibilities, the production manager of Division A actually communicates with many other people in the organization, such as other managers, support units, the headquarters staff, and people who are simply friends and acquaintances.

In extreme situations, the production manager, with all these other communication sources available, may not pay adequate attention to messages received from the general manager; this is especially likely to occur when the production manager is evaluated on production efficiency rather than on overall performance. The realities of management control system design cannot be understood without recognizing the importance of the relationships that constitute the informal organization.

The culture of an organization is not just a factor that is present in the organization, and which we need to take as it comes. Culture can also be changed, and input control practices, such as value statements, can therefore be implemented to try to change the culture. This requires, however, that we understand more fully what we mean with 'organizational culture' and to delineate it from other meanings of culture – for example, to describe differences between countries and nations. The following examples of culture description in various organizations at least attest to the importance that organizations attach to culture.

**Real World Example:** Below are some examples of how firms describe the importance of organizational culture in their annual reports. These examples demonstrate in particular how the organization wants its culture to be seen by others. For example, the cultural characteristics that dominate the banking industry, as documented in Luyendijk's account of the London City, are typically informal and hidden rather than formal and disclosed. Yet these statements are at least partly informative about some of the actual cultural characteristics of the organization that communicates them.

**Beiersdorf Annual Report (2012): Our Employees & Our Values**[24]

*Beiersdorf's success has many faces. Our dedicated employees and unique corporate culture are our most important assets.*

*Beiersdorf employs some 17,000 people at over 150 affiliates worldwide. Each and every one of them contributes to the company's success and continuing development. To ensure that this remains the case, we aim to focus even more on our values in the future – openness, trust, international orientation, and a sincere and straightforward corporate culture in which teamwork and, above all, mutual respect are of central importance.*

***Courage and Openness***

*Courage, openness, and determination are key factors for growth in a dynamic market. This is why we aim to motivate our employees to improve their performance every day by giving them challenging tasks and plenty of individual responsibility.*

***Flexibility and Speed***

*New technologies, new products, and getting ideas to market more quickly are vital – as is always making sure you are that little bit faster than the competition. Beiersdorf offers its employees lean structures, flat hierarchies, and flexibility, letting them turn their passion and creativity into successful innovations and developments – and to bring them to market.*

***Responsibility and Teamwork***

*For over 130 years, our corporate culture has encouraged our employees to champion their own ideas and convictions and to take responsibility for themselves and their teams. At Beiersdorf, the suggestions and decisions of each and every employee help contribute to the company's success.*

[24] http://annualreport2012.beiersdorf.com/bdf/index_en.php#

***Transcending Boundaries and Borders***

*Beiersdorf is growing globally. Our brands are at home in the truest sense of the word in over 150 countries. For example, NIVEA – the company's core brand – is seen as a local product in a large number of countries. We will successfully continue on this course in the coming years by investing further in internationalizing the company – and in our employees.*

**Siemens Annual Report (2018): Our Company's Values and Business Conduct Guideline[25]**

*Our Company's values and Business Conduct Guidelines In the 171 years of its existence, our Company has built an excellent reputation around the world. Technical performance, innovation, quality, reliability, and international engagement have made Siemens a leading company in electrification, automation and digitalization. It is top performance with the highest ethics that has made Siemens strong. This is what the Company will continue to stand for in the future.*

*The Business Conduct Guidelines provide the ethical and legal framework within which we want to maintain our successful activities. They contain the basic principles and rules for our conduct within our Company and in relation to our external partners and the general public. They set out how we meet our ethical and legal responsibility as a Company and give expression to our corporate values of being 'Responsible' – 'Excellent' – 'Innovative'.*

**Volvo (2020): Code of Conduct – Volvo Group[26]**

*Why do we have a Code? At Volvo Group we want to conduct business ethically and in compliance with the law.*

*Doing business this way is the right thing to do. It builds trust with our customers as well as with society which enhances our commercial success. And it helps us avoid situations that might lead to adverse legal issues or damage to our reputation. This Code of Conduct clearly states the expectations for how we do business – not just in a few locations, but everywhere we operate. The Code is what we stand for and what we expect from you.*

*[. . .]*

*NON-DISCRIMINATION: Volvo Group values a diverse workforce and expects hiring managers to observe applicable laws against discrimination. Employment decisions like hiring, pay, title, promotion, discipline, termination, or working conditions should be based on a person's ability or performance, not irrelevant personal factors.*

*For You, This Means:*

- *Do not practice discrimination; instead,*
- *Evaluate candidates based on talent, skill, and experience.*

*Speak up if you see discrimination, or believe you have been unfairly discriminated against.*

*[. . .]*

*MODERN SLAVERY AND CHILD LABOR: The Volvo Group does not tolerate any forms of modern slavery, including forced, bonded or compulsory labor, or human trafficking. We respect children's right to personal development and education, and we do not use child labor.*

*For You, This Means:*

- *Ensure that we do not use or support modern slavery, including by suppliers or other business partners. If you are a manager, ensure that your employees have freely chosen their jobs and are free to leave under their terms of employment and law.*

---

[25] https://assets.new.siemens.com/siemens/assets/public.1580482594.5c242542-e991-4b97-af63-090ad509be74.2019-sag-bcg-en.pdf

[26] https://www.volvogroup.com/content/dam/volvo/volvo-group/markets/global/en-en/about-us/our-values/code-of-conduct-and-other-policies/Code-of-Conduct-EN-new.pdf

- *If you hire, observe the minimum employment age in your country. Never hire children under 15, even if it is permitted by local law.*
- *Do not use young workers (ages 15-18) for work that is hazardous or poses risks to their individual development or their physical or mental health.*

## Social values matter (a lot) for management control system design and use

The theme of organizational and societal culture is fascinating and deep. However, we should be careful not to attribute everything that deviates from what we expect to see, or like to see, to 'culture'. In many discussions, the word culture is used to explain human behaviour, or, worse, to excuse it. Such excuses take a form of 'this is not the way we do it' or 'this type of control practice does not fit our culture'. Such claims may be right sometimes, but we should take the time to investigate better and in more detail what is meant by the general label 'culture' that is invoked. We can leave the sociological label of culture behind, and make use of some more detailed insights from social psychology. Here it is emphasized that 'people organizations' care for the social and ethical environment in which they work. We have strong reasons to believe that people work better, work harder, work smarter and work more in line with the official strategy of the organization if they work in environments in which they are appreciated and able to interact with others in a constructive and ethical way. This is why social and ethical qualities of the working environment are not just elements that are 'nice to have', and that we should use when they are there, but play a crucial role in management control systems and should be handled carefully. While being part of the organizational culture, we need to understand what it is from this cultural environment that has a positive effect on control via the positive effects it has on people's motivation and effort. There are three social values of direct importance to management control system design and use that we explore in more detail now.

The first is interpersonal trust, which we already mentioned briefly in a previous section. To trust somebody means that you believe in the honesty and goodness of the other person's intentions, to such an extent that you find yourself able to rely on their judgements and, to some extent, to put your faith in their hands. When interpersonal trust is high, people are more open and honest to one another, they show greater commitment to others and to the organization, and they are more motivated to do their work in the right way. Trust, therefore, is a more specific element of a larger organizational culture whose presence immediately adds to the goals of good management control. This also means that organizational practices that reduce interpersonal trust should be avoided. This, in particular, goes for those management control system elements which signal that managers and employees are not trusted, since, as the sayings go, trust 'comes on foot and leaves on horseback' and 'trust is a two-way street'. These expressions signify that people are inclined to reciprocate trust and lack of trust.

A second factor is empathy.[27] Empathy relates to the experience people have with regard to knowing one another's emotions and feelings. People have a natural capacity for empathy in that, without too much analysis, they are often able to explain behaviour as coming from some internal problem and therefore read the intentions of another's behaviour. People with good empathetic skills are able to understand what the other is doing and why, and to put themselves, so to speak, in the shoes of somebody else, take their perspective and therefore understand their motivations. Empathy is therefore often considered as a sort of social 'glue' that emotionally connects people. Organizations that take human social interactions seriously and that invest in the type of control practices that enable such mutual empathy are therefore also increasing the chances that managers will work 'well' because empathy contributes to good cooperation and good collegiality, and thus control.

---

[27] Davis, M.H. (1983) Measuring individual differences in empathy: evidence for a multidimensional approach. *Journal of Personality and Social Psychology*, 44(1): 113.

A third factor is organizational citizenship. This, often overlooked, element of organizational culture is studied in sociology, and deals with the small behaviours that people display in the workplace. Organizational citizenship relates to the extent to which managers and employees act as good citizens. Citizenship shows in the micro-behaviours of bringing one another cups of coffee, cleaning one's desk, repairing a stuck copying machine and helping one another out in the little everyday challenges of time management. Although it is hard to influence organizational citizenship through management control systems, it is important to note that these micro-behaviours do translate to overall positive culture in the sense that they create a feeling of collegiality and togetherness. Absence of this kind of citizenship may signal absence of a good and productive culture. Together with trust and empathy, organizational citizenship is typically the kind of variable that we easily overlook when designing management control systems, but which, at the end of the day, very much determines the success of these systems.

### *Ethics matter (a lot) for management control system design and use*

Last, but not least, we devote attention here to the role of ethics. Rather than referring to ethics only globally, as we did when we mentioned it previously, we need to devote some detailed attention to ethics for two reasons. First, over the past decades there has been an increasing interest in the field of management and business in the topic of ethical and unethical behaviour. Discussions about ethical and unethical behaviour have reached a peak in reaction to recent crises in modern business. Both the dotcom crisis in the early years of this century and the more recent 2007–2008 banking crisis spurred many to blame individuals and groups of individuals for their unethical behaviour. However, as we have seen, such blame-placing is often complicated, especially when the wrongdoings are the outcome of interactions between many people. In the banking crisis in particular, it is clear that although it is relatively easy to argue what went wrong, it is more difficult to invoke ethics to specify who exactly was wrong and why exactly that person was wrong. Analyses of the financial crisis seemed to suggest that there was no evidence of everybody acting unethically, at least that people were not deliberately seeking financial chaos. However, when judging their behaviours based on these chaotic outcomes, everybody may need to carry some of the blame. The reason for such difficulties in ethical judgement is that there is an enormous difference between the general idea of good and bad that we apply every day to all kinds of situations and a more analytical understanding of what it means to be good or bad. For example, although we generally judge it ethically bad for managers to lie about their performance, for example if they want to obtain a higher bonus than is warranted based on their true performance, we need to understand what it is about this lying that makes it bad. Some psychologists argue that almost everybody engages in some form of lying everyday. Some of these lies are insignificant or motivated by the fact that telling the truth can be hard and very painful. We can understand a little bit better what it is to have a judgement about good or bad if we realize that our opinions and our judgements are based on different ideas of what it is to be good or bad. For our purposes, it is useful to make a distinction between three kinds of moral reasoning that we apply in the design and use of management control systems. These are called deontic ethical reasoning, virtue-based ethical reasoning and consequence-based ethical reasoning (see the Real World Example).It is important for us to realize that these different forms of the ethical reasoning do not give us easy recipes to judge the certain act as good or bad, but rather to be aware of the ethical logic we apply. There are many examples in which these different kinds of reasoning lead to different conclusions. It is important to understand that people differ in the way they come to these judgements, and seeing where they come from may have a positive effect on the resolution of potential differences of opinion about certain courses of action. For example, if somebody judges a certain act to be morally wrong, understanding the way in which this judgement was produced could point to a shared understanding of what is right and wrong in a certain case.

***Real World Example:*** The field of ethics and ethical analysis goes back to the early days of human writing. In Western culture, great contributions have been made by Greek philosophers. Ethics is an important basis for religious and spiritual thought, such as in the teachings of Confucius. Here we can provide only a brief overview of some of the main forms of ethical reasoning. Note that these ethical reasoning styles can and do conflict, and should be seen as tools for the analysis of how people reason, rather than as a tool to solve ethical dilemmas.

**Deontic ethical reasoning**

The first category of ethical reasoning emphasizes that what is good or bad depends on what people do. There are certain acts that are simply good in themselves. For example, 'telling the truth' and 'not lying' are good things in principle. This type of ethical reasoning uses generic and general principles that people in their behaviour could or should adhere to. It is their duty to behave so, and that is why we talk of 'deontic' ethics because the Greek word 'deon' means duty or obligation. So when people justify their actions as being 'good' or condemn actions as 'bad', they do so based on the nature of the action itself. 'Cheating', 'stealing' and 'gossiping' are bad things in themselves, and go against the duty that people have to play fair, to respect others' property, and to talk honestly and positively about one another.

**Virtue-based ethical reasoning**

Another view on ethical reasoning is labelled 'virtue ethics'. Here the concern is to evaluate goodness or badness by arguing what a virtuous person would do. It is not the action itself that is evaluated as being good or bad, but the focus lies on the intention the actor had when performing the action. We can think of a long list of characteristics that a virtuous person has or must have, and much religious and spiritual thought focuses on stating such characteristics. A person must be honest, sympathetic, brave and prudent, but since there is no limit to these kinds of characteristics, it is sometimes hard to judge what a virtuous person would or should do in any specific situation.

**Utilitarian (consequence-based) ethical reasoning**

Utilitarian, or consequentialist, ethical reasoning does not focus on the quality of the act or the qualities of the actor, but rather looks at the results of the action. Typically, the argument is that an action is good when and because it delivers a certain positive outcome. Many argue that this kind of reasoning is a good way to explain the dominance of economic thought in business and society. Economics looks at actions from a utility-maximizing perspective, and its only criterion of judging whether certain decisions and choices are good or bad is by whether they serve the goal of utility maximization.

## *Social, cultural and ethical considerations may point to some no-go zones for management control systems*

These elements of the organizational and cultural environment are important to understanding how human behaviour comes about and what, therefore, we should try to stimulate in our design of management control systems. However, they also provide limits to what management control systems could or should try to achieve. One such limit concerns individual privacy. It is important to note that the way we ask managers and employees to behave in an organization requires them to show personal involvement and to share, formally and informally, a lot of personal information. Organizations know a lot about their managers and employees, including their abilities, their performance levels and their type of personality. When being employed or going up for promotion, formal ability and personality tests may be part of the process. It is a continuous debate, which is addressed differently across time and across cultures and countries, how far organizations can ethically go in measuring personal details. Organizations have access to a lot of formally collected information, given by consent, but the availability of informally collected information is increasing exponentially. The rise of social media, and the development of technology for the online real-time collection of physical data, such as face recognition, extends the scope of management control systems immensely. Boundaries between professional commitment and private life are becoming permeable, and the practical question is how far management control systems can go in measuring these elements of human personality and behaviour if they want to remain effective. Even if such measurements are informative about what people do and how they behave, or don't behave, vis-à-vis organizational objectives, ethical and social considerations may advise against their progression. Across the globe, views differ widely on the acceptability of such measures, which can partly be explained by the culture of a particular country being more individualistic or collectivist. Individualistic cultures seem to place a greater emphasis on privacy protection and protection of the self. Collectivist cultures seem more comfortable with the sharing of personal details. However, given the globalization of firms and the associated mix of cultural opinions, it will be agreed that what levels of privacy should be maintained is worthy of explicit consideration. The introduction of the Social Credit System in China (see the Real World Example) is a highly significant and intriguing example. This is not only because of ethical and social considerations but also pragmatic ones. Management control systems that conceive managers and employees as automatons that respond to programmed cues, rather than human beings with social, ethical and cultural norms, will lose their effectiveness immediately.

***Real World Example:*** Much has been said about China's Social Credit System (SCS) and its implications for individuals. Far less discussion has taken place on how it will affect business, even though the potential disruptions are substantial and wide-reaching. While the lack of awareness about the scale of this system and its effects on daily operations is understandable to an extent, the overwhelming absence of preparation by the European business community is deeply concerning.

As an organization here to serve European business and sound alarm bells when radical change is on the horizon, the European Chamber felt an urgent need to publish this report on China's impending, all-encompassing, technological regulatory system, in an attempt to knock the blinkers off. It is no exaggeration to say that the Corporate SCS will be the most comprehensive system created by any government to impose a self-regulating marketplace, nor is it inconceivable that the Corporate SCS could mean life or death for individual companies.

Aimed at full implementation by the end of 2020, the Corporate SCS uses real-time monitoring and processing systems to collect and interpret big data, which facilitates immediate detection of compliance, and raises or decreases a company's 'score'. Higher scores can mean lower tax rates, better credit conditions, easier market access and more public procurement opportunities for companies. Lower scores lead to the opposite, and can even result in blacklisting.

So, what does this mean for European businesses in China?

In some respects, this is good news. Equal enforcement of regulations should become a reality as numbers are crunched by impartial algorithms, before the system then pumps out a rating for each individual firm. It could also mean an end to blanket enforcement in areas like environmental protection. After having invested in world-class emissions control systems, European companies that have until now been routinely shut down alongside non-compliant competitors on heavily polluted days should be able to continue production while polluters will see their scores plummet.

In other areas, the Corporate SCS will bring major new challenges. Small and medium-sized enterprises (SMEs) will struggle to find the resources that compliance demands. Keeping pace with ever-changing regulations and ratings standards will be extremely draining. This issue poses a threat to downstream producers as well, with the flow of supplies being disrupted as their SME suppliers fight to keep their heads above water.

The level of compliance of business partners will also affect a company's score, which will necessitate tighter monitoring of each link in the supply chain. Monitoring concerns do not end there either, as individual ratings of a company's legal representative and high-ranking management will also impact company results. This will require European companies to consider monitoring the individual behaviour of employees, a major taboo for many.

[. . .]

For better or worse, China's Corporate SCS is here to stay and businesses in China need to prepare for the consequences, and they need to start now.

[. . .]

We hope that together, we can help to raise awareness and ensure that our member companies will live by the score, not die by the score.

Jörg Wuttke, President, European Union Chamber of Commerce in China

*Source:* European Chamber of Commerce (2019) *The Digital Hand.*

## Summary

A management control system is defined as comprising a combination of control practices designed and implemented by top managers to increase the probability that lower-level managers and employees will *behave* in ways consistent with the organization's mission, goals and strategies. Designing and using sound and effective management control systems therefore cannot be done if we do not understand human behaviour well enough to be able to explain what causes human behaviour and what inhibits human behaviour. Therefore we need to know, and be able to predict, the effects of individual control practices and their combinations. But we also need to understand that human behaviour is complex and multifaceted. This is already the case when we look at humans individually, as humans differ substantially in their abilities, competencies and preferences. Control practices are hardly ever designed and used for individual managers, so we also need to understand their effects on humans in the social context of an organization. Each control practice should thus be evaluated by its effect on both individual managerial behaviour as well as managers' collective and cooperative behaviours. This immediately forces us to apply many and multiple perspectives to human behaviour and actions. In this chapter, this complexity was illustrated by referring to the financial crisis of 2007–2008. We then sketched three models of human behaviour that originate in the social scientific disciplines of economics, psychology and sociology, respectively. Since management control system design is not about the scientific understanding of humans per se, but rather about designing and using management control systems that work in practice, we attempted to combine and summarize these insights into a more practical model. We sketched the management control system view of human behaviour by emphasizing the elements of such behaviour on which management control systems can be practically designed. Among these elements, the focus on human motivational forces is a dominant one. While demonstrating the many ways in which human motivation can be stimulated, we also demonstrated that management control system design and use is confronted by dilemmas and trade-offs. In addition, given the many possibilities this motivational focus provides, we also need to understand that technological sophistication and ingenuity may exceed human cognitive, social and ethical boundaries. Clearly, management control systems that are technically possible are not always desirable, from a functional or ethical point of view. In particular, the role of ethics needs to be highlighted, as ethical considerations have gained importance in management control system debates in response to the financial crisis. The Real World Vignette at the start of the chapter demonstrates the difficulty of making ethical judgements, and our discussion of various types of ethical reasoning explains this.

## Suggested additional reading

Azjen, I. and Fishbein, M. (1980) *Understanding Attitudes and Predicting Social Behavior.* Englewood Cliffs, NJ: Prentice-Hall.

Bendickson, J., Muldoon, J., Liguori, E. and Davis, P.E. (2016) Agency theory: the times, they are a-changin', *Management Decision*, 54(1): 174–93.

DesJardins, J. (2020) *An Introduction to Business Ethics.* McGraw-Hill.

Endenich, C., & Trapp, R. (2018). Ethical implications of management accounting and control: A systematic review of the contributions from the Journal of Business Ethics. *Journal of Business Ethics,* 1-20.

Kahneman, D. (2011) *Thinking, Fast and Slow.* New York: Farrar, Straus and Giroux.

Rilling, J.K. and Sanfey, A.G. (2011) The neuroscience of social decision-making, *Annual Review of Psychology,* 62: 23–48.

Shim, J.K., Siegel, J.G., Dauber, N. and Levine, M.H. (2019) *Corporate Controller's Handbook of Financial Management 2019–2020.* Wolters Kluwer.

# Case 3.1

# A matter of ethics?*

**by Frank G.H. Hartmann**

## Management control issues

Considering that management control is very much about making sure that managers align their behaviours with the goals and objectives of the firm, this also means that we need to understand what drives human behaviours. In this chapter we proposed several views on managerial (human) action, and we discussed some ethical guidelines and boundaries that we should adhere to in the design and use of management control systems.

Please consider the following short case descriptions and formulate an opinion on 'what to do' in each case. Explicitly consider how the various views on management action and the alternative theories on human ethics we discussed may affect your answer, and may thus explain why people can diverge largely in their evaluations of the cases. If it helps you in addressing this issue, consider yourself as having a senior role in the staff accounting department of the firm.

1. You discover that management is using bribe money to attract some contracts in a country that your company is not yet present in. The move towards this country is part of the strategy. After some investigations, you find out that the practice of bribe money is considered 'part of the game' in that country.
2. You notice that the company you work for is manipulating the emission tests of the car types it produces, in order to pass environmental regulations. After some internal discussions, you understand that this is common practice across the car industry. However, you also find out that eventual fines could jeopardize the company.
3. You are told that you will not get any bonus payment for the current year due to the financial problems of the firm. However, you find out that bonuses are still paid to those above you in the organizational hierarchy. Commenting on this practice, your direct superior suggests to you to stay silent, not to put your future fortune in the firm 'at risk'.
4. You notice that the pricing policies of your consumer product sales firm tend to be a bit weird. Most of the products sell at a price that ends with '99', and you wonder what effect that has on consumer behaviour. You also notice that bargain prices are sometimes compared to prices that were never 'actual', suggesting that consumers are not as advantaged as they think.
5. You notice a change in the menus of the restaurant at your firm. Without much notice, or 'democracy', the menus have become largely vegetarian and the growth in provision of vegan options has come at the expense of your favourite dishes. You also notice that it is very hard to talk about this openly.

* This case was written by Professor Frank G.H. Hartmann, Radboud University.

# Case 3.2
# Do not fool yourself*

**by Frank G.H. Hartmann**

## 'Figures don't lie, but liars figure'

This is an old saying, suggesting that while the numbers that management accounting reports may be truthful on an individual basis, they may still be used to provide a picture of reality that is distorted.

### Diversity management at Markratek Inc.

Markratek Inc., a global firm that develops, produces and sells safety equipment for the energy industry, has disclosed the following statement on diversity management (excerpt) in its 2020 annual report:

> *Markratek aims to be a leader in its market segment when it comes to the diversity of its employees. For every position in the firm, we offer equal opportunities to women and men.*

During 2020, the HR director of Markratek, Lilian Rose-Sheppard, reviews the new policies on diversity management she installed in 2018. Her eyes are drawn to the hiring figures, aggregated globally. Markratek, apparently, attracted 912 applicants in 2019. Of these, 544 were male, and Markratek hired 240 males (44 per cent of applicants). Of these applicants, 368 were female, of which Markratek hired 114 females (31 per cent of female applicants). In total Markratek hired 68 per cent males and 32 per cent females. Lilian is amazed. Although these figures are somewhat better than in 2018, they suggest that Markratek still has a long way to go.

However, before drawing any definitive conclusions, she asks one of her employees to provide a more detailed overview of the hires per area of activity (called 'sector'). Exhibit 1 provides this overview.

**EXHIBIT 1** Overview of hires per sector

| | Men | | Women | |
|---|---|---|---|---|
| **Markratek Inc. hires per sector** | **Applicants** | **Hired** | **Applicants** | **Hired** |
| Production and maintenance | 166 | 100 | 22 | 18 |
| Accounting and legal | 112 | 72 | 6 | 4 |
| Marketing | 66 | 24 | 118 | 34 |
| Sales | 84 | 28 | 76 | 28 |
| Logistics and supplies | 40 | 12 | 78 | 20 |
| Other | 76 | 4 | 68 | 10 |
| Total | 544 | 240 | 386 | 114 |

## Questions

1 Has there been a gender bias in the selection of new employees by Markratek Inc. overall?

2 Has there been a gender bias in the selection of new employees by sector in Markratek?

3 What inconsistency do you observe between the overall analysis and the analysis per sector? Can you explain this apparent inconsistency?

---

* This case was written by Professor Frank G.H. Hartmann, Radboud University.

## Suggested reading

Bickel, P.J., Hammel, E.A. and O'Connell, J.W. (1975) Sex bias in graduate admissions: data from Berkeley, *Science*, 187(4175): 398–404.

# Case 3.3

# Decision support systems and ethics*

**by Ted Welten**

## Discussion and decisions about the Brent Spar oil platform

This quote from Shell appeared in the German press on 27 June 1995:

> *We will change. We have learned that public opinion could not understand our arguments. But not only that. We now also realize that we have to listen more and better to our customers. Even if it hurts, only he who learns his lesson has the future.*

What happened? Let's take a look . . .

### Brent Spar

Brent Spar was a North Sea oil storage and tanker loading platform in the Brent oilfield, operated by Shell UK, with a pipeline connection to the oil terminal at Sullom Voe in Shetland. It was installed in June 1976.

Brent Spar was 482 ft (147 m) high and 95 ft (29 m) in diameter, and displaced 66,000 tonnes. The storage tank section had a capacity of 300,000 barrels of crude oil.

### *Economic lifetime ended. What to do? Shell's decision . . .*

The storage facility had continued in use, but by September 1991 was considered to be of no further value. The end of its economic lifetime had been reached, which meant that the costs of operating the asset were greater than the revenues, despite the fact that the technical lifetime could have been expanded.

Shell had two serious options for disposal:

1. *Onshore dismantling:* The first option involved towing the Brent Spar to a shallow-water harbour to decontaminate it and recycle the materials used in its construction. Any unusable waste could be disposed of on land. Technically, this option was more complex and presented a greater hazard to the workforce. This option was estimated to cost £41 million. There was some concern that the facility would disintegrate in shallow coastal water, having a much more economically and environmentally significant effect.
2. *Deep-sea disposal:* The second option involved towing the decommissioned platform into deep water in the North Atlantic and sinking it. The facility would then fall to the seabed and release its

---

* This case was written by Assistant Professor Ted Welten, Erasmus University Rotterdam.

contents over a restricted area. The cost of this option was estimated at between £17 million and £20 million.

Shell proposed that deep-sea disposal was the best option for the Brent Spar, arguing that its decision had been made on sound scientific principles and data. Dismantling the platform on-shore was more complex from an engineering point of view than disposal at sea. Shell also cited the lower risk to the health and safety of the workforce with deep-sea disposal. Environmentally, Shell considered that sinking would have only a localized effect in a remote deep-sea region that had little resource value. Shell acknowledged that sinking the Brent Spar at sea was also the cheaper option.

Its decision was supported by the British Government.

*Reaction of Greenpeace*

Greenpeace organized a worldwide, high-profile media campaign against this plan, occupying Brent Spar for more than three weeks.

Encouraged by Greenpeace, German drivers decided to avoid Shell's fuel pumps en masse, resulting in a widespread boycott of Shell service stations, with incidentally some physical attacks and an arson attack on a service station in Germany. Even then-Chancellor Helmut Kohl criticized Shell's decision to give the Brent Spar, which still contained oil residues and heavy metals, a seaman's grave. Kohl wiped out his British colleague John Major at the summit conference of seven major industrialized countries (G7). The dumping of the Brent Spar and the approval the British Government gave for this, was, said Kohl, 'a miserable example of European environmental policy'.

Shell saw with disappointment that its sales figures fell as a result of a decision made in England. Some pump owners saw their customers fall by half.

*Shell's altered decision taken under pressure*

In the face of public and political opposition in northern Europe, Shell abandoned its plans to dispose of the Brent Spar at sea – while continuing to stand by its claim that this was the safest option, both from an environmental and an industrial health and safety perspective.

It released the following statement on 20 June 1995:

> *Shell's position as a major European enterprise has become untenable. The Spar had gained a symbolic significance out of all proportion to its environmental effect. In consequence, Shell companies were faced with increasingly intense public criticism, mostly in Continental northern Europe. Many politicians and ministers were openly hostile and several called for consumer boycotts. There was violence against Shell service stations, accompanied by threats to Shell staff.*

*Conflicting interests and arguments*

Shell and Greenpeace obviously had conflicting interests. To motivate their points of view, they used different arguments. Both organizations claimed to have made their decision taking into account as many arguments as possible. But where did these arguments came from? Were the arguments of both Shell and Greenpeace taken out of context and was each emphasizing only its part of the problem? And why, if they are referring to the same facts, do these arguments differ?

To give two examples:

1. Greenpeace's own reputation suffered during the campaign, when it had to acknowledge that its assessment of the oil remaining in the Brent Spar's storage tanks had been grossly overestimated.
2. And Shell presented many arguments to defend its decision to sink the Brent Spar. The fact that this was the cheapest solution was one of them. As Shell is a for-profit company, could this be the dominating factor?

*General business principles of Shell*

Shell formulated its General Business Principles in 2014. Principle 5 is as follows:

5. *Health, Safety, Security and the Environment*

   *Shell companies have a systematic approach to health, safety, security and environmental management in order to achieve continuous performance improvement.*

   *To this end, Shell companies manage these matters as critical business activities, set standards and targets for improvement, and measure, appraise and report performance externally.*

   *We continually look for ways to reduce the environmental impact of our operations, products and services.*

## Questions

1. Discuss the ethical point of view for Shell.
2. Discuss the ethical point of view for Greenpeace.
3. Discuss the existence of information asymmetry between Shell and Greenpeace from an agency theory perspective.
4. Do you think that Shell's formulated General Business Principle 5 will bring the (ethical) positions of Shell and Greenpeace together? Why? Why not?
5. How would you design a management control system that takes ethical issues into consideration?

## References

Schwartz, K. (1998) De harde lessen van de Brent Spar voor Shell en Greenpeace, *Trouw*, 29 January. Available at: https://www.trouw.nl/nieuws/de-harde-lessen-van-de-brent-spar-voor-shell-en-greenpeace~b3cdab63/ (accessed 7 May 2020).

Shell, Brent Spar dossier. Available at: https://www.shell.co.uk/sustainability/decommissioning/brent-spar-dossier.html (accessed 7 May 2020).

Shell, Our values. Available at: https://www.shell.com/about-us/our-values.html (accessed 7 May 2020).

Wikipedia, Brent Spar. Available at: https://en.wikipedia.org/wiki/Brent_Spar (accessed 7 May 2020).

# Case 3.4
# Cultural issues: Netflix culture*

**by Professor Ted Welten**

## The organization

Netflix, founded in 1997 by Reed Hastings and Marc Randolph, is a production company and media-services provider. The company's key business is a subscription-based streaming service that offers customers an online collection of films and TV series. This includes content produced inhouse as well as a variety of content from other sources. Netflix has more than 148 million subscribers and is available worldwide, except in North Korea, Syria and mainland China. Its headquarters is in Los Gatos, California, but the company has offices in South Korea, Japan, Brazil, the Netherlands and India.

## Seven aspects of the Netflix culture

Netflix formulated and published a 128-page cultural deck slide that is accessible to everybody on the internet; it has been viewed millions of times.

Patty McCord was chief talent officer at Netflix between 1998 and 2012. She was responsible for the cultural deck slide of the Netflix culture. According to Patty, the Netflix approach to talent and culture was basically based on common sense.

Let's take a look at the most important elements of these cultural aspects of Netflix . . .

### 1. Values

Netflix does not rely on well-formulated values on paper, but on what it calls the *real* company values, which are shown by who gets rewarded, promoted or let go.

These company values are the *behaviours* and *skills* that Netflix particularly *values* in its employees, and can be described in terms of nine values that should be inherent in these employees, as described below.

1 *Judgement:* You are able to balance out different (contra dictionary) aspects and make a wise decision. You look at the problem analysis and find a solution accordingly. You are strategically focused and can decide what must be done now and what must be done in a later stage.

2 *Communication:* You are a good listener, try to understand and then come up with a reaction. You excel in speech and writing, treat people with respect, also when they have a different status or opinion and stay calm in stressful situations.

3 *Impact:* You can handle a lot of work, perform strong, you are more result oriented than action oriented and you don't overthink a problem, but act quickly.

4 *Curiosity:* You are a quick learner, understand the broader context and contribute outside your specialty.

5 *Innovation:* You discover practical solutions to hard problems by thinking outside the box and come up with new ideas and simplify complexity.

6 *Courage:* You say what's on your mind, make tough decisions, take smart risks and question actions that are inconsistent with our values.

---

* This case was written by Assistant Professor Ted Welten, Erasmus University Rotterdam.

7 *Passion:* You are inspirational, are involved in the success of the company, you celebrate wins and are persistent.

8 *Honesty:* You tell people what you think to their face and admit your mistakes and are not political.

9 *Selflessness:* You are more focused on the interest of Netflix than your own, you help colleagues and share information openly. There is a goal congruence between the organizational and individual goals.

An important aspect of these values is the possible mismatch between the values you're talking up and the behaviours you're modelling and encouraging. It's a waste of time to articulate ideas about values and culture if you don't model and reward behaviour that aligns with those goals. In the management control literature this is known as the 'tone at the top'.

This comes down to basic psychology: if people say one thing and do another, you should always look at what people do and not what they say they will do.

As leaders build a company culture, they need to be aware of subcultures that might require different management.

### 2. High performance

Netflix focuses heavily on team performance that consists of great-performing individuals. Don't confuse a team with a family. Compare it to a pro sports team, not a kids' recreational team. A great workplace is working with the best of the best.

The job of a coach at every level of Netflix is to hire, develop and cut smartly, so it has stars in every position. Netflix calls it the keeper test that managers use: 'Which of my people, if they told me they were leaving in two months for a similar job at a peer company, would I fight hard to keep at Netflix?'

Netflix measures people by how much, how quickly and how well they get work done – especially to deadlines.

Even if you've hired people who want to perform well, you need to clearly communicate how the company makes money and which behaviours will drive its success.

Netflix eliminated formal job reviews and has conversations about performance as an organic part of its work. Netflix calls these 360-degree reviews: people are asked to identify things that colleagues should stop, start or continue.

Only after they've done the work of envisioning the ideal outcome and the skill set necessary to achieve it should they analyse how well their existing team matches what they need. This is a principle that within the manufacturing world is known as a greenfield study: if you were to design a production factory from scratch, what machines would you invest in? You can compare this blueprint to the actual situation and take it in to consideration when you replace a machine.

Netflix promotes honesty about performance and treats people like adults, so if people are not performing well, it tells them. People often know more about their own (negative) situation than they think.

Netflix continually tells managers that building a great team is their most important task.

### 3. Freedom and responsibility

Most companies increase the number of rules and regulations as they grow. Netflix decided to go in the opposite direction: minimize rules – and let the increasing chaos be handled by ever more high-performance people.

Flexibility is more important than efficiency in the long term. At least in a creative environment it is cheaper to fix problems when they occur than to prevent them by implementing all kind of procedures. It is important to fix problems quickly. And high performers make very few errors.

The Netflix organization had learned that if it asks people to rely on logic and common sense instead of on formal policies, most of the time it will get better results and at lower cost. If you're careful to hire people who will put the company's interests first, who understand and support the desire for a high-performance workplace, 97 per cent of your employees will do the right thing. Most companies spend endless time and money writing and enforcing policies to deal with problems the other 3 per cent might cause.

As far as its vacation policy is concerned, instead of shifting to a formal system, Netflix went in the opposite direction: salaried employees were told to take whatever time they felt was appropriate.

Also, the company has a travel and expense policy that is five words long, 'Act in Netflix's best interests', instead of formulating rules.

With the right people, instead of a culture of process adherence, you need a culture of freedom and responsibility, innovation and self discipline.

### 4. Context, not control

The best managers figure out how to get great outcomes by setting the appropriate context, rather than by trying to control their people. This means that you set the boundaries and give the employees the freedom to make their own decisions. This is the basic condition for decentralization of responsibilities and competencies.

The basic premise for managers is: When you are tempted to 'control' your people, ask yourself what context you could set instead.

High-performance people will do better work if they understand the context and are given the freedom to operate according to their own insight.

### 5. Highly aligned, loosely coupled

The team and its members should look into the same direction (highly aligned) but have enough freedom to excel on an individual level (loosely coupled). Teamwork effectiveness is dependent on high-performance people and good context (discussed under point 4). Employees should all focus on the same goals and strategy, but are free to fill in their contribution.

The result will be that the Netflix goal will be able to grow, be flexible and be controllable, even if the size is big.

### 6. Pay top of market

Netflix is paying its employees at the top of the market, because that is in line with the high-performance culture. The reason is simple: one outstanding employee gets more done and costs less than two adequate employees, so Netflix strives to have only outstanding employees.

Netflix approaches this at the individual level in three different ways:

1. Pay them more than anyone else likely would
2. Pay them as much as a replacement would cost
3. Pay them as much as we would pay to keep them if they had a higher offer from elsewhere.

The Netflix principle comes down to giving employees a big salary as this is the most efficient form of compensation, so no bonuses or free stock options.

It is possible within Netflix to trade off a part of your salary for stock options, which can be executed under favourable conditions. So then your effort may be reflected in the performance of Netflix, measured by the stock price.

### 7. Promotions and development

Within Netflix there are two necessary conditions for promotion:

1. *Job has to be big enough:* Netflix might have an incredible manager of something, but we don't need a director of it because job isn't big enough. So you cannot get a promotion if the job stays the same.
2. *Person has to be a superstar in current role:* In a way, this person has reached the top of the job, but not the top of his capabilities.

These employees have the opportunity to get the next-level job at a peer firm that knows their talents well.

## The downside of the culture at Netflix

Being a member of one of these 'dream teams' at Netflix isn't the perfect fit for everyone. Some people prefer to work at companies more orientated to seniority and stability. The model at Netflix works for those who value consistent excellence in their colleagues.

Netflix isn't the perfect company to work for and doesn't have to be. The CEO is creating 'better entertainment at lower cost and greater scale than the world has ever seen' and succeeding at it. There is no excuse for a prospective employee who has done their research on Netlix' values and the way it operates, to join the company if they disagree with the way things work.

A high-performance culture isn't necessary to build a successful company – there are many companies without a well-defined company culture that are slowly, but steadily growing. But Netflix is a company that does not want to grow slowly and steadily. If you want to build a company that is innovative, disruptive and has rapid growth and attracts and keeps the best performers, then you need to deliberately define the culture that you want to create. But these strong cultures are demanding and prospective and current employees should analyse the company culture honestly and gauge whether they fit within the values and expectations and want to commit or continue to commit to that culture.

## Concluding remarks about the Netflix culture

Netflix depends on a culture that supports rapid innovation *and* excellent execution.

Netflix needs a culture that supports effective teamwork of high–performance people.

Netflix needs a culture that avoids the rigidity, politics, mediocrity and complacency that infect most organizations as they grow.

## Questions

1 In this chapter three models of managers were discussed. Explain which model is the most applicable to Netflix. Are the three principles of the management control model of managers applicable to Netflix? Why? Why not?

2 In this chapter the relevance of culture in organizations is discussed. How would you describe the culture of Netflix? Compare this to a more traditional business culture.

3 Discuss the cultural dimensions of Netflix.

4 Discuss the negative aspects of the Netflix culture.

5 How does Netflix cope with the global cultural differences between countries and customers?

6 Can you elaborate on the ratio of intrinsic versus extrinsic motivation that is relevant for the Netflix culture? Relate this to the seven cultural aspects described in this case.

## References

McCord, P. (2014) How Netflix reinvented HR, *Harvard Business Review,* January–February. Available at: https://hbr.org/2014/01/how-netflix-reinvented-hr (accessed 7 May 2020).

Netflix, Reference guide on our freedom & responsibility culture. Available at: https://igormroz.com/documents/netflix_culture.pdf (accessed 7 May 2020).

Putter, B. (2018) Netflix's company culture is not for everybody and that's exactly how it should be, *Forbes,* 4 December. Available at: https://www.forbes.com/sites/brettonputter/2018/12/04/netflixs-company-culture-is-not-for-everybody-and-thats-exactly-how-it-should-be/#ee8dbec1880e (accessed 7 May 2020).

# Case 3.5
# 'In control' at FBS Executive Education*

**by Frank G.H. Hartmann**

## At the end of the first week

John Simpson was sitting at his desk on 5 April 2015, after his first week as freshly appointed Dean of Executive Education at FBS Executive Education. He had not expected that so much would happen in such a short time. The 25 colleagues in the Executive Education department had awaited his arrival for some months, and John's reputation of being straightforward, outspoken and not easy to please had preceded him. They were well aware of the fact that John's arrival was the result of disappointing financial and operational results over the past decade. FBS's overall strategy had stated that executive education should be 'turned around'. Moreover, with the appointment of John, who was a fully active research professor, a line of successive interim directors ended. These temporary directors had few long-term incentives and had accomplished too little. While inviting the stability John would bring, the departmental colleagues were also anxious about what this would mean for them personally. On top of this, John had had an interesting conversation with Winston Carpenter, one of his fellow statutory directors. Winston asked John why on earth he had taken up the role of Dean of Executive Education. Did John not know what a mess it was? Did he not realize that life as an academic was so much easier and more comfortable? This promised to be an interesting journey . . .

## FBS Executive Education

FBS Sealand University was the business school of Sealand University, founded in 1955. FBS called itself a full-service school, as it organized a wide range of degree and non-degree programmes. Degree programmes were those leading to an academic degree, such as a BSc, MSc or PhD. These programmes were funded with public money. Non-degree programs were organized in the Executive Education department. The customers of these programmes were either firms that wanted to have internal management education, or individual customers who would enrol in short-term management courses. These latter programmes were called 'open' since they were basically offered to everybody. The internal programmes were called 'customized', since these were specifically designed for a firm having a specific need. Traditionally, FBS Executive Education has focused on these customized programmes. These often came with a turnover of several hundred thousand euros. However, competition was fierce, and since the financial crisis of 2008, average turnover had dropped significantly. Moreover, since many of these programmes required entry into a tendering process, with chances of investing in programme design for 'nothing', the attractiveness of the customized market was severely weakened. This had led to the decision to increase efforts towards open programmes, which were considered easier to design and organize.

## FBS governance and management

Morgan Lawson was Dean of FBS. He had first announced that he wanted to be a hands-off type of leader, and during his period as Associate Dean had shown himself to be a laissez-faire, laissez-passer type of leader. As Dean, this did not change. Rather his strategic vision simply amounted to 'get higher in the rankings'. As any international business school, FBS had realized more and more that being ranked

---

* This case was written by Professor Frank G.H. Hartmann, Radboud University.

**EXHIBIT 1** The structure of the school

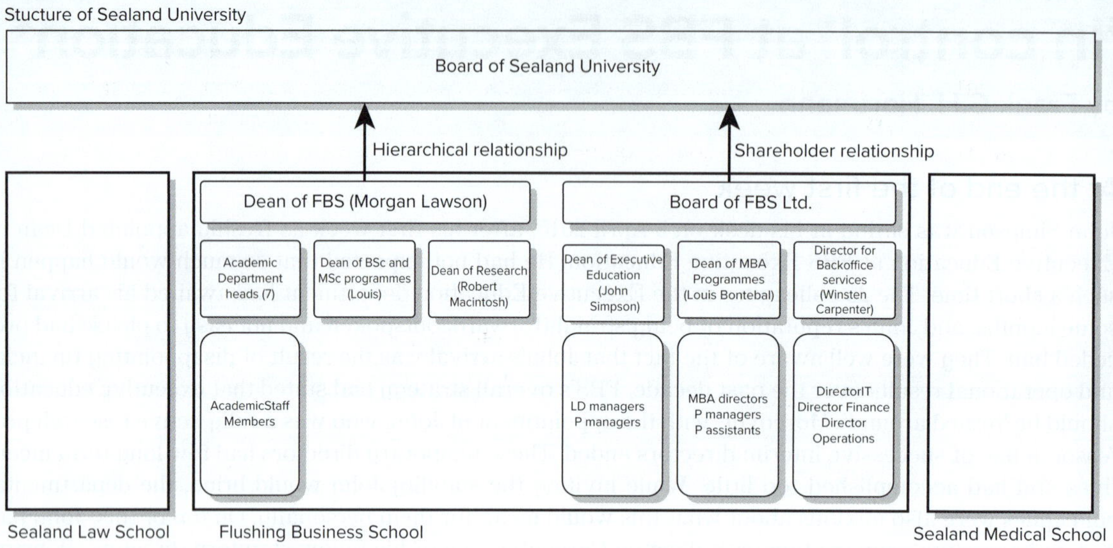


highly meant a lot. Students choose their universities increasingly based on rankings, and MBA students in particular would look for a university that was highly ranked, to get a better bang for their buck and increase their chances of entering the labour market catapulted by the school's rank. The ranking system was quite complicated, but for example the influential *Financial Times* ranking would score the school, taking various objective and subjective factors into account. It would look at the several parts of the school, including research output, and would also weigh the customer satisfaction of students and professionals enrolled in MBA and executive programmes. Thus, the aim to be ranked better, combined with the pressure to secure the expensive research programmes, with declining tax money, gave the general idea of 'being ranked higher' a strong push towards improving the commercial MBA and executive programmes.

This structure of the school (Exhibit 1) had been in place since 2005. In that year, a so-called 'three-party agreement' was signed between the board of the university, the (former) Dean of FBS and the (former) board of FBS Ltd. This was done to create a 'united school' as the new direction for the school was then baptized. This short agreement simply stated that 'all parties should work towards the common goal of FBS'. This agreement had been necessary, since FBS Ltd and the 'public' organization have a rather different legal status. Both were governed by the board, but in a different way. The three statutory directors of FBS Ltd were in principle accountable only to the board of the university. However, this agreement suggested that the Dean of FBS also had supervisory powers in FBS Ltd. The organizational structure at FSB Ltd. had, over the past decade, changed quite a bit, due to the diverging opinions of successive interim directors. When John sat down to figure out the structure at FSB Executive Education (Exhibit 2), he decided it did not make much sense.

## FBS incentives

Academic staff members at FBS were evaluated on both teaching and research, but it was well understood that making it at FBS was based on one's research output. FBS had adopted a system of a limited number of academic journals in which publications were rewarded with points. Over a rolling period of five years, everybody was expected to publish three papers in those journals that ranked highest in each field. If not, somebody would lose research time, with the danger of getting stuck in a vicious cycle that would result in full-time teaching. Researchers would earn up to 60 per cent of their time in research.

Under this system, research blossomed at FBS, at least in quantitative terms. What you measure is what you get, Robert Macintosh, Dean of Research at FSB, argued, triumphantly.

Under the 'united school' principle, FBS wanted more of its own academics in both the MBA and executive programmes. First, such internal sourcing would keep more financial benefits inside, improving the financial position of the school. Second, having FBS programmes being in fact taught by non-FBS academic staff just did not seem right. Third, having FBS academic staff engage in teaching for professional practitioners would expose them to the business problems of these practitioners, which would enhance the relevance of research. Louis Bontebal, who was both the Dean of Education at the public part of FBS and Dean of the MBA programme in FSB Ltd. strongly pushed for more 'internal sourcing'.

But bridging the academic with the practical was more easily said than done. First, many academics simply lacked the ability to teach in front of executives. Their teaching style was geared towards a much younger audience, and much of their knowledge was inspired by theoretical problems rather than the practical challenges of real managers. Second, the enormous pressure to publish in the up-or-out system provided little incentive for academics to spend time on additional teaching. This teaching was additional, since it was often very hard to plan a year in advance. Third, academics felt that teaching for an MBA and executive audience was underpaid. Under the rather strict rules of the university there was a cap on the amount of extra salary that people could get. As the rate per teaching hour was in fact quite high, that cap was reached easily, especially by the relatively small group of excellent executive lecturers.

## The business processes at Executive Education

Within Executive Education, the two main roles were those of the Account and Programme Managers (APMs) and of Programmes Assistants (PAs). APMs were responsible for designing programmes, together with academic staff, and for supervising their execution. Given the history, most APMs were experienced in customized programmes, which enabled them to spend enormous amounts of time on getting it right. Open programmes required a different skill, and the combination of customized and open programmes spelled a challenge to their organizing skills. APMs were responsible for planning, organizing and supporting programme execution. Their supervisor was Carol Woods. They had to plan their work at very short notice. Although there was a rough calendar of programmes, it changed constantly due to the unpredictability of customized programmes and the cancellations of open programmes

**EXHIBIT 2** The structure of Executive Education in 2015

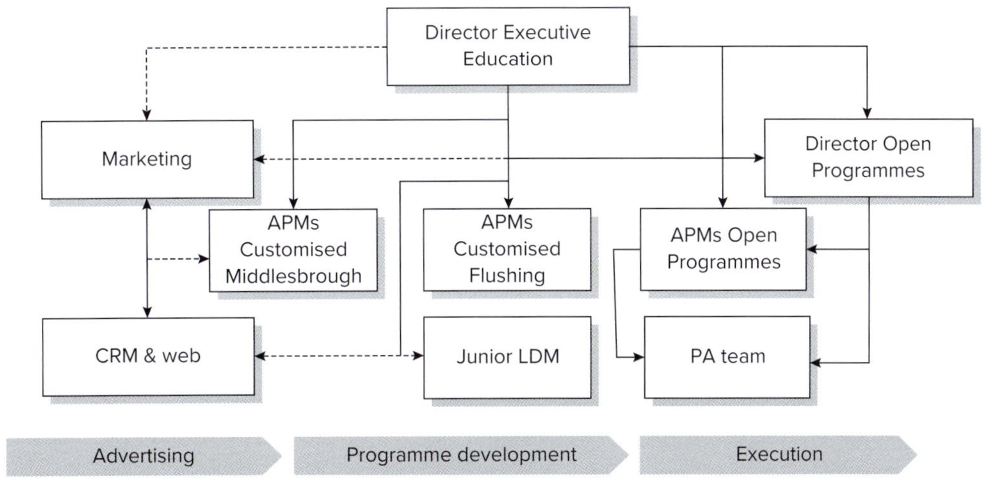

that did not get filled. APMs and PAs were allocated over programmes on an ad hoc basis, and based on a subjective judgement of their availability. APMs were more or less independent and self-organized. Three years ago, Executive Education had opened a separate sales office in Middlesborough, a town located an hour's drive from Flushing, to work on attracting clientele from Middlesborough's large population of headquarters of large international firms. But little turnover had resulted from that.

Marketing and sales of programmes was restricted to the use of a CRM system that contained all the names of people that had participated in the past. In addition, online media (LinkedIn and Twitter) were used once new open programmes were launched. Customized programmes were not actively acquired, but given the good name of FBS, still a considerable amount of requests (to enter a tender, develop a programme, suggest an idea) were made during the year.

## The challenge

FBS strategy had called for a 'turnaround' of Executive Education. Certainly, profitability was a problem, although John had a hard time establishing how big that problem really was. Back-office costs were not allocated to MBA and Executive Education programmes, and the costs allocated from the public school were opaque. They consisted of fees for marketing services and other central support. Also, the profitability of the external Executive Education department was simply not known. But more important than this lack of management was the way the business processes within the department were organized. Much time seemed spent on activities that did not produce value to FBS Ltd.

**EXHIBIT 3** Financial developments 2010–2014 (€m)

| | 2010 | 2011 | 2012 | 2013 | 2014 |
|---|---|---|---|---|---|
| MBA CM* | 3.5 | 3.6 | 3.2 | 3.8 | 3.6 |
| ExEd CM* | –1.3 | –1.8 | –0.8 | –1.4 | –1.2 |
| Back office | –1.2 | –1.2 | –1.3 | –1.4 | –1.5 |
| Charges from FBS public to FBS Ltd | –0.5 | –0.6 | –0.7 | –0.7 | –0.8 |
| BV net profit | 0.3 | –0.0 | 0.4 | 0.3 | 0.1 |

*CM = contribution margin

### Discussion points

Where did all the hours go? Something needed to be changed for sure. What were the goals of Executive Education anyway, and what would be the right management control system to help achieve those goals? And, above all, where to begin?

Part 2

# Management control systems: applying organizational architecture

In Part 1, this book presented a fundamental view on both the meaning and significance of management control systems, and the stakeholders that such systems should satisfy. In this second part of the book we take a closer look at throughput controls in the form of the various structural choices that need to be made by top management, and choices related to the organization's set of rules, such as policies and process descriptions. The fact that we devote the whole of this part of the book to organizational architecture highlights an important message we want to send: management control systems are about so much more than performance measurement and incentives. The throughput controls that make up the organizational architecture are the 'skeleton' around which output controls are designed, and top managers need to pay close attention to these throughput control practices.

Chapter 4 discusses how the assignment of responsibility to the different organizational units is an important step towards ensuring the effectiveness of the management control system. We introduce and discuss four types of so-called responsibility centre, which are organizational units headed by managers responsible for the unit's performance. These are revenue centres, expense centres (also often referred to as cost centres), profit centres and investment centres. For each of these centres, the chapter provides definitions, a general description and issues of importance when deciding on which centre is appropriate for a particular organizational unit.

Chapter 5 discusses some of the principal challenges in managing responsibility centres, namely transfer pricing, corporate service pricing and shared service centres. Transfer pricing is about how to devise a satisfactory method of accounting for the transfer of goods and services from one responsibility centre to another in organizations that have a significant number of these transactions. Another principal challenge in managing responsibility centres is how to avoid task redundancies at each responsibility centre because of, for instance, the additional personnel and record-keeping required in each unit. One new promising form of gaining efficiency is the concept of shared service centres, in which a subset of 'non-core' business functions are concentrated into a new business unit – that is, the shared service centre.

Chapter 6 reflects on the 'silo'-based view created by a too narrow focus on responsibility centres by highlighting a number of additional structural choices that need to be made by top management, as well as the need for integration between units. These choices concern whether an organization should be organized according to a functional structure, a business unit structure, a matrix structure or a 'project' type of structure. The chapter discusses, for instance, lean management, the waterfall method for projects and agile project management, and corresponding policies and process descriptions.

Chapter 7 further reflects on the 'silo'-based view by highlighting the need for top managers to extend the notion of organizational architecture beyond the company's borders. We discuss various types of cooperation, such as strategic alliances and joint ventures. Compared with coordinating activities within an organization in which hierarchical authority is one important basis for control, inter-organizational coordination takes place between legally independent organizations where there is no clear formal hierarchical authority in place.

# Chapter 4

# Responsibility centres

## Learning objectives

After reading this chapter, you should be able to:

1 Define the four standard types of responsibility centre.

2 Explain and apply the criteria for deciding what type of responsibility centre a particular organizational unit should be.

3 Explain the main characteristics of revenue centres and how they are evaluated.

4 Explain the main characteristics of engineered and discretionary expense centres and how they are evaluated.

5 Explain the main characteristics of profit centres and how they are evaluated.

6 Explain the main characteristics of investment centres and how they are evaluated.

## Real world vignette: Volkswagen and Dieselgate

It's unlikely that anyone can have missed the Volkswagen emissions scandal described in Chapter 2, also known as Dieselgate. Following this crisis, Volkswagen initiated many different changes. For instance, it launched a group-wide unit responsible for research and development, and its trucks and buses unit was separated into different responsibility centres. A company representative quoted in the *Financial Times*, said: 'The new structure streamlines group management, systematically leverages synergies in the individual operating units, and speeds up decision-making.'[1] What Volkswagen in effect did was to change

[1] *Financial Times*, Volkswagen makes sweeping changes to management and structure. Available at: https://www.ft.com/content/9a0b092c-3e48-11e8-b7e0-52972418fec4

the responsibility structures within the company. This is not surprising. *Responsibility centres* – that is, organizational units headed by managers who are responsible for their activities – are the important 'skeleton' of a management control system in a large company. Once the skeleton is set, the 'flesh' of the management control system, in the form of, for instance, budgeting, performance measurement systems and incentive programmes, can be developed. Assigning responsibility needs to be an important consideration when designing a management control system.

## Introduction

In Chapter 1, we defined a management control system as comprising a combination of control practices designed and implemented by top managers to increase the probability that lower-level managers and employees will behave in ways consistent with the organization's mission, goals and strategies. We also discussed that these control practices could usefully be divided into three types, labelling these input controls, throughput controls and output controls. In this chapter we will take a closer look at throughput controls: control practices that direct lower-level manager and employee behaviour through formal delegation of decision-making responsibility, and by specifying how behaviours are to be performed or not performed. More specifically, we look at how top managers can control the behaviours of lower-level managers and employees by designing appropriate structural arrangements or, as we call it in this book, an appropriate 'organizational architecture'. One important consideration is to do with designing appropriate responsibility centres. Should the various organizational units be responsible for only revenues (revenue centres) or only costs (expense centres) or both revenues and costs (profit centres) or also assets employed (investment centres)? As such, *the assignment of responsibility* to the different organizational units is an important and vital step to ensure the effectiveness of the management control system in large organizations. This tends to be forgotten by many top managers, who want to start directly with budgeting and the design of performance measurement systems and incentives. However, effective budgeting and measurement of performance requires assignment and acceptance of responsibility of performance. Thus, the creation of *responsibility centres* – that is, organizational units headed by managers responsible for the unit's performance – constitutes an important 'skeleton' of a management control system and the assignment of responsibility to these units should reflect the organization's mission, goals and strategies. There are four standard types of responsibility centre: revenue, expense (also often referred to as cost), profit and investment. They reflect the different degrees of financial decision-making authority that the top managers have delegated to the lower-level managers and employees.

We begin this chapter by describing the nature of responsibility centres in general and the basic criteria for choosing which type of responsibility centre to use for a particular organizational unit. We then discuss each of the four standard types of responsibility centre. We focus on the considerations involved in assigning *financial responsibility* (in terms of expenses, revenues, profit and assets employed) to organizational subunits. This involves discussing, to some extent, the financial measures to be used for performance evaluation of the responsibility centres. In Chapter 9 we provide more details on how to measure and evaluate financial performance, and how to supplement financial measures with non-financial performance measures in the evaluation of the organization's responsibility centres.

## Responsibility centres

*A responsibility centre is an organizational unit that is headed by a manager who is responsible for its activities.* In a sense, an organization is a collection of responsibility centres, each of which is represented by a box on the organization chart. These responsibility centres form a formal hierarchy. At

**FIGURE 4.1** Reading organizational structures using the concept of responsibility centres

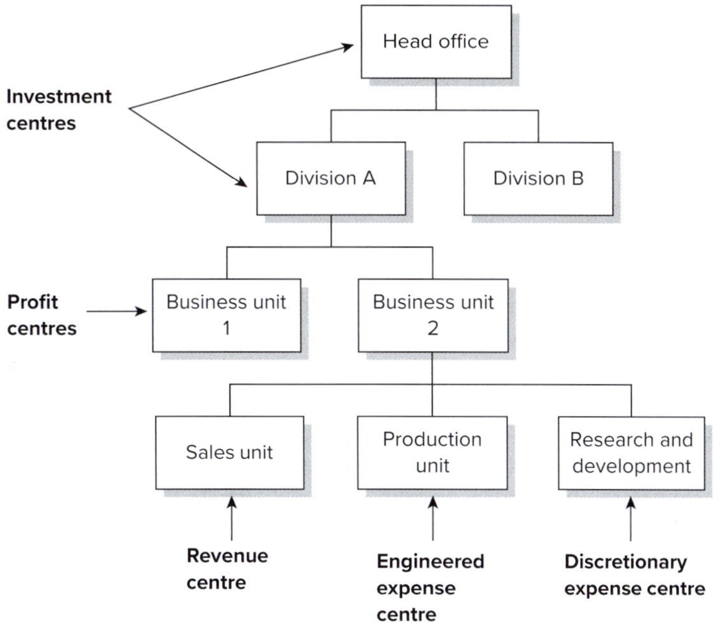


the lowest level are the centres for sections, work shifts and other small organizational units. Departments or business units comprising several of these smaller units are higher in the hierarchy. From the standpoint of top managers, the entire organization is a responsibility centre, though the term is usually used to refer to organizational units within the company. Figure 4.1 provides an example of an organization chart, illustrating how the four standard types of responsibility centre are matched with the different units in the hierarchy to reflect the responsibilities of the managers running each unit. In this way, *organizational structures can be 'read' using the concept of responsibility centres.*

A responsibility centre exists to accomplish one or more *objectives.* The company as a whole has a mission, goals and strategies. Because every organization is the sum of its responsibility centres, the idea is that if each responsibility centre meets its objectives, the mission, goals and strategies of the organization will have been achieved. But how can managers analyse what type of responsibility to assign to their different organizational units? Figure 4.2 illustrates a basic model for analysing assignment of responsibility to managers. As shown in the model, the key is to start with an analysis of the *core operation* of

**FIGURE 4.2** Responsibility centre

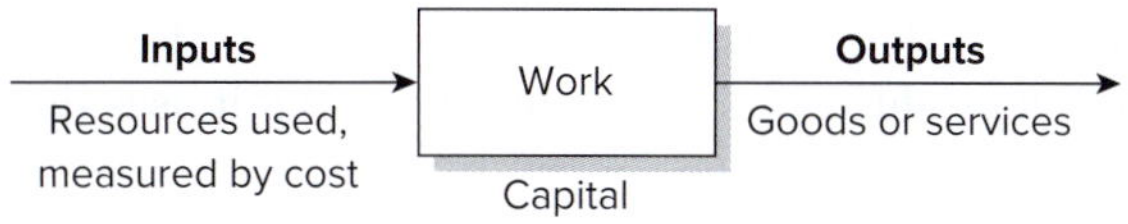

every responsibility centre. Responsibility centres receive *inputs*, in the form of materials, labour and services. Using working capital (e.g., inventory, receivables), equipment and other assets, the responsibility centre performs its particular function, with the ultimate objective of transforming its inputs into *outputs*, either tangible (i.e., goods) or intangible (i.e., services). For instance, in a production plant, the outputs are goods. In other organizational units, such as human resources (HR), transportation, engineering, accounting and administration, the outputs are services.

The products (i.e., goods and services) produced by a responsibility centre may be furnished either to another responsibility centre, where they are inputs, or to the outside marketplace, where they are outputs of the organization as a whole. Revenues are the amounts earned from providing these outputs.

Responsibility centre managers are responsible for ensuring the optimum relationship between inputs and outputs. In some centres, the relationship is causal and direct, as in a production department, for example, where the inputs of raw material become a physical part of the finished goods. Here, control focuses on using the minimum input necessary to produce the required output according to the correct specifications and quality standards, at the time requested, and in the quantities desired.

In many situations, however, inputs are not directly related to outputs. Advertising expense is an input that is intended to increase sales revenue; but as revenue is affected by many factors other than advertising, the relationship between increased advertising and any subsequent increase in revenue is rarely demonstrable, and management's decision to increase advertising expenditures is typically based on judgement rather than data. In research and development (R&D), the relationship between inputs and outputs is even more ambiguous; the value of today's R&D effort may not be known for several years, and the optimum amount that a given company should spend for R&D is indeterminable.

Much of the input that responsibility centres use can be stated as physical measurements – hours of labour, reams of paper and kilowatt hours of electricity. In a management control system these quantitative amounts are translated into monetary terms; money is a common denominator that allows the value of several different resources to be combined or compared. The monetary value of a given input is ordinarily calculated by multiplying a physical quantity by a price per unit (e.g., hours of labour × a rate per hour). The resulting monetary sum is called 'expense'; this is the way a responsibility centre's input is commonly expressed. Expense is a monetary measure of the amount of resources used by a responsibility centre.

Note that inputs are resources used by the responsibility centre. Patients in a hospital or students in a school are not inputs. Rather, inputs are the resources that the hospital or school uses to accomplish the objective of treating patients or educating students. It is much easier to measure the cost of inputs than to calculate the value of outputs. For example, annual revenue may be an important measure of a profit-oriented organization's output, but this will not express all that the organization did during that year. Inputs such as R&D activity, HR training, and advertising and sales promotion may not affect output in the year in which they occur. Nor is it possible to measure accurately the value of the work done by a public relations department, a quality control department or a legal department. In non-profit organizations, there may be no quantitative measure of output whatsoever; a university can easily measure the number of students who graduated, but not how much education each of them acquired. Many organizations do not even attempt to measure the outputs of such responsibility centres. Others use an approximation, while acknowledging its limitations.

The concepts of input, output and expenses can be used to explain the meaning of *efficiency* and *effectiveness*, which are the two criteria by which the performance of a responsibility centre is judged.

*Efficiency is the ratio of outputs to inputs, or the amount of output per unit of input.* Responsibility Centre A is more efficient than Responsibility Centre B (1) if it uses fewer resources than Responsibility Centre B but produces the same output or (2) if it uses the same amount of resources but produces a greater output.

Note that the first criterion does not require that output be quantified; it is only necessary to judge that the outputs of the two units are approximately the same; if so, assuming both centres are performing their jobs in a satisfactory manner and the respective jobs are of comparable magnitude, the unit with the lower inputs (i.e., lower expenses) is the more efficient. In the second criterion, however, where the input is the same but the output differs, some quantitative measure of output is required; this is a more difficult calculation.

In many responsibility centres, efficiency is measured by comparing actual expenses with some standard of what those expenses should have been at the measured output. Though this method can be somewhat useful, it has two major flaws: (1) recorded expenses are not precise measures of the resources actually consumed; and (2) the standard is merely an approximation of what ideally should have happened under the prevailing circumstances.

In contrast to efficiency, which is determined by the relationship between input and output, *effectiveness is determined by the relationship between a responsibility centre's output and its objectives.* The more this output contributes to the objectives, the more effective the unit. Both objectives and outputs are difficult to quantify, so effectiveness tends to be expressed in subjective, non-analytical terms – for example, 'Unit A is doing a first-rate job, but Unit B has slipped somewhat in recent years.'

Efficiency and effectiveness are not mutually exclusive; every responsibility centre ought to be both efficient and effective – in which case, the organization ought to be meeting its mission, goals and strategies in an optimum manner. A responsibility centre that has carried out its responsibilities with the lowest possible consumption of resources may be efficient, but if its output fails to contribute adequately to the attainment of the organization's mission, goals and strategies, it is not effective. If a credit department handles the paperwork connected with delinquent accounts at a low cost per unit, it is efficient; but if, at the same time, it is unsuccessful in making collections (or needlessly antagonizes customers in the process), it is ineffective.

In summary, a responsibility centre is efficient if it does things right, and it is effective if it does the right things.

## Types of responsibility centre

There are four standard types of responsibility centre, classified according to the nature of the monetary inputs and/or outputs that are measured for control purposes: *revenue, expense, profit* and *investment.* Their respective characteristics are shown in Figure 4.3. In revenue centres, output is measured in monetary terms and the manager is responsible for revenue only. In expense centres, inputs are measured in monetary terms and the manager is responsible for expenses only. In profit centres, both revenues (output) and expenses (input) are measured and the manager is responsible for profit. Finally, in investment centres, the relationship between profit and assets employed is measured and the manager is responsible for both assets employed and profit.

One common misunderstanding when we talk to top managers is that all responsibility centres should fit exactly into one of these four standard types. We therefore want to emphasize that these are four 'ideal' types; in practice many responsibility centres do not (and should not!) fit exactly into one of these four standard types. For example, a manager of a revenue centre is often also responsible for some expenses, such as salaries for the sales personnel, and sometimes is also responsible for working capital in the form of accounts receivables. Manufacturing units are often treated as expense centres, yet these managers typically influence revenues because timely delivery and product quality are important for customer satisfaction. Nevertheless, the four standard types of responsibility centre are very useful as a starting point when top managers think about how to assign responsibility in their organizations.

**FIGURE 4.3** Types of responsibility centre

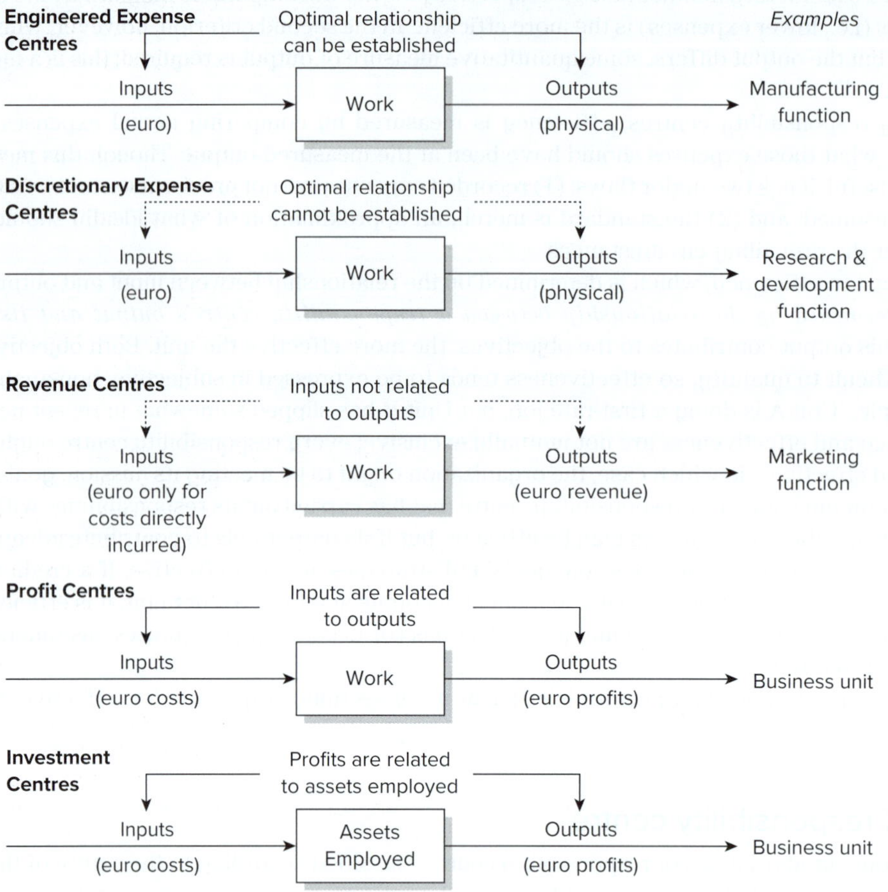


## Criteria for assigning responsibilities

When deciding how to assign responsibilities, *the core operations of the unit and the measurement possibilities of input and output*, as discussed above, are the starting point. The *organizational structure* in general – that is, functional, business unit or matrix organization as will be discussed in Chapter 6 – should also be taken into account. Decisions on how to allocate responsibilities are intimately related to a company's organizational structure. In addition, the *controllability principle* is important. This principle states that managers should be assigned responsibility only for the revenues, expenses and/or assets employed that are within their control. For instance, top managers might not decide on all capital investments for a particular unit, even if these investments can be reliably measured for the unit. In this case, the unit should not be an investment centre because the manager cannot influence the investment decisions. The controllability principle is important for motivational purposes. It tends to be demotivating for managers to be held responsible for factors that they cannot influence. Sometimes, *specific strategic concerns* also affect the choice of responsibility centre. In hotels committed to a superior service, such as Hilton Hotels, the staff in reception are those who interact most frequently with customers. Here Hilton may take specific strategic concerns into consideration when deciding on what type of responsibility centre the reception unit should be. Strategic concerns may also affect the measurement used in the responsibility centres. A company committed to being a technological leader, such as Apple, might not include R&D expenses in the evaluation of its profit centre managers as this may lead to too little spending on R&D activities, which in the end may threaten Apple's competitive position.

We now move on to review the four different types of responsibility centre.

## Revenue centres

*In a revenue centre, output (i.e., revenue) is measured in monetary terms, but no formal attempt is made to relate input (i.e., expense) to output.* (If expense was matched with revenue, the unit would be a profit centre.) Typically, revenue centres are marketing and sales units in which the manager neither controls the cost of the product or service they market, nor the investments made in the unit.

**Real World Example:** Adidas is one of the best-known brands globally. It has a number of different sales units. Recently it has been engaged in econometric modelling and found that its individual sales units were not solely driving their own business unit sales. As its global media director said: '[A]lthough we believed that football [advertising] was going to drive football sales, actually it wasn't; football was driving running sales, running was driving Originals, Originals was driving training.' So the different sales and marketing units need close cooperation to maximize sales for Adidas.

*Source:* Spary, S. (2019) Adidas: we overlooked traditional media's ability to drive ecommerce sales, *Campaign*, 16 October. Available at: https://www.campaignlive.co.uk/article/adidas-overlooked-traditional-medias-ability-drive-ecommerce-sales/1662365 (accessed 30 April 2020).

When evaluating the manager of a revenue centre, actual sales or orders booked are measured against budgets or quotas. Thus, control of a revenue centre depends on the effective establishment of a reference point to which the actual revenues can be compared.[5] In practice, there are few 'pure' revenue centres. Most revenue centres incur sales and marketing expenses and the manager is often also held responsible for the expenses incurred directly within the unit, but the primary measurement of how well the unit has performed is revenue. Focusing primarily on revenue rather than profits is considered a simple and effective way to motivate salespeople to attract and retain customers.

However, focusing primarily on revenue has been criticized for creating undesirable consequences for the company as a whole, by downplaying the link between the sales unit and other organizational units. In general, if the manager is held responsible for revenue alone, there is little incentive to manage expenses and working capital wisely. And the vast majority of organizations would probably argue that marketing and sales decisions have a profound impact on expenses incurred elsewhere in the organization. Salespeople may, for instance, promote a wide range of products, which leads to increased working capital, and high inventory ordering and carrying costs. In addition, it might be tempting for salespeople to give customers extended credit terms in exchange for a somewhat higher price, which will increase revenue but may not be profitable for the company as a whole because more assets employed will be tied up in working capital in the form of accounts receivables. Furthermore, when products and services differ in terms of profitability for the company as a whole, a sole focus on revenues gives the sales staff little incentive to promote the most profitable products/services. In these situations, the performance reviews of managers of revenue centres should include an appraisal of how well they carry out these additional responsibilities.

[5] Chapter 9 deals in detail with different ways of establishing such reference points, for instance, through budgeting or benchmarking.

There are also other issues relating to common revenues that may require consideration. In some situations two or more organizational units may participate in a successful sales effort; ideally, each centre should be given appropriate credit for its part in the transaction. For example, a salesperson from Revenue Centre A may be the main company contact with a certain customer, but the orders the customer finally places may be for products carried by Revenue Centre B. The Unit A salesperson would not be likely to pursue such orders if all resulting revenues were credited to Unit B. Similarly, a bank customer with an account in Branch C may prefer to do some business with Branch D, perhaps because it is more conveniently located. Branch D may not be eager to service this customer if all the revenue so generated is credited to Branch C.

Many organizations do not devote a great deal of attention to solving these common revenue problems. They take the position that the identification of precise responsibility for revenue generation is too complicated to be practical, and that sales personnel must recognize they are working not only for their own unit but also for the overall good of the company. Other companies attempt to untangle the responsibility for common sales by crediting the unit that takes an order for a product handled by another unit with the equivalent of a brokerage commission or a finder's fee (or, as in the case of a bank, by granting explicit credit to the branch that performs a service even though the account of the customer being served is maintained at another branch).

It is important to note that when controlling revenue centres, financial metrics are often complemented by non-financial performance measures. For example, additional important indicators of the performance of a revenue centre are customer satisfaction and loyalty, and growth in market share. In Chapter 9, we discuss how financial and non-financial performance measurement can be combined.

## Expense centres

*Expense centres are responsibility centres whose inputs are measured in monetary terms, but whose outputs are not.* Expense centres are also often called cost centres in many organizations. There are two general types of expense centre: engineered and discretionary. These labels relate to two types of expense. *Engineered expenses* are those for which the 'right' or 'proper' amount can be estimated with reasonable reliability – for example, a factory's costs for direct labour, direct material, components, supplies and utilities. *Discretionary expenses* (also called managed expenses) are those for which no such engineered estimate is feasible. In discretionary expense centres, the expenses incurred depend on management's judgement of what is appropriate.

### Engineered expense centres

Engineered expense centres have the following characteristics:

- Their input can be measured in monetary terms.
- Their output can be measured in physical terms.
- The optimum monetary amount of input required to produce one unit of output can be determined.

Engineered expense centres are usually found in manufacturing operations. Warehousing, distribution, trucking and similar units within the marketing organization may also be engineered expense centres, as may certain responsibility centres within administrative and support departments – for instance, accounts receivable, accounts payable and payroll sections in the finance department, and personnel records and the cafeteria in the HR department. Such units perform repetitive tasks for which standard costs can be developed. These engineered expense centres are usually located within departments that are discretionary expense centres.

***Real World Example*:** ABB operates in more than 100 countries and has around 147,000 employees. The company describes its manufacturing units in the following way: 'Manufacturing at ABB ranges from assembly of customized industrial robots to advanced production of electrical switches and breakers. From generator to user, our products support the efficient use of electric power in industrial, commercial and residential applications.'

*Source:* ABB (n.d.) Manufacturing: producing a better world. Available at: https://new.abb.com/careers/opportunities/where-do-i-fit-in/manufacturing (accessed 30 April 2020).

In an engineered expense centre, output multiplied by the standard cost of each unit produced measures what the finished product should have cost. The difference between the theoretical and the actual cost is measured to evaluate the performance of the expense centre.

We emphasize that engineered expense centres have other important tasks not measured by expenses alone; the managers are responsible for the quality of the products and the volume of production, as well as for efficiency. Therefore, the type and level of production are prescribed, and specific quality standards are set, so that manufacturing expenses are not minimized at the expense of quality. Moreover, managers of engineered expense centres may be responsible for activities such as training and employee development, which are not related to current production; their performance reviews should include an appraisal of how well they carry out these responsibilities.

There are few, if any, responsibility centres in which all cost items are engineered. Even in highly automated production departments, the use of indirect labour and various services can vary with management's discretion. Thus, the term 'engineered expense centre' refers to responsibility centres in which engineered expenses predominate, but it does not imply that valid engineered estimates can be made for each and every expense item.

## Discretionary expense centres

Discretionary expense centres include administrative and support units (e.g., accounting, legal, industrial relations, public relations, HR), R&D operations and most marketing activities.

***Real World Example:*** H&M describes its marketing department as 'our own global advertising agency, where we create all of our multi-channel campaigns and produce our marketing materials. This is where our brand is built and nourished – making sure everyone loves fashion at a great price just as much as we do.'

*Source:* H&M (n.d.) Careers: marketing: Available at: https://career.hm.com/content/hmcareer/en_au/workingathm/what-can-you-do-here/corporate/marketing.html (accessed 30 April 2020).

The output of these centres cannot be measured in monetary terms. For instance, the results of R&D activities are difficult to measure quantitatively. There is output in the form of patents, new products or new processes, but the relationship of output to input is difficult to appraise on an annual basis because the completed 'product' of an R&D group may involve several years of effort. Thus, inputs as stated in an annual budget may be unrelated to outputs. Furthermore, even when such a relationship can be established, it may not be possible to estimate reliably the value of the output. And even when such an evaluation can be made, the technical nature of the R&D function may defeat management's attempt to measure efficiency. A brilliant effort may come up against an insuperable obstacle, whereas a mediocre effort may, by chance, result in a bonanza.

The term 'discretionary' does not imply that management's judgement as to optimum cost is capricious or haphazard. Rather, it reflects management's decisions regarding certain policies: whether to match or exceed the marketing efforts of competitors; the level of service the company should provide to its customers; and the appropriate amounts to spend for R&D, financial planning, public relations and a host of other activities.

One organization may have a small headquarters staff, while another organization of similar size and in the same industry may have a staff 10 times as large. The top managers of each company may each be convinced that their respective decisions on staff size are correct, but there is no objective way to judge which (if either) is right; both decisions may be equally good under the circumstances, with the differences in size reflecting other underlying differences in the two organizations.

Furthermore, top management's view as to the proper level of discretionary expenses is always subject to change, especially when revenues go down, or when new management takes over.

***Real World Example:*** In February 2020, Danske Bank announced its plans to cut 400 jobs globally. Karsten Breum, head of HR at Danske, commented: 'Today, we are discontinuing 400 positions across the Group, and we are taking a number of initiatives to adjust and simplify parts of our organization.' The lost jobs are primarily within staff and back-office functions – that is, within discretionary expense centres.

*Source:* Danske Bank (2020) Danske Bank discontinues 400 positions and lays off app. 230 employees across the Group. Available at: https://danskebank.com/news-and-insights/news-archive/press-releases/2020/pr27022020 (accessed 30 April 2020).

In a discretionary expense centre, the difference between budget and actual expense does not incorporate the value of the output. If actual expenses do not exceed the budget amount, the manager has 'lived within the budget', but because, by definition, the budget does not purport to predict the optimum amount of spending, living within the budget does not necessarily indicate efficient performance. Thus financial control in a discretionary expense centre is quite different from that in an engineered expense centre. In the latter, the objective is to become cost competitive by setting a standard and measuring actual expenses against this standard. By contrast, the main purpose of a discretionary expense budget is to control expenses by allowing the manager to participate *in the planning*, sharing in the discussion of what tasks should be undertaken and what level of effort is appropriate for each. Thus, in a discretionary expense centre, financial control is primarily exercised at the planning stage *before* the expenses are incurred.

In the planning stage for discretionary expense centres there is often a problem of goal congruence. Typically, managers of, for instance, administrative and R&D units strive for functional excellence. Superficially, this desire would seem to be congruent with company goals; but, in fact, much depends on how one defines excellence. Although a manager of a discretionary expense centre may want to develop the 'ideal' system, programme or function, the ideal may be too costly relative to the additional profits that perfection may generate. The 'perfect' legal staff, for example, will not approve any contract that contains even the slightest flaw, but the cost of maintaining a staff large enough to guarantee this level of assurance may outweigh the potential loss from minor flaws. At worst, a striving for 'excellence' can lead to 'empire building' or to 'safeguarding one's position' without regard to the welfare of the company.

The problem with goal congruence implies that top management should make budgetary decisions for discretionary expense centres that differ from those for engineered expense centres. For the latter, top management decides whether the proposed operating budget represents the unit cost of performing its task efficiently. Its volume is not a major concern; this is largely determined by the actions of other responsibility centres; for instance, the marketing department's ability to generate sales. By contrast, top management formulates the budget for a discretionary expense centre by determining the magnitude of the job that needs to be done. Thus control of a discretionary expense centre depends on the effective establishment of a reference point to which the actual expenses can be compared. As the budget of the discretionary expense centre often serves as the reference point, companies put a lot of effort into budget preparation. A more thorough discussion on budgeting, including criticism and alternatives to using budgets, is provided in Chapter 8.

The primary job of a discretionary expense centre's manager is to obtain the desired output. Spending an amount that is 'on budget' to do this is considered satisfactory; spending more than that is cause for concern; and spending less may indicate that the planned work is not being done. In discretionary centres, as opposed to engineered expense centres, the financial performance report is not a means of evaluating the efficiency of the manager. If these two types of responsibility centre are not carefully distinguished, top management may erroneously treat a discretionary expense centre's performance report as an indication of the unit's efficiency, thus motivating those making spending decisions to expend less than the budgeted amount, which, in turn, will lower output. For this reason, it is unwise to reward managers who spend less than the budgeted amount. Control over spending can be exercised by requiring the superior's approval before the budget is overrun. Sometimes, a certain percentage of overrun (say, 5 per cent) is permitted without additional approval.

It is important to note that control over discretionary expense centres often is achieved primarily through non-financial performance measures. The best indication of the quality of service for some discretionary expense centres may be the opinion of their users. As previously stated, in Chapter 9 a more thorough discussion of non-financial performance measurement is provided. In addition, for basic research activities, alternative procedures are often employed. In some organizations, basic research is included as a lump sum in the research programme and its budget. In others, no specific allowance is made for basic research as such, but there is an understanding that scientists and engineers can devote part of their time (perhaps 15 per cent, or one day a week) to explore in whatever direction they find most interesting, subject only to the informal agreement of their supervisor. Google, for instance, is known for such an approach.

## Profit and investment centres

This section discusses profit centres and investment centres – that is, the two most far-reaching forms of formal decentralization. When a responsibility centre's financial performance is measured in terms of profit (i.e., by the difference between the revenues and expenses), the centre is called a *profit centre.* Profit is a particularly useful performance measure because it allows higher-level managers to use one comprehensive indicator rather than several (some of which may be pointing in different directions). Thus, profit is an important measure of effectiveness. Furthermore, because profit is the difference between revenue (a measure of output) and expense (a measure of input), it is also a measure of efficiency. Thus, profit measures both effectiveness and efficiency. When such an overall measure exists, it is not necessary to determine the relative importance of effectiveness versus efficiency, and this is one important explanation for why so many top managers often strive to turn as many units as possible into profit or investment centres.

For some units, profit is compared with the assets employed in earning it. We refer to this type of responsibility centre as *investment centres.* Focusing on profits without considering the assets employed to generate those profits is often an inadequate basis for control. Except in certain types of service organization, in which the amount of assets employed is insignificant, an important objective of a profit-oriented company is to earn a satisfactory return on the assets employed. A profit of €1 million in a company that has €10 million of assets employed does not represent as good a performance as a profit of €1 million in a company that has only €5 million of assets employed, assuming both companies have a similar cost of capital.

Unless the amount of assets employed is taken into account, it is difficult for top managers to compare the profit performance of one unit with that of other units, or with similar outside companies. Put simply: comparing absolute differences in profits is not meaningful if units use different amounts of assets employed; clearly, the more assets used, the greater the profits should be. Such comparisons are used to judge how well managers are performing and to decide how to allocate resources. This means that investment centre managers have two financial performance objectives. First, they should generate adequate profits from the assets at their disposal. Second, they should invest in additional resources only when the investment produces an adequate return. (Conversely, they should divest if the expected annual profits of any resource, discounted at the company's cost of capital, are less than the cash that could be realized from its sale.) The purpose of relating profits to assets employed is to motivate unit managers to accomplish these objectives.

***Real World Example:*** The multinational company Siemens has a number of different divisions, all profit or investment centres. Some examples are the Digital Factory Division (offers its customers a comprehensive portfolio of hardware and software products) and the Power and Gas Division (offers its customers a broad spectrum of products and solutions for the environmentally compatible and resource-saving generation of power from fossil fuels and renewable sources of energy).

*Source:* Siemens (n.d.) Our businesses. Available at: https://new.siemens.com/us/en/company/about/businesses.html (accessed 30 April 2020).

In practice, companies use the term 'profit centre', rather than 'investment centre' to refer to both types of responsibility centre. We agree that an investment centre is a special type of profit centre, rather than a separate, parallel category. However, we also want to emphasize that there are many problems involved in measuring the assets employed. This topic warrants a separate discussion (see Chapter 9 on how financial measures can be used for evaluating performance).

Although the degree of delegation may differ from organization to organization, complete authority for generating profits and assets employed is never delegated to a single segment of the business. Thus, when analysing profit and investment centres, it is important to analyse the conditions for delegating profit and assets employed responsibilities. For instance, many management decisions involve proposals to increase expenses with the expectation of an even greater increase in sales revenue. On a more general level, many decisions involve expense/revenue trade-offs and profit/asset employed trade-offs. Before it is safe to delegate such trade-off decisions to a profit or investment centre manager, two conditions should exist:

1. The manager should have access to the *relevant information* needed for making such decisions.
2. There should be some way to *measure* the effectiveness of the trade-offs the manager has made.

A major step in creating profit and investment centres is to determine the lowest point in an organization where these two conditions prevail. All responsibility centres fit into a continuum ranging from those that clearly should be profit centres or investment centres to those that clearly should not. Top management must decide whether the advantages of giving profit and asset employed responsibilities offset the disadvantages, which are discussed below. As with all management control system design choices, there is no clear line of demarcation.

## Advantages and difficulties of profit and investment centres

Establishing organizational units as profit or investment centres provides the following advantages:

- The *quality of decisions* may improve because they are being made by managers closest to the point of decision. For instance, the speed of operating decisions may be increased because they do not have to be referred to top managers. In addition, profit and investment centre managers, subject to fewer corporate restraints, are freer to use their imagination and initiative. At the same time, top managers, relieved of day-to-day decision making, can concentrate on broader issues.

- Because profit and investment centres are similar to independent companies, they provide an excellent *training ground* for general management. Their managers gain experience in managing all functional areas, and top managers gain the opportunity to evaluate their potential for higher-level jobs.
- *Profit consciousness* is enhanced because managers who are responsible for profits will constantly seek ways to increase them. Because their output is so readily measured, profit and investment centres are particularly responsive to pressures to improve their competitive performance. (A manager responsible for marketing activities, for example, will tend to authorize promotion expenditures that increase sales, whereas if this manager is responsible for profits he or she will be motivated to make promotion expenditures that increase profits.)

**Real World Example:** The well-known Swedish company, IKEA, is famous for its cheap products but also because all IKEA stores have an in-house restaurant where Swedish dishes, such as meatballs, and other meals can be bought for just a few euros. But when asked about the restaurants, IKEA officials are quick to point out that they are important as 'customers buy less on an empty stomach'. In fact, due to the massive volume of people visiting, the restaurants are *profit centres* of their own.

*Source:* Kirbyson, G. (2012) Home, Swede home: a visit to IKEA's birthplace before its arrival in Winnipeg. Available at:http://www.winnipegfreepress.com/opinion/fyi/home-swede-home-164986286.html (accessed 14 June 2013).

The creation of profit and investment centres may, however, cause difficulties:

- Decentralized decision making will force top managers to rely more on formal reports than on personal knowledge of an operation, entailing some *loss of control*. For instance, if top managers are more capable or better informed than the average profit centre manager, the quality of decisions made at the unit level may be reduced.
- *Friction* may increase because of arguments over the appropriate transfer price (see Chapter 5), the assignment of common costs, and the credit for revenues that were formerly generated jointly by two or more business units working together. For instance, organizational units that once cooperated as functional units may now be in competition with one another. An increase in profits for one manager may mean a decrease for another. In such situations, a manager may fail to refer sales leads to another unit better qualified to pursue them; may hoard personnel or equipment that, from the overall company standpoint, would be better off used in another unit; or may make production decisions that have undesirable cost consequences for other units.
- Divisionalization may impose *additional costs* because of the additional management, staff personnel and record-keeping required, and may lead to task redundancies at each profit or investment centre.
- Competent *general managers* may not exist in a functional organization because there may not have been sufficient opportunities for them to develop general management competency.
- There may be too much emphasis on *short-run profitability* at the expense of long-run profitability. In the desire to report high current profits, the profit or investment centre manager may skimp on research and development (R&D), training programmes or maintenance. This tendency is especially prevalent when the turnover of profit or investment centre managers is relatively high. In these circumstances, managers may have good reason to believe that their actions may not affect profitability until after they have moved to other jobs. Thus it is often important to also use non-financial measures when evaluating profit and investment centre managers (see Chapter 9).

## Turning functional units into profit centres

When talking to top managers, we see a strong desire among them to turn also some of their functional units into profit centres. It can sometimes be desirable to constitute one or more of the functional units – for example, marketing, manufacturing and service operations – as profit centres. There is no guiding principle declaring that certain types of unit are inherently profit centres and others are not. Top managers' decision as to whether a given unit should be a profit centre is based on the amount of *influence* (even if not total control) that the unit's manager exercises over the activities that affect the bottom line.

A marketing unit, for instance, can be turned into a profit centre by charging it with the cost of the products sold. This requires transfer pricing policies (which are discussed further in Chapter 5). The transfer price provides the marketing manager with the relevant information to make the optimum revenue/cost trade-offs, and the standard practice of measuring a profit centre's manager by the centre's profitability provides a check on how well these trade-offs have been made. The transfer price charged to the profit centre should be based on the standard cost, rather than the actual cost, of the products being sold. Using a standard cost base separates the marketing cost performance from that of the manufacturing cost performance, which is affected by changes in the levels of efficiency that are beyond the control of the marketing manager. When should a marketing activity be given profit responsibility? When is the marketing manager in the best position to make the principal cost/revenue trade-offs? This often occurs where different conditions exist in different geographical areas – for example, a foreign marketing activity. In such an activity, it may be difficult to control centrally such decisions as how to market a product; how to set the price; how much to spend on sales promotion, when to spend it, and on which media; how to train salespeople or dealers; and where and when to establish new dealers.

The manufacturing unit is, as previously discussed, usually an expense centre, being evaluated on performance versus standard costs and overhead budgets. This measure can cause problems, however, because it does not necessarily indicate how well the manager is performing all aspects of the job. For example:

- A manager may skimp on quality control, shipping products of inferior quality in order to obtain standard cost credit.
- A manager may be reluctant to interrupt production schedules in order to produce a rush order to accommodate a customer.
- A manager who is measured against standards may lack the incentive to manufacture products that are difficult to produce – or to improve the standards themselves.

Therefore, where performance of the manufacturing process is measured against standard costs, it is advisable to make a separate evaluation of such activities as quality control, production scheduling and make-or-buy decisions. In addition, one way to measure the activity of a manufacturing unit in its entirety is to turn it into a profit centre and give it credit for the selling price of the products minus estimated marketing expenses. Such an arrangement is far from perfect, partly because many of the factors that influence the volume and mix of sales are beyond the manufacturing manager's control. However, it seems to work better in some cases than the alternative of holding the manufacturing operation responsible only for costs. Some researchers maintain that manufacturing units should not be made into profit centres unless they sell a large portion of their output to outside customers; they regard units that sell primarily to other business units as pseudo profit centres on the grounds that the revenues assigned to them for sales to other units within the company are artificial. Some companies, nevertheless, do create profit centres for such units. They believe that, if properly designed, the system can create almost the same incentives as those provided by sales to outside customers.

Service and support units (such as units for maintenance, information technology, transportation, engineering, consulting, customer service and similar support activities) can all be made into profit centres. These may operate out of headquarters and service corporate divisions, or they may fulfil similar functions within business units. They charge customers for services rendered, with the financial objective of generating enough business so that their revenues equal their expenses. Usually, the units receiving these services have the option of procuring them from an outside vendor instead, provided the vendor can offer services of equal quality at a lower price.

When service units are organized as profit centres, their managers are motivated to control costs in order to prevent customers from going elsewhere, while managers of the receiving units are motivated to make decisions about whether using the service is worth the price.

## Constraints on profit and investment centre authority

Finally, we want to highlight that when talking to profit and investment centre managers it is clear that many of them are not in a position to fully influence revenues and costs. When a profit or investment centre manager's authority is constrained in various ways, this ought to be reflected in a profit or investment centre's operation and evaluation. To realize fully the benefits of the profit and investment centre concepts, the manager would have to be as autonomous as the president of an independent company. As a practical matter, however, such autonomy is not feasible. If an organization were divided into completely independent units, it would lose the advantages of size and synergy. Furthermore, top managers would be abdicating their own responsibility. Consequently, responsibility centre structures represent trade-offs between unit autonomy and corporate constraints. The effectiveness of a profit or investment centre is largely dependent on how well these trade-offs are made.

***Real World Example:*** The German airline Lufthansa announced in December 2019 that it planned to restructure operations by making the core brand a separate profit centre. It was inspired by IAG, which runs British Airways, Iberia, Vueling and Air Lingus, as separate profit centres. In short, Lufthansa wants the different operations to be more independent and entrepreneurial, to make profits for the company.

*Source:* Reuters (2019) Lufthansa to create holding structure, manage core brand separately. Available at: https://www.reuters.com/article/lufthansa-restructuring/lufthansa-to-create-holding-structure-manage-core-brand-separately-idUKL8N28L2PV (accessed 30 April 2020).

It is useful to think of managing a profit or investment centre in terms of control over three types of decision: (1) the product decision (what goods or services to make, and sell); (2) the marketing decision (how, where and for how much are these goods or services to be sold); and (3) the procurement or sourcing decision (how to obtain or manufacture the goods or services). If a manager controls all three activities, there is usually no difficulty in assigning profit responsibility and measuring performance. In general, the greater the degree of integration within an organization, the more difficult it becomes to assign responsibility to a single profit centre for all three activities in a given product line – that is, if the production, procurement and marketing decisions for a single product line are split among two or more units, separating the contribution of each unit to the overall success of the product line may be difficult.

The constraints imposed by top managers can be grouped into two types: (1) those resulting from strategic considerations; (2) those resulting because uniformity is required.

Most organizations retain certain decisions, especially financial decisions, at the top management level, at least for domestic activities. Consequently, one of the major constraints on profit and investment centres results from corporate control over new investments. Units must compete with one another for a share of the available funds. Thus, a profit centre could find its expansion plans thwarted because another unit has convinced higher-level managers that it has a more attractive programme. Top managers also impose other constraints. Each profit or investment centre has a 'charter' that specifies the marketing and/or production activities that it is permitted to undertake, and it must refrain from operating beyond its charter, even though it sees profit opportunities in doing so. The maintenance of the proper corporate image may also require constraints on the quality of products or on public relations activities.

Organizations impose some constraints on profit and investment centres because of the necessity for uniformity. One constraint is that they must conform to corporate accounting and management control systems. This constraint is especially troublesome for units that have been acquired from another company and that have been accustomed to using different systems. Corporate headquarters may also impose uniform pay and other personnel policies, as well as uniform policies on ethics, vendor selection, computers and communication equipment, and even the design of the unit's letterhead.

In general, corporate constraints do not cause severe problems in a decentralized structure as long as they are dealt with explicitly. It is the responsibility of top managers to discuss the necessity for the constraints with profit and investment centre managers so they understand and (hopefully) accept them with good grace.

## Summary

A responsibility centre is an organizational unit that is headed by a manager who is responsible for its activities. There are four standard types of responsibility centre classified according to the nature of the monetary inputs and/or outputs that are measured for control purposes: revenue, expense, profit and investment. They reflect different degrees of financial decision-making authority that the top managers have delegated to the unit managers. In practice, there are also hybrids that do not fit exactly into one of these standard types.

In this chapter, we described the general considerations to be applied when deciding what type of responsibility centre is appropriate for a particular organizational unit. The core operations of the unit and the measurement possibilities of input and output are the starting point for the analysis. The general organizational structure should also be taken into account. In addition, the controllability principle is important. This principle states that managers should be assigned responsibility only for the revenues, expenses and/or assets employed that are within their control. Sometimes, specific strategic concerns also affect the choice of responsibility centre.

In a revenue centre, typically a sales unit, output is measured in monetary terms, but no formal attempt is made to relate input to output. When evaluating the manager of a revenue centre, actual sales or orders booked are measured against budgets, and control depends on the effective establishment of a reference point to which the actual revenues can be compared. There are two general types of expense centre: engineered and discretionary. In engineered expense centres, typically a manufacturing unit, it is possible to estimate the 'right' amount of expenses that should be incurred to produce a given level of output. The difference between the theoretical and the actual expenses is measured to assess the performance of the expense centre. In discretionary expense centres, on the other hand, budgets describe the amounts that can be spent, but it is not possible to determine with precision the optimum levels of these expenses. Typical examples are R&D and administrative units. Financial control is primarily exercised at the planning stage before the expenses are incurred, by allowing the manager to participate in the budget preparation and in the discussion of what tasks should be undertaken. A profit centre is an organizational unit in which both revenues and expenses are measured in monetary terms. In an investment centre, the manager is responsible for both the profit generated and the assets used to generate the profit. In setting up a profit or investment centre, an organization devolves decision-making power to those lower levels that possess relevant information for making expense/revenue and profit/assets employed trade-offs. This move can increase the speed of decision making, improve the quality of decisions, focus greater attention on profitability and provide a broader measure of management performance, among other advantages.

## Suggested additional reading

Burkert, M., Fischer, F.M. and Schäffer, U. (2011) Application of the controllability principle and managerial performance: the role of role perceptions, *Management Accounting Research*, 22: 143–59.

Huang, W. (2019) Optimizing the management control system for responsibility centers. In *Built on Value* (pp. 275–301). Singapore: Palgrave Macmillan.

Kaplan, R.S. (2007) *The Demise of Cost and Profit Centers.* Boston, MA: Harvard Business School Publishing, Article Reprint No. B0701A.

Kirby, J. (2002) The cost center that paid its way, *Harvard Business Review*, April: 31–41.

# Case 4.1

# BookWorm*

**by Ebba Sjögren**

Eleanor Ehrman is the owner and CEO of BookWorm, a chain of book stores with 50 locations in Stockholm, Malmö and Gothenburg. In addition to the BookWorm stores, the company also has a publishing division, specializing in forensic and medical crime novels.

For some time, Eleanor has thought about converting part of each store into a café. One basic idea behind launching the cafés is to keep customers in the store and provide them with the possibility of browsing books. Both of these things might indirectly contribute to increased book sales. In addition, because the BookWorm stores are typically located in central locations, it is possible to make money by *not* having customers leave BookWorm to sit in a nearby café. Most importantly, however, Eleanor wants to use the cafés to showcase BookWorm's own publications and special launches from other publishers. One source of inspiration has been the initiative by the Stockholm regional manager to organize events together with a number of local book clubs in conjunction with the announcement of the winner of the annual Nobel Prize in Literature. In the fiercely competitive book business, the Nobel event has raised the profile of the BookWorm chain. According to Michael Hawerman, Stockholm regional manager, the Nobel events may have also resulted in increased business – in addition to exposure in local and national press.

At present, BookWorm is organized into two divisions: publishing and stores. The stores division, in turn, is set up with three regional managers, each of whom is responsible for a geographic region: east (Stockholm), west (Gothenburg) and south (Malmö). In addition, the company headquarters has a small corporate staff that is organized into three functional units: accounting, marketing and HR. Both the publishing and stores divisions operate as investment centres; the logic behind this is that the tough competition from online bookstores and international publishing houses necessitates managers to have considerable autonomy – but to be very careful in how they manage both expenses and revenues.

The question that Eleanor is grappling with is how to organize the café operations. She sees the following alternatives:

- Integrate cafés into the existing stores division structure.
- Make cafés a central corporate unit within the BookWorm organization.

## Questions

1 Characterize the form of responsibility centre that is inferred or appropriate given the two alternative ways of organizing cafés.

2 Which form of responsibility centre is the best alternative to pursue, in light of Eleanor's purpose in creating the cafés?

* This is a fictional case for education purposes only, prepared by Associate Professor Ebba Sjögren, Stockholm School of Economics. 

# Case 4.2
# MoreSki*

**by Malin Lund**

MoreSki, a company based in Finland, manufactures and sells cross-country and downhill skis. The company operates two factories, in Åbo and Tammerfors, each manufacturing different stages of the ski production. Near the factory in Åbo, there is also a unit devoted to research and development, in particular focusing on the wax used in ski production. Company-level departments such as marketing, accounting, finance and personnel are located in Stockholm. The sales department focusing on the Scandinavian market is situated in Vanda. Recently, the company decided to expand and target the European market whereby an additional sales unit was established near to the corporate-level functions in Helsinki. The company deploys neither transfer prices nor non-financial performance measures. All managers and the CEO stress the importance of financial aspects manifested in the annual budgets.

## Questions

1 Describe how the various activities at MoreSki are organized into units. Ensure that you relate your description to the general characteristics and evaluation of responsibility centres.

2 In this question, your task is to discuss and analyse the situation at MoreSki on the basis of the following quotes made by the CEO, who is also the majority shareholder of the company:

*The good news this year is that the production managers will hit their target. And up until recently I have been quite satisfied with the sales managers because they have been selling like crazy. However, now suddenly they seem to drown in customer complaints about quality and delays. We have even lost some of our key customers. It is a disastrous development.*

*More generally I have another thing bothering me. No one in this company seems to care about profit. I constantly have to remind the unit managers of the importance of profit but they seem to be totally incapable of taking decisions of their own in order to enhance profitability. I don't think they really understand this and it takes a lot of my energy to stress this obvious matter all the time.*

Ensure that you relate your analysis and discussion to the current responsibility centre structure from question 1.

*Helpful hint: Divide your answer into:*

a The CEO's statement concerning the sales and production units

b The CEO's statement concerning profit consciousness in the company.

* This is a fictional case for education purposes only, prepared by Malin Lund, Stockholm School of Economics. 

# Case 4.3
# BreathEZ*

**by Ebba Sjögren**

BreathEZ Inc. is a pharmaceutical company that markets products for the treatment of asthma. The company has an existing portfolio of products that will all lose their patent protection in the next five to ten years. When the patents expire, it will be possible for anyone to manufacture and sell the active substances, and the expectation is therefore that prices for these drugs will decrease by up to 90 per cent. In order to secure additional sources of income, it is vital for the company to develop new products that can be patented. However, because of current fierce competition, it is also necessary to make ongoing, but smaller improvements to existing products until they lose their patent protection. Both new discovery and refinement of existing products is the responsibility of the research and development (R&D) department.

Unfortunately, the R&D department has financially and operationally underperformed for a number of years. A recent evaluation concluded that the budget had been consistently overspent by 5–10 per cent per annum. In addition, the milestones for commercializing new discoveries have lagged by an average of six months. The refinement of existing products, however, has consistently met its targets. The R&D department is currently run as a profit centre, with income generated in two main forms. Each refinement of an existing product is contracted and run as a separate project paid for by an internal customer, in the form of the marketing and sales department. New discovery projects are run in a similar fashion, based on a contract that specifies milestones and timelines. The only difference is that the internal customer is the CEO, because the size of funding is much larger and the question of whether or not to continue individual development projects is a strategic decision.

The CEO is not satisfied with the performance of the R&D department. One idea is that the current choice of responsibility centre structure is less appropriate. However, the CEO is unsure about the arguments for and against.

## Task

You have been asked to analyse the situation and discuss what might be a better form of responsibility centre, and why.

*Please note:* As part of your answer, you are expected to (1) characterize the two forms of responsibility centre (profit centre and your proposed form); and (2) discuss at least three *generic* advantages and disadvantages with profit centres and the proposed form of responsibility centre that are *specifically* relevant in the present case.

---

* This is a fictional case for education purposes only, prepared by Associate Professor Ebba Sjögren, Stockholm School of Economics. 

# Case 4.4

# Responsibility structure within the Volvo Group*

**by Johan Åkesson and Mikael Cäker**

## Introduction

This case discusses the challenges of creating a responsibility structure within the Volvo Group, one of the world's largest manufacturers of trucks, buses, construction equipment and industrial engines. The company, with headquarters in Gothenburg, Sweden, has more than 100,000 employees, production facilities in 18 countries and a global market presence. Volvo Group shares are listed on Nasdaq OMX in Stockholm, Sweden. We will examine the progress of the Group over the past 10 years – a period that has included different phases under different managers. We will focus on the strategic changes that were decided at the starting point of the last, and ongoing, phase around 2016.

First, here is some more information about the Group and its position, after which we will dig deeper into its strategies.

Based on net sales the truck business dominates, but synergies, linked to for example joint production of engines and other components, create economies of scale for the other business areas like Buses, Construction Equipment and Volvo Penta (see Exhibit 1).

**EXHIBIT 1** Share of net sales by business area

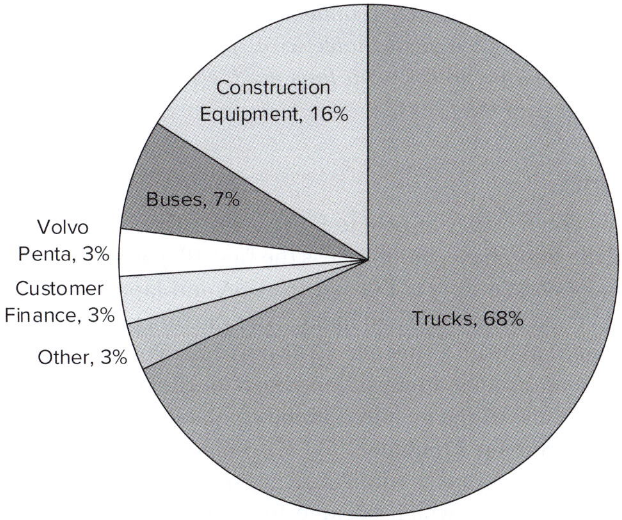


*Source:* Volvo Group Annual Report 2015.

* This case was written by Johan Åkesson and Dr Mikael Cäker, Gothenburg University.

**EXHIBIT 2** Share of net sales by market

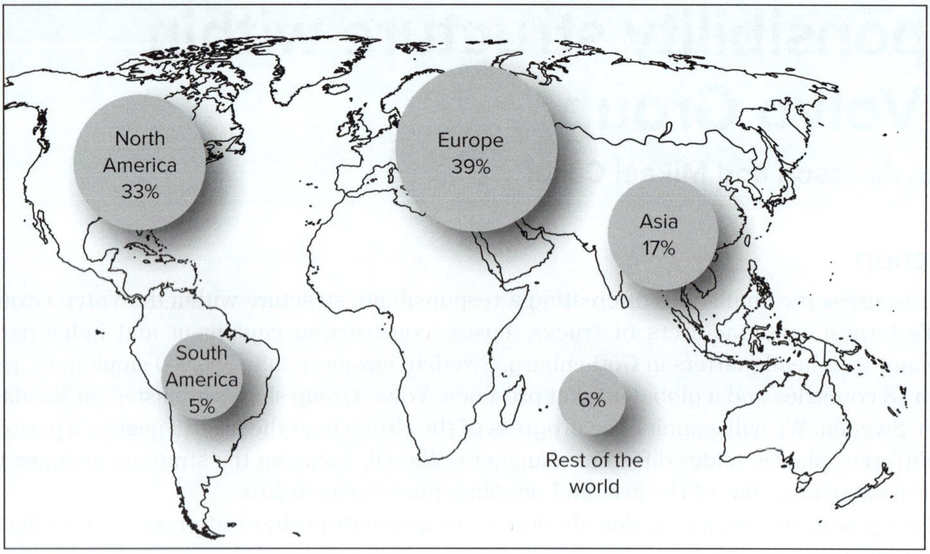


*Source:* Volvo Group Annual Report 2015.

The Volvo Group has achieved a global market presence in this millennium and its mission is:

*Driving prosperity through transport solutions*

*The Volvo Group's mission statement expresses a broad ambition – to drive prosperity. Our customers provide modern logistics as the base for our economic welfare. Transport supports growth, provides access for people and goods and helps combat poverty. Modern transport solutions facilitate the increasing urbanization in a sustainable way. Transport is not an end in itself, but rather a means of allowing people to access what they need, economically and socially.*

*Source:* Volvo Group Annual Report 2016.

## History and background

During the past 20 years, after Volvo Cars was sold to Ford in 1999, the Volvo Group has passed through different strategic phases. In the first phase, more or less the first 10 years, the group expanded the business mainly by the acquisition of competitors in Europe, the USA and Japan, while later Volvo both made acquisitions and created joint ventures in China and India. After the first phase, the Volvo Group achieved a global presence in all major markets with either a local brand or the Volvo brand. Acquired brands were mainly organized under the Group Trucks organization which, during this period, included both manufacturing and sales operations. Some of the acquired brands expanded the offer of other already existing business areas: Volvo Construction Equipment (VCE), Volvo Buses, Volvo Penta and of course Financial Services, which provided customers with financing solutions for the products' life cycle.

In the following consolidation phase, which became formally explicit from 2012, focus shifted to work on some necessary restructuring, increased cost-efficiency measures and an extensive product renewal programme, mainly for the trucks business. Cost efficiency was achieved by gaining synergies, especially through increased operational efficiency within the truck divisions, like joint procurement,

**EXHIBIT 3** Organizational chart, Volvo AB

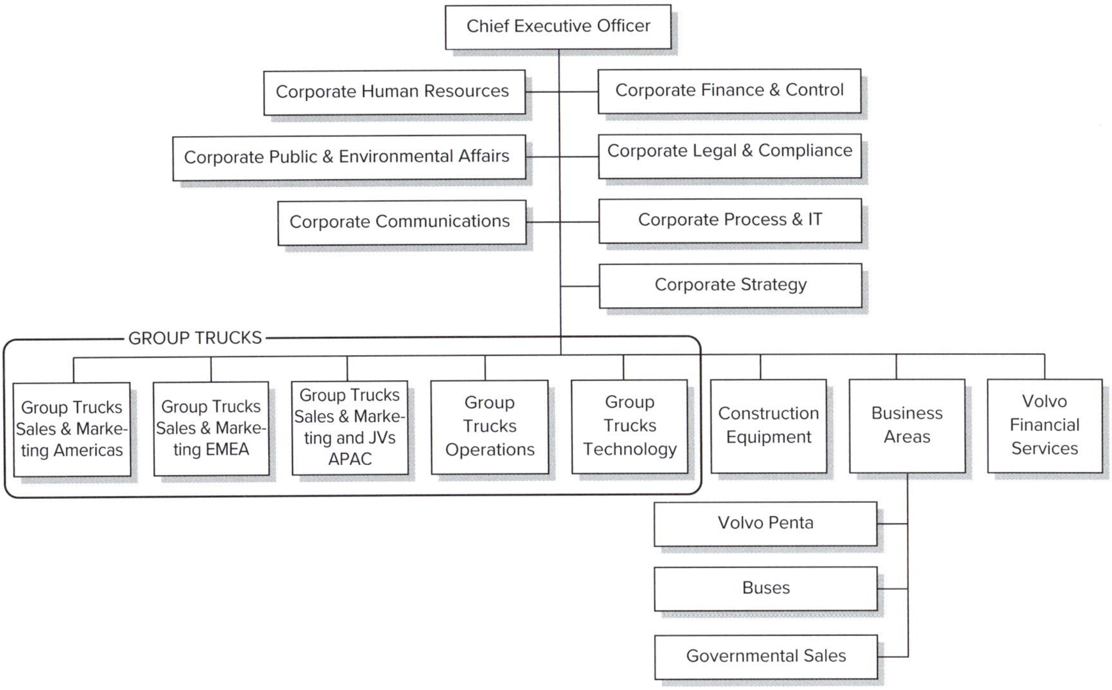


*Source:* Volvo AB Annual Report 2012.

better utilization of manufacturing plants, and so on. Using Volvo terms, this phase was about 'streamlining and merging all brands to an efficient Volvo Group' (Annual Report 2014).

CEO Olof Persson explained the phase, saying: '. . . to achieve this, we are focusing on turning volumes into profit and capturing potential for increased efficiency' (Annual Report 2014). Efforts towards optimization of the sales and service channels for all brands also gave increased efficiency. A company-wide concept to drive continuous improvement along the value chain was developed during this phase and implemented under the title VPS: Volvo Production System. An overall aim was to minimize productivity losses and gain economies of scale. Over the years, more or less all manufacturing plants have been certified to different VPS standards. There are some similarities between VPS and more commonly known LEAN concepts.

As a basis for the ongoing management control process, the company identified five key focus areas, which were all linked to the overall target of creating a more profitable business – for example, strengthen customer partnerships, creating global teams of employees across businesses and reducing costs by more efficient internal processes. Linked to the focus areas, 20 strategic objectives were determined and each of these was clearly defined and connected to both financial and non-financial key performance indicators (from now on called PM-indicators). Each strategic objective had a defined responsible party and was broken down into local targets and PM-indicators in the organizational structure. In summary, the management control process was vertical in its structure and PM based to a rather detailed level. Each organizational unit was supposed to know its role in the process and how to increase internal efficiency. This was supported by responsibility for coordination and production planning at a high level.

All units within Group Trucks Operations (GTO) were coordinated in a global production system, in order to be able to handle increased demands on quality and delivery from customers. GTO coordinated production together with the different sales and marketing units, and assigned production schedules for the various plants around the globe.

## Part 1

### New organization and ideas for a new responsibility structure

As we join the Volvo Group in this case, it is entering the third strategic phase in its history. Martin Lundstedt, the new CEO, has during his first year – which he calls 'a year of travelling' (Annual Report 2016) – identified a need for change. Martin writes in his CEO comments:

> *We have identified improvement areas such as speeding up decision-making and strengthening our agility to adapt to market volatility. Our tools for achieving this include decentralizing decisions and accountability. One step in this direction was the implementation of a brand-based organization for our truck business. Each of the brands now has responsibility for its own commercial development and profitability. Moving more responsibility into the regions is something we will continue to drive within our 10 business areas – the goal is to have as much of the daily decision making as close to the customer as possible.*

It was obviously time to reorganize in order to benefit from the full effect of a global presence for all the brands and a more efficient value chain. The new structure is a sort of matrix organization based on brand-based business areas and truck divisions, in order to secure an efficient production process, from R&D and purchasing to assembled products. The business areas have sales units or representatives in all major regions of the world.

**EXHIBIT 4** Organizational chart, Volvo Group

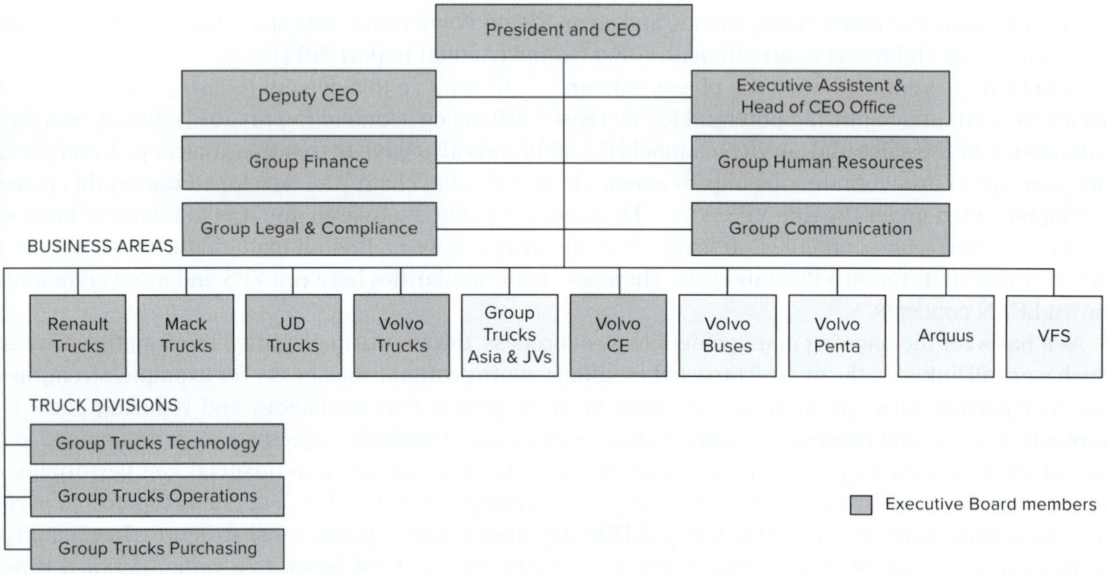


*Source:* Volvo Group Annual Report 2017.

The joint truck divisions – Technology, Operations and Purchasing – are, in terms of number of employees, the dominant part of the company. Within the Group Trucks divisions, all R&D projects, manufacturing and purchasing are synchronized in order to gain economies of scale and, at the same time, customer flexibility for the different needs of the business areas (i.e., the different brands).

## Questions

1 Given the new organization of the Group, and the intention of the new strategy, what financial responsibility do you think should be assigned to the truck divisions and the truck-related business areas, and what are the pros and cons of your choice?

2 Manufacturing and selling trucks is capital intensive. How do you look upon delegating capital employed in the responsibility structure?

## Part 2

This second part of the case concerns the largest unit of the truck divisions, Group Trucks Operations (GTO), which is a global industrial structure with approximately 60 production plants in 18 different countries around the world. Some plants are focused on assembly, others on parts of the powertrain for a truck, and so on. An important part of the operations is of course logistics and the optimization of inventory.

The core of the GTO division's top-down control was, from 2012 onwards, based on 60 financial and non-financial performance indicators (from now on referred to as PM-indicators), which made up the cornerstone of top-down control. These PM-indicators were concerned with many different aspects – e.g., HR, engineering, quality, sales and logistics – and were supposed to reflect the entire organization of GTO. The PM-indicators were used to follow developments in the respective plant, and as input to analysis and performance evaluation by the management group of the division. One plant could be accountable for approximately 30 of these PM-indicators. The overall aim was to increase manufacturing efficiency for producing trucks within the Group, regardless of brand.

## Question

3 Volvo Group's new organization and strategy (2016) wanted all units – including GTO, of course – to support the strategic change from growth to profitability. What implications do you think this should have for GTO's management of its different plants, which were previously run as engineered expense centres, based on full standard cost models for components complemented by multiple PM-indicators?

## Part 3

This part of the case is about one unit within GTO: the engine plant located in the small town of Skövde, Sweden. The Skövde plant dates back to the middle of the nineteenth century when the foundry was inaugurated. The first engine was assembled in 1907 and, in the late 1920s, Volvo became an important customer. During the 1930s Volvo acquired the company and today the plant is a proud production facility supplying the business areas within the Volvo Group with diesel engines and components. The plant has approximately 3,000 employees.

The Skövde plant is organized into three functions (Exhibit 5), which reflect the three main processes when building an engine: from foundry, via machining to assembly. Back in 2012, it was mandatory to utilize all the 30 financial and non-financial performance indicators (from now on called PM-indicators) that were used by GTO to control the plant, as well as in the internal management of the Skövde plant. With the arrival of a new plant manager, the management team at Skövde concluded that

**EXHIBIT 5** Overall structure of the Skövde plant

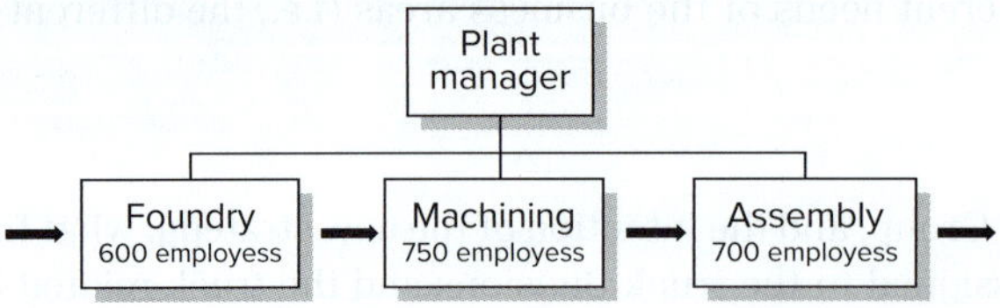


*Source:* Company internal data.

it was impossible to use all 30 PM-indicators. The factory manager initiated negotiations with superior management at the GTO level, suggesting that the Skövde plant should continue to report the 30 PM-indicators, but disregard them in the internal management process. Instead, the management team at the Skövde plant should decide on a number of areas that they considered critical for managing the plant. The suggestion was accepted after negotiations with superior management. The resistance came from different central staff functions, which feared that their interests would be set aside.

In 2013, the management team of the Skövde Plant agreed on six areas for PM-indicators: Fixed Cost, Variable Cost, Safety, Quality, Delivery and Sustainability. These six areas were to be considered at function, department and unit level (the three hierarchical levels within the plant) to the extent this was relevant (fixed cost was measured only on a function level). How the six areas were measured varied throughout the organization; this was suggested by each management group accountable, and agreed upon in discussion with the superior level. This had the benefit of a high degree of relevance of each measure for the local management group, but it was complicated to break down and trace an

**EXHIBIT 6** Organization of the Skövde plant

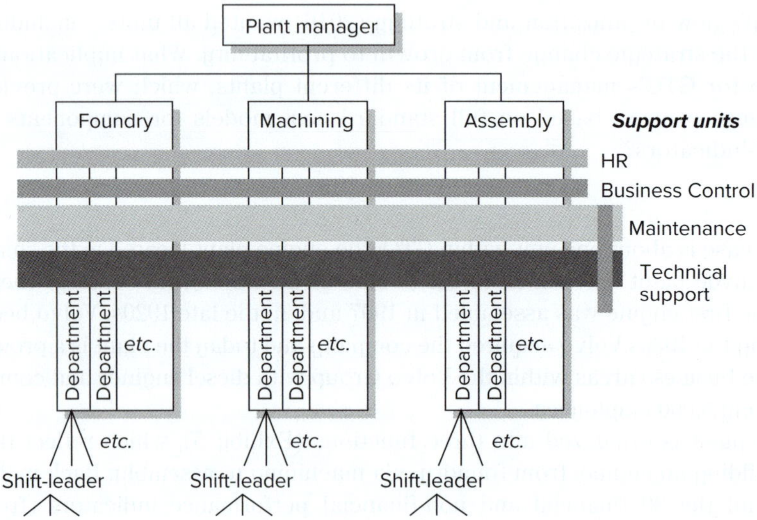


*Source:* Company internal data.

outcome at plant level down to function or department. For example, 'Sustainability' could be measured by energy consumption in one department and emissions in another. Another distinctive feature of the management process was the business reviews. Reports on PM-indicators were not used for 'control-at-a-distance'. Instead, the PM-indicators were presented, analysed and discussed at monthly business review meetings, headed by superior managers. At these meetings, accountable managers presented the story behind the PM-indicators, by using other more detailed indicators and verbal stories, and suggested how to move forward.

Top management at the plant were satisfied with the management process, and the factory delivered on its objectives during the three-year period up to 2016.

## Question

4 Discuss whether the management team at the Skövde plant should change the management control system within the plant as a consequence of the new organization and strategy at Volvo in 2016?

# Case 4.5 Grand Jean Company*

**by Joseph G. San Miguel**

The Grand Jean Company was founded in the mid-nineteenth century. The firm survived lean years and the 1929 depression largely as the result of the market durability of its dominant product – blue denim jeans. Grand Jean had been a market leader with 'wash-and-wear', bell-bottom and flared jeans, and modern casual trousers. By 1989 it was one of the world's largest clothing manufacturers. It offered a wide variety of dress and fashion jeans for both men and boys, and a complete line of trousers for women. It enjoyed a reputation for reasonably priced, quality trousers. The company sold 40 million pairs of trousers last year.

## Production

In each of the last 30 years, Grand Jean sold virtually all its production and often had to begin to ration its trousers to buyers as early as four months prior to the close of the production year. The company owned 25 manufacturing plants. The plants' capacity varied, but the average output was about 20,000 pairs of trousers per week. With the exception of two or three plants that usually produced only blue denim jeans, the plants produced various types of trousers. The firm augmented its own production capacity by contracting with independent manufacturers. Currently, there were 20 such contractors making all lines of Grand Jean's trousers (including blue denim jeans). Last year contractors produced one-third of the total number of pairs of trousers sold by Grand Jean.

Tom Wicks, vice president for production operations (see the organization chart in Exhibit 1), commented on the firm's use of outside contractors: 'The majority of these contractors have been with us

* Adapted (with permission) by Professor Joseph G. San Miguel from a case prepared by Professor Charles T. Horngren, in *Cost Accounting*, 5th edn, Prentice-Hall, Inc. © Charles T. Horngren and Joseph G. San Miguel.

**EXHIBIT 1** Grand Jean Company organization chart

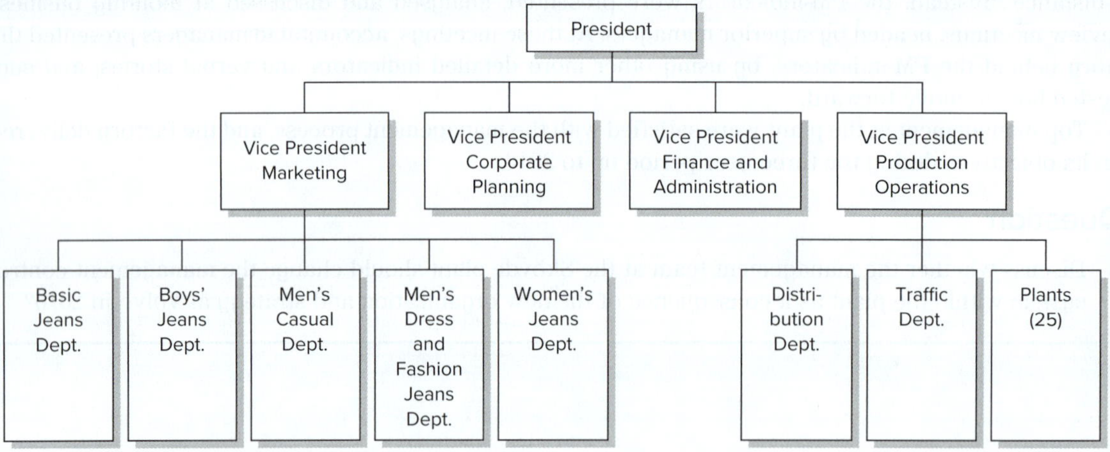


for five years or more. Several of them have served Grand Jean efficiently and reliably for over 30 years. In our eagerness to get the trousers made, we understandably link with some independents who don't know what they are doing and are forced to go out of business after a year or so because their costs are too high. Usually we can tell from an independent's experience and per unit contract price whether or not he's going to survive.

'Contract agreements are made by me and my staff. The ceiling or maximum price we are willing to pay for each type of pairs of trousers is very well established by now. If a contractor impresses us as being both reliable and capable of making quality trousers, we will pay him that ceiling. If we aren't sure, we might bid a little below that ceiling for the first year or two, until the contractor proves himself.'

Due to intense domestic and foreign competition, the failure rate in the garment industry was quite high. Hence, new entrepreneurs often stepped in and assumed control of existing facilities.

## The control system

Mr Wicks continued: 'We treat our 25 plants as expense centres. Operations at each plant have been examined thoroughly by industrial and cost engineers. You know, time-and-motion studies and all. I'm quite proud of the standard times and costs we have in place. We have even developed learning curves that tell us how long it will take production of a given type of trouser to reach the standard hours allowed per pair after initial start-up or a product switch-over. We know the rate at which total production time per pair reaches standard for every basic style of trousers we make. We use this information for budgeting a plant's cost. The marketing staff estimates the quantity of trousers of each type it wants produced each year. That information is used to divide total production among the plants. If possible, we like to put one plant to work for a whole year on one type of trouser. That saves start-up and change-over costs. Since we can sell all we make, we try to keep our plants at peak efficiency. Unfortunately, the marketing folks always manage to complicate production schedules with a lot of mid-year changes in trouser needs, so this objective is difficult to meet.

'The plant budgeting begins with me and my staff determining what a plant's quota (in pairs of trousers) for each month should be for one year ahead of time. We look at the plant's past performance and add a little to this because we expect people to improve around here. These yearly budgets are updated at the end of each month in light of the previous month's production. If a plant manager beats this budget figure, we feel he has done a good job. If he cannot meet the quota, his people have not been working at what the engineers feel is a very reasonable level of speed and efficiency. Or possibly absenteeism or worker turnover, big problems in our plants, have been excessively high. When the quota has not been reached, we want to know why and want the problem corrected as quickly as we can.

'Given the number of pairs of trousers that a plant actually produces in a month, we can determine the number of standard labour hours allowed for that month. We compare this figure against the actual labour hours to determine how a plant manager performed as an expense centre. I phone every plant manager each month to give prompt feedback on either satisfactory or unsatisfactory performance.

'We also look for other things in evaluating a plant manager. Have his community relations been good? Are his employees happy? The owners of this company are very concerned about these factors.'

An annual bonus constituted the core of Grand Jean's reward system. Mr Wicks and his two chief assistants rated each plant manager's performance on a 1-to-5 scale, where 5 was the highest rate. At year-end, Grand Jean's top management determined a bonus base by evaluating the firm's overall performance and profits for the year. The bonus base had been as high as $10,000. The performance rating for each member of Grand Jean's management cadre was multiplied by this bonus base to determine a given manager's bonus. For example, a manager with a 3-point rating would receive a $30,000 bonus.

Grand Jean's management group included many finance and marketing specialists. The case writer noted that these personnel, who were located at corporate headquarters, were consistently awarded higher ratings by their supervisors than were plant managers. This difference consistently approached a full point.

The five marketing departments listed in Exhibit 1 under the vice president of marketing are treated as revenue centres. Marketing forecasts are used to set sales unit and sales dollar targets. The performance of marketing department managers is measured on the basis of meeting these targets. To meet changing consumer demand, frequent changes in product mix were necessary. The sales force sells all types of jeans within an assigned territory. Their compensation consists of salary plus 8 per cent sales commissions. Commissions represent roughly half the average salesperson's compensation. The customers are retail stores and clothing distributors. For marketing department performance assessment, the sales of each line of trousers are assigned to the respective marketing department (i.e., basic jeans, etc.). Marketing department managers participated in the company's bonus system.

## Evaluation of the system

Mia Packard, a recent business school graduate, gave the case writer her opinions regarding Grand Jean's production operations and its management control procedures: 'Mr Wicks is one of the nicest executives I've ever met, and a very intelligent businessman, but I really don't approve of the system he uses to evaluate his plant managers. On a recent plant visit as part of my company orientation programme, I accidentally discovered that the plant manager was 'hoarding' some of the trousers produced over quota. He does this in good months to protect himself against future production deficiencies. That plant manager was really upset that I stumbled upon his trouser storehouse. He insisted that other managers did the same thing and begged me not to tell Mr Wicks. This is odd behaviour for a company that usually has to turn away orders near the end of the year! I suspect that most plant managers aren't really pushing for maximum production. If they do increase output, their quotas are going to go up, and yet they won't receive any immediate monetary rewards to compensate for the increase in their responsibilities or requirements. If I were a plant manager, I wouldn't want my production exceeding quota until the end of the year.

'Also, Mr Wicks worked his way up the ranks of the company. He was a very good plant manager himself and feels that everyone should run a plant the way he did. For example, in Mr Wicks' plant there were 11 workers for every supervisor or member of the office and administrative staff. Since then, Mr Wicks has elevated this supervision ratio of 11:1 to some sort of sacred index of leadership efficiency. All plant managers aim for it and, as a result, usually understaff their offices. Because of this, we can't get timely and accurate reports from plants. There simply aren't enough people in the offices out there to generate the information we desperately need when we need it!

'Another thing! Some of the plants have been built within the last five years and have much newer equipment. Yet there is no difference between the standard hours determined in these plants and the older ones. The older sewing machines break down more often, require more maintenance, and probably aren't as easy to work with.'

## Questions

1 How would you describe the goal(s) of the company as a whole? Is this, or are these, the same as the goal(s) of the company's marketing organization and the company's 25 managers of manufacturing plants? Explain.

2 Evaluate the current management planning and control system for the manufacturing plants and the marketing departments. What are the strengths and weaknesses?

3 One plant manager recommended that plants be operated as profit centres because this would overcome some of the problems discovered by Mia Packard and the case writer. This plant manager commented, '[My] competitor is the nearby independent manufacturer that makes the same trousers for Grand Jean as my plant makes. And this outsider might also make trousers for Grand Jean's competitors. Because of the competitive market, only the best-managed plants survive in this business. Therefore, like the outside company's manager I should have bottom-line responsibility and be rewarded accordingly.' Do you agree or disagree with the profit centre concept for Grand Jean's 25 manufacturing plants? How would this approach affect the plant managers' decisions, performance, etc.?

4 If Grand Jean's manufacturing plants were treated as profit centres, three alternatives were suggested for recording revenues for each plant:

   a Use the selling price recorded by Grand Jean's sales personnel for trousers sold to retailers and distributors.

   b Use full standard manufacturing cost per unit plus a 'fair' fixed percentage mark-up for gross profit.

   c Use the average contract price Grand Jean paid outside companies for making similar trouser types.

   Evaluate these three alternatives. Which one would you recommend? Why is your selection the best one?

# Chapter 5

# Control with transfer prices and shared service centres

## Learning objectives

After reading this chapter, you should be able to:

1. Explain the four objectives that an appropriate transfer pricing system should accomplish.
2. Qualitatively and quantitatively explain different transfer pricing methods.
3. Explain the key considerations involved in the administration of transfer prices.
4. Explain the main characteristics of shared service centres.
5. Explain the management control challenges related to shared service centres.

## Real world vignette: Glencore

Transfer prices are the prices that one part of an organization charges to another part to pay for goods and services delivered. In large companies the issue of transfer pricing is an internal challenge about how to set those prices to be acceptable to the managers of the organization's different responsibility centres. Transfer pricing thus plays an important part in aligning these centres to reach the overall goals of the organization. But transfer prices are also important in another way for large for-profit companies that have operations in different countries. Transfer prices affect profit levels, and therefore tax payments, when these responsibility centres are subsidiaries and separate entities for legal and tax purposes. With some subsidiaries located in offshore, lower-tax countries, nations face the risk that transfer pricing is used to lower overall tax payments. Organizations run the risk of being fined for tax evasion. National authorities around the globe are increasingly scrutinizing the transfer prices used by companies and seeking to establish that such prices are 'at arm's length'. This means that the prices are exactly as they would be when dealing with an unrelated company. As such, transfer pricing is an important management control system topic, both to align managerial behaviours across centres and to comply with tax authorities.

### *Glencore wins transfer pricing court case with Australian Tax Office (ATO)*

Glencore plc is a British multinational commodity trading and mining company. Glencore describes itself as one of the world's largest global natural resource companies, and a major producer and marketer of more than 60 commodities. The group's operations comprise around 150 mining and metallurgical sites and oil production assets. Its headquarters are in Baar, Switzerland. Glencore's Australian subsidiary has operated the Cobar copper mine, which is located in the New South Wales state, since 1998. It sold the copper concentrate that was taken from the mine to its parent company in Switzerland. The price paid for this concentrate was originally set at a 'market-related' price, but this policy was changed in February 2007. At that time, a new 'price-sharing agreement' was entered into. This agreement based the price paid by the Swiss parent company to its Australian subsidiary on the London Metals Exchange commodity price. This basis price was adjusted for a price-sharing percentage as the basis for the transfer price. The ATO argued that this new price-sharing agreement meant that the prices paid to the Australian subsidiary were less than the returns under the the original market-related pricing method, or under some other arm's length agreement. The ATO's commissioner alleged that this caused a shift in profit resulting in additional tax owed of A$92.6 million. Australia's Federal Court, however, found that Glencore had used a price that was in conformity with the arm's length principle.[1]

## Introduction

As pointed out in Chapter 4, organizational architecture is oriented towards designing an optimal organizational structure, and organizations often strive to create responsibility centres in the form of profit or investment centres. Few managers would question this development, and the advantages – for instance, from a motivational point of view – that such a clear allocation of responsibility can be explained by the way we understand human motivation (see Chapter 3). As such, a relatively clear-cut discussion has been provided on the role and function of responsibility centres, where revenue centres, expense centres, profit centres and investment centres are created. Designing such centres is related to what we in this book label 'organizational architecture', but their functioning also depends on the use of appropriate performance measures and reports for each of these centres. From a management control systems point of view, this implies that there are *principal challenges in managing responsibility centres*. Even if a certain structure is optimal from an architectural perspective, it does not function by itself, but requires management control practices that are able to guide the interactions between the centres. Obviously, the structural design is not intended to create responsibility centres that are free to do what they want. Rather, the challenge is to orchestrate the actions of such centres to achieve the organizational mission, goals and strategies by joint effort. One critical challenge here is how to account for goods and

---

1 https://www.glencore.com/media-and-insights/news/Third-Quarter-2019-Production-Report; https://www.duffandphelps.com/insights/publications/transfer-pricing/transfer-pricing-times-september-2019/australia-court-rules-favor-glencore-transfer-pricing-case; https://www.reuters.com/article/us-australia-glencore-tax/glencore-wins-transfer-pricing-court-battle-with-australian-tax-office-idUSKCN1VO05S (accessed 1 October 2019).

services that are delivered from one unit to the other. Surely, the optimal internal transfer of goods and services is crucial for an organization's coherence. But such transfers cannot happen for free, which is why management control systems should include the practices that ensure that consumers of such goods and services pay the producers appropriately. This chapter deals with three such management control practices, namely *transfer pricing*, *corporate service pricing* and *shared service centres.* Transfer pricing is about how to devise a satisfactory method of accounting for the transfer of goods and services from one profit centre to another in organizations that have a significant number of these transactions. In the first part of the chapter, we discuss various approaches to arrive at transfer prices for transactions between profit centres, and the system of negotiation and arbitration that is essential when transfer prices are used.

Corporate services pricing mainly concerns the way in which the company's expenses of central and overall services, such as marketing, administration and research, are borne by responsibility centres. Typically, these services are provided to the benefit of many, if not all, responsibility centres within the company. Therefore, the costs of these services should be recognized in these units' profit and loss statements. In the second part of the chapter, we discuss how such services can be priced. There are similarities, of course, between the pricing of corporate services and generic transfer pricing. However, many of the services provided by the central services department are not easily identifiable. They are overhead costs. This means that many companies 'price' these services in a very generic and rough way, which is commonly addressed as (overhead) cost allocation.

Such services are often of vital importance to the organization's well-being and coherence. Moreover, they often require a level of professionalism and expertise that would be too costly to organize in every responsibility centre. This, for example, goes for HR and tax services, which can benefit from economies of scale and require expert professionals. Therefore, another principal challenge in managing responsibility centres is how to optimally organize such central services and how to make sure that responsibility centres do not over- or under-consume them. One way of dealing with this issue is to apply the concept of shared service centres. It is, in fact, an organization architectural approach in which a subset of 'non-core' business functions are concentrated into a new organizational unit that forms the shared service centre. Shared service centres need to price their services much in the same way as regular transfer prices are applied, and many of the transfer pricing issues are directly applicable. However, shared service centres bring some additional management control system challenges that have to do with the centralized nature of the centre and the related importance of guaranteeing value for money to the other responsibility centres.

## Transfer pricing

Transfer pricing concerns how to devise a satisfactory method of accounting for the transfer of goods and services from one responsibility centre to another in companies that have a significant number of these transactions. For instance, if two or more profit centres are jointly responsible for product development, manufacturing and marketing, each should share in the revenue generated when the product is finally sold. The transfer price is the mechanism for distributing this revenue. The transfer price should be designed so that it accomplishes the following objectives:

- It should provide each responsibility centre with the relevant information it needs to determine the *optimum trade-off* between company costs and revenues.
- It should induce *goal-congruent* decisions – that is, the system should be designed so that decisions that improve responsibility centre profits will also improve company profits.
- It should help measure the *financial performance* of the individual responsibility centres.

- The system should be *simple* to understand and *easy* to administer.
- It should be *acceptable to the tax authorities* if the two responsibility centres are located in two different tax jurisdictions.

Designing transfer pricing systems is a key management control system topic for most organizations.

## Transfer pricing methods

Some writers use the term 'transfer price' to refer to the amount used in accounting for *any* transfer of goods and services between responsibility centres. We use a somewhat narrower definition and limit the term *transfer price* to the value placed on a transfer of goods or services in transactions in which at least one of the two parties involved is a *profit centre* or *investment centre*. Such a price typically includes a profit element because an independent company normally would not transfer goods or services to another independent company at cost or less. Therefore, we exclude the mechanics for allocating costs in a cost accounting system in our discussion of transfer prices; such costs do not include a profit element. The term '*price*' as used here has the same meaning as it has when used in connection with transactions between independent companies. This also reflects in the single most important question that tax authorities have about such internal prices. Do they sufficiently reflect that price that two independent companies would have agreed on? The term 'arm's length' reflects this independence, as it denotes the arm's length handshake between two business partners, rather than a more intimate embrace that is not 'at arm's length' between family members. (The Real World Example discusses arm's length transfer pricing.)

***Real World Example:*** The Organisation for Economic Co-operation and Development (OECD) is an international non-governmental organization (NGO) that advises on national policies and international trade arrangements. One of its topics of interest is international taxation, and its policy recommendation on transfer pricing is an important international benchmark. The OECD Transfer Pricing Guidelines for Multinational Enterprises and Tax Administrations 2017 proposes detailed policies and principles for establishing transfer prices by companies and tax authorities in the evaluation of such prices. Two relevant policy statements are as follows:

1. *Arm's length principle:* The international standard that OECD member countries have agreed should be used for determining transfer prices for tax purposes. It is set forth in Article 9 of the OECD Model Tax Convention as follows: where 'conditions are made or imposed between the two enterprises in their commercial or financial relations which differ from those which would be made between independent enterprises, then any profits which would, but for those conditions, have accrued to one of the enterprises, but, by reason of those conditions, have not so accrued, may be included in the profits of that enterprise and taxed accordingly.
2. *Arm's length range:* A range of figures that are acceptable for establishing whether the conditions of a controlled transaction are arm's length, and are derived either from applying the same transfer pricing method to multiple comparable data or from applying different transfer pricing methods.

*Source:* OECD transfer pricing guidelines for multinational enterprises and tax administrations 2017. Available at: https://read.oecd-ilibrary.org/taxation/oecd-transfer-pricing-guidelines-for-multinational-enterprises-and-tax-administrations-2017_tpg-2017-en#page23 (accessed 7 May 2020).

### Fundamental principle

The transfer pricing issue is actually about pricing in general, modified slightly to take into account factors that are unique to internal transactions. *The fundamental principle is that transfer prices should be similar to the prices that would be charged if the products were sold to outside customers or purchased from outside vendors*. Applying this principle is complicated by the fact that there is much disagreement in the literature as well as in practice as to how outside selling prices are established. Classical economics literature states that selling prices should be equal to marginal costs, and some authors advocate a transfer price based on marginal cost.[2] This is unrealistic for transfer pricing. Few companies follow such a policy in arriving at either selling prices or transfer prices. Delivering at marginal costs would effectively reduce the delivering unit to an expense centre, which may effectively reduce that unit manager's motivation for efficiency. It may also diminish the manager's motivation to deliver internally at all, especially when external prices are better. Note again that also the tax authorities will not accept a price that does not contain a profit margin as it would have in 'arm's length' contracts, even if it will often accept a small price difference that reflects that companies may save marketing costs, as well the risk of bad debtors when selling and sourcing internally.

When the profit or investment centres of a company buy products from, and sell to, one another, two decisions must be made periodically for each product:

1. Should the company produce the product inside the company or purchase it from an outside vendor? This is the *sourcing decision*.
2. If produced inside, at what price should the product be transferred between profit/investment centres? This is the *transfer price decision*.

Transfer price systems can range from very simple to extremely complex, depending on the nature of the business. We start with the ideal situation and then describe increasingly complex situations.

## The ideal situation

A *market price*-based transfer price will induce goal congruence if all the following conditions exist. Rarely, if ever, will they all exist in practice. The list, therefore, does not set out criteria that must be met to have a transfer price. Rather, it suggests a way of looking at a situation to see what changes should be made to improve the operation of the transfer price mechanism.

- *Competent people:* ideally, managers should be interested in the long-run as well as the short-run performances of their responsibility centres. Staff involved in negotiation and arbitration of transfer prices must also be competent.
- *Good atmosphere:* managers must regard profitability, as measured in their income statements, as an important goal and a significant consideration in the judgement of their performance. They should perceive that the transfer prices are just.
- *A market price:* the ideal transfer price is based on a well-established, normal market price reflecting the same conditions (quantity, delivery time and quality) as the product to which the transfer price applies. The market price may be adjusted downwards to reflect savings accruing to the selling unit from dealing inside the company. For example, there would be no bad debt expense, and advertising and selling costs would be smaller.
- *Freedom to source:* alternatives for sourcing should exist, and managers should be permitted to choose the alternative that is in their own best interests. The buying manager should be free to buy from the outside, and the selling manager should be free to sell outside. In these circumstances, the transfer price policy simply gives the managers of each profit centre the right to deal with either insiders or outsiders at their discretion. The market, therefore, establishes the transfer price. This method is optimal if the selling profit centre can sell all its products to either insiders or outsiders, and if the buying centre can obtain all its requirements from either outsiders or insiders. From a company point of view, the relevant cost of the product is the market price because that is the amount of cash that has been forgone by selling inside. The transfer price represents the opportunity cost to the company.

[2] Hirschleifer, J. (1956) On the economics of transfer pricing, *Journal of Business*, July: 172–84.

- *Full information:* managers must know about the available alternatives, and the relevant costs and revenues of each.
- *Negotiation:* there must be a smoothly working mechanism for negotiating 'contracts' between responsibility centres.

If all these conditions are present, a transfer price system based on *market prices* would induce goal-congruent decisions, with no need for central administration. However, this is rarely the case in practice. In the next subsection, we consider situations in which not all of these conditions are present.

## Constraints on sourcing

In practice, freedom to source might not be feasible or, if it is, might be constrained by corporate policy. We now consider the situations in which profit centre managers may not have the freedom to make sourcing decisions, and the implications of constraints on sourcing on the appropriate transfer pricing policies.

### *Limited markets*

In many companies, markets for the buying or selling profit centres may be limited. There are several reasons for this. First, the existence of internal capacity might limit the development of external sales. If most of the large companies in an industry are highly integrated, as in the pulp and paper industry, there tends to be little independent production capacity for intermediate products. Thus, these producers can handle only a limited amount of demand from other producers. When internal capacity becomes tight, the market is quickly flooded with demands for the intermediate products. Even though outside capacity exists, it may not be available to the integrated company unless this capacity is used on a regular basis. If the integrated company does not purchase a product on a regular basis, it might have trouble obtaining it from the outside when capacity is limited.

Second, if a company is the sole producer of a differentiated product, no outside source exists. Third, if a company has invested significantly in facilities, it is unlikely to use outside sources unless the outside selling price approaches the company's variable cost, which is not usual. For practical purposes, the products produced are captive. Integrated oil companies are good examples of this. The producing unit may be required to send the crude oil to the refining unit, even though the former could potentially sell the crude oil in the open market.

Even in the case of limited markets, the transfer price that best satisfies the requirements of a profit centre system is the *competitive price.* Competitive prices measure the contribution of each profit centre to the total company profits. In the case of an integrated oil company, use of crude oil market prices is the most effective way to evaluate the extracting and refining units as if they were stand-alone businesses. If internal capacity is not available, the company will buy outside at a competitive price. The difference between the competitive price and the inside cost is the money saved by producing rather than buying. Moreover, a competitive price measures how well a profit centre may be performing against competitors.

How does a company find out what the competitive price is if it does not buy or sell the product in an outside market? Here are some ways:

- If *published market prices* are available, they can be used to establish transfer prices. However, these should be prices actually paid in the marketplace, and the conditions that exist in the outside market should be consistent with those that exist within the company. For example, market prices that apply to relatively small purchases (e.g., a 'spot' market) would not be valid for measuring what is essentially a long-term commitment.
- Market prices may be set by *bids.* This generally can be done only if the low bidder stands a reasonable chance of obtaining the business. One company accomplishes this by buying about one half of a particular group of products outside the company and one half inside the company. The company puts *all* the products out to bid but selects half to stay inside. It obtains valid bids because low

bidders can expect to get some of the business. By contrast, if a company requests bids solely to obtain a competitive price and does not award contracts to the low bidder, it will soon find that either no one bids or that the bids are of questionable value.

- If the *selling profit centre* sells similar products in *outside markets*, it is often possible to replicate a competitive price on the basis of the outside price. For example, if a manufacturing profit centre normally earns a 10 per cent profit over standard cost on the products that it sells to outside markets, it can replicate a competitive price by adding 10 per cent to the standard cost of its proprietary products.
- If the *buying profit centre* purchases similar products from the *outside market*, it may be possible to replicate competitive prices for its proprietary products. This can be done by calculating the cost of the difference in design and other conditions of sale between the competitive products and the proprietary products.

### Excess or shortage of industry capacity

Suppose the selling profit centre cannot sell to the outside market all it can produce – that is, it has excess capacity. The company may not optimize profits if the buying profit centre purchased from outside vendors while capacity is available on the inside.

Conversely, suppose the buying profit centre cannot obtain the product it requires from the outside while the selling profit centre is selling to the outside. This situation occurs when there is a shortage of capacity in the industry. In this case, the output of the buying profit centre is constrained and, again, company profits may not be optimal.

If the number of internal company transfers is small or if the situation is temporary, many companies let buyers and sellers work out their own relationships without central intervention. Even if the number of internal company transfers is significant, some senior managers still do not intervene on the theory that the benefits of keeping the profit centres independent offset the loss from sub-optimizing company profits.

Some companies allow either the buying or the selling profit centre to appeal against a sourcing decision to a central person or committee. For example, a selling profit centre could appeal against a buying profit centre's decision to buy a product from outside when capacity was available inside. In the same way, a buying profit centre could appeal against a selling profit centre's decision to sell outside. The person or group (called an *arbitration committee*) would then make the sourcing decision on the basis of the company's best interests. In every case, the transfer price would be the *competitive price*. In other words, the profit centre is only appealing against the sourcing decision. It must accept the product at the competitive price.

A word of caution is in order at this point: given the option, buying profit centres in some companies prefer to deal with an outside source. One reason for this is the perception that outside sources provide better service. Another reason is the internal rivalry that sometimes exists in divisionalized companies. For whatever reason, management should be aware of the strong political overtones that sometimes occur in transfer price negotiations. There is no guarantee that a profit centre will voluntarily buy from the inside source when excess capacity exists.

To conclude, even if there are constraints on sourcing, the market price is the best transfer price. *If the market price exists or can be approximated, use it.* However, if there is no way of approximating valid competitive prices, the other option is to develop *cost-based* transfer prices. These are discussed in the next section.

In arriving at the transfer price, companies typically eliminate advertising, financing or other expenses that the seller does not incur in internal transactions. This is similar to the practice when two outside companies arrive at a price. The buyer ordinarily will not pay for cost components that do not apply to the contract.

## Cost-based transfer prices

If competitive prices are not available, transfer prices may be set on the basis of cost plus a profit, even though such transfer prices may be complex to calculate and the results less satisfactory than a market-based price. Two decisions must be made in a cost-based transfer price system: (1) how to define cost and (2) how to calculate the profit mark-up.

### The cost basis

*The usual basis is standard costs.* This is a relatively simple principle, which is easy to understand and administer. Actual costs should not be used because this would mean that production inefficiencies will be passed on to the buying profit centre. If standard costs are used, however, an incentive is also still needed to set tight standards and improve standards. A related question is how the standard costs should be calculated – for instance, whether full (absorption) costing or activity-based costing principles should be applied. These latter may help cost reductions that benefit both supplier and buyer and the overall firm. We emphasize that an efficient cost-based transfer pricing system builds on the fact that accepted and proper costing systems are in place. As such, transfer pricing and costing are intimately related topics. Crucial to both is that the standard costs are based on a realistic level of production. Standard costs will be too high if production is estimated too low.[3]

### The profit mark-up

In calculating the profit mark-up, there also are two decisions: (1) what the profit mark-up is based on and (2) the level of profit allowed.

The simplest and most widely used base is a *percentage of costs.* If this base is used, however, no account is taken of capital required. A conceptually better base is a *percentage of investment,* but calculating the investment applicable to a given product may pose a major practical problem. If the historical cost of the fixed assets is used, new facilities designed to reduce prices could actually increase costs because old assets are undervalued.

The second problem with the profit allowance is the amount of profit. Senior management's perception of the financial performance of a profit centre will be affected by the profit it shows. Consequently, the profit allowance should approximate the rate of return that would be earned if the business unit was an independent company selling to outside customers. The conceptual solution is to base the profit allowance on the investment required to meet the volume needed by the buying profit centres. The investment would be calculated at a 'standard' level, with fixed assets and inventories at current replacement costs.

## Upstream fixed costs and profits

Transfer pricing can create a significant problem in integrated companies. The profit centre that finally sells to the outside customer may not even be aware of the amount of upstream fixed costs and profit included in its internal purchase price. Even if the final profit centre is aware of these costs and profit, it might be reluctant to reduce its own profit to optimize company profit. Methods that companies use to mitigate this problem are described below.

### Agreement among business units

Some companies establish a formal mechanism whereby representatives from the buying and selling units meet periodically to decide on outside selling prices and the sharing of profits for products with significant upstream fixed costs and profit. This mechanism works only if the review process is limited

[3] It is important to have a thorough knowledge of costing when designing cost-based transfer pricing systems. For discussions on full (absorption) costing and activity-based costing, we refer to traditional management accounting textbooks. In this book we focus on the transfer pricing considerations.

to decisions involving a significant amount of business to at least one of the profit centres; otherwise the value of these negotiations may not be worth the effort.

### *Two-step pricing*

Another way to handle the setting of transfer prices is to establish a transfer price that includes two charges. First, a charge is made for each unit sold that is equal to the *standard variable cost* of production. Second, a periodic (usually monthly) charge is made that is equal to the *fixed costs* associated with the facilities reserved for the buying unit. One or both of these components should include a profit margin and the buying party should also compensate the selling party for the risk of holding a certain capacity. For example, assume the conditions in Table 5.1. We assume that a wellness centre operates a hotel as a profit centre, which buys meals for its guests from the restaurant, which is also a profit centre.

**TABLE 5.1** Two-step pricing: assumed situation

| Restaurant (supplier) | Meals |
|---|---|
| Expected monthly sales to hotel | 5,000 meals |
| Variable cost per unit | £5 |
| Monthly fixed costs assigned to product | £20,000 |
| Investment in working capital and facilities | £1,200,000 |
| Competitive return on investment per year | 10% |
| One way to charge these lunches to the hotel is at a price per unit, calculated as follows: | |
| | **Transfer price for lunch** |
| Variable cost per unit | £5 |
| *Plus* fixed cost per unit | £4 |
| *Plus* profit per unit* | £2 |
| Transfer price per unit | £11 |

*Note:*
* 10% of monthly investment per unit $\frac{(£1{,}200{,}000/12) \times £0.10}{£5{,}000}$

In this method, the transfer price of £11 per unit is a variable cost as far as the hotel is concerned. However, the company's variable cost for the lunches is £5 per unit. Thus, the hotel does not have the right information to make appropriate short-term marketing decisions. If the hotel knew the company's variable costs, for example, it could take business at less than its normal price under certain conditions.

Two-step pricing corrects this problem by transferring variable cost on a per-unit basis, and transferring fixed cost and profit on a lump-sum basis. Under this method, the transfer price for meals would be £5 for each unit that the hotel purchases, plus £20,000 per month for fixed cost, plus £10,000 per month for profit:

$$(£1{,}200{,}000/12) \times 0.10$$

If transfers of meals in a certain month are at the expected amount of 5,000 units, under the two-step method the hotel will pay the variable cost of £25,000 (5,000 units × £5 per unit), plus £30,000 for fixed costs and profit: a total of £55,000. This is the same amount it would pay the restaurant if the transfer price was £11 per unit (5,000 × £11 = £55,000). If transfers in another month were less – say, 4,000 units – the hotel would pay £50,000 ([4,000 × £5] + £30,000) under the two-step method, compared with the £44,000 it would pay if the transfer price was £11 per unit (4,000 × £11). The difference is its penalty for not using a portion of the restaurant's capacity that it has reserved. Conversely, the hotel would pay less under the two-step method if the transfer was more than 5,000 units in a given month. This represents the savings the restaurant would have because it could produce the additional units without incurring additional fixed costs.

Under two-step pricing, the company's variable cost for meals is identical to the restaurant's variable cost for this product, and the hotel will make the correct short-term marketing decisions. The hotel also has information on upstream fixed costs and profit relating to meals, and it can use this data for long-term decisions.

The fixed-cost calculation in the two-step pricing method is based on the capacity reserved for the production of meals that are sold to the hotel. The investment represented by this capacity is allocated to product A. The return on investment that the restaurant earns on competitive (and, if possible, comparable) products is calculated and multiplied by the investment assigned to the product.

In the example, we calculated the profit allowance as a fixed monthly amount. It would be appropriate under some circumstances to divide the investment into variable (e.g., receivables and inventory) and fixed (e.g., plant) components. A profit allowance based on a return on the variable assets would be added to the standard variable cost for each unit sold.

Some points to consider about the two-step pricing method are as follows:

- The monthly charge for fixed costs and profit should be negotiated periodically and will depend on the capacity reserved for the buying unit.
- Questions may be raised about the accuracy of the cost and investment allocation. In some situations, assigning costs and assets to individual products is not difficult. In any event, approximate accuracy is adequate. The principal problem usually is not the allocation technique; it is deciding how much capacity to reserve for the various products. Moreover, if capacity is reserved for a group of products sold to the same business unit, there is no need to allocate fixed costs and investments to individual products in the group.
- Under this pricing system, the manufacturing unit's profit performance is not affected by the sales volume of the final unit. This solves the problem that arises when marketing efforts by other business units affect the profit performance of a purely manufacturing unit.
- There could be a conflict between the interests of the manufacturing unit and those of the company. If capacity is limited, the manufacturing unit could increase its profit by using the capacity to produce parts for outside sale, if it is advantageous to do so. (This weakness is mitigated by stipulating that the marketing unit has first claim on the capacity for which it is contracted.)
- This method is similar to the 'take or pay' pricing that is used frequently by public utilities, pipelines and coal-mining companies, and in other long-term contracts.

### Profit sharing

If the two-step pricing system just described is not feasible, a *profit sharing system* might be used to ensure congruence between business unit and company interests. This system operates as follows:

1. The product is transferred to the marketing unit at standard variable cost.
2. After the product is sold, the business units share the contribution earned, which is the selling price minus the variable manufacturing and marketing costs.

This method of pricing may be appropriate if demand for the manufactured product is not steady enough to warrant the permanent assignment of facilities, as in the two-step method. In general, this method does make the marketing unit's interest congruent with the company's. One mechanism that such a system would endorse is that the production and sales managers meet and decide on the production plan together. Their typical focus on efficiency and effectiveness respectively may create the largest profit to the company.

Implementing such a *profit sharing system* produces several practical problems. First, there can be arguments over the way contribution is divided between the two profit centres, and senior management might have to intervene to settle these disputes. This is costly and time-consuming, and works against a basic reason for decentralization – namely the autonomy of business unit managers. Second, arbitrarily dividing up the profits between units does not give valid information on the profitability of each unit. Third, as the contribution is not allocated until after the sale has been made, the manufacturing unit's contribution depends on the marketing unit's ability to sell as well as the actual selling price. Manufacturing units may perceive this situation to be unfair.

### *Two sets of prices*

In this method, the manufacturing unit's revenue is credited at the outside sales price and the buying unit is charged the total standard costs. The difference is charged to a headquarters account and eliminated when the business unit financial statements are consolidated. This transfer pricing method can be used when there are frequent conflicts between the buying and selling units that cannot be resolved by one of the other methods. Both the buying and selling units benefit under this method. This practice is sometimes called *dual-rate transfer pricing.*

However, there are several disadvantages to the system of having two sets of transfer prices. First, the sum of the business unit profits is greater than overall company profits. Senior management must be aware of this situation when approving budgets for the business units and subsequently evaluating performance against these budgets. Second, this system creates an illusive feeling that business units are making money, while, in fact, the overall company might be losing money. Third, this system might motivate business units to concentrate more on internal transfers where they are assured of a good mark-up at the expense of outside sales. Fourth, there is additional book-keeping involved in first debiting the headquarters account every time a transfer is made and then eliminating this account when business unit statements are consolidated. Finally, the fact that conflicts between the business units would be lessened under this system could be viewed as a weakness. Sometimes, conflicts over transfer prices signal problems in either the organizational structure or other management systems. Under the two-sets-of-prices method these conflicts are smoothed over, thereby not alerting senior management to these problems.

## Administration of transfer prices

We have so far discussed how to formulate a sound transfer pricing policy. In this section we discuss how the selected policy should be implemented – specifically, the degree of negotiation allowed in setting transfer prices, methods of resolving transfer pricing conflicts and classification of products according to the appropriate method. Negotiations can be costly in terms of time and energy, and create little value in themselves.

### Negotiation

In most companies, business units negotiate transfer prices with one another – that is, transfer prices are not set by a central staff group. Perhaps the most important reason for this is the belief that establishing selling prices and arriving at satisfactory purchase prices are among the primary functions of line management. If headquarters controls pricing, line management's ability to affect profitability is reduced. Also, many transfer prices require a degree of subjective judgement. Consequently, a negotiated transfer price is often the result of compromises made by both buyer and seller. If headquarters establishes transfer prices, business unit managers can argue that their low profits are due to the arbitrariness of the transfer prices. Another reason for having the business units negotiate their prices is that they usually have the best information on markets and costs and, consequently, are best able to arrive at reasonable prices.

**Real World Example:** Business Unit Aalto and Business Unit Helsinki are both part of the same Finnish company. Suppose the Aalto unit has an opportunity to supply a large quantity of a certain product to an outside company at a price of $100 per unit. The raw material for this product would be supplied by Business Unit Helsinki. The Helsinki unit's normal transfer price for this material is $35 per unit, of which £10 is variable cost. The Aalto unit's process cost (excluding raw material) plus a normal profit is $85, of which £50 is variable cost. The Aalto unit's total cost plus normal profit, therefore, is $120; at this amount, the selling price of $100 is not attractive. Rejecting the contract would be dysfunctional for the company as a whole because both business units have available capacity. The two units, therefore, should come together to negotiate a lower price for the raw material so that both units will make a contribution to their unit profit by engaging in the transaction that is profitable from the company's point of view.

If, instead of two business units within a single company, one company had an offer to sell raw material to another company that had a similar sales prospect, the two companies should negotiate in the same fashion. The fact that a transfer price was involved in the first example does not affect how reasonably managers should behave.[4]

Business units must know the ground rules within which these transfer price negotiations are to be conducted. In a few companies, headquarters informs business units that they are free to deal with one another or with outsiders as they see fit, subject only to the qualification that, if there is a tie, the business must be kept inside. If this is done, and there are outside sources and outside markets, no further administrative procedures are required. The price is set in the outside marketplace, and if business units cannot agree on a price, they simply buy from, or sell to, outsiders. In many companies, however, business units are required to deal with one another. If they do not have the threat of doing business with competitors as a bargaining point in the negotiation process, headquarters staff must develop a set of rules that governs both pricing and sourcing of intra-company products.

Line managers should not spend an undue amount of time on transfer price negotiations, so these rules should be specific enough to prevent negotiating skill from being a significant factor in determining the transfer price. Without such rules, the most stubborn manager will negotiate the most favourable prices.

## Arbitration and conflict resolution

No matter how specific the pricing rules, there may be instances in which business units will not be able to agree on a price. For this reason, a procedure should be in place for arbitrating transfer price disputes. There can be widely different degrees of formality in transfer price arbitration. At one extreme, the responsibility for arbitrating disputes is assigned to a single executive – the financial vice-president or executive vice-president, for example – who talks to the business unit managers involved and then verbally announces the price. The other extreme is to set up a committee. Usually such a committee will have three responsibilities: (1) settling transfer price disputes; (2) reviewing sourcing changes; and (3) changing the transfer price rules when appropriate. The degree of formality employed depends on the extent and type of potential transfer price disputes. In any case, transfer price arbitration should be the responsibility of a high-level headquarters executive or group, because arbitration decisions can have an important effect on business unit profits.

Arbitration can be conducted in a number of ways. With a formal system, both parties submit a written case to the arbitrator. The arbitrator reviews their positions and decides on the price, sometimes with the assistance of other staff offices. For example, the purchasing department might review the

[4] David Solomons (1968) discussed a similar example in Chapter VI of his book, *Divisional Performance: Measurement and Control*. Homewood, IL: Richard D. Irwin. He concluded that the transfer pricing system would be dysfunctional because Division A would reject a contract that was in the best interests of the company. He did not mention the possibility of negotiation, and his conclusion was, therefore, incorrect.

validity of a proposed competitive price quotation, or the industrial engineering department might review the appropriateness of a disputed standard labour cost. As indicated above, in less formal systems the presentations may be largely verbal.

It is important that relatively few disputes should be submitted to arbitration. If a large number of disputes are arbitrated, this indicates the rules are not specific enough or are difficult to apply, or the business unit organization is illogical. In short, this is a symptom that something is wrong. Not only is arbitration time-consuming to both line managers and headquarters executives, but arbitrated prices often satisfy neither the buyer nor the seller. In some companies, submitting a price dispute to arbitration is so cumbersome that very few are ever submitted. If, as a consequence, legitimate grievances do not surface, the results are undesirable. Preventing disputes from being submitted to arbitration will tend to hide the fact that there are problems with the transfer price system.

Irrespective of the degree of formality of the arbitration, the type of conflict resolution process that is used will also influence the effectiveness of a transfer pricing system. There are four ways to resolve conflicts: forcing, smoothing, bargaining and problem solving.[5] The conflict resolution mechanisms range from conflict avoidance through forcing and smoothing, to conflict resolution through bargaining and problem solving.

## Product classification

The extent and formality of the sourcing and transfer pricing rules depend to a large extent on the number of internal transfers and the availability of markets and market prices. The greater the number of internal transfers and the availability of market prices, the more formal and specific the rules must be. If market prices are readily available, sourcing can be controlled by having headquarters review make-or-buy decisions that exceed a specified amount.

Some companies divide products into two main classes:

1. *Class I* includes all products for which senior management wishes to control sourcing. These would normally be large-volume products: products for which no outside source exists; and products over whose manufacturing, for quality or secrecy reasons, senior management wishes to maintain control.
2. *Class II* is all other products. In general, these are products that can be produced outside the company without any significant disruption to present operations, and products of relatively small volume, produced with general-purpose equipment. Class II products are transferred at market prices.

The sourcing of Class I products can be changed only by permission of central management. The sourcing of Class II products is determined by the business units involved. Both the buying and the selling units are free to deal either inside or outside the company.

Under this arrangement, management can concentrate on the sourcing and pricing of a relatively small number of high-volume products. Rules for transfer prices would be established using the various methods described in the preceding section, as appropriate.

# Corporate services

In this section we describe some of the problems associated with charging business units for services furnished by corporate staff units. It is important to first make a distinction in these services, based on whether decentralized units have control over the consumption of these services.

[5] Lawrence, P.R. and Lorsch, J.W. (1967) *Organization and Environment.* Homewood, IL: Richard D. Irwin, pp. 73–8.

## Corporate services and cost allocation

For some corporate services, individual business units can simply not decide on the amount of services they consume. This is because those services can not be individuated, but rather are delivered to the company overall. Business units therefore often have no control over the consumption. This is the case for services that are necessary for the company to function, and which may even be invisible to the decentralized units. For example, central accounting is required for the company to keep and maintain its financial records, and to be able to publish financial performance to the shareholders, the tax authorities and other stakeholders. Other examples of such necessary activities are those in public relations, general, marketing, and (basic) research and development. These services are necessary to be able to run the company at all, and are thus provided to the benefit of all. Even if business units can identify those services, their consumption is still implicit, and cannot be enhanced or decreased. To these units, these services are literally a form of 'overhead activity'. It is a matter of continued theoretical and practical debate how companies should deal with the costs of these services. There are arguments for and against allocating these costs to the decentralized business units.

Arguments for the allocation of costs of corporate services mainly focus on three benefits that such cost allocations may bring with them. First, cost allocations enable the calculation of accurate cost prices of goods and services produced in the decentralized unit. If we define costs as the total value that is consumed by producing a good or service, leaving corporate service cost outside the cost causes an under determination of the real cost of that good or service. Second, cost allocation may make decentralized unit managers aware of the existence of the service and may encourage them to use the service. If a corporate service, like marketing, may benefit the unit, its unit manager may be incentivized to involve corporate marketing, rather than hire a marketing firm (at extra cost). Third, allocating corporate service cost to decentralized firms creates a healthy tension between central and non-central managers. If these cost allocations become too high, and decentralized managers object, this provides a strong signal that some form of cost reduction may be necessary. This is important, since for some corporate services it is hard to establish the right activity level.

Arguments against the allocation of corporate service costs are mainly based on the argument of controllability. If decentralized managers cannot control the consumption of corporate services, or cannot affect the amount of costs allocated, then those allocated costs may be perceived as a sort of corporate tax that is not informative, or, worse, that feels like a punishment as it reduces bottom-line profit. Of course, this very much depends on the level of transparency about the kind of service whose costs are allocated, and the cost allocation method. Typically, cost allocation of corporate services can be done using rather rough, so-called *allocation bases.* These costs can be distributed over units based on financial parameters (turnover, cost level, profit level) or some other quantitative metric (number of employees). When these allocation bases are considered to be arbitrary by the decentralized manager, they are the source of disappointment and debate. Clearly, it pays to invest in finding relevant allocation bases, which try to connect certain corporate activities with an appropriate allocation key. Thus it makes more sense to allocate corporate HR costs using 'employees' as the basis rather than 'floorspace', but in many cases, finding the right basis is a matter of a detailed analysis, in line with principles of *activity-based costing.*

Note that despite the difficulties in deciding on whether or not to allocate costs from corporate services to decentralized units, tax authorities will scrutinize situations in which corporate taxes are reduced because of no, or too little, allocation. Thus, for tax purposes, some form of allocation is required if corporate and decentralized units operate in different tax jurisdictions.

## Corporate services and pricing

For other types of services, identification may be easier, and pricing them enables them to be treated in much the same way as discussed for the transfer of goods and services described earlier.

For these types of services, two types of transfer may exist:

1 For central services that the receiving unit must accept but can at least partially control the amount used (this relates to the controllability principle discussed in Chapter 4)
2 For central services that the business unit can decide whether or not to use.

## Control over amount of service

Business units may be required to use company staff for services such as information technology (IT) and research and development (R&D). In these situations, the business unit manager cannot control the *efficiency* with which these activities are performed but can control the *amount* of the service received. There are three schools of thought about such services.

The first holds that a business unit should pay the *standard variable cost* of the discretionary services. If it pays less than this, it will be motivated to use more of the service than is economically justified. On the other hand, if business unit managers are required to pay more than the variable cost, they might not elect to use certain services that senior management believes are worthwhile from the company's viewpoint. This possibility is most likely when senior management introduces a new service such as a new project analysis programme. The low price is analogous to the introductory price that companies sometimes use for new products.

A second school of thought advocates a price equal to the standard variable cost plus a fair share of the standard fixed costs – that is, the *full cost*. Proponents argue that if the business units do not believe the services are worth this amount, something is wrong with either the quality or the efficiency of the service unit. Full cost represents the company's long-run costs, and this is the amount that should be paid.

A third school advocates a price that is equivalent to the *market price*, or to the standard full cost plus a profit margin. The market price would be used if available (e.g., costs charged by a computer service bureau); if not, the price would be the full cost plus a return on investment. The rationale for this position is that the capital employed by service units should earn a return just as the capital employed by manufacturing units does. In addition, the business units would incur the investment if they provided their own service.

## Optional use of services

In some cases, management may decide that business units can choose whether to use central service units. Business units may procure the service from outside, develop their own capability or choose not to use the service at all. This type of arrangement is most often found for such activities as IT, internal consulting groups and maintenance work. These service centres are independent; they must stand on their own feet. If the internal services are not competitive with outside providers, the scope of their activity will be contracted or their services may be outsourced completely.

In this situation, business unit managers control both the *amount* and the *efficiency* of the central services. Under these conditions, these central groups are profit centres. Their transfer prices should be based on the same considerations as those governing other transfer prices. Obviously, the question whether or not to allow such external sourcing must be explicitly addressed. Not only may external sourcing damage economies of scale, but becoming dependent on external suppliers may have various drawbacks. For example, it may involve sharing sensitive (marketing) information, and may also lead to risk associated with the external supplier's reliability in terms of delivery, as well as engaging with a supplier which has an inferior market reputation.

## Simplicity of the price mechanism

The prices charged for corporate services will not accomplish their intended result unless the methods of calculating them are straightforward enough for business unit managers to understand them.

Computer experts are accustomed to dealing with complex equations, and the computer itself provides information on the use made of it on a second-by-second basis and at low cost. There is sometimes a tendency, therefore, to charge computer users on the basis of rules that are so complicated that a user cannot understand what the effect on costs would be if he or she decided to use the computer for a given application or, alternatively, to discontinue a current application. Such rules are counterproductive.

## Shared service centres

**Real World Example:** Credit Suisse provides companies, institutional clients and private clients worldwide with advisory services and products within the areas of private banking, investment banking and asset management. On its website, the company emphasizes the importance of its shared service centres for providing high-quality and cost-effective corporate services and business support for the bank's three divisions. Credit Suisse calls these centres 'Business Delivery Centres'. Credit Suisse operates shared service centres in India, the USA and Poland. One area embodies finance, operations and IT; another provides legal and compliance support to help protect the reputation of the bank; a third comprises human resources (HR), corporate communications, corporate branding and advertising.

*Source:* Credit Suisse Wroclaw. Available at: https://www.credit-suisse.com/microsites/careers-wroclaw/en.html (accessed 1 October 2019).

As highlighted in the Introduction to this chapter, one principal challenge in managing responsibility centres is how to avoid task redundancies at each profit centre because of, for instance, the additional management, staff personnel and record-keeping required in each unit. Many large companies have experienced a huge build-up of support service staff when they expanded their operations into new countries and regions. Business units in different countries often operated independently, with their own systems and processes for support services. Over time companies have come to realize that this may be an expensive and inefficient way of managing support activities. As a result, many companies have implemented *shared service centres* in which *a subset of 'non-core' business functions are concentrated into a new business unit*. Many public-sector organizations, such as municipalities, hospitals and universities, have also started to use this concept.

The introduction of a shared service centre is a strategic and long-term decision taken by top management. Support services, previously spread across a decentralized organization or performed in a centralized unit controlled by top management, are now structured into a separate unit – that is, the shared service centre, which provides support services to the company's various divisions, regions and business units. What is considered non-core naturally differs between organizations, but common areas for developing shared service centres are HR management, accounting/finance, legal advisory and IT. Often organizations start by turning repetitive transaction processing activities, such as accounts payable, accounts receivable or payroll, into a shared service centre.

**Real World Example:** Barclays Bank is a well-known user of shared service centres. When it implemented a shared service centre for HR, the bank reduced its company-wide costs related to HR by 50 per cent. Previously these support services were performed in its six operating divisions.

*Source:* Hogg, J. (2003) Getting the most from an HR shared service centre, *Strategic HR Review*, 2: 32–5.

According to their proponents, shared service centres are seen as an improved way of structuring and managing support services, and the intention is to capture the best aspects of both centralization and decentralization. The centres are argued to *generate the advantage of economies of scale (cost reduction) from centralization* as the bundling of the development, maintenance and use of services implies that the costs can be shared among the business units. The job of the shared service centre is to find the best way to perform the support activities, and the cost savings can then be passed on to each of the business units. The implementation of shared service centres has also been found to *improve clarity about strategic alignment* due to a simpler organizational communication structure. This enables the business units to concentrate on their respective strategic tasks. Business unit managers' time is freed up as non-core processes now are performed by shared service centres. In addition, *customer focus and quality (service improvement)* advantages from decentralization will be enhanced as the support activities are considered core by the shared service centre manager. This means that managers and employees can become experts in the specific area and really focus on achieving good customer service, quality of the services and transferring knowledge between business units. Finally, these centres enable employees to build up *specialized knowledge* in fields of management support that would be impossible, or simply too expensive, without the explicit definition of a centre. Given the increasing complexity of almost all areas of business support – be it HR, tax, financial reporting or legal – building expertise is vital. As an added benefit, the creation of such centres of support excellence will attract and keep professionals in these fields, by offering a rewarding and challenging working environment.

However, it is important to bear in mind that the concept of shared service centres has also received heavy criticism. Many shared service projects fail, or end up costing much more than originally planned. Since standardization is often a key feature in shared services, there is a risk that customer demand (with a need for variety) will suffer. Variations in, for instance, HR and IT, are difficult to force into standardized processes. As a result, customers' perception of the quality of the services may decrease. In addition, critics argue that the companies often implement shared service centres instead of investigating what can be gained from redesigning the existing service flow. These redesigns are argued to generate cost savings and increased quality of service, and to be much easier to implement than a shared service centre solution. Nevertheless, as mentioned above, shared service centres are increasingly being implemented in private- and public-sector organizations. Management control is a critical component in such implementations, and below we describe the management control considerations related to shared service centres. We will return to the challenges of running and controlling shared service centres in the last section of this chapter.

## Management control systems and shared service centres

*Shared service centres are not the same as centralized service units.* Head office concerns should not dominate. A shared service centre should be a relatively free and independent unit within the organization that ideally is located close to the internal customers. The service delivery should be negotiated between the unit and its internal customers (the various business units). The centres are intended to respond faster and to be more flexible to various needs from the internal units than centralized service units. Compared to outsourcing the support activities to an external party, shared service centres allow organizations to maintain control of the technical and organizational arrangements and expertise.

Shared service centres normally *operate as either an expense centre or a profit centre with full responsibility for financial performance and quality of services.* Historically, shared service centres were often expense centres, as the focus has been on cost reduction. However, the trend now is more business like shared service centres with profit responsibility centres to motivate the centre managers to find value-adding activities (see Chapter 4). Most shared service centres operate on a break-even basis, but some are encouraged to make profits. In either case, they are normally not given a fixed budget, but rather are *financed by the fees charged to the business units* for services. The fees provide an incentive for the shared service centre to know its internal customers' requirements and deliver services at a cost that the customers are willing to pay.

The service centre takes its strategic direction from top management, but more importantly forms close relationships with the business units it serves. Thus, from a management control perspective, the task of influencing shared service centre management to perform efficiently and effectively is largely delegated from top management to business unit managers. This is a major difference compared with a centralized service unit largely controlled by top management.

However, top management is still important in a number of dimensions. First, *what are considered core and non-core activities is often not easy to decide* and may even change over time with technological developments. Top management needs to carefully decide which activities are best suited to being turned into shared service centres. Second, top management needs to *explain and justify clearly why shared service centres are implemented* as they are often met with resistance. Employees working with these support activities at the various business units feel threatened and are afraid of losing their jobs. Top management should, for example, benchmark the cost of the organization's support services against those of other leading companies. They should also ensure that a steering committee is formed with line and staff representation from the various business units.

Third, top management needs to decide *if the business units should be permitted to purchase support services outside the company*, and *if the shared service centre should also be allowed to sell its services to outside customers*. These are two delicate and important questions. In practice, the answer to both questions is normally no – that is, business units need to use the support services provided by the shared service centre and the centre cannot have outside customers. One useful piece of advice is to use the services for some years and then decide whether outside competition is needed. If shared service centres cannot meet business units' needs in a satisfactory way, then the units may be permitted to purchase services outside the company.

One concern often raised if internal customers are not permitted to buy the services from outside is whether there will be sufficient incentives for the shared service centre to worry about performance. In practice, this is not often seen as a big problem. The shared service centre management is normally dedicated to creating good value for their internal customers, and the fact that there is always a risk of outsourcing the entire function to an external party normally provides enough incentive for the centre managers.

A key management control issue for shared service centres is *determining the level of service the business units are willing to pay for, and the price for the services*. A balance must be found between service quality (accessibility, responsiveness, timeliness, accuracy) and cost. The service centre must provide support services to the business units that will satisfy them. Services need to be broken down into specific deliverables that are formally stated in an internal contract called a *service level agreement*. This is a written contract where the type and scope of services are negotiated between the shared service centre and its internal customers – that is, the business units.

The service level agreement specifies what services will be provided at what cost, deadlines and quality standards, and it is important to ensure that both the shared service centre and the business units understand their respective responsibilities. Often top management becomes involved if there are disputes between the shared service centre and the business units over appropriate transfer prices. The service level agreement should also specify how the performance of the centre will be measured and evaluated. It is important to measure the performance of the shared service centre not only in

**FIGURE 5.1** Development of shared service centres

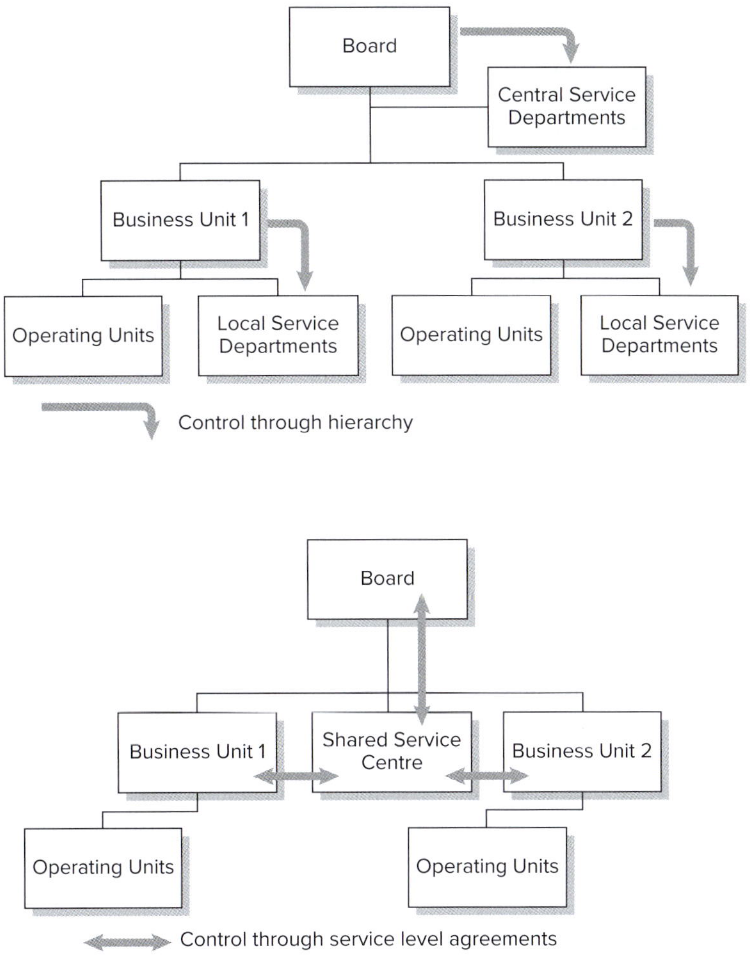


financial terms, but also to include *non-financial measures* such as internal customer satisfaction, productivity, response times, deadlines and quality. In the absence of an external market, the performance measures should be linked to benchmarking if possible, to challenge the shared service centre to improve continuously.

In sum, the development of shared service centres (see Figure 5.1) is motivated by management's desire to integrate units that provide corporate services to profit from economies of scope, to concentrate those services profiting from economies of scale, and to centralize the provision of these services so that they are controlled by contracts and service level agreements, rather than through a dispersed hierarchy. Notably, once shared service centres are formed successfully in this way, they may be candidates for outsourcing to become an independent, outside, service firm. However, whether outsourcing is a good step or not depends on the strategic criticality of the services provided. Controlling such outside service firms is further discussed in Chapter 7.

## Management control system challenges arising from interdependent responsibility centres

In this final section of this chapter, we will summarize the discussion on intra-firm delivery of goods and services by highlighting some management control system challenges arising from interdependent responsibility centres. We can understand these challenges better if we refer back to the various models of human behaviour that we discussed in Chapter 3. Below we will argue that when using the economic model of human behaviour, there is no way to completely ensure that responsibility centre managers work in the best interests of the organization. This means that the management control practices we have discussed in this chapter, which are mainly based on the economic model, need to be supplemented by those suggested by the psychological and sociological model of human behaviour.

### The agency problem revisited

Clearly, in the economic model of human behaviour, the 'splitting up' of a firm into different responsibility centres is a prime example of an agency relationship and immediately leads to the solutions that we have discussed in this chapter for how to govern internal transfers of goods and services. The agency theory model points us to the importance, and necessity, of formal contracts, between the top managers and the managers of responsibility centres on the one hand, and between managers of different responsibility centres for the transfer of goods and services on the other. Our discussion of the right way to establish transfer prices, and indeed of the right way to allocate corporate service costs, was informed by the importance of formal contracts, endorsed by the economic model. Even when we suggested that sometimes corporate costs are not allocated, this was justified by economic considerations. Sometimes, it just is not worth the administrative trouble to specify what unit has consumed what service. However, economic theory also points out that even with the best contracts, and the most extensive management control systems, the so-called agency problem cannot be completely solved (see the following Real World Example).

***Real World Example:*** In their best-selling book, *Freakonomics*, Steven Levitt and Stephen Dubner discuss the benefits (or lack of) of hiring a real estate agent to sell your house. Hiring an agent to perform some activity that benefits you is the almost perfect example of a relationship between a principal and agent that features in economic agency theory. In a way, your hiring an agent to work for you can be seen as you 'decentralizing' by delegating some work to another. Obviously, the big management control question would be: What should the contract between you and the real estate agent look like to make sure that the agent works in your favour, and that you are, so to speak, 'in control'? Levitt and Dubner argue that the typical system in which you pay a provision, for example of 6 per cent of the house price, provides some alignment between you and the agent. The better price you get for the house, the more the agent gets, and vice versa. However, when comparing the prices agents get for houses they sell for others, as agents, and when they sell their own houses, as owners, there is a remarkable difference. Real estate agents keep their own houses on the market an average of 10 days longer and settle for a selling price that is 3 per cent higher than comparable houses they sell for their clients ($10,000 for a $300,000 home). Levitt and Dubner suggest that the incentives may not be so aligned after all. Suppose that the 6 per cent commission is split between the seller's agent and the buyer's agent, and then the agent must also give half of the 3 per cent commission to the agency the agent works for. Then only 1.5 per cent of the commission remains as incentive. So, while getting this $10,000 more for you as owner is quite a bit, the agent's commission on this extra sum is only $150 for an extra 10 days of work. From this, you could draw the conclusion that an incentive contract that is aligned in design, may not solve all agency problems. Decentralization is costly (and should result in benefits that outweigh these costs).

*Source:* Levitt, S.D. and Dubner, S.J. (2009) *Freakonomics.* William Morrow Paperbacks.

## Managing the service level agreement

A similar and sometimes even more visible challenge occurs around the transfer of services, as many experiences with shared service centres show. In short, it is one thing to define and price corporate services, and create a systematic process of negotiating, signing and executing *service level agreements*, and quite another to make such agreements work as efficient management control practices. Many firms experience problems and frustration with many of the steps in the process of defining services, negotiating about service levels in terms of quantity and quality, setting prices and in dealing with deviations from the contract.

- *Level of specification of the agreement:* Shared service centre logic dictates that services are specified and priced in advance. But the nature of many services is such that such specification is problematic.
    - Services are sometimes needed on an ad hoc basis – for example, when a takeover opportunity in a business unit calls for the immediate attention of the tax department. How to arrange the availability for such immediate assistance?
    - Services are sometimes small and insignificant when taken individually, but when taken together amount to a great effort – for example, processing one application is not much work for a central HR department, but many such individual tasks may add up to a massive amount of work. Who can foresee what capacity is needed and who takes the risk of unused capacity?
    - Many services have important quality characteristics that are difficult to specify in advance – for example, asking the central legal department for advice on a complex business transaction is not simply a matter of asking to 'spend a certain amount of time' on figuring things out, but rather asking for 'sound advice'. However, it is hard to define what 'sound advice' really is, which means that disputes over qualitative aspects of arrangements are hard to avoid. How to make sure that services meet the quality standards of the consuming party?
- *Price setting:* Related to the complexity of specifying the full range of services that will be needed is the challenge to price these services. In fact, price setting for such services from the supplier side involves both determining the cost price of a service as well as a profit mark-up. Technically, these prices can be determined by applying appropriate cost accounting principles, but charging for services at full cost plus a profit mark-up may cause internal services to be expensive. In particular, when units are forced to use services provided by an internal shared service centres, this may cause dissatisfaction and stagnation of internal processes.
- *Dealing with deviations from the agreement:* As in all business transactions, it may occur that services are not provided in line with the contract according to the consuming unit. This may be the case if services are not delivered, are delivered late, or do not meet the agreed quality standards. Addressing such deviations is not easy, when the shared service centre is relatively autonomous, as is most often the case. Shared service centres are not vertically controlled as is the case of central service departments, which are managed by the board in a more or less direct sense. Shared service centre logic, however, entails that control is organized horizontally. Control by hierarchy and

authority is replaced by control through contracting and negotiation. However, since the contracts between business units and the shared service centre are internal contracts, they differ from contracts signed between independent market parties, and typical sanctions available to market parties are absent here.[6]

As we emphasized at the beginning of this section, organizational issues related to dealing with internal delivery and pricing of goods and services are traditionally discussed using the economic model of human behaviour. Here the focus lies on throughput and output controls. However, the principles of good management control system design offered by the other, psychological and sociological, perspective also have practical relevance. As to the latter, decisions about sourcing internally and externally may be affected by the perceived importance of belonging to the same company. Preferences for internal supply may be, rightly, driven by concerns about shared values and integrity. These are clearer from the psychological and sociological perspective, and emphasize that input controls have, and should have, an impact on these matters.

## Transfer prices and tax

It was mentioned in this chapter's opening Real World Vignette that tax compliance is a serious concern for multinational organizations. Such compliance is, first and foremost, a legal matter, as compliance is legally enforceable and lack of compliance may have serious negative financial consequences. However, tax compliance is also more and more becoming a prime matter of corporate social responsibility.[7] As we discussed in Chapter 2, the stakeholder model strongly endorses the payment of fair amounts of corporate tax. Overall, this provides a trilemma to top management concerning the adoption of transfer pricing models and techniques.

1 Top management may want to use the transfer pricing system that maximizes shareholder value by reducing immediate tax-related expenses. Reducing the overall tax burden is an acceptable goal to companies, and many countries are in fact trying to attract companies, and associated economic growth, via tax rates.
2 From a management control system perspective, top management should endorse transfer pricing systems that optimize managerial decision making. This has been the underlying principle in our discussion of transfer pricing techniques in this chapter. Obviously, good management control system design also benefits shareholder value creation, even if only in the longer run.
3 From a legal tax perspective, transfer pricing systems should adhere as much as possible to the 'arm's length principle'. And although companies can argue for their particular arrangements, since the 'arm's length' principle allows for some flexibility, the associated administrative and procedural burden to defend a certain transfer pricing system may force companies to settle for simple and tax-compliant systems that are suboptimal from a management control system perspective, as academic research has shown.[8] This makes transfer pricing techniques in their pure and optimal form often less applicable from a management control system perspective only.

---

6 Knol, A., Janssen, M. and Sol, H. (2014) A taxonomy of management challenges for developing shared services arrangements, *European Management Journal*, 32(1): 91–103.

7 Sikka, P. (2010) Smoke and mirrors: corporate social responsibility and tax avoidance, *Accounting Forum*, 34(3–4), September: 153–68. Taylor & Francis.

8 Cools, M. (2014) Transfer pricing: insights from the empirical accounting literature. In *Management Control and Uncertainty* (pp. 14–29). London: Palgrave Macmillan.

## Summary

From a management control system point of view, there are principal challenges in managing responsibility centres. This chapter has dealt with three such challenges, namely transfer pricing, corporate service pricing and shared service centres. Transfer pricing is about how to devise a satisfactory method of accounting for the transfer of goods and services from one profit centre to another in companies that have a significant number of these transactions. In complex organizations, devising a transfer price system that ensures the necessary knowledge and motivation for optimum decision making can be difficult. Two decisions are involved in designing a transfer price system. First is the sourcing decision: should the company produce the product inside the company or purchase it from an outside vendor? Second is the transfer price decision: at what price should the product be transferred between profit centres?

Ideally, the transfer price should approximate the normal outside market price, with adjustments for costs not incurred in internal transfers. Even when sourcing decisions are constrained, the market price is the best transfer price. If competitive prices are not available, transfer prices may be set on the basis of cost plus a profit, even though such transfer prices may be complex to calculate and the results less satisfactory than a market-based price. Cost-based transfer prices can be made at standard cost plus profit margin, or by the use of the two-step pricing system.

A method of negotiating transfer prices should be in place and there should be an arbitration mechanism for settling transfer price disputes, but these arrangements should not be so complicated that management devotes an undue amount of time to transfer pricing. There are probably few examples in complex organizations of completely satisfactory transfer price systems. As with many management control design choices, it is necessary to choose the best of several less than perfect courses of action. The important thing is to be aware of the areas of imperfection and to ensure that administrative procedures are employed to avoid sub-optimal decisions.

One new promising form of gaining efficiency in managing responsibility centres is the concept of shared service centres, in which a subset of 'non-core' business functions are concentrated into a new business unit. Common areas for developing shared service centres are HR management, accounting/finance, legal advisory and IT. Shared service centres generate the advantage of economies of scale (cost reduction) from centralization, and the advantage of customer focus and quality (service improvement) from decentralization.

A shared service centre is a relatively free and independent unit within the organization that normally operates as a profit centre, financed by the fees charged from the business units, and with full responsibility for financial performance and quality of services. The service centre takes its strategic direction from top management, but more importantly forms close relationships with the business units it serves. Top management needs to carefully decide which activities are best suited to being turned into shared service centres and explain clearly why shared service centres are implemented, as they are often met with resistance. Other important management control system considerations are whether the business units should be permitted to purchase support services outside the company, and if the shared service centre should be allowed to sell its services to outside customers too. The service centre and the business units need to find a balance between service quality (e.g., accessibility and timeliness) and cost. For this reason, service level agreements are an important control practice. It is also important to measure the performance of the shared service centres not only in financial terms, but to include also non-financial measures such as internal customer satisfaction and productivity.

## Suggested additional reading

Bergeron, B. (2003) *Essentials of Shared Services*. Hoboken, NJ: John Wiley & Sons, Inc.

Cools, M., Emmanuel, C. and Jorissen, A. (2008) Management control in the transfer pricing tax compliant multinational enterprise, *Accounting, Organizations and Society*, 33: 603–28.

Crow, S. and Sauls, E. (1994) Setting the right transfer price, *Management Accounting*, 76(6): 41–7.

Feinschreiber, R. (1998) *Transfer Pricing Handbook*. New York: John Wiley & Sons, Inc.

Henshall, J. and Donegan, R. (2019) *Global Transfer Pricing: Principles and Practice*. Bloomberg.

Hirshleifer, J. (1956) On the economics of transfer pricing, *Journal of Business*, 29(3): 172–84.

Kaplan, R.S. and Anderson, S.R. (2007) *Time-Driven Activity-Based Costing: A Simpler and More Powerful Path to Higher Profits*. Boston, MA: Harvard Business School Press.

Rugman, A.M. and Eden, L. (2017) *Multinationals and Transfer Pricing*. London: Routledge.

Schulz, V. and Brenner, W. (2010) Characteristics of shared service centers, *Transforming Government: People, Process and Policy*, 4(3): 210–19.

# Case 5.1
# SLA contracting: the big three shared services centres (SSCs)*

**by Ted Welten**

As firms look at avenues to improve their performance, one emerging way to cuts costs and streamline processes is the outsourcing of tasks to shared services centres (SSCs). These centres, often in countries with lower labour costs but adequate talent pools, perform operational tasks – like accounting, IT, payroll and human resources – utilized by multiple departments in organizations. This is also the case with the so-called 'Big Four' accounting and advisory firms. Let's take a look at three of them.

## SSC EY

EY's shared services centre (SSC) started its operations in 2002 in Thiruvananthapuram, India, in a highly professional and technology-centric environment. The centre has been successfully serving a multitude of industries through 19 EY Middle East offices in 15 countries.

The SSC is equipped with an excellent workplace setting and facilities that match international standards. The resources, knowledge and skills, along with world-class telecommunications network and easy connectivity around the globe, provide the right backdrop to effectively address challenging business objectives.

The highly skilled and experienced professional staff at the centre, comprising chartered accountants, business and management professionals and engineers, possess vast knowledge and expertise in a variety of areas. Their versatility and experience have enabled the centre to work successfully with clients from sectors ranging from banking and capital markets, oil and gas, real estate, insurance, media and entertainment to technology and telecommunications. The centre regularly follows various workforce development programmes, translating development into enhanced value, quality and client satisfaction.

The centre's quality management system meets high industry standards. This has enabled it to fully optimize its information security management and quality of work in line with the international code of practice for information security management (ISM). The centre manages client information and data in a highly secured environment, meeting all the security norms of ISM. Industry recognitions and certifications, such as SEI CMM L3, ISO 9001:2000, ITIL, PCMM and BS7799, stand testimony to the quality the centre has been delivering since its inception.

ASG and EY recently signed a service level agreement (SLA), formalizing their partnership on a number of international aviation consultancy projects. ASG has partnered with EY to provide industry-leading consultancy services to EY clients. Incorporated in Ireland in 2015, ASG's primary goal is to provide high-quality, cost-effective and responsive training, consultancy and services to the aerospace and defence sectors. The company boasts a wide range of professional aerospace expert consultants, each of whom has been carefully selected for their direct operational, oversight and regulatory experience, and insights from both public and private sectors, to deliver real value and an outstanding customer experience. ASG is also an approved Air Training Organization IE.ATO.012 of the European Aviation Safety Agency (EASA).

* This case was written by Assistant Professor Ted Welten, Erasmus University Rotterdam.

## SSC PwC

PwC has announced the opening of a shared delivery centre (SDC) in Lviv, Ukraine. The SDC plans to employ more than 350 staff members and will support PwC in the delivery of its audit, advisory and tax services. The Lviv location is the third shared services centre that PwC has established in the CEE region, including its shared delivery centre in Katowice, Poland, which employs 1,700 people and serves 50 countries in the firm's network.

Though there are already a number of shared service centres in the western Ukrainian city, the new PwC centre is, according to the firm, the first one to carry out high value-added professional services. 'Opening the Service Delivery Centre in Lviv is a key element of our development strategy, not just in Ukraine but across CEE,' said Richard Pollard, country managing partner of PwC Ukraine. 'The location was selected after thorough analysis. Lviv met all our expectations: access to highly educated local talent, convenient location, open business environment, significant opportunities for innovation, not to mention the growing role of Ukraine in the regional business community.'

Cross-border cooperation will be a large part of the centre's operations, helping Ukraine build stronger ties in the European and global business community. The centre will also help advance Ukraine's regional development goals, providing more than 350 professional jobs, excellent working conditions, and good educational and career opportunities for young talent.

## SSC Deloitte

Deloitte has opened its first and only European regional service centre in Romania.

Deloitte has been present in Romania since 1992. Over the ensuing 25 years, the firm has provided auditing, advisory, legal, financial consulting, risk management and tax services, as well as other related services to public and private industry clients in the region. The professional services giant presently employs 600 people in its three offices, in Bucharest, Cluj and Timisoara.

With the launch of its new European services centre, located in the northern part of the Romanian capital, Bucharest, the firm has already added 100 IT consultants to its staff, with more to come over the next three years.

Satya Swaroop Roddam, managing director of Deloitte's technology arm in Romania, said of the new office, 'The decision to open our technology centre in Bucharest shows a recognition of Romania's IT talents and of the local IT market's dynamics. I am confident that this regional service centre will become a global reference point and will offer IT talents in Romania the opportunity to develop their skills by engaging in major international projects.'

The European regional service centre in Bucharest joins the other three Deloitte technology centres in the world. These are found in Hyderabad (India), Belfast (Northern Ireland) and Orlando (USA).

## Discussion questions

1. Compare the SSCs of the three accounting firms and discuss the similarities and differences.
2. Discuss the dimensions that management has to decide, as discussed in this chapter, for all three SSCs in the case.
3. How is the quality of the services of the three SSCs guaranteed?
4. What are essential points that should be settled in the SLA? Do these differ in the three cases? Why? Why not?

## References

ASG (n.d.) ASG and EY sign service level agreement (SLA) to create a formalised partnership for a number of consultancy projects. Available at: https://www.asg.ie/latest-news/asg-and-ey-create-formal-partnership-for-consultancy-projects (accessed 7 May 2020).

Consultancy.eu (2017) Deloitte creates 700 jobs with European service centre in Romania, 4 May. Available at: https://www.consultancy.eu/news/36/deloitte-creates-700-jobs-with-european-service-centre-in-romania (accessed 7 May 2020).

Consultancy.eu (2018) PwC seeking 350 professionals for new shared delivery centre in Ukraine, 20 June. Available at: https://www.consultancy.eu/news/1206/pwc-seeking-350-professionals-for-new-shared-delivery-centre-in-ukraine (accessed 7 May 2020).

EY.com (n.d.) Homepage. Available at: https://www.ey.com/em/en/about-us/shared-services-center (accessed 7 May 2020).

# Case 5.2

# SLA control and reinforcement: Vodafone*

**by Ted Welten**

Vodafone Shared Services (VSS) creates value for Vodafone by optimizing quality and efficiency. It has matured over the past 10 years, delivering value to its partners and contributing significantly to the customer experience.

Established in 2006, VSS has evolved from being a single entity into a multi-functional and multi-location organization, which currently covers centres across Hungary, Egypt, India and Romania, with more than 20,000 professionals.

In recent years, VSS has transformed its approach from being a reliable service provider to becoming a strategic partner with a focus on value and business outcomes, and has become a key lever for Vodafone to drive cost saving programmes across group and local markets.

Vodafone is doing this by effectively enabling the Vodafone strategy and playing a key role in delivering cost optimization, innovation and higher levels of profitability.

## VSS vision

Lead the change for Vodafone as a strategic partner, to create a competitive edge and improve profitability.

This will be realized by utilizing the following value drivers.

## VSS value drivers

1 *Maximize cost arbitrage:* Continue to optimize footprint, increase VSS penetration and expand P&S portfolio.

2 *Enhance productivity:* Do it better and smarter through leveraging business excellence and automation technologies.

3 *Capitalize on knowledge:* Leverage VSS's diverse experience and telecommunications know-how to deliver innovative business solutions and services that identify new opportunities for Vodafone.

* This case was written by Assistant Professor Ted Welten, Erasmus University Rotterdam.

## Portfolio of services

Today, VSS own a wide portfolio of services, supporting Vodafone group and local markets. These cover various capabilities, including: finance, supply chain, customer operations, sales and marketing, product development and management, Legal, Fraud, Credit and Collection, HR, Technology, Networks and Business Intelligence.

## Some elaborations on the vision and value drivers of VSS

Vodafone's shared services centre, like many other SSCs, has arisen from the demand to improve the quality of services and reduce costs. Many SSCs start from the finance organization. Often parts of IT and HR follow, for example. Success is determined by a good relationship with the functional owners within the organization: think of the leaders of finance, HR or IT. The SSC must deliver what they need. The focus of SSCs has shifted in recent years. They not only provide more back-office functions, but the SSC is changing into a global business services organization that is increasingly adding value.

Naturally, every SSC knows the processes like no other over time. Digitization ensures that these processes run faster and more efficiently. The global business services organization has an enormous amount of data that can be used to improve business results.

It doesn't stop after you transfer processes from the organization to offshore locations. You have to keep innovating. In recent years, global business services have continuously focused on further optimization of processes and workflows. Now digitization is a dominant topic and much use is made of robotic process automation and artificial intelligence to further accelerate and optimize processes. That is why a good relationship with the IT organization is crucial. In society there are concerns about solutions such as robotic process automation, but the share of transactional work is decreasing, which makes the jobs of people within Vodafone teams more interesting, and means the creativity of people can be used more.

The transition into a global value organization is preceded by something, such as continuous management of service excellence and performance management. A good relationship with the company's executive committee is essential. Your customer is there. This customer mindset must be clearly anchored in all teams of the global business service organization. In addition, you should not fall into a role as a supplier, but always fully understand the challenges of the business. The business and the directors, in turn, must continue to trust the global business centre, without interfering too much with its internal organization.

A global business services organization should be run as a company within a company; only then can you continuously optimize. It must always be better and more cost efficient than in the original situation. That seems to be primarily a technology game, but you always need creative people who can make connections and devise applications to implement improvements.

An SSC will be more and more a sparring partner for the business. For example, the shared service centre of Vodafone is regularly asked to support operating companies, the country branches, in optimizing onshore processes and to help them with digitization. That is a result of all the expertise accumulated in our centres. It also helps that you have the confidence of the board. We are not the body that the strategy will come up with or implement, but we can provide input.

A global business services organization can focus more on developing assets that can be used throughout the organization and that add value. This can be achieved through an agile-based collaboration, where innovations are implemented through trial and error on a small scale and, when proven successful, applied in a larger part of the organization.

You often see that the retained organization tends to push the shared service centre in the supplier's corner. In some retained organizations that is still the state of affairs. But in many places the SSC is changing at a rapid pace: repetitive tasks are fully automated, more and more complex work is being added, such as market research, content creation, digital marketing. It is conceivable that a shared service centre will gradually become more intertwined with the business in the future; think of a scenario where it does not matter where you do the work. For some activities you will find the best talent in India and others closer to the business.

What remains is the distinction between core business strategy, direct sales and marketing, and support processes. Within a shared service centre you can think and experiment with the use of new technology such as chatbots, so that the costs of operations are reduced while the quality remains up to date, and often even increases. It is crucial that the board realizes that the SSC can no longer be based on the old concept of repetitive standard work and scaling up.

## Questions

1 Explain why Vodafone uses a shared service centre to implement its strategies and realize its goals.

2 Compare the SSC as discussed in this chapter with the structure and content of the Vodafone SSC. What are the similarities and differences?

3 In general, an SLA is formulated to ensure price and quality. Vodafone does not discuss the use of an SLA. How does Vodafone guarantee quality and price?

4 How are responsibilities and competences divided between the offshore SSC and the onshore businesses?

## References

Bouwer, E. (2018) Ellen van Essen (Vodafone) over het nieuwe shared service center, Mgmt. *Scope,* 1 November Available at: https://managementscope.nl/magazine/artikel/1185-ellen-van-essen-vodafone-shared-service-center (accessed 7 May 2020).

Vodafone (n.d.) Vodafone shared services. Available at: https://www.vodafone.com/what-we-do/services/vodafone-shared-services (accessed 7 May 2020).

# Case 5.3 Transfer pricing trouble at galeria glassworks *

**by Frank G.H. Hartmann**

'This is weird,' Nicolai exclaimed, after his telephone conversation with his colleague Orsolya Tóth in early 2019. As director of the Polish subsidiary branch of a European firm called KK (Klasyczny Kryształ) Spólka z.o.o., he had been concerned about the way headquarters was managing its subsidiaries. KK had been part of the Galeria group for seven years now. Nicolai was convinced that Galeria headquarters really would need to look into the ways the goods and services that Galeria group members supplied to one another were priced. 'If only these were invoices,' Nicolai told his local marketing manager Kamilla, 'then I could refuse to pay them or refuse their services. But what can I do now? I need to use the goods and services from within the group, so I am simply obliged to pay up.'

---

* This case was written by Professor Frank G.H. Hartmann, Radboud University.

## Galeria Glassworks

Galeria Glassworks had started as a local Spanish manufacturer of glasses and vases in 1928. Going through moderate growth for some decades, Spain's entrance to the European Union in 1980, and the further European unification in later decades, made Galeria a true European player. Galeria specialized in luxury glass and metal tableware, having been able to position itself in the top market segment. It would typically face competition from companies like Alessi, Hutschenreuther and Iittala. Growth had gone in jumps, in line with economic tides. With the extension of the union with Eastern European countries it became active in takeovers. Galeria had a good feel for the quality and potential of many national firms. Based on an explicit strategy of combining the quality and originality of local craftsmanship with the economies of scale of cooperation at the European level, Galeria had been able to grow into a group of five subsidiaries: in Spain, Poland, Slovakia, Hungary and the Czech Republic (Exhibit 1). Each of these subsidiaries contained a production unit and a wholesale office. Some had a small product development unit. They were each run like profit centres and bottom-line profit was an important yardstick for evaluating unit managers, as well as for Nicolai.

**EXHIBIT 1** Galeria's six subsidiaries

| Location | | Focus on | Tax rate |
|---|---|---|---|
| Czech Republic | KN (Kuchyňské Nádobí) SRO | Flatware<br>Serveware | 19% |
| Hungary | KE (Konyhai Elektronika) KFT | Flatware<br>Electronic ware | 9% |
| Poland | KK (Klasyczny Kryształ) Spólka z.o.o. | Drinkware<br>Serveware | 19% |
| Slovakia | KP (Kuchynský Porcelán) SA | Chinaware | 21% |
| Spain | GE (Galeria Espana) SRL | Dinnerware<br>Drinkware | 25% |

Typically, Galeria's total product portfolio was spread over the subsidiaries, such that each was responsible for the development and sales of a selected set of products, often a product family. Given the history, each local production unit was specialized in a limited number of such products and product families. However, Galeria encouraged the subsidiaries to come up with new products and product ideas, to face competition and provide full coverage of customer needs. Increasingly, this called for international cooperation between the subsidiaries.

## The issue

Nicolai Wi niewski had risen to this challenge. He and his team had developed a new series of tableware that would combine classical design with modern technology. It would feature a matching set of traditional objects on luxury dining tables (plates, cups, glasses and cutlery), with various electronic products in the kitchen (food processors, coffee machines, juicers and slow cookers). Nicolai had imagined that people often had open kitchens and that matching styles would be an interesting offer. He was considering quotes from three suppliers of food processors. KK needed to buy its central mechanical part, consisting of the motor, the rotating machinery and the metal tools from outside its own unit. It would then assemble this into a full machine. The quotes received from Galeria's own Hungarian KE, and two external suppliers are presented below. One external supplier was a Chinese company, known for excellent value for money. The other external supplier was from Germany, and known for high quality but had quoted a very attractive price. The offers (per 1,000 machines) are shown in Exhibit 2.

Nicolai had made a rather detailed budget for the new machine, and estimated that its sales price would be €180. Other components would cost €32,000 and further production (machine and labour) costs would be approximately €80,000, of which €20,000 should be considered variable. Based on this budget he reasoned that sourcing from China was his best option. However, when Orsolya, general director of the Hungarian branch KE, found out about Nicolai's intention, she grabbed the phone. She told Nicolai outright that she was very disappointed. She also showed him the note that her KE colleagues had made to prepare the offer to KK. She summarized to Nicolai that she estimated the standard manufacturing costs to be €66,000, of which €34,000 could be seen as variable. Also she informed that of this €34,000, she would have to source €17,400 worth from KN. KN would supply a major part of the metal tools that would be engineered by KE: 'That's what is so great about our company – we are full service, and can supply our needs internally.' Orsolya also suggested that Nicolai contact his colleague at KN to understand its costing and pricing structure. 'The more we keep inside, the better it is,' she argued. And Nicolai found out that the €17,400 worth sourced from KE to KN consisted of €13,930 full manufacturing costs, of which only €4,300 were variable. Orsolya also mentioned the corporate tax rate, which was lower in Hungary than Poland, 'such that it would be good for the company if I charge you high prices'.

**EXHIBIT 2** The suppliers' offers

| Supplier | Cost per 1,000 machines |
|---|---|
| KE | €90,000 |
| China | €76,000 |
| Germany | €56,000 |

Nicolai also found out that both KE and KN were very eager to pursue this deal. Probably they had some overcapacity, and Nicolai wondered whether he could negotiate a better price, or still go ahead with the China offer.

## Questions

1 What should Nicolai do?

2 What is the best decision for Galeria overall?

3 Analyse this problem, in terms of:
   - a The performance indicators used in Galeria
   - b The freedom individual subsidiaries have to source outside
   - c The role of headquarters in setting pricing policies.

4 Should headquarters interfere, when considering:
   - a The financial importance of this product
   - b The longer-term consequences
   - c The optimal responsibility centre structure of a firm like this
   - d The relevance of tax rate differences.

5 To what extent does your analysis depend on the strategic importance of the new initiative? To what extent does it hinge on the financial impact of the new transaction, both in the short run and the long run?

# Case 5.4

# North Country Auto, Inc.*

**by Mark C. Rooney**

George G. Liddy, part owner of North Country Auto, Inc., was feeling pretty good about the new control systems recently put in place for his five department managers (new and used car sales, service, body and parts departments). Exhibit 1 describes each department. Mr Liddy strongly believed in the concept of evaluating each department individually as a profit centre – but he also recognized the challenge of getting his managers to 'buy in' to the system by working together for the good of the dealership.

**EXHIBIT 1** North Country Auto, Inc. departmental structure

**New car sales and used car sales**

The new and used car sales departments each had a sales manager. They shared six salespeople. In addition, these departments shared an office manager and clerks. The managers were paid a flat salary, plus a fixed sum per new or used vehicle sold, and a percentage of their department's gross profit (calculated as sales minus cost of vehicles sold). When the owners and the managers agreed on annual unit volume and margin goals, the dollar weights were set to make each portion approximately one-third of the manager's expected total compensation. The owners claimed that this type of dual incentive bonus structure allowed the managers flexibility in targeting margins and volume. George Liddy maintained, 'If the margins are low, the sales manager can try to make it up in volume.' The sales force was paid strictly a commission on gross profit. Many dealerships in the area were changing sales compensation to a flat salary plus a partial commission on gross profits generated.

The new car sales manager was responsible for recommending to Liddy new model orders and inventory mix among the three product lines. He also had the authority to approve selling prices and trade-in allowances on customer transactions. Typically, the new car manager was allowed to transfer the trade-in at blue book. However, if the car was obviously of below average quality, the used car department was asked for its estimate of value. The used car manager was responsible for controlling the mix of used car inventory through buying and selling used vehicles at wholesale auto auctions.

**Service**

The service department occupied more than half of the building's usable square footage and was the most labour-intensive operation. Service comprised 11 bays with hydraulic lifts, one of which was used for the oil change operation. The department employed a manager, ten technicians, three semi-skilled mechanics, two counter clerks and three office clerks. The manager was paid a flat salary plus a bonus on the department's gross profit on labour hours billed (computed as labour dollars billed minus total wages of billable technicians and mechanics). Service revenue consisted of labour only. No mark-up for parts was realized by the service department. The bonus portion was planned to be approximately 50 per cent of the manager's salary. The technicians, mechanics and clerks were all paid a flat salary, regardless of actual hours billed. The technicians required speciality training to perform factory-authorized work on each of the specific lines. Sending a technician to school cost about $4,000 over a two-year period. The owners estimated that a new hire could cost as much as $10,000 in non-billable overruns on warranty jobs, where reimbursement was limited to standard allowable labour hours. Of the ten techs, four were certified for Ford, three for Saab and three for Volkswagen. George Liddy and Andrew Jones contemplated reducing the cost of idle time by cross-training, but were averse to risks of turnover among highly skilled labour. Retraining costs could triple when one person quit.

* This case was written by Mark C. Rooney (T'90), under the supervision of Professor Joseph Fisher. 

The primary sources of service department revenue were warranty maintenance and repair work, non-warranty maintenance and repair work, used car reconditioning, and the oil change operation. Warranty work was reimbursed by the factories at their prescribed labour rates, which were typically as much as 20 per cent lower than the rates charged directly for non-warranty work. Lower margins on warranty work were a potential problem for the dealership if it dissuaded the service manager from delivering prompt service to recent buyers. During times of near capacity utilization, the manager would be motivated to schedule higher-margin non-warranty jobs in place of warranty work.

**Parts**

The parts department consisted of a manager, three stock-keepers and two clerks. The parts manager was paid a flat salary plus a bonus on department gross profits (computed as total parts sold less cost of parts). The parts manager was responsible for tracking parts inventory for the three lines, and minimizing both carrying costs and 'obsolescence'. The owners defined obsolescence as a part in stock that was not sold in over a year. Mr Liddy estimated that as many as 25 per cent of the parts-on-hand fell into this category. Days supply of parts (inventory turnover) averaged 100 days for the industry. The manager had to be an expert on the return policies, stock requirements and secondary market of three distinct and unrelated lines of merchandise. It was the parts manager's job to use factory return credits most effectively and identify outside wholesale opportunities so as to minimize large write-downs. Local wholesalers would pay as much as 80 per cent of dealer cost for old parts.

Demand for parts was derived almost completely from other departments. Dollar sales volume in parts broke down as follows: 50 per cent through service, 30 per cent through the body shop, 10 per cent wholesale and 10 per cent over-the-counter retail. Similar to service work, parts needed in warranty work were reimbursed at rates as much as 20 per cent less than prices charged for non-warranty work.

**Body shop**

The body shop consisted of a manager, three technicians and a clerk. The manager, like the others, was paid a flat salary plus a bonus on departmental profitability. To keep the shop in business in the long run, North Country Auto needed to invest an additional $50,000 in new spray-painting equipment. As it was, the body shop was showing a loss after allocation of fixed overhead. Gross margins as high as 60 per cent could be attained, but rework and hidden damage beyond estimates tended to drive them down to closer to 40 per cent.

**Oil change operation**

The dealership's oil change business operated under the nationally franchised 'Qwik Change' logo, using one bay in the service department and one of the semi-skilled mechanics. Volume averaged 68 changes per week. The operation was not evaluated as an independent profit centre but as a means of filling unused capacity in the service department. The oil change franchise paid for all equipment, reducing the dealership's out-of-pocket investment to $500. After direct labour, direct parts and the franchise fee, the dealership made about $10.00 on each oil change priced at $21.95. The owners were willing to devote an extra bay to this operation if volume warranted.

## Background

North Country Auto, Inc. was a franchised dealer and factory-authorized service centre for Ford, Saab and Volkswagen. Multiple franchises were becoming more common in the 1980s. But the value of multiple franchises did not come without costs. Each of the three manufacturers used a different computerized system for tracking inventory and placing new orders. They also required their dealerships to maintain an adequate service facility with a crew of trained technicians that, in turn, necessitated carrying an inventory of parts to be used in repairs. Exhibit 2 gives balance sheet data with a breakout of investment for each product line.

The dealership was situated in an upstate New York town with a population of about 20,000. It served two nearby towns of about 4,000 people, as well as rural areas covering a 20-mile radius. North Country began operations in 1968, and in 1983 moved one mile down the road to its current 6-acre lot, 25,000 square-foot facility. It was owned as a corporation by George Liddy and Andrew Jones, who were both equally active in day-to-day operations. Mr Liddy purchased an interest in the dealership from a previous partner in 1988. Mr Jones had been part owner since the start of the business. Whereas Mr Liddy

**EXHIBIT 2** Balance sheet

| NORTH COUNTRY AUTO, INC. Balance sheet, 31 October 1989 (Dollar figures in 000s) | | | |
|---|---|---|---|
| **Assets** | | **Liabilities and equity** | |
| Cash | $ 32 | Accounts payable | $ 73 |
| Accounts receivable | 228 | Notes payable – vehicles | 1,294 |
| Saab inventory | 253 | Long-term debt | 344 |
| VW inventory | 243 | | |
| Ford inventory | 773 | Total liabilities | 1,711 |
| Used cars | 231 | | |
| Saab parts | 75 | | |
| VW parts | 75 | | |
| Ford parts | 226 | | |
| Body shop materials | 6 | Stockholders' equity | |
| Other current assets | 89 | Common stock | $ 400 |
| | | Retained earnings | 205 |
| Property & equipment | 85 | | |
| – net* | | | |
| ($377m gross) | | | |
| Total | $2,316 | Total | $2,316 |

* North Country leases both the land and the building.

focused his energies on new and used car sales, Mr Jones concentrated on managing the parts, service and body shop departments – commonly referred to as the 'back end' of a dealership.

The owners were determined to maintain a profitable back end as a hedge against depressed sales and lower margins in vehicles sales. In an industry characterized by aggressive discounting fuelled by a combination of high inventories, a more educated consumer and a proliferation of new entrants, alternative sources of cash flow were crucial. Industry analysts were estimating that fewer than 50 per cent of the dealers in the US would make a profit on new car sales in 1990. Overall net profit margins were expected to fall below 1 per cent of sales (*Wall Street Journal*, 11 December 1989).

## George Liddy's challenge

Before George Liddy bought into the dealership, all the departments operated as part of one business. Department managers were paid salaries, and a year-end bonus determined at the owners' discretion based on overall results for the year and a subjective appraisal of each manager.

George Liddy believed this system did not provide proper motivation for the managers. He believed in decentralized profit centres and performance-based compensation as superior models of control. He instructed each of his departmental managers (new, used, service, body and parts) to run his/her department as if it were an independent business. He knew that the success of the profit centre control system was dependent upon the support of his managers. They must understand the rationale for allocating costs to their departments and believe that they had reasonable control over profitability. The managers' bonuses in 1989 were calculated on the basis of departmental *gross* profits. Expenses below the gross profit line were not considered in the bonus calculation. They were told only, in a statement outlining their responsibilities, to exercise 'judicious control over discretionary expenses'. Implementing a more comprehensive control system tied to actual departmental net profits would require that Liddy break down costs traditionally regarded as general overhead into separate activities associated with specific departments. His strategy with the managers involved a gradual phasing in over the next few years of an 'almost' full-cost allocation system, where each department manager would eventually have responsibility for all controllable costs incurred in the department. Fixed expenses, such as interest expense, would be allocated by Liddy for his own decisions, but would not be used in the managers' bonus calculations.

The gradual changeover would allow Liddy, who was new to the dealership, time to become more knowledgeable about the intricacies of North Country Auto's accounting records. He did not want to lose credibility because of perceived arbitrary cost allocations. Exhibit 3 gives a breakdown of department profitability on an 'almost' full-cost basis.

**EXHIBIT 3** Financial statement

**NORTH COUNTRY AUTO, INC. Financial statement, 31 October 1989 (10 months) (Dollar figures in 000s)**

| | New | Used | Service | Body | Parts |
|---|---|---|---|---|---|
| Sales | $6,558 | $1,557 | $ 672 | $231 | $1,417 |
| Gross profit | 502 | 189 | 421 | 145 | 361 |
| Number of units (vehicles, repairs or parts) | 474 | 390 | 9,795 | 406 | 40,139 |
| Direct selling (commission & delivery) | $ 96 | $ 25 | n/a | n/a | n/a |
| Indirect labour | 162 | 74 | $ 237 | $ 64 | $ 156 |
| Department advertising | 91 | 30 | 19 | 2 | 3 |
| Policy work – parts & service (giveaways & rework) | 29 | 12 | 14 | 12 | 1 |
| Supplies & utilities | 22 | 18 | 19 | 28 | 12 |
| Depreciation | 3 | 1 | 15 | 5 | 2 |
| Rent | 89 | 22 | 67 | 13 | 9 |
| Profit before common expenses | $ 10 | $ 7 | $ 50 | $ 21 | $ 178 |
| Other expenses: | | | | | |
| Interest (on new inventory) | $ 110 | | | | |
| Other interest | 21 | | | | |
| Owners' salary | 65 | | | | |
| Insurance | 35 | | | | |
| Net operating profit | $ 35 | | | | |

**Notes to financial statement**

1. New car sales and gross margins (000s) break down as:

| | Sales | Gross profit | # units |
|---|---|---|---|
| Ford | $3,114 | $193 | 243 |
| Saab | 1,502 | 90 | 73 |
| VW | 1,794 | 117 | 158 |
| Financing fees* | 148 | 102 | n/a |
| | $6,558 | $502 | 474 |

2. Used car sales and margins break down as:

| | Sales | Gross profit | # units |
|---|---|---|---|
| Retail | $1,045 | $212 | 177 |
| Wholesale | 423 | (59) | 213 |
| Financing fees* | 89 | 36 | n/a |
| | $1,557 | $189 | 390 |

* Financing fees consist of income that the dealer earns on dealer-sourced auto loans. It also includes the dealer's commission on service contracts and extended warranties sold through the dealership.

3. Notes payable for vehicles is a revolving line of credit secured by new car inventory. Payments to the bank are due upon sale of each vehicle financed in inventory. This liability has been reduced over the past 10 months by approximately $1.5 million.
4. Indirect labour consists of department managers, clerks, book-keepers and work involving tasks directly related to the activities in a specific department. It does not include sales commissions or billable employees in the back end.
5. Departmental advertising is assigned to departments based on actual ads placed.
6. Policy work consists of dealer concessions made to customers arising from disputes over dealer-installed options on new vehicles, warranty coverage or cost of repairs. These costs are allocated to the departments in which they occur.
7. Depreciation is allocated by historical cost of leasehold improvements or equipment in each department.
8. Rent is allocated by square footage used by each department, adjusted for the value of the space.
9. Interest expense is treated as a common expense for the purpose of keeping investing and financing costs separate.
10. Insurance consists of both umbrella liability and property damage for the dealership as a whole. Because of the multiple types of coverage included, and the bundled pricing, it is not feasible to break out coverage costs by department.
11. Approximately 75 per cent of the fixed costs in the used car department related closely to retail vehicle sales and approximately 25 per cent to wholesale sales.
12. Total number of parts sold during the year = 40,139 parts; total number of service orders undertaken during the year = 9,795 orders.
13. Using the above financial statement, North Country determined the following allocations for overhead expenses:

| | |
|---|---|
| New: | $835/vehicle = $396,000/474 vehicles |
| Used: | $665/vehicle = $157,000 × 0.75/177 vehicles |
| Parts: | $32 = $183,000/40,139 parts = 4.55/part × 7 parts |
| Body: | (2 brake kits, 1 lock assembly, 4 tune-up parts) |
| Service: | $114 = $371,000/9,795 orders × 3 orders |
| | (lock, brakes, tune-up) |

In addition to finding a way to effectively track departmental performance, George Liddy had to devise a sensible system for transfer pricing. Though Mr Liddy believed that each department at North Country theoretically could operate as an independent business, he acknowledged that a complex inter-relationship existed among the profit centres in the course of normal business transactions. A recent new vehicle purchase illustrates the potential problems that could arise.

Alex Walker, manager of the new car sales department, sold a new car for $14,150. This purchase was financed by a cash down-payment of $2,000, a trade-in allowance of $4,800 and a bank loan of $7,350. The dealer's cost was $11,420, which included factory price plus sales commission.

The manager of the used car sales department, Amy Robbins, examined the trade-in vehicle. The trade-in had a wholesale guidebook value of $3,500. The guidebook, published monthly, was, at best, a near estimate of liquidation value. Actual values varied daily with the supply–demand balance at auto auctions. These variances could be as much as 25 per cent of the book value.

Ms Robbins believed that she could sell the trade-in quickly at $5,000 and earn a good margin, so she chose to carry it in inventory instead of wholesaling it for a value estimated to be $3,500. Mr Walker, in turn, used the $3,500 value in calculating his actual profit on the new car sale.

In performing the routine maintenance check on the trade-in, the service department reported that the front wheels would need new brake pads and rotors, and that the rear door lock assembly was jammed. The retail estimates for repair would be $300 for the brakes ($125 in parts, $175 in labour) and $75 to fix the lock assembly ($30 in parts, $45 in labour). Cleaning and touch-up (performed by the service department as a part of the service order for lock and brake) would cost $75. The service department also recommended that a full tune-up be performed for a retail price of $255 ($80 in parts, $175 in labour).

The repair and tune-up work was completed and capitalized at retail cost into used car inventory at $705. These mechanical repairs would not necessarily increase wholesale value if the car subsequently were sold at the auction. The transfer price for internal work recently had changed from cost to full retail equivalent. The retail mark-up for labour was 3.5 times the direct hourly rate and about 1.4 times for parts.

George Liddy was concerned that the retail transfer price of the repairs in conjunction with his plan to eventually allocate full costs to each department (as illustrated in Exhibit 3) might encourage the used car sales manager to avoid the possibility of losses in her department by wholesaling trade-in cars that could be resold at a profit for the dealership. This might also hurt the dealership by making its deals less attractive for new car customers.

Knowing how important it was to maintain credibility with each of the departments, Liddy called a meeting with the three department managers. He decided to use the recently completed new car sale to illustrate the effect this transaction would have on departments' profits. In his presentation, Mr Liddy laid out the transaction and allocation of profits and costs. After this presentation, Mr Liddy asked for the reactions of his department managers.

Alex Walker was the first to chime in, 'I understand that the allowance above book value on the trade-in cannot be accounted for as profit. However, the real issue is how to set the price between me and Amy when we transfer the trade-in. I refuse to be responsible for any loss that might arise if the trade-in vehicle is liquidated at auction for an amount less than the wholesale guidebook value. Her department should be accountable for its valuation errors.'

Amy Robbins vehemently disagreed. 'My department should not have to subsidize the profits of the new car sales division.'

Liddy quickly jumped into this deteriorating argument, 'Obviously, we need to carefully consider how to set the price between the new and used car departments and who should be responsible for unexpected losses.'

'Another item that concerns me,' Robbins went on, 'is using full retail price for parts and labour used in the repairs of trade-ins. Given under-utilized capacity in service, I do not understand why I am charged full price. It doesn't make sense for the service department to mark up on projects undertaken for new and used car departments within our own dealership. I can't see how we can make profits when one part of our company sells to another.'

Robbins added, 'When I am unsure of the actual retail value, I tend to wholesale rather than take a risk of a negative margin at retail. However, when I do this, we may be losing as an organization as a whole.'

'I agree with Amy on this,' stated Walker, 'and I have the same problem with dealer-installed options. When I am charged full price for options, I have no incentive to try to sell these items.'

'Hold on,' said the service department manager. 'I make my profit by selling service, and these are the prices I would charge for outside work. To sell service for a lower price inside defeats the purpose of this profit centre idea. But I do have a problem with getting full price for parts. The demand for parts is derived almost completely from service, and we are dependent on parts for quick delivery for repairs.'

Liddy jumped back in: 'Obviously, we are dependent on each other for quality and prompt service. We need to make sure that, as each of you maximizes profits in your departments, you do not negatively affect other departments.'

Liddy continued, 'I am also concerned about the impact of capitalizing trade-in repairs rather than expensing immediately. We all know that wholesale values drop with each publication of the new guidebook. I am afraid that, when a car is slow to sell, we might be reluctant to sell the car at a loss, even though we should. Car inventory ties up cash, and a key measure of departmental success is our inventory turnover [average industry inventory turnover was 75 days for new cars and 45 days for used cars]. In conclusion, while I think the profit centre concept makes good sense for this business, I am concerned about the frictions that are taking place between the departments.'

## Questions

1. Using the data in the transaction, compute the profitability of this one transaction to the new, used, parts and service departments. Assume a sales commission of $250 for the trade-in on a selling price of $5,000. (Note: Use the following allocations [new, $835; used, $665; parts, $32; service, $114] for overhead expenses while computing the profitability of this one transaction. These overhead allocations are also shown as Note 13 in Exhibit 3.)
2. How should the transfer-pricing system operate for each department (market price, full retail, full cost, variable cost)?
3. If it were found one week later that the trade-in could be wholesaled for only $3,000, which manager should take the loss?
4. North Country incurred a year-to-date loss of about $59,000 *before* allocation of fixed costs on the wholesaling of used cars (see Note 2 in Exhibit 3). Wholesaling of used cars is theoretically supposed to be a break-even operation. Where do you think the problem lies?
5. Should profit centres be evaluated on gross profit or 'full cost' profit?
6. What advice do you have for the owners?

# Case 5.5

# Transfer pricing in international firms: interaction of control and tax*

by Ted Welten

## Part 1: The Unilever transfer pricing dispute

The Kenya Revenue Authority (KRA) discovered in 2003 that Unilever was selling its Nairobi (Kenya)-produced Omo washing powder and Close-Up toothpaste at higher prices in Kenya than in Uganda.

The Income Tax Department ruled against the multinational in September 2003 for diverting part of its profits to its Ugandan subsidiary, resulting in lower taxes for Kenya. Unilever Kenya Ltd appealed against this KRA decision in 2003 by going to the High Court.

Both Unilever Kenya and Unilever Uganda had signed a contract in 1995 in which it was agreed that Unilever Kenya committed to produce on behalf of Unilever Uganda and deliver to it products according to the contract. This was the case during 1995 and 1996.

According to the KRA, Unilever Kenya charged lower prices to Unilever Uganda than it charged its domestic buyers and importers not related to Unilever Kenya.

For the years 1995 and 1996 the KRA concluded that sales made by Unilever Kenya to Unilever Uganda were not at what are called 'arm's length' prices – which means that any transaction between two entities of the same firm should be priced as if the transaction were conducted between two unrelated parties. It appeared that Unilever Kenya charged lower prices to Unilever Uganda compared to the domestic buyers of Kenya and importers that were independent from Unilever Kenya.

The KRA noted that the prices of Unilever Uganda (which had exclusive marketing rights) were approximately 25 per cent lower than those offered to the independent third parties in Kenya who exported to Tanzania, and Unilever was therefore violating the arm's length principle, because prices between related parties must be the same as if those parties were not related.

### *Kenya Income Tax Act*

Two articles in the Kenya Income Tax Act are relevant in this context.

Section 18(3):

> *Where a non-resident person carries on business with a related resident person and the course of that business is so arranged that it produces to the resident person either no profits or less than the ordinary profits which might be expected to accrue from that business, if there had been no such relationship, then the gains or profits of that resident person from that business shall be deemed to be the amount that might have been expected to accrue if the course of that business had been conducted by independent persons dealing at arm's length.*

Section 18(6) implies that the two companies were related due to the fact that Unilever plc participated directly and/or indirectly in the management, control or capital of the business of the two subsidiaries.

---

* This case was written by Assistant Professor Ted Welten, Erasmus University Rotterdam.

The KRA examined sales accounts and invoices and found major differences in prices offered to related parties against local customers and independent (third-party) exporters of the same commodities to the Tanzanian market.

But the KRA faced a two-sided obstacle. First there were few people on the KRA staff who were familiar with these transactions. Second, there was inadequate regulatory framework in place to deal with transfer pricing.

The Kenyan High Court ruled in 2005 in favour of Unilever, with the argument that there was no Kenyan transfer pricing legislation and therefore Unilever, as a major manufacturer and distributor of popular, fast-moving consumer goods like Omo, was right to apply internationally recognized principles in setting its transfer pricing policy.

### The reaction of the KRA

Because the KRA lost the case, it had to rethink how to approach similar cases and was forced to suspend audits of other companies. The result was a lot of regulatory changes to restrain firms that were not committing to their tax obligations.

The KRA developed national rules on transfer pricing in the 2006/7 financial year as a self-evaluation tool to be used by companies going forward. Before this was implemented, the KRA had to drop a similar case against Sara Lee.

The KRA formed a transfer pricing team in 2008 to deal with transfer pricing audits, and resumed these audits in 2009. It admitted that it struggled with this, even though Kenya has been among the most aggressive cases.

## Part 2: OECD Task Force on Tax and Development work on transfer pricing

The Organisation for Economic Co-operation and Development (OECD) had the following two reasons for creating the task force:

1. To reduce the risk of tax base erosion and profit shifting (BEPS) for developing countries because, due to globalization, they are more often trading and investing across borders
2. Because most developing countries have no or limited fully effective transfer pricing regimes in place to deal with risks arising from BEPS, these countries encounter serious tax revenue 'losses' as a consequence.

The task force developed a successful transfer pricing assistance programme in 2011 for developing countries, in cooperation with the European Commission and the World Bank Group.

### The importance of transfer pricing for developing countries

With reference to point 1 above, multinational enterprises (MNEs) are responsible for two-thirds of all cross-border transactions that are conducted within companies of one group. It is obvious that such cross-border trade and investment is essential to economic development. On the other hand, developing countries must be able to collect profit taxes from the activities from these MNEs without discouraging or disturbing international trade and investment.

A transfer price is an internal selling price that a member or business unit of the MNE charges to another member or business unit of the same MNE. This is relevant when members of the same MNE conduct transactions with one another (e.g., purchases of inputs, transfers of assets). These transactions are registered in their accounts and are the basis for the calculation of their taxable profits. Therefore, the transfer prices that are used by different entities of an MNE directly influence the profit and thus the tax they pay in each country in which they operate. To illustrate, let's look at a transfer pricing example of three companies of the same MNE, which operate in three different countries.

**EXHIBIT 1** Example of a transfer pricing transaction between companies belonging to same MNE and operating in three different jurisdictions

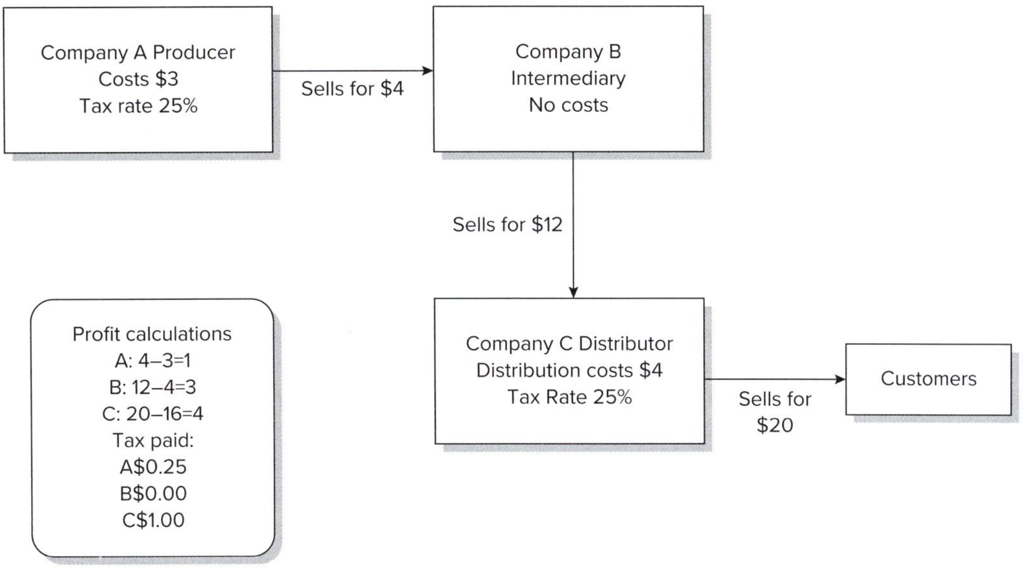


Exhibit 1 shows producer A, intermediary B and distributor C. Company B buys goods from company A for $8 and sells them to company C for $24. Company B generates a significant amount of profit without any economic activity and without incurring costs. Besides this, company B is located in a no-tax country and thus does not pay any taxes on its profit.

This example raises the question of whether a transfer price has been set between companies A, B and C according to the ' arm's length' principle . If this is not the case, the countries where producer A and distributor C are located miss significant potential revenues and therefore taxes.

## Two sides of the same coin

On the one hand, transfer pricing is a normal business feature of transactions between different responsibility centres of the same organization, both national and international. It is part of doing business. On the other hand, there is the phenomenon of artificial profit shifting, and companies use the transfer price system as a means to reduce their global tax bill by shifting profit to low tax-rate countries. Exhibit 1 illustrates this. This concerns both developing and developed countries alike.

Profit shifting has two consequences. First, when profit is transferred to another country it denies the country of origin its essential tax revenues. Second, and even more severe, it shows a kind of 'tone at the top' problem. If well-known companies avoid paying taxes, why should other companies and citizens not do the same? The tax system may be considered unfair, and there is the risk that it may be considered illegitimate and incredible, and consequently that people will no longer obey tax laws.

An important element of developing standards and guidance on transfer pricing for developing countries is the feedback from these countries into the standard-setting process of the OECD and treating this feedback seriously. In this way, developing countries are permitted by the OECD to have a say on the BEPS.

The OECD has been asked by its member countries, non-members and the G20 to take the initiative on BEPS and advise on an international tax system to address the challenges of tax revenues, tax sovereignty and tax fairness. Transfer pricing regulation within tax legislation has been introduced by most OECD and many non-OECD countries. They want to make sure that reported MNE profits in their own country are in line with internationally accepted principles and that they have the possibility to deal with any inappropriate or abusive transfer pricing by MNEs. The transfer pricing rules that have been adopted are in line with the 'arm's length' principle. However, there are relatively few developing countries that have implemented fully effective transfer pricing regimes. Most developing countries that have some kind of legislation do not have the administrative, technical and auditing capacity to conduct effective and efficient audits.

### The transfer pricing programme of the Task Force on Tax and Development

To deal with the latter, the OECD's Task Force on Tax and Development began a programme in 2011 to support developing countries to implement or strengthen their transfer pricing rules. The countries were given assistance to implement measures to protect their tax bases, and to create certainty and consistency for companies by defining rules that stimulate a transparent and predictable investment climate.

These OECD support initiatives have been put in place in Botswana, Cambodia, Colombia, Ethiopia, Ghana, Jamaica, Kenya, Malawi, Morocco, Peru, Rwanda, Sri Lanka, Tunisia, Vietnam, Zambia and Zimbabwe. A regional project is under way in the Economic Community of West African States (ECOWAS) region (including Nigeria and Senegal).

The OECD, European Commission and World Bank Group have been working together on different projects to make sure that support is coherent and coordinated. Other partners, such as GIZ, SECO and the tax administrations/ministries of finance of developed countries, are also involved in the OECD project. The result is that support has been created for wider financial governance reform and country-specific approaches.

### Transfer pricing programmes: results to date

There have already been visible results in all of the countries where the programme has been operating.

#### *A few examples*

In Colombia, transfer pricing adjustments were realized due to audits of multinational enterprises, and this resulted in increased revenues: from US$3.3 million in 2011 to over US$33 million in 2014. The Tax and Development programme contributed by means of practical advice. Colombia also improved its transfer pricing legislation, which is in line with international standards. The programme provided input and advice to Colombia on the drafting of the new legislation. Colombia is strengthening its advance pricing agreement (APA) programme to create a more certain and transparent investment climate, and the programme is assisting with that.

In Kenya, in 2012, the tax administration initiated a significant training programme for its staff on advanced transfer pricing topics. The Tax and Development programme supported the development and delivery of this training programme, which is aligned with Kenya's needs and auditors' level of knowledge. The result was that the Kenyan Revenue Authority (KRA) realized an increase in the number of audit cases completed and in revenue collected, while the number of cases going to dispute resolution also rose. Revenue collection from transfer pricing audits has risen from US$ 52 million for 2012 to US$ 107 million for 2014. In addition, the KRA introduced an APA programme, which realized a more certain and transparent investment climate.

In Vietnam similar results were achieved: an increase in the number of audits conducted by the tax administration from one in 2012 to 40 in 2013. This led to transfer pricing adjustments of US$ 110 million by the end of 2013. In 2014, Vietnam's tax administration realized more than 100 audits, which resulted in revenue collection of US$ 40 million. The programme also supported the Vietnamese government with organizational changes in the tax administration and legislation, APAs, safe harbours and thin capitalization.

Zambia improved its transfer pricing legislation, and new regulations and transfer pricing documentation rules will be introduced in the near future. Revenue from audits increased from US$ 3.22 million in 2012 to US$ 7.91 million in 2013.

Botswana, Jamaica, Sri Lanka and Zimbabwe are starting the process of revising transfer pricing legislation and regulations that conform to international standards.

### Next steps

The results discussed above show that progress is possible and there is also a growing demand for these types of programme.

One of the longest-lasting bodies is the Tax Inspectors Without Borders (TIWB) initiative to consolidate the impact of the programmes. TIWB is a joint initiative of the OECD and the United Nations Development Programme (UNDP) supporting countries in building tax audit capacity. These experts also advise around the world about transfer pricing issues.

For example, in Ghana, transfer pricing specialists from the Netherlands tax administration were deployed on behalf of TIWB and are working alongside tax administration auditors to increase their knowledge, experience and abilities. The same goes for Albania, Malawi, Rwanda, Lesotho and Senegal. These countries also benefit from TIWB deployments from the United Kingdom, Italy and France.

## Questions

1 Explain the 'arm's length' principle.

2 Explain why Kenya was denied taxes according to the Income Tax Department.

3 Apparently, Unilever was acting within the law when it decided not to follow the 'arm's length' principle. Explain this.

4 Was Unilever acting ethically by violating the 'arm's length' principle?

5 Discuss the OECD Task Force's part in realizing the implementation of the arm's length principle in Kenya.

6 Can international transfer pricing be controlled by the management control instruments of a firm?

### References

Nyabiage, J. (2012) Court case changed KRA's view on transfer pricing, africog.org, 4 September. Available at: https://africog.org/court-case-changed-kra-s-view-on-transfer-pricing-by-jevans-nyabiage/ (accessed 7 May 2020).

OECD (n.d.) Developing capacity in BEPS and transfer pricing. Available at: https://www.oecd.org/ctp/tax-global/developing-capacity-in-beps-and-transfer-pricing.pdf (accessed 7 May 2020).

# Chapter 6

# Organizational structure and cross-functional integration

## Learning objectives

After reading this chapter, you should be able to:

1. Explain the concepts of differentiation and integration, and how they relate to each other.
2. Discuss the pros and cons of different organizational structures.
3. Describe the basic principles behind lean management.
4. Explain what a project is and describe the major phases in project management.
5. Describe the difference between waterfall planning and agile management of projects.

## Real world vignette: The Czech restaurant

Back in 1989 an important event occurred: the so-called Iron Curtain that separated Eastern Europe from Western Europe, socialism from capitalism, dictatorship from democracy, came down. This meant that people, even from the same families, who had been separated from one another for decades, could meet again. But it also meant that tourists from the West could easily visit countries formerly behind the Iron Curtain.

Czechoslovakia, which we will concentrate on here, abolished visa requirements for tourists from 1 August 1990. This meant that the country was not ready for all the tourists that suddenly flooded in, and it became a problem. For example, when people got hungry and wanted to have a meal there were basically only two types of restaurant in the centre of Prague at the time: small cosy ones that were fully booked for the next two weeks, and larger, less cosy restaurants that could take many more guests. Many tourists had no choice but to go to the latter kind of restaurant, where the procedure was always the same. The following story is based on the author's personal experience.

First, we had to wait a long time for a waiter to take us to a table. We could see that there were plenty of empty tables, but we were not allowed to sit down until the waiter showed us to the table. Often the lines with customers waiting for a table went well out into the street. Finally, the waiter showed us to a table and when the waiter did that, we tried to order beers, because it was very hot and we were thirsty. But we did not get any beer from the waiter. Instead, another person came up and asked us what we wanted to drink. We ordered two beers and they were swiftly delivered to us.

Then, after a while, another person came along and asked us what we wanted to eat. Basically, we had three or four standard menus to choose from. We had to stick to one of these for the entire meal, so could not for instance choose the entrée from one menu, main course from another and dessert from a third. We ordered one of the menus and eventually got our food. After a while we had finished our beers and wanted new ones. So, we tried to order more beer from the person who delivered the main course. Needless to say, we did not get any beer – not until we had the brilliant idea to order our beers from the person that had brought us the first ones.

The dinner went on and when we tried to order coffee from the person bringing the dessert, we of course did not get any. Obviously, we had to order that from the person we had ordered the beer from! Finally, we wanted to pay and asked first one of the persons, then the other, for the bill. However, we did not get a bill until we asked the waiter who had showed us to the table . . .

## Introduction

It would be easy to explain the level of customer service in our Czech restaurant example in terms of the lack of competition in a socialist plan economy. And that is probably a valid explanation, not least when it comes to restaurants – a visit to a restaurant in Prague today is a very different experience. But it does illustrate a very common problem in many organizations, namely lack of integration. Let us have a look at a modern illustration of this in the Real World Example . . .

***Real World Example:*** A customer in one of the major banks in the Nordic countries wanted to buy a new car. To finance it, he wanted to increase the loan on his house. So, the customer did what he always did in a situation like this – he phoned his personal bank clerk. However, the customer did not know that the bank had made some changes concerning customer contacts. The changes included increased digitalization and a change from a personal bank clerk to a whole team that served the customer, depending on what matter the customer wanted help with. Some matters were not even handled by the team any more, but by a completely different department.

Anyway, due to these changes, the customer could not talk to his personal bank clerk but was now directed to customer service instead. However, customer service could not help the customer with this particular matter and said that they would ask one of the personal bank clerks to call him back. Later a personal bank clerk phoned the customer. However, the personal bank clerk regrettably informed the customer that they could not increase the loan on the house, and therefore recommended a private loan instead. But, unfortunately, the personal bank clerk no longer handled private loans and had to direct the customer to call customer service instead. The customer called customer service to apply for a private loan . . .

The root of the lacking customer service in these two examples is probably as old as organizations. It is called 'division of labour' and was thoroughly described as early as 1776 by Adam Smith on the very first page of his famous book *The Wealth of Nations*. The division of labour is usually described as something positive, since it is a way to increase productivity. In the example given by Adam Smith, the process of making pins is broken down into 18 separate tasks performed by different workers, that way making productivity 50 times higher than when one person performed the whole process. The problem, though, is that when the process is broken down people will not get an overview of the whole process and they may not even know how the way they perform their task influences other people working further along in the process, including what problems they may cause.

Integration problems may occur inside one department due to the division of labour (as discussed in detail later, under lean management), but are probably even more common between responsibility centres (as discussed in Chapter 4, and further elaborated on below, in the section on organizational structure). So, even if the division into responsibility centres has a number of advantages (for instance, when it comes to the controllability principle, see Chapter 4), it also often creates integration problems between the responsibility centres, and these problems may cost organizations huge amounts of money, as Case 6.2 illustrates. In short, the responsibility centre structure referred to in Chapter 4 risks creating too much of a 'silo' mentality in an organization.

As we have seen in the examples already described, a lack of integration may be very frustrating for customers, because they are not only interested in the food and the drinks or getting loans. They are interested in the whole customer experience and getting prompt service. They do not want to have to speak to several people before they finally get the service they are after.

Another way of putting this is to say that every organization has two basic needs, namely *differentiation* and *integration.*[1] Differentiation in this context refers to the need for special competence in different areas, and has been thoroughly discussed in Chapter 4 in relation to the four standard types of responsibility centres. An organization may for instance need competence in management, technology, manufacturing, sales, IT, HR and finance. Integration refers to the need for people with different competencies to cooperate towards some kind of common goal or purpose.

***Real World Example:*** Imagine a football team. What does it need? The first thing we think of is probably good players; players that can score goals. But it not only needs players who can score goals, it also needs a good goalkeeper, good defence players, players who assists the one who scores, and so forth. Every good football team needs players with different skills, since a team that consists only of players who are good at scoring and not much else is not likely to win many games.

However, it is not enough to have good players, even if you have players that are good at more or less every important skill in football. The players also need to function together as a team, which is harder to achieve the bigger the egos in the team. A football team may have the best players in the world, but if they cannot play together they may still lose to a team that is really well integrated. Likewise, a very well-integrated team may well beat a team with much better players (see Case 6.1 for more examples).

All organizations need both differentiation and integration, but in some organizations differentiation is more important and in others integration is more important. In some organizations both needs are very important, and that may pose a bit of challenge. This is because the higher the differentiation, the harder it is to achieve integration.

Let us say that we have lots of highly skilled employees from two very different specialities (or responsibility centres); this could be engineers and sales people, doctors and nurses, or programmers and consultants. It is harder to integrate these two groups compared to less skilled employees from two groups that are more similar to each other. The reason for this is that highly skilled and educated people are more influenced by what they have studied, compared to people with lower levels of education. This means that they tend to reason in a certain way, and even talk in a certain way, which often makes it difficult for different professions to communicate very well. Just as in the football example, we may also have an 'ego' problem with highly skilled professionals, which makes the problem even more severe.

[1] Lawrence, P.R. and Lorsch, J.W. (1967) *Organization and Environment: Managing Differentiation and Integration.* Boston, MA: Harvard University.

Still, many successful organizations are very good at both differentiation and integration. However, the way the management control system is designed in organizations means that it often tends to favour differentiation (that is, a 'silo'-based structure with different responsibility centres) rather than integration because of its mainly vertical character, as illustrated in Case 6.2.

Imagine a manufacturing department that is an engineered expense centre (as discussed in Chapter 4). The most important performance measures of the department are volume produced and cost in relation to that figure, because the unit manager believes that these are the most important performance criteria for the unit. In fact the unit manager is even thinking of moving the expense centre to a low-cost country far away, in order to lower the costs even more.

However, if we look at this from an integration perspective we might see it quite differently. Then other aspects, such as product quality and ability to deliver quickly, may be more important than volume and costs. Because if we see it from the sales unit's perspective, volumes are less important unless it can get the right product at the right time – what the customers want, when they want it. Costs are also less important if customers are dissatisfied with quality. And, from the quality and fast delivery perspectives, it might actually be a disaster to move the department to a low-cost country from where it will take weeks just to ship the products.

So, whether volumes and costs or quality and fast deliveries will be the dominating performance measures in the management control system will have a big impact on the integration in the company. Volumes and costs are typical measures of a traditional, more financially oriented, management control system, whereas quality and fast deliveries may be important measures in, say, a balanced scorecard as discussed in Chapter 9.

As a first step to dive deeper into these matters we need to take a closer look at how organizations can be structured. These choices when it comes to throughput control have important implications for the other control practices that are part of the organization's management control system. These implications can be understood in terms of the tension between differentiation and integration. We will then discuss lean management, which is a management model with the major purpose to strengthen integration by prioritizing flow efficiency over resource efficiency. Finally, we are going to take a look at projects, which can be seen as a structural solution that temporarily integrates the specific competencies needed to carry out the task of the project.

## Organizational structure

One important throughput control to direct the behaviours of lower-level managers and employees is the selection of the organizational structure. This discussion relates to the discussion about responsibility centres in Chapter 4, but here we are going to focus on the overriding idea behind the division into responsibility centres. The organizational structure that is chosen also has a substantial impact on the tension between differentiation and integration. Although organizations come in all sizes and shapes, their structures can be grouped into three general categories:

1. A *functional* structure in which each manager is responsible for a specified function such as production or marketing
2. A *business unit* structure in which business unit managers are responsible for most of the activities of their particular unit, and the business unit functions as a semi-independent part of the company
3. A *matrix* structure in which functional units have dual responsibilities, to both a functional manager and a business unit manager. A matrix structure, therefore, can be seen as a mix between the functional and the business structures.

Abbreviated organization charts for each type are shown in Figure 6.1.

**FIGURE 6.1** Three types of organizational structure

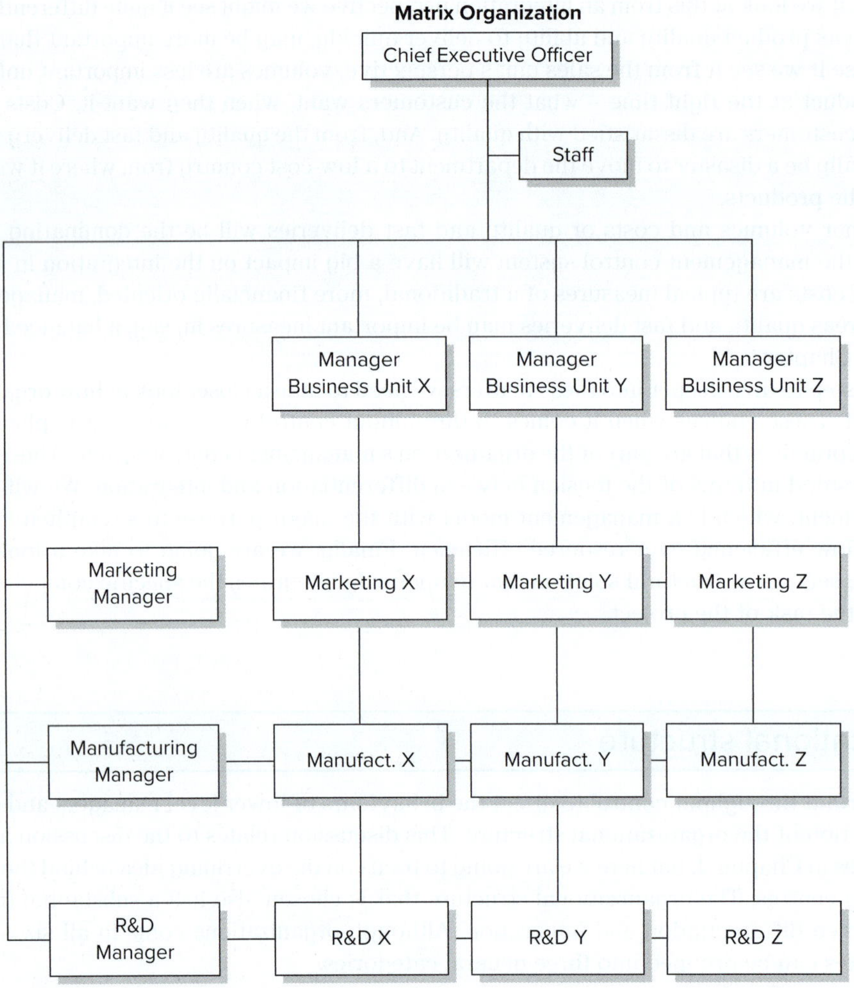

## Functional organizations

The rationale for the functional form of organization involves the notion of a manager who brings specialized knowledge to bear on decisions related to a specific function, in contrast with the general purpose manager who lacks that specialized knowledge. A skilled marketing manager and a skilled production manager are likely to make better decisions in their respective fields than a manager who is responsible for both functions. Moreover, the skilled specialist should be able to supervise employees in the same function better than the generalist would, just as skilled top managers should be able to provide better supervision of lower-level managers in the same or a similar function. Also, a functional structure takes advantage of economies of scale to a greater degree than do other structures, since all similar tasks are conducted in one department or unit. Thus an important advantage of a functional structure is efficiency. Another advantage is competence development, since managers and employees develop their skills through learning from one another.

However, there are also several disadvantages to a functional structure. In a functional organization there is no unambiguous way of determining the effectiveness of the separate functional managers (e.g., the managers of marketing and production) because each function contributes jointly to the organization's final output. Therefore, there is not an accurate way to measure what fraction of profit was contributed by each. Similarly, at lower levels in the organization, there is no way to determine how much of the profit was earned respectively by several production departments, the product engineering department and the sales office.

Also, if the organization consists of managers in one function, who report to managers in the same function, who in turn report to managers in that function, then a dispute between managers of different functions can be resolved only at the top, even though it may have originated at a much lower organizational level. For example, the marketing department may want to satisfy a customer's need for a certain quantity of a product even if it requires overtime work by the manufacturing department, the cost of which the manufacturing department may be unwilling to incur. Theoretically, such a dispute would have to be settled by headquarters, even though it may involve just a single branch sales office and one small department of a single manufacturing plant. Taking the issue up through several levels in the organization and then communicating the decision down to the level where it originated can be time-consuming and frustrating.

Functional organizations tend to create 'silos' for each function, thereby preventing cross-functional coordination in areas such as new product development. To sum up, a functional structure often supports efficiency and competence development related to differentiation, but it does not support integration between the different functions. In an organization like this, which is very common, we tend to get the problem that 'the left hand doesn't know what the right hand is doing'.

## Business units

The business unit form of organization is designed to solve problems inherent in the functional structure. A business unit, also called a division, is responsible for all the functions involved in producing and marketing a specified product line. Business unit managers act almost as if their units were separate companies. They are responsible for planning and coordinating the work of the separate functions – ensuring, for example, that the plans of the marketing department are consistent with production capabilities – and for resolving the disputes that arise between these functions. Their performance is measured by the profitability of the business unit. This is a valid criterion because profit reflects the activities of all the functions in the whole business unit.

Although business unit managers exercise broad authority over their units, headquarters reserves certain key prerogatives. At a minimum, headquarters is responsible for obtaining funds for the company as a whole, and for allocating these funds to the various business units in accordance with its determination as to their best use. Headquarters also approves budgets and judges the performance of business unit managers, sets their compensation and, if the situation warrants, removes them. Finally, headquarters establishes the 'charter' of each business unit – that is, the product lines it is permitted to make and sell and/or the geographical territory in which it can operate, and, occasionally, the customers to which it may sell.

Headquarters also establishes company-wide policies, which, depending on the wishes of the chief executive officer (CEO), may be few and general, or may be codified in several thick volumes of manuals. Headquarters staff offices may assist the business units in production and marketing activities, and in specialized areas such as human resources, legal affairs, public relations, and controller and treasury matters. These headquarters functions are crucial; without them, the business units would be better off as separate companies.

An advantage of the business unit form of organization is that it provides a training ground in general management. The business unit manager should demonstrate the same entrepreneurial spirit that characterizes the CEO of an independent company.

Another advantage of this type of structure is that because the business unit is closer to the market for its products than is headquarters, its manager may make sounder production and marketing decisions than headquarters, and the unit as a whole can react to new threats or opportunities more quickly. Offsetting these advantages is the possibility that each business unit's staff may duplicate some work that in a functional organization is done at headquarters. Business unit managers are presumably generalists, but their subordinates are functional specialists, and they must deal with many of the same problems addressed by specialists both at headquarters and in other business units as well. In some cases, the layers of business unit staff may cost more than the value gained by the structure.

Moreover, since the people working with, for instance, R&D in the company are scattered around in different business units, they are much less likely to learn from one another. If one engineer in business unit X has an idea, it may not only be beneficial for business unit X, but also for business units Y and Z. However, with a business unit structure there is a significant risk that a long time will pass before business units Y and Z get to know about it, if they get to know about it at all. This means that functional competence development normally suffers.

On the other hand, since, for instance, the engineers in R&D now come closer to both marketing and manufacturing, they are likely to increase their competence in those fields. This means that they get a better understanding of the problems and issues faced in both marketing and manufacturing, and therefore can take those issues better into consideration when they conduct their daily job. While functional competence development often suffers in a business unit organization, cross-functional competence development – popularly referred to as T-shaped skills – often benefits from it.

From an integration point of view this means that cross-functional integration is very likely to increase, while integration within the functional areas is very likely to decrease, in a business unit organization compared to a functional one. Still, the business unit is likely to have its own functional departments and we will probably have integration problems between these functional departments, even with a business unit structure.

## Matrix organizations

The idea with a matrix is to achieve good integration in both the functional and business unit dimensions. It tries to combine the advantages with both the functional and business unit structures, and when this succeeds it is often a major advantage for the organization.

In a matrix organization each operational unit manager has two managers. If we take the Marketing X department, the manager of this department reports both to the Marketing manager and the Business unit X manager. While the Marketing X manager is responsible for increasing the integration between the different marketing units, the Business unit X manager is responsible for increasing the integration in the business unit. If these two managers cooperate well the matrix often functions well.

However, if these two managers behave in a more competitive way, this will probably be frustrating for everybody in the Marketing X department, who may well find themselves in a situation where they have to handle contradicting orders from the managers in these two dimensions. It is often difficult to follow orders and live up to the expectations of one manager; having to follow partly contradicting orders and live up to partly different expectations from two managers is practically impossible.

A matrix structure is much more complex than a functional or business unit structure and requires a rather high level of maturity among managers. This means that even if the idea behind a matrix structure is very good in theory and that it sometimes works very well, it is as often a practical reality that it does not work well at all.

## Lean management

As stated above, a traditional management control system with a focus on designing an appropriate organizational structure and corresponding responsibility centres is often vertical in nature and may even decrease horizontal integration across functional units. We are therefore now going to take a closer look at a management philosophy that is more focused on the horizontal, process dimension than the vertical, hierarchic dimension. This philosophy takes the integration needs as an important point of departure. Even if there are many different, and often comprehensive, definitions of lean management, the very heart of the philosophy is to emphasize horizontal integration. It could thus be said to have the same perspective as the business unit structure discussed earlier, although on a lower, more operational level. However, what we need to remember is that even in a business unit, the structure inside the business unit tends to be functional and the same integration problems may occur in such an organization, but at a lower level.

First, though, let us go back to when lean ideas started to spread across the world. In the 1990s many Western companies faced fierce competition from East Asian competitors from South Korea, Singapore, Taiwan and especially Japan. This was the case in many industries, not least in the car industry. For some reasons Japanese cars were both cheaper and of a higher quality compared to Western cars. One consequence of this was that the Western companies started to look at how the Japanese, and particularly Toyota, produced cars. This, in turn, resulted in a large number of Japanese- and Toyota-inspired management concepts dominating development efforts in the West. These included concepts such as just-in-time (JIT), total quality management (TQM), process management and lean production – concepts that all had the goal of strengthening integration in organizations.

***Real World Example:*** One of the most important issues in a Western car manufacturing plant before lean production was to keep the assembly line running. Huge amounts of money had been invested in building the assembly line and this meant that the line cost money even when it stood still. So, in order to keep the costs down they had to keep the lines running no matter what. This meant that if somebody detected a quality issue with the cars in the assembly line, they did not stop the line because that would be too expensive. Instead, the cars with quality problems were sent to another department that fixed the problems. Even if this made sense, the difficulty was that these rework departments grew bigger and bigger until they were almost as big as the ones actually producing the cars on the production lines.

In Toyota, on the other hand, a production department that fixed errors after the actual manufacturing process would be regarded as waste. When workers at a Toyota assembly line detect a quality problem, they pull a cord that stops the whole line. The problem is solved before the assembly line is started again. In a Toyota plant, the assembly line is stopped several times a day. This means that the capacity utilization of the Toyota assembly line is not as high as in the old Western plants, but instead it has a number of other advantages. The most obvious of course is that you do not need another department to fix all the problems afterwards. With the Toyota system it is also less likely that a quality problem will be missed and less than perfect cars delivered to customers (even if this has happened to Toyota too). And, since all problems are dealt with directly instead of later, there is no risk of a mix-up between cars that need to be adjusted and the kind of adjustments they need.

*Source:* Womack, J.P., Jones, D.T. and Roos, D. (1991) *The Machine that Changed the World: The Story of Lean Production.* New York: Harper Perennial.

## Resource efficiency vs. flow efficiency

One way to describe the basic difference between the traditional management control systems used in the old Western car plants in the example above, and lean management control systems is that while traditional management control systems are focused on resource efficiency, lean management control systems are focused on flow efficiency.[2] Resource efficiency means that capacity utilzation in every part of the process, and for all the resources (people, machines, etc.), should be as close to 100 per cent as possible. It never reaches 100 per cent because people need breaks, and machines need maintenance and repairs, but the closer you get without wearing people or machinery out, the better it is. In the Real World Example that described the assembly line, this means keeping the assembly line running as much as possible. The workers work in shifts, breaks for maintenance are carefully planned and the assembly line is not stopped unless there is a very good reason for it.

However, if we focus on flow efficiency instead, what really matters is that the car is produced and delivered as quickly as possible. This means that sending cars to another department for adjustments after the assembly line is not just considered a waste of money, it is also a total waste of time. So, everyone needs to do things right the first time, and when somebody detects that somebody is not doing things right the first time, this needs to be remedied as quickly as possible.

***Real World Example:*** Many women worry about whether they might have breast cancer or not at some point in their lives (the most common form of cancer for women). The cause for the worry is usually that they felt a lump or something irregular in one of their breasts. However, a lump may be perfectly harmless, so they need to have the lump examined to know if they have cancer or not. We are going to take a closer look at the examination processes of two women with these worries. Let's call them Karen and Eve.

Karen goes to see her doctor, who also thinks that the lump needs to be properly examined and says that he will send her to the breast clinic. Still very worried, Karen returns home to wait for a letter with an appointment at the breast clinic. After a week she has still not received any letter and calls the doctor. After some time in a telephone queue she gets to talk with a nurse, who promises to look into it. Some days later Karen finally gets the letter with an appointment the following week. She goes to the breast clinic where they give her both X-ray and mammography examinations. Home again, she gets another letter after 10 days, with an appointment scheduled with a different doctor this time. The doctor can still not say if Karen has cancer or not, but she tells Karen that she wants to send her to do another test. Karen becomes even more impatient and calls the clinic that will be performing the test. It turns out that it has already booked a date for her, but that it is two weeks away. She wants to get an earlier date, but unfortunately the clinic is fully booked, so she waits two weeks for the test to be performed. Karen then has to wait for another letter with an appointment to see the doctor. Exactly six weeks after she went to see the first doctor she meets the second doctor again, who will tell her whether or not she has cancer.

Eve is as worried as Karen, but at least she has heard that there is a 'one-step breast clinic' at the hospital in her home town. She decides to visit the clinic, where she is first examined by a nurse and then a doctor. The doctor wants to conduct further examinations and tests – as it turns out, exactly the same as they did on Karen. However, all the examinations and tests are done at the clinic and Eve does not need to return home in between. Eve has to wait a little while for the examinations and then to see the doctor again. When the doctor informs her as to whether or not she has cancer, just two hours have passed since she arrived at the clinic.

[2] These concepts, and the example below, are taken from Modig, N. and Åhlström, P. (2012) *This is Lean: Resolving the Efficiency Paradox.* Stockholm: Rheologica Publishing.

The process that Karen went through is based on resource efficiency logic. Whoever she is going to meet or whatever she is going to do, she must wait until a specific point in time. This is because, according to this logic, it is very important to utilize the capacity in the form of doctors, nurses and medical equipment as much as possible, and this is achieved through scheduling the resources and having the people queue for a time in the schedule. This way they can examine as many patients as possible, given the available capacity. Or, the other way around, this way they can keep the costs for the different resources to a minimum, given the number of patients that they have.

In Eve's case we are talking about another type of logic altogether: a flow logic. What is important here is to finish the process as quickly as possible. This also means that the resource utilization of the equipment probably is quite low. On a day when lots of women have discovered a lump in their breast, the clinic is probably fully occupied, but on other days it may have much less to do. This means that, with this logic, you tend to need higher capacity, which requires greater investment. On the other hand, Eve probably values the service higher than Karen does the service she experienced. Not only did Eve get the results much quicker and did not need to suffer from the uncertainty for long, she did not have to visit doctors and places scattered all around town.

Moreover, if Eve has cancer the chances that they can cure it may very well increase the sooner they can start the treatment. Another advantage with Eve's examination process is that the risk of administrative problems decreases drastically. In Eve's process they only had to handle one patient at a time, while in Karen's they had to handle hundreds of patients that either waited to get an appointment or who had a booking. The risk of mix-ups or that patient's papers get mislaid or filed in the wrong place is of course considerably higher in Karen's case. Moreover, in Eve's case it is much easier for the people working in the process to talk to one another, which makes it much easier to straighten out questions, solve problems and learn how to do things in order to avoid problems later in the process.

All this means that even if the costs for capacity are higher in Eve's case, her process may still be cheaper because we need fewer people to administrate the queue and the bookings, fewer administrative mistakes are made, and it might be easier and cheaper to cure the cancer.

The same basic logic can be applied to many different industries. So far, we have discussed car manufacturing and diagnosing breast cancer. Let us now have a look at a manufacturing plant not suited to an assembly line. It might be a process that involves casting, drills, lathes and milling machines. Let us also assume that these operations are performed in sequence. If we then apply resource efficiency logic we do not want to invest more in machinery than necessary, and we want to utilize the machines as much as we can. This means that we do not want the operators of one type of machine to have to wait for the operators of the previous type of machine in the process. If the operators are going to be able to work all the time, there needs to be a stock of pieces to work on all the time. Then we get a process where the pieces are cast by one department and put in stock for the second department, eventually taken out of stock by the second department, drilled and put in stock for the third department, and so on. This way, as illustrated in Figure 6.2, we may get high resource utilization, but we also get stocks of pieces or queues of patients waiting for the next activity. In the diagram the arrows symbolize the flow of pieces (or people) between the different activities and stocks (or queue).

However, if we use flow efficiency logic we do not like this at all. Because in a process like this the pieces spend most of their time in stock, which is seen as waste and results in very long lead times, just as in Karen's case above. There are many problems related to long lead times, according to this logic:

- *Costs:* The material ties up capital and therefore costs money when in stock. The stock also requires space, transport and administration, which also costs money. In Karen's case the cost was her uncertainty, which meant she probably could not perform her job very well, if at all, and the costs of administrating the bookings, etc.
- *Quality*: If there are quality issues with the pieces coming from the casting department, the operators in the drilling department would not detect this until they had worked their way through the

**FIGURE 6.2** Resource and flow efficiency

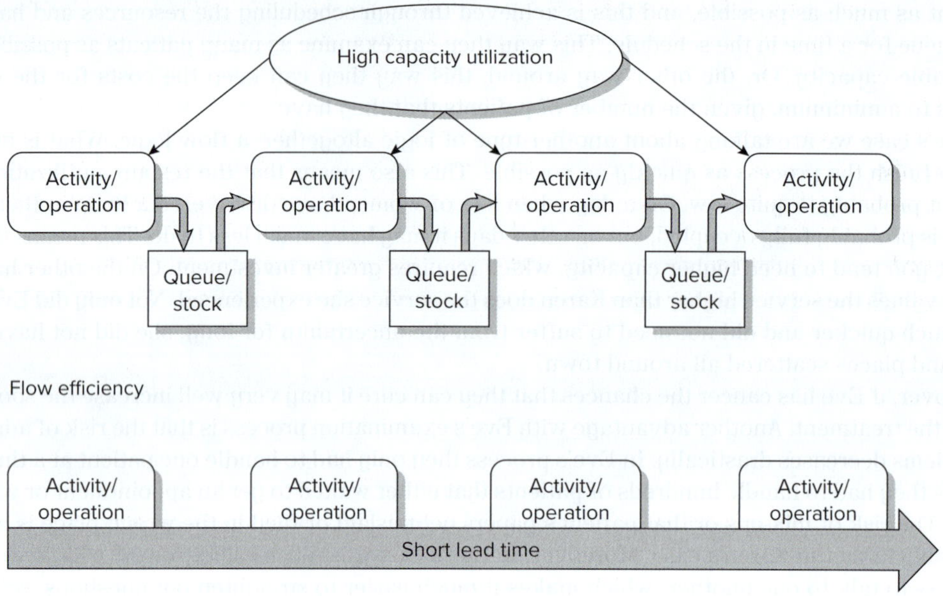


whole stock that they have at a certain point in time. This means that the casting department may very well continue to produce pieces with quality issues for quite some time. Likewise, if the department performing a test on Karen did something wrong this would probably not be detected until she met the doctor again, which means that they may very well have continued to make the same mistake for weeks.

- *Waste:* If the demand for the product is low or if the customers change preference regarding some aspect of the product, the company will probably end up with a large stock of both finished products and unfinished pieces, which is more or less worthless. This is not a problem that we usually have in service industries though, such as in Karen's case.
- *Flexibility:* If a customer is in urgent need of a certain product that the company does not have in stock, it will probably not be able to deliver this product in time due to the long lead times. Likewise, if Karen's cancer needs to be treated quickly, the lead time of this process does not help her.

## Lean implementation

As we have said, the origins of lean management can be found in Japan, and especially at Toyota. The concept spread across the world, particularly among car manufacturers in the 1990s. Then manufacturing companies in many other industries followed and lean became the dominant management concept in the manufacturing industries. However, the actual implementation of lean differed considerably, not least when it came to the management control systems aspects of the implementation.

In the literature, the lean concept is described as a combination of input, throughput and output controls, but it is not unusual that only one or perhaps two of these types of control are focused on the actual implementation of lean. In particular, throughput control in the form of process descriptions often seems to be favoured in many implementations, often at the expense of input controls that establish the values behind lean, such as customer focus, communication and integration. This often results in a situation where employees are more concerned with following the process descriptions than considering the needs of the customer or communicating with other employees working in the same process. The risk that the process lacks integration and that the customer is less than satisfied thus remains.[3]

There is a great irony in this because if you focus only on throughput control it is not really lean management, but more resembles Fordism or scientific management. This means that many organizations that want to implement lean instead implement the system that lean outperformed.

In later decades the lean trend has spread to service industries and public services, and it has had a considerable influence in health care. However, the effects have been mixed, from successful implementations like the one-step breast clinic to less fruitful ones. The latter examples, often associated with an excessive focus on throughput controls, have also tended to give lean management a bad name. Many people tend to think that even if lean, as they know it, may be suited to manufacturing, it is far too mechanistic for, say, health care. As a consequence, lean management as a concept is not used as much as before, even if the ideas behind it are still very much alive in many organizations.

## Projects

### What is a project?

*A project is a set of activities intended to accomplish a specified end result and which starts and ends at a particular time.*

A project team is thus a solution to two needs. The first need is to have an organizational unit that is temporary; it exists only until it has fulfilled its task and is then dissolved. The other need is to have a number of competencies that normally may not work together; competencies that are needed for the special task that the project is formed to carry out. This often means that competencies from different functional departments are cooperating in the team, thus creating a temporary integration between different professions and departments. However, the integration effect does not stop when the project does, as people from different departments have got to know one another better and have reached a better understanding of one another's situation and challenges during the project.

Projects include construction projects, the production of a sizeable unique product (such as a turbine), rearranging a plant, developing and marketing a new product, consulting engagements, audits, acquisitions and divestitures, research and development work, development and installation of information systems, and many others.

A project begins when management has approved the general nature of what is to be done and has authorized the approximate amount of resources that are to be spent in doing this work. The project ends when its objective has been accomplished, or when it has been cancelled. The construction of a building and the renovation of a building are projects; the routine maintenance of a building is not. The production of a television 'special' is a project; the production of a nightly television news broadcast is an ongoing operation. An organizational change to improve motivation among employees is a project, day-to-day management with the same purpose is not.

Projects vary greatly. At one extreme, a project may involve one or a few persons working for a few days or weeks, performing work similar to that done many times previously – for example, an annual financial audit that is conducted by a public accounting firm. At the other extreme, a project may involve thousands of people working for several years, performing work unlike they have ever done before, as was the case with the project to land the first men on the moon. The discussion here does not describe

---

[3] For an example, see Case 6.4.

either of these extremes. Rather, it focuses on projects that have a formal control organization and that consume enough resources so that a formal management control system is necessary. Extremely complex first-of-a-kind projects have more complicated control problems than those described here, although the general nature of these problems and the appropriate management control system are similar.

The characteristics of projects make the management control of projects different from the management control practices of ongoing activities. Described below are some of these characteristics that apply to most, but not necessarily all, projects.

- *Single objective:* A project usually has a single objective; ongoing operations have multiple objectives. Although the project manager also makes decisions that affect the future, the time horizon is the end of the project. Project performance can be judged in terms of the desired end product; operating performance should be judged in terms of all the results that the manager achieves, some of which will not be known until a year or more later.
- *Organizational structure:* In many cases, the project organization is superimposed on an ongoing operating organization, and its management control system is superimposed on the management control system of that organization.
- *Focus on the project:* Project control focuses on the project, whose objective is to produce a satisfactory output, within a specified time period and at an optimum cost. In contrast, control in ongoing organizations focuses on the activities of a specified time period, such as a month.
- *Less reliable standards:* Performance standards tend to be less reliable for projects than for ongoing organizations. Although the specifications for one project and the method of producing it may be similar to those for other projects, the project design literally is used only once.
- *Different rhythm:* The rhythm of a project differs from that of ongoing operations. Most projects start small, build up to peak activity, and then taper off as completion nears and only clean-up remains to be carried out. Ongoing activities tend to operate at the same activity level for a considerable time.

## Project selection

The decision to start a project or not is usually based on some sort of assessment of the costs and benefits of the project. In some cases, these costs and benefits can be quantified with a rather high degree of certainty, in others the certainty is so low that there is no point in even trying. If we take a project with a paying customer, the revenue becomes easier to predict. If we have a fixed-price contract, we know exactly what revenue we will get and all the uncertainty is related to the costs. But if we have a cost-reimbursement contract we know what profit margin we are going to get, since the customer has agreed to pay for all the costs plus a profit margin. The latter type of contract is often beneficial for the seller but does on the other hand move all the financial uncertainty over to the customer.

However, many projects do not have an external customer and the benefits may be reaped over a very long period. In this case, the decision to start the project becomes an investment decision. In some cases the benefits can still be predicted with some certainty – for instance, if the project will decrease production costs or increase revenues. In these cases a capital budgeting technique can be used in order to compare the costs of the project with its future benefits. Common techniques for this are the payback method, internal rate of return and discounted cash flow.

In other projects, such as change of information systems, reorganization, improvements in the working environment or, indeed, development of the management control system, the benefits are almost impossible to quantify. This means that a more qualitative assessment has to be done. A very important aspect of this assessment is, if and to what extent the project will support the strategy of the company. In fact, this is a very important criterion even when the benefits can be quantified. In other cases the organization may not have a choice whether to start the project or not – for instance, if it is an answer to new legal requirements concerning environmental issues or compliance.

## Cost, time and quality

Ideally a project is completed on time, does not spend more money than budgeted and produces very good results. However, this does not happen regularly, and one reason for this could be that the targets set before the start of the project were highly unrealistic. This could in turn have been the result of lacking information, high uncertainty or quite simply that the managers who initiated the project were far too optimistic. For better or for worse, many projects would never start if the people in charge had more realistic expectations.

It is therefore important to set the priorities before the project starts, especially since there are inherent conflicts in practically every project. One way to set priorities is using the *project management triangle*, which illustrates how priorities are set considering quality, time and cost. The idea with this is that depending on the project and the goals of the project, the three different aspects are not equally important. The project management triangle is illustrated in Figure 6.3.

***Real World Example:*** Imagine the project of building a new sports arena for the Olympic Games. In this case, it is of course crucial that the arena is finished in time for the games. It does not matter how good the arena is or how cheap it is, if it is not finished on time it will still be considered a failure. In some cases, the construction company has been accused of compromising the safety of workers to get sports arenas finished on time. In other cases, the construction workers have decided to go on strike to raise their wages during such projects, of course knowing that their employer is in a very bad position to negotiate.

Then imagine that the government grants a sum of money for a project with the purpose to increase integration in a number of suburbs outside a large city. In this case the project manager knows exactly how much money can be spent on the project. Moreover, a request for more money would probably be a very long and complicated process. A good idea would therefore be to compromise on time and quality rather than on costs, and to try to get the best results possible given the amount of money available. And perhaps, if the results are good enough, the government may be generous and grant more money in the future.

Finally, imagine the construction of a nuclear plant. In this case it is not a very good idea to compromise on quality and safety. Time and costs may also be very important, but probably not as important as safety. It does not matter how fast or how cheaply it can be built, if it is not safe. If there is even the smallest risk that what happened in Chernobyl in 1986 can happen again, it should not be built at all.

In the cases described in the Real World Example there is always one dimension that simply cannot be negotiated. This may not be the case in other projects, but some aspects are still more important than others. In Figure 6.3 a cross is placed close to costs and very far from time. This means that this particular project can

**FIGURE 6.3** The project management triangle

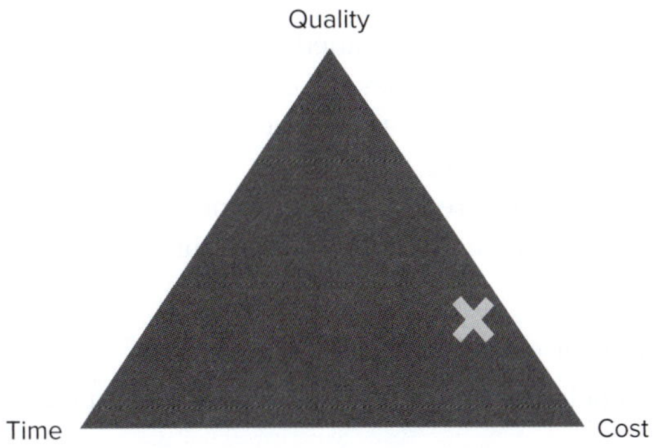

only, to a small extent, be compromised on costs and to a larger extent on quality, whereas time does not seem very important at all. This means that we should not spend money on activities to speed up the project, such as the hiring of expensive consultants. Nor should we hesitate to delay the project if it means producing a better result. However, we should be more careful with spending, even if the spending would create better results.

## Project budgeting

Cost estimates for most projects tend to be less accurate than those for manufactured goods because projects are less standardized, and cost information that has been accumulated for similar work is therefore not as valid a basis for comparison. Nevertheless, if a contractor has performed similar work in the past, the costs incurred on these work packages provide a starting point for estimating the costs of the new project. For some work, industry norms, or rules of thumb, have been developed that are useful in estimating costs.

Obviously, no one knows what actually will happen in the future, therefore no one knows for sure what future costs will actually be. In estimating what these costs are likely to be, two types of unknown must be taken into account. The first type is the *known unknowns*. These are estimates of the cost of activities that are known to be going to occur, such as digging the foundations for a house. The nature of the task is known, and the costs, although unknown, often can be estimated within reasonable limits on the basis of past experience. If unexpected rock or other conditions are encountered, however, these estimates may turn out to be way off the mark.

The other unknowns are the *unknown unknowns*. For these activities, the estimator does not know that they are going to occur, and obviously, therefore, has no way of estimating their cost. Work stoppages, destruction caused by storms or floods, delays in receiving materials, accidents and failure of government inspectors to act in a timely manner are examples. A fixed-price contract usually states that costs caused by such events are added to the fixed price.

In using cost estimates in the evaluation phase, the impossibility of estimating the cost of unknown unknowns must be recognized. Their actual costs may range from zero up to any amount whatsoever. There is no definable upper limit. If the contract does not provide that all these costs are added to the fixed price, the estimator should include a contingency allowance for them.

## Project planning

A project is performed only once and even if there are other similar projects there are still often differences that make each project unique. This makes the planning of the activities, or the throughput controls, extremely important for the success of the project. Therefore, we are going to focus a bit more on this part and we are going to present two different strategies for project planning. We will start with the traditional strategy for project planning, sometimes referred to as the *waterfall* method, and we will then take a look at the allegedly more flexible *agile* method.

### *The waterfall method*

With the waterfall method the whole project is planned in detail, and in sequence, before the project work starts. Then, when the project starts, the activities fall down in a constant flow like a waterfall, hence the name. This is done in order to make sure that no important activity is forgotten and that the different activities are performed in the optimal order.

Several throughput control practices are available for constructing the time schedule for the project; one example of such a tool is CPM (critical path method). In this method, each control practice has three basic steps:

1. Estimating the time required for each activity
2. Identifying the interdependencies among activities (which activity must be completed before the next activity can be started)
3. Calculating the critical path.

Collectively, these are techniques for *network analysis.* A network diagram consists of a number of subgoals that must be completed to accomplish the project, and lines joining these goals to one another. The estimated time to carry out each activity is shown on the network diagram. An activity connecting two events, say A and B, indicates that the activity leading to B cannot be started until event A has happened. Thus a network diagram shows the chronological sequence in which events must be completed to complete the whole project.

Computer programs are available for analysing project networks. They identify the *critical path* – i.e., the sequence of events that has the shortest total time to complete the project. The nature of the critical path is shown in Figure 6.4. To complete event B, event A must first be completed; this requires two weeks. A–B requires an additional five weeks. Then B–C requires an additional three weeks to complete the project. This is the critical path, and it is 10 weeks long. Note that to complete event B, activity X–B must also be undertaken, with an estimated time of four weeks. However, activity B–C cannot be started until both A–B and X–B have been completed. X–A and A–B require a total of seven weeks; and X–B, which requires only four weeks, can be performed at any time during this seven-week period. Activity X–B is said to have three weeks of *slack.*

There are several management control system implications in the concepts of critical path and slack. First, in the control process, special attention must be paid to those activities that are on the critical path, while less attention needs to be paid to slack activities. Second, in the planning process, attention should be given to possibilities of reducing the time required for critical path activities; if such possibilities exist, the overall time required for the project can be reduced. Third, it may be desirable to reduce critical path times by increasing costs, such as incurring overtime, but additional money should not be spent to reduce the time taken by slack activities.

## Agile project management

In project management, there is a debate going on similar to the beyond budgeting debate described in Chapter 8. Just as in that debate, the value of making very thorough and detailed plans when everybody knows that most of it will be revised anyway, is questioned. Another argument that can also be heard in that debate is that those detailed plans tend to decrease the *flexibility* in the project. Flexibility is important for both external and internal reasons. One external reason that is frequently mentioned is that the customers, or whoever defines the planned outcome of the projects, change their minds. Even if this change is rather small, it may still create quite a lot of work when it comes to revising the detailed project plan.

Internal reasons for flexibility may have something to do with a particular technical solution in a development project that turns out not to be working as well as it was thought it would when the project was planned. In this case it may cost a lot of time and money to hold on to this particular solution instead of trying to find a better one. It may also reduce the quality of the final product that is developed.

**FIGURE 6.4** Critical path (X–A, A–B and B–C indicate critical path)

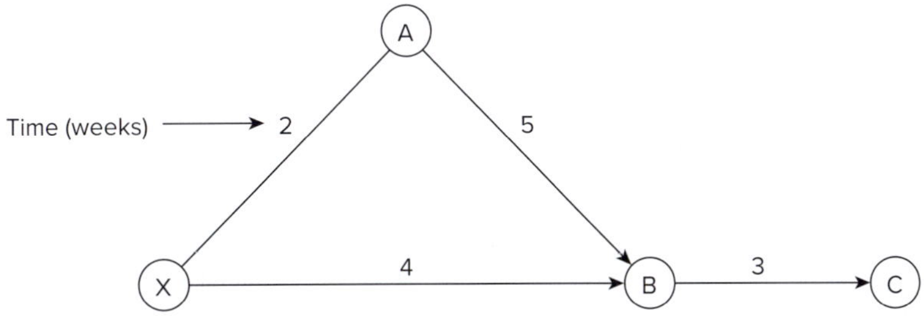

**FIGURE 6.5** Traditional and agile project planning

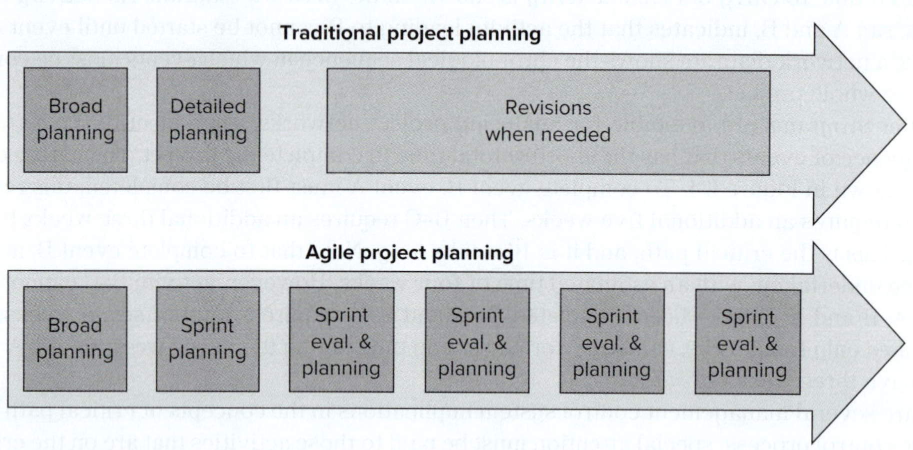


The main idea in agile project management (at least with the common *Scrum* method) is to plan the whole project in only broad terms and then plan in detail for only a short part of the project (a so-called *sprint*) at a time. When the sprint is over, it is evaluated (a *sprint evaluation*) and only then is the next sprint planned. An important input to the *sprint planning* of the next sprint is, of course, the experiences acquired in previous sprints. External changes, such as changed customer demands, are, of course, also taken into account in the sprint planning. However, only minor changes are allowed during the sprints. A sprint takes between a day and a month, depending on the type of project. The difference in the planning between agile and traditional project management is illustrated in Figure 6.5.

***Real World Example:*** In a survey carried out one year after the implementation of agile project management (in the form of the Scrum method) at Yahoo! some interesting figures can be found. A majority of the employees thought that agile project management was an improvement with regard to a range of issues, namely productivity, team morale, adaptability, accountability, collaboration and cooperation. As many as 81 per cent of the respondents thought agile project management was an improvement with regard to collaboration and cooperation, while most of the other issues had improved according to 50–65 per cent of employees. The figure for productivity was 68 per cent and the average estimated increase in productivity was 36 per cent. The figures for employees who thought that agile project management made these issues worse were all between 1 and 9 per cent.

*Source:* Deemer, P., Benefield, G., Larman, C. and Vodde, B. (2009) *The Scrum Primer.* Available at: http://cs.union.edu/~striegnk/courses/csc497/scrumprimer.pdf (accessed 14 March 2013).

But agile project management is not just about a different planning system, and a good summary of the values behind it can be found in the *Manifesto for Agile Software Development*,[4] as reproduced here in Figure 6.6. The manifesto clearly shows that agile project management has its roots in software development, but there is nothing to prevent us from taking out the word software and putting in product or whatever the intended end outcome of the project is.

[4] Various contributors (2001) *Manifesto for Agile Software Development.* Available at: http://agilemanifesto.org/ (accessed 22 November 2019).

**FIGURE 6.6** The Agile Manifesto

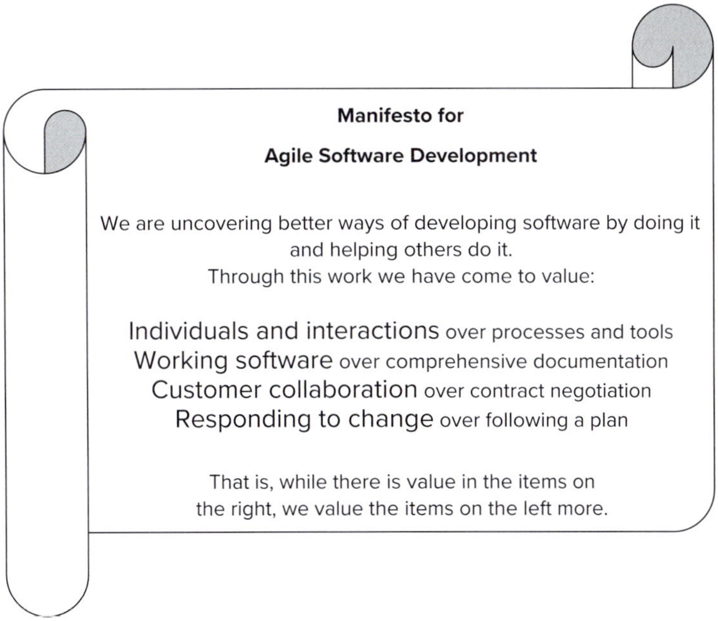


We have already discussed the importance of flexibility and *responding to change*, but let us take a look at the other items. *Individuals and interactions* is another crucial aspect of agile methods and there are a number of ways in which this is addressed:

- An agile team does not have a project manager in the traditional sense, because this person is working to create favourable conditions for the team rather than leading its work. In an agile team everybody is expected to take responsibility for the work and the outcome.
- Face-to-face contact is very important in an agile team and the members are preferably sitting in the same room in order to facilitate the communication.
- Meetings are very frequent in agile project management. Apart from the sprint evaluations and planning meetings, an agile team has a short meeting every day when everybody can have their say.
- One of the most important qualities for an agile team member is social competence. It is just as important as the technical competence required in the project.

Working software, or *working on the project*, in order to make it more general, is considered more important than working on the documentation and the project bureaucracy. This may be seen as something rather obvious, but in many cases the bureaucracy takes so much time that the actual project work suffers.

Finally, *customer collaboration* is another focused aspect of agile methods. This is, of course, very important if the project's end result is going to be in line with the demands and needs of the customer. It is also important for the project team to get information about changed demands from the customer as soon as possible in order to react to the new demands rather than work to satisfy the old ones. It is also possible that a good collaboration leads to the finding of solutions that are favourable for both parties.

A potential downside with agile project management is the loss of a feeling of being 'in control'. In traditional methods you have a plan that covers the project from beginning to end, whereas with agile methods you may not know what is going to happen next month, next week or even tomorrow. Knowing what is going to happen gives a sense of control, but the question is: is it only a *sense* of control or actually being in control? One may argue that if the plan is going to be revised, perhaps several times, it gives a feeling of being in control rather than actually being in control. Still, we should not underestimate how important the *feeling* of being in control can be to many people. However, if and when people start to appreciate the benefits of agile project management, this will also contribute to the feeling of being in control. This is at least the case with an old research colleague of ours who has recently been working as CEO for a software company and who once said something like this:

> *When we use agile project management the projects are finished in time, the costs do not exceed the budget and they reach their goals.*

## Project evaluation

Up until now, this chapter has focused on throughput controls, but in the case of projects it is important to highlight that we also have important output control implications. A project can be evaluated at different points in time. It can be evaluated during the project in order to make sure that the project is on track and that it is not costing too much. It can be evaluated after it is finished to check that it achieved its goals. It can also be evaluated several years after the project is finished, especially if the positive effects of the project are of a more long-term nature.

## Evaluation after the project

The evaluation of performance in executing the project has two aspects:

1. An evaluation of project management
2. An evaluation of the process of managing the project.

The purpose of the former is to assist in decisions regarding project managers, including rewards, promotions, constructive criticism or reassignment. The purpose of the latter is to discover better ways of conducting future projects. In many cases, these evaluations are informal. If the results of the project were unsatisfactory and if the project was important, a formal evaluation is worthwhile. A formal evaluation of a highly successful project may also identify techniques that will improve performance on future projects.

Because work on a project tends to be less standardized and less susceptible to measurement than work in a factory, evaluation of a project is more subjective than evaluation of production activities. It resembles the evaluation of marketing activities in that the effect of external factors on performance must be taken into account. A judgement about whether actual accomplishment was satisfactory under the actual circumstances encountered is highly subjective.

When actual costs exceed budgeted costs, there is said to be a cost overrun. To some, this implies that actual costs were too high. An equally plausible conclusion, however, is that the budgeted costs were too low. If the higher costs resulted from changes in the scope of the project or from non-controllable factors, the explanation is that there was an underestimate of costs, rather than excessive actual costs. Interpretation of the cost reports is complicated by the need to analyse both the budget and the actual costs.

A common error in analysing costs is to assume that the budget represents what the costs should have been. It does not. At best, the budget estimates what the cost should have been *based on the information that was available at the time it was prepared.* This information is rarely an accurate reflection of conditions that will be encountered on the project; to the extent that it is inaccurate, the budget does not reflect what the costs should be. Moreover, budget numbers are estimates made by human beings, and they are based, in part, on judgements and assumptions. Although reasonable people can differ in their judgements and assumptions, only one set of conclusions is incorporated in the budget.

## Evaluation of results

The success of a project cannot be evaluated until enough time has elapsed to permit measurement of its actual benefits and costs. This may take years. Unless the impact can be specifically measured, such an evaluation may not be worthwhile. Furthermore, there is no point in attempting to evaluate a project unless some action can be taken based on this analysis.

For many projects, the evaluation of results is complicated by the fact that the expected benefits were not stated in objective, measurable terms, and the actual benefits were also not measurable. In these cases, a quantitative cost–benefit analysis is not feasible, and reliance must be placed on judgements by knowledgeable people about the project's accomplishments. This is the situation in the majority of projects undertaken by governments and non-profit organizations, many research and development projects undertaken by staff units, and projects whose objective is to improve safety or eliminate environmental deficiencies.

Part of the evaluation should be a comparison of the actual results with the results that were anticipated when the project was approved. The anticipated results were based on certain assumptions (e.g., for a new product: size of the market, market share, competitors' reactions, inflation), and these assumptions should have been documented during the process of approving the project. Unless the need for such documentation was recognized, the record is likely to be incomplete or vague.

## Summary

Every organization has two basic needs: the need for differentiation and the need for integration. Differentiation refers to the need for competence in different fields, while integration refers to the need to make people with different competencies cooperate. The greater the differentiation in an organization, the more difficult it is to create integration. Still, many successful organizations manage to create both.

An organization can be organized according to a functional structure, a business unit structure or as a matrix. All of these forms have pros and cons, but the functional structure in particular tends to inhibit integration. The matrix structure is an attempt to combine the pros of both a functional and business unit structure. It may work very well, but often tends to create confusion.

Lean management is a Japanese- and Toyota-based management concept that prioritizes integration and flow efficiency over resource efficiency. This means that fast processes are more important than having a high capacity utilization. However, actual implementations of lean differ regarding what types of controls they emphasize. Some implementations that mostly focus on throughput controls actually tend to be more in line with scientific management than lean.

A project is a set of activities with a start and an end, whose purpose is to achieve specific goals. A project team is often a temporary unit integrating different competencies from different departments that are needed for the task. It tends to go through certain phases, such as project selection, project budgeting and planning, and project evaluation. It is often wise to decide how important the aspects of quality, time and cost are in the project.

The traditional way to plan projects is the waterfall method, where the whole project is planned in detail before it starts. However, a more flexible way to manage projects, agile project management, has become increasingly popular. With this method the whole project is planned in very broad terms, whereas only the the next short phase is planned in detail.

## Suggested additional reading


Highsmith, J.A. (2010) *Agile Project Management: Creating Innovative Products*. Upper Saddle River, NJ, Addison-Wesley.

Lawrence, P.R. and Lorsch, J.W. (1967) *Organization and Environment: Managing Differentiation and Integration*. Boston, MA: Harvard Business School Press.

Liker, J.K. (2004) *The Toyota Way: 14 Management Principles from the World's Greatest Manufacturer*. New York, McGraw-Hill.

Meredith, J.R. and Mantel, S.J. (2017) *Project Management: A Strategic Managerial Approach*. New York: Wiley.

Mir, F. (2019) The Interactive Use of Management Control Systems and Project Performance: An Empirical Examination of IT projects. Paper, University of Guelph.

Modig, N. and Åhlström, P. (2012) *This is Lean: Resolving the Efficiency Paradox*. Stockholm: Rheologica Publishing.

Womack, J.P., Jones, D.T. and Roos, D. (1991) *The Machine that Changed the World: The Story of Lean Production*. New York: Harper Perennial.

# Case 6.1
# Miracle on ice!*

**by Göran Nilsson**

When the chances of different sport teams are discussed by fans and journalists, a frequently discussed aspect is of course the quality of the players in the team. In professional sports it is not unusual to even compare the sums that the teams have paid for their players. The more you have paid, the better the team and the greater the chance of winning, seems to be the logic. This does of course make sense since teams are more willing to pay money for good players that can help them win than for average players. The same logic can be applied to national teams – the more valuable players, the better the team – even if these teams do not pay for the players.

Still, it is not unusual that teams that, from this perspective, should not stand a chance actually perform very well and sometimes even win. One example of a team that did not stand a chance is the Icelandic football (soccer) team in the UEFA Euro 2016 tournament. Apart from defeating the Netherlands twice during the qualification campaign, Iceland also defeated England in round 16 of the tournament. This was not only despite the English players being worth substantially higher amounts of money, but also despite the difference in the number of football clubs and football players in the two countries. England has 40,000 football clubs, which is more than any other country. Iceland has fewer than 400,000 inhabitants and could not come close to the English figure even if everybody in Iceland played football!

Another recent sensation occurred in the Ice Hockey World Championships in 2019. A common measure of the quality of the teams in this tournament is how many players they have from the National Hockey League (NHL) in North America, since it is considered the best league in the world. While the teams from Canada, the United States, Russia and Sweden were totally dominated by players from the NHL, Finland had just two. Moreover, the Finnish team consisted of 19 young debutants, who had never played a world championship before. Needless to say, nobody thought that Finland would have any chance whatsoever in this tournament. However, after victories over, among others, Sweden, Russia and Canada, they became world champions!

One of the biggest sensations in the Olympic Games also occurred in ice hockey and has been documented several times, including in the Disney film, *Miracle.* During the Winter Olympics at Lake Placid in 1980, the so-called Red Machine from the Soviet Union was a huge favourite. Not only had the team won gold in the previous four Games, but also professional players from the NHL were not allowed to participate. This meant, among other things, that the US team would consist of young and inexperienced college players, probably not that different from the Finnish team in 2019. On the plus side, the US Olympic Committee granted the team enough money to make it possible for them to play together for the whole season leading up to the Winter Olympics.

Still, on paper, the young American players did of course not stand a chance against one of the best teams in the world in any sport. Therefore, it was hardly surprising that the team lost to the Soviets with a score of 10–3 during an exhibition game that took place before the tournament. However, when the tournament started the US team forced a draw against Sweden and resoundingly defeated Czechoslovakia. As the game against the Soviet team approached, the tension was definitely growing. We also need to remember that this was a match between the two superpowers during the Cold War. The Soviet Union had invaded Afghanistan the year before and the United States would for this reason boycott

* This case was written by Dr Göran Nilsson, Uppsala University.

the summer Olympics in Moscow later the same year. The political situation thus increased the tension even more.

The miracle happened: the United States won the game against the Soviet team with a score of 4–3 in an exceptionally exciting game. Later it also defeated Finland and won gold. The victory was later voted the greatest sports moment of the twentieth century in the US magazine *Sports Illustrated*.

## Questions

1. Can you give more examples of sports teams that should not have stood a chance, but performed exceptionally well or even won?
2. Is it pure chance when these things happen? If not, how can we explain them? What possible factors make these teams so successful?
3. If we believe there are factors explaining the success, can we use this knowledge to improve, not only sport teams, but also other types of organization?

# Case 6.2 The washer*

**by Göran Nilsson**

I (one of the authors of this book) once worked in a company with a rather traditional organizational structure and performance measurement system. This meant that the sales department was a revenue centre, R&D was a discretionary expense centre and manufacturing consisted of several engineered expense centres. You could also argue that the purchasing department was an engineered expense centre, since its main performance measure was the price difference. The price difference measured the cost of purchased material and components compared to the calculated price. The formula for the measure looked like this:

***Price difference = Volume (Calculated cost – actual cost)***

This meant that the lower the cost compared to the calculated cost for a certain item, and the larger the volume of this item, the bigger the price difference. The idea behind the price difference was thus quite simple: motivate the purchasers to buy things cheap! The cost of purchased material was also very important since it was the biggest cost item in the company.

So it was hardly surprising that the purchasers changed supplier for a washer (a small thin metal plate with a hole in the middle, not a washing machine!) that we bought in large quantities, when they found one that was cheaper. Even if the price was only half a cent (€0.005) cheaper, it should not be ignored, especially since we bought large quantities of the washer. The immediate effect was of course that the price difference increased, but unfortunately that was not the only effect. As it turned out, the washers from the new supplier were not made with the same precision as those from the old supplier.

This also created problems in manufacturing since a large number of products that included the new washer did not work as they should. As a consequence of this, a large number of products were scrapped

* This case was written by Dr Göran Nilsson, Uppsala University.

and a large number had to be adjusted, which meant significant costs for scrapping and rework. Apart from these costs another significant cost was that for totally messing up the production planning in the department.

It became my task to calculate the costs of the problems. I could find the costs for scrapping and rework, but not the costs for messing up the planning, in the accounting system. Eventually I reached a figure of about €500,000, which equalled a normal year's profit for the organization.

All of these costs appeared in the manufacturing department and it goes without saying that the performance of this department was appalling during this period. However, we already know that the performance of the purchasing department increased somewhat.

## Questions

1 This problem could be seen as a consequence of lacking cross-functional integration, in this case between purchasing and manufacturing. What other type of similar problems do you think could arise – for instance, between other departments like R&D and manufacturing, R&D and sales, and between manufacturing and sales?

2 Do you have any personal experience of this sort of problem originating from lack of integration? It could be from a job, doing group assignments, from a sports club, etc.

3 Why do you think this particular problem occurred in this company?

4 If you were the CEO of this company, what would you do to prevent similar problems from occurring in the future?

# Case 6.3

# The Motorway PPP*

**by Salman Ahmad, Ciaran Connolly and Istemi Demirag**

## Introduction

Since the 1980s and 1990s, Europe has experienced major shifts in how public services are delivered. These shifts were chiefly the result of government reforms aimed at making public-sector organizations and public services delivery more efficient and effective by adopting private-sector management models and marketization. The United Kingdom (UK), which is recognized as a 'pace setter' in pursuing such reform agendas, witnessed an aggressive privatization era during the 1980s.[1] This was succeeded by a new approach for public infrastructure procurement, namely public–private

* This case was authored by Professor Salman Ahmad, Aston University, Professor Ciaran Connolly, Queen's University Belfast, and Professor Istemi Demirag, Tallin University of Technology.

[1] Jupe, R. (2011) The modernisation and fragmentation of the UK's transport infrastructure, *Financial Accountability & Management,* 27(1): 43–62. Jupe, R. (2012) The privatization of British Energy: risk transfer and the state, *Accounting, Organizations and Society,* 37(2): 116–29.

partnerships[2] (PPPs).[3] Since 1992, when PPPs were officially launched in the UK, this model has remained popular among successive governments, having delivered up until now close to 700 infrastructure projects in the transport, health, education, prison and waste-management sectors, with a capital value of approximately £60 billion.[4]

Under a PPP arrangement, a government department procures construction and life-cycle operation and maintenance (O&M) services from the private sector. The private-sector partner in a PPP is a consortium or 'special purpose vehicle' (SPV), which then subcontracts the finance, design, construction, maintenance and soft services (Exhibit 1). As the client, the procuring government department has to develop project objectives a priori, which are operationalized through the contractual management control systems.

## The Motorway PPP (MPP)

The UK's transport sector of roads was the earliest adopter of PPPs for procuring toll motorways under the central government's Highways Agency. However, subsequent road PPPs addressed broader

**EXHIBIT 1** Organization of a typical UK PPP*

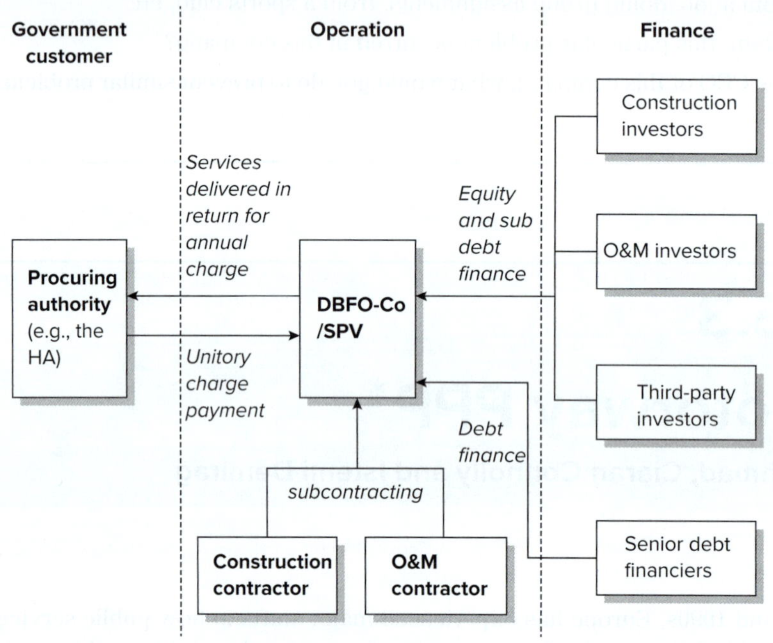


*Source:* Adapted from HM Treasury (2003) PFI: Meeting Investment Challenge, HM Treasury, London, p. 37.

[2] Broadbent, J. and Laughlin, R. (2004) PPPs: nature, development and unanswered questions, *Australian Accounting Review*, 14(33): 4–10. Florio, M. (2014) Contemporary public enterprises: innovation, accountability, governance, *Journal of Economic Policy Reform*, 17: 201–8. Warner, M.E. and Bel, G. (2008) Competition or monopoly? Comparing privatization of local public services in the US and Spain, *Public Administration*, 86(3): 723–35.

[3] Popularly known in the UK as the Private Finance Initiative (PFI) or, in some sectors, DBFO (design, build, finance and operate) contracts. The term PPP is used in this case study to refer to the PFI and the case at hand.

[4] Private Finance Initiative and Private Finance 2 projects; 2018 Summary Data, HM Treasury, May 2019. Available at: https://assets.publishing.service.gov.uk/government/uploads/system/uploads/attachment_data/file/805117/PFI_and_PF2_FINAL_PDF1.pdf (accessed 25 May 2020).

government objectives for the sector, particularly for acquiring solutions to increasing accidents on the strategic roads network. The largest of these later tranches of road PPPs is the Motorway PPP (hereafter the MPP). The MPP was signed as a 30-year contract during the late 2000s, with the government's rationale for signing off the project being:

> *The MPP is one of the busiest motorways in Europe with some sections carrying up to 200,000 vehicles per day . . . the level of congestion leads to . . . risk of accidents.* (Business Case)

To improve commuters' safety from accidents on the project road, the SPV was awarded a PPP contract for widening (constructing) some sections of the motorway, together with O&M over a 30-year period for the entire project road (including certain bridges and tunnels).

## Operationalizing commuters' safety-related management controls in the MPP

The MPP has completed the construction phases, which included widening works linked to availability-based payments for the SPV. The construction work has been delivered on time and to budget. During the ongoing O&M phase, for achieving commuters' safety, the SPV is assigned to mitigate risks of severe accidents (termed in the contract as KSI – Killed or Serious Injury accidents) by developing and implementing strategic safety plans. The SPV has the option to apply to the Highways Agency for funding to assist with the implementation of these safety plans, in which case they are recognized as Safety Improvement Schemes (Exhibit 2).

The Highways Agency is not obliged under the contract to fund safety proposals submitted by the SPV. Rather, the private funding of such proposals is emphasized as a desirable route, incentivized through certain key performance indicators (KPIs) that the Highways Agency applies on an annual basis for determining whether the SPV is entitled to a bonus. This scorecard, which is called the Proactive Management Review (PMR), is one of the subsystems within the MPP's management control system that is deployed over the O&M phase. For example, one of the scoring criteria under the PMR requires the SPV to propose solutions and plans 'often without calling on additional funding from the HA', while another PMR performance parameter emphasizes that the SPV should 'understand and work within the HA's budget constraints'.

**EXHIBIT 2** Commuters' safety KPIs assigned to the SPV over the O&M phase

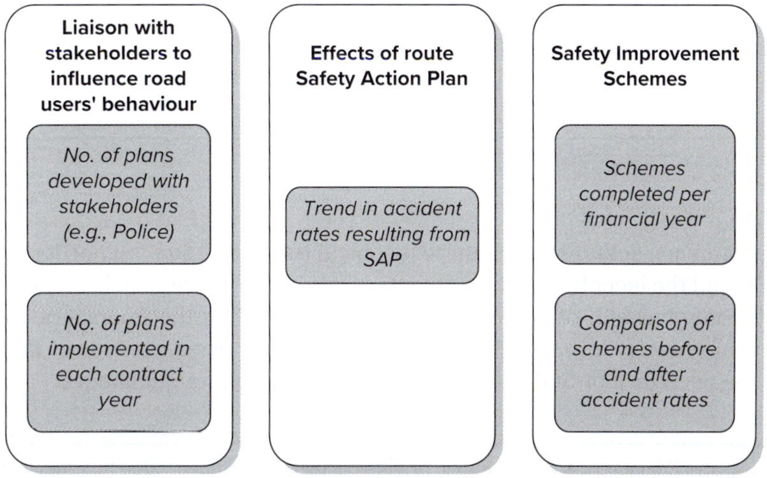

However, the contractors, as commercial organizations, will self-fund safety plans only when they can anticipate a positive financial return for their shareholders and lenders. A cost–benefit analysis would thus require comparing the budgeted cost of the safety plans with the financial incentives (bonuses) the contractors could be awarded if the operationalization of the plans leads to a reduction in the KSI accidents to or below the annual target.

Presently, there is only one KSI-related financial incentive deployed during the O&M phase. This is known as the Safety Performance Adjustment (SPA), and it awards an annual penalty or bonus to the SPV for either failing or achieving the KSI targets respectively. The SPA is capped at £1,000,000 annually (as a penalty or bonus) by the Highways Agency because it is believed that the contractors have limited influence on reducing KSIs on the MPP as they can only oversee the engineering and thus the amount is capped as a risk-management strategy. The MPP's contract manager at the Highways Agency was of the view that 'There will be a high risk premium if we don't cap the incentive. They do not control drivers' behaviour, or enforcements of rules, such as speed limits etc., nor are they authorized to educate the road users – these are things which governments do.'

Although, safety plans are produced each year by the SPV in order to conform to the KPIs (Exhibit 2), they are frequently not implemented. Capping the SPA to an annual bonus of £1,000,000 was considered to be inadequate and a disincentive by the CEO of the SPV: '. . . if they were giving us £10 million or £15 million or £20 million each year then I think you could see a big difference'.

The operationalization of the SPA has had a further dysfunctional effect. The underlying formula, which was developed a priori, was not tested before the commencement of O&M and therefore has unintentionally resulted in persistent deductions over several years (Exhibit 3). The formula compares the relative decline in KSI accidents on the MPP with certain comparator roads, however it does not take into account (for rewarding the contractors) any decrease in annual KSIs on the MPP itself.

**EXHIBIT 3** Financial impacts of operationalizing SPA from the start of the O&M phase

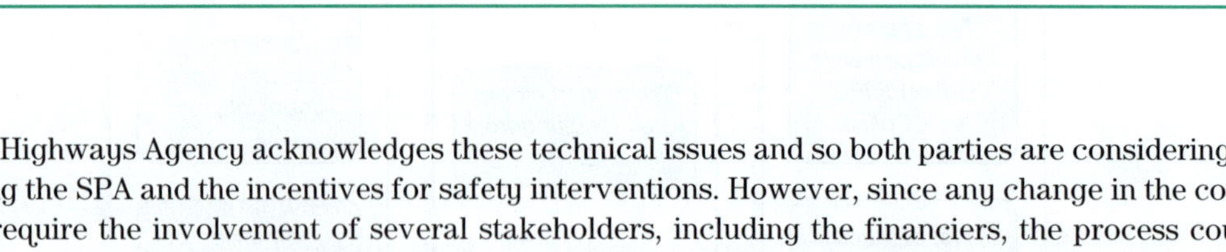


Financial impacts of operationalizing SPA from the start of O&M phase.

The Highways Agency acknowledges these technical issues and so both parties are considering renegotiating the SPA and the incentives for safety interventions. However, since any change in the contract would require the involvement of several stakeholders, including the financiers, the process could be cumbersome and inefficient. Also, UK PPPs are relatively centralized in terms of their governance[5] and, ultimately, it is the Secretary of State for Transport that approves any changes.

[5] Steijn, B., Klijn, E.H. and Edelenbos, J. (2011) Public private partnerships: added value by organizational form or management? *Public Administration*, 89(4): 1235–52.

## Tasks

Accounting technologies, such as management control systems, can constitute power to govern at a distance for state authorities.[6]

1 In light of this notion, and the policy aim of the UK and other European governments of providing more and better services through PPPs, discuss how and why management accounting, and in particular management control systems, could enable the realization of the 'partnership' ideal.

2 Consider yourself as an independent, third-party management consultant for the MPP. With regard to operationalizing commuters' safety objectives:

   a Prepare a report that outlines the shortcomings in the existing commuters' safety-related elements of management control systems.

   b Propose a commuters' safety-related management controls conceptual model, which should include relevant KPIs, performance measurement and performance management (i.e., incentive) elements.

3 Explain whether the O&M phase of PPPs reflects the recursive nature of contracting, requiring consistent recourse by the public- and private-sector parties to collaboration and practices of social control (i.e., 'trust'). Your answer should refer to the need to address the contentions regarding dysfunctional elements of the management controls tied to the commuters' safety objective.[7]

---

[6] Kurunmäki, L., Lapsley, I. and Miller, P. (2011) Accounting within and beyond the state, *Management Accounting Research*, 1(22): 1–5. Marques, L., Ribeiro, J.A. and Scapens, R.W. (2011) The use of management control mechanisms by public organizations with a network coordination role: a case study in the port industry, *Management Accounting Research*, 22(4): 269–91. Miller, P. and Rose, N. (1990) Governing economic life, *Economy and Society*, 19(1): 1–31. Walker, S.P. (2016) Revisiting the roles of accounting in society, *Accounting, Organizations and Society*, 49: 41–50.

[7] The following literature may be useful for you in developing your answers to questions 2 and 3 below: Chung, D. (2016) Risks, challenges and value for money of public–private partnerships, *Financial Accountability & Management*, 32(4): 448–68.

# Case 6.4

# The cross-functional integration project*

**by Angela Liew and Julia Harrison**

The late 1990s was a golden era for tech companies, not least those connected to the mobile phone industry. In those days the giants in the business were Ericsson and Nokia, but there were also many smaller producers as well as suppliers to the phone producers, who all wanted a slice of the cake. Allgon Mobile Communication (AMC) was one of these companies. It was set up at the beginning of the 1990s and grew considerably throughout the decade. Around the turn of the century, it was a market-leading manufacturer of antennas for mobile phones, with a 10 per cent share of the global market, a turnover of around €100 million and 400 employees.

---

* This case was written by Dr Angela Liew, Senior Lecturer, University of Auckland, and Dr Julie Harrison, Associate Professor, University of Auckland.

Even though the firm had grown rapidly, it was still entrepreneurial in nature, informal and not particularly structured. Due to the strong expansion, there was constant and strong pressure on the organization, and the focus was on solving concrete and urgent problems. One of the employees described the culture well with the statement: 'Here, everybody is running around with a screwdriver in their back pocket!' Many of the employees, especially in R&D, were engineers straight out of university and in their first job. However, most of them moved on after a year or two, seeking challenges more technically advanced than antennas.

Formal organizational affiliation, top-down hierarchy and follow-up systems were less important, and the organizational structure could be described as a matrix. One dimension consisted of functions and heads of the various functions, such as marketing, development and manufacturing, while the other and definitively strongest dimension consisted of cross-functional teams based around customers, markets or types of products. The customer teams consisted of a global account manager and a project leader, both from marketing, a radio frequency and a mechanical engineer, both from R&D, and a production engineer from manufacturing. The global account manager was the formal leader of the team. The team members all sat together in the same room, got to know one another very well and the teams became very tight.

In a fast-growing organization like this, there is likely to be a lot of problems and this was no exception. Top management identified three major problems all related to product development:

1. The lead time for product development projects was considered too long. This was important for several reasons, but one important reason was the large number of development projects in the company.
2. The design of the antennas frequently resulted in major problems in manufacturing. The young engineers in R&D lacked experience of manufacturing and rarely took manufacturing aspects into consideration when designing the antennas.
3. Projects with the aim of developing new technological solutions were carried out to only a very limited extent, since all the customer teams were occupied with developing antennas for customers.

At the beginning of the project, top management therefore decided to improve the cross-functional integration of the time-to-market process (TTM). The TTM was mainly the product development process; it started with a new product request or idea and finished when the new antenna was ready to put into manufacturing. It included several departments but was mainly included in the tasks of the customer teams. In addition, top management appointed a team consisting of 12 individuals who started formulating the overall objectives for the entire TTM project:

- Maximized net present value in product development projects
- Shorter lead times for product development projects
- Increased customer satisfaction at an average of four on a five-point scale
- Increased employee satisfaction at an average of four on a five-point scale.

### Task

Imagine that you are a member of the team with the task of improving the cross-functional integration of the TTM process in order to achieve the goals you have formulated. Develop a plan for what you want to change and how you are going to do it, as well as what you do not want to change. For information that is not included in the case you are free to make assumptions. Just be explicit about these assumptions in your answer.

# Case 6.5
# New product development at Big Fish*

**by Angela Liew and Julie Harrison**

## Introduction

Nancy Shen, the chief executive officer of Big Fish, has recently completed a strategic review of the company's operations and identified new product development (NPD) as the company's most important contributor to growth and profitability. Nancy is concerned that NPD in Big Fish is currently conducted in an ad hoc fashion, and no one person seems to have the full picture of what new products are being developed or when they are likely to be launched. She has also discovered that a formal approval process for new products seems to be absent and some new ideas being developed are not aligned with Big Fish's strategy. She thinks part of the problem is due to different functional groups in Big Fish competing against one another for limited company resources. Nancy has decided to restructure the NPD processes by adding a formal approval process and establishing a separate NPD Technologists team, with the goal of improving the strategic alignment of Big Fish's NPD processes.

## Background

Big Fish is a vertically integrated seafood company that rears, farms, develops and processes its own-branded sea-farmed fish products. It is a medium-sized firm with more than 425 employees and an annual turnover in excess of $100 million. Big Fish produces 8,500 tonnes of fish each year, half of which are sold locally while the other half are exported.

Big Fish's strategic vision is twofold. First, the company wants to sell lucrative value-added fish products, such as high-grade whole fish, premium fish fillets and ready-to-eat smoked fish products. Second, the company wants to grow its local and worldwide market share. NPD has been identified as a key driver for both strategic goals. Senior management believe that developing and selling innovative, value-added ready-to-eat fish products will help the company achieve its strategic vision. Big Fish wants to sell fish products that are the 'star attraction' of a meal and not just an ingredient for other dishes.

Although NPD was identified as critical strategically, Big Fish has only limited NPD resources to invest. Accordingly, only some of the new ideas proposed can proceed as working projects. Nancy and her senior management team consider it unwise to invest in projects that are assessed as loss-making, unless there are compelling strategic reasons to do so. However, under the existing NPD system there is no process for identifying the best allocation of resources across new projects.

The company is currently structured into functional teams as shown in Exhibit 1, with no separate department responsible for NPD.

As shown in Exhibit 1 the structure of Big Fish before the establishment of a separate NPD function consisted of four senior managers in charge of aquaculture (rearing and farming fish), processing, finance and marketing. All senior managers report directly to the CEO. The middle management team report to the senior managers and there are 11 departmental managers: the Freshwater Hatchery Manager, responsible for hatching new fish; the Seawater Aquafarm Manager, responsible for farming the fish; the Fish Performance Analyst, responsible for analysing the hatchery and aquafarm production results; the Fresh

---

* This case was written by Dr Angela Liew, University of Auckland, and Dr Julie Harrison, University of Auckland.

**EXHIBIT 1** Big Fish's organizational chart before restructuring

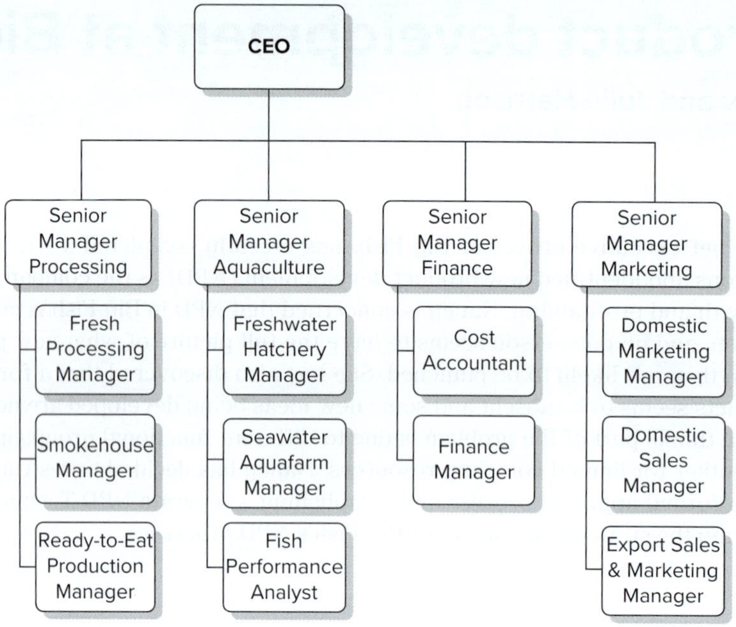


Processing Manager, responsible for the 'gill and gut' of whole fish, then filleting and grading processes; the Smokehouse Manager, responsible for the value-added hot and cold smoking processes; the Ready-to-Eat Production Manager, responsible for slicing and packaging the products; the Domestic Marketing Manager, responsible for local marketing activities aimed at generating future sales; the Domestic Sales Manager, responsible for current sales in the domestic market; the Export Sales & Marketing Manager, responsible for current and future export sales; the Cost Accountant, responsible for product costing and cost control; and the Finance Manager, responsible for accounting revenues and expenses.

## New product development

Innovation in NPD can be regarded as a continuum from incremental (minor) innovation through semi-radical innovation to radical (major) innovation. Innovation relates to both the business model of the company and its technical capabilities. If both are changed, an innovation is radical; if only one is changed, an innovation is semi-radical; if no material change is made to either, then it is an incremental innovation. Whether innovation is regarded as incremental or radical is defined with reference to a particular company's business, irrespective of the types of products produced in the same industry, other industries or different countries. For example, a radical innovation for a UK company would include the development of a new product sold in the US only if the UK company had not previously produced a similar product. A change in business model might involve drastically changing an existing distribution channel, or setting up a new distribution channel. Similarly, a stuffed chicken meal is a standard product in the poultry industry, but a stuffed fish fillet could be a radical innovation in a seafood company if it has not previously produced a similar product. In contrast, incremental innovation encompasses only minor changes to existing products – for example, if dill-flavoured fillets are currently produced, a new pesto-flavoured fillet would be incremental if the company does not need to make any significant changes to its production processes or business model.

In broad terms, the NPD process involves generating new ideas, evaluating ideas and selecting ideas for further development, developing prototypes, piloting new products and launching new products in the market.

## Problems with the existing NPD system

Under the existing NPD system new products can be developed by any functional team, but most new ideas are initiated by the marketing department, often in response to requests from customers. Like many firms in the food industry, most of Big Fish's new products are only slight variations or adjustments to its existing products, such as changing the packaging size, volume or flavour. For example, the most successful new products launched in the last three years were (1) the pesto-crusted smoked fillet, which uses the same production processes and packaging as an existing dill-crusted smoked fillet; and (2) the Christmas whole smoked fillet, which uses an intermediary whole smoked fillet produced from the existing smoking process and a new packaging pouch to create the new product.

New ideas can be proposed by anyone in Big Fish in any of the departments, however ideas are usually proposed by teams working in the Sales and Marketing Department or within the Processing Department. The selection of new ideas to develop can be made by any of the senior management team but is, mostly, done by the Marketing and Processing Senior Managers. In a small number of cases, ideas are proposed direct to the CEO. This happens when staff are trying to impress Nancy with their 'fancy' new ideas. In some cases, staff have been known to shop ideas around all the senior managers and the CEO to try to get their 'pet projects' developed.

Because decisions are made by any of the senior management team or the CEO no one has a complete view of the NPD decisions made, which projects are being approved and how the projects are progressing. The Marketing Senior Manager tends to approve only those new products closely aligned to what he knows is performing in the market, to ensure success. The Processing Senior Manager tends to approve only those new products based on what his factory employees can easily produce with minimal changes to the production processes and machineries. As the food industry is serving what is by nature an unadventurous market, where consumers have conservative tastes and refrain from trying new innovative food products, senior managers have been inclined to make conservative decisions in order to minimize the risk of failure.

The first problem Nancy encountered when she decided to review NPD at Big Fish was a lack of data. To begin her review she had to collate information from interviews with the senior managers and from her own records. The information collected is shown in Exhibit 2. Nancy wanted to measure how many new ideas were generated, but she could locate no record of all the ideas proposed, because new ideas were usually proposed in an ad hoc manner and in private meetings. However, she was able to collate a reasonable estimate of the number of new ideas developed, the number of new products launched into the market, the number of successful products[1] and the average time from the start of development to the product launch.

**EXHIBIT 2** Big Fish's NPD statistics for the past three years

| Year | New ideas proposed | New ideas developed | New product launch | Successful[1] products | Average time from idea to launch |
|---|---|---|---|---|---|
| 2020 | ? | 37 | 18 | 2 | 23 months |
| 2019 | ? | 39 | 19 | 2 | 23 months |
| 2018 | ? | 40 | 20 | 2 | 24 months |

[1] Nancy defined a successful product for this data collection as one that was still on the market three months after the launch date.

Currently, Big Fish works on the development of approximately 40 new products each year. Of these, about 20 are launched into the market, and only two products are still on the market after three months. While the level of NPD activity is viewed positively by Big Fish, the success rate of converting new ideas into successful products in the market is regarded as low. In addition, the average time between idea generation and market launch is almost two years, compared to industry standards of six to twelve months for less radical new food products.

Nancy thinks the most pressing problem is the low success rate for new products. In the food industry it is vital to refresh food brands by releasing successful new products on a regular basis, but these new products are effective only if they can last in the market for more than 12 months. Also of concern is the long lag time from idea generation to product launch. Nancy is keen to reduce this time to be in line with industry standards. Further, she has identified a significant number of new products that fail to launch because of a lack of evaluation during the development stage, which leads to retailers rejecting projects as unsuitable. Similarly, there are significant cost overruns with some new products when retailers request changes to packaging or labelling after the products are launched, which involves scrapping already purchased packaging materials and developing customer-approved packaging. Nancy thinks both these problems could easily be solved by talking to retail customers before launching new products. Finally, there are a large number of stalled product ideas, where the team developing those ideas have lost interest and moved on to other more interesting projects, and there appears to be no control over these decisions to abandon development.

With all this in mind, Nancy has reviewed all the new project ideas developed in the past three years and identified the following problems with the process:

- No detailed records are kept for all the parts of the NPD process, and there appeared to be no follow-up on abandoned or stalled projects.
- Limited or no product and market evaluation was conducted either during the development stage or after products were launched to assess the reasons for success/failure of new products.
- There was no communication with customers during the product development stage to measure the likely demand for the products or specific customer requirements.
- Some ideas developed related to low-volume or low-margin products were not in line with the company's strategic goals of high-value-added and high-volume products.
- Some ideas developed by the marketing team were rejected by the production team as not feasible using existing machinery and processes.
- There was no central review of new product ideas with approval to develop provided by different senior managers, depending on where the ideas originated.
- There was no systematic process for allocating resources (both people and funding) to new product ideas.
- Functional managers felt they were competing for resources and were reluctant to be involved in NPD where ideas had not originated in their own departments.
- Some ideas that had been rejected in previous years due to strategic misalignment continued to be worked on as new projects. The most prominent of these 'bad ideas' was the development of a fish stock soup additive. While customers had asked for this product, there are a large number of similar products already on the market, and margins and fish volume consumption on these types of products are low. Despite this, this same idea has been regularly recycled.
- Some functional managers lobbied Nancy direct to get approval for 'pet projects', especially when their own senior managers were likely to reject, or had rejected, the ideas.
- The 'success rate' for new products – that is, the number of new ideas that resulted in successful new products launched on the market – was very low.
- The time from idea generation to product launch was, on average, more than two years, which was viewed as unacceptable.

### New production development: implementing a new system

Given the importance of NPD to Big Fish, Nancy's first decision following her review was to set up a separate NPD Technologists team. This new team is responsible for coordinating and providing technical and administrative support for new projects. Freddy Roberts was employed as the new technology senior manager and his first task was to establish a new management control system for NPD.

Exhibit 3 shows the organizational chart for Big Fish following the restructuring.

Following the establishment of the NPD Technologists team, Freddy's first major decision was to implement a structured NPD process that was a 'stage-gate' embedded information technology (IT) system. The stage-gate process is a widely adopted NPD practice for managing the progress of individual projects. The stage-gate process is subdivided into a number of NPD stages and gates. Stages comprise investigation and development work activities; gates are set times in the development process when the gatekeepers meet, discuss and decide on the progression or termination of ideas and projects (referred to as 'gate meetings'). The new IT system comes with the default full classic stage-gate model built in it. This model has six stages and five gates, and was designed for radical innovation.

All new ideas proposed within Big Fish are recorded and tracked using the new IT system. Freddy is responsible for the day-to-day monitoring of the new IT system for NPD. The senior management team and Nancy have access to a dashboard that details progress in all the stages and this information is reviewed regularly as part of the monthly senior management meetings.

Exhibit 4 shows the stage-gate process implemented by Freddy.

Freddy and Nancy decided the best approach to implement the new system would be to form a Gatekeeper Group that had members from all the functional departments. Accordingly, the group comprises all the senior managers from the four divisions of Big Fish, plus Freddy as Technology Senior Manager. This group is responsible for approving new ideas as projects, and for deciding whether the projects can continue to the next stage or be terminated. The inclusion of every divisional senior

**EXHIBIT 3** Restructured organizational chart for Big Fish

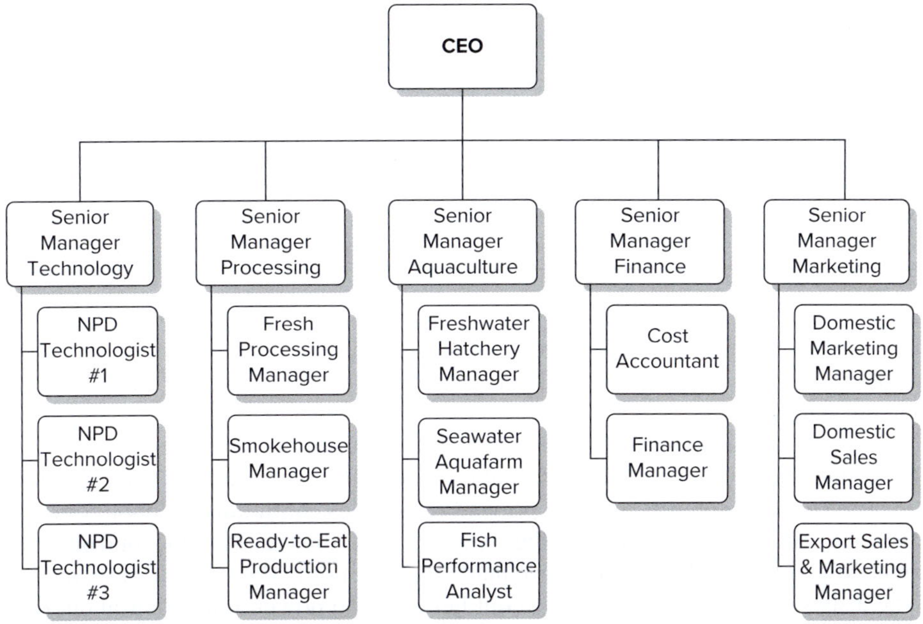

**EXHIBIT 4** Original stage-gate process embedded in Big Fish's IT system

| Embedded Stage-Gate Process | Stage/Gate | Description |
|---|---|---|
| Stage 1 | Discovery stage | New ideas for consideration in the first screen/gate are submitted by anyone in Big Fish from any level of the company |
| Gate 1 | Idea (first) screen | The Gatekeeper Group evaluate all new ideas for fit with Big Fish's strategy, and for product and market viability |
| Stage 2 | Capture idea and scoping | For the approved new ideas passing Gate 1, information is collected and the development of the idea scoped |
| Gate 2 | Second screen | The Gatekeeper Group evaluate the approved ideas using the new information collected in Stage 2 |
| Stage 3 | Build business case | For the approved new ideas passing Gate 2, detailed business plans are prepared, including financial analysis and legal compliance review |
| Gate 3 | Go to development | The Gatekeeper Group assess the business cases for the approved ideas and select the ideas to commit substantial financial resources to in the development stage |
| Stage 4 | Development | For the new ideas passing Gate 3, prototypes are developed to assess if selected ideas can be produced |
| Gate 4 | Go to testing | The Gatekeeper Group assess the prototypes and select those to proceed with further development |
| Stage 5 | Testing | For the approved prototypes passing Gate 4, market testing is performed including providing prototypes to customers to evaluate, and trial production of the new product is performed for estimated sales orders and production rates |
| Gate 5 | Go to launch | The Gatekeeper Group assess the customer feedback and sales and financial projections, and make a final decision on whether to launch the product |
| Stage 6 | Launch | For the approved new products passing Gate 5, manufacture and market launch |

manager as a gatekeeper reflected all the company leadership, both in body and in spirit. Gatekeepers are responsible for the gates; the NPD Technologists team is responsible for managing all the work performed in the stages.

Nancy, who had been responsible for the decision to establish the new NPD group, is not officially a gatekeeper in the new technology-driven decision process. However, she has been appointed chair of the NPD process. This decision was made to prevent employees continuing to lobby Nancy to promote their pet projects. However, Nancy considers she is, nevertheless, still in control and can exert authority over NPD if she thinks decisions are made that are not in the best interests of the company. However, she insists that the process is not about her exerting power, but rather about doing what is right for Big Fish. Nancy thinks it unlikely she will need to exert her authority given the consensus decision-making in the gate meetings, which ensures all senior management are equally involved in NPD resource allocation decisions. She strongly believes that her surrendering of a critical position in the Gatekeeper Group increases the morale of senior management so they feel more responsible for the decision-making process.

Under the new system Nancy can log into the IT system to read and learn about the findings and progress related to each project. In this way she can monitor all the new projects' progress quietly and remotely. Also, statistics on the number of ideas evaluated and their current status are collected and easily viewable thanks to a new project dashboard that has been installed on Nancy's computer and those of all the other senior managers. Nancy thinks this high visibility of NPD projects will help motivate her senior management team.

Occasionally, Nancy also comes to the gate meetings unexpectedly. To her, physical presence is a way to show her support to employees. She also expresses her opinions on decisions while she is at the gate meetings even though she is, technically, not a gatekeeper and has no voting rights.

Big Fish has endured many launch failures in the past that the NPD Technologists and senior management believed could have been avoided had they had more complete information about their local processes. Under the new system senior management are able to encourage employees to identify issues and share their knowledge to help improve the success rate of new product launches. The new IT system has also provided them with a methodological approach to consider as many local aspects as possible so that a more complete picture of production or of the launch outcome can be constructed.

To date (the system has been fully operational for nine months), the new NPD process has been successful in providing complete records of all new ideas generated, monitoring developing ideas, implementing new evaluation procedures, and eliminating problems with retailer refusal or reworking of products after launch. This has increased the number of successful products launched and Nancy is satisfied that the new system has been a success. However, the NPD Technologists team members have adhered closely to the whole prescribed stage-gate process as they are worried they might fail to conduct some important investigation activities if they do not follow the full classic project model. Nancy is concerned that although there is better oversight of NPD and the rate of successful products has improved, the problems related to the time to launch products have not been addressed. Further, some of the gatekeepers are getting frustrated by all the steps in the process, and one of them was recently overheard saying, 'Why do I have to jump through all these hoops when all I want to do is change the flavour of a product?'

Nancy wonders if it is time to start tweaking the new system.

## Questions

1 Discuss whether NPD processes are better suited to the waterfall method or agile method of project management.

2 From a lean perspective, explain whether you think the stage-gate process is a flow-efficiency or resource-efficiency system?

3 Discuss how you think cross-functional issues contributed to Big Fish's NPD problems under its old system of project management.

4 Explain how you think the gate meetings can provide matrix decision-making within Big Fish's functional organizational structure? What problems in the original NPD process do you think these meetings will or will not solve?

5 Consider the current full classic stage-gate process used by Big Fish and the problem(s) it has not addressed. How could an agile approach be used to simplify the stage-gate process to better reflect the types of new products being developed and to speed up the NPD process?

# Chapter 7

# Management control systems and inter-organizational relationships

## Learning objectives

After reading this chapter, you should be able to:

1. Explain the main drivers behind the development and increased importance of inter-organizational relationships.
2. Explain the common forms of inter-organizational relationships.
3. Explain the differences between traditional 'internal' management control systems and inter-organizational management control systems.
4. Explain the main changes to an organization's internal management control practices needed to promote better inter-organizational relationships.
5. Explain the main ways to achieve the joint development of inter-organizational management control practices with key customers and/or suppliers.

## Real world vignette: Ducati

The Italian motorbike producer, Ducati, experienced a severe financial crisis and, in order to survive, had to achieve a major turnaround.[1] When searching for ways to reduce costs, an analysis of its internal productivity found that it could be increased by 20 per cent. Without an inter-organizational perspective on management control systems, the company would most likely have focused its efforts on internal productivity improvement efforts. However, on closer inspection, Ducati found that the increase in internal

[1] This vignette is based on information in Bocconcelli, R. and Håkansson, H. (2008) External interaction as a means of making changes in a company: the role of purchasing in a major turnaround for Ducati, *IMP Journal*, 2: 25–37.

productivity would reduce its product costs by only 4 per cent because purchased components accounted for 80 per cent of its product costs. The conclusion drawn from this was that it would be impossible for Ducati to make the turnaround by itself. Ducati had close inter-organizational relationships with some of its suppliers and realized that these suppliers were the key to a successful turnaround.

Ducati's suppliers deliver a number of customized subsystems to Ducati, which then assembles them into a motorbike. As such, Ducati's production is spread over many highly specialized production sites, each owned by other companies. Ducati's higher-level managers concluded that they had to mobilize the suppliers if the company was to achieve a turnaround. Instead of trying to pressure its suppliers into reducing their prices by threatening to change suppliers, Ducati developed a more intimate cooperation with some of its suppliers, to combine forces to reduce costs and to increase the efficiency of their combined production. Ducati needed to describe and analyse all the activities and related costs and revenues between itself and its suppliers. And, in collaboration with its close suppliers, Ducati achieved its turnaround and overcame the financial crisis.

This case is an example of where the traditional (internal) view of management control systems developed so far in this book is of little help, making it necessary for Ducati to apply an inter-organizational view of management control systems. Ducati's inter-organizational relationships with suppliers were the key to achieving sustained competitive advantage. The key aspects of Ducati's costs in this situation were not those of its own internal operations or the overall prices paid for its purchases. Instead, the key costs for Ducati were those involved in the interplay between its own operations and those of its close suppliers. Companies like Ducati need to think systematically with regard to how to develop efficient and effective inter-organizational management control systems.

## Introduction

In Chapter 1, we explained that an important aspect of throughput controls is the organizational architecture. That is, one way to control the behaviours of lower-level managers and employees is to systematically design appropriate structural arrangements for the organization's mission, goals and strategies. In this chapter we discuss one such structural arrangement, namely whether organizations should engage systematically in formal cooperation with other organizations and form, for instance, joint ventures or outsourcing arrangements. Inter-organizational relationships, defined as various forms of cooperation between independent organizations, have increased in popularity during recent decades. As a consequence, today's organizational landscape is characterized to a large extent by more and more specialized organizations that limit themselves to just a few operations that contribute only a minor part of the eventual offering that is acquired by end customers. For many companies, such as Ducati, a few core suppliers and customers are responsible for a significant proportion of the costs and revenues. One explanation for this development is that the requirements of customers have grown more complex and changed so that they can rarely be satisfied by buying conventional or generic products. Organizations have become, by choice or by necessity, highly dependent on specific suppliers and customers, and well-functioning cooperation is often seen as key to achieving sustainable competitive advantage.

'Inter-organizational relationships' is a general term that encompasses several different forms of cooperation, such as joint ventures, supply chain initiatives, strategic alliances and outsourcing relationships. The increase in the number and importance of inter-organizational relationships imposes new demands on top managers, who need to rethink the notion of organizational architecture and as such the very design of management control systems. So far in this book, we have discussed traditional 'internal' management control practices mainly focused on internal activities within the organizational boundary. In terms of throughput controls (more specifically the organizational architecture), there has been a clear hierarchical authority structure between top managers, managers of the various responsibility centres and the rest of the employees in the company. As the Ducati case illustrates, the significance of inter-organizational relationships makes it necessary for managers to *extend the notion of organizational architecture beyond the company's borders.* This begs the question: How can top managers design management control practices to achieve well-functioning cooperation with the organization's important customers and suppliers? This view of control, henceforth called *inter-organizational management control systems,* is conceptually different from traditional (internal) management control systems. Compared with coordinating activities within an organization in which hierarchical authority is one important basis for control, inter-organizational coordination takes place between legally independent organizations where there is no clear formal hierarchical authority in place.

This chapter starts by detailing some of the most common types of inter-organizational relationship, as well as introducing and explaining the main drivers behind the increased formation of these relationships. Thereafter, inter-organizational management control systems are discussed. First, we describe how each organization individually can develop its internal management control practices to account better for inter-organizational relationships. Second, we discuss how organizations jointly can develop inter-organizational management control practices aimed at facilitating cooperation between the organizations.

## Increased importance of inter-organizational relationships

There are a number of factors that, in combination, can be seen as the main drivers behind the development and increased importance of inter-organizational relationships. Two of the most commonly mentioned factors are *globalization,* and *rapid technological transformation and increased technical complexity of products and services.* Through globalization the speed of transformation of existing customer structures and the emergence of new business opportunities have increased dramatically. Organizations face globalized markets that are much larger than before, but at the same time they also meet fierce global competition. To remain competitive in a globalized world, organizations need to have fast and efficient access to customers to be able to develop new products quickly. As such, the development of existing relationships to form close long-term inter-organizational relationships with key customers, sometimes called lead users, has become an important tool for achieving success in a globalized world. These lead users are actively involved in the supplying organization's product development processes.

***Real World Example:*** ABB Robotics is a business unit of ABB, a large multinational company. It develops, manufactures and sells robots, and is one of the world's largest robot manufacturers. Important customers are car manufacturers, such as General Motors, Volvo and Peugeot. When ABB Robotics developed some of its robots, General Motors and ABB Robotics embarked on joint projects involving key specialists such as project coordinators, engineers, purchasers and sales representatives. Engineers from ABB Robotics gained important knowledge by observing how General Motors organized the production and handled smaller robot-related problems. In addition, ABB Robotics' engineers described the General Motors staff as being extremely knowledgeable, with useful ideas about how to improve robots and about future trends.

*Source:* Carlsson-Wall, M. (2011) Targeting target costing: cost management and inter-organizational product development of multi-technology products. PhD thesis, Stockholm School of Economics.

Another important factor is the rapid technological transformation and increased technical complexity of products and services that has been taking place. This has made it difficult for organizations to maintain in-house expertise in every potentially relevant technical area. For instance, organizations often have products in which many technologies need to be coordinated, with the result that hardly any organizations can rely solely on their own technological expertise. An organization cannot be on the technological forefront in every area, and needs to develop close inter-organizational relationships with its suppliers to be able to exploit their knowledge when developing its products or services. Thus, it often makes sense for an organization to outsource some activities to suppliers who are experts in the area concerned. A Swedish survey conducted in the engineering industry showed that more than 65 per cent of production units with more than 500 employees had outsourced the production of a product or component during the previous three years.[2] It is also increasingly common to outsource functions other than production – for example, information technology (IT), maintenance, development and internal auditing. Through outsourcing, the organization may avoid the risks, costs and probable lengthening of lead times associated with in-house development in an unfamiliar field. Its use is often justified by the need for organizations to focus on their core competencies, but it is increasingly apparent that organizations perceive outsourcing as a means of gaining access to a supplier's know-how with the intention of improving product quality. However, outsourcing is successful only when the cooperation with the suppliers functions smoothly, and hence the organization needs to develop close inter-organizational relationships with these suppliers.

In summary, it can be said that organizations today develop inter-organizational relationships to handle globalization, worldwide competition, rapid technological development and more complex products. Collaboration with suppliers and customers enables organizations to share the fixed costs and risks associated with technological and product development, to enhance their core competencies, to gain access to complementary competencies and to increase the speed of market entry. As such, both increased revenues and decreased costs can provide the motives for forming inter-organizational relationships. Some organizations enter into inter-organizational relationships in an attempt to increase revenue by gaining access to complementary resources, to improve product development and to get better access to customers. Other organizations attempt to decrease costs by achieving economies of scale by engaging in joint research projects and/or joint marketing or production activities. It has been shown that the increased formation of inter-organizational relationships, either through the development of existing relationships to make them closer and longer term, or through the formation of new inter-organizational (outsourcing) relationships, are ways for organizations to stay competitive in a rapidly changing world. It is important, however, to stress that there is also a 'dark side' to inter-organizational relationships. Powerful customers have been found to exploit suppliers, sometimes forcing them to share confidential information about their costs. So one must remember that engaging in close inter-organizational relationships offers both opportunities and risks for the organizations.

***Real World Example:*** French retail giant Carrefour has expanded its operations to Kenya. There it has been accused of exploiting suppliers and was ordered to review all its supply agreements. In particular, it had to excise some items from supplier contracts that were said to give Carrefour unfair competitive advantage on the Kenyan market.

*Source:* KSN Reporter (2020) Carrefour under fire for exploiting suppliers, *KSN News*, 19 February. Available at: https://ksnmedia.com/2020/02/carrefour-under-fire-for-exploiting-suppliers/ (accessed 8 May 2020).

## Types of inter-organizational relationship

Organizations engage in a variety of inter-organizational relationships. Apart from the inter-organizational relationships between customers and suppliers described earlier, there are also more formalized forms

[2] Bengtsson, L., Berggren, C. and Lind, J. (eds) (2005) *Alternativ till outsourcing [Alternatives to Outsourcing]*. Malmö: Liber.

of inter-organizational relationship. *Technology licensing* offers the opportunity for one organization to exploit the know-how of another by paying a fee or royalty based on sales. As such, technology licensing is seen by many managers as a way of getting rapid access to technology at a low cost. Compared with in-house development, this type of licensing is assumed to reduce development costs, speed up product development times and result in a faster market entry. However, one potential drawback compared with, for instance, outsourcing is a loss of control over operational issues such as pricing and product quality.

*Strategic alliances* typically take the form of an agreement between two organizations to co-develop a new technology, product or service with specified goals and to a predetermined timetable. A strategic alliance can be viewed as a long-term inter-organizational relationship that does not have an ultimate (individual) decision-making authority, and that aims to improve the competitive position and performance of the organizations involved through the sharing of resources. *Joint ventures* are even more formal than strategic alliances and involve setting up a new organization with two (or more) parent companies as its owners. A joint venture involves a distinct operating entity with an authority structure deriving from the combination of resources provided by the parent companies, which then share the ownership and control. These formalized forms of inter-organizational relationship are often established between a buyer and supplier, but can also be developed by potential competitors. An example of this is the collaboration between Volvo and Mitsubishi in forming NedCar, the Dutch car manufacturing company.

We now understand why inter-organizational relationships have moved up the organizational agenda and are perceived as important concerns for top managers. Inter-organizational relationships pose unique control problems as compared with traditional management control systems within organizations. In inter-organizational relationships, control encompasses the separately owned organizations and thus there is no longer a superior authority with the right to impose hierarchical control. In the next section, inter-organizational management control systems are discussed.

## Inter-organizational management control systems

As the Ducati case at the beginning of this chapter illustrates, many organizations are, financially and operationally, highly interdependent with specific customers and suppliers. Close cooperation with these organizations thus becomes an important factor for success. In the previous chapters in the book, we have implicitly assumed a particular organizational architecture where the organization in question has control over, or at least is responsible for, all the costs that arise within its boundary, and that the organization has little, if any, control over what happens outside this boundary. When we now relax this assumption, there is a need for inter-organizational management control systems. Inter-organizational management control systems may be divided into two parts:

1. *Changes of an organization's internal management control practices* to account for better inter-organizational relationships
2. *The joint development of inter-organizational management control practices* with key customers and/or suppliers.

We will deal with these in turn.

### Changes to an organization's internal management control practices

When top managers become aware of the strategic importance of inter-organizational relationships, they often focus on joint development of inter-organizational management control practices with their customers and suppliers. However, many managers forget that they also need to analyse how their internal management control practices can be adapted to account better for inter-organizational relationships. Without such adaptation, cooperation with customers and suppliers is likely to suffer as employees tend to focus their efforts on internal activities and resources. We describe various ways in which an organization's internal management control practices can be adapted to account better for inter-organizational relationships.

### Changing throughput controls: working capital management

Working capital is defined as current assets (e.g., accounts receivables and inventory) less current liabilities (e.g., accounts payables). Traditionally, working capital management has been performed mainly from a single organization's point of view. This has often led to large and powerful organizations squeezing their smaller customers with decreased payment terms and/or squeezing their smaller suppliers with increased payment terms. In effect, small suppliers often act as 'banks' to their large customers.

In taking *an inter-organizational perspective on working capital management*, there are obvious problems with transferring credit risks and capital costs to small suppliers and customers. As many working capital efficiencies are zero-sum games where one organization gains and another loses, the organizations that lose are often the small suppliers and customers with a relatively high cost of capital. These organizations often have difficulties getting cash, which means a risk for a less financially stable supplier and customer base. This together with quality problems and delays will most likely lead to total costs being higher in the end.

If organizations want well-functioning and effective cooperation, there is a need for an alternative view on working capital management. One implication is the importance of first starting with the organization's internal processes before the organization tries to squeeze its (small) customers and suppliers. Can the company improve the internal routines for invoice handling, for example? This might create working capital efficiencies without impacting on the cooperation with customers. In addition, with an inter-organizational perspective on working capital management, large and powerful companies should focus on reducing costs for working capital for the whole supply chain by sharing information and resources. One way to achieve this could be to ensure that small suppliers have access to credit. The large customers (with a relatively low cost of capital) may act as 'banks' to small suppliers (with a relatively high cost of capital) to reduce the capital costs for the supply chain as a whole.

**Real World Example:** The large consumer products company, Unilever, applies an inter-organizational perspective to its working capital management. Unilever's head of global sales and operations, Martin Jarvis, argues that improving working capital on the backs of suppliers is usually counterproductive. For instance, Unilever deals with numerous tea suppliers in Kenya, Sri Lanka and Indonesia, whose cost of capital often is higher than Unilever's. Unilever focuses on reducing working capital for the entire supply chain by sharing information and resources. Unilever works with its financial service providers to ensure its suppliers have access to credit at Unilever rates. According to Unilever's calculations, working capital fell 40 per cent, or about $2 billion, over a period of four years.[3]

### Changing output controls: overlapping responsibilities

One common problem for organizations that want to increase focus on inter-organizational relationships is that cooperation gets too little priority because lower-level managers and employees continue to focus on their internal activities. The reason for this is that the output controls in place foster such behaviour because the assigned responsibilities and the corresponding performance measures relate primarily to the organization's internal activities. One novel way to overcome this problem and increase focus on inter-organizational relationships is to create units with *partially overlapping responsibilities*.

[3] Reason, T. (2005) Capital ideas: the 2005 Working Capital Survey, *CFO Magazine*. Available at: http://www.cfo.com/article.cfm/4315504 (accessed 14 June 2013).

This means that various responsibility centre managers, in addition to the 'internal' performance measures, are also evaluated on measures that relate to the actions of important customers and suppliers – that is, measures that are not controlled by the unit but can be influenced through its interaction with customers and suppliers. The manager responsible for a sales unit can, for instance, be evaluated and rewarded through the customers' actions. A measure of the performance of the sales unit would then be whether customers start to use a particular feature (which is important for the organization) in their operations. The sales units need to build well-functioning inter-organizational relationships with their customers in order to be able to influence the outcome of these 'inter-organizational' performance measures. As such, overlapping responsibilities are likely to increase focus on inter-organizational cooperation. If a company has different sales units responsible for different customers, these sales units are likely to act as their customers' voices within the organization. If the different customers have different needs, the sales units will attempt to get the maximum amount of attention paid to their own customers' needs.

***Real World Example:*** Swedish cellular telecommunications company, Ericsson, has developed close inter-organizational relationships with customers such as Vodafone, Telia, Orange and France Telecom. To increase focus on cooperation Ericsson created units with partially overlapping responsibilities, where the individual units were evaluated on measures that could not necessarily be controlled by the unit. For example, Ericsson's customer unit for Telia was measured on actions related to Telia. As such, Ericsson's customer units were, to some extent, evaluated and rewarded based on the outcome of their customers' actions. One manager within the customer unit responsible for Telia, for example, was evaluated on how successful he had been in persuading Telia to use a new software feature in its operations. The overlapping responsibilities led to increased focus on inter-organizational cooperation with important customers as Ericsson's customer units acted as its customer's voice within Ericsson and tried to influence Ericsson's development units to meet its customer's needs.

*Source:* Based on information in Håkansson, H. and Lind, J. (2004) Accounting and network coordination, *Accounting, Organizations and Society*, 29: 51–72.

### *Changing output controls: target costing and rank-based rewards*

Originating in Japan, target costing has been the object of increased attention in the West since the 1990s and has become a central output control practice for product development. It is claimed that 70–80 per cent of product costs are committed during development, and target costing aims to reduce costs already 'on the drawing board'. Successful adaptations of target costing include Toyota, Olympus and Caterpillar. The concept, and its underlying logic, have been proven to be as important in the relationship between organizations that act as suppliers and customers in an overall supply chain.

The starting point and underlying logic of target costing is captured in the target costing equation:

**Estimated selling price − desired profit = target cost**

The equation demonstrates how the target cost is the cost at which the organization can afford to sell the product and still make enough profit to satisfy its shareholders. The estimated selling price is based on assumptions of what customers are willing to pay for the product. The goal of target costing is to ensure that unprofitable products are never launched. Traditionally, target costing has focused on internal activities. Development projects are organized using cross-functional teams, which analyse current costs and see if they can attain the target cost. When there is a mismatch, the teams are forced to seek alternative solutions. If the target cost cannot be met, the organization must choose between closing down the project or identifying other positive effects for the product portfolio or specific customers.

Taking an inter-organizational perspective on target costing brings to the fore *the importance of involving suppliers and customers in the target costing process.* As illustrated in the Ducati case, when key technologies and a large portion of costs are located outside firm boundaries, collaboration with suppliers becomes crucial for financial success. Well-functioning inter-organizational cooperation with customers gives the organization important input on future trends that needs to be taken into account during product development, as well as trade-offs between additional costs and what it is expected to add in terms of value for the customer. In addition, target costing becomes a tool for reducing the overall cost of a product with the help of all the organization's departments and suppliers. Costs of new products may be reduced by examining all possible ideas that might bring about cost reductions in the product's planning, research and development, and prototyping phases. The involvement of suppliers is crucial because supplier costs are often a large part of the total product cost.

**Real World Example:** Nissan works closely with its suppliers during product development because supplier costs represent more than 80 per cent of the total vehicle target cost. The vehicle target cost is divided into its smallest elements, with each part and component having specific objectives for functionality and allowed cost. Nissan integrates its suppliers in this planning process. As a result, target costing affects the cost consciousness of both Nissan and its suppliers. In this way, Nissan coordinates its cost reduction efforts within its own departments and suppliers through target costing processes.

*Source:* Carr, C. and Ng, J. (1995) Total cost control: Nissan and its UK supplier partnerships, *Management Accounting Research*, 6: 347–65.

Formalized buyer–supplier interactions in target costing processes to identify opportunities for joint cost reduction often imply involving the buyer's and the supplier's design teams in the joint management of costs. On the basis of empirical studies conducted in Japanese manufacturing companies, research[4] has identified three different types of target costing approach: *functionality–price–quality trade-offs*, *inter-organizational cost investigations* and *concurrent cost management.*

Functionality–price–quality trade-offs were used to resolve relatively minor cost overrun problems, where limited interactions between organizations' design engineers were sufficient to resolve the problems. The only way to reduce costs to the target level was to relax functionality and/or quality specifications in ways that would be acceptable to the buyer. The estimated cost savings obtained in this way were in the range 0–5 per cent. When more significant changes to the product design were required, inter-organizational cost investigations were used. More intense interactions between the organizations' design engineers were then needed, and various redesigns of the product were performed to make it more cost-efficient. The cost savings from this technique were estimated to be in the range of 5–10 per cent. Finally, concurrent cost management was used when fundamental changes in both the buyer's product and the supplier's components were needed. The design teams from the collaborating organizations met frequently to discuss the design changes that the supplier could make. The supplier is involved early in the design process, and cost savings in the range of 10–15 per cent were estimated.

Another way of motivating suppliers to produce cost savings and quality improvements is to use *rank-based rewards.* Suppliers are then ranked into categories – for instance, A, B or C. Rank A suppliers are the excellent suppliers and, therefore, the organization engages in close and long-term relationships with them. Rank B suppliers may be used as capacity buffers. Inter-organizational relationships with

[4] Cooper, R. and Slagmulder, R. (2004) Interorganizational cost management and relational context, *Accounting, Organizations and Society*, 29: 1–26.

rank C suppliers, on the other hand, are not expected to endure and will be terminated unless considerable improvements become evident. The logic with rank-based rewards is that suppliers who achieved relatively high performance increased their chances of being awarded a more profitable assignment in the future.

### Changing throughput and output controls: value flow charts and profitability analysis of customer relationships

A central issue for managers when attempting to analyse inter-organizational relationships is how a relationship should be conceptualized. Increasingly, more and more organizations tend to view each individual inter-organizational relationship as an element within a *network of relationships*. This is a setting that involves the simultaneous handling of a set of interconnected relationships that are interdependent. Interactions in an inter-organizational relationship between organizations A and B can have an influence through *network effects* on another inter-organizational relationship between, for instance, organizations A and C. Thus, network effects imply that changes in the inter-organizational relationship between an organization and, for example, one of its suppliers can also affect the organization's other relationships with suppliers and customers. The opposite is also the case, so that any one of the organization's inter-organizational relationships may be affected by events taking place within the interconnected network of relationships.

Interdependencies mean that operations, investments, cash flows, costs and revenues are intimately connected between specific organizations across a business network. Many relationships have similar requirements and an organization may be able to combine relationships that can benefit from a single investment in facilities or knowledge. The outcome of investments in one relationship will often appear as decreased costs or increased revenues in other relationships. Consequently, an organization's throughput and output control practices need to be adapted to account for network effects. For instance, the managers need to ensure that the organization's internal information system can capture both the direct effects on the other organization in the inter-organizational relationship, and also the network effects on and from the other inter-organizational relationships in the network. Obtaining a complete model for all these direct and indirect effects is impossible, and the organization needs to focus on the most important interconnections.

One way to account for network effects is to use throughput controls in the form of *value flow charts* to provide a network picture of the organization's interconnected inter-organizational relationships. The names and locations of key suppliers and customers may be shown on the value flow chart along with, for instance, the connections between the suppliers, the flow of materials and each supplier's added costs. Value flow charts will work as guidelines to help the (buying) organization understand that the costs in the inter-organizational relationship with a supplier are often not only driven by the buying organization's costs and the supplier's costs, but also by how the inter-organizational relationship relates to other relationships. Decisions on adding new products may, for example, be analysed in terms of the consequences they would have on the organization's overall costs that mainly depend on what and how the supplier's other customers bought. Thus, through a value flow chart, the scope of the costs to include in the analysis can be expanded to include network effects in the form of the costs of interconnected organizations in the network.

***Real World Example:*** A German car manufacturer, anonymized here as Eurocar, introduced a value chain flow chart (Figure 7.1) that visualized the car manufacturing network. It presented the network members involved in the production of a particular component or system and the cost occurrence at the different stages of the material flow in the network. The value chain flow chart was prepared by Eurocar in cooperation with the Tier 1 supplier, which in turn involved the Tier 2 or Tier 3 suppliers.

**FIGURE 7.1** Eurocar value chain flow chart

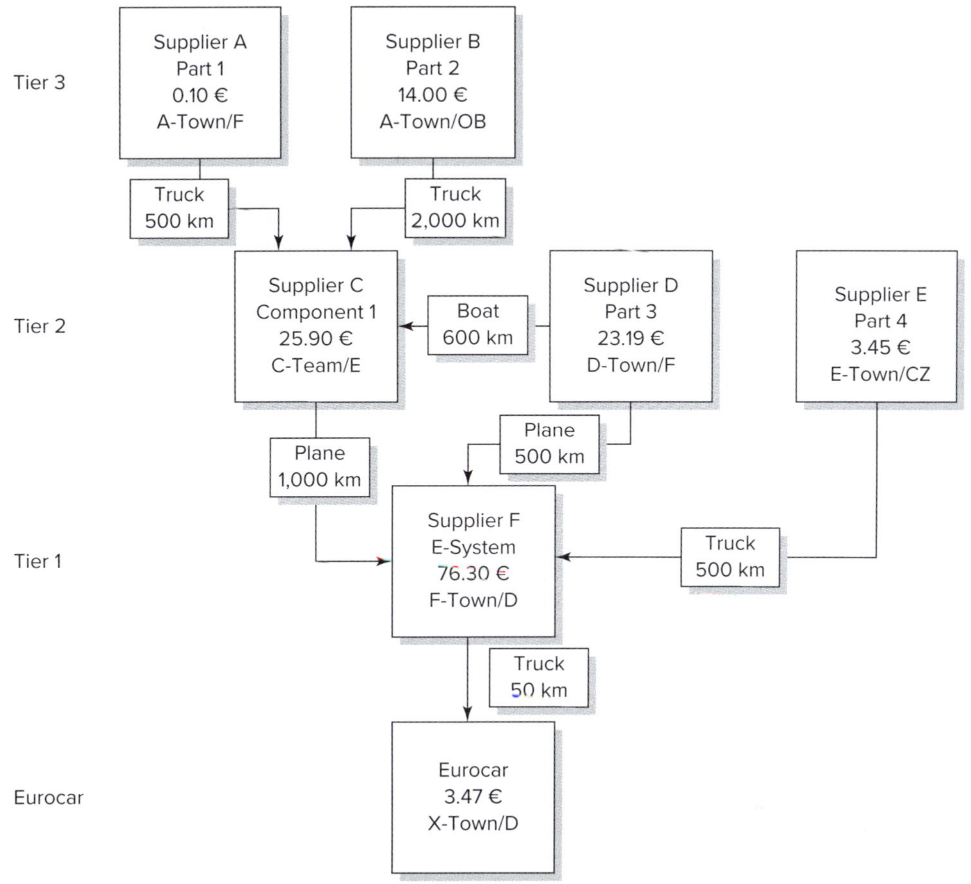


*Source:* Kajüter, P. and Kulmala, H.I. (2005) Open-book accounting in networks: potential achievements and reasons for failures, *Management Accounting Research*, 16: 179–204.

Another example of the importance of accounting for network effects is when an organization designs output controls in the form of *profitability analysis of customer relationships* that account for long-term investment and indirect benefits. These customer relationships impose specific demands on the organization's customer profitability evaluation because they create high direct costs but generate low direct revenues. The existence of these inter-organizational relationships is rather motivated in accounting terms by the revenues that these relationships can generate indirectly in and through other relationships. These customers can, for instance, be involved in joint product development and provide input for cost reductions that improve the profit margin on products sold to numerous other customers. If these key customers were evaluated without incorporating network effects, they would appear highly unprofitable. However, the customer profitability analysis needs to extend beyond the annual time period typically used in accounting and incorporate benefits from connected relationships. Measuring the investments and indirect benefits from all the organization's customer relationships will however be a complex and expensive task. Therefore, only a few key customer relationships can be evaluated in this way.

In summary, when applying an inter-organizational perspective on management control systems, there are a number of changes to an organization's internal management control practices that should be implemented. These involve creating units with partly overlapping responsibilities, conducting target costing in close cooperation with suppliers and customers, applying an inter-organizational perspective on working capital management and designing management control practices that account for network effects. However, organizations also need to jointly develop inter-organizational management control practices aimed at facilitating cooperation between the organizations. These are discussed next.

## The joint development of inter-organizational management control practices

In parallel to changing their internal management control practices to account for better inter-organizational relationships, top managers need to work out how to jointly develop inter-organizational management control practices (input, throughput, output) with key customers and/or suppliers.

### *Inter-organizational input controls*

Well-functioning cooperation is largely dependent on *trust* between people in the cooperating organizations. Research on inter-organizational management control systems has shown that level of trust among managers and employees is an important influence on behaviour in inter-organizational relationships. Trust is the expectation by one party in an inter-organizational relationship that the other party will behave in a predictable and acceptable way. Trust may stem from previous experiences, or it may gradually develop in an inter-organizational relationship through learning and adaptation. Unless a certain level of trust is established between the cooperating organizations, it will be difficult for the people involved to agree on common goals, or to work together in teams. As such, a high level of trust makes it easier to agree on the measures to be taken and the procedures to be adopted in a relationship, thereby facilitating the process of finding acceptable inter-organizational output and throughput controls. Trust also improves the sharing of information (such as is needed, for instance, in open-book accounting) and makes it easier to have common development projects, which are important factors for successful inter-organizational relationships.

Inter-organizational input controls should therefore be designed to increase the level of trust. This can be done by holding regular meetings and establishing a joint means of resolving disputes to ensure that any conflicts that arise in the inter-organizational relationship are sorted out quickly. The sharing of accounting information can also help in building trust and commitment. In addition, the selection of a 'partner' is brought forward as key if a successful inter-organizational relationship is to be achieved. Prior experience of working together and evidence of 'matching' cultures are criteria often used when choosing a partner for an inter-organizational relationship. Once the inter-organizational relationship is established, a consideration of the preferences of both organizations when making joint decisions is likely to lead to the creation of shared meaning and visions in the relationship. As it takes time to build a common culture, it is important that managers of both organizations are dedicated to the task and that they initiate activities with this aim in mind. Without such support and involvement, it is difficult to have a successful cooperation. Other ways of building trust include ensuring that there are open communication channels between the employees in the respective companies and focusing on developing personal relationships between key people in each company. When entering into important cooperation with suppliers and customers, managers tend to forget these input control practices. This is dangerous as many inter-organizational relationships fail due to mistrust between the organizations.

### *Inter-organizational throughput controls*

*Inter-organizational throughput controls* are also important for well-functioning cooperation. These control practices first specify how the two organizations should act and then evaluate whether the specifications have been followed. Common throughput controls in inter-organizational relationships are policy documents and procedures. They set out what is considered acceptable behaviour and specify the roles of the different actors in the relationship. Formal documents are important for describing the agreements made between the organizations and the methods that have to be followed throughout the cooperation. People from both organizations in the inter-organizational relationship should meet regularly to develop and discuss the guidelines for joint projects, the routines to be used to reduce costs and the actions to be taken to increase revenues. In inter-organizational relationships, there is often a need to clarify how everyone should behave as well as having a forum for communication; meetings provide an ideal opportunity for both clarification and communication. A more formalized forum for clarification and dispute resolution is to implement an '*alliance board*' with top managers representing both organizations. The alliance board decides on the rules to be followed in the inter-organizational relationship and the routines to be established.

Supply chain management is a broad term that encompasses the integration of key business processes from end user through original suppliers that provide products or services, and the management of multiple inter-organizational relationships across the supply chain. This means that continuous information flows and planning and control of operations are critical to effective supply chain management. *Value chain analysis* has been put forward as the preferred inter-organizational throughput control practice for companies that operate an integrated supply chain. Value chain analysis is used to analyse, coordinate and optimize linkages between interdependent activities in the value chain. In such a process the whole value chain, from raw materials to end product, is broken down into strategically relevant segments, enabling the managers to gain a better understanding of cost behaviour and the sources of differentiation. Value chain analysis was developed as a reaction to the traditional focus on maximizing the difference between the organization's purchasing costs and selling price. This traditional analysis ignores the linkages in the wider value chain such as the exploitation of linkages with suppliers and customers.

Thus, the idea with value chain analysis is to increase the understanding of the linked chain of value-creating activities that runs from basic raw materials to end-use customers in order to understand better how the activities can be carried out in more efficient and effective ways. Figure 7.2 displays the essence of a value chain. As shown, different parts in the value chain are often performed by different organizations – that is, raw material suppliers, a manufacturer and various retailers, and as such there is clearly an inter-organizational aspect involved in value chain analysis.

A value chain analysis is performed in a number of steps. First, the value chain is decomposed into strategically relevant activities. Cost drivers are then identified for each activity, which form the basis for assigning the revenues, costs and assets to the activities. Finally, organizations should use the information to control cost drivers better than competitors do, or to reconfigure the value chain. This means that value chain analysis can contribute to a sustainable competitive advantage either by reducing costs, while keeping value constant, or by increasing value, while keeping costs constant.

Value chain analysis has traditionally been described as being performed by one organization. Taking an inter-organizational perspective on value chain analysis, however, brings to the fore that the analysis may be performed jointly by both buyers and suppliers in collaboration. This means that different organizations need to share cost and performance information, which creates a joint analysis of the value chain that integrates financial data from multiple organizations. When the analysis is performed by one organization alone, assumptions need to be made about buyers' and suppliers' activities and costs. As such, the benefit of a joint value chain analysis is higher accuracy of the financial data, as a larger

**FIGURE 7.2** Example of a value chain

Raw material ⟶ Manufacturer ⟶ Retailers ⟶ End customers

amount of financial information will be based on actual numbers instead of assumptions. Conducting a joint value chain analysis requires trust between the collaborating organizations to safeguard against misuse of the sensitive financial information that is being shared.

**Real World Example:** The large UK retailer, Sainsbury's, together with its key suppliers, used value chain analysis to manage the supply chain and to identify opportunities to reduce supply chain costs. A Supply Chain Development Group, with representatives from Sainsbury's and its core suppliers, was formed that initiated activities for improving the supply chain. Senior managers from the different organizations met yearly to exchange information and present the changes they were implementing in the supply chain. For all suppliers a standard categorization of activities and cost drivers was used. As such, the value chain analysis used and integrated the cost and activity information of both Sainsbury's and its core suppliers. The suppliers were free to choose whether or not they wanted to be involved in the joint value chain analysis. The participating suppliers were required to collect the cost data and cost driver quantities themselves, and to deliver the data to Sainsbury's. The model gave suppliers' cost information to Sainsbury's, which it used to benchmark the suppliers and to monitor costs. The activity costs of each supplier were benchmarked against the average of all the suppliers so that potential areas for improvement could be targeted. The value chain analysis provided benefits to Sainsbury's and its suppliers mainly in the form of identifying possibilities for individually or jointly improving processes and reducing costs.[5] However, as has already been noted, there may also be a 'dark side' to these initiatives, since Sainsbury's has also been accused of exploiting suppliers.

*Source:* Smithers, R. (2019) Workers exploited at farms supplying UK supermarkets: report, *Guardian*, 10 October. Available at: https://www.theguardian.com/business/2019/oct/10/workers-exploited-at-farms-supplying-uk-supermarkets-report (accessed 8 May 2020).

### *Inter-organizational output controls*

When organizations enter into long-term inter-organizational relationships, one of the most important factors for successful cooperation is handling *appropriation concerns*. Appropriation concerns denote whether both organizations feel that they receive a fair share of the benefits of the relationship, motivating both organizations to cooperate and to put greater effort into the relationship. The starting point when handling appropriation concerns is that the two organizations jointly decide on the goals of the inter-organizational relationship and appropriate inter-organizational output controls in the form of *inter-organizational performance measures* that reflect whether or not the goals are being achieved. Often there is a mix of financial and non-financial measures. Quality and cost measures are commonly used, along with productivity measures. If possible, some measuring may be conducted by an independent third party to increase confidence in the measures. Some collaborating organizations also develop a *joint reward system* where it is specified in detail how, for instance, jointly developed cost reductions in either of the organizations should be divided between the two parties. Another benefit of jointly developed inter-organizational performance measures is that they facilitate the coordination of joint activities and guide the people in the organizations towards what are perceived to be important goals for the collaboration.

**Real World Example:** In a newly established alliance between a supplier of railway safety systems and the company responsible for rail infrastructure in the Netherlands, a number of inter-organizational performance measures were used. Some examples were measurement of cost reductions and ordering quantities. The two companies also developed a financial incentive system to ensure that the financial results from the inter-organizational relationship were shared fairly between them.

*Source:* Dekker, H.C. (2004) Control of inter-organizational relationships: evidence on appropriation concerns and coordination requirements, *Accounting, Organizations and Society*, 29: 27–49.

[5] Dekker, H.C. (2003) Value chain analysis in interfirm relationships: a field study, *Management Accounting Research*, 14: 1–23.

In addition to inter-organizational performance measures and joint reward systems, *open-book accounting* can be used to assist the two organizations to achieve efficient and effective co-operation. Open-book accounting was initially associated with Japanese companies, but the technique has spread rapidly throughout the world. Open-book accounting builds on the simple logic that one or both of the organizations in a relationship 'open their books' and disclose financial and/or non-financial data that had previously been kept within the organization. The financial data can be in the form of details on revenues, material costs, salaries and various indirect costs such as transportation. The non-financial data may concern productivity, lead times, delivery precision, future development projects and ethical guidelines. The financial and non-financial data may be exchanged on a daily, monthly or yearly basis, and may concern products, services, processes, customers or projects, depending on what the organizations agree upon.

The core idea with open-book accounting is that the increased transparency and the extensive flow of information between the organizations will enable them to successfully develop each other's operations. Often, benefits come in the form of identification and realization of cost reductions in production. Other benefits relate to better adaptation of the different organizations' operations to each other. In this way, open-book accounting serves to identify additional cost reduction opportunities through collaborative efforts that could not be discovered by the individual organizations acting on their own.

In practice, open-book accounting is often one-sided, with a strong customer requiring its supplier to give it access to financial and non-financial information, thereby enabling it to become actively involved in improving its supplier's operations. However, it is not self-evident that a supplier will share sensitive data on, for instance, costs, revenues, lead times and delivery precision. If the customer misuses this financial and non-financial transparency, the supplier is in trouble. As previously discussed, a high level of trust needs to be established and, in a sense, the system of open-book accounting can be self-regulating, as a customer who misuses such transparency will have problems establishing new open-book accounting arrangements with other suppliers.

***Real World Example:*** A German car manufacturer initiated open-book accounting in its network of inter-organizational relationships with suppliers. The suppliers were invited to share cost data with the car manufacturer. Open-book accounting was supported by ongoing work in cross-functional and cross-company teams, and technical support to the suppliers was provided free of charge by the car manufacturer.

*Source:* Kajuter, P. and Kulmala, H. (2010) Open-book accounting in networks, in H. Håkansson, K. Kraus and J. Lind (eds) *Accounting in Networks*. New York: Routledge, pp. 211–32.

## Summary

Inter-organizational relationships, defined as various forms of cooperation between independent organizations, have proliferated in recent years as a result of increased globalization, and the rapid technological transformation and increased technical complexity of products and services. The formation of inter-organizational relationships is one important way for organizations to stay competitive in a globalized and rapidly changing world. The most common form of inter-organizational relationship is customer/supplier relationships. One typical development is that ongoing customer/supplier relationships evolve to become closer and more long term in their nature. Another development has been the establishment of new inter-organizational relationships through outsourcing activities that were previously performed in-house. Other common forms of inter-organizational relationship are technology licensing, strategic alliances and joint ventures.

The increased importance of inter-organizational relationships produces the need for managers to find ways to manage and control their inter-organizational relationships. Inter-organizational management control systems are conceptually different from traditional (internal) management control systems in which hierarchical authority is one important basis for control. Inter-organizational coordination, on the other hand, takes place between legally independent organizations where there is no clear formal hierarchical authority in place. Inter-organizational management control systems consist of two parts. First, we have the *changes to an organization's internal management control practices* to account better for inter-organizational relationships. These changes include: (a) throughput controls in the form of an inter-organizational perspective on working capital management; (b) output controls in the form of overlapping responsibilities, target costing and rank-based rewards; and (c) redesigning throughput and output controls to account for network effects. Second, there is the *joint development of inter-organizational management control practices* with key customers and/or suppliers. This includes: (a) inter-organizational input controls in the form of joint meetings and partner selection processes; (b) inter-organizational throughput controls such as policy documents and value chain analysis; and (c) inter-organizational output controls in the form of inter-organizational performance measures, joint reward systems and open book accounting. All in all, the well-designed inter-organizational management control system is one of the most important factors contributing to successful cooperation between organizations.

## Suggested additional reading

Caglio, A. and Ditillo, A. (2012) Opening the black box of management accounting information exchanges in buyer–supplier relationships, *Management Accounting Research*, 23: 61–78.

Carlsson-Wall, M., Håkansson, H., Kraus, K., Lind, J. and Strömsten, T. (eds) (2018) *Accounting, Innovation and Inter-Organisational Relationships*. New York: Routledge.

Hofmann, E. and Kotzab, H. (2010) A supply chain-oriented approach of working capital management, *Journal of Business Logistics*, 31: 305–30.

Stouthuysen, K., Van den Abbeele, A., van der Meer-Kooistra, J. and Roodhooft, F. (2019) Management control design in long-term buyer–supplier relationships: unpacking the learning process, *Management Accounting Research*, 45: 100643.

# Case 7.1
# Ramirent*

by Kalle Kraus

Ramirent provides a broad product portfolio of high-quality and unmanned reliable rental equipment in 13 countries in Northern, Central and Eastern Europe. On its homepage[1] it states the following:

> *Sound business depends on good relationships with customers, suppliers and other cooperation partners. That is why we at Ramirent place such great importance on creating and maintaining good relationships with those around us. There are many good opportunities to meet and exchange viewpoints, e.g. informational meetings, customer meetings and study tours. During such relationship-building, the topic of discussion is not always machinery and technical solutions. Social gatherings are an important part of business relations, but we feel that it is important that this takes place in such a way as not to be questioned by outsiders.*

### Task

Analyse Ramirent's actions in terms of inter-organizational management control.

* This case was written by Professor Kalle Kraus, Stockholm School of Economics.

1 Ramirent, homepage. Available at: http://www.ramirent.com/portal/en/sustainability/code_of_ethics_/our_relationship_with_customers__suppliers_and_cooperation_partners/ (accessed 14 June 2013).

# Case 7.2
# Working capital management*

by Kalle Kraus

Many European countries are in a recession, and manufacturers and other large companies have become increasingly interested in working capital management. According to a treasury benchmarking study conducted by the Association of Finance Professionals, 55 per cent of the companies surveyed had expanded their treasury department's role over the past few years. As a consequence, large and powerful companies are demanding more time to pay their suppliers. Procter & Gamble, for instance, plans to shift its payment terms from 45 days to 75 days.[1]

### Task

Taking an inter-organizational perspective on working capital management, analyse this current development.

* This case was written by Professor Kalle Kraus, Stockholm School of Economics.

1 Blanchard, D. (2013) Finance: manufacturers' big squeeze puts pressure on suppliers, *Industry Week*, 6 May. Available at: http://www.industryweek.com/finance/finance-manufacturers-big-squeeze-puts-pressure-suppliers (accessed 14 June 2013).

# Case 7.3
# Outsourcing Unilever*

**by Frank G.H. Hartmann**

The following excerpt from Unilever's website[1] states that it has awarded its global HR outsourcing contract to Accenture:

> *This [announcement] follows the announcement in April [2006] of an outsourcing contract to Accenture for its European IT operation, and in December last year [2005] for its European financial transactional services to IBM.*

The Human Resources contract sees Unilever outsourcing the transactional and administrative parts of the function globally. The contract covers transactional, administrative and HR IT systems support for activities such as recruitment and resourcing, reward, training and performance management.

The outsourcing programme is part of the company's One Unilever initiatives to increase leverage of its scale, improve its marketplace competitiveness, deliver functional excellence and create a more competitive cost structure, allowing it to focus on its consumers and customers.

Unilever intends to minimize the impact on people by transferring staff to Accenture, early retirement, exploring alternative roles, natural attrition and through voluntary programmes.

Unilever has a great deal of experience of managing change and, as well as dealing with people issues sensitively and professionally, it is committed to working closely with the relevant employee representatives and works councils.

Sandy Ogg, Unilever's chief HR officer, said: 'This global outsourcing deal represents a major strategic choice for Unilever. We believe that it is best for our business if we concentrate on our core competencies and transfer what is our back office and make it into someone else's front office. We can also leverage Accenture's capabilities and expertise. This deal allows us to create a simpler, more agile Global HR function to better support Unilever's growth agenda.'

John Zealley, managing partner of Accenture's European Consumer Goods & Services Practice, said: 'This agreement should help support Unilever as it strives to transform its business. By outsourcing functions such as human resources to Accenture, Unilever should benefit from increased efficiencies, decreased costs and greater global standardization.'[2]

## Questions

1. What are the control problems that Unilever faced? What additional benefits is the relationship with Accenture likely to offer beyond solving Unilever's control problems?
2. Why do you think Unilever decided that 'internal' management control system changes to solve these control problems were unlikely to be cost effective?
3. What are potential threats to the outsourcing relationship between Unilever and Accenture? How has this relationship developed over the last couple of years?

---

* This case was written by Professor Frank G.H. Hartmann, Radboud University.

[1] https://www.unilever.com/

[2] Unilever (2006) Unilever awards HR outsourcing contract to Accenture, *Unilever News*, 6 June. Available at: http://www.unilever.com/mediacentre/pressreleases/2006/UnileverawardsHRoutsourcingcontracttoAccentu200666131159.aspx (accessed 14 June 2013).

# Case 7.4
# The clothing industry supply chain*

**by Nandita Farhad and Andrea Fried**

Today, the clothing industry is one of the most important industries in the world economy. It has an annual export value of US$175 billion[1] and annual revenues of more than US$3 trillion, which accounts for 2 per cent of total global manufacturing. It could be ranked the world's seventh-largest economy if it were ranked on the basis of individual countries' GDP[2]. Trade estimates from *The Economist* (2017) suggest that this industry will continue to attract large-scale investment, and to generate trade, revenue and employment worldwide as demand for clothing increases across the globe.

In England, at the end of the eighteenth century, textiles were produced by importing high-quality, low-price cotton from India (Marks, 2015). Around that century, the Indian subcontinent (India, Pakistan, Sri Lanka, Bangladesh) was the largest supplier of cotton, while the West was the producer of textiles and clothing. After the 1950s the clothing industry started to shift from the Western countries due to increased costs of production and wages. In today's world, the Indian subcontinent supplies both textiles and clothing around the world as it has the competitive advantage due to its high agricultural production per-acre yield, low cost of living and relatively low wages (Marks, 2015). Clothing brands and retailers from the Western hemisphere now buy goods and services from independent suppliers and manufacturers based in the Indian subcontinent. Thus, on the one hand, clothing brands and retailers can keep the cost of production low, as they do not have to make direct capital investment or commit to the direct control of labour (Bartlett & Ghoshal, 1989). On the other hand, the supplier countries get the benefits of increasing export growth, employment opportunities for their people, tax revenues and growth opportunities for domestic firms (Ghemawat & Hout, 2008).

Independent suppliers and manufacturers produce clothing based on designs sent to them by Western clothing brands' and retailers' designers. Gap, H&M, Inditex, Topshop and many other clothing brands serve 'demanding' markets for low-cost fashionable clothing in the fastest response time, known as 'fast fashion'. Also, retailers such as Walmart, Sainsbury's and Tesco sell a year-round supply of everyday clothes at discount prices. They have contracts directly with consumers and order their products from those suppliers who offer the cheapest prices (Ashby *et al.*, 2012). In addition, the brands' and retailers' preference for trade is based on negotiated bilateral quotas, and restrictions and opportunities affecting textile and clothing imports between the countries of major clothing suppliers and advanced economic zones, such as the EU, United States, and so on (Hasan, 2013). Those supplier and manufacturer countries that enjoy quota-free access and duty-free entry to the EU market under the European Commission's Generalized Scheme of Preferences (GSP)[3] have greater prospects for trade. Sometimes the governments of clothing supply and manufacturing countries offer different facilities, such as no customs duty or a duty-drawback facility on importing fabrics, to support the industry. Moreover, government can also keep regulation and intervention to a minimum, to encourage the rapid growth of the industry.

---

* This case was written by Postdoctoral researcher Nandita Farhad and Associate Professor Andrea Fried, Linköping University.

1 https://www.economist.com/blogs/economist-explains/2017/04/economist-explains-6

2 https://www.mckinsey.com/industries/retail/our-insights/the-state-of-fashion
https://www.economist.com/blogs/economist-explains/2017/04/economist-explains-6

3 European Commission under their Generalized Scheme of Preferences (GSP) allows developing and least developed countries to pay fewer or no duties on exports to the EU market and contributing to their growth, Available at: http://trade.ec.europa.eu/tradehelp/everything-arms

In general, the relationship between buyers (i.e., brands and retailers) and suppliers (i.e., manufacturers) is called a supply chain (Cavusgil *et al.*, 2008). Clothing supply chains (see Exhibit 1) start from natural (e.g., cotton, wool) and synthetic (e.g., polyester, nylon) fibre production, and proceed through the growing, harvesting and cleaning of fibres. Fibres are converted into yarn through spinning. Yarns are turned into fabric through weaving or knitting. Fabrics are dyed and finished to produce textiles. Textiles are used by clothing manufacturers to produce ready-made garments. The manufacturers work as assemblers, engaging in basic cutting–making–trimming, quality checking, packaging and labelling, as specified by the brands and retailers (Allwood *et al.*, 2006). The manufacturers can be the direct suppliers of their finished products to brands and retailers. There can be also suppliers who buy clothing from the manufacturers and sell it on to the brands and retailers.

The suppliers ask the manufacturers to make sample clothing for the brands based on their particular design and recommended fabrics, in order to negotiate a trading deal with the brands and retailers. Once a trading deal has confirmed, brands' designers send a technical sheet, known as a 'tech pack', that includes information like measurements, size, materials, accessories, number of pieces, and so on, for each particular product to be bulk-produced. Based on the requirements of the tech pack, the manufacturers acquire the necessary textiles/fabrics and materials to make the garments. In the computer-aided design (CAD) studio, the clothing patterns are aligned with different sizes and sent to the computer-aided manufacturing (CAM) department. After this, the marker templates for the patterns are printed using a plotter and sent to the cutting section for the textile to be cut based on the marker. Next the cutting pieces are sent for sewing. Clothing production normally consists of cutting, sewing, trimming, ironing and packaging units. The manufacturer then delivers the products to the distribution warehouses of the brands and retailers using hired logistics support.

The global clothing supply chain is characterized by a labour-intensive manufacturing process (Perry *et al.*, 2015), short-term relationship between buyers and suppliers (Cooke & He, 2010), and a complex buyer-driven global production network (Winter & Lasch, 2016). Due to the complexity in terms of the sheer numbers of actors involved across national boundaries, it is very difficult to map at full scale an entire clothing industry supply chain – starting from the fibre-yarn producers in the upstream of the supply chain via the brands and retailers in the downstream of the supply chain, who sell the clothing to the end consumer. The dynamism of clothing industry supply chains arises from the adding and dropping of individual suppliers and manufacturers of clothing (including fibre, yarn, fabric, textiles) depending on the evolving needs and demands of consumers. Frequent changes in ownership and management within the individual companies also contribute to the complexity of the supply chain.

The individual companies in the supply chain face different kinds of challenges depending the stage in the supply chain to which they belong. For example, the fibre and yarn production process requires intensive use of land and water resources, and can involve child labour and animal welfare issues, as well as resource scarcity and the struggle for fair pricing of the products. Fabric and textile production can be responsible for a significant environmental impact because of its use of excessive energy and toxic chemical products, as well as risks to the health and safety of workers (Brito *et al.*, 2008). The desire for lower-cost clothing manufacture can lead to social concerns related to working conditions, workers' rights and the fair treatment of workers (Allwood *et al.*, 2006). In addition, distribution to retailers and consumers

**EXHIBIT 1** The clothing industry supply chain

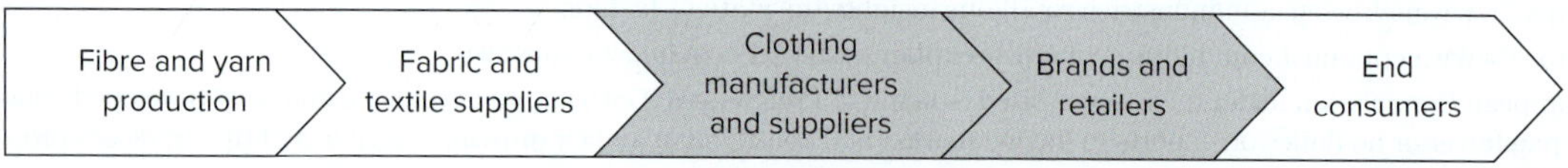

causes carbon emissions and the release of greenhouse gases (Eltayeb *et al.*, 2011). For this reason, ecological and social impacts are commonly observable in the clothing industry supply chain (Fried, 2020).

Non-governmental organizations (NGOs) and activists monitor and report the environmental and social impacts of the clothing industry. They blame brands and retailers for not taking enough measures to deal with these (Taplin, 2014). They have even targeted brands and retailers through 'naming and shaming' – organizing public demonstrations and running media campaigns to promote consumer awareness. Media reports and academic research reveal that more and more consumers are showing an interest in sustainable fashion. However, many consumers of fast-fashion brands and the generic discount retailers that provide a low-price alternative, do not care about sustainable production and do not want to pay higher price for clothing (Vringer *et al.*, 2015).

The poor working conditions at clothing manufacturers in Bangladesh and elsewhere in the subcontinent are regularly reported on in the international news media – in particular after the Rana Plaza factory building collapsed in Bangladesh in 2013, killing 1,134 people and injuring more than 2,500. The media and anecdotal evidence from earlier research claimed that Primark, Benetton, Walmart and some other large Western brands had sourced their clothing from manufacturers located in the Rana Plaza building (Manik *et al.*, 2013; Passariello & Banjo, 2013; Reinecke & Donaghey, 2015). Despite this, in 2013 – a year plagued by instability thanks to the Rana Plaza collapse – clothing retailer brand Primark's revenue increased by 44 per cent (Rochan, 2013). Today, Primark is one of the fastest-growing clothing retailers in the UK, with more than 200 large outlets. Marks & Spencer (M&S) is planning to increase its sourcing from Bangladesh to a total of $1 billion, up from the existing $800 million (RMG-Bangladesh, 2017). H&M, one of the top buyers of apparel, is also increasing the amount it sources in Bangladesh, where it currently has 265 suppliers (Apparel_Views, 2017).

However, media coverage and the increasing attention demanded by activists are putting the brands and retailers in the spotlight for their failure to guarantee sustainable production in the countries from which they source their products. Such pressures have encouraged clothing brands and retailers to assess the risk of sourcing where a supplier is located. To do so, they use a country risk matrix that indicates different risk categories, such as safety of infrastructure (including buildings), fire and electrical safety, the safety of the production process and the level of turnover with a supplier. The scale of risk varies significantly in different production locations, which is why clothing brands and retailers are now not only looking for locations that can provide cheap production, but are also seeking lower risk. Some brands and retailers have started to disclose the names and addresses of their Tier 1 suppliers[4] on their official web pages, to promote transparency.

Clothing brands and retailers also play a dominant role when engaging with suppliers and manufacturers in terms of specified suppliers' contracts. The brands and retailers have a formal written policy, known as a code of conduct, for their suppliers, stating their position of responsibility, which is also provided on corporate web pages. Codes of conduct describe the provision of ethical standards and sustainable production – for instance, no child or young labour, no forced labour, no harassment or abuse, no discrimination, only authorized employment, fair wages, working hours, compensation for voluntary overtime, freedom of association and collective bargaining, occupational health and safety, environmental protection and anti-corruption measures. It is mandatory for suppliers and manufacturers to follow codes of conduct.

However, the provisions in codes of conduct constitute only the minimum standards to be achieved, not the maximum objectives. Some suppliers may not even feel encouraged to take responsibility for following these minimum standards. Despite the increasing number of brands and retailers who are issuing codes of conduct, their effective implementation is practised by only a small number of companies. Many brands and retailers delegate the responsibility for ensuring compliance with codes of conduct to their suppliers. Just because codes of conduct are documented, this does not guarantee that the

[4] First-tier suppliers send materials or products directly to the buyers. Suppliers that send materials or products to the first-tier supplier is called second-tier suppliers, and so on.

manufacturers will automatically follow all the provisions stated therein. When approaching new suppliers and in consultation with current suppliers, some brands (not all) will evaluate their suppliers' compliance with codes of conduct. However, problems often arise regarding the common understanding of a code due to cultural differences or its 'top down' implementation.

Brands and retailers usually order products through third-party trading agents from the manufacturer's country of production (Farhad, 2019). These trading agents are known as 'buying houses', and their job is to buy from the suppliers or manufacturers and sell to the brands and retailers. In the recent past, brands and retailers have faced diverse problems related to different suppliers because of the series of accidents that have occurred in their premises. Many brands and retailers have set up subsidiaries in their production countries and call these the 'brand's liaison office'.

Fifty Shades of Colour (FSC)[5] is one such global brand that has built a subsidiary in Bangladesh. The responsibility of this subsidiary is to coordinate production, control quality, monitor the risks of production by addressing sustainable issues, and negotiate the conflicting interests between brands and suppliers. The subsidiary consists of a sourcing division responsible for product merchandising, a finance unit, a human resource and administration department, and a responsible sourcing team for monitoring the compliance of suppliers (see Exhibit 2). The sourcing unit has three teams: a merchandising team,

**EXHIBIT 2** The internal structure of Fifty Shades of Colour's subsidiary

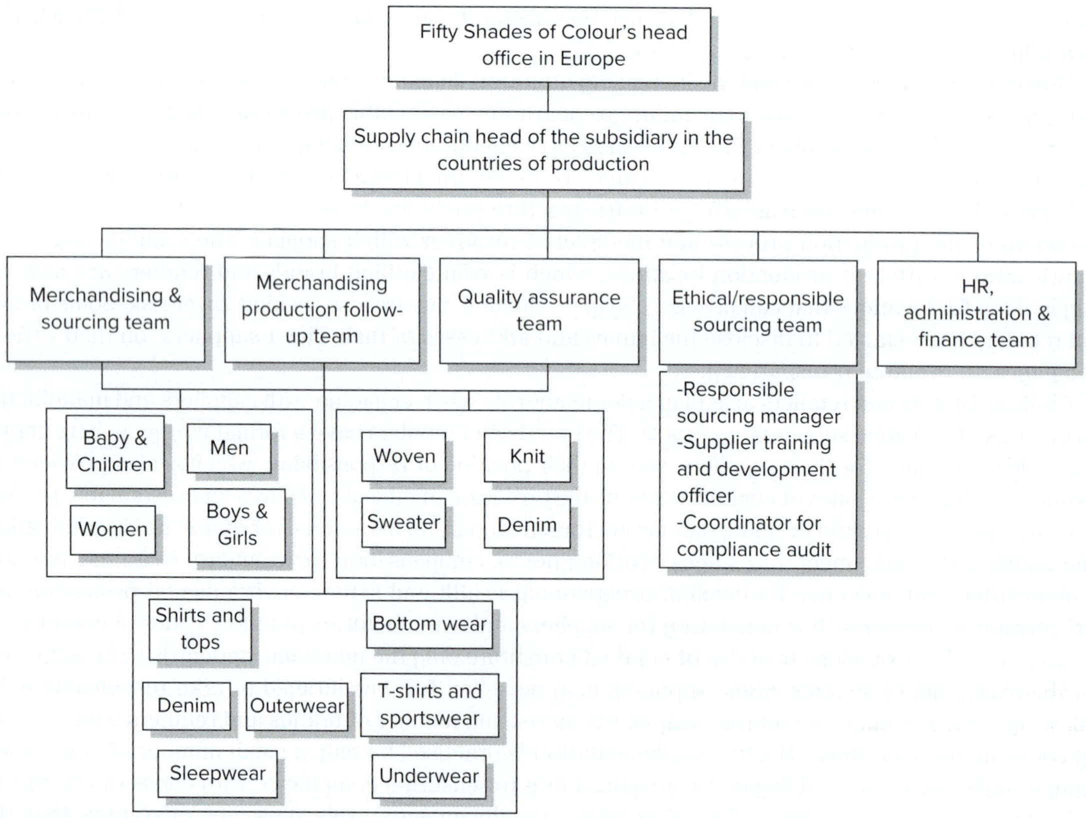


[5] Fictional name

who place orders to the suppliers or manufacturers; another team of merchandisers to follow up production; and a quality assurance team to ensure the quality of the clothing made by the manufacturer. The merchandising team is composed of small clusters based on the items, products or fabrics they order from the manufacturers. This is because some manufacturers can produce only clothing that is woven or knitted, or sweaters, while others may have expertise only in making 'bottom wear' (e.g., jeans, trousers) in denim.

The responsible sourcing team in FSC's subsidiary is a special team for ethical sourcing. In this team there are three people involved. Their task is to verify whether or not a large number of manufacturers (more than 200) are complying with the code of conduct. On the other hand, the merchandising team wishes to emphasize lower price, quality and on-time delivery of the products when selecting a manufacturer. The responsible sourcing team does not approve an order if a manufacturer does not follow the code of conduct. The subsidiary's merchandising team can place an order only after getting a positive assessment regarding a manufacturer from the responsible sourcing team. However, having few people working in the responsible sourcing team means that it takes a long time to assess manufacturers and therefore to negotiate a trade order.

The responsible sourcing team also coordinates compliance audits of manufacturers. It carefully evaluates a manufacturer's state of compliance by analysing the compliance audit data. It monitors the manufacturers progress towards compliance and offers training according to the manufacturer's need. To develop suppliers, it also provides guidelines and organizes discussion sessions with regard to codes of conduct. In addition, the FSC's responsible sourcing managers have autonomy when it comes to conflict management in compliance issues.

Despite its benefits, having this subsidiary increases the costs of management for FSC. Moreover, FSC's subsidiary does not always have the required personnel and technical expertise to investigate all the compliance issues in the manufacturer's premises, especially electrical, structural and fire safety, security and health hazard issues.

### Tasks

1 Assess the risks and opportunities faced by the buyers (e.g., brands and retailers), as well as the suppliers (e.g., manufacturers) in the clothing industry.

2 Explain how the identified risks can be handled through using inter-organizational management control practices.

### References:


Allwood, J. M., Laursen, S. E., Malvido de Rodríguez, C. & Bocken, N. M. P., 2006. *Well- dressed? The Present and Future Sustainability of Clothing and Textiles in the United Kingdom.* Cambridge: Biffaward Programme on Sustainable Resource Reuse, University of Cambridge Institute for Manufacturing.

Apparel_Views, 2017. Swedish firms keen to increase investment in Bangladesh RMG. *Apparel Views.* [Online] Available at: http://www.apparelviews.com/swedish-firms-keen-invest-bangladesh-rmg-industry/ [Accessed 21 January 2019].

Ashby, A., Leat , M. & Hudson-Smith, M., 2012. Making connections: a review of supply chain management and sustainability literature. *Supply Chain Management: An International Journal,* 17(5)(5), pp. 497–516.

Bartlett, C. A. & Ghoshal, S., 1989. *Managing Across Borders: The Transnational Solution.* s.l.:Harvard Business School Press.

Brito, M. P. D., Carbone, V. & Blanquart, C., 2008. Towards a sustainable fashion retail supply chain in Europe: Organisation and performance. *International Journal of Production Economics,* 114(2), pp. 534–55.

Cavusgil, S. T., Griffith, D. A. & Xu, S., 2008. Emerging themes in international business research. *Journal of International Business Studies,* 39(7), pp. 1220–1235.

Cooke, L. F. & He, Q., 2010. Corporate social responsibility and HRM in China: a study of textile and apparel enterprises. *Asia Pacific Business Review,* 16(3), p. 355–376.

Eltayeb, T. K., Zailani, S. & Ramayah, T., 2011. Green supply chain initiatives among certified companies in Malaysia and environmental sustainability: Investigating the outcomes. *Resources, Conservation and Recycling,* 55(5), pp. 495–506.

Farhad, N. 2019. *Supply chain governance for social sustainability: A study of the ready-made garment industry in Bangladesh.* Linköping : Department of Industrial Management, Linköping University.

Fried, A. (ed.) 2020. *Understanding deviance in a world of standards.* Oxford, Oxford University Press.

Ghemawat, P. & Hout, T., 2008. Tomorrow's Global Giants – Not the Usual Suspects. *Harvard Business Review,* 86(11), pp. 80–88.

Hasan, J., 2013. The competitiveness of Ready Made Garments Industry of Bangladesh in post MFA era: how does the industry behave to face the competitive challenge? *British Journal of Economics, Management & Trade,* 3(3), p. 296–306.

Manik, A. J., Greenhouse, S. & Yardley, J., 2013. Western firms feel pressure as toll rises in Bangladesh. *The New York Times.* [Online] Available at: http://www.nytimes.com/2013/04/26/world/asia/bangladeshi-collapse-kills-many-garment-workers.html [Accessed 1 March 2019].

Marks, B. R., 2015. *The Origins of the Modern World: A Global and Environmental Narrative from the Fifteenth to the Twenty-First Century.* 3rd ed. s.l.:Rowman & Littlefield Publishers.

Passariello, C. & Banjo, S., 2013. Retailers debate reparations for Bangladesh factory deaths. *Wall Street Journal.* [Online] Available at: https://www.wsj.com/articles/retailers-meet-to-set-reparations-for-bangladesh-factor [Accessed 20 January 2019].

Perry, P., Wood, S. & Fernie, S., 2015. Corporate social responsibility in garment sourcing network: factory management perspectives on ethical trade in Sri Lanka. *Journal of Business Ethics,* 130(3), pp. 737–752.

Reinecke, J. & Donaghey, J., 2015. After Rana Plaza: building coalitional power for labour rights between unions and (consumption-based) social movement organisations. *Organization,* 22(5), pp. 720–740.

RMG-Bangladesh, 2017. Marks & Spencer to lift B'desh apparel import. *RMG Bangladesh.* [Online] Available at: http://rmgbd.net/marks-spencer-to-lift-bdesh-apparel-import/ [Accessed 21 January 2019].

Rochan, M., 2013. Primark Profits Jump 44% Despite Criticism Over Rana Plaza Disaster. *International Business Times.* [Online] Available at: http://www.ibtimes.co.uk/ab-foods-primark-earnings-profit-514mm-george-519633 [Accessed 20 1 2019].

Taplin, M. I., 2014. Who is to blame? A re-examination of fast fashion after the 2013 factory disaster in Bangladesh. *Critical perspectives on International Business,* 10(1/2), pp. 72–83.

Winter, S. & Lasch, R., 2016. Environmental and social criteria in supplier evaluation - Lessons from the fashion and apparel industry. *Journal of Cleaner Production,* Volume 139, pp. 175–190.

Vringer, K. et al., 2015. *Sustainable Consumption Dilemmas - OECD Environment,* Working Paper No. 84, Available at: http://www.oecd-ilibrar: Organisation for Economic Co-operation and Development, OECD. https://doi.org/10.1787/5js4k112t738-en.

# Case 7.5
# J.L. Apparel Limited*

by Nandita Farhad and Andrea Fried

*Source:* Pinar Alver/Shutterstock

J.L. Apparel Limited[1] is a ready-made garment factory situated in Gazipur, 25 kilometres from Dhaka, the capital of Bangladesh (shown in the image). It is located in a factory hub. There are approximately 15 factories around J.L. Apparel. The roads surrounding J.L. Apparel's factory are puddled with water and thick mud, and very difficult to drive on. The trucks transporting goods to and from the factories make the road conditions even worse. Bad road conditions have been a common obstacle for all factories in the area, 'but no one cares, no one wants to be the first to take action. There is huge rivalry and competition between us [the factories] as we compete to sell our garments to the same global brands,' said Amir Sadat, the managing director of J.L. Apparel.

Amir has been working for J.L. Apparel from the very beginning. In 2002, the company was created by two bothers. The name J.L. came from the first letters of the brothers' names: Jewel and Liton. At the start, it was a small factory with just 60 employees, while today it has more than 3,500. J.L. Apparel sells garments to major global brands and retailers. 'Now the owners [the two brothers] live abroad and visit the factory once a year for three to four months,' states Amir. A management committee runs the company; it includes a managing director and several deputy managing directors.

Amir is setting at his office desk in the factory, drinking small sips from his tea cup and expressing his frustration. 'I am extremely under pressure. On the one hand, the owners only come to take their profit. They do not want to be bothered with managerial problems. They rely on me and my colleagues in the management team. On the other hand, the brands are constantly putting pressure on us to reduce the prices of our products, so that they can increase their profit margin. Consequently, we are bound to reduce the CMT [cutting, making and trimming] costs for the garments.' Amir attempts to negotiate with the brands to set a price per piece for the garments, but most of the brands want to pay a price per order for a bundle of garments, say 10,000 T-shirts. Due to this price pressure from the brands, the only way a manufacturer like J.L. Apparel can cut CMT costs to pay lower and lower wages to its employees. In addition, J.L. Apparel wants its employees to work overtime. As the regular wage is low, employees involved in cutting, making, trimming, ironing, packaging and loading clothes, also feel the need to earn some extra money by working overtime.

---

* Case written by Postdoctoral researcher Nandita Farhad and Associate Professor Andrea Fried, Linköping University.

[1] A fictitious company name.

[2] Clean Clothes Campaign, Rana Plaza. Available at: https://cleanclothes.org/campaigns/past/rana-plaza (accessed 11 May 2020).

## Subcontracting

*Source:* humphery/Shutterstock

After more than 1,100 people were killed by the collapse of the Rana Plaza factory building in Bangladesh, the global brands (Joe Fresh, Kik, Mango, Primark, Texman, and so on)[2] that sourced from the factory not only provided compensation to the victims, but also tightened controls on manufacturers. It was an enormous surprise for many global brands that their clothing was found in the wreckage of Rana Plaza. The brands only then realized that some of their manufacturers were involved in subcontracting. These manufacturers were taking more orders from the brands than they could produce. Because of this limited capacity, a manufacturer or supplier then delegates some part of an order to other manufacturers (see Exhibit 1). For instance, J.L. Apparel attracts an order for 20,000 T-shirts from a brand, with the order valued at $30,000, but has capacity (including machines and people) to make only 10,000. It will thus need to call on subcontractors to fulfil the order. So the company commissions a few other small manufacturers to produce 5,000 T-shirts each at a price of only $2,500, or even less. Some of these commissions are even awarded to sweatshops. Sweatshops, like that pictured, are local tailor shops, often located in tiny rooms of just 12–40 square metres, where five to ten people work, without proper lighting or ventilation.

Sweatshops usually do not comply with any codes of conduct and the brands do not want J.L. Apparel to subcontract to sweatshops or any other manufacturers without their authorization. J.L. Apparel has to inform a brand about any subcontractors (e.g., Manufacturing factory A in Exhibit 1). The brand would then check whether this subcontractor complies with its code of conduct and, if appropriate, authorize the supplier order.

**EXHIBIT 1** A supply chain that includes manufacturing factories subcontracting without authorization[3]

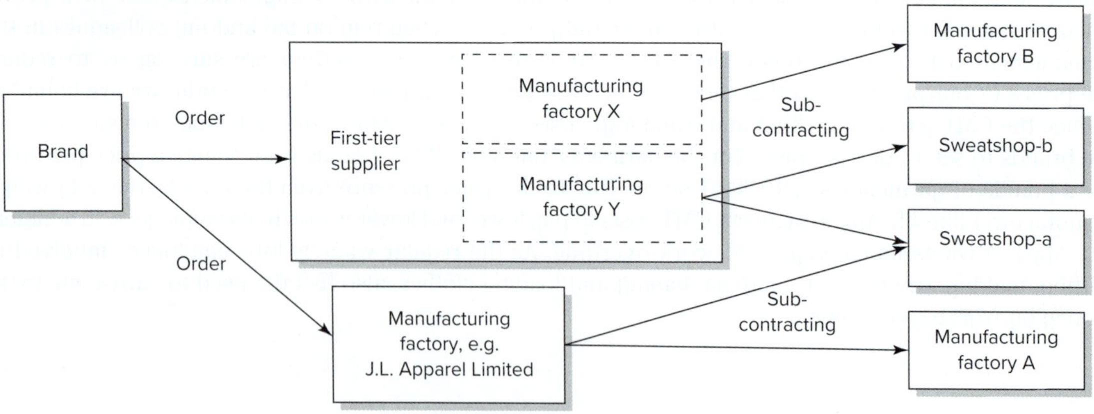


[3] Farhad, N. (2019) *Supply Chain Governance for Social Sustainability: A Study of the Ready-Made Garment Industry in Bangladesh.* Linköping: Department of Industrial Management, Linköping University, p. 117.

Says Amir Sadat, 'After the Rana Plaza incident – because of the strong media campaign for ethical sourcing – brands became very strict about unauthorized subcontracting. If they find out we are subcontracting, they will just cancel all the orders they have placed.' Along with being strict about subcontracting, the brands demand that every manufacturer needs to be audited to check to what extent it is following the specified codes of conduct.

## Auditing

Generally, auditing includes assessment of J.L. Apparel's performance with regard to health and safety conditions, wages and benefits – basically, everything that is stated in the brands' codes of conduct. From 2014, following the Rana Plaza disaster, fire, electrical and building safety audits were also required. J.L. Apparel is expected to coordinate and cooperate with such monitoring activities.

Amir states: 'Currently, we are producing for four big brands. All of the brands have separate codes of conduct and distinct auditing requirements. The number of audits has increased dramatically following the Rana Plaza incident. I have to spend a lot of time coordinating with the brands.' Amir has to deal with specific, sometimes conflicting, auditing requirements, as the following list of requirements from several brands illustrates.

- **Brand A** prefers to conduct an audit using its in-house 'responsible sourcing team'. This team performs both a final and in-line product quality assurance audit. J.L. Apparel does not have to pay any fees for these audits, which are carried out by the brand itself. The responsible sourcing team evaluates J.L. Apparel's compliance with the brand's code of conduct. However, the final auditing report can be biased because of the interdependence between Brand A and J.L. Apparel: J.L. Apparel is needed for production.
- Until 2011, **Brand B** had been performing the audits itself. Today, however, it prefers to use third-party auditors from a private auditing firm. Third-party auditors are specialists who are recognized as competent by Brand B. Third-party auditors consider, among other criteria, environmental issues, building and fire safety, internal management systems, and so on. J.L. Apparel must provide unrestricted access to its premises to permit investigation of all relevant documents. Amir says: 'I don't feel comfortable sharing confidential documents with the third-party auditors.' Despite this, J.L. Apparel bears the costs of the auditing.
- **Brand C** performs both in-house and third-party audits. Its in-house responsible sourcing team conducts interviews with front-line workers, asking the factory management not to provide any answers to the employees. The responsible sourcing team checks compliance with and without prior notification. Brand C also sends third-party auditors to J.L. Apparel once a year to audit technical issues, such as environmental, building and fire safety issues. J.L. Apparel has to pay for the third-party audits, but Brand C covers the costs of the in-house auditing.
- **Brand D** demands certification from accredited monitoring organizations such as the Supplier Ethical Data Exchange (Sedex).[4] Brand D is a founding member of Sedex; it therefore relies on this certification. Sedex conducts audits after receiving a registration fee from manufacturers such as J.L. Apparel. Based on Sedex certification, Brand D selected J.L. Apparel as its supplier. Brand D's in-house auditors now carry out one or two follow-up audits every year. Brand D checks the compliance of J.L. Apparel's security system, as well as factory capability and capacity, in order to verify its compliance with the subcontracting requirements. J.L. Apparel has to pay fees to Sedex for this audit, whereas it does not need to pay for the in-house audit by Brand D.

---

[4] The Supplier Ethical Data Exchange (Sedex) is a non-profit membership organization that provides certification to the organization upon assessment and evaluation. Sedex was founded by a group of brands and retailers from the UK to drive convergence in social audit standards and monitoring practices, to deliver improvements in responsible and ethical business practices in global supply chains. Available at: https://www.sedexglobal.com/about-us/governance/

## Ranking

Auditing provides vital information on how key aspects of labour practices have been addressed by a manufacturer. However, the ranking based on the audit data can be confusing for a manufacturer, when different brands rank manufacturers in different ways.[5] Amir says: 'J.L. Apparel received a "red" score from Brand A, a "C rating" from Brand B, a low standard from Brand C, and I am not sure about the rating from Brand D. It could be medium–high risk, maybe not termination as we have started to take the necessary actions based on its requirements.' Later, he describes the ranking systems of the four brands as follows.

- **Brand A** uses a colour-coded system to rate its manufacturers. Green represents high performing, while amber stands for average performing. Orange means needs improvement on minor issues and needs to be re-audited every six months following the original inspection. Red stands for needs improvement on major critical issues and must be re-inspected within four months.
- **Brand B** practises alphabetical coding from A–E, where an A rating means compliance, a B rating means low risks, a C rating means medium risks, a D rating stands for major critical issues but time for improvement, and an E rating means termination.
- **Brand C** uses a 'high–medium–low–critical' standard-based coding, where a high standard signifies compliance with codes of conduct; medium means up to 10 minor violations of codes, which need to be audited once every two years; a low standard means up to 10 major violations or more than 10 minor violations, which require annual audits; a critical standard signifies non-compliance, which is directly subject to termination of the contract.
- **Brand D** uses assessment based on 'low–medium–high' risk, where low risk means no non-compliance, medium risk meets the criteria of 'acceptable with issues,' and requires audits every six months, while a high risk assessment requires audits every three months, with an immediate 'need for improvement' or 'pending termination', and termination of the supplier contract if no initiatives towards improvement are taken.

Amir claims that, 'brands terminated contracts with two of our neighbouring factories, as they could not satisfy the requirements of the brands, meaning they were not able to follow the codes of conduct'. However, he continues: 'I believe brands are eager to work together with us to improve the workplace rather than terminate the contract.' Therefore, a 'red' or 'low' compliance status means manufacturers are not directly terminated, but rather are given a chance to improve.

### Reward systems

Since J.L. Apparel performed well according to Brand B and Brand D regarding compliance, good quality and on-time delivery, there is the chance that Brand B will order higher quantities at a higher price, while Brand D may promise to continue to trade with the manufacturer for the next five years. In contrast, after analysing the audit reports, Brand A and Brand C found that J.L. Apparel did not perform well, and therefore both brands provided training and recommendations for improvement. After giving sufficient time and training the brands will conduct another follow-up audit. However, if J.L. Apparel fails and again does not comply with the codes of conduct, orders from these brands may be cancelled and the contracts terminated. 'Sometimes we fear losing business, so we do not feel like sharing openly records of wages and overtime with the brands,' Amir states.

He explains further that it is very challenging for him and the management committee to undergo so many different types of audit per year. They need to rearrange their existing administrative and reporting activities to meet the audit requirements of the different brands. He continues: 'the frequent changes

[5] Gey, R. and Fried, A. (2018) Meta-structuring for standards: how organizations respond to the multiplicity of standards, in K. Jakobs (ed.) *Corporate and Global Standardization Initiatives in Contemporary Society* (Ch. 11, pp. 252–76). A volume in the book series Advances in Human and Social Aspects of Technology (AHSAT). USA: IGI Global.

**EXHIBIT 2** Internal structure of J.L. Apparel Limited

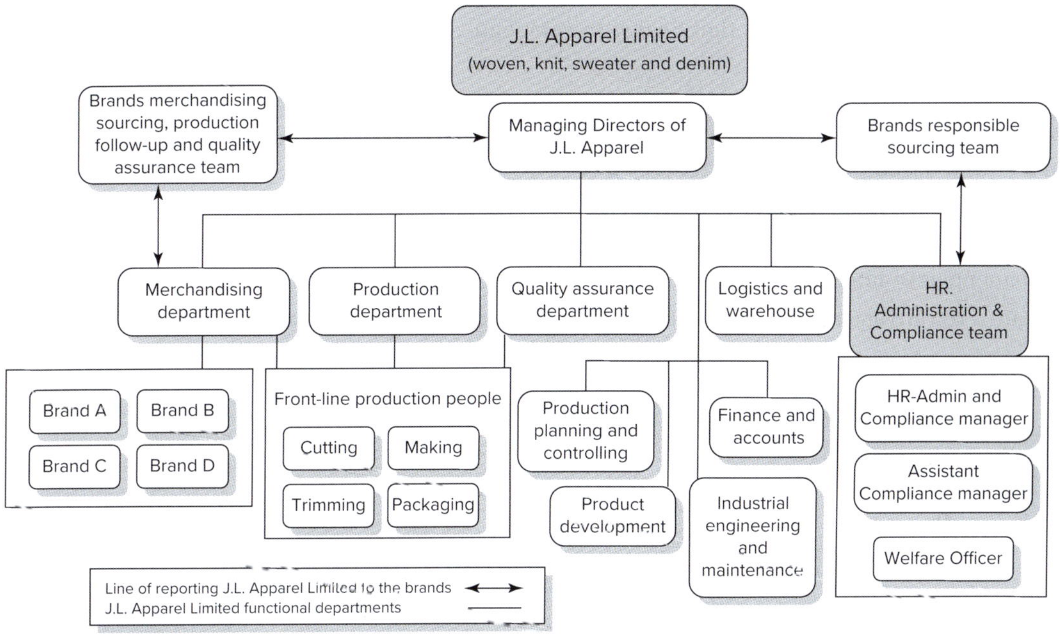


incur 40 per cent more cost and time, and the brands do not shoulder any of these costs. We are a 100 per cent export-oriented business and time management is the biggest challenge here, as we have to deliver products just in time. The preparation of all the documents for the audits takes time and makes it difficult for me to meet production deadlines.' To deal with this, J.L. Apparel recently changed its organizational structure (see Exhibit 2).

## Structure

Today, J.L. Apparel's organizational chart includes units for merchandising, production, quality assurance, logistics/warehouse, and human resources/administration (see Exhibit 2). The merchandising unit coordinates interactions with the responsible sourcing teams of the four brands. The production department incorporates production units, such as cutting, making, trimming, packaging. The quality assurance team is responsible for inspecting the quality of products. Then there are other functional units – for example, production planning and control, product development, industrial engineering and maintenance, finance and accounting, logistics and warehouse management.

The compliance team is new. Says Amir, 'Previously, one or two people in the HR department used to handle the production workers' problems. After the Rana Plaza incident, and due to the brands' requirements, we had to form a compliance team linked with our HR and administration department.' The compliance team will carry out compliance procedures and communicate with the brands' responsible sourcing teams. The compliance team has a compliance manager, an assistant compliance manager and a welfare officer. Together they are responsible for organizing and providing the necessary documents and records for audits. The welfare officer in the compliance team is responsible for observing all kinds of workplace facilities, including the canteen, sanitation, drinking water, childcare facilities for front-line employees, and so on.

In the end, Amir Sadat acknowledged with sadness that there is a general knowledge gap among the factory managers as to how to achieve compliance: 'The factory owner, and senior and mid-level managers, have limited understanding of compliance. There are no courses available in universities' business administration departments that deal with compliance issues.'

## Questions

1 Analyse the brands' engagement in output control in the form of overlapping auditing responsibilities and a rank-based evaluation system.

2 Evaluate which financial and non-financial responsibilities are appropriate for manufacturers.

3 Identify the changes in the internal management control system that are necessary for the successful management of inter-organizational relationships.

4 Create a reward system for brands that could motivate J.L. Apparel Limited to improve its compliance.

PART 3

# Management control systems: the performance management process

In this part of the book we deal primarily with output controls – i.e., making managers and employees accountable for certain results, through planning, measuring and following up on important performance targets. We discuss budgeting and forecasting in Chapter 8, the design and use of financial and non-financial performance measures in Chapter 9, incentive systems in Chapter 10, and risk management in Chapter 11. There is no standard definition of performance management, but generally it is understood

The performance management loop

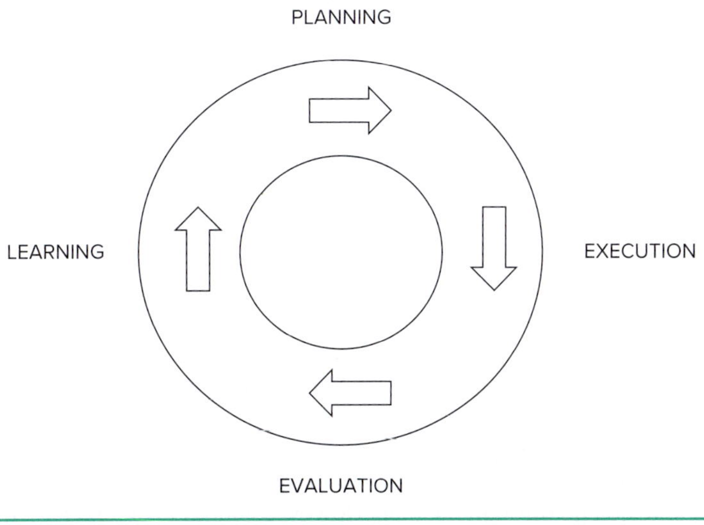

to be the name for the control practices used to make sure that the planned activities are performed and set goals are met in organizations. Performance management can be, and often is, used on several levels, from the company level to the individual level. A very important part of performance management is planning and the setting of goals, and another is feedback that is given regularly. Often when we think of performance management we therefore think of a number of activities performed over and over again in a loop. Which activities are included in the loop depends on who we ask, but generally the following activities are included in some form: planning, execution, evaluation and learning (as shown in the diagram).

***Real World Example:*** Imagine that you start to worry about your physical health. You may have spent far too much time lately watching Netflix and HBO series, and playing *World of Warcraft* and *League of Legends*, and your body has suffered because of it. So, you decide that you are going to do something about it (planning), more specifically go to the gym and run regularly. You even make a schedule of how many times a week you are going to do it, how long you are going to spend in the gym and what distance you are going to run. You even set goals including how fast you will be able to run and perhaps how much weight you are going to lose.

Then you try to live up to your ambitious goals (execution) and after a month you decide that you are going to evaluate how you have done. The evaluation involves asking yourself questions like: Have I followed my schedule? Do I run faster now than I did at the beginning of the month? Have I lost weight? After some months you will probably start to see a pattern and, based on that pattern, it is probably a good idea to think about a number of issues such as: Do I feel better? Do I need more discipline? Should I increase, change or perhaps stop the exercise altogether? Should I focus more on changing my McDonald's and Coke diet instead? Depending on what your answers are to those questions (learning) you may want to draw up a new plan that you will try to stick to in the future.

The *planning* phase involves a lot of discussions and decisions regarding a number of aspects, from what activities we are going to see through to how well we are going to perform in a certain period. This could include activities like cutting a deal with a new customer, developing a new product for this customer and building a new production line for this new product, including investments in machinery and the hiring of people. It may also include figures on revenues for different customers, costs for every department, as well as the profitability of the whole company. Much of the planning often takes place during the autumn when the budget is prepared for the next year, but often also before every quarter of a year when a new forecast is prepared. The planning phase also involves the setting up of goals and targets that usually can be measured with different performance measures.

The *execution* phase involves the daily operations and trying to see to it that you follow the plan. At least in the short term, this is the most important phase because you can spend a lot of time planning and evaluating, but it is not much use if you do not see the plan through. Having said that, it is not always a good idea to see the plan through – for instance, if unforeseen changes makes the plan obsolete or if it turns out to be unrealistic.

The *evaluation* phase is when the outcome is compared to the plan, deviations are analysed, performance is discussed and feedback given. Evaluation is also usually linked to some form of appraisal of the job done by the individual or the manager of the evaluated responsibility centre. It is not unusual that the appraisal is linked to some kind of reward or bonus, in order to motivate managers and employees. Although these incentives are quite popular, they are also often criticized, and we will dig deeper into this issue in Chapter 10. However, the appraisal may also create anxiety, especially when there are substantial negative deviations from plan.

The last phase, the *learning* phase, is in the long term perhaps the most important phase. The reason for this is that a major idea behind conducting this loop is that you improve your performance and do a little bit better every time you go through the loop. However, judging from managers that we meet this is far from always the case. Many organizations spend a lot of time on planning, execution and evaluation, but considerably less time on learning.

Planning, execution, evaluation and learning are all important aspects to take into account when designing and using budgeting practices (Chapter 8), performance measurement systems (Chapter 9), incentive systems (Chapter 10) and risk management (Chapter 11).

# Chapter 8

# Budgeting and forecasting

## Learning objectives

After reading this chapter, you should be able to:

1. Explain the different roles of budgeting.
2. Explain top-down and bottom-up budgeting, as well as tight and loose budgetary control.
3. Explain what budget gaming is and what factors might influence it.
4. Discuss the critique against budgeting.
5. Discuss the proposed alternatives to budgeting, including their potential benefits and limitations.

## Real world vignette: Budgeting in practice[1]

Peter used to work as a controller or, as his formal title actually read, budget manager, for a mid-sized manufacturing company, FHP Motors (fractional horsepower motors). As its name suggests the organization manufactured motors, or more specifically electric motors and related products. Major customers included Flymo, Siemens, Volvo, Saab and Jaguar. The company had earlier belonged to the Electrolux group but was now part of an Electrolux/AEG joint venture, with its headquarters in Oldenburg, Germany, to which Peter reported.

Every year when Peter returned to work after the summer holiday he had to get the budget process started. He knew from experience that if he did not start it as soon as possible, the budget would not be completed in time. The budget process took most of his time during the autumn months, but it also

[1] This vignette is based on the personal experience of one of the authors and a longer description of the case is available in Case 8.3.

involved a large number of other people. Basically every manager, every salesperson, several production engineers and accountants were involved in the process. They never calculated the working hours that they spent on budgeting but it was certainly a considerable number. After having put in all these hours, it was always a big relief to be able to hand over the completed budget to the chief executive officer (CEO) some time in late October or early November. Finally done! However, as it turned out they were never done when they first thought they were. They were not finished because now the next phase started, a phase that included several iterations of parts of the budget process and adjustments of the numbers.

Once the budget really was completed, its main use was to compare the budget figures with the actual results for each month and to find deviations. This was something that was done internally for each department, especially for the manufacturing departments. But Peter would say that this was mainly used by the German headquarters to check that the company was performing according to plan. Every month the CEO had to go to Germany to present the result. But before she did so she used to sit down with Peter and go through all the numbers. Peter actually thought that she was a bit picky because she wanted an explanation for practically every deviation worth mentioning. But he soon understood why she asked these questions. The CEO did it because she would probably be asked the same questions at German headquarters and she wanted to be able to give them good answers.

Peter found this a bit frustrating for two reasons. The first was simply that it was quite difficult to answer all the questions. But, more importantly, he thought that a lot of time was spent on explaining details to the group managers, time that could have been spent internally in order to improve the results. But there was not much time for that. In fact, the worse the organization was performing, the more time they had to devote to supplying headquarters with information and the less time they had to devote to the organization.

However, some months into the new year, people started to say that the circumstances had changed in a way that had not been foreseen and that the budget was not relevant any more. For this reason the company also produced so-called forecasts three times a year for the remainder of the year. These forecasts were similar to the budget but made on a less detailed level. The organization then mainly compared the outcome for the previous month with the latest forecast. However, even if they now had a more relevant forecast, they still had to analyse deviations to the budget and this could be a real challenge, especially since the budget was no longer a relevant comparison.

## Introduction

To plan or not to plan, that is the question; or maybe we should say: to plan a lot or not to plan a lot, that is the question. Budgeting has traditionally meant a lot of planning. If we take the example of the overhead budget in the Real World Vignette, this included hundreds of cost accounts multiplied by dozens of cost centres, which meant that thousands of cost items were budgeted for every year. The sales budget included several products multiplied by a large number of customers, which meant that both volume and price had to be budgeted for hundreds of items. When all these cost and sales items are compared with the outcome, the reliability of the budget is often rather weak. As the saying goes, 'The only thing we do know when we complete a budget is that it is not going to be met.' However, that does not necessarily mean that budgeting is a bad idea; we will return to this.

An alternative to planning ahead might be to be extremely flexible and quick when it comes to reacting to changes in the environment. If an organization is changing slowly, it also has to start a change process early in order to get the changes implemented at a certain time, and this will, of course, require managers to look ahead and plan. But it will also require that the future to some extent is predictable, otherwise it will be hard to know what to plan and when to carry out what was planned. If the environment, on the other hand, is unpredictable and uncertain, planning becomes a much more difficult task. If the future is very unpredictable, it might even be better not to plan ahead but to wait and see what happens before deciding what to do. If the organization is then fast and flexible enough, it will still be able to adjust to the changes ahead of its competitors.

***Real World Example:*** When you are planning a holiday you may want to do several different things: spend time on the beach, go shopping, visit museums, restaurants and clubs. Some of these activities are more dependent on the weather than others and the weather is, of course, more uncertain in some countries than in others. If you go to, say, Spain, it is probably less uncertain than if you go to, say, Britain. This means that you probably can plan your visit to Spain in detail in advance and then follow that plan. It probably does not matter which days you had planned to spend on the beach, because the sun probably shines every day.

But if you go to Britain, you may end up spending a day full of showers on a beach in Brighton if you stick to the plan. So this makes it much harder to plan the trip ahead and it seems like a much better idea to decide what to do on a certain day when you know what the weather is going to be like. If you rely on the weather forecast you can still plan some days ahead, but weather forecasts may also be wrong and you may still end up getting soaked. Maybe the best solution is to wait and see what the weather is like and then decide if you are going to the beach or to a museum, and if the weather changes during the day maybe you should be flexible and switch activities?

Still, an overwhelming majority of organizations do use some kind of planning tool such as the budget. The budget is the very heart of the management control system in many organizations and a lot of attention is devoted to preparing the budget (planning), acting on the budget (execution) and following up the budget (evaluation). Often, but not always, the budget is linked to a more long-term plan like a strategic plan, a business plan or a five-year plan. Such a long-term plan is of course related to even higher uncertainty, but may also give a strategic direction when preparing the budget. If the budget is not linked to a strategic plan, there is a significant risk that the budget preparation mostly becomes an exercise in trend extrapolation.

## The roles of budgeting

One reason why the budget is so popular is that it can fulfil a number of different roles. Generally, those roles can be understood by referring to the top-down and bottom-up roles of management control systems that we addressed in Chapter 1, for instance related to motivation, communicating and coordinating. Different organizations use budgeting in different roles, and often also in several roles in one particular organization. Therefore, let us take a look at some of the possible roles of budgeting. Many of these roles can, of course, also be accomplished by other control practices, but we now focus on how budgeting can contribute to them. Without having the ambition to cover every possible role for budgeting, the roles can be divided into four groups, namely planning, accountability, process and ritual.

We have already touched on the *planning* role. Planning involves, of course, deciding what the organization is going to do, or at least try to do, during the budgeted period. This may include what is going to be produced and sold, which new products or services are going to be developed, which marketing campaigns are going to be executed and which organizational changes are going to be implemented.

An important part of the planning role is *resource distribution*. Given that it is known what the organization is going to do, it is also possible to estimate how much resource every department will need in order to fulfil the plan: what it will cost for research and development (R&D) to develop new products or services, what it will cost for operations to produce them, and what it will cost to execute marketing plans, and so on. The budget is in this sense a tool to distribute resources.

Another important part of the planning role is *coordination*, which relates to cross-functional management (see also Chapter 6). Budgeting is a way to ensure that all parts of the organization follow the same plan, including that R&D develops the same products that the marketing and operations departments are preparing to market and sell. The plans can succeed only if all these different departments fulfil their part of the plan.

The next role the budget often has is related to *accountability*. Managers at different levels prepare budgets for their respective part of the organization. Once this budget is approved the same managers are also expected to fulfil this budget; they are made accountable for it. The managers can hardly guarantee that they will meet the budget, but when they do not they should be able to explain and justify the reasons for the deviations. After all, the deviations might very well be due to circumstances that are outside the manager's control.

The accountability role includes, at least, two different purposes, namely *monitoring* and *motivation*. Monitoring is about superiors checking that their subordinates stick to the budget and relates to agency theory (discussed in Chapter 3). This is exactly what the superiors in the Oldenburg headquarters did and did thoroughly in the Real World Vignette. They checked, on a very detailed level, if we were performing in accordance with the budget or not. As it turned out, quite often we were not and they then required plausible explanations and justifications for the deviations. This was probably the most important role of the budget in that particular case.

Motivation through the budget is achieved mainly through the setting of goals, which relates to goal-setting theory (also discussed in Chapter 3). If managers or employees have specific goals to strive for, this often increases their motivation, especially if they have set up these goals themselves. Usually, some kind of reward is also tied to achieving the goals, whether it is a bonus, a rise in salary, the possibility of promotion or just the fact that you do not have to explain to your superior why you failed to meet the budget. However, as we will discuss further in Chapter 10, external rewards do not always increase motivation and some researchers even claim that they may reduce it!

This leads us to an important aspect of the accountability role, namely that the monitoring and motivation roles may well be in conflict, at least if we believe in self-determination theory (again discussed in Chapter 3). The reason for this is that too much monitoring may decrease the intrinsic motivation that managers and employees feel to reach a certain goal, if they sense that it reduces their autonomy.[2]

***Real World Example:*** It was a sunny Saturday morning some time in the late 1990s. There was a high demand for lectures about the balanced scorecard from all types of organization and on this particular day Emma was on her way to Sweden's Young Investors to give a lecture about it. What made this lecture stand out from all the other ones was the positive feedback she got after the lecture when the listeners came up to her, asked questions, discussed topics that arose or just wanted to say what an interesting lecture it was. It was not that she did not receive any positive feedback on other lectures she gave, because she did, but this was on another level and it made her wonder why.

Maybe she got the answer there and then, because at the end a person that she recognized as one of her students came up to her and said, 'That was much more interesting now than when I heard you give the same lecture at school and was sitting there thinking about the exam!' So, when students heard the lecture as part of a course and knew there was going to be an exam that monitored what they had actually learned about the balanced scorecard, they were not very motivated, but when they heard more or less the same lecture during their free time and were not going to be monitored at all, they were very motivated. You might think that they would be more motivated when they were going to have an exam that would decide what grade they got on the course, which, in turn, might even influence their future careers, but they were actually much more motivated when they were not monitored at all!

---

[2] This phenomena is often referred to as motivation crowding – extrinsic motivation crowds out intrinsic motivation – and is explained in Chapter 10. The Real World Example that follows may very well also be an example of this.

According to the *process* role, the benefits of the budget are not so much tied to the actual budget as to the budgeting process. The usefulness of the actual budget may very well be limited, since a number of circumstances may change after it has been prepared. But that does not rule out the possibility that a number of useful activities were performed during the preparation of the budget. These activities may include, for example, *reflection* and *communication*, and they relate to the learning phase of performance management.

Most managers today have a very busy schedule; there is normally a large number of urgent matters that require their attention. Usually it is difficult to find enough time for all these urgent matters and finding time for less urgent issues, issues that in a longer-term perspective may be very important, is often even more difficult. But the budgeting task may actually make managers sit down and think about matters (reflection) that are important also in a longer-term perspective. When they sit down and think about it, they will probably also conclude that they do not have all the answers themselves, but are dependent on other people. Hopefully, they will then talk to these people (communication), whether they are customers, suppliers, other managers or employees. These activities may actually prove to be extremely valuable, even if the actual budget turns out to be of less value.

The fourth role the budget may have is that of a *ritual*. When the budget has become a ritual, it means that it is no longer used as a well thought through management control practice but for other reasons. One such reason may be *habit*. Most organizations have been budgeting for as long as anyone can remember and, in some cases, may even have forgotten why they do it, but since they are so used to doing it, they do not consider the possibility of not doing it. Budgeting has become an activity that is taken for granted.

Another possible reason for preparing a budget, even if it is not used for controlling, may be *legitimacy*. Many organizations would not be seen as very professional or efficient if they did not prepare budgets. A stock-listed company may need to prepare a budget in order to show its shareholders that it is 'in control' of its business, including revenues and costs. A public service organization may, apart from any other reasons, need to prepare a budget in order to convince taxpayers that it is taking good care of their money. If it does not, there is a risk that the media may claim that it is not being managed in an efficient way and does not have any control over its spending.

Both habit and legitimacy relate to the sociological model of human behaviour (discussed in Chapter 3) and the need to behave in a way that is in line with one's identity, as well as considered normal and acceptable by others.

The different roles of the budget can be linked to the different phases of performance management, as discussed in the opening section to this part of the book. With mainly a planning role, the planning phase of course becomes most important, whereas with an accountability role the evaluation becomes very important. With a process role the focus is to a large extent on learning. The planning phase also becomes important from this perspective, while the evaluation phase becomes much less important. If we mainly have a legitimacy role what matters is that we show figures that are politically wise, but there is no need to overdo the work involved in the budgeting process.

## The parts of the budget

The traditional budget contains a number of building blocks that with some variations occur in the budget in most organizations. We now take a closer look at some of these building blocks.

### Revenue budgets

A revenue budget consists of unit sales projections multiplied by expected selling prices. Of all the elements of a profit budget, the revenue budget is the most critical, but it is also the element that is subject to the greatest uncertainty. The degree of uncertainty differs among companies, and within the same company the degree of uncertainty differs at different times. Companies with large backlogs or companies whose sales volumes are constrained by production capacity will have more certainty in sales projections than companies whose sales volumes are subject to the uncertainties of the marketplace. The revenue budget is usually based on forecasts of some conditions for which the sales manager cannot be held responsible. For example, the state of the economy must be anticipated in preparing a revenue budget, but the marketing manager obviously has no control over it. Nevertheless, effective advertising, good service, good quality and well-trained salespeople influence the sales volume, and the marketing manager does control these factors.

## Budgeted production cost and cost of sales

The standard material and labour costs of the planned volume level of a standard mix of products are shown in the budget. Production managers make plans for obtaining quantities of material and labour. They also develop production schedules to ensure that the resources needed to produce the budgeted quantities are available.

The budgeted cost developed by the production managers may not be for the same quantities of products as those shown in the sales budget; the difference represents additions to or subtractions from the finished goods inventory. Nevertheless, the cost of sales reported in the summary budget is the standard cost of the products budgeted to be sold. Similarly, the budgeted cost of sales in wholesale and retail establishments is not necessarily the cost of the goods that will be purchased in the budget year. Control over the amounts that may be purchased is obtained by detailed 'open to buy' authorizations made during the year, rather than by the amounts shown in the budget. As is the case with manufacturing companies, the difference between purchases and sales represents additions to or decreases in inventory.

## Marketing expenses

Marketing expenses are expenses incurred to obtain sales. A considerable fraction of the amounts included in the budget may have been committed before the year begins. If the budget contemplates a selling organization of a specified number of sales offices with specified personnel, then plans for opening or closing offices, and for hiring and training new personnel (or for laying off personnel) must be well under way before the year begins. Advertising must be prepared months in advance of its release, and contracts with the media are also placed months in advance.

Logistics expenses are usually reported separately from order-getting expenses. They include order entry, warehousing and order picking, transportation to the customer and collection of accounts receivable. Conceptually, these expenses behave more like production costs than marketing costs – that is, many of them are engineered costs. Nevertheless, many companies include them in the marketing budget because they tend to be the responsibility of the marketing organization.

## G&A expenses

These are general and administrative (G&A) expenses of staff units, both at headquarters and at business units. Overall, they are discretionary expenses, although some components (such as book-keeping costs in the accounting department) are engineered expenses. In budget preparation, much attention is given to these categories; because they are discretionary, the appropriate amount to authorize is subject to much debate.

## R&D expenses

The research and development (R&D) budget uses either of two approaches, or a combination of them. In one approach, total amount is the focus. This may be the current level of spending or it may be a larger amount, in the belief that more can be spent in good times, if the company expects an increase in sales revenue or if there is a good chance of developing a significantly new product or process. The alternative approach is aggregating the planned spending on each approved project, plus an allowance for work that is likely to be undertaken even though it is not currently identified.

Many companies decide to spend a specified percentage of sales revenue on R&D, but this percentage is based on a long-run average – that is, R&D spending is not geared to short-run changes in sales volume. To permit R&D spending to reflect the short run could have undesirable effects on the R&D organization; hiring and organizing researchers is a difficult task, and, if spending fluctuates in the short run, inefficiencies are likely.

### Income taxes

Although the bottom line is income after income taxes, some companies do not take income taxes into account in preparing the budgets for business units. This is because income tax policies are determined at corporate headquarters.

### Capital budget

The capital budget states the approved capital projects, plus a lump-sum amount for small projects that do not require high-level approval. It is usually prepared separately from the operating budget and by different people. During the year, proposals for capital expenditures are considered at various levels within the organization, and some are finally approved.

At budget time, the approved projects are assembled into an overall package and examined in total. It may turn out that this total exceeds the amount that the company is willing to spend on capital projects; if so, some projects are deleted, others are reduced in size and others are deferred. For the projects that remain, an estimate of the cash that will be spent each quarter is prepared. This is necessary in order to prepare the cash flow statement.

### Budgeted balance sheet

The budgeted balance sheet shows the balance sheet implications of decisions included in the operating budget and the capital budget. Overall, it is not a management control device, but some parts of it are useful for control. Operating managers who can influence the level of inventories, accounts receivable or accounts payable are often held responsible for the level of those items.

### Budgeted cash flow statement

The budgeted cash flow statement shows how much of the cash needs during the year will be supplied by retained earnings and how much, if any, must be obtained by borrowing or from other outside sources. It is, of course, important for financial planning. As its name indicates, the cash flow statement shows the inflows and outflows of cash during the year, usually by quarter. In addition, the treasurer needs an estimate of cash requirements for monthly (or even shorter) intervals as a basis for planning lines of credit and short-term borrowing.

## The budgeting process

Now we know which parts a budget usually consists of we are going to take a closer look at the actual process of budgeting. We are going to look at preparing a budget, as well as evaluating the outcome compared to the budget. Both these activities may be conducted in a more top-down or more bottom-up manner. Finally, we are also going to take a look at one of the well-known, but also unintended, parts of the budget process, namely budget gaming.

## Budget preparation

A budget preparation process is either 'top down' or 'bottom up'. With top-down budgeting, top management sets the budget for the lower levels. With bottom-up budgeting, lower-level managers participate in setting the budget numbers.

*Top-down budgeting* may be conducted in such a way that top management first draw up the budget or at least decide on the aggregated figures in the budget. The budget is then broken down to a more detailed level by the controlling or budget function and sent out to the managers who are responsible for the different items in the budget. All these managers have to do is to check the figures to see if they find them realistic or not. If they find the figures reasonably realistic they probably accept them. If they do not they can protest against them, which usually means that they have to provide very good arguments as to why the figures are unrealistic. It is then up to the controlling department to decide what changes are going to be included in the budget before they consolidate it and send it to the top management, who still have the last word when it comes to accepting any changes. This type of process is illustrated in Figure 8.1.

The benefits of a top-down process are that it is relatively fast and the top managers can control the end result. With a top-down process, top managers can decide what they want the budget to show, based on how well they think the organization is going to perform or what figures they think it might be tactical to present in the budget. The major drawback, though, is that lower-level managers and employees have provided very little input to the budget process or, in other words, their budget participation is very low. Therefore, the top-down approach is more common in public service organizations than companies, organizations where it is more or less known from the beginning of the year how much money can be spent.

Research has shown that budget participation (i.e., a process in which lower-level managers are both involved and have influence over the setting of budget numbers) has positive effects on their motivation for two reasons:

1. There is likely to be greater acceptance of budget goals if they are perceived as being under the managers' personal control, rather than being imposed externally. This leads to higher personal commitment to achieve the goals.
2. Budget participation results in effective information exchanges. The approved budget amounts benefit from the expertise and personal knowledge of the lower-level managers, who are closest to the product/market environment. Further, lower-level managers have a clearer understanding of their jobs through interactions with top management during the review and approval phase.

**FIGURE 8.1** Top-down budgeting

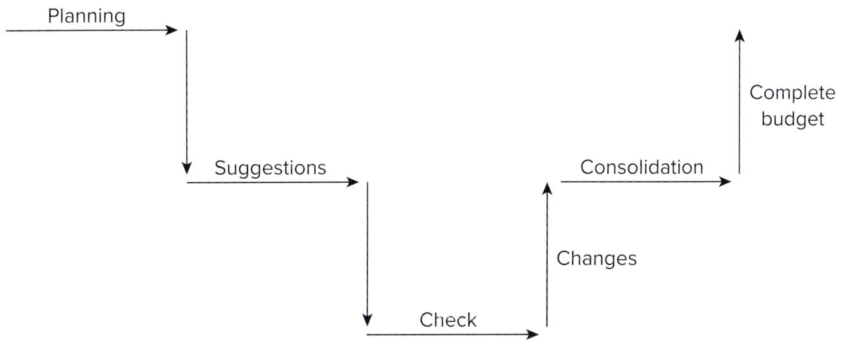


*Source:* Bergstrand, J. (2009) *Accounting for Management Control.* Lund: Studentlitteratur.

Budget participation is especially beneficial for responsibility centres that operate in dynamic and uncertain environments because managers in charge of such responsibility centres are likely to have the best information regarding the variables that affect their revenues and expenses.

In *bottom-up budgeting*, the participation and involvement of lower-level managers, and even ordinary employees, is much higher. All managers make their own assessment of how well they think they are going to perform based on the budgeting guidelines they have received. They then send their budget figures to the controlling department, which consolidates them into a complete budget, which is then sent to top management. This process is illustrated in Figure 8.2.

This approach is much more likely to generate commitment to meet the budgeted objectives. It may also be more realistic because of all the specific information about the circumstances in every responsibility centre, possessed by those who participate in the budgeting. However, there is also a considerable risk that lower-level managers might want to include buffers in the budget figures in order to make the goals more easily achievable. It is also quite likely that the figures in the consolidated budget are not in line with top management's predictions or, indeed, ambitions.

Because of the limitations of these two approaches, a third method, which was used in the FHP Motors case in the Real World Vignette, is often applied in practice. This approach may be referred to as *iterative budgeting* (Figure 8.3). It starts out exactly like bottom-up budgeting, but is then repeated once or more until top management is content with the consolidated budget figures. Usually this means that some or all of the responsibility centre managers have to revise their figures in some direction in order to reach, for example, another profit figure in the budget. However, due to time limitations the revisions may also be made by the controlling department – for example, by reducing all costs by a certain percentage. The revision does often include negotiations between lower-level managers and top management.

With this method, the budget process can get the lower-level managers involved in the process and at the same time ensure that the figures are in line with top management's intentions. However, even if this type of budgeting for these reasons is preferred in a lot of organizations, it also features a number of drawbacks. First, this method tends to take a long time, and even if many more people are involved in the budget process, the revisions made may well undermine the commitment created by making people participate. If, for example, cost centre managers make the best possible predictions of the overhead costs they will have next year and then are told to reduce them perhaps several times, their commitment to the revised figures is likely to drop.

Another problem arises if this approach is deployed every year and the managers know that there will be a revision, where they usually have to lower their costs or increase their sales. Then the managers are

**FIGURE 8.2** Bottom-up budgeting

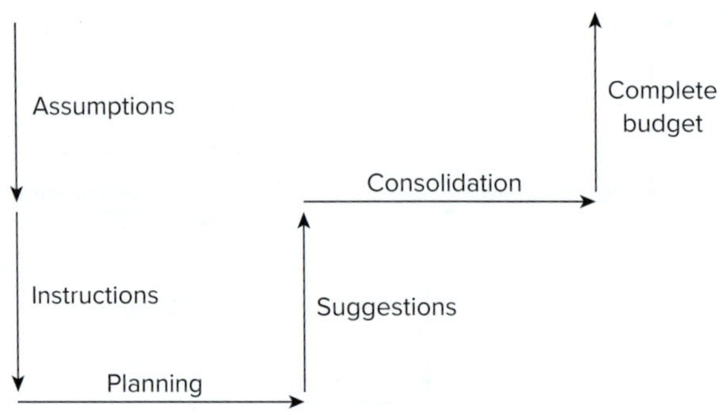


*Source:* Bergstrand, J. (2009) *Accounting for Management Control.* Lund: Studentlitteratur.

**FIGURE 8.3** Iterative budgeting

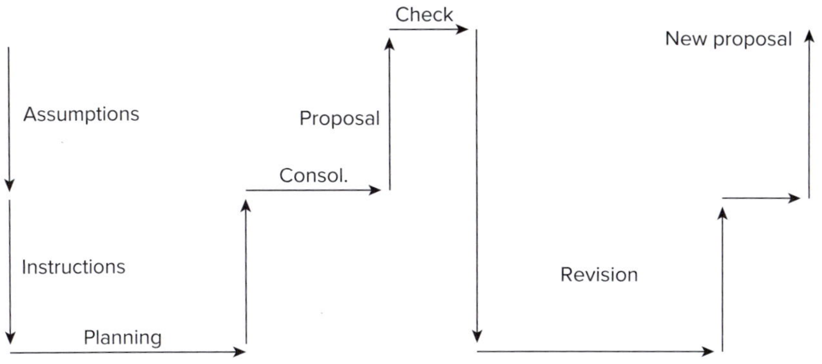


*Source:* Bergstrand, J. (2009) *Accounting for Management Control.* Lund: Studentlitteratur.

quite likely to try to put in some slack or a buffer in the first round, by making the figures worse than they actually expect them to be. If they are then asked to revise them maybe the figures will end up where they wanted them in the first place. However, this is of course something that top management and the controller are aware of and try to prevent, for example by exposing slacks and buffers, or by making ever higher demands in terms of revisions. In the worst-case scenario the budget process becomes a game where managers at different levels try to trick one another the best way they can. This leads us into the area of budget gaming and tactical behaviour, which we will discuss below.

## Budget evaluation

The perhaps most important characteristic of a budget process is if the evaluation is made in a top-down or bottom-up manner. These types of budget evaluations are often referred to as *tight* and *loose budgetary control.*

Tight budgetary control consists of a strict evaluation with little acceptance of deviations. If there are still deviations from the budget (and there almost always are), the evaluated manager had better have a good explanation for why they occurred and plans for how to prevent them from occurring again. The outcome may also be linked to some kind of reward or punishment, like receiving a bonus or not, being promoted or not, or quite simply having to go through the evaluation meeting, which may be a more or less pleasant experience. Often the evaluation experience is related to a certain degree of anxiety on the part of the evaluated manager.

In loose budgetary control, there is a mutual understanding that the budget was just a guess, although hopefully an educated guess, made several months earlier without the full information available today. For this reason the budget meeting becomes less of an top-down evaluation and more of a constructive discussion regarding how the evaluated unit has performed, what can be learned from it and what improvements can be made in the future. The evaluated manager thus feels less put up against the wall and more supported, and often even strengthened, compared to the case with tight control.

To what extent tight and loose budgetary control are used often determines how people behave in the organization. Tight budgetary control often strengthens discipline and makes people do what they are told, whereas loose budgetary control rather makes people willing to make decisions, take the initiative and be creative. This makes tight budgetary control related to mechanistic control and loose budgetary control related to organic control (as discussed in Chapter 2), even though you may not have a budget at all in an organic system. It also implies that tight control is more appropriate with a low-cost strategy as well as in a stable and certain environment, while loose control is more appropriate with a differentiation strategy and in a dynamic and uncertain environment. However, there is also a risk that especially tight budgetary control creates more gaming in the organization, which we will look into next.

## Gaming and tactical behaviour

*Budget gaming* is a complicated topic that has been the subject of much research over the years. Gaming refers to behaviour that does not necessarily have the sole purpose of improving control in an organization; it can be beneficial in helping both individual goals and departments' goals. Budget gaming usually refers to a wish to show budget figures that are either better or worse than the lower-level manager actually believes is the most likely outcome for the budgeted period. Showing higher revenues and/or lower costs is called *exposure*, and showing lower revenues and/or higher costs is called *hedging*. Budget gaming depends on a number of complicated factors and their interplay; we will take a look now at some of these factors.

### *Budgetary control*

As we have already mentioned, to what degree top management deploys tight or loose budgetary control tends to influence lower-level managers' tactical behaviour to a large extent.

Tight budgetary control deployed by top management usually leads to a higher amount of gaming, especially hedging, on the part of the lower-level managers, while loose budgetary control usually leads to a lower amount. This is because if lower-level managers have slack in the budget, it is more likely that they can avoid negative deviations. This way they can avoid criticism and the trouble of explaining the deviations to top management. Moreover, they will probably also look better in the eyes of top management; after all, they do seem to value meeting budget goals highly. It may very well even influence the future careers of lower-level managers.

However, loose budgetary control may also lead to a higher amount of gaming under some circumstances. This is because loose budgetary control probably makes it easier for lower-level managers to behave tactically, because the top managers are less likely to discover gaming. In the case of tight budgetary control, the lower-level managers may have more reason to indulge in gaming, but it is probably also more difficult to get away with it, because the top managers are likely to put more effort into uncovering that type of behaviour.

### *Profitability*

The economic situation in the organization is something that may well influence the tendency for gaming. If the profitability or economic situation is particularly bad, the lower-level managers may want to show a more positive picture of the future than they actually believe themselves. This is because if they produce a negative budget, the top managers may decide to close down this part of the organization. Another reason is that showing a realistic budget under very bad circumstances may make the lower-level managers look bad in the eyes of top management. It may appear as if the lower-level managers have given up and as if they are not even trying to fix the bad situation.

Likewise, if the economic situation is looking extremely good, it may be better to show good but slightly more modest goals in the budget. The reason for this is that the top managers may well be satisfied with reasonably good figures and if the lower-level managers can then show even better results, the reaction from top management is likely to be very positive. If, on the other hand, the lower-level managers show very good figures in the budget and then fail to live up to them, the top managers may be disappointed even if they still show a satisfying result.

However, just as in the previous example, the effect can be the opposite in that gaming decreases during a bad economic situation. This is because the top managers may be more alert to attempts at gaming during bad times and this may make the lower-level managers less willing to take the risk that is involved in gaming.

#### *Uncertainty*

Uncertainty in the organization's environment – for example, regarding future demand – may very well influence the propensity of gaming in one direction or the other. One possible effect is that the lower-level managers want to create more buffers in the budget that they can use if something negative happens. However, this also depends on how risk averse the lower-level managers are, to which we return shortly.

#### *Reward system*

A performance-based reward system is very likely to create tactical behaviour in general and this also applies to budget gaming. The most obvious example would be that the lower-level managers create slack in the budget, slack that will make it more likely that they will meet the budget goals and receive bonuses. But there are also many other ways that the gaming can manifest itself, depending on the reward system as well as the risk aversion of the lower-level managers.

#### *Personality*

We have already touched upon risk aversion of the lower-level managers and that it is likely to influence the gaming. A more risk-willing manager is probably more likely to indulge in exposure in the budget preparation, whereas a more risk-averse manager is more likely to indulge in hedging. Exposure means that the manager takes a higher risk in not being able to meet the budget, but an optimistic budget may also be seen as a sign of ambition on the part of the lower-level manager, something that may draw the attention of top management.

## Beyond budgeting

### Critique against budgeting

When we discuss budget gaming and tactical behaviour we get closer to the critique against budgeting. That budgeting is very common among all types of organization does not mean that everybody thinks it is such a good idea. Particularly during the 1990s, there was a very lively debate concerning the future of budgeting – a debate often led by what was referred to as the 'beyond budgeting movement'. The majority of the voices in this debate, and certainly the most vocal ones, were very critical of budgeting.[3] The fact that most organizations seem to have carried on with budgeting after this intense debate is really interesting. However, whether this is because the budget critics were wrong, or if it is a sign of organizations lacking ability to change their management control systems, is very difficult to say. In either case, we are going to take a look at some of the arguments against budgeting.

#### *Budgets create internal gaming and myopia*

We have already discussed the gaming problem. The believers in the budget, and there are many of them, tend to think that this is a cost worth taking in order to gain all the benefits from budgeting. The critics, on the other hand, tend to think that the negative effects of gaming make a strong argument against budgeting.

Another effect of budgeting is myopia, which refers to sub-optimization and short-termism. Sub-optimization means that budgeting makes managers and employees focus on what is best for their

---

[3] See, for example, Hope, J. and Fraser, R. (2003) *Beyond Budgeting: How Managers Can Break Free from the Annual Performance Trap.* Boston, MA: Harvard Business School Press.

small part of the organization rather than what is good for the whole organization, which relates to the silo problem discussed in Chapter 6. Because managers are made accountable for the performance of their own department or responsibility centre in the budget, rather than for the performance of the whole organization, sub-optimizations may very well occur.

Short-termism means that managers become mainly occupied with short-term performance and focus very much on showing good figures in their next report, rather than focusing on the long-term performance of the organization. This is also a plausible risk given that the performance is usually evaluated against the budget quite frequently, often monthly. Some critics also state that the budget tends to be so focused on financial numbers that it makes both sub-optimization and short-termism even worse.[4]

### *Budgeting is too resource consuming*

Another common criticism of budgeting is that it is time-consuming and that resources could have been used in a better way. The way the budget has usually been prepared and followed up undoubtedly consumes a lot of time and resources. Whether the resources could have been used in a better way is a much harder question to answer, though. However, there is no reason why organizations could not prepare and use the budget in a much less detailed, simplified way. Still, there is a conflict between preparing a very simplified budget and involving a large part of the organization in the budgeting process.

### *Calendar year is not a good time period*

The fact that budgets traditionally have been prepared for the next calendar year is also something that has been criticized. Some say that 12 months is too long a period to plan for because the environment changes so much during such a long period. Others are more concerned that the actual budget is made for 12 months, while the budget revisions or forecasts are made only for the rest of the year. This means that at 1 January the organization has a plan for the following 12 months, while at 1 October the plan only covers the following three months. Why organizations need a 12-month plan in January but only a three-month plan in October is certainly a very relevant question. However, just as with the previous point of critique, there is no reason why an organization cannot prepare budgets for time periods other than a calendar year.

### *It is impossible to make a reliable budget these days*

That it is impossible to make a reliable budget these days when the world is changing probably faster than ever, is an argument very much in line with the previous one; that 12 months is too long a period to plan ahead. However, now the critics are saying that it is no use making plans at all in a world increasingly characterized by virus crises, climate crises, refugee crises or financial crises. Some even say that when the budget period finally starts – perhaps four months after the budget preparation process commenced – the budget is already obsolete. This argument is very much in line with the discussion about 'to plan or not to plan' at the beginning of this chapter, as well as the example of making a plan of which days you are going to spend on the beach when you go to Britain on holiday.

### *The budget makes organizations less flexible*

The argument that budgets may make organizations less flexible is, of course, related to the fast-changing world we live in. If we do make a plan there is a risk that we are setting our minds to follow it and, if we do that, we may also find it harder to be flexible and change our plans. If we set our minds to one alternative we tend to stop thinking of others. But if we do not set our minds, if we do not make a plan, we are more likely to consider different alternatives. This is, of course, a problem if the world is changing, because what seemed like a very good idea when we made the plan might not be so good after the changes.

---

[4] Financial versus non-financial performance measures is a topic that is discussed in Chapter 9.

However, this argument is not only about changing circumstances; it also relates to the improvement work that hopefully is performed in the organization. As many critics have pointed out, the budget is in many cases an extrapolation of the previous years' performance and budgets. When managers prepare their budgets for the next year, they are often looking at how they performed last year, what the budget is for this year and how they think they are going to perform this year.[5] Based on this information they then decide on the budget for next year. This makes it likely that next year's budget is quite similar to previous years' performance and budgets, and it may make managers think more in terms of business as usual than about new ways of doing things.[6]

### *Contradicting roles*

As we have discussed earlier in this chapter the budget is often made with several roles in mind and even if this is one of the strengths of budgeting, it is also one of its problems. If we want the budget to be motivating we may want to make a so-called stretch budget. A stretch budget is an optimistic budget made to make managers and employees walk an extra mile to reach the goal. But if we want the budget to be a realistic forecast so that we distribute the appropriate amount of resources to different parts of the organization, we should not have any stretch goals. And if we want to make a more political budget, aiming at legitimacy, it might be wise to make a more conservative budget and not expose ourselves. Or it might under other circumstances be a better idea to make a very optimistic budget, even more optimistic than the stretch budget, if we otherwise fear that we might be closed down. Preparing a budget that fulfils all the different roles is often a challenge and sometimes impossible. In the latter case we may end up with budgets that are good for, say, political reasons, but they are not motivating at all, nor do they help us to plan for the future.

The 'beyond budgeting' movement not only criticized the traditional budgeting performed in most organizations, it also suggested alternatives. However, the movement did not limit itself to theoretical alternatives, because a large number of organizations also changed their formal planning system. If the theoretical development was led by Britain, the majority of the practical examples were found in Scandinavia. The alternative management control system that evolved consists of a number of strategies and methods that altogether are said to serve organizations working in a dynamic and changing world. Some of those strategies and methods are detailed in the following section.

## Rolling forecasts

The heart of the new planning method, and something that most organizations that followed the beyond budgeting trend did, was to move from budgeting to making so-called rolling forecasts. The main differences between traditional budgets and rolling forecasts are as follows:

- *Calendar year:* A rolling forecast does not limit itself to a calendar year as a traditional budgeting system usually does (see Figure 8.4). It may be prepared any time during the year and it may cover any time period. The word 'rolling' indicates that the rolling forecasts usually overlap one another. If a rolling forecast is prepared for the next 12 months, the next rolling forecast is often prepared after just three months and covers the last nine months of the previous forecast and an additional three months. This is illustrated in Figure 8.5.
- *Level of detail:* A rolling forecast is often prepared in much less detail than the traditional budget. It may be focused on a number of key performance indicators (KPIs) and the aggregated budget, and is also much less concerned about individual costs or sales items. In this sense rolling forecasts are

---

[5] Remember that when managers prepare the budget for coming year, they do not yet know the outcome for the present year.

[6] This is a problem that zero-based budgeting tried to prevent. Zero-based budgeting is about starting the budgeting process from scratch and not looking at previous years' figures. However, as it turned out, it was not very easy to apply in practice.

**FIGURE 8.4** A traditional budgeting system with one budget and three forecasts each year

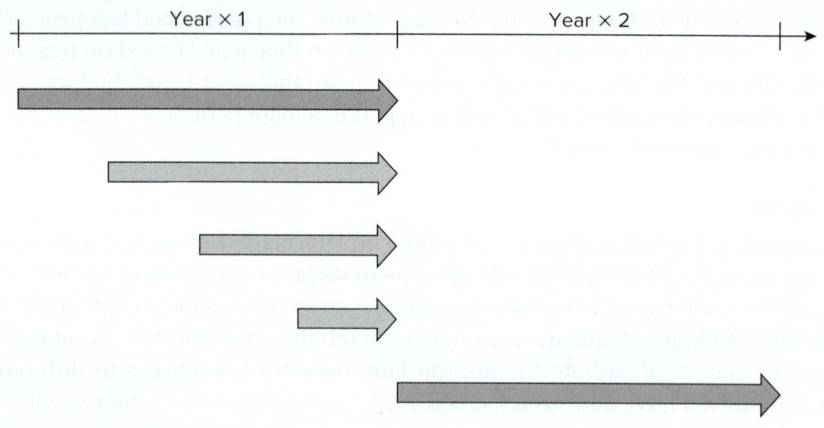


**FIGURE 8.5** Rolling forecasts with four 12-month forecasts each year

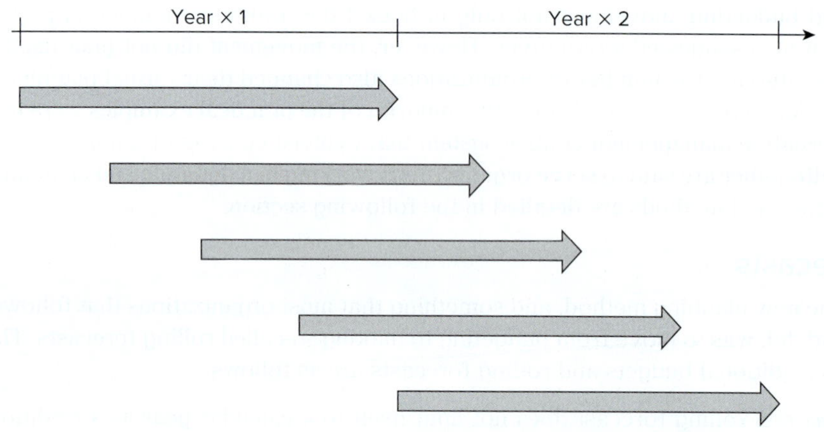


similar to traditional budget revisions, often performed quarterly in many organizations. These revisions were often referred to as forecasts and that is probably why they have been named rolling forecasts instead of rolling budgets. However, the level of detail varies and sometimes the rolling forecasts are as detailed as the budget.

- *Frequency:* Rolling forecasts are often, just like the budget, updated regularly. A common frequency is to update it once every quarter of a year. This is more frequent than the budget, which is usually updated once a year, but it is not more frequent than is the case in many companies, which prepare one budget and three forecasts every year. However, in some organizations the forecast is not updated regularly, but rather when the conditions have changed to an extent where the old forecast is no longer considered relevant.

***Real World Example:*** Volvo was one of the companies that changed its formal planning routines when the beyond budgeting debate was at its most intense. In Volvo's case, headquarters stopped asking for a budget from business units and subsidiaries. Instead, it started to ask subsidiaries for a number of KPIs whenever it thought it needed them, which was usually when the previous forecast was made obsolete by changing circumstances. The headquarters then made a new forecast based on the KPIs received. This made the planning process much more flexible in two ways. First, the company could now make a new forecast whenever it thought there was a need for it, instead of because it was a certain time of the year. Second, it could now prepare a new forecast much more quickly than with the old planning system. Instead of devoting months to preparing a budget, it could now make a new forecast in a matter of a week.

- *Commitment:* Sometimes, but far from always, a rolling forecast is regarded just like a forecast. This means that nobody is accountable for achieving the figures in the forecast. But it is not uncommon that the forecast is regarded as a commitment to the same degree as the budget. In some cases the forecast is partly a commitment and partly a forecast.

***Real World Example:*** The white goods producer, Electrolux, also changed its formal planning system following the debate in the 1990s.[7] But instead of making forecasts whenever management thought they were going to need them, as at Volvo, Electrolux made them every quarter for the following 12 months. It also decided that the forecast for the first quarter was a commitment, whereas the forecast for the remaining three quarters was just a best guess. The motivation behind this was that it would not be possible to make a commitment for more than three months, considering how quickly circumstances change.

- *Evaluation:* Depending on whether the forecast is just a forecast or, in fact, also a commitment, the evaluation of the outcome is also likely to differ. If it is a commitment, the evaluation is not likely to differ much from that of a budget. The lower-level manager is held responsible and asked for explanations for deviations from the forecast. But if it is regarded as only a forecast there may not be any evaluations at all, but more of a discussion as to what can be learned from the outcome. However, even if the forecast is said to be just a forecast, there is always a risk that top managers still choose to evaluate lower-level managers as if it were a commitment. In this case the forecast is in fact seen as a commitment, even if top managers say that it is not.

In the debate, rolling forecasts are sometimes accused of being just another word for budgets, meaning that the actual use of them does not differ much from the use of the budget. In some cases this may very well be true. If we look at the differences discussed above we can conclude that if the forecast is prepared in as much detail as the budget, if the forecast is updated regularly rather than when needed and if the forecast is a commitment that is thoroughly evaluated, then it is quite similar to budgeting. In this case, it is not very likely that so-called rolling forecasts will solve any of the problems related to budgeting described above, except the problem of the calendar year.

However, if it is not detailed at all, done only when needed and seen only as a forecast and not evaluated, the difference from traditional budgeting is substantial. Let us take a look at a company that at least claims that its forecasting process differs considerably from budgeting.

[7] Based on Ax, C. and Johansson, C. (2001) Budgetlös styrning eller lös budgetstyrning? In O. Herolf and P. Westman, *Ekonomistyrning*. Stockholm: Ekerlids förlag.

***Real World Example:*** We are going to take a closer look at Atlas Copco Industrial Technique and its planning process.[8] The business unit that is part of the Atlas Copco group delivers tools and systems mainly to other manufacturing companies. The planning process is a continuous (rolling) process based on a number of key drivers such as market trends and changes at customer level. The process includes the setting of goals and targets as well as the making of forecasts.

Goals that represent ambitions with a three-year horizon are set. But instead of deciding a certain number that should be reached at a certain moment in time, they are relative. This means that development is compared with the development of competitors, and the development of internal units is compared with that of other units.

The goals are then broken down into yearly targets that are important to reach in order to achieve the more long-term goals. The targets are then broken down to action plans and performance measures that can be followed up.

The forecasts are also made with a one-year horizon, expressing where the organization expects to be in 12 months. The forecasts are continuously updated and always made for the next 12 months. However, the forecasting process during the autumn is the most thorough, taking about two months.

The plans are followed up during three meetings every year. The meetings are described more as dialogues than as evaluations with the purpose of blaming or praising managers for their performance. It is more important to reflect on and learn from the outcome, as well as to find solutions for the future.

## Targets, forecasts and resource allocation

In the Atlas Copco example, it had separated goal setting from forecasting to make two different processes. This is similar to a planning model suggested by the Beyond Budgeting Round Table (BBRT) and used by the Norwegian oil company Statoil, nowadays called Equinor. In this model the processes for target setting, forecasting and resource allocation are separated. The main reason for this is that these different functions of the traditional budgeting process are in conflict with one another (as discussed above). Target setting is about setting ambitious and motivating targets to make people try harder, forecasting is about giving a realistic description of the future, while resource allocation is about deciding how much money different parts of the organization are allowed to spend. This model is illustrated in Figure 8.6 and the Real World Example.

***Real World Example:*** At Statoil,[9] targets were set as a number of KPIs. If possible these should be relative and Statoil used two KPIs that were relative to a chosen group of competitors. These were relative return on average capital employed and relative shareholder return. With the first KPI, the target was to be above the average of the peers in the group; with the second, the target was to be among the top third in the same group.

While the targets were set to be ambitious, the forecasts were set to match the expected outcome. This means that there will be a gap between targets and forecasts. Therefore the forecast was not a commitment. Statoil claimed that it did not perform rolling forecasts, but dynamic forecasts. This means that it did not prepare a new forecast at a given point in time, but when it thought it was needed. New events and new information were factors that triggered the need for a new forecast. Also, it was the local units that decided when a new forecast was needed, not the head office.

When evaluating the KPIs, the forecasts were compared with the targets in order to see whether or not the targets were going to be met. The purpose of this was to make the process more forward looking and less focused on explaining historical variances.

---

8 Based on Kullvén, H. (2018) *Management of an Industrial Company: Atlas Copco Industrial Technique.* Lund: Studentlitteratur.

9 Bogsnes, B. (2016) *Implementing Beyond Budgeting: Unlocking the Performance Potential,* 2nd edn. Hoboken, NJ: Wiley.

Concerning resource allocation, Statoil tried to move away from decisions regarding expenditure being based on the question 'Do we have a budget for it?' Many managers thought that this was the most difficult aspect of this planning model, but they tried to do this with a mix of values based on frugality and different types of, often relative, KPIs. How different units dealt with this issue varied a great deal.

This is illustrated in Figure 8.6.

**FIGURE 8.6** The planning model at Statoil

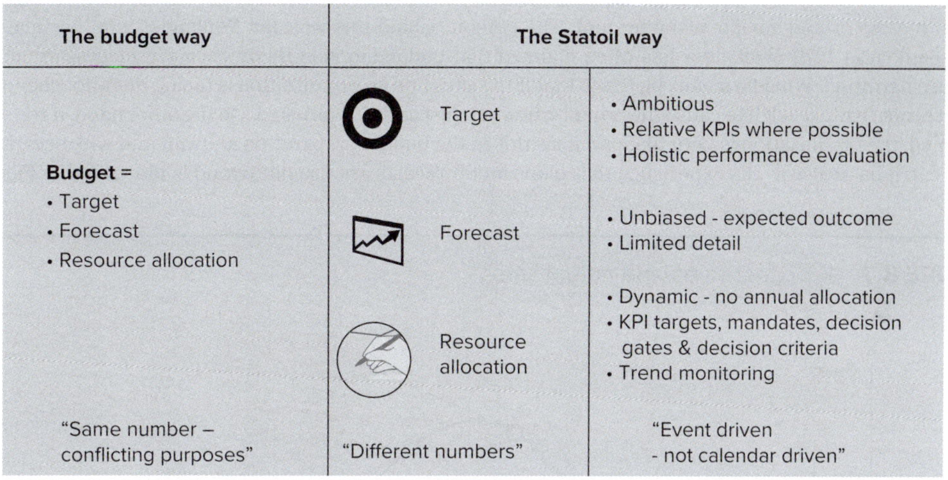


*Source:* Bogsnes, B. (2016) *Implementing Beyond Budgeting: Unlocking the Performance Potential*, 2nd edn. Hoboken, NJ: Wiley.

When studying this model it seems reasonable that it would deal with the problem with the contradicting roles of the budget. But the question is to what extent it solves other problems like budget gaming and resources consumed by the process. Regarding the latter issue, it seems reasonable that working with KPIs is much less time-consuming than working with the enormous amount of data in the traditional budgeting process. But the fact that this model suggests working with three plans instead of one surely must increase the amount of time spent on it.

Also, one can expect that sooner or later some top manager would think that it would be great to have a detailed analysis of all the deviations to all three plans carried out regularly – something that would turn the controlling job into a complete nightmare! But if the top managers remain disciplined and do not interfere more than they are supposed to, the chance that this model may offer advantages compared to traditional budgeting increases.

## The Handelsbanken way

Despite the alternatives to budgeting presented above, a much earlier and probably better-known company that abandoned the budget is Swedish bank, Handelsbanken. But not only was Handelsbanken much earlier than the previous examples, as it abandoned the budget in the early 1970s, it was also far more radical than the examples above, since Handelsbanken does not do any budgets or forecasts at all.

***Real World Example:*** Handelsbanken has made quite a name for itself through its outspoken resistance to budgeting. Not only has the bank become very well known in Scandinavia, it is also frequently mentioned in the British and European beyond budgeting literature, and it has even stirred up some interest in North America.[10] A factor that has probably also contributed to the interest in the company is its outstanding profitability record. Handelsbanken has received a higher return on equity (ROE) than the average returns of its competitors for almost 50 years, the competitors being the other large banks operating in the same market as Handelsbanken. For quite some time this meant Swedish banks, but it eventually came to include banks in the other Nordic countries, and now also includes British and Dutch banks as Handelsbanken has expanded into those markets too.

Unlike practically every other example in the beyond budgeting debate, Handelsbanken abandoned budgeting as early as 1970. Handelsbanken also abandoned formal planning altogether and did not replace the budget with rolling forecasts or any similar planning tool. The person behind this was Jan Wallander who became CEO of Handelsbanken in 1970. Wallander has often claimed that budgeting is in the best case unnecessary and in the worst case harmful.[11] What he means by this is that if the situation an organization is facing does not change much, a budget is not really needed because the organization can just carry on as usual. On the other hand, if the situation is changing, the organization is very likely to miss this in the budget preparation anyway and will, because of the budget, carry on as usual. His experience that plans and forecasts are usually wrong is illustrated in Figure 8.7.

**FIGURE 8.7** Forecast sales and actual sales

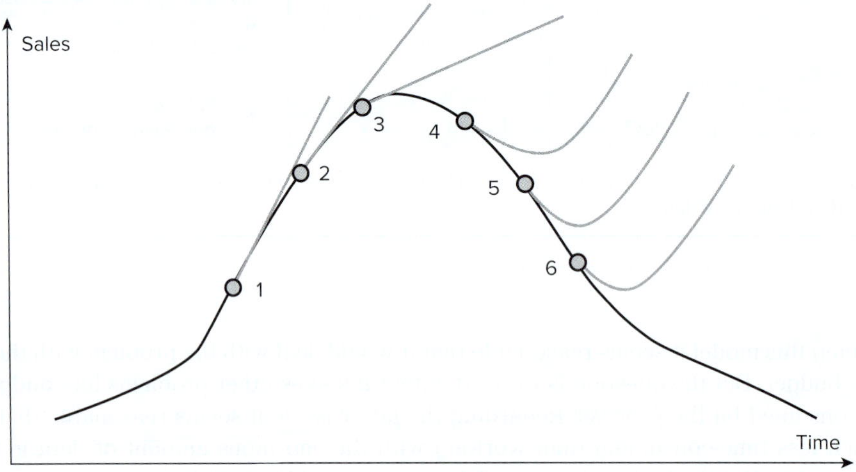


*Source:* Wallander, J. (1979) *Om prognoser, budgetar och långtidsplaner (On forecasts budgets and long-term planning)*. Stockholm: Sv. Handelsbanken.

This diagram, which is based on Wallander's experience as a member of the board in a number of different companies, illustrates how forecasts tend to relate to actual sales. The black curve illustrates how the sales actually turned out for a product/business unit/company during a time period. The grey lines illustrate how forecasts made at certain times tend to look. At point 1 sales have begun to rise quickly and in the forecast it is predicted that they will continue to do so. The forecast at point 2 is

[10] See, for example, Lindsay, R.M. and Libby, T. (2007) Svenska Handelsbanken: controlling a radically decentralized organization without budgets, *Issues in Accounting Education*, 22(4): 625–40.

[11] See, for example, Wallander, J. (1999) Budgeting – an unnecessary evil, *Scandinavian Journal of Management*, 15(4): 405–21.

similar to the one at point 1, but at point 3 sales are not increasing as much as at points 1 and 2. The forecast will, therefore, predict that sales will continue to increase, but not at the same pace as before. All these are just trend projections of the present development when the forecasts are made. At points 4, 5 and 6 the situation is different because now sales have started to fall. In this situation the forecast will probably indicate that sales will continue to fall for some time – sales do not increase just because forecasts are made – but also that they will start to rise again after a while because the fall is only temporary! According to Wallander these errors are being made systematically when we make forecasts, budgets or plans.

But what is Handelsbanken using instead and what does its management control system look like? Well, the management control system implemented by Jan Wallander does have some interesting features that we are going to take a look at.[12]

- *Benchmarking:* Instead of comparing the outcome with a budget or predetermined target, Handelsbanken is comparing its performance with past performance and competitors' performance, very much in line with the relative targets advocated by the beyond budgeting movement. Benchmarking is also used extensively internally in Handelsbanken and the goal for every branch is to be among the top 50 per cent of performers in Handelsbanken. Of course, all branches can never be among the top 50 per cent of performers, but they can all strive for this.
- *Planning:* Handelsbanken does plan. What it does not is to put up absolute targets in those plans. A very important plan in every Handelsbanken branch is the activity plan. In this plan issues like which products or customer segments to focus on next year are stated. There are just no figures telling us how much the sales of a certain product or a certain segment are going to increase.
- *Decentralization:* An important part of the Handelsbanken management control philosophy is decentralization. At Handelsbanken, 'the branches are the bank' and they are allowed a very large degree of autonomy. The logic behind this is that it is the branches that are closest to the customers and so they are the ones who should make strategic decisions about which direction to take in order to meet customer needs. For this reason, Handelsbanken has not yet, unlike most other banks, started to cut down on the number of branches.
- *Management compensation:* Unlike managers in most banks in many Western countries, Handelsbanken's managers do not have individual performance-based bonuses. The reason for this is quite simply that they do not believe these kinds of systems work. But what they do have is a profit-sharing system where every employee gets an equal share of the profit placed in a retirement pension fund.
- *Culture:* Another important aspect of the Handelsbanken example is the input controls in the form of the corporate culture. Apart from the focus on decentralization and branches, it also includes a very strong cost consciousness. This is believed to be the main reason why Handelsbanken for many years has managed to be more cost efficient than its competitors. However, this cost advantage has decreased of late. Still, they are very conscious about the culture at Handelsbanken and almost every manager is recruited internally, in order not to jeopardize the culture. One expression of the strong culture is also the very low turnover of personnel.

As we can see, some of these factors, such as decentralization and relative targets, are very much in line with the beyond budgeting movement. This is hardly surprising because Handelsbanken has been a strong inspiration to the movement. But Handelsbanken does appear to go one step further than most other beyond budgeting companies. The main difference is of course that Handelsbanken does not do any forecasts at all, but – just like Atlas Copco and Statoil – it has relative targets. The bank of course also needs some kind of plan for resource allocation to staff units, and so on. In Handelsbanken this is done

---

[12] More information regarding this highly interesting company can be found in Case 8.5.

in negotiation with the business parts of the company and the staff units do not get more resources than they are allowed by the business managers. This is in line with the idea that the business parts of the organization are seen as customers to the different staff units.

## Summary

Budgeting is at the heart of many management control systems and it may fulfil a number of different roles, such as planning, monitoring, creating motivation, as well as reinforcing reflection and communication. Sometimes it may also be done out of habit or to create legitimacy for the budgeting organization.

The budgeting process can be executed in a top-down or bottom-up manner. The top-down way is quick and top management has control over which figures will appear in the completed budget. The bottom-up way takes more time, but may result in more realistic figures, as well as commitment to the budget among lower-level managers and employees. In practice, however, we often find a combination of the two ways, which is called iterative budgeting.

The budget evaluation can be more or less tight or loose. Tight budgetary control implies very little acceptance of deviations and is intended to create discipline. Loose budgetary control implies more of a constructive discussion and tends to support the confidence of the evaluated manager.

The budgeting process often includes elements of gaming, which refers to tactical behaviour on the part of the evaluated manager. Gaming refers to when managers show figures other than those they actually believe to be the most likely outcome. Showing too positive figures, called exposure, is more likely to happen if the managers fear that their unit will perform very badly or if they have risk-willing personalities. Showing too negative figures, called hedging, is more likely to happen if the managers think they will perform very well, if they have a risk-averse personality, if a reward is tied to meeting the budget or if the top managers tend to react badly on negative deviations.

Gaming is one aspect for which budgeting has been criticized. Other criticisms include: it may create sub-optimization and short-termism; it is time-consuming; it is difficult to predict the future in today's changing world; budgets may make organizations less flexible; and the roles of the budget are to some extent in conflict.

The beyond budgeting movement has, therefore, suggested that budgeting should be abandoned and replaced with rolling forecasts. However, in some cases working with rolling forecasts is not that different from traditional budgeting. Another suggestion is to separate the budgeting process into three different processes, namely target setting, forecasting and resource allocation. This will probably solve the problem with the contradicting roles of the budget, but it is less certain if it will solve problems with, for instance, budget gaming.

The most radical suggestion, however, is to abandon budgets and forecasts altogether, as Handelsbanken has done. Handelsbanken has successfully for almost 50 years deployed an alternative management control system including strong decentralization, relative targets and a profit-sharing system. This has been supported by a solid culture of cost-consciousness.

## Suggested additional reading

Bogsnes, B. (2016) *Implementing Beyond Budgeting: Unlocking the Performance Potential*, 2nd edn. Hoboken, NJ: Wiley.

Hofstede, G. (1967) *The Game of Budget Control*. Assen: Van Gorcum & Co.

Hope, J. and Fraser, R. (2003) *Beyond Budgeting: How Managers Can Break Free from the Annual Performance Trap*. Boston, MA: Harvard Business School Press.

Matějka, M., Merchant, K.A. and O'Grady, W. (2020, in press) An empirical investigation of beyond budgeting practices, *Journal of Management Accounting Research*. doi: 10.2308/jmar-19-010.

Libby, T. and Lindsay, R.M. (2010) Beyond budgeting or budgeting reconsidered? A survey of North American budgeting practice, *Management Accounting Research*, 21(1): 56–75.

Wallander, J. (2003) *Decentralisation – Why and How to Make it Work: The Handelsbanken Way*. Stockholm: SNS Förlag.

# Case 8.1
# Tight budgetary control*

by Frank G.H. Hartmann

## The 2020Q1 corona crisis

Jessica was staring down the numbers her controller had prepared for her 2020Q1 performance review, which was due in a couple of days. She was slightly disconcerted. Jessica has been sales manager of a large European web shop selling consumer electronics. She is part of the management team of the subsidiary office located in Vienna, Austria, and her sales area includes a couple of countries in Eastern Europe. As sales manager she reported to the local CEO. Over the past few years, she had been getting used to a steady increase in sales of packages of 4G phones and subscriptions, whereas sales of other items had been relatively stable. As Chinese brands were becoming more popular, due to their good quality-to-price ratio, the general optimism for a continuation of this trend in 2020 had been expressed in the sales budget Jessica had prepared for 2020.

## The budget for 2020Q1

As usual, this budget (see Exhibit 1) had been prepared in close cooperation with the controlling department at head office, and then signed off by Jessica's local CEO. Local business units were expected to project increasing sales in number of both new customers and overall sales, and the CEO carried the overall responsibility for making 'the bottom line'. The forecasts for 2020 also included expected sales of new 5G phones, many of which were supplied by China's top manufacturers, Huawei and Xoami.

**EXHIBIT 1** Budget 2020Q1 (all amounts in €000s)

| Budget 2020Q1 | Jan | Feb | March | Q1 | | Difference (%) |
|---|---|---|---|---|---|---|
| | | | | Budget | Actual | |
| Turnover mobile phones | 270 | 270 | 270 | 810 | 624 | −23.0 |
| Contract value old subscriptions | 650 | 650 | 650 | 1.950 | 1.948 | −0.1 |
| Contract value new subscriptions | 100 | 110 | 120 | 330 | 240 | −27.3 |
| Other products (aggregated) | 830 | 830 | 830 | 2.490 | 2.525 | 1.4 |
| Total turnover | 1.850 | 1.860 | 1.870 | 5.580 | 5.337 | −4.4 |
| Costs of goods sold | 162 | 162 | 162 | 486 | 423 | −13.0 |
| Gross margin 1 | 1.688 | 1.698 | 1.708 | 5.094 | 4.914 | −3.5 |
| Marketing expenses fixed | 75 | 75 | 75 | 225 | 234 | 4.0 |
| Marketing expenses variable | 40 | 60 | 40 | 140 | 190 | 35.4 |
| Other expenses | 500 | 500 | 500 | 1.500 | 1.498 | −0.1 |
| Gross margin 2 | 1.073 | 1.063 | 1.093 | 3.229 | 2.993 | −7.3 |

The outbreak of coronavirus (COVID-19) around the turn of the year had simply not been foreseen in the sales budget Jessica had prepared the year before. Now it had started to hit hard (see Exhibit 2).

* This case was written by Professor Frank G.H. Hartmann, Radboud University.

**EXHIBIT 2** Expected coronavirus impact on tech shipments

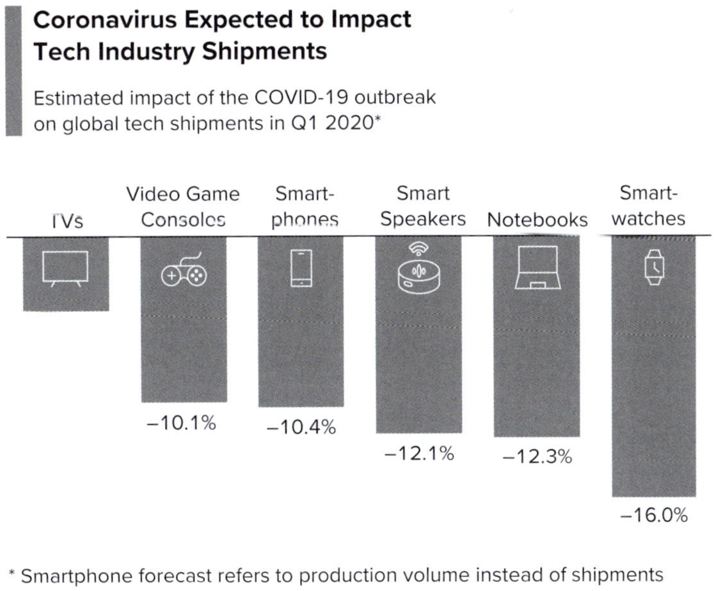


*Source:* Richter, F. (2020) Coronavirus expected to impact tech industry shipments, *Statista*, 20 February. Available at: https://www.statista.com/chart/20894/estimated-impact-of-the-covid-19-outbreak-on-global-tech-shipments/ (accessed 11 May 2020).

Whereas the results for January and February had still shown some growth, sales had dropped dramatically in March 2020 due to the simple fact that her Chinese suppliers had had to cut down on production. Market demand was intact, Jessica estimated, but she had simply been unable to meet demand due to supply issues. Fortunately, sales of Samsung phones were still up, as Samsung production had not been affected by the epidemic. The reason for this was that Samsung had closed its remaining production site in China at the end of 2019. China's main brands were heavily affected, however, with production and sales more than 10 per cent lower than in 2019.

Obviously, Jessica and her country sales team had tried to counter the adverse effects of this drop by trying to turn customers' attention to non-Chinese brands, such as Samsung and Sony. They had also tried, through ad hoc marketing campaigns, to compensate for the drop in phone sales with turnover in other product groups, but she was not sure she had been very successful and feared she would face a tough talk with her CEO, Laura. Not only had the turnover target not been reached, but also the budget for commercial activities had been overrun.

Laura was known to be a fair leader, and very well informed about the ups and downs of the mobile communications business, but her style of performance management was widely known as being very 'numbers oriented'. Laura had expressed more than once how important she felt 'keeping the budget' was and that those 'brave enough to submit ambitious budgets should be brave enough to defend them'. Laura's leadership style was also known for applying 'tight budgetary control'. Laura argued that in this competitive business, the focus on the budget was essential to 'keeping things on track'. She argued that she felt that 'once we let go of the budget, everything could run out of hand'. For her, good management control essentially came down to good budgetary control.

## Questions

1 How does tight budgetary control differ from loose budgetary control?

2 How do you think Laura evaluated Jessica's performance in Q1?

3 How could Jessica respond?

4 State the advantages and disadvantages of revising the budget for the coming quarters of 2020.

# Case 8.2

# Rolling forecasts or budgets? New wine in old wineskins?*

**by Paul Thambar**

Esther Kerr, chief financial officer, MutualBank, was in her office on Monday morning reflecting on the planning meeting she had to attend later in the week. One of the key items on the agenda for the meeting was the annual budget for 2020 (Exhibit 1) which her team had pulled together in collaboration with two business units and four support units.

**EXHIBIT 1** Annual budget 2020 and related information

| | Budget 2020 $000 | Actuals 2019 $000 | Budget 2019 $000 |
|---|---|---|---|
| **Net Interest Income** | | | |
| Interest income | 382,560 | 373,590 | 363,720 |
| Interest expense | 187,213 | 175,324 | 170,000 |
| **Net Interest Income** | **195,347** | **198,266** | **193,720** |
| **Expenses** | | | |
| Employee benefits | 80,368 | 76,112 | 71,456 |
| Marketing | 12,003 | 11,286 | 12,357 |
| Occupancy | 9,000 | 8,092 | 10,242 |
| Administration | 35,679 | 31,156 | 30,235 |
| Communication | 6,534 | 5,489 | 7,218 |
| **Total Expenses** | **143,584** | **132,135** | **131,508** |
| **Net Profit before Tax** | **51,763** | **66,131** | **62,212** |
| Tax expense (30%) | 15,529 | 19,839 | 18,664 |
| **Net Profit after Tax** | **36,234** | **46,292** | **43,548** |

* This case was written by Dr Paul Thambar, Monash University.

| Drivers and data | Budget 2020 | Actuals 2019 | Budget 2019 |
|---|---|---|---|
| **Home Loans** | | | |
| Number of approvals | 23,355 | 24,906 | 24,248 |
| Approvals $000 | 12,752,000 | 12,453,000 | 12,124,000 |
| Average size $000 | 546 | 500 | 500 |
| Average rate % | 3 | 3 | 3 |
| Interest income | 382,560 | 373,590 | 363,720 |
| Number of staff | 600 | 578 | 569 |
| Average employee benefit $000 | 134 | 132 | 126 |
| Number of marketing campaigns | 240 | 226 | 309 |
| Average marketing spend $000 | 50 | 50 | 40 |
| Average occupancy costs $000 | 15 | 14 | 18 |
| Average administration costs $000 | 59 | 54 | 53 |
| Average communications costs $000s | 11 | 9 | 13 |

As a recent graduate of a well-regarded MBA programme, where one of the courses she had taken was accounting, Esther had been challenged by faculty and a guest industry presenter to consider doing away with traditional budgets in favour of rolling forecasts. All the factors identified to support rolling forecasts over budgets (e.g., flexibility targets, more relevant performance measurement, use of accounting and non-accounting information, measures and targets) made sense to Esther, but she knew that her colleagues, in particular her CEO, were committed to the current practice of budgeting, and making a change to rolling forecasts would require Esther to mount a pragmatic case.

MutualBank (MB) is a small member-owned bank located in the regional city of Newcastle, about two hours north of Sydney, Australia. MB was established in 1912 as a small credit union and has grown through mergers with other like-minded credit unions. MB has one business unit, Home Loans, and four support units, Finance, Human Resources, Information Technology and Marketing. Each of the business and support units reports to a general manager, who forms part of the Senior Leadership Team (SLT) of MB along with Esther and the CEO. Each of the general managers has a business analyst with a commercial and finance background, who collaborates with Esther and her small finance team to prepare and deliver the annual budget.

As she sat in her office thinking about budgets and rolling forecasts, Esther remembered a paper she had read where the author vehemently argued in favour of companies adopting rolling forecasts and doing away with budgets. The authors suggested a number of factors that favour rolling forecasts over budgets, including more flexibility to change and adapt the business to external environmental conditions, encouraging innovation and collaboration within the company, fewer incentives for gaming performance, providing more relevant performance measures and targets, better-targeted incentives to encourage high performance among managers and staff, and greater sensitivity and focus on customer needs. She remembered reading in the paper about cases in northern Europe of companies successfully transitioning from annual budgets to rolling forecasts, but she also realized that many companies in other parts of the world, including Australia, still favoured the annual budget, with many senior executives reluctant to make the move to rolling forecasts completely.

As Esther was mulling over the issue of rolling forecasts, there was a knock on her door and her finance manager, Ruth Sivam, came in to check on any last-minute questions and issues that Esther had about the annual budget and the SLT meeting in the afternoon. Esther asked Ruth to sit down, then she

**EXHIBIT 2** Rolling forecast–driver data

| 2020 rolling forecast – drivers | Monthly avg. |
|---|---|
| Loan size $000 | 546 |
| Loan approvals $000 | 12,752,000 |
| Loan rate % | 3 |
| Number of staff | 600 |
| Employee benefits $000 | 134 |
| Number of marketing campaigns | 240 |
| Average marketing spend $000 | 50 |
| Average occupancy costs $000 | 15 |
| Average administration costs $000 | 59 |
| Average communications costs $000 | 11 |

outlined her concerns about budgets and rolling forecasts. Ruth agreed with Esther's concerns and also raised another issue, which she had noticed featuring prominently in her LinkedIn feed recently. She mentioned that many of her accounting connections were raising and discussing the issue of driver-based forecasts (e.g., Exhibit 2), and how drivers could be identified and developed for each of the key items of revenue and expenses. Ruth described a driver-based approach to rolling forecasts, with an example. She suggested that revenue from Home Loans was driven by a number of drivers – number of approvals, average size of a home loan and the average unit price (i.e., interest rate) on a home loan. Ruth suggested that each of these drivers needed to be estimated to develop a revenue budget for Home Loans. She then mentioned that a rolling forecast approach would allow these drivers to be estimated more frequently and would therefore lead to more realistic revenue projections.

Esther was a decisive manager, a trait that had helped her to rise rapidly through the executive ranks to become a CFO at a youngish age, and she made another decision that would have great ramifications for her, her team and MB. She asked Ruth to develop a short paper on rolling forecasts, including driver-based approaches to estimating key revenue and expense items. She also requested that the short paper identify the issues and challenges involved in moving MB away from budgeting to rolling forecasts, and include a high-level implementation plan. She also requested Ruth to review the annual budget and prepare a rolling forecast for 2020 by month. As Ruth got up to leave Esther and work on the matters discussed, Esther picked up her phone and rang her CEO's executive assistant to request a meeting that afternoon to provide an update on her decisions in relation to budgets and forecasts.

## Questions

1 To help Ruth and Esther, develop a list of key issues (at least five) in support of rolling forecasts. Provide a justification for each issue.

2 Evaluate and discuss the role of drivers in developing rolling forecasts, and describe at least three challenges in working with drivers.

3 Create a rolling forecast for 2020 from the information provided in Exhibit 2 and the Appendix.

4 Identify and discuss at least two alternative drivers for each item of revenue and expense in the 2020 budget and provide a simple argument (two sentences) for each of your choices.

5 Evaluate and discuss the role of non-accounting information, with examples, in rolling forecasts.

## APPENDIX Driver-based budgeting

A recent development in budgeting and forecasting has been the use and integration of non-accounting information to more reliably and sustainably predict revenues and costs. Variously labelled as driver-based budgeting, driver-based forecasting, predictive planning and active planning, this innovation has been argued by practitioners to be an advance on the 'fixed form' budgeting traditionally carried out by organizations and management accountants. In this case, we use the term driver-based budgeting.

The concept of driver-based budgeting is a simple one despite the fancy label. The term driver is used almost in the same way as drivers are used in activity-based costing (ABC). A driver is either resource-related or activity-related non-accounting information that helps with the improved prediction of budget values for any item of revenue or costs. A simple example will help you to understand the concept . . .

Take the issue of predicting revenues from home loans in our case. Think about how a home loan sale takes place. A person or people, say John and his partner Mary, need funds to purchase an apartment in their city. They call their local bank's call centre and speak with its home loans sales consultant, Sally. Next, they arrange to meet with Sally to complete an application form and to provide relevant documents to support key personal information (e.g., payslips to support their personal incomes, utility bills to support power costs). Once the application is completed, Sally arranges for the application to be assessed by the credit risk department, and then a decision is made to either approve and grant the funds to John and Mary or to decline. Therefore, a key piece of non-accounting resource-related driver of home loans revenue would be the number of loan inquiries received by the bank in a specific period (e.g., a week or a month). The underlying assumption here is that a certain percentage of these loan inquiries would be converted into actual home loan sales and related revenue. So, in a driver-based budgeting process, the amount of home loan inquiries would be estimated by looking at the number of inbound calls into the bank's call centre and /or the number of appointments taken by home loan consultants. These key pieces of non-accounting information are referred to as drivers.

Other examples of drivers include number of staff (driver for salary costs), floor area rented in a building (driver for rental costs) and number of training courses attended by staff (driver for training costs). Take each item of revenue and costs to think about relevant non-accounting information that could be used as drivers.

# Case 8.3
# Budgeting at FHP Motors*

**by Göran Nilsson**

## The company

FHP Motors was formed around 1990 as a joint venture between the Swedish company Electrolux and the German company AEG. The idea was to group together a number of former AEG and Electrolux companies producing similar products, to make them bigger and more competitive. The products were, as the name suggests FHP motors – that is, products that included FHP motors. The term FHP motors means electric motors with an effect less than one horsepower, FHP standing for 'fractional horse-power'. Neither the former AEG nor Electrolux companies had performed very well on their own, prior to the merger. This meant that there was something of a threat hanging over the joint venture from the start. If it did not succeed it might spell the end for all the companies in the venture. The former

* This case was written by Dr Göran Nilsson, Uppsala University.

Electrolux part of the company was named FHP Elmotor and Peter worked as budget manager for that company from before the merger up until 1994.

FHP Elmotor was a mid-sized company in the Swedish countryside, with a turnover of around SEK 400 million and between 300 and 400 employees. Many of the employees had worked there for a long time, especially the blue-collar workers, and the general education level was low. In fact, the company was one of the oldest in Sweden, originally founded by Walloon smiths in 1655. Many Walloons moved from Belgium to Sweden in the seventeenth century and it was they that started the industrialization of Sweden. The culture in the company and in the small village where it was located could definitely be described using the Swedish word *brukskultur*, which refers to the culture in a rural area with a long industrial history and tight-knit societies.

Its major customers included Flymo, to which it supplied motors for hover-type lawn mowers, Volvo, Saab and Jaguar, all of which were supplied with wiper systems, and Electrolux, which among other things was supplied with food processors. FHP also got a new customer in Siemens, to which it sold ignition coils. This was the only customer it secured as a result of the joint venture. It was a rather big customer, of course, but not necessarily a very profitable one. FHP Elmotor was organized around the different types of products, in production departments. Up to the formation of the joint venture it was not doing very well. There was very strong price pressure from customers. This was especially true for the Swedish car industry, which had to handle fierce competition from Japanese car manufacturers and a global recession at the same time. It did not help that general cost levels in Sweden were high at the time, as a result of the high inflation during the carefree 1980s.

## Budget preparation

Since this used to be an Electrolux company it continued to follow Electrolux routines in the budgeting process. The main difference was that FHP now reported to Oldenburg, Germany, where the HQ of FHP Motors was located. For some reason all the people at HQ were Germans and most of them, perhaps all, had a background at AEG. It is difficult to say if this made group management more distrustful of FHP than the other companies in the group, but they to some extent got that feeling.

Peter always took his summer holiday late since he had to finish all the reports on the outcome of the first six months before he could go away. This also meant that he did not get back until one of the last weeks in August and he knew that he had to get the budget preparation started if they were going to get the budget ready in time. One consequence of this was that they never really had any time to sit down and discuss if they were going to make any major change to the budget preparation process – it was always the same procedure as last year.

The one thing Peter did the very first day back from his holiday was to write and send out instructions to everybody who should participate in the budget preparation. This included a large number of people, such as:

- Three salesmen who budgeted price and volume for every product to every customer; this included hundreds of items that were handled in huge spreadsheets
- Two purchasers who budgeted the prices on all the components bought from the suppliers; this included thousands of items
- Dozens of people who were responsible for different cost centres budgeted the overhead costs for every single account on every cost centre; this also included thousands of items
- A couple of production engineers budgeted the labour time for every operation for every product, also a large number of items
- All the department managers budgeted the investments for every department, but it was in fact more a wish-list than a budget and the CEO then decided which investments to include in the budget.

So far the process was very much in line with budgeting theory since it involved a large number of people, which is supposed to create commitment towards the budget. In some cases all these people followed

Peter's instructions and delivered the figures according to the schedule, but in others he had to remind them once or several times before he got them. Apart from the items mentioned above, Peter also budgeted a number of items himself, such as depreciation, interest and all the items in the balance sheet. Other things that he did himself were a cash flow analysis and a calculation of return on net assets (RNA). With the help of the salespeople, he also divided up all the figures so that they had a budget for every month.

Some time in early November the first version of the budget was usually ready. This version was presented to the CEO and she was usually not too impressed by the figures Peter presented to her. The usual criticism was that she could not show these figures to HQ in Germany because the profit was too low, but it also sometimes happened that she thought the profit was too high. Either way, Peter's impression was that her main concern was whether the figures were in line with the expectations of the people at HQ, and not so much whether they were realistic or not. Or maybe she was thinking of what profit level it might be smart to show HQ from a tactical perspective? Anyway, Peter always did a first revision of the budget after this meeting. Sometimes this revision included the salespeople and the people responsible for cost centres, who often had to raise sales volumes and prices and lower overhead costs. This often involved rather specific demands, such as increase prices by 2 per cent or cut costs by 7 per cent.

However, this was rarely the final revision. The next step was that the CEO presented the budget to HQ and even though Peter had tried to make the figures more in line with their demands, they were rarely satisfied. Usually he had to revise the budget again in the same direction as the first revision, only more so. Sometimes this meant involving, for instance, the salespeople again, but sometimes he did it somehow without involving them. It even sometimes happened that he had to make several revisions since HQ was still unsatisfied. Of course, all these adjustments, often done for political reasons, reduced the likelihood of the final budget being very realistic.

Since Peter did this practically every year, there was of course a great risk that the people involved in budget preparation would add buffers to their figures to compensate for the adjustments they knew would come. It is hard for Peter to say to what extent they did this, because this was not something they were very likely to tell him about, but he would definitely say that the salespeople in particular were very conservative with both volumes and prices. They did not want to risk putting figures in the budget that they could not live up to. This meant that there was definitely a certain amount of gaming in the process. Not only did salespeople and cost centre managers want to have a certain buffer, the CEO probably did too. The people at HQ, on the other hand, wanted Peter to have very ambitious, stretching goals, probably hoping that they would make them work very hard to reach them.

## Forecasting

When they finally did have a budget and the new year commenced, it usually did not take long until somebody said that the budget was obsolete. The argument was that the circumstances now had changed so much since the budget figures were set, it was no longer relevant. The solution to this problem was that Peter and others made three so-called forecasts during the year. They always did the forecasts at the same points in time, one before the start of every new quarter, regardless of changes on the market or otherwise.

One difference between the budget and a forecast was that they did a forecast for the remainder of the year and not for a full year; the forecasts always ended 31 December. Another difference was that they did not do a forecast in as much detail as a budget. One example is the overhead budget, which originally included thousands of items, whereas the forecast was limited to a simple assumption in line with 'x per cent over budget'. However, the sales forecast was as detailed as the budget and still included hundreds of items.

## Evaluation

Almost every month (the exceptions were January and July) Peter did a follow-up, and compared the actual outcome with the budget and the forecast if there was one. To start with, he just prepared the reports and did not bother to analyse them very much. However, the CEO soon started to have meetings with Peter to go through the figures in detail every month. At first, Peter was a little irritated that she had to ask for reasons for every deviation worth mentioning. Not only did Peter find it difficult to answer her questions, he also wondered why she had to know everything in such detail. He thought the CEO was supposed to deal with bigger, strategic issues!

However, Peter soon realized that she asked him these questions because she got the same questions from group management in Oldenburg. She went down to Oldenburg almost every month to present and explain the monthly figures to group management. It soon became clear that they exercised very tight budgetary control and demanded good explanations for all deviations of a certain size. If the CEO failed to explain why they had a certain deviation, it probably made her look as if she was not in control of the company.

Peter therefore started to phone every manager with a deviation he thought he would be asked about, and asked them for the reason. Then he could answer the questions he got, and the CEO could answer the questions she got in Oldenburg. However, this was often still not enough, and the group managers demanded more thorough analyses of different issues. This meant that they spent quite a lot of time just trying to analyse and explain their figures. An interesting observation was that the worse they were doing, the more time they spent explaining it. This is hardly surprising – the managers would of course be more concerned the worse they were performing. But it also meant that the worse they were performing, the less time they had to do something about it since they were so occupied with HQ's questions.

This situation was by no means new to Peter though. Even before they became part of FHP they were exposed to very tight budgetary control with very little acceptance of deviations from plan. In those days they reported to an Italian business area manager located in Turin. Not only did that manager pay much attention to their monthly reports, he often called the CFO and Peter's closest boss, and asked for some kind of analysis or figures that he needed first thing next morning. He often made these calls between five and six in the afternoon, when Peter and the others were getting ready to go home. But he not only called the accounting department, he also often called the CEO at home in the morning during her breakfast, too, and told her what he wanted her to do during the day.

This was not just annoying because breakfasts and evenings were destroyed, but also because his requests prevented Peter and the others from doing the jobs they were there to do. So the CEO called a manager in the Electrolux group she knew, and who had a position above the Italian manager in the group hierarchy, and complained about the situation. The result of this was that this manager called the business area manager in Turin and told him to back off. He did so, eventually, but not before making some angry calls to the CEO where he told her that *someone is going to pay for this!* This was also the time when Peter learned some four-letter words in Italian, some of which he still remembers. However, when it came to the managers at HQ in Oldenburg there was no longer anyone they could call, even if they wanted to.

Another issue was that they not only had to explain the deviations from the latest forecast, which had been prepared a couple of months earlier, the controller at HQ also had them explain any deviations from the budget – which might have been prepared a year ago. This was actually a bit baffling. First of all Peter did not understand why they should analyse deviations to a budget that everybody seemed to agree was no longer relevant. Second, it was actually quite challenging to come up with explanations on a very detailed level for what often was a completely different scenario. Peter does know that the group managers did ask very specific questions concerning the deviations from the latest forecast, but he is not sure whether they also asked about the deviations from budget. Maybe his counterpart at HQ just wanted to know this so that she would be able to answer should she get a question about it from the group managers.

The evaluation did not stop at company level with the CEO going to Oldenburg. She also performed this internally in the organization, with a special focus on the different production departments. However,

Peter cannot say much about this evaluation since he did not participate in it, even if he often helped the department managers to understand the figures. What Peter also did was a presentation of the performance of the production departments at weekly management group meetings. Each week the meetings focused on one of the production departments and one point on the agenda was their financial performance. However, one problem with this presentation – and probably with all the financial performance evaluations – was that they all involved rather old figures. This meant that the production managers had usually forgotten about whatever happened all those weeks ago. They were concerned with their present problems, not the problems they'd had a month ago.

The reason why the figures were old was that they did not close the books until two weeks into the new month. Then Peter had to compile the different reports and he always had to prioritize the reports going to HQ – they did not appreciate it if he reported late – before he could compile the internal reports. This meant that it was not until two and a half to three weeks into the new month that they were ready, which would be how old the report for the production department at the first management group meeting would be. The report for the production department presented at the meeting the week after that would be one week older and the report presented two weeks later would be over a month old.

## Questions

1. What do you think are the most important pros and cons of the budgeting process in this case?
2. Would you like to change the budgeting/control process in the company? If so, how and why? If not, why do you not want to change it?
3. What other changes to the organization and management control would this require/would you suggest? If you would not suggest any other changes, why not?
4. What do you think are the main obstacles to changing budgeting and management control in the company?

# Case 8.4

# Beyond budgeting in a medical company*

**by Knut Fahlén**

## The company

The medical company that is the subject of this case operates globally, with around 10,000 employees in more than 40 countries. Total revenue in the previous accounting year had been €2,000 million and operating profit €500 million, giving an operating margin (EBIT) of 25 per cent. Organic growth has been between 8 and 10 per cent during the past 10 years. The company began operating in Sweden in 1960, and enjoyed stable global growth and profitability until the great recession of 2008, when growth suddenly came to a halt and it had to dismiss 500 employees. The company estimated that its owners, even though the company made a small profit, earned about €50 million less between 2008 and 2009 than might otherwise have been possible.

---

* This case was written by Dr Knut Fahlén, Ekan Management.

**EXHIBIT 1** Results 2005–2015 showing revenue, organic growth and profitability

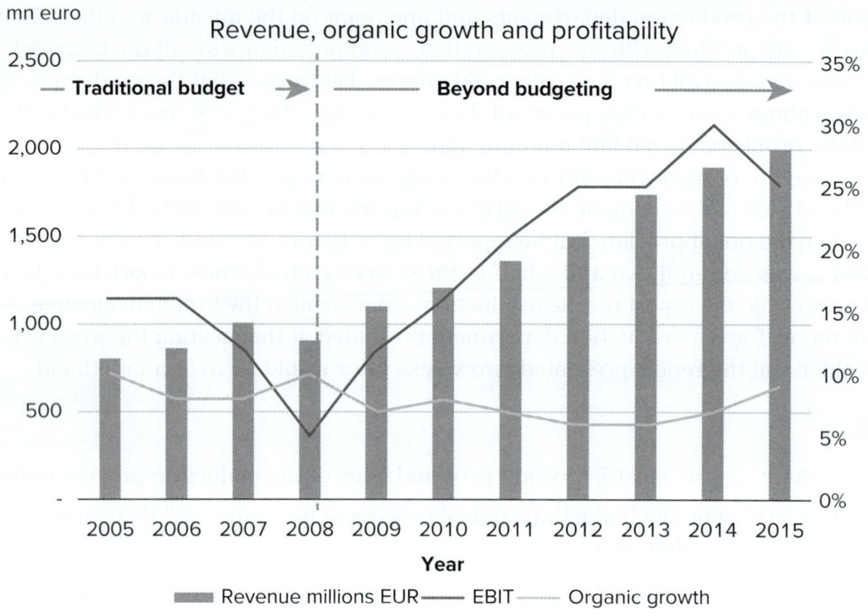


The company's four main business areas are medical treatment in the sectors of heart failure treatment (pharma) and oncology (pharma), wound and skin care (tech) and urology care (tech). It also has smaller businesses within vitamins and nutrition, and software to support doctors in the tech area. Its products are sold in more than 100 countries. The company has production facilities in five countries in Europe, the USA and China; 50 per cent of its market is in Europe, 35 per cent in other developed countries and 15 per cent in emerging markets.

The company is organized into two divisions – pharma and medtech – and each of these has separate businesses for marketing, sales, product development and manufacturing. The main office coordinates group finance, business legal issues and communications to the market. Prior to 2009, decisions made in the operating business units followed a classic command-and-control structure, with some responsibilities organized as a matrix to coordinate operations and business between business areas, market areas and product segments.

## The case for change

The transition from a traditional budget-driven company began at the time of the Lehman Brothers collapse. This was in late 2008, when the company found out that the reality was not even near the budget that was adopted the previous year. The question the CFO asked was whether budget variances (both higher cost and lower revenue) were due to poor budgeting or whether bad performance led to bad financial results that deviated from the budget plan. After several discussions, looking for literature about better ways to manage the budget, it was found that the main problem was too detailed a budget. Top management initiated a project to change the company's management model towards a more dynamic management model based on the 'beyond budgeting' concept. One of the first initiatives undertaken was to read the literature about the concept and redefine the importance of strategy. The vice-president and CFO of the company explain it this way:

> *We had corporate strategies, business strategies, IT strategies, HR strategies, financial strategies and other strategies. We asked ourselves: How many strategies do we really need? The answer was that we needed a comprehensive strategy and a strategy for each of the three business areas. So, for us it was a total of four strategies and not more than that.*

Now, no one has a strategy only for their business, or just for its own sake. They argued that if they had a human resources (HR) strategy, it would mean that they would be an HR company, but they are not. They are a company in the medical industry and that is what they should have a strategy for. Every other part of the business needs a plan that supports corporate and business strategies.

They continued with analysing the rolling trends for critical financials, like revenue, salaries, material, R&D, marketing, sales, facilities and administration. On a high level this helped them establish long-term ambitions in the first quarter of 2009. Shortly after that, quarterly rolling forecasts were established using different techniques to extrapolate trends into forecasts and scenarios. Alongside this they decided when and how they should meet to facilitate a flexible resource allocation. At the end of 2009 they developed ways to reward good performance. During the change, they concluded that they had spent too much time on details instead of seeing the bigger picture. They were also focusing more on decisions already taken, and guarded old routines and habits with sand-bagging and other dysfunctional behaviour. With the new management model they wanted to be more forward-looking, agile and more innovative. They concluded that they not only had to change the budget process but also had to leave behind the traditional hierarchical organization based on command and control and be more decentralized, giving employees and business units greater autonomy.

The problems were similar to the usual challenges faced by traditional budgeting:

- The budget was disconnected from strategy.
- The budget was time-consuming to prepare.
- The budget was often outdated when ready.
- The budget led to wrong and dysfunctional behaviour.

To communicate the change they used a lot of quotes, like Steve Job's 'We don't hire smart people to tell them what to do, we hire smart people so that they can tell us what to do', and Charles Darwin's 'It is not the strongest of the species that will survive, it is the one most adaptive to change', as guidelines. These quotes made sense to others in the organization and helped get those resistant to change slowly but surely onboard.

## The separation of the budget processes

Making dynamics and adaptation to change happen means transforming the budget process, which involves three sometimes conflicting purposes, into three separate processes. In the traditional budget targets, forecasts and decisions about resource allocation converge on one and the same number, although the processes can be influenced by conflicting objectives and motives. Each of the processes should be developed and adopted in a way that is consistent with an organization's external and internal environment, and accounts for where in the organization the processes are used.

By separating the processes and numbers there will be natural gaps between forecasts, targets and strategies. This creates an urge to act in accordance with changed conditions. It also creates a need for innovation and adaptation, when the goal is to reduce the gap instead of hiding or negotiating for targets that are easy to reach.

### Managing strategic resource allocation and other decisions

The company's new management model incorporated a description of the dynamic resource allocation process. As long as capital was not a scarce resource, it communicated that resources were always available for current operations, and that resources could be assigned to projects or invested in anything specific at any time of the year. However, this dynamic allocation of resources scared many in the organization, which meant that there was a huge risk of cost overruns.

The process was, though, proven to be both efficient and flexible, and there was a shift in mindset in relation to the traditional management model. Instead of asking the question 'Do I have the budget for this?', those accountable asked 'Is this the right thing to do?' Decisions were taken in line with the strategy, and in accordance with established principles and values. Through trust and transparency, management at the company became more dynamic. The company no longer uses just one budget number but works with three numbers and different ways to analyse and define portfolios. Those three numbers are:

1 The decided resource allocation needed (e.g., 1,000) is the expected (calculated) cost or allocation needed when analysing profitability for a market, product or any other initiative. This number might be called a first forecast, and everyone knows that the number might change during the project period.
2 Next there is a lower, more ambitious number (e.g., 900), which is the target for cost – the cost the one accountable for a market, product or project is striving to achieve.
3 A higher estimate (e.g., 1,100) can be used if the trend shows that more resources are required than the first forecast and decided allocation indicates.

The management then has to work with the process and improve it by closing gaps and acting in accordance with reality every day, week and month of the year. Thus managers work with a reality that they can control and be accountable for. The concept of fixed budgets decided by someone far away from the actions no longer makes sense and has almost disappeared.

With this new way of managing decisions everyone could also see what was going on at the group level. Business areas are given better conditions and opportunities to make quick decisions, and managers in the company no longer ask, 'Do we have the budget for this?' when it comes to allocating resources. Instead, they ask, 'Is this the right thing to do?' They can also make investments 24 hours a day instead of once a year as the traditional model would require. Instead of having costs locked into a budget they had more control over fixed and variable costs since variable costs were treated as variable. By following costs on a rolling basis they also could visualize and predict the leverage and business risk for the different businesses.

Changing the idea of costs as something bad to the idea that costs are good as long as revenue is higher, also helped to change the general mindset in the organization.

### Managing the future with forecasts and trends

When it came to forecasting, the company left the traditional yearly cost-control perspective in favour of emphasizing long-term value creation. Forecasts were adapted to each unit's operational conditions, ability to predict the future and time to react. Thus, the time horizon no longer focuses on the last day of the fiscal year, 31 December. Costs and cost control used to consume most of financial controllers' and managers' time during the autumn, and revenues were usually set as targets from managers higher up in the hierarchy. The value-creating mindset was built by a new corporate strategy that looked three to five years ahead, and the four business areas had plans that looked two to three years ahead. To make this easier to understand, plans were translated into bulleted lists with a maximum of 10 items top management wanted the entire organization to focus on over the next cycle. Each business unit was then given 10 bullet points on which to work. At the same time, the group's management team made information open and transparent to everyone in the organization. Data for the past three years was visualized and forecasts calculated automatically. This resulted not in biased or negotiated numbers, but predictions based on the latest information. Added to this, managers provided other intelligence necessary to facilitate good decision making.

Specifically, forecasting was adjusted to each business unit and organizational level's ability to act and predict. Forecasting was presented as a three-year (yearly average), 12-month total, and three-month (monthly average) rolling monitoring of revenue, total cost and three to five key performance indicators (KPIs) (see targets, below). The three-year rolling monitoring created a yearly moving average that could be compared to the yearly moving total covering the past 12 months. These moving numbers set the long- and medium-term trend, which was extrapolated using three mathematical forecasts:

1 The future will continue at the same pace as the last 12 months' momentum.
2 The future will continue at the same pace as last year's actuals.
3 The future will continue at the same pace as the last three years' momentum.

These long- and medium-term forecasts were complemented by short-term analysis of seasonal variations, monitoring the last three-month moving average. Two depictions of these trends are presented in Exhibit 2 for one of the business areas.

The new way of monitoring numbers created a more forward-looking and action-oriented organization, where the aim was to reduce the gap between a realistic forecast and an ambitious goal for costs. To make internal communications easy to understand the chart shows actual trend lines in green, targets with a red dot and forecast with a small dashed black line (not depicted in Exhibit 2).

New reports are updated weekly and monthly. Additionally, management meetings are held weekly, monthly and quarterly at various levels in the organization. The aim at these meetings is to move the focus forward, away from explanations of historical variances. This does not mean that the company does not care about the actual numbers. It is the comparison with the outdated reference point in the

**EXHIBIT 2** Rolling 12-monthly (darker line) and rolling three-monthly average (lighter line) revenue per month for one of the units (local currency)

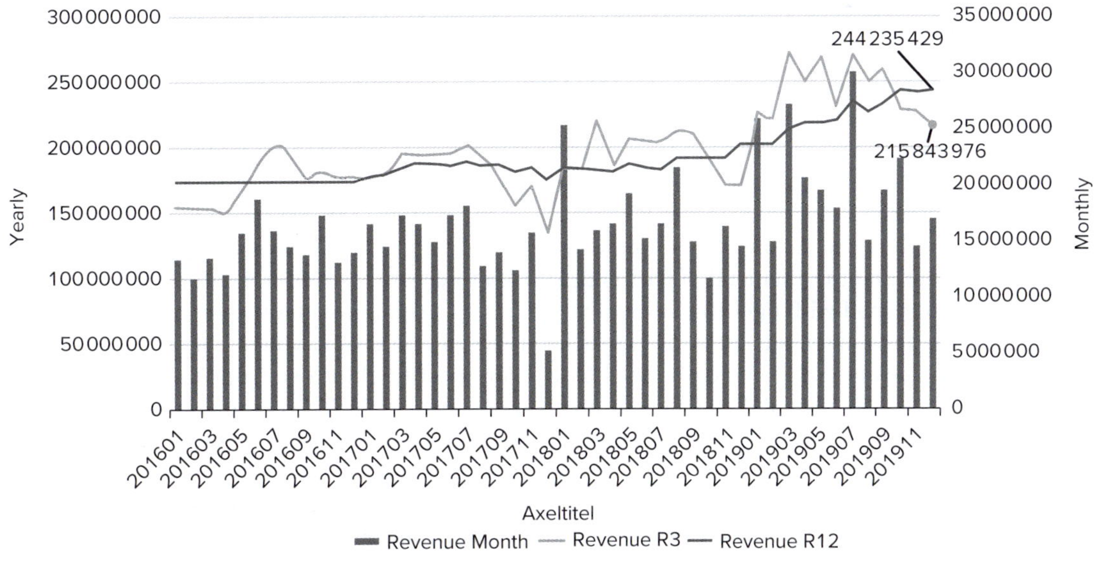


*Note:* 244,235,429 is the latest actual yearly total and 215,843,976 is the short-term monthly revenue multiplied by 12, giving the short-term trend depicted in light grey.

traditional annual budget that has been removed. For managers this results in answering one of the following two questions:

1 *If the trend is moving towards the red dot (target):* What are the risks things will change and how can (and should) risks be prevented and/or managed?
2 *If the trend is moving in the wrong direction from the red dot (target):* What action(s) should be initiated to get it back on track to meet the target?

Since status (actuals, trends and forecasts) are updated and reported on a rolling basis, a better view of reality and trends is provided, compared to using a traditional January–December picture, where the image on average is always half empty.

The management model based on rolling monitoring of 'key value drivers' and rolling forecasts is forward looking and this way of analysing trends and forecasts leverages the ability to act quickly and remain dynamic throughout the year.

The initial problem – to find relevant trends and targets at each level of the organization where decisions are made – leads to the conclusion that it is better to see if business is doing approximately right and moving in the desired direction, instead of analysing variances from an outdated plan.

When trends move in the wrong direction, caused by unpredicted external events, collaboration and actions can be taken immediately, instead of waiting for explanations or discussions about who is to blame. An unexpected example of disruption occurred early in 2015, when oil prices fell sharply. This immediately affected the company's markets in Angola and Brazil, and within a month resources were reallocated to other markets and operations. According to the CFO, this would probably not have happened had the company continued to operate using the traditional management model. In that case managers would have defended the variation from the plan for a long time and continued to argue for explanations to prove that the business would turn around.

Perhaps they would have acted six months after the first signs of a disturbance, a declining market or anything else, which would have meant greater losses than necessary.

### Managing with targets and indicators

Under the traditional management model, the major focus is on absolute financial numbers on a yearly basis. This could be in the form of a profit and loss statement showing a company's revenues and expenses during a given period, or its balance sheet or cash flow statement. Focal performance indicators may include return on capital employed, equity or total capital, to show profitability. And there may be indicators showing liquidity, solvency or leverage, to obtain a picture of the company's financial strength or vulnerability. These financial numbers are often lagging since they are created after the associated products have been marketed, or the actions and activities have taken place – sometimes long before the closing of the financial records. To put more focus on operations management, management and the financial department started to create a set of indicators where financial numbers were combined with operational numbers, such as sales per employee or cost per hour.

After 2009 the new management strategy focused sharply on cost savings, but with clear signals that it was not a question of 'going on a diet'. As a result, profitability rose from a modest 4 per cent in 2008 to 10 per cent in 2009 and 20 per cent in 2010 (see Exhibit 1). The company had, in just three years, become a world leader in the industry in terms of profit, growth and sustainability, a position that has since been further strengthened. To reach this position, it not only changed its decision process and method of forecasting, but also started to benchmark KPIs, comparing its own performance with that of competitors and making internal comparisons between the various business units. This represents a marked change from customary practice, where everyone is compared against fixed, negotiated financial targets, established in the autumn of each year and followed up on 31 December the following year.

Before the company changed to this new management model it had all the KPIs in the world but felt that it had lost sight of the bigger picture. The KPIs were too detailed with respect to planning and monitoring of performance, and the company had lost the speed and ability to act quickly in response to important events. The work done to produce a traditional budget forced it to play an annual game with additional resources beyond those previously negotiated, and prevented the business from achieving a broader and more strategic perspective.

Objectives and targets used to be cascaded down through the organization, but that approach was changed. In fact, the target process looks different in different parts of the company. At the group level, for example, it is more of a continuous process, where strategic themes are discussed when there is a need for this or at larger strategy conferences, usually held every six months. The strategic objectives at group level describe how to define success from a medium- to long-term perspective. What it means for a business unit or team varies, and depends on the rhythms of those concerned. Well-established strategic objectives do not change, unless they involve major strategic changes initiated by top management. To test the quality of the strategy and targets, questions such as the following are discussed:

- Is the target reflecting the overall aim of our ambition and strategy, and does it refer to areas that are both important and need to be changed?
- Does the target give clear guidance and set a direction?
- Is the target written in understandable language, free of too many buzzwords?
- Are the targets altogether supporting the overall objectives, their causes and effects, through the four perspectives of the balanced scorecard?
- Is the time horizon right?

The exact number of targets varies, but there are many hundreds of targets and indicators. However, each employee or group has only a few to relate to, based on their needs in the organization. The strategic process at the company involves the whole organization and not just the 'strategic top'. In the process, targets and KPIs are defined in relation to specific business units, and this is where objectives and actions are monitored and addressed.

The planning horizon varies for different activities and parts of the organization because not everyone has the same opportunity to predict the future or the ability to react. When monitoring trends associated with relevant indicators and measures, the focus is on the future, with the purpose of learning. Strategic objectives are translated from the corporate vision and strategy, not cascaded mechanically, into targets and indicators that a business unit, team or employee can influence in practice. It may seem contradictory but at the company *the target aimed for is not the actual target.* The target is what it wants to achieve, and that is to get the best possible performance under the prevailing circumstances. The company wants to understand what motivates and is behind good (or bad) performance. Thus it is not simply a matter of finding some perfect number that reveals the whole truth, but finding indicators. As for the issue of the 'right' number of indicators, there is no correct answer. It depends on how many strategic objectives there are and how quantifiable the business is. It also depends on the quality of the strategic objectives and actions. Normally, the company measures between five and ten indicators per person or group, with about 300 in total used across the entire organization.

As a rule of thumb, a good indicator discloses a relationship between performance and resource use in comparison with a peer. Moreover, a good indicator focuses on an area that can be influenced, and where there is need for change or improvement. The selection of indicators is reviewed regularly to ensure that they fit the company's strategic direction. This may involve, for example, product areas to develop, which markets to develop or how resources can best be allocated under the circumstances.

## Reporting

Reporting has changed from a focus on absolute financial targets set at the top of the organization to reporting on trends and actions undertaken by local subsidiaries, delivering the results. The new decentralized organization manages reports in the following way:

1. Reports are designed with respect to information management and local teams need to make the right decisions according to what they can influence.
2. Forecasting focuses on big, important numbers instead of detailed variance analysis, as was the case with traditional budgets. This means that numbers are approximately right instead of exactly right or wrong.
3. The monitoring and forecasting process, and the reflections it brings, are considered important for the whole team, but the numbers themselves are not necessarily considered important per se.
4. A business unit or team using information owns that information, which means it is fully responsible for its accuracy, especially when it comes to forecasting. This is crucial and makes people more accountable compared to the old way, where numbers were decided and cascaded down by someone else.
5. All numbers relating to the organization are available to everyone, so everyone knows where the overall business is heading.

## Incentives

Finally, the company discarded the traditional reward model for individual bonuses in favour of a model that is more collective. It also started to judge performance in relation to how others perform rather than by comparing it with a predetermined target (budget). One of the main purposes of the management model is to describe and evaluate performance in a good way. In the traditional management model this is considered too simple. Performance is considered 'good' if the delivery agrees with the negotiated and contracted numbers in a plan, even if the plan is outdated or the numbers have been proved wrong. Instead of evaluating performance against a fixed number, the company introduced a model using the symbols thumb up (green) and thumb down (red), where green denotes above-average performance and red below average. This might seem an unfair model since circumstances like market size, how established customers are, and so on, differ. To compensate for this, the model also compares the rate of change (progress). This makes it harder for managers acting in mature markets and with mature products to perform, and comparatively easier for those managing tougher (newer) markets and products. The collective incentive scheme is there for all employees and is based on how the company performs compared with its competitors. There is also a maximum incentive, which is set to about one month's salary.

As a complement to collective financial bonuses and rewards, the company introduced awards. Awards are given to any manager, team or individual that has performed well during any period of time. The use of awards was introduced to celebrate the successes management saw but couldn't express. To test performance and determine whether an award could be given to someone, top, middle and team managers have a checklist that consists of three questions with accompanying guidelines.

1. *Has delivery contributed to the organization's strategic objectives?* Just looking at a number is not interesting here. If internal or external circumstances – the reality around an organization – have influenced performance, this has to be considered. Maybe performance that looks like a rather mediocre result is, in fact, very good given the circumstances. Events such as natural disasters, competitors going out of business or changes in exchange rates must be considered. Maybe the performance wasn't that good or bad after all.

2 *How difficult or ambitious was the assignment?* Imagine two teams where one has an ambitious and difficult assignment but fails to deliver and the other has a less ambitious or difficult assignment that can easily be achieved. In such a case the first team should not be punished while the second one is rewarded.

3 *Are the results sustainable over the long term and has there been any issue with sub-optimization, or were shortcuts taken to perform?* It is always important to know how employees have behaved to achieve a goal.

## Results in terms of finance, culture, innovation and sustainability

The new management model has completely changed the culture in the organization. In fact it is now the culture and desire for the whole company to perform and achieve relatively ambitious financial goals, without focusing on the numbers, that is the drive. Along with rolling monitoring and forecasting for relevant financials and other indicators, the model continuously takes the pulse of every business unit. This means that management have decoupled the hierarchy in the organization with newly developed and decentralized decision-making processes.

The management model is supported by strong values, and locally responsible teams and decentralized decision-making support the culture. By changing not only the organization but also the management process, employee behaviour changed. And when the behaviour changed so did the culture. This is an example of how the management process goes hand in hand with organization, leadership and culture. To summarize, here are some of the learnings from the company:

- Cost for external marketing activities reduced by 15 per cent, with a positive impact on sales
- Cost for R&D, manufacturing and administration decreased
- Reduced time for (unnecessary) planning and number-crunching
- More time to focus on the business
- Increased transparency
- Changed mindset overall
- Increased trust and collaboration within the organization
- More fun.

Today, the company is not only one of the most profitable medical companies in the world, its employees are also more satisfied than those in comparable companies. According to a study in the *Harvard Business Review*, the company is one of the most innovative companies in the world. *Forbes* ranks the company in the top 25 of the world's 100 most innovative companies. Even customers (patients) have ranked the company number one six years in a row (2012–2018). The company is also ranked among the best for sustainability, among other things, by the Dow Jones Sustainability indices, Storebrand and the FTSE4Good Index. The latter organization also assesses the working environment.

## Questions

1 Why do you think costs fell rather than rose when the management model replaced the traditional budget with three separate processes?

2 Give examples of different designs of resource allocation process for any chosen company. What are the challenges and why?

3 What is a good performance? Discuss different ways of defining a good performance and how this might drive people to perform better or worse.

4 How long do you suggest forecasting and planning horizons should be in a company and why? Suggest and justify for two or three different industries, and at strategic, tactical and operational levels.

5 In Exhibit 2 you can follow the long-term trend (rolling 12-month) and short-term trend (rolling three-month average). As you can see, the short-term trend is deviating from the long term. What will your action be when analysing these trends and why?

# Case 8.5 Svenska Handelsbanken*

by Hamish Scott

## Sustaining growth in a decentralized organization

In late summer 2007, Lars Kahnlund sat in his office in Stockholm and looked through the statistics before him. He had recently become the head of the mortgage business area for Handelsbanken, the Swedish-based international banking group. Outside the window the early evening traffic was already ferrying commuters down Kungsträdgårdsgatan and across the bridges to their homes. But Lars knew that, with the monthly President's Meeting to be held tomorrow, he needed to work out what he would say to his colleagues around the table.

With more than 15 years' experience in operational roles at the bank, Lars knew that when he'd accepted the job of head of mortgages for the entire group just three months ago he was facing a completely different set of challenges from those he had faced recently as a regional director. The role gave him ongoing general management duties – as CEO of the mortgage business, Stadshypotek AB – but it was the responsibility for leading the development of mortgages across all countries that was the major task.

Handelsbanken has a distinctive culture and an approach to decentralization that gives all of the power to the branches and regions. The result has been an unrivalled record of shareholder value creation, customer satisfaction and employee satisfaction.

When Pär Boman, the new CEO, recently took over he declared he would strengthen the hand of the head office product heads, and appointed Lars to take a grip of mortgages. He wanted proactive development, a faster speed to market and better exploitation of emerging opportunities.

With market share in mortgages in Sweden around 25–30 per cent, Lars knew that the Swedish business would have difficulty accepting a different way of working. He looked once more at the statistics in the report before him. The facts were certain and the conclusion was clear. There was an opportunity for everyone to raise their performance. But he knew that the facts and figures were not the challenge for him.

### *Forty years of steady growth*

For 40 years Swedish-based banking group Svenska Handelsbanken (SHB) has been steadily growing beyond its core. Describing itself as a 'universal bank' it seeks to cover a full range of financial services, from corporate transactions to basic retail and consumer banking, life assurance, mutual funds, investment banking and trading.

With an operating profit of €2.1 billion in 2007, SHB is a mid-sized banking group – approximately one-sixth of the size of British-based giant RBS at that time.

But SHB is notable for a number of things:

- Its cost-efficiency – it has the lowest cost–income ratio of any major bank in Europe
- Its financial robustness – it was the only major Swedish bank to avoid seeking government support in the late 1980s and is faring better than many in the crisis that began in 2007

---

* This case was written by Hamish Scott, Ashridge and North Network Ltd. It is intended to be used as the basis for class discussion rather than to illustrate either effective or ineffective handling of a management situation. The case was made possible by the co-operation of Handelsbanken. 

- Its strong organic growth – it has generally shied away from major transactions and instead built its growth on branch openings and product launches
- Its track record of creating shareholder value – the bank has outperformed its Scandinavian rivals on most measures, including return on equity, total shareholder return and earnings per share; it has had a higher return on shareholders' equity than the average of its peer group for 36 years running; it produced an annual total shareholder return of 24 per cent between 1979 and 2001 – a rate 33 per cent higher than its nearest direct rival
- Its credit management – it has lower loan losses than its competitors
- Its customer satisfaction consistently scores higher than that of its rivals.

But most notable is its operating model and approach to people and processes. It employs an approach to customers, to products and service, to internal decision making and planning, to the management of its own people, and to control and risk management, that stands out in today's industrial landscape.

### Activities

Over the past 15 years, full-range banking operations have been developed in Nordic countries other than Sweden (where SHB has almost 460 branches): as at end 2007, Handelsbanken had 39 branches in Denmark, 44 in Finland and 46 in Norway. Since 2000 it had been developing quickly in Great Britain, where it had 42 branches by the start of 2008. In addition there are 20-plus branches in other countries, such as the USA, Germany and Singapore.

Handelsbanken Capital Markets handles corporate finance, trading in the equity, money and foreign exchange markets, debt capital financing, correspondent banking and trade finance.

Handelsbanken Asset Management handles mutual funds. Handelsbanken Finans offers financing services alongside the banking services of the branch offices and Handelsbanken Liv covers life assurance. Handelsbanken is also Sweden's largest telephone bank, with more than 300,000 customers.

Handelsbanken is strong when it comes to mid-size and smaller companies, and is one of the two leading banks in Sweden for tier-one customers.

### Evolution of SHB

In its early years, Svenska Handelsbanken AB confined its operations to the city of Stockholm. In the first half of the twentieth century, it was the foremost financier of Swedish heavy industry.

By the mid-1960s, Handelsbanken had not only become the largest bank in all of Scandinavia, it was also a leader among Swedish banks in recognizing the increasing importance of international markets. Major Swedish companies had always conducted much of their business abroad, but the lack of a Swedish banking presence in those countries meant that foreign banks wound up supplying their credit needs. In 1964 Handelsbanken joined with three other Scandinavian banks – Kjobenhavns Bandelsbank of Denmark, Den Norske Creditbank of Norway and Kansallis-Osake-Pankki of Finland – to establish Nordfinanzbank in Zürich and Banque Nordique du Commerce in Paris. The main aim was to help Swedish companies capitalize on foreign markets.

Handelsbanken continued to prosper and expand its foreign operations in the 1970s. It took a merger between Stockholm's Enskilda Bank and Skandinaviska Bank in 1972 to overtake it as Scandinavia's largest bank. In 1970, Handelsbanken participated in the formation of Nordic Bank Limited in London, along with Den Norske Creditbank and Kansallis-Osake-Pankki. In 1974 it opened a representative office in Moscow, responding to increased trade between Sweden and the Soviet Union. The following year, it established a subsidiary in New York, Nordic American Banking Corporation, devoted largely to import and export financing for North and South American clients doing business with Nordic countries. And in 1978, it set up a subsidiary bank in Luxembourg, Svenska Handelsbanken SA, Luxembourg.

By the early 1980s, Svenska Handelsbanken no longer needed consortium partners to carry out its international business and in 1982 it established its own merchant banking subsidiary in London, Svenska

International. The next year, it sold its interest in Nordic Bank Limited to Den Norske Creditbank. In 1984 it formed a subsidiary in Singapore, Svenska Handelsbanken Asia Limited, and sold much of its stake in Nordfinanzbank to Kansallis-Osake-Pankki, giving its Finnish partner a controlling interest. In 1985, it sold its 25 per cent share of Nordic American Banking Corporation to Den Norske Creditbank. And in 1989 it opened an office in Norway.

During the 1980s, as major corporations set up their own in-house financing units, Handelsbanken gradually took over more big-ticket finance business from the former kingmaker of industry, Skandinaviska Enskilda Banken (SEB). It also began to profit on the smaller end of the domestic market and started to look into international, integrated markets.

Together with SEB, Handelsbanken was the only large Swedish bank to survive the country's banking crisis in the early 1990s without having to be bailed out by the government. In fact that economic crisis triggered renewed growth efforts. In 1990, the bank made the acquisition of the Swedish Skanska Banken and Norway's Oslo Handelsbank. Stavanger Bank, another Norwegian operator, was purchased in 1991. In 1992, Handelsbanken expanded its life insurance holdings when it acquired the life insurance company RKA (its name was quickly changed to Handelsbanken Liv). The flurry of Nordic acquisitions continued throughout the decade.

The bank expanded its service base by taking its business to the internet in 1997. In 2000, Handelsbanken had 200,000 registered internet customers, about 20 per cent of its customer base. The bank also offered internet customers the opportunity to pay their bills electronically.

### Goals and performance

Handelsbanken defines its goal in terms of having higher profitability – as measured by ROE – relative to its peer group.

As the bank struggled to recover after a severe crisis in the late 1960s, it set its sights high and made an undertaking to its shareholders and analysts: it would outperform its industry's average profitability year after year. See the Appendix for the list of peers against which Handelsbanken benchmarks its performance.

By 2007, the bank had met that goal every year since 1972. In that year, shareholders earned 23 per cent on equity.

Profitability is always given higher priority than volumes. And customer satisfaction is always given higher priority than short-term profitability. As one branch manager explained, 'We invest in long-term relationships with customers. If they are happy, then we keep them and they tell others. If that happens, then we grow. If we grow, we create shareholder value.'

### Decentralization: the branch is the bank

Handelsbanken is strongly decentralized, with the branches being the focal point for the development and delivery of strategy. Responsibility for earning profits, and for controlling costs, rests with the managers of the 660 branches. The branch managers are given the freedom to decide which products to emphasize in their own market, how to resource the branch, how to market it and how to keep the cost ratio in line.

Branches also serve corporate clients in their areas. The branch located closest to the head office of an international corporate giant will be the one that handles all of that firm's needs. So in addition to lending to employees of, say, Ericsson, the branch takes the lead in arranging multi-million-dollar financing for the corporate group itself. And, at the end of each quarter, all of those decisions show up in the branch's profit-and-loss statement.

In a recent presentation to Morgan Stanley, new CEO Pär Boman explained that 'the branch is the bank'. Running every aspect of the local branch, the manager, not the head office, handles local advertising, sets pay levels, prices product and chooses which product to push.

'Our branch manager position has been likened to that of an entrepreneur,' says Lennart Francke, former CFO. This leaves the branch manager with responsibility for all his revenue and all his cost.

Yes – *all* his cost – because even most head office cost allocations of group-wide services are put into the branch managers' domain. All cost allocations are scrutinized each year by a committee of central and branch staff – inaccurately named the Planning Committee. Each manager of a central department who wishes to allocate cost to the branches must make an application to this committee and convince it of the appropriateness of the amount and the value for money of the service that he is delivering to the branches. If the committee decides that the cost allocation is too high or the service level too highly specified, or the service is poor value for money compared with what is available on the open market, then the transfer price is reduced to what the branches agree with, and the central department budget holder falls into 'loss' or under-recovery. The department then has a fixed time to get back to break-even – by cost reduction or finding something else to do for which the branches *will* pay.

The bank has always been determined to cut out unnecessary layers of bureaucracy. The branch managers, in addition to having a large amount of control and responsibility, have an almost direct route to the bank's chief executive. The only level between the branch managers and the bank's CEO is a group of 11 regional managers.

With spans of control being so wide, there is almost no chance of micro-management. The regional managers are assisted by area managers but these positions have no line authority over the branches.

### Positioning and focus

Handelsbanken's preferred approach is to focus on certain customer types – those that value the service Handelsbanken branches deliver. When CEO Pär Boman describes the bank's growth model, he refers to 'cherry picking customers'.

Magnus Uggla, head of the UK regional bank since 2000, explains that the bank is not interested in vanilla products or competing on product or price. 'Everything can be copied,' he declares. 'Service is the only sustainable advantage.'

With the customer in focus – not individual products – the branch starts with the question of the customer needs. 'Other banks come up with great products and sell them to customers . . . even if they don't really need them. We think if we do that then we will compromise the customer relationship,' says Pat Hanlon, branch manager, Birmingham, UK. His manager for personal banking, Tony Hall, likens it to selling pizza: 'We start with the basic pizza and ask the clients what toppings they want on it.'

### Attitude to risk

The bank has a cautious approach to lending and risk. Its branches are clear that the bank aims to deal with the borrowers that offer the least risk and the best chance of repayment.

This may restrict its ability to grow quickly, but the bank has an unashamedly long-term perspective. This approach has given it a financial robustness that stood it in good stead during the banking crisis of the late 1980s when it was the only major Swedish bank to avoid even discussing government support. 'We lost money but it could have been a lot worse if it hadn't been for our stance,' says Lennart Francke.

Boman explains that the Handelsbanken approach is to have 'no macro bets'.

Paradoxically, this control of risk is not achieved through portfolio management control from the bank leaders in Stockholm. Francke explains that when he was in charge of credit (control of lending) for the group he didn't direct so much as add up how much the branches had lent to this or that industry.

With no heavy central controls, it is at branch level that the risk is managed; the portfolio of loans is mostly created by a series of decisions in branches, not lending decisions from above. Each branch manager is responsible for his own lending decisions and only a few very large ones need to be referred for approval. Even when they do require approval from above, the accountability is clear: 'If it goes wrong, it's my decision, my customer, my situation to fix,' says Pat Hanlon. He explains that there is little time or money spent on paperwork to win internal arguments or central credit teams double-checking branch work or trying to shift responsibility to someone else when a loan goes bad.

This sense of ownership relies on the 'church tower' principle: a branch manager should be able to see all his customers from the top of the tower. 'On my way to work, if I see that the car dealer has started to cut his prices, I know that I need to go and talk to him about his trading and the loan I have made to him,' said one manager.

### Planning and decision making

In 1971, under the guidance of then-CEO Jan Wallander, SHB abandoned most forms of long-range economic forecasting and budgeting. Writing in his own book about the bank's guiding principles, *The Handelsbanken Way*, Wallander explained that decentralization is fundamental and that:

> *Annual budgeting should be abolished. It makes decentralisation impossible and suffers from a fundamental fault. The problems it is supposed to solve can be dealt with in a much simpler and more effective way.*

Ten years later, president Jan Ekman announced that the policy had produced results above the industry average. 'Forecasting is an exercise in meaningless impossibilities,' he wrote in *Euromoney* magazine.

Regions and branches, in effect, set their own targets: they decide the improvements they want to make and strive to beat their peers – other regions and branches in the Handelsbanken group.

There is no top-down goal setting. When Magnus Uggla, regional head for the UK, receives the plans from his branches, he explains that he looks at them out of interest but doesn't add them up to make a regional plan. The plans produced by the branches are 'a working tool for the branch'.

Regional banks are compared using ROE as a measurement. Branches compete with one another on their cost-to-income ratio as well as on profit per employee and total profit. When the C/I ratio is calculated at branch office level, branch offices are charged with a capital cost based on how much of the bank's risk-bearing capital their business volumes consume. Standings are prominently displayed in what the company refers to as 'league tables'.

According to Wallander, now the honorary chairman, 'We just communicate to people the average and a ranking that shows which branches are above and which are below. The system works on its own. Managers know what is "acceptable" performance; you can't linger in the depths of the league table for long. Peer pressure plays an important part in this process. No branch manager wants to let down the regional team'.[1]

The regional offices monitor the performance of the branches – transaction volumes, fluctuations in numbers of customers, customer profitability, branch profits, cost patterns, productivity, and so on – and if they notice that a branch is underperforming over a period of time, someone contacts that branch to see if it needs help.

The short lines of control benefit Handelsbanken: 'Other banks have access to the same technology, so the difference must be down to how we work,' says Ame Martensson, the bank's CEO in the 1990s and its chairman until recently. 'Problems are transparent; they are not hidden within the nooks and crannies of management layers and allowed to fester.'

Rolling cash forecasts, prepared every quarter, are produced by the finance department and seen by the CFO and the CEO only. If a problem is apparent, they make clear that steps need to be taken to ensure adequate liquidity.

### Cost and operational management

A decade ago, then-CEO Arne Martensson explained to *The Economist* that Handelsbanken has 'a culture of thrift'.

With branch managers focused on managing their own profit lines, they attend to their costs as an owner would do. No sweeping head office policies attack cost lines, just the day-to-day, incremental

[1] Hope, J. and Fraser, R. (2003) Who needs budgets? *Harvard Business Review*, February. Available at: https://hbr.org/2003/02/who-needs-budgets (accessed 12 May 2020).

advances of people who take pride in their numbers . . . and their position in the league tables. Uggla points to a branch that decided to use second-hand furniture in the office to save money, and another that opted to vacuum clean its own carpets and save the cost of cleaners. Little by little, this stream of initiatives has built Europe's most efficient bank.

Writing in the *Harvard Business Review*, Fraser and Hope[2] reported that experienced managers at the company expected an increase in the number of workers when unit heads were given staffing authority, but the opposite happened. They found that the approach facilitated smart decisions about resource management and growth. 'In a traditional budgeting system, inflexible cost targets can have the perverse effect of limiting the amount of business a unit takes on. At Handelsbanken, branches have the authority to decide whether the income generated by, say, opening many new accounts is worth the higher costs those accounts will entail.' The clear priority is profit, not revenue.

A head office coordinated campaign to streamline systems is being led by Katarina Berner Froesdal, who as head of infrastructure is charged with overseeing all changes to systems and operational processes. The project is entitled KLOS ('scratch' in Swedish) to signify what the bank wants to do to any itches! Typically for Handelsbanken, this project has been driven by the branches, which were simply asked: 'What would make your life simpler and easier?' In the first three months after launch in February 2007, 700 ideas were generated by the branches. Berner Froesdal and her team then began working their way through a list of 400 improvements – big and small scratches – which had been identified. 'My job is to make the branches' lives easier by trimming out things that the centre does that slow down the branch. . . . so they can focus on the business of servicing customers,' she explains. 'But,' she adds, 'the project does not have its own investigation or development resources – it is totally dependent on the regular organization being involved and taking responsibility.'

As a former branch manager, Berner Froesdal is clear about where the responsibility should sit. Her selling initiative – SALJ – is designed to increase cross-selling, but 'if they don't want to use it, they don't have to,' she says. Central initiatives can get in the way and add cost, she modestly explains. She recalls the three-week wait for central credit approval in 1972. 'Now it can be three minutes!' she beams. Attributing the faster speed and lower cost to the local powers of the branches, she adds: 'If a branch manager knows someone is a good customer, he should be able to tell him he can have the money on the spot. What can head office add to that?'

### Service and selling

An annual poll conducted by the Stockholm School of Economics has found Handelsbanken's clients more satisfied than those of other banks each year since 1989.[3]

As well as an engrained passion for service, the factors driving this performance are empowerment and multi-skilling. People are trained and able to cross-sell all products; indeed, every branch member has been accredited to sell insurance. And because half of Handelsbanken's staff have lending authority, customers receive answers quickly.

When *Privata Affärer*, a periodical for private finances, named Svenska Handelsbanken Bank of the Year in 2001, the award was explained as follows: 'At a time when many banks are closing branches, Handelsbanken stands out as a bank which offers good personal service at branch offices and combines an extensive branch network with free banking services over the internet. Loyal customers have every opportunity of negotiating better conditions for themselves. This year, Handelsbanken has also opened up for increased competition by removing mutual fund charges and allowing customers to move their pension savings.'

Stories of good service abound. But, as Francke explains, they are mostly about the small things, 'everyday service', rather than extraordinary feats or amazing new products.

---

[2] Hope, J. and Fraser, R. (2003) Who needs budgets? *Harvard Business Review*, February. Available at: https://hbr.org/2003/02/who-needs-budgets (accessed 12 May 2020).

[3] Euromoney.

### Marketing

In contrast to the approach at many other financial services companies, Handelsbanken dispenses with a central marketing function (except in the case of product launches) and sales targets.

Big marketing investment is eschewed in favour of word of mouth – there are no widespread campaigns.

Handelsbanken describes a 'network effect'. Here is an explanation from the UK: 'A local accountant introduces us to a client. We lend him £200K. The client's solicitor's wife starts to bank with us and borrows £500K. The solicitor's firm now borrows £8 million. The solicitor's brother starts to bank with us. The accountant starts to bank with us. The client's IFA makes contact with us. The IFA introduces a client who now borrows £1.5 million. The client introduces his "best friend".'

Pat Hanlon, branch manager, Birmingham, UK, explains that approximately 80 per cent of his personal accounts have introduced a client.

### Current product development process

Products are developed from the bottom up: a branch identifies new, unmet needs as a result of its dealings with customers. It escalates these needs with its regional bank, the regional head sanctions work or raises the need with the head office product heads. All work to develop product is re-routed out to the branches. Any major investment needs to be a group decision.

Product heads have traditionally seen their role as supportive to the branches.

Berner Froesdal explains that the product heads compete for the time of the branch offices. They certainly do not insist on their support.

### Geographical development: in the UK

New geographies are an important route to growth for Handelsbanken.

The bank began branch office operations in the UK in 1994 with just two branches focused on serving Nordic corporate clients who wanted support in that country. Based in London and Manchester, they operated a quite different model from that used in their home market.

By the end of the 1990s, the bank decided to import its Swedish model: the 'universal bank' proposition delivered from decentralized branches.

'It was practically just lifted over the North Sea and put down on UK soil,' recalls Francke. The aim from day one was to build a well-spread, low-risk portfolio without compromising on margins.

'In Sweden we target towns with a minimum of 10,000 people, but in the UK I have seen a list of over 900,' says Uggla. With this choice of target towns Handelsbanken's main criterion for where to set up became the location of potentially good branch managers. 'When it comes to where we open, it's a question of finding the right person . . . In that respect we are quite opportunistic.'

So, after an initial search in the UK, the bank identified someone it wanted as a branch manager – a man called Colin Kirk – and set up in Nottingham because that was where he had good contacts.

If the bank finds someone who looks like its target profile, and he or she has good contacts, *and* if they are based in a city or town that is on the hit list, then it sets up there. Simple as that.

Uggla explains that he is looking for a branch manager with 20–30 years' banking experience – ideally with the same bank – who is frustrated with the responsibility he/she is currently being given. At first it was hard to convince people, but now that the bank has developed critical mass and some reputation, it is getting easier to find good people.

Word of mouth in the UK is also driving revenue growth: the majority of new business comes from recommendations and personal introductions.

To this end, PR is vital for Handelsbanken. Its Bristol branch benefited from this press comment in 2005:

> *More people are complaining about the service they get from banks than ever before. One Bristol bank has set out to change all this by focusing on what customers really want. Clifton Life, 2005*

By 2007 the UK business had reached sufficient size to be split into two regional banks. Uggla takes the south and the new regional head for the north will report direct to the bank's CEO.

### Pay and incentives

With a very few exceptions, no one in the bank's 10,600-strong workforce is offered an annual personal bonus based on their own – or their branch's performance. This sort of incentive – common to banking and indeed all other industrial sectors – has been rejected in favour of a form of profit sharing that pays out on the bank's group-wide performance.

Each year the bank assesses its ROE performance compared with that of its peers. Any profit that can be associated with performance above the average performance of the peers is split in three and one-third is distributed to employees. But here's the twist: the allocation is made equally across all staff who worked in the bank that year – the regional head getting the same as a junior teller – and the allocation is made to a trust called the Oktogonen Trust, in which employees of Handelsbanken hold all the shares. No cash. And the shares can be sold only in the event of retirement.

So, the eventual payment depends upon length of tenure only, not on salary. Any employee leaving after 25 years' service would currently receive about SEK2.5 million, or £200,000.

One other thing: the Oktogonen's biggest investment in its SEK20 billion portfolio is in . . . Handelsbanken stock.

So the performance of the bank indirectly drives the value of the retirement nest egg of each member of staff. And – with Oktogonen's 10 per cent shareholding giving it two seats on the board of the bank as one of the two biggest investors in Handelsbanken stock – the performance of the bank is driven by the interests of the staff.

Individual and unit rewards consist of peer recognition and praise.

Such a global bonus payout could be expected to give a free ride to managers who perform poorly, but employees report that the team-based approach means that peer pressure soon applies.

The bank's overall performance is the chief motivation of the staff. Which means that the sort of internal competition that plagues so many decentralized organizations melts away. Branches feel safe sharing information about customers and even passing on business to the branch that can deliver best service. The league tables are important, but the long-term satisfaction of customers – and the value they will bring to the bank – is the overriding and unifying motivation.

The long-term nature of the incentive means that those motivated by short-term financial rewards will not be drawn to the bank. Salaries are significantly higher than in rival firms: the bank is keen to pay a fair price for the best people. But few people join the bank for the immediate pay prospects. 'It's a way of life thing,' explains Tony Hall. 'Here I get a good job, a chance to make decisions, and get respect. My wife would kill me if I left Handelsbanken.'

### People and culture

'When identifying branch managers we look for frustrated entrepreneurs and ask them to risk their reputation and our money.' This is how the UK business explains its recruitment policy.

The decentralized set-up brings out the best in a certain kind of person. 'We look for people with an inner drive,' says Francke. Typical 'Handelsbankers' obviously need to be self-starting, confident in their abilities and committed to service.

'We want people who like people,' explains one other senior executive when describing how the service position of the bank requires a certain kind of employee.

Long-term tenure is expected – indeed targeted. Handelsbanken's model has a certain style and not everyone gets it. The role of the boss is important: 'We want leaders to grow their people; that's a very important part of their culture,' says Uggla.

Looking back to the Skånska Banken acquisition in Sweden in 1990, Francke reckons it took three years before the acquired people had figured out – and bought into – the Handelsbanken approach. 'Some feel uncomfortable not being told what to do,' he said.

And, it seems, head office people need to know their place. The power is definitely with the branch. 'I wouldn't dare tell a branch what to do,' Lars Kahnlund declared soon after taking up his new job running mortgage products across the group. Indeed, as one branch manager makes clear: 'If I don't want to do it, it won't happen.'

### The President's Meeting

So, with years of experience of working within the business, Lars Kahnlund knew that making his new role successful would require more than smart plans for the products. He would have to win over his peers to a different way of working. And the forthcoming President's Meeting was the place to make his first pitch.

As he sat at his desk, he pondered the following questions . . .

1. How do I get the business to accept a firmer, more directive approach? How do I make sense of my role?
2. How do I make the most of the culture we have, the systems we have, the structures and skills we have? What do I try to change to push the development of products and opportunities in my product area?
3. How do I get my colleagues to work with me on this?
4. Above all, what do I say tomorrow at the President's Meeting?

**APPENDIX** Handelsbanken profitability at a glance, 2007

| Profit statement – highlights | (SEK m) | (Euro m) |
|---|---|---|
| Net interest income | 15,608 | 1,653 |
| Net fee and commission income | 7,745 | 820 |
| Net gains/losses on financial items at fair value | 3,054 | 324 |
| Risk result – insurance | 151 | 16 |
| Other income | 568 | 60 |
| **Total income** | **27,126** | **2,874** |
| Staff costs | –7,528 | –797 |
| Other expenses | –4,840 | –513 |
| **Total expenses** | **–12,368** | **–1,310** |
| **Profit before loan losses** | **14,758** | **1,563** |
| Loan losses, net | –27 | –3 |
| Disposal prop. equipmt/intang. assets | 1 | 0 |
| Discontinued operations | 4,651 | 493 |
| **Operating profit, incl. discont. op.** | **19,383** | **2,053** |
| **Key financial metrics** | | |
| ROE total operations, actual tax % | | 23.3 |
| ROE total operations, after standard tax % | | 20.9 |
| C/I ratio before loan losses, total operations % | | 40.5 |
| Earnings per share total operations | 24.84 | 2.63 |

*Source:* Handelsbanken Annual Report 2007.

## Peer group analysis

The banks to which SHB compares ROE to calculate if and how big an allocation should be made to the Oktogonen Foundation are:

- In Sweden – Nordea, Swedbank, SEB
- In Finland – OKO Bank
- In Norway – DnB NOR
- In Denmark – Danske Bank, Jyske Bank, Sydbank
- In the UK – HSBC, Barclays, Lloyds TSB, RBS, HBOS.

## Examples of league tables

**Branch network in Sweden, 2003**

*Most profitable*

| Place 0312 | 0212 | RegB | C/I before loan losses % | Change | C/I after loan losses % | Operating income SEK m | Operating Profit mSEK | Operating Profit/D mSEK |
|---|---|---|---|---|---|---|---|---|
| 1 | (17) | RC | 11.8 | –3.4 | 11.3 | 113.4 | 100.1 | 3.8 |
| 2 | (2) | RC | 12.7 | 0.3 | 12.5 | 90.3 | 78.8 | 9.4 |
| 3 | (7) | RC | 16.5 | –7.3 | –77.9 | 97.5 | 81.4 | 6.6 |
| 4 | | RV | 19.1 | –8.2 | 82.5 | 36.9 | 29.9 | 4.8 |
| 5 | (1) | RM | 19.2 | 7.1 | –11.7 | 102.9 | 83.1 | 7.0 |
| 6 | (20) | RC | 20.8 | –6.4 | 20.7 | 91.6 | 72.6 | 5.3 |
| 7 | (12) | RM | 22.4 | –4.0 | 22.0 | 41.4 | 32.1 | 5.2 |
| 8 | (8) | RV | 23.0 | –1.2 | 21.0 | 49.9 | 38.4 | 4.8 |
| 9 | (3) | RV | 23.1 | 0.8 | 22.5 | 48.8 | 37.6 | 5.0 |
| 10 | (18) | RM | 23.6 | –0.3 | 23.9 | 44.8 | 34.3 | 3.5 |
| 11 | (4) | RS | 24.1 | 2.3 | 29.1 | 66.4 | 50.4 | 4.1 |
| 12 | (10) | RC | 24.3 | –1.0 | 21.4 | 90.6 | 68.6 | 4.1 |
| 13 | | RC | 24.3 | –12.4 | 21.3 | 68.7 | 52.0 | 4.2 |
| 14 | (11) | RM | 24.5 | –1.1 | 25.6 | 80.7 | 60.9 | 4.8 |
| 15 | (5) | RC | 24.5 | 3.8 | –27.1 | 49.5 | 37.4 | 3.0 |
| 16 | (15) | RV | 24.9 | –0.7 | 24.3 | 83.1 | 62.4 | 4.5 |
| 17 | (9) | RC | 25.4 | 2.1 | 25.2 | 82.5 | 61.5 | 3.8 |
| 18 | | RM | 25.7 | –2.7 | 29.2 | 58.1 | 43.2 | 4.3 |
| 19 | (6) | RM | 26.2 | 3.9 | 26.4 | 52.8 | 38.9 | 3.5 |
| 20 | (16) | RM | 26.4 | –0.2 | 27.1 | 46.4 | 34.1 | 3.5 |
| Average | | | 21.4 | –0.4 | 12.3 | 69.8 | 54.9 | 4.6 |

**Regional banking units, 2005**

*League table*

| 2005 January–September | | | | | |
|---|---|---|---|---|---|
| | Operational profit SEK m | | +/− | Return on equity % | |
| Region | 2005 | 2004 | % | 2005 | 2004 |
| R9 | 298 | 237 | 26% | 19.6 | 17.3 |
| R2 | 680 | 578 | 18% | 18.8 | 18.3 |
| R1 | 395 | 356 | 11% | 18.6 | 18.0 |
| R5 | 801 | 766 | 5% | 17.3 | 18.0 |
| R6 | 1382 | 1306 | 6% | 17.2 | 17.6 |
| R7 | 1020 | 973 | 5% | 16.9 | 16.9 |
| R11 | 626 | 558 | 12% | 16.5 | 18.4 |
| R4 | 1738 | 1779 | −2% | 15.8 | 17.1 |
| R3 | 1442 | 1453 | −1% | 14.6 | 15.7 |
| R8 | 130 | −27 | . . . | 12.3 | . . . |
| R10 | 231 | 231 | 0% | 10.6 | 10.3 |
| Specialist units and subsidiaries | 2310 | 1932 | | | |
| **SHB Group** | 11055 | 10142 | 9% | 17.1 | **16.6** |

## Customer satisfaction

*Press release, 10 October 2007*

**Handelsbanken tops customer satisfaction poll**

This week, the Swedish quality index company, Svenskt Kvalitetsindex (SKI), presented its annual customer survey of Swedish banks.

For the tenth year in succession Handelsbanken continues to top the polls for customer satisfaction in both the corporate and private sectors among the Swedish clearing banks.

**Customer satisfaction: private sector**

| Banks | 2007 |
|---|---|
| Handelsbanken | 74.1 |
| Swedbank | 70.4 |
| SEB | 69.9 |
| Nordea | 67.3 |
| Average for banks | 71.3 |

**Customer satisfaction: corporate sector**

| Banks | 2007 |
|---|---|
| Handelsbanken | 71.9 |
| SEB | 71.5 |
| Swedbank | 70.7 |
| Nordea | 68.1 |
| Average for banks | 71.4 |

# Chapter 9

# Financial and non-financial performance measurement systems

## Learning objectives

After reading this chapter, you should be able to:

1. Explain the general considerations involved in selecting financial and non-financial measures.
2. Explain the pitfalls when choosing financial measures, including the advantages and disadvantages of return on investment (ROI), residual income (RI) and economic value added (EVA®).
3. Explain the pitfalls when choosing non-financial measures.
4. Explain what a balanced scorecard (BSC) is and in which ways it differs from a simple laundry list of financial and non-financial measures.
5. Explain the main issues to consider when implementing a balanced scorecard.

## Real world vignette: BMW

More and more companies realize that relying solely on financial measures when evaluating company and responsibility centre performance is often inadequate and can, in fact, be dysfunctional for several reasons. BMW Financial Services is an important part of the BMW group, financing a large part of the new BMW vehicles sold. It is well known for using the balanced scorecard (BSC) when evaluating performance. A BSC is a performance measurement system that systematically *combines strategically important financial and non-financial measures*. It is argued that the BSC has enabled BMW Financial

Services to steer its performance in a world-class strategic direction. John Christman, one of BMW Financial Services' top managers, explains:

> *The balanced scorecard links our objectives, initiatives, and metrics to our strategy while communicating our priorities to every member of our company. Today our BSC programme includes linkages to our project approval process, budgeting methodology, compensation system, technology initiatives, training programmes, and even our community involvement and charitable contribution efforts. Our results have been excellent, with an uninterrupted history of growth and a successful strategy implementation that continues today, consistent with the first plans established over six years ago. Profits are up, return on assets is up, and assets have grown each year.*[1]

John Christman's description of how BMW Financial Services uses the BSC illustrates that performance measurement systems, such as the BSC, are not simply a collection of financial and non-financial measures. There are important links between the measures and mission, goals and strategies, between measures and incentive systems, and between measures and company culture. If used properly, the BSC can become a powerful performance measurement system, contributing to good *current* as well as *future* performance.

## Introduction

In the introduction to Part 3 of the book, we defined performance management as the outcome control practices used to make sure that planned activities are performed and set goals met in organizations. If budgets (Chapter 8) are seen by managers as a cornerstone of performance management, an organization's performance measurement system is definitely seen as an equally important cornerstone. It involves all the activities in the previously mentioned performance management loop: planning, execution, evaluation and learning. Designing and using appropriate *performance measurement systems* is thus seen by many managers as a core element of a well-functioning management control system. There is a famous expression that we hear over and over again from top managers, but also from many lower-level managers and employees: 'What gets measured gets done.' One central question therefore becomes: How well are the organization as a whole and its various organizational units performing? To be able to answer this question managers need to decide which dimensions of performance the organization seeks to develop. Dimensions of performance are specified as *measures* that quantify performance financially and/or non-financially, thereby identifying factors that are crucial to the company's success. By comparing the outcome of the chosen performance measures against appropriate targets, top managers can assess the performance of the organization and its sub-units. In addition, performance measurement systems provide important feedback to managers and employees on whether or not their efforts have been successful, thereby fostering motivation and learning within the company.

Using financial and non-financial measures is meaningful only if the outcome of a certain measure is compared with a valid target (or 'standard' as some managers call it). A target answers the question 'What is a good enough outcome of a particular performance measure?' For example, an organization decides to use customer satisfaction as an important non-financial performance measure. If the target is set to be 85 per cent, this means that a customer satisfaction outcome of 90 per cent is more than good enough, whereas an outcome of 70 per cent is not good enough. As discussed in Chapter 8, a negotiated

[1] Previously available at https://www.thepalladiumgroup.com/Results/hof/Pages/HofViewer.aspx?MID=7.

predetermined target, if carefully prepared and coordinated, is the most commonly used target. Continuous improvements and benchmarking are other ways to arrive at an appropriate target (as the Handelsbanken case in Chapter 8 illustrates). Managers, who often primarily focus on the design and use of the measures as such, tend to forget that an essential step in measuring performance is to continuously examine *the validity of the target.*

The goal of performance measurement systems is to help managers and employees understand, implement and refine the organization's mission, goals and strategies. The measures can be seen as helping top managers assess whether the organization is 'on track'. One difficulty when designing appropriate performance measurement systems is to *decide which measures to focus on.* Research shows that a mix of financial and non-financial measures is preferred since relying solely on financial measures is inadequate and can, in fact, be dysfunctional, for several reasons. But there are a myriad of financial and non-financial performance measures available. When it comes to financial measures, we have, for instance, revenues, expenses, earnings before interest expenses and taxes, return on investment (ROI), residual income (RI) and economic value added (EVA®). Examples of non-financial measures are customer satisfaction, churn rate, employee satisfaction, various quality measures, lead time, delivery precision, market share and number of development projects started. Research shows that human brains can process and remember only a limited number (studies in cognitive psychology, for instance, indicate seven to nine items of information simultaneously) of measures at the same time. So managers have to be *selective* when deciding on the appropriate mix of financial and non-financial measures. When making these difficult choices, three criteria have proved to be of help: the representational criterion, the measurement systems criterion and the user criterion.[2]

The representational criterion relates to how well a measure captures goal-congruent behaviour and strategically important dimensions in a striking manner. Top managers need to carefully evaluate each selected financial and non-financial measure with this criterion in mind and ask questions such as: Is this measure 'good-to-have' (and maybe used simply because we 'have always measured it') or 'need-to-have' (that is, strategically important)? Do we really measure the lower-level manager and employee behaviour we think we do, or is there a big risk that they take short-cuts and/or engage in goal-incongruent behaviour to maximize the outcome of the chosen measure? For instance, some managers witness that when they introduce a quality measure for a certain product some units start to reclassify certain quality defects as acceptable that, before the measure was introduced, would have caused the product to be 'logged' as not acceptable in terms of quality.

The measurement systems criterion concerns the quality of how the data for the measure are captured, transformed and used. Top managers need to ask the following questions: Can we verify the data used for this measure with a reasonable degree of certainty? Is there a lack of personal bias when the data are collected? Can the measure easily be compared between different units? In other words, do the different units collect data in the same way and 'define' the measure in the same way? How much is needed in terms of resources for this measurement? For instance, do we have adequate systems for providing us with reliable data? Financial measures usually 'score high' on this criterion since the organization normally has reasonably standardized systems for collecting financial data. With non-financial measures it is more difficult since they often require manual data collection, and units may 'define' and collect data on, for instance, customer satisfaction in different ways. Recent developments in digitalization and big data provide new opportunities for managers to handle some of the challenges posed by the measurement systems criterion.

The user criterion refers to the extent to which the measure is adapted to the attributes and prerequisites of those being measured – i.e., the lower-level managers and employees (the 'users'). Top managers need to ask the following questions: To what extent is a particular measure accepted by the lower-level

---

[2] Johansson, S.E. and Östman, L. (1995) *Accounting Theory: Integrating Behaviour and Measurement.* London: Pitman.

managers and employees as a 'good measure' of their performance? Is the measure simple enough so they understand why to use it? Do we as top managers apply the controllability principle and actually use measures that the lower-level managers and employees perceive they can influence? Non-financial measures normally 'score high' on this criterion since they are perceived as less abstract by lower-level managers and employees, and are more closely related to what they perceive they can influence. Financial measures are often criticized based on the user criterion as many lower-level managers and employees do not understand how they are related to their day-to-day work. The user criterion is closely related to the 'enabling' role of management control systems, which was introduced in Chapter 1. For performance measurement systems to have an enabling role, top managers need to design them to help maintain or enhance the skill set, job motivation and organizational commitment that lower-level managers and employees aim to contribute to the organization. The lower-level managers need to perceive performance measurement systems as something that supports them, that they can use to identify problems, prioritize issues and develop innovative ideas.

In the coming sections, we will return to these criteria when we discuss the use of financial and non-financial measures. We will first discuss pitfalls when using financial measures for investment centres in particular when it comes to the representational and user criteria. We will then discuss pitfalls when using non-financial measures. Finally, we will discuss how non-financial and financial performance measures can be systematically integrated. Special attention is given to the balanced scorecard (BSC), a widely adopted performance measurement system that combines strategically important financial and non-financial measures.

## Pitfalls when using financial measures

The choice of appropriate financial measures is a natural starting point for many managers. This is linked to the management considerations involved in assigning *financial responsibility* to organizational sub-units discussed in Chapter 4. The *controllability principle* was emphasized, stipulating that responsibility centre managers should be evaluated based on financial measures that are within their control. As discussed in the previous paragraph, this principle is related to the user criterion, and often serves as a general guideline for top managers when they select financial measures for revenue, expense, profit and investment centres. For instance, if the responsibility centre manager cannot influence the invested capital, the manager's unit should be structured as a profit centre and evaluated based on a profit measure, and not on measures such as return on capital employed (ROCE). Applying the controllability principle also brings to the fore the existence of a revenue, expense, profit and investment centre continuum – that is, responsibility centres are often not 'pure' profit centres or investment centres. If managers can influence inventory and accounts receivables but not the investment in non-current assets, we suggest that they are evaluated based on appropriate profit measures combined with measures reflecting inventory and accounts receivables. They will not be in charge of a 'pure' investment centre, but they will be evaluated on the capital components that can be influenced. Research shows that the non-application of the controllability principle leads to decreased motivation and increased role stress, which may result in dysfunctional behaviour by the responsibility centre managers.[3] This implies that effective performance measurement requires assignment and acceptance of responsibility for performance (as stated in the user criterion). Below we discuss two common pitfalls when using financial measures.

[3] See, for example, Burkert, M., Fischer, F.M. and Schäffer, U. (2011) Application of the controllability principle and managerial performance: the role of role perceptions, *Management Accounting Research*, 22(3): 143–59.

## Pitfall 1: What profit should we use?

We know from experience that the performance of the profit centre manager is especially challenging as they may be evaluated by five different measures: (1) contribution margin; (2) direct profit; (3) controllable profit; (4) earnings before interest and taxes (EBIT); or (5) net income. The nature of these measures is indicated by the income statement example in Table 9.1 and each one is discussed below.

**TABLE 9.1** Example of a profit centre income statement

| | | Profitability measure |
|---|---|---|
| Revenue | €1,000 | |
| Cost of sales | 600 | |
| Variable expenses | −180 | |
| **Contribution margin** | **220** | **(1)** |
| Fixed expenses incurred in the profit centre | −90 | |
| **Direct profit** | **130** | **(2)** |
| Controllable corporate charges | −10 | |
| **Controllable profit** | **120** | **(3)** |
| Other corporate allocations | −20 | |
| **Earnings before interest and taxes (EBIT)** | **100** | **(4)** |
| Taxes | −40 | |
| **Net income** | **€60** | **(5)** |

### *1. Contribution margin*

The contribution margin (€220 in Table 9.1) reflects the spread between revenue and variable expenses. The principal argument in favour of using it to measure the performance of profit centre managers is that if fixed expenses are beyond their control, managers should focus their attention on maximizing contribution. The problem with this argument is that its premises are inaccurate; in fact, almost all fixed expenses are at least partially controllable by the manager, and some are entirely controllable. As discussed in Chapter 4, many expense items are discretionary – that is, they can be changed at the discretion of the profit centre manager. Presumably, top management wants the profit centre to keep these discretionary expenses in line with amounts agreed on in the budget formulation process. A focus on the contribution margin tends to direct attention away from this responsibility. Further, even if an expense, such as administrative salaries, cannot be changed in the short term, the profit centre manager is still responsible for controlling employees' efficiency and productivity. A related measure is contribution margin ratio – that is, contribution margin/revenues (€220/€1000 = 22 per cent in Table 9.1). Contribution margin ratio allows better comparisons between profit centres because differences in size are handled.

### *2. Direct profit*

This measure (€130 in Table 9.1) reflects a profit centre's contribution to the general overhead and profit of the corporation. It incorporates all expenses either incurred by or directly traceable to the profit centre, regardless of whether or not these items are within the profit centre manager's control. Expenses incurred at headquarters, however, are not included in this calculation. A weakness of the direct profit measure is that it does not recognize the motivational benefit of charging headquarters costs.

### 3. Controllable profit

Headquarters expenses can be divided into two categories: controllable and non-controllable. The former category includes expenses that are controllable, at least to a degree, by the business unit manager – information technology services, for example. If these costs are included in the measurement system, profit will be what remains after the deduction of all expenses that may be *influenced* by the profit centre manager (€120 in Table 9.1). A major disadvantage of this measure is that because it excludes non-controllable headquarters expenses it cannot be directly compared with either published data or trade association data reporting the profits of other companies in the industry.

### 4. Earnings before interest and taxes (EBIT)

In this measure (€100 in Table 9.1), all corporate overhead costs are allocated to profit centres based on the relative amount of expense each profit centre incurs. There are two arguments against such allocations. First, as the costs incurred by corporate staff departments – such as finance, accounting and human resource management – are not controllable by profit centre managers, these managers should not be held accountable for them. Second, it may be difficult to allocate corporate staff services in a manner that would properly reflect the amount of costs incurred by each profit centre.

There are, however, three arguments in favour of incorporating a portion of the corporate overhead costs into the profit centres' performance reports. First, corporate service units have a tendency to increase their power base and to enhance their own excellence without regard to their effect on the company as a whole. Allocating corporate overhead costs to profit centres increases the likelihood that profit centre managers will question these costs, thus serving to keep headquarters spending in check. Second, the performance of each profit centre will become more realistic and more readily comparable to the performance of competitors who pay for similar services. Finally, when managers know that their respective centres will not show a profit unless all costs, including the allocated share of corporate overhead, are recovered, they are motivated to make optimum long-term marketing decisions to pricing, product mix and so on, that will ultimately benefit (and even ensure the viability of) the company as a whole.

It is also worth mentioning a related measure of profit: earnings before interest, taxes, depreciation and amortization (EBITDA). This measure is primarily related to financial accounting but is also increasingly used internally in numerous organizations. In Table 9.1 we do not have specific information about depreciation and amortization (i.e., depreciation on non-current intangible assets)[4] to calculate EBITDA. By excluding depreciation and amortization, EBITDA is a more 'cash flow like' measure than earnings before interest expenses and taxes.

**Real World Example:** When one of the leading retail companies in the Nordic region, ICA, presented its financial performance, one of the main focus areas was the EBIT development. For the fourth quarter of 2019, the EBIT was SEK1,267 million, which was 7.3 per cent higher than for the same period in 2018. ICA talks about this in terms of a solid EBIT development.[5]

### 5. Net income

Here, companies measure the performance of domestic profit centres according to the bottom line – the amount of net income after income tax. There are two principal arguments against using this measure: (1) after-tax income is often a constant percentage of the pre-tax income, in which case there would be no advantage in incorporating income taxes; and (2) because many of the decisions that affect income

4 Non-current assets are also sometimes referred to as fixed assets.

5 https://www.icagruppen.se/globalassets/3.-investerare/5.-rapporter/arkiv---finansiellt/engelska/2020/0146.-year-end-report-2019/200206_icagruppen_presentation_eng_q4.pdf.

taxes are made at headquarters, it is not appropriate to judge profit centre managers on the consequences of these decisions.

There are situations, however, in which the effective income tax rate does vary among profit centres. For example, foreign subsidiaries or business units with foreign operations may have different effective income tax rates. In other cases, profit centres may influence income taxes through their instalment credit policies, their decisions on acquiring or disposing of equipment, and their use of other generally accepted accounting procedures to distinguish gross income from taxable income. In these situations, it may be desirable to allocate income tax expenses to profit centres not only to measure their economic profitability but also to motivate managers to minimize tax liability.

Each type of profitability measure described in Table 9.1 is used by some companies. Most companies include some, if not all, of the costs discussed earlier in evaluating their managers, whether or not these are under their control. For example, many multinational corporations measure the performance of managers of foreign subsidiaries in their domestic currency. Performance therefore is affected by fluctuations in the value of the domestic currency relative to the host currency – a matter wholly beyond the individual manager's control.

If one considers the measurement of the manager alone, the solution often becomes evident: *Managers should be measured against those items they can influence, even if they do not have total control over those items.* This means that special attention is given to the user criterion. In the typical organization, these items probably include all expenses incurred directly in the profit centre. Managers should be measured on an after-tax basis only if they can influence the amount of tax their unit pays, and items that they clearly cannot influence, such as currency fluctuation, should be eliminated.

## Pitfall 2: Should we use ROI or RI for investment centres?

As already discussed in Chapter 4, in many organizational units, the managers cannot only influence profit, but can also influence the assets employed in earning it. The sum of the assets employed in an investment centre is called the investment base. We discuss two primary methods of relating profit to the investment base: (1) the percentage *return on investment*, referred to as ROI,[6] and (2) *residual income*, called RI.[7] In our examination of the alternative treatments of assets and the comparison of ROI and RI, we are primarily interested in how well the alternatives serve the purposes of providing information for sound decision making and measuring an investment centre's financial performance. As we shall see, there are significant practical difficulties involved in creating a system that focuses on assets employed in addition to the focus on profits.

Table 9.2 shows a hypothetical, simplified set of an investment centre's financial statements; it will be used throughout this analysis. (In the interests of simplicity, income taxes have been omitted from this table. Including income taxes would change the magnitudes in the calculations that follow, but it would not change the conclusions. We have also assumed that all current assets are non-interest bearing and that all non-current assets are interest bearing.) The table shows the two ways of relating profits to assets employed; namely, ROI and RI.

*ROI is a ratio.* The numerator is earnings before interest and taxes, as reported on the income statement. The denominator is assets employed. In Table 9.2, assets employed is calculated as total assets less current liabilities in the business unit. *RI is a euro amount, rather than a ratio.* It is found by subtracting a capital charge from the earnings before interest and taxes. This capital charge is found by

[6] ROI is the general term used throughout this chapter. Common versions are return on assets, ROA and return on capital employed, ROCE.

[7] RI is the general term used throughout this chapter. In the later parts of this chapter, we also discuss a more advanced version of residual income; namely, EVA® (a trademark of Stern Stewart & Co).

**TABLE 9.2** Investment centre financial statements

| Balance sheet (€000s) | | | | |
|---|---|---|---|---|
| **Current assets** | | | **Current liabilities** | |
| Cash | | €50 | Accounts payable | €90 |
| Receivables | | 150 | Other current | 110 |
| Inventory | | 150 | | |
| Total current assets | | **350** | Total current liabilities | **200** |
| **Non-current assets** | | | **Non-current liabilities** | **100** |
| Cost | €650 | | **Corporate equity** | **400** |
| Depreciation | −300 | | | |
| Book value | | **350** | | |
| **Total assets** | | **€700** | **Total liabilities and equity** | **€700** |
| **Income statement** | | | | |
| Revenue | | | | €1,000 |
| Expenses, except depreciation | | €−850 | | |
| Depreciation | | −50 | | −900 |
| Earnings before interest and taxes | | | | 100 |
| Capital charge (€ (700 − 200) × 10%) | | | | −50 |
| Residual income (RI) | | | | 50 |
| Return on investment (ROI) = 100/500 = 20% | | | | |

multiplying the amount of assets employed by a rate, which is 10 per cent in Table 9.2. In equation form, ROI and RI are measured as follows:

$$\textbf{ROI} = \textbf{Earnings before interest and taxes/Assets employed}$$

$$\textbf{RI} = \textbf{Earnings before interest and taxes} - \textbf{Capital charge}$$

where

$$\textbf{Capital charge} = \textbf{Cost of capital} \times \textbf{Assets employed}$$

Corporate headquarters normally sets the cost of capital (i.e., the interest rate) used to calculate the capital charge, and since we in this book primarily are interested in the behavioural consequences of ROI and RI we will not go into detail about these calculations (see any corporate finance textbook for such information).

An RI above zero is good as the investment centre then creates value, and the higher the RI, the more value is created. As the formula shows (RI = earnings before interest and taxes − (cost of capital × assets employed)), when RI is positive, the investment centre has generated a 'true' profit – that is, a profit high enough also to cover the cost of all capital employed to produce those profits.

## RI versus ROI

Research shows that most companies worldwide, employing investment centres, evaluate them on the basis of ROI rather than RI. There are two apparent benefits of the ROI measure. First, related to the measurement system criterion, it is a comprehensive measure in that anything that affects financial statements is reflected in this ratio. In addition, it is a common denominator that may be applied to any organizational unit responsible for profitability, regardless of size or type of business. The performances of different investment centres may be compared directly with one another. ROI data are also available for competitors and can be used as a basis for comparison.

***Real World Example:*** The international steel company SSAB describes that 'realization of the strategic growth targets combined with the improved efficiency as a result of continuous improvement is the platform to achieve our financial target of industry-leading profitability'. The organization has set up ambitious ROCE targets – for instance, the unit Tibnor should have a ROCE of more than 15 per cent in 2022.[8]

Second, related to the user criterion, ROI is simple to calculate, easy to understand and meaningful in an absolute sense. For example, an ROI of less than 5 per cent is considered low on an absolute scale, and an ROI of over 25 per cent is considered high. In addition, the ROI measure is seen as easy to communicate internally because it can be disaggregated through the DuPont formula. As previously mentioned, ROI = earnings before interest and taxes/assets employed. By multiplying both the nominator and the denominator with sales, we get the following: ROI = (earnings before interest and taxes/sales) × (sales/assets employed). Because (earnings before interest and taxes/sales) is called profit margin and (sales/assets employed) is called capital turnover, we find that ROI = profit margin × capital turnover. A low capital turnover implies that the business unit needs a lot of invested capital to produce revenues and profits. Through the DuPont formula, ROI can graphically be shown as different curves in a diagram, which many managers find very powerful for communication purposes.

As shown in Figure 9.1, the four curves in the diagram represent different levels of ROI, from 5 to 20 per cent. It shows, for instance, that an investment centre can produce a ROI of 10 per cent by having a profit margin of 20 per cent and a capital turnover of 0.5. Another investment centre with a profit margin of only 10 per cent can nevertheless also produce a ROI of 10 per cent if the capital turnover is 1.0. Here we see that profit margin alone is an inadequate basis for comparison if investment centres differ in capital turnover. As a result, investment centre managers need to consider the effects that their decisions have on the income statement (i.e., profit margin) as well as on the balance sheet (i.e., capital turnover), and often weighing trade-offs between the two. The diagram in Figure 9.1 graphically brings to the fore these trade-offs and is often used internally when investment centre managers communicate financial performance with employees, or when different investment centres are compared with one another or with outside competitors.

The euro amount of RI does not provide such a basis for comparison, and thereby 'scores lower' when it comes to the user criterion. Nevertheless, we want to stress that when it comes to the representational criterion, the RI approach has some very important inherent advantages. There are three compelling reasons, all related to achieving goal-congruent behaviour, to use RI over ROI. First, with RI all investment centres have the same profit objective for comparable investments. The ROI approach, on the other hand, provides different incentives for investments across investment centres. For example, an investment centre that currently is achieving a ROI of 30 per cent would be reluctant to expand unless it is able to earn a ROI of 30 per cent or more on additional assets; a lesser return would decrease

[8] https://www.ssab.com/company/investors/ssab-as-an-investment.

FIGURE 9.1 ROI – function of profit margin and capital turnover

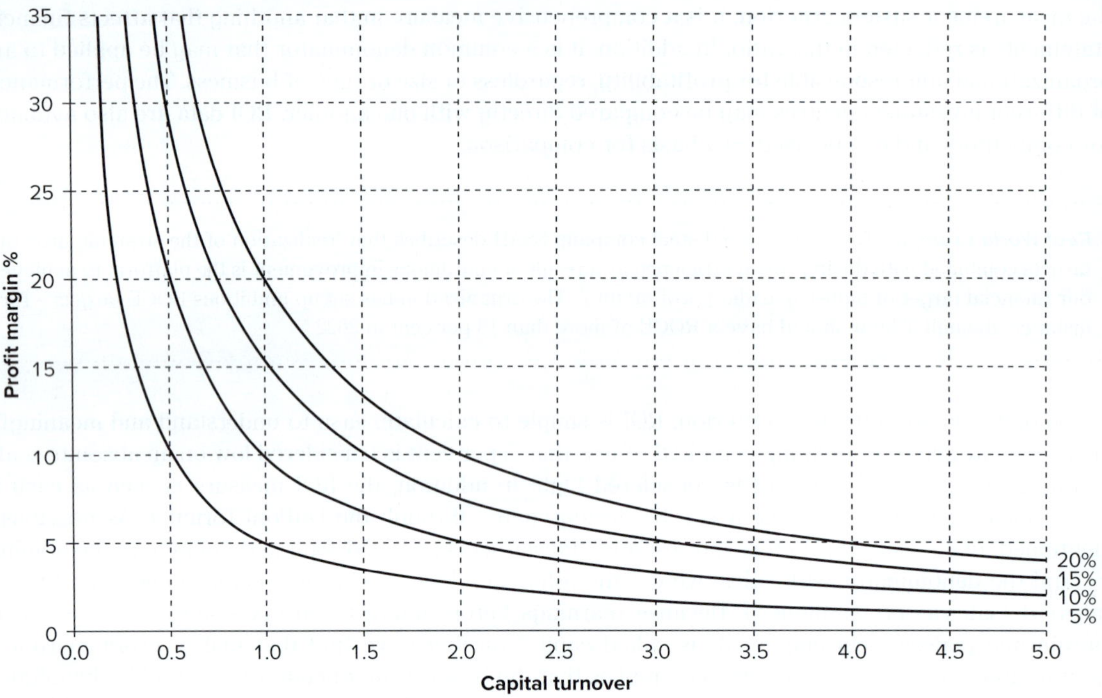


its overall ROI below its current 30 per cent level. Thus, this investment centre might forgo investment opportunities whose ROI is *above* the cost of capital but *below* 30 per cent.

Similarly, an investment centre that currently is achieving a low ROI – say, 5 per cent – would benefit from anything over 5 per cent on additional assets. As a consequence, ROI creates a bias towards little or no expansion in high-profit investment centres while, at the same time, low-profit units are making investments at rates of return well below those rejected by the high-profit units.

Second, decisions that *increase* a centre's ROI may *decrease* its overall profits. For instance, in an investment centre whose current ROI is 30 per cent, the manager can increase its overall ROI by disposing of an asset whose ROI is 25 per cent. However, if the cost of capital tied up in the investment centre is less than 25 per cent, the absolute euro profit after deducting capital costs will decrease for the centre.

The use of RI as a measure deals with both these problems. They relate to asset investments whose ROI falls between the cost of capital and the centre's current ROI. If an investment centre's performance is measured by RI, investments that produce a profit in excess of the cost of capital will increase RI and, therefore, will be economically attractive to the manager.

A third advantage of RI is that different interest rates may be used for different types of asset. For example, a low rate may be used for inventories while a relatively higher rate may be used for investments in non-current assets. Furthermore, different rates may be used for different types of non-current assets to take into account different degrees of risk. In short, using RI is consistent with the framework used for decisions about capital investments and resource allocation, and thereby helps create goal congruence between top managers (having the overall organizational perspective) and investment centre managers (acting in the interests of their individual investment centres). It follows that the same type of asset may be required to earn the same return throughout the company, regardless of the particular investment centre's profitability. Thus, investment centre managers should act consistently when deciding to invest in new assets.

***Real World Example:*** The SKF Group is a leading global supplier of products, solutions and services within, for instance, rolling bearings and lubrication systems. SKF's financial performance management model is a residual income model called total value added (TVA), promoting greater operating profit, capital efficiency and profitable growth. TVA is the operating profit, less the pre-tax cost of capital in the country where business is conducted. The company claims that the TVA performance for the group correlates well with the share price trend over a longer period. Variable salary schemes are primarily based on this model.

*Source:* SKF Annual Report 2011, p. 53.

Differences between ROI and RI are illustrated with the example provided in Tables 9.4 and 9.5. Assume that the company's cost of capital is 10 per cent. Table 9.4 shows two investment centres' earnings before interest and taxes and assets employed, and the calculations of ROI and RI.

**TABLE 9.3** Problems with using ROI

| | Investment centre A | Investment centre B | Company as a whole |
|---|---|---|---|
| Earnings before interest and taxes | 7,200 | 8,600 | 15,800 |
| Assets employed | 55,400 | 34,400 | 89,800 |
| ROI | 13% (7,200/55,400) | 25% (8,600/34,400) | 18% (15,800/89,800) |
| RI | 1,660 (7,200 − 0.1 × 55,400) | 5,160 (8,600 − 0.1 × 34,400) | 6,820 (15,800 − 0.1 × 89,800) |

**TABLE 9.4** Problems with using ROI (continued)

| | Investment centre A + investment | Investment centre B + investment |
|---|---|---|
| Earnings before interest and taxes | 11,400 (7,200 + 4,200) | 12,800 (8,600 + 4,200) |
| Assets employed | 75,400 (55,400 + 20,000) | 54,400 (34,400 + 20,000) |
| ROI | 15% (11,400/75,400) YES to investment since ROI increases (from 13% to 15%) | 23.5% (12,800/54,400) NO to investment since ROI decreases (from 25% to 23.5%) |
| RI | 3,860 (11,400 − 0.1 × 75,400) YES to investment since RI increases (from 1,660 to 3,860) | 7,360 (12,800 − 0.1 × 54,400) YES to investment since RI increases (from 5,160 to 7,360) |

Now assume that there is an investment proposal with the following numbers: earnings before interest and taxes of €4,200 and assets employed of €20,000. This means the ROI is 21 per cent (€4,200/20,000) and the RI of the investment is €2,200 (€4,200 − 0.1 × 20,000). Thus, this investment is clearly beneficial for the company as a whole. However, as shown in Exhibit 9.4, if the managers of the company's two investment centres are evaluated based on ROI, they will come to different conclusions as to whether or not to carry through the investment. The manager of investment centre A will say yes because ROI increases, but the manager of investment centre B will say no because ROI decreases. This is clearly not in the best interests of the company, and thus the ROI measure 'scores low' with regards to the representational criterion.

RI corrects these inconsistencies. The investment, multiplied by the cost of capital, is subtracted from the earnings before interest and taxes. Here, both investment centre managers will say yes to the investment, because RI increases for both units. More generally speaking, if any of the two investment centres earns more than 10 per cent on added assets employed, it will increase its RI. In this way the financial decision rules of the investment centres will be consistent with those of the company – i.e., RI 'scores high' on the representational criterion.

In relation to the user criteria, RI also solves the problem of differing profit objectives for the same asset in different investment centres and the same profit objective for different assets in the same unit. The method makes it possible to incorporate in the measurement system the same decision rules used in the planning process: the more sophisticated the planning process, the more complex the RI calculation can be. For example, assume the capital investment decision rules call for a 10 per cent return on general purpose assets and a 15 per cent return on special purpose assets. Investment centre non-current assets can be classified accordingly, and different rates applied when measuring performance. Managers may be reluctant to invest in improved working conditions, other sustainability and environmental activities or other social goals if they perceive them to be unprofitable. Such investments will be much more acceptable to investment centre managers if they are expected to earn a reduced return on them.

In view of the disadvantages of ROI, it seems surprising that it is so widely used. We know from personal experience that the conceptual flaws of ROI as a financial performance measure are real and contribute to goal-incongruent behaviour by investment centre managers. We are unable to determine the extent of this goal incongruence, however, because few managers are likely to admit its existence and many are unaware of it when it does exist. We strongly advocate considering the use of RI, instead of ROI, as a financial performance measure when measuring an investment centre's financial performance. RI, however, does not solve all the representational criterion problems of measuring profitability in an investment centre. This is because both ROI and RI approaches normally use book values from the financial accounting reports when estimating the asset base to be used in the calculations.

Economic valued added (EVA®), an advanced version of RI, focuses, among other things, on the measurement problems of intangible non-current assets. EVA® proponents suggest that a number of *accounting adjustments* need to be performed to arrive at 'better' measurement of profit and assets employed than if book values of intangible non-current assets are used (as in the RI approach). They provide a list of about 160 different adjustments that could be used but emphasize that, in most cases, only 20–25 adjustments are necessary, and as few as 5–10 adjustments are actually made in practice. Some of these key adjustments are related to the treatment of intangible assets – for instance, the capitalization of research and development (R&D) expenses, the capitalization of market-building expenses and the adding back of goodwill amortization. Thus, the EVA® of a unit is calculated with the following formula: EVA® = adjusted net operating profits after taxes − (cost of capital × adjusted assets employed).[9]

Some companies tend to be R&D-intensive (e.g., pharmaceutical firms such as AstraZeneca spend huge amounts on developing new products). Capitalizing intangible assets such as R&D and then amortizing them over a selected life would change how the investment centre manager views these expenditures. By accounting for these assets as long-term investments, the investment centre manager will gain less short-term benefit from reducing outlays on such items. For instance, if R&D expenditures are expensed immediately, each euro of R&D cut would be a euro more in pre-tax profits. On the other hand, if R&D costs are capitalized, each euro cut will reduce the assets employed by one euro; the capital charge is,

[9] Note that, for simplicity reasons, in this chapter we have often ignored taxes. When calculating EVA®, however, it is emphasized that tax should be deducted from operating profits.

therefore, reduced only by one euro times the cost of capital, which has a much smaller positive impact on EVA®. For these reasons, with regards to the representational criterion, EVA® is considered a superior measure of performance of investment centres than RI, especially if the company has a lot of intangible non-current assets.

The same reasoning can be applied to market-building expenses, which are of high importance to companies that are marketing-intensive (e.g., consumer products firms such as Unilever spend huge amounts on advertising). By capitalizing marketing expenses the investment centre manager will gain less short-term benefit from reducing outlays on such items, in the same way as with the R&D expenses.

***Real World Example:*** Diageo plc, whose portfolio of brands includes Burger King, Guinness and Häagen-Dazs, used EVA® (an advanced version of residual income) to help make business decisions and measure the effects of management actions. An EVA® analysis of Diageo's returns from its liquor brands led to a new emphasis on producing and selling vodka, which, unlike Scotch, does not incur ageing and storage costs.

*Source:* Shand, D. (2000) Economic value added, *Computerworld*, 30 October, p. 65; Gregory Millman (2000) CFOs in tune with the times, *Financial Executive*, July–August, p. 26.

## Pitfalls when using non-financial measures

In addition to the specific pitfalls with advanced financial measures such as ROI, there is a general criticism of relying too much on financial measures when analysing performance. One main reason for this more general criticism of financial measures is that they are defined as *lagging* measures, which means that they are historical; they focus on what has happened. Non-financial measures, on the other hand, are defined as *leading* in that they also relate to the means to reach future profitability; they are indicators of whether the current financial performance is also sustainable in the future. Brand recognition, new product pipeline, and growth in new markets or sales channels, for instance, all point to trends that can predict future performance. We also want to stress that for non-profit organizations, non-financial measures are even important on a stand-alone basis (and thus for these types of organization we do not even need the 'leading and lagging' distinction to make an argument for the importance of non-financial measures).

Relying solely on financial measures is therefore inadequate and can, in fact, be dysfunctional. First, focusing on financial measures alone may encourage managers to take short-term actions that may be wrong in the long run. In other words, a manager may deliver inferior-quality products to customers to meet sales targets, which will adversely affect customer goodwill and future financial performance. These are errors of *commission*.

Second, managers may not undertake useful long-term actions to obtain short-term profits. For instance, they may not make investments that promise long-term benefits because they hurt short-term financial results. A common example is managers investing inadequate money in innovation and sustainability; these investments must often be expensed in the year in which they are incurred but their benefits show up later. In other words, managers may propose 'safe' investments in existing products and services instead of high-risk projects in emerging, new and more environmentally friendly products and services that may produce high returns in the future. These are errors of *omission*.

Third, and as already mentioned in the discussion about the user criterion, financial measures are often perceived as too abstract by many employees. It is easier for them to see the links between what they do in their daily work and the outcome of non-financial measures. A focus on financial measures only therefore risks decreasing employee motivation and makes it more difficult for top managers to have a nuanced discussion about performance of a particular responsibility centre with lower-level managers and employees. Therefore, it needs to be emphasized that the use of non-financial measures is also needed at all levels in the organization.

As with financial measures, there is a large variety of non-financial measures to choose from. To get some structure, we provide some examples grouped around customer-oriented measures, business process-oriented measures, employee-oriented measures, and innovation- and environment-oriented measures.

### Customer-oriented measures

- *Bookings:* In most organizations, some aspect of sales volume is a key variable. Ideally, this is sales orders booked, because unexpected changes in this variable can have future repercussions throughout the business. Because bookings precede sales revenue, this is a better indicator than sales revenue itself. A decrease in this variable signals that adjustments to marketing activities may be warranted – in the hope of increasing sales or production activities, or both – to change operating levels.
- *Market share:* Unless the market share is watched closely, deterioration in the unit's competitive position can be obscured by reported increases in sales volume that result from overall industry growth.
- *Key account orders:* In business units that sell to retailers, the orders received from certain important accounts – large department stores, discount chains, supermarkets, mail-order houses – may give an early indication of the entire marketing strategy's success.
- *Customer satisfaction:* This can be measured by customer surveys, 'mystery shopper' approaches and number of complaint letters.
- *Customer retention:* This can be measured by the lengths of customer relationships.
- *Customer loyalty:* This can be measured in terms of repeat purchases, customer referrals and sales to the customer as a percentage of the customer's total requirements for the same product or service.

### Business process-oriented measures

- *Capacity utilization:* Capacity utilization rates are especially important in businesses in which fixed costs are high (e.g., paper, steel, aluminium manufacture). Similarly, in a professional organization, the percentage of the total available professional hours that is billed to clients – *sold time* – is a measure of fixed-resource utilization. In a hotel, the percentage of rooms occupied each day – *occupancy rate* – is the capacity utilization measure.
- *On-time delivery:* Over time, this measure has increased its importance since more and more customers expect products to be delivered and services to be performed fast and without delays.
- *Quality:* Indicators of quality include the number of defective units delivered by each supplier, number and frequency of late deliveries, number of parts in a product, percentage of common versus unique parts in a product, percentage yields, first-pass yields (i.e., percentage of units furnished without rework), scrap, rework, machine breakdowns, number and frequency of times production and delivery schedules were not met, number of employee suggestions, warranty claims, field service expenses, number and frequency of product returns, and so on.

### Employee-oriented measures

- *Number of training hours completed per employee:* The employees are considered to be many companies' most important assets. If the company also wants to be successful in the future, the employees need to be properly trained and have the competency required for current operations but also for future challenges.
- *Employee retention index:* Recruitment is often costly and time consuming, and the loss of important competence may hit an organization hard if experienced managers and employees leave.
- *Employee satisfaction:* This can be measured by employee surveys.
- *Employee health:* This can be measured by total number of sick days or number of sick days per employee per quarter/year.

### *Innovation and environment-oriented measures*

- *Number of new products/services launched* and/or *Percentage of sales from new products or services:* Organizations need to continuously renew their product or service portfolio. It is often tempting for managers to focus on established products and services to reap short-term financial benefits. Measuring the number of products/services launched indicates whether the organization also invests for the future.
- *Number of development projects started:* Before any new products or services can be launched, there is often extensive development work needed.
- *The environment:* This can be measured in terms of $CO_2$ emissions from, for instance, energy, in operations and transport of goods. Other measures are continuous reduction of water consumption and reduction of total waste in relation to sales.

When there is such a huge variety of non-financial measures to choose from, it is important to keep in mind that, as with financial measures, there are a number of pitfalls when using non-financial measures. These are discussed below.[10]

## Pitfall 1: Not validating the causal links

Comparing performance measurement systems to an instrument panel on a dashboard provides important insights about the mix of financial and non-financial measures needed in a management control system: a single measure cannot control a complex system; and too many critical measures make the system uncontrollably complex. A performance measurement system, such as a dashboard, has a series of measures that provide information about the operation of many different processes. Some of these measures tell the manager what *has* happened; for instance, net profit is currently £1 billion and return on capital employed (ROCE) is 12 per cent (lagging measures). Other measures tell the manager what *is* happening and give an indication of what *will* happen in the future, such as the non-financial measure of an on-time delivery percentage of 70, the number of product development projects started and the number of new products launched (leading measures). Behind the idea of lagging and leading measures is the notion of cause-and-effect – that is, improving a non-financial measure will, and should (given that we talk about for-profit organizations), lead to better future financial performance. Improving on-time delivery will, it is hoped, increase customer satisfaction and eventually also financial performance. Research shows, however, that many organizations do not develop such causal models and of those who do so, few go on to prove that actual improvements in non-financial performance actually affect future financial results.

Many managers seem to simply rely on their preconceptions about what 'should' be important to customers, suppliers and employees. Take the non-financial measure 'employee turnover'. Many managers would argue that this is a very good measure to use since high employee retention would indicate a high level of satisfaction and motivation, which would lead to better customer service and eventually higher profitability. But evaluating this reasoning from a representational criterion point of view, it may well be equally plausible that this holds true only for some of the employee groups. Research from a fast-food chain however showed that for that particular organization, what distinguished profitability between different units was the turnover among managers, not among lower-level workers. Thus, if organizations do not investigate basic causality, they cannot determine the relative importance of the non-financial measures they use and risk spending money on costly initiatives that will not lead to the intended results.

---

[10] The discussion of pitfalls when using non-financial measures is based on the extensive research conducted by Christopher Ittner and David Larcker. See Ittner, C.D. and Larcker, D.F. (2003) Coming up short on nonfinancial performance measurement, *Harvard Business Review,* 81(11): 88–95.

### Pitfall 2: Forgetting to consider the system support when choosing non-financial measures

As already discussed, one important aspect of the measurement system criterion is for managers to consider the system support needed to get reliable data without using too great an amount of resources (money or employee hours). Especially when choosing non-financial measures, managers tend to forget that the effectiveness of a particular non-financial measure will be compromised if the organization has little system support for the collection of the information needed regarding the chosen measure. Managers need to think carefully about the costs associated with measuring. Organizations often realize, after having launched a new set of non-financial measures, that some measures need to be abandoned because the information required is too costly, not possible to find or differs too much in quality between different units.

Take customer satisfaction as an example. Many managers have told us that in their eagerness to use this measure, employees have called their customers monthly to ask if they are satisfied. After some time, the customers have complained to the top managers, asking: 'Why do you call us all the time to see if we are satisfied? If we are not, we will definitely let you know.' Here, an alternative measure, such as customer retention, might be a more effective way of capturing whether or not customers are satisfied.

When it comes to many other non-financial measures, such as for instance quality measures, it is often found that responsibility centres within the same organization use different methodologies to measure the same thing, such as product quality. Such inconsistencies make it hard for top management to assess overall progress or to compare the performance of the various responsibility centres, something that is key to 'scoring high' on the measurement systems criterion.

### Pitfall 3: Not setting the right performance targets

At the beginning of this chapter, we emphasized that managers tend to forget that an essential step in measuring performance is to continuously examine the validity of the target. This is especially important to consider when using non-financial measures, since spending huge amounts of resources on improving a particular measure might not be worthwhile when it often produces diminishing financial returns. Researchers investigated a telecommunications company for which customers' switching costs were minimal. The company aimed for 100 per cent customer satisfaction and spent lots of resources to achieve this target. But over time it was discovered that a strong relationship between satisfied customers and sales was true only up to a certain point. Customers who were 100 per cent satisfied often did not spend much more money than those that were only 80 per cent satisfied. This meant that it was not efficient to spend the extra resources to move up from 80 to 100 per cent satisfied customers. It is important that companies make the effort in thoroughly thinking through what an appropriate target should be for the non-financial measures.

## The balanced scorecard: an 'enabling' performance measurement system

So far in this chapter we have concluded that organizations should have a mix of financial and non-financial measures that need to be carefully selected in order to avoid the many pitfalls we have discussed. And since research shows that human brains can process and remember only a limited number of measures at the same time, managers need to keep the number of measures down, as well as find ways to organize the information in a systematic way. The balanced scorecard (BSC) is the best-known example of a performance measurement system that blends financial and non-financial measures. It was launched by Robert Kaplan and David Norton in 1992, and surveys suggest that the BSC is widely adopted among both private- and public-sector organizations.[11] This is reinforced by case studies on BSC applications in, for instance, the USA, the UK, Finland, Denmark, Sweden, Australia and the Netherlands.[12] A number of well-known companies and organizations use the BSC, such as British Telecommunications (BT), DaimlerChrysler, Lloyds Bank, Siemens, the UK Ministry of Defence and Volvo Financial Services.[13] When it was launched, a key argument was that the BSC was a tool that could help managers choose an appropriate mix of financial and non-financial measures, which would avoid the pitfalls discussed above. The BSC would guide the managers in selecting measures that together 'score high' on the representational, measurement systems and user criteria. It would make it possible for the organization to have a truly 'enabling' performance measurement system – that is, a system that supports lower-level managers and employees, that they can use to identify problems, prioritize issues and develop innovative ideas. According to Kaplan and Norton, this 'enabling' role has to do with responsibility centres being assigned goals and critical success factors (they set out what needs to be done to be successful – for instance, good leadership, engaged employees), which are then measured from the following four perspectives:

1. Financial perspective – how do we look to shareholders? (lagging measures)
2. Customer perspective – how do customers see us? (leading measures)
3. Internal business perspective – what must we excel at? (leading measures)
4. Innovation and learning perspective – can we continue to improve and create value? (leading measures, often with a more long-term horizon than the measures in the customer and internal business perspectives)

Figure 9.2 shows a graphical representation of a BSC. With the organization's mission, goals and strategies as the starting point, strategic goals are set for each perspective, critical success factors are decided on and appropriate performance measures developed.

It is important to note that the four perspectives suggested by Kaplan and Norton should be seen as a template, and many companies have found it useful to adapt them. Organizations are wise to design a scorecard that best expresses their mission, goals and strategies. Many public-sector organizations add a society perspective, while many companies add the employee perspective. In recent years, the debate around climate change has changed how many organizations use the BSC, with the environment and sustainability-related dimensions playing a key role in its design. We illustrate this below in the Real World Example from Atlas Copco's BSC, where environment-related issues play an important role. The number of measures is not clear-cut. Whereas Kaplan and Norton suggest the inclusion of four to seven measures in each perspective, many organizations have tried many more than that, with only limited success. The general advice is to choose as few measures as possible in each perspective (given the limited human brain capacity discussed above) and that managers should, as far as possible, be held responsible only for results that are reasonably within their control.

---

[11] See, for instance, Hoque, Z. and James, W. (2000) Linking balanced scorecard measures to size and market factors: impact on organizational performance, *Journal of Management Accounting Research,* 12(1): 1–17; Kald, M. and Nilsson, F. (2000) Performance measurement at Nordic companies, *European Management Journal,* 18(1): 113–27; Speckbacher, G., Bischof, J. and Pfeiffer, T. (2003) A descriptive analysis on the implementation of balanced scorecards in German-speaking countries, *Management Accounting Research,* 14(4): 361–88.

[12] See, for instance, Andon, P., Baxter, J. and Chua, W.F. (2007) Accounting change as relational drifting: a field study of experiments with performance measurement, *Management Accounting Research,* 18(2): 273–308; Malina, M.A. and Selto, F.H. (2001) Communicating and controlling strategy: an empirical study of the effectiveness of the balanced scorecard, *Journal of Management Accounting Research,* 13(1): 47–90; Olve, N.G., Petri, C.J., Roy, J. and Roy, S. (2003) *Making Scorecards Actionable: Balancing Strategy and Control.* Hoboken, NJ: John Wiley & Sons.

[13] Balanced Scorecard Institute (n.d.) Balanced scorecard adopters. Available at: https://balancedscorecard.org/bsc-basics/about-the-balanced-scorecard/balanced-scorecard-adopters/ (accessed 5 June 2020).

**FIGURE 9.2** The balanced scorecard

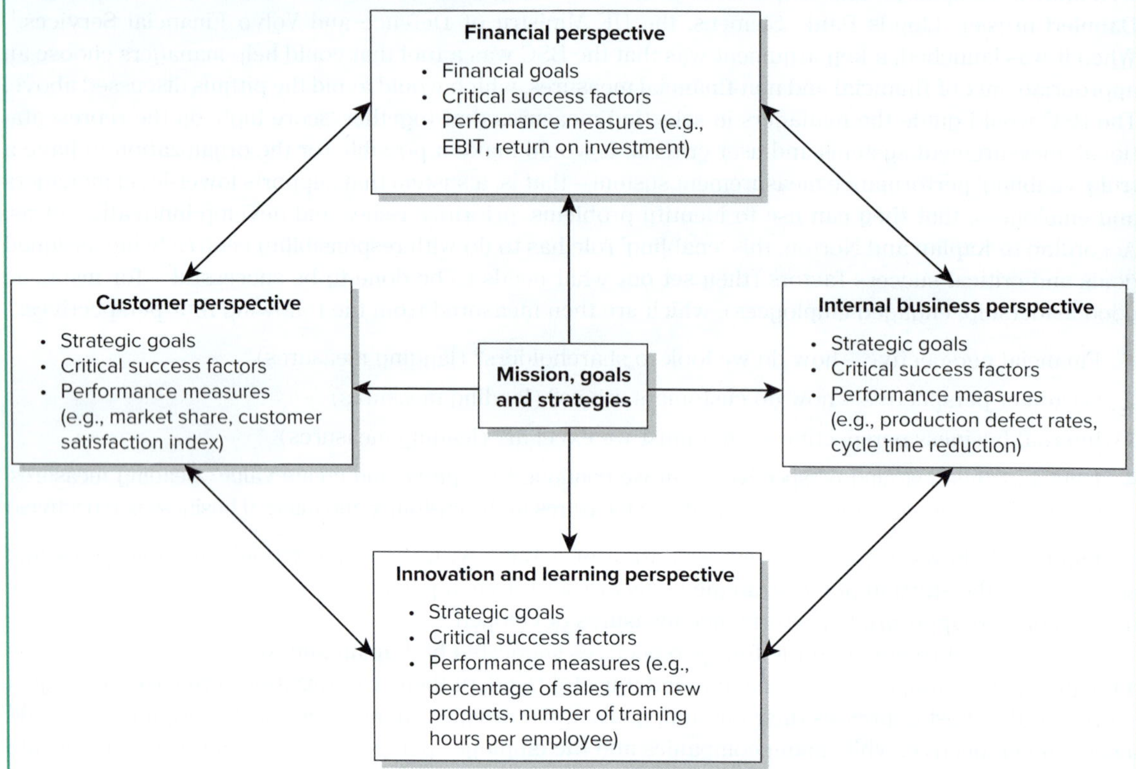


We want to emphasize that the BSC as a tool is more than a way to simply measure financial and non-financial performance. Before the BSC became popular, obviously many organizations already measured financial and non-financial performance. However, the popularity of the BSC, in itself not the most complicated concept, can be explained by a number of factors related to its claimed contribution to performance measurement. Even if these claims have not all been met, they still serve as a concrete illustration of how top managers consider an ideal system of performance measures. First, by *systematizing* the various measures into a number of *perspectives*, the BSC fosters a balance among different strategic measures in an effort to achieve goal congruence, which encourages employees to act in the organization's best interests. This aspect is directly targeting the representational criterion. By requiring managers to select a number of critical measures within each of the perspectives, and by emphasizing that each perspective should be given equal consideration, it forces managers to focus attention on the critical areas of business. As such, the scorecard gives managers a fast but comprehensive view of the business, presented in a single management report. The BSC helps to safeguard against sub-optimization by forcing managers to focus on all four perspectives together. This allows them to see whether improvement in one perspective has been achieved at the expense of another. The different perspectives also suggest a way for managers to mentally organize the large number of performance measures that may otherwise lead to measurement overload.

Second, the *link between mission, goals, strategies and performance measurement* is emphasized in the BSC: once they are formulated, they should be translated into specific strategic objectives and critical success factors that can be classified within each of the four perspectives. Thereafter, appropriate performance measures should be selected to report and monitor the success in achieving these objectives. As such, the BSC helps to link overall strategic objectives with lower-level objectives that can be observed and affected at different organizational levels. This aspect is directly targeting the user criterion. With these measures, all employees can understand how their actions affect the company's mission, goals and strategies. In other words, the measures in the scorecard must be strategy-specific and, therefore, organization-specific. While a generic performance measurement framework exists, there is no such thing as a generic scorecard. The scorecard measures are linked from top to bottom and tied to specific targets throughout the entire organization. Thus, an important advantage of the BSC is that it forces managers and employees to think clearly about their mission, goals and strategies, and to specify quite clearly the timescales in which they hope to achieve their strategic objectives.

Third, the scorecard also emphasizes, either explicitly or implicitly, the idea of *cause-and-effect relationships* among measures. By presenting and debating the cause-and-effect relationships, an organization will understand how non-financial measures (e.g., product quality) drive financial measures (e.g., revenue). Figure 9.3 presents an example of how the measures may link to one another in a cause-and-effect relationship. Better selection, training and development of manufacturing employees (measured in terms of 'manufacturing skills') are assumed to lead to better product quality (measured in terms of 'first-pass yields') and better on-time delivery (measured in terms of 'order cycle time'). These improvements, in turn, are assumed to lead to improved customer loyalty (measured through 'customer satisfaction surveys'), which is assumed to lead to enhanced sales (measured in terms of 'sales growth').

**FIGURE 9.3** Example of cause-and-effect relationships among measures

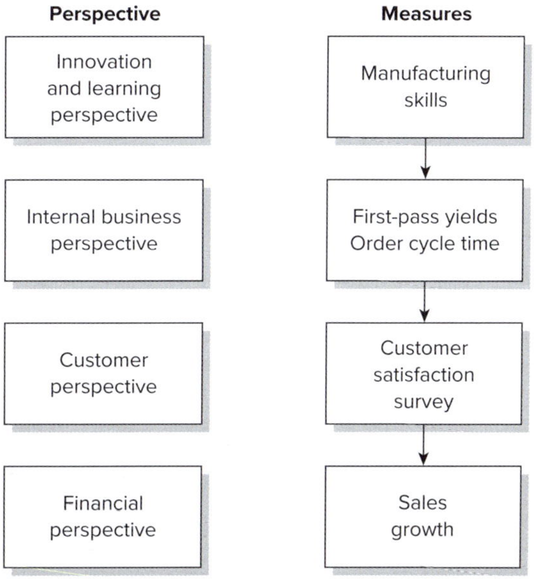

This idea of explicit cause-and-effect relationships was launched to emphasize that the BSC was not introduced solely as a performance measurement system, but also as an aid to strategy refinement by improving communication, setting organizational goals and providing feedback on strategy. The whole idea with the BSC is to start with the mission, goals and strategies, which are then broken down into: how the organization differs in a number of perspectives, what the critical success factors are and how to measure them. Going from the mission, goals and strategies down to the measurements in this way, it is most likely that many issues relating to strategy will be discussed. Kaplan and Norton themselves used the concept of *strategy maps* to highlight this aspect of the BSC.[14] The main difference between strategy maps and the original BSC model (as presented in Figure 9.2) is that the links between the measures – that is, how certain factors lead to other factors – are made explicit in strategy maps. When the measures and links are made explicit in the strategy map, the map aids visualization of the strategy of the organization. Research has shown that the way financial and strategic goals are communicated is important for the effectiveness of managers' strategy implementation work. The more clearly managers understand the objectives assigned to them, the more effective they are at implementing them. And providing a graphic representation of the relationships between the different goals and measures via a strategy map enhances such understanding. But designing strategy maps not only implies choosing

***Real World Example:*** Figure 9.4, which depicts a business area in telecommunications company Ericsson, shows a simplified example. The real scorecard included many more measures.

**FIGURE 9.4** Simplified strategy map for a business area at Ericsson

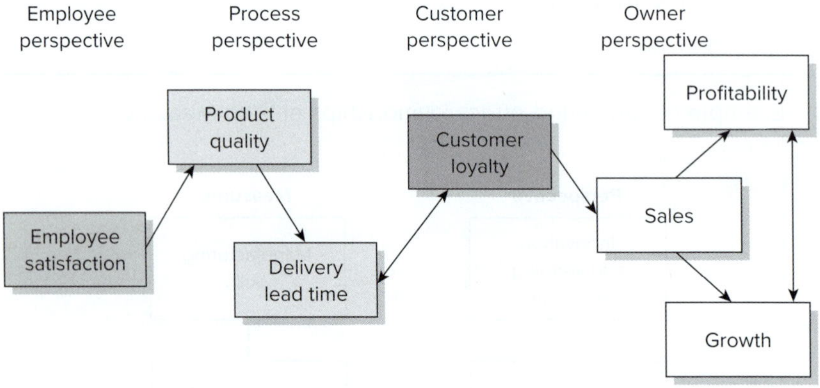


As we can see in this example, employee satisfaction is important, partly because it will lead to higher product quality. Satisfied employees are believed to produce better equipment for telecoms operators. Product quality, in turn, is believed to lead to faster implementation and, therefore, delivery of the equipment. Fast deliveries are very important for Ericsson as its customers, telecoms operators, cannot afford to have two parallel systems working at the same time, which means that when they close the old system the new system has to work. And the higher the product quality, especially in terms of software, the faster they can finish the implementation. If they finish the implementation on time, the customers are likely to return to Ericsson next time. Returning customers will, of course, lead to high sales, and this might very well lead to high profitability and growth.

[14] Kaplan, R.S. and Norton, D.P. (2004) *Strategy Maps: Converting Intangible Assets into Tangible Outcomes.* Boston, MA.: Harvard Business School.

performance measures and defining how they are related, but also includes strategy formulation, because the designing of the maps becomes an important input in the formulation of strategy. Managers were found to engage more strongly with goals communicated using a strategy map than they did with equivalent goals communicated without such maps.[15]

In summary, the BSC is not simply a laundry list of financial and non-financial measures. It systematizes strategically important financial and non-financial measures in four perspectives, and the individual measures in the scorecard should – preferably explicitly – be linked together in a cause-and-effect way as a tool to implement and, at times, also refine the organization's mission, goals and strategies.

***Real World Example:*** Atlas Copco is a world-leading provider of sustainable productivity solutions. It offers customers innovative compressors, air treatment systems, vacuum solutions, industrial power tools and assembly systems, and power and flow solutions. Atlas Copco develops products and services focused on productivity, energy efficiency, safety and ergonomics. The company was founded in 1873 and has a global reach spanning more than 180 countries. In 2019, it had revenues of about €10 billion and 39,000 employees worldwide. It is well known for its consistently strong profitability – for instance, reporting a ROCE of 30 per cent for 2019. Recently, Atlas Copco has significantly increased its focus on sustainability. For example, more than 1,000 of its suppliers were audited for safety, health, environment and ethics, and Atlas Copco reports 10 per cent reduced water consumption and 12 per cent reduced $CO_2$ emissions from energy in operations and transport of goods. Its CEO, Magnus Rahmström, stresses that the strategy of Atlas Copco is to deliver long-term growth and customer value in a sustainable way. He stated in the company's 2019 Annual Report:

> *It is said by many that 2020 is the start of the 'decade for action' for achieving the Sustainable Development Goals (SDGs) set by the United Nations, and I agree. Our goals for sustainability, launched in early 2019 with 2018 as the baseline, set the direction for Atlas Copco being part of the solutions for many years to come. They help to ensure that we create value for all stakeholders and that is the right way to grow for our company.*

**FIGURE 9.5** Graphic display of Atlas Copco's balanced scorecard

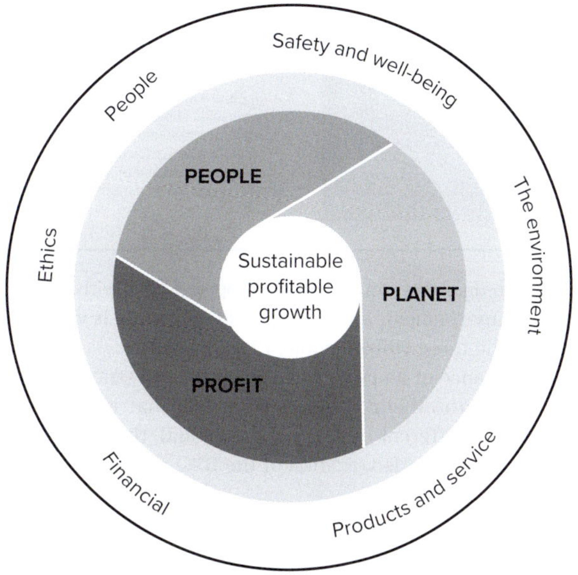


[15] Cheng, M.M. and Humphreys, K.A. (2012) The differential improvement effects of the strategy map and scorecard perspectives on managers' strategic judgments, *Accounting Review*, 87(3): 899–924.

**FIGURE 9.6** Details of Atlas Copco's balanced scorecard

| | | Goals |
|---|---|---|
| **Financial** | Our growth is sustainable and profitable | –Revenue growth measured over a business cycle. Target: 8% per annum. Growth should primarily be organic, supported by selective acquisitions.<br>–Sustained high return on capital employed by constantly striving for operational excellence and generating growth.<br>–Earnings as dividends to shareholders. Target: about 50% |
| **People** | Our culture of collaboration and inclusion drives our success | –The degree to which Atlas Copco employees agree there is opportunity to learn and grow should be above the global benchmark and continuously increase.<br>–The degree to which Atlas Copso employees agree we have a work culture of respect, fairness and openness should be above the global benchmark and continuously increase.<br>–Atlas Copco should have 30% female employees at year end 2030.<br>Additional information on page 36 |
| **Ethics** | We are known for ethical behavior, openness and respect | –All employees sign the Business Code of Practice.<br>–All employees are trained in the Business Code of Practice.<br>–All managers in risk countries lead trainings in the Business Code of Practice.<br>–All significant suppliers sign the Business Code of Practice.<br>–All significant distribbutors sign the Business Code of Practice.<br>Additional information on page 40 |
| **Products & Service** | Our products create lasting value and make a positive impact | –All projects for new or redesigned products have clear and specific targets for reduced environmental impact by 2021.<br>–Projects for new and redesigned products achieve significantly reduced environmental impact. Target to be defined.<br>Additional information on page 35 |
| **Safety & Well-being** | The way we work contributes to our safety and well-being | –The degree to which Atlas Copco employees agree that the company takes a genuine interest in their well-being should continuously increase.<br>–Atlas Copco should have a balanced safety pyramid, meaning that more near misses than minor injuries, and more minor injuries than recordable injuries are reported.<br>Additional information on page 39 |
| **Environment** | Our processes minimize our impact on the environment | –$CO_2$ emissions from energy in operations and transport of goods in relation to cost sales should be reduced with 50% by 2030.<br>–Continuous reduction of waste in relation to cost of sales.<br>–Continuous reduction of water consumption in relation to cost of sales.<br>–Continuous increase of significant direct suppliers with an approved environment management system.<br>Additional information on page 42 |

In order to deliver on this strategy, Atlas Copco has developed a BSC with six perspectives: financial, people, ethics, products and service, the environment, and safety and well-being. It visually displays these as a number of circles (see Figure 9.5), under the three labels People, Planet, Profit.

Atlas Copco stresses the importance of an integrated sustainability strategy, backed by ambitious goals, for being able to deliver greater value to all stakeholders in a way that is economically, environmentally and socially responsible. The goals have different time horizons: annual, three-year, a business cycle, and by 2030 for the longer-term ambitions. The overall visualization of the BSC in Figure 9.5, is then made more concrete in the actual BSC, as seen in Figure 9.6.

*Source:* Atlas Copco Annual Report 2019.

The better these relationships are understood, the more readily each individual in the organization will be able to contribute directly and clearly to the success of that organization. As such, *the process of designing, developing and implementing the BSC is valuable in itself,* as it forces managers and employees to think of the linkages between performance measurement and the organization's mission, goals and strategies. In the Real World Example we introduce Atlas Copco's BSC as a way to clarify what a BSC can look like in practice and also to highlight how this tool is useful in systematically integrating issues related to our biggest challenges today: the environment and climate change.

The Atlas Copco BSC offers an excellent example of how this tool can be used to systematically integrate sustainability into the performance measurement system. As suggested by Kaplan and Norton, the generic BSC has been adapted to fit the specific needs of Atlas Copco. The only original perspective that remains is the financial perspective. The other five perspectives are named so as to fit the mission, goals and strategies of Atlas Copco. Some targets are set on an annual basis and some on a more long-term basis to make explicit the various time horizons every organization needs to work with. And, importantly, sustainability is not simply 'another perspective' in the BSC, it is firmly integrated via the people, ethics, products and service, safety and well-being, and environment perspectives. As Atlas Copco puts it: 'Atlas Copco's focus areas for sustainability are implemented in the daily operations, supported by policies, training material and monitoring tools. Concrete targets and key performance indicators are used to continuously measure performance in relation to the goals set in these areas. Progress in relation to the [performance measures] contributes to the achievement of the UN Sustainable Development Goals.'[16] This clearly resonates with the stakeholder view, as discussed in Chapter 2.

## Issues related to implementing a BSC

By now it should be clear that the BSC is a popular and widely used tool to ensure the successful design and use of 'enabling' performance measurement systems. There are, however, a number of issues, which are discussed below, to consider when implementing performance measurement systems such as the BSC. If not properly dealt with, these issues could limit the usefulness of the BSC.

### *Top management commitment and employee involvement*

Successful implementation of a BSC requires the participation and support of top managers in combination with the involvement of lower-level managers and employees throughout the organization. Although the controller may be responsible for overseeing its development, it is a task for the entire top management team, lower-level managers and employees. For a single-industry firm (e.g., Ryanair), the scorecard may be developed at the corporate level and then cascaded down to functional levels and below. However, for a multi-business firm (e.g., General Electric), the scorecard may first be developed at the business unit level. It is important that functional departments within a business unit should have their own scorecards, and that the business unit scorecard and the scorecards below that level should be aligned. As a final step, for a multi-business unit organization, a corporate-wide scorecard should be developed to address, among other things, synergies across business units. Irrespective of whether the scorecard is cascaded down from the corporate level, or first developed at the business unit level, employees need to be involved in the implementation process. When choosing implementation teams, for instance, it is important to involve people from different departments and at different hierarchical levels. The scorecard needs to be perceived as relevant to the actual activities of the people at the level to which it is addressed. This speaks directly to the user criterion and is critical for successful BSC implementation. For a performance measurement system to have an enabling role, it needs to be designed to help lower-level managers and employees maintain or enhance the skill set, job motivation and organizational commitment that lower-level managers and employees aim to contribute to the organization. The lower-level managers need to perceive performance measurement systems as something that supports them, that

[16] Atlas Copco Annual Report 2019, p. 12.

they can use to identify problems, prioritize issues and develop innovative ideas. When implementing the BSC, organizations need to be aware of the fact that successful implementation requires a delicate balance between scorecard templates that are tailored to the specific characteristics of particular business units and the need to create an overall coherence between the scorecards at the various organizational levels.

### *Review measures and results frequently*

Once the BSC is up and running, it must be consistently and continually reviewed by top management (as part of the learning dimension in the performance management loop discussed at the beginning of Part 3 of the book). The organization should look for the following:

- How is the organization doing according to the financial (lagging) measures?
- How is the organization doing according to the non-financial (leading) measures?
- How have the organization's mission, goals and strategies changed since the last review?
- How have the scorecard measures changed?

Many companies do not have a formal mechanism for updating the measures to align with changes in mission, goals and strategies. As a result, they continue to use measures based on yesterday's strategy. Additionally, measures often build up inertia, particularly as people get comfortable using them. We emphasize the need to continuously review the scorecards and, when needed, to abandon strategically irrelevant measures and add new measures that better reflect the company's mission, goals and strategies. Such reviews of the scorecard, where each perspective should be given equal consideration, also show that top managers are serious about the importance of both financial and non-financial measures, and give the responsibility centre managers and employees important feedback on their performance. The reviews also provide top management with important information from the lower-level managers and employees about how the BSC is perceived – for instance, whether certain measures need to be abandoned and others added because the company's mission, goals and strategies have changed or because they 'score low' on the representational, measurement systems and/or user criteria.

There is no guarantee that future profitability will follow target achievements in any non-financial area. This is a serious problem because there is an inherent assumption that future profitability does follow from achieving individual non-financial measures. Identifying the cause-and-effect relationships among the different measures (as illustrated in Figure 9.3) is easier said than done. This is a problem when we try to develop proxy measures for future financial performance. It is important for companies to understand that the links between non-financial measures and financial performance are not well understood, and to frequently review and discuss whether the proposed cause-and-effect relationships are still valid.

### *Avoid measurement overload and reflect on the link to incentive systems*

How many critical measures can one manager track at one time without losing focus? As we have already discussed, there is no right answer to this question, except to say that it is more than 1 and less than 50! If the number is too few, it means that the manager is ignoring measures that are critical to monitoring strategy execution. If there are too many measures, the manager may risk losing focus in trying to do too many things at once. As previously mentioned, Kaplan and Norton suggest the inclusion of four to seven measures per perspective. The main message is to carefully think through the number of measures and be as selective as possible.

A complication when using the BSC is that most top managers are well trained and adept with financial measures and they also keenly feel pressure regarding the financial performance of their organizations. In the case of for-profit organizations, shareholders are vocal, and boards of directors frequently apply pressure on the shareholders' behalf. For non-profit organizations, whether the budget is balanced or not is under tough public scrutiny. This pressure may overwhelm the long-term, uncertain payback of the non-financial measures. Poorly designed incentive programmes create additional pressure. Many companies implement a BSC but continue to reward managers on financial measures only. This is a severe problem as all perspectives in the scorecard should be given equal consideration and can disrupt goal congruence, causing managers to be more concerned about financial measures than any other measure. There needs to be executive commitment to the BSC, and top managers must show that they truly believe in the idea – for instance, by basing reward systems on the outcome of both financial and non-financial measures. Some companies combine financial and non-financial measures into a single report and give weights to the individual measures when calculating, for instance, how much bonus should be paid. But most scorecards do not assign explicit weights across measures. Without such weights, it becomes difficult to establish trade-offs between financial and non-financial measures, and there is a risk that the BSC becomes just another paper product and that the financially focused and often short-term-oriented performance measurement continues. The relative weights given to the different scorecard perspectives in management reward systems reveal what the organization truly values. The importance of reward systems is further discussed in Chapter 10, which is fully devoted to this matter.

## Summary

One central question for top managers is: How well are the organization as a whole and the various responsibility centres performing? Performance measurement systems form the basis for such assessment. By comparing the outcome of the chosen performance measures with appropriate performance targets, managers can assess the performance of the organization. In the first part of this chapter we discussed general considerations when designing and using financial and non-financial performance measures. Managers need to pay careful consideration to the representational, measurement systems and user criteria. We then discussed pitfalls when using financial and non-financial measures. In an investment centre, for instance, the manager is responsible for both the profit generated and the invested capital used to generate the profit. From a representational criterion point of view, RI is superior to ROI when measuring the financial performance of investment centre managers, but nevertheless ROI is more often used in practice.

However, relying solely on financial measures is inadequate and can, in fact, be dysfunctional for the organization. And since the issue of climate change is our biggest challenge, organizations need ways to systematically integrate sustainability in their performance measurement systems. In the final part of the chapter, we therefore discussed how a widely adopted performance measurement system tool, the balanced scorecard (BSC), can help organizations. It operates on the assumption that financial measures alone are not sufficient to operate an organization and that special attention must be paid to developing sophisticated, non-financial measures. The key belief behind the scorecard is that measurement will drive change as the organization conforms to what is being measured. The BSC systematizes the performance measures into a number of perspectives. Financial, customer, internal business processes, and learning and innovation are the four perspectives suggested in the original BSC model, but recently these generic perspectives have been modified to better take into account sustainability. There are many issues that a company needs to consider when trying to implement a BSC, such as top management commitment and employee involvement, reviewing measures and results frequently, and avoiding measurement overload.

## Suggested additional reading


Bedford, D.S., Bisbe, J. and Sweeney, B. (2019) Performance measurement systems as generators of cognitive conflict in ambidextrous firms, *Accounting, Organizations and Society*, 72: 21–37.

CIMA (2005) A practitioner's guide to the balanced scorecard. Available at: http://www.cimaglobal.com/Thought-leadership/Research-topics/Management-and-financial-accounting/A-practitioners-guide-to-the-balanced-scorecard2/ (accessed 1 June 2020).

CIMA (2013) *Corporate Social Responsibility and Innovation in Management Accounting*, 9(1), February. Available at: https://www.cimaglobal.com/Documents/Thought_leadership_docs/Research%20Funding/Corporate-social-responsibility-innovation-management-accounting.pdf (accessed 1 June 2020).

Ittner, C.D. and Larcker, D.F. (2003) Coming up short on nonfinancial performance measurement, *Harvard Business Review*, 81: 88–95.

Kaplan, R.S. and Norton, D. (1996) *The Balanced Scorecard: Translating Strategy into Action*. Boston, MA: Harvard Business School Press.

Kraus, K. and Lind, J. (2010) The impact of the corporate balanced scorecard on corporate control: a research note, *Management Accounting Research*, 21: 265–77.

Parmenter, D. (2019) *Key Performance Indicators*. New York: Wiley.

# Case 9.1 MedalRain*

## by Ebba Sjögren

MedalRain Inc. manufactures trophies and prizes for professional and amateur sports events. The company operates three factories, in Hamburg, Berlin and Nuremberg. The three factories are very independent. They manufacture three different product ranges using dedicated machinery, and each has a dedicated procurement function and sales force to sell its specific products. There is no overlap in the markets targeted by the three product ranges.

Until recently, the company has operated the factories as profit centres. However, the CEO and CFO have now decided to make them into investment centres.

As part of making the factories into investment centres, MedalRain is thinking about what might be an appropriate means of evaluating their performance. The management team is considering return on investment (ROI) and economic value added (EVA®). The management team is aware of some of the generic advantages and disadvantages with the two metrics. However, in order to understand the potential practical consequence of using ROI versus EVA® when comparing the three factories, the management team has asked the CFO to comment on a few company-specific issues.

## Questions

1 What is the difference between a profit centre and an investment centre? Do you think that the CEO and CFO have made an appropriate decision when deciding to make the factories into investment centres? Why, or why not?

*Note:* As part of your answer, you must characterize both profit centre and investment centre *and* describe the main advantage with investment centres.

2 Describe how ROI and EVA® are affected by the circumstances listed below. Comment on the consequences this could have for the performance evaluation of the three factory managers.

*Helpful hint:* As part of your answer, you may want to relate the possible consequences for performance evaluation to the generic advantages and disadvantages.

a The Hamburg factory is three times the size of the Berlin and Nuremberg factories.

b The Hamburg and Berlin factories are thinking about making considerable investments in new machinery in the next two years, while the Nuremberg factory is planning on continuing to operate its fully depreciated – but still functional – machines.

c Unlike the other two facilities, the Nuremberg factory produces and markets high-end trophies that are manufactured using patented processes and materials. The factory invests 10 per cent of sales in R&D annually.

---

* This is a fictional case for education purposes only, prepared by Associate Professor Ebba Sjögren, Stockholm School of Economics. 

# Case 9.2

# TurnAround*

**by Malin Lund**

TurnAround produces paper-based consumer products such as diapers, incontinence products, female hygiene products, and various consumer tissues such as cleaning napkins and toilet paper. TurnAround is organized into three business units: adult care, family care and child care. The managers of these units are responsible for most of the activities of their particular unit and are currently evaluated on 'earnings before interest expenses and taxes'. For a couple of years, corporate profitability has declined and a new CFO was appointed. She suggested a redesign of the entire management control system, beginning with changes to the management control structure: 'We are in a business where low margins are common so we also need to address the assets employed. The divisions should be responsible for profit, including marketing, but also for the assets employed in their business unit,' she said. This also brought to the fore the issue of how to measure the performance of the established investment centres. The CEO knew that return on investment (ROI) was a quite common performance measure in other organizations and suggested the use of that measure. However, the CFO emphasized that residual income (RI) or economic value added (EVA®) were more appropriate performance measures for investment centres. She estimated that the cost of capital to be used in the RI calculations was 12 per cent and the cost of capital to be used in the EVA® calculations was 11 per cent. The CFO also made a few initial adjustments of the financial accounting numbers to be used when calculating EVA®. These adjustments were primarily related to capitalizing R&D expenses and brand-building activities. The financial figures of the three divisions are shown in Exhibit 1.

**EXHIBIT 1** Financial figures for the three divisions

| | Child care division | Adult care division | Family care division |
|---|---|---|---|
| Non-current assets (book value) | 1600 | 1600 | 1750 |
| Non-current assets (adjusted) | 3800 | 3100 | 2100 |
| Working capital (book value) | 110 | 700 | 2000 |
| Working capital (adjusted) | 1300 | 1000 | 2200 |
| Earnings before interest expenses and taxes (book value) | 650 | 720 | 850 |
| Adjusted net operating profit after taxes | 550 | 525 | 650 |

* This is a fictional case for education purposes only, prepared by Malin Lund, Stockholm School of Economics. © Malin Lund.

## Questions

1 a Calculate ROI for the three divisions and analyse the levels. Make explicit your calculations.

b Calculate RI for the three divisions and analyse the levels. Make explicit your calculations.

c Calculate EVA® for the three divisions and analyse the levels. Make explicit your calculations.

2 Compare, analyse and discuss the results of question 1a when calculating the performance of the divisions via the three approaches (ROI, RI, EVA®).

3 The CEO and the CFO of TurnAround also want some additional information about the three approaches (ROI, RI, EVA®). Explain and discuss the potential benefits and drawbacks related to each approach.

# Case 9.3

# Setting an appropriate target: continuous improvement or benchmarking?*

**by Kalle Kraus**

The CEO of a medium-sized company turns to you for advice. She tells you: 'I went to a big conference where everyone talked about "new ways" of setting targets. As you know, we have always used *pre-set negotiated targets* in my company. Take customer satisfaction as an example. Should the target be (a) at least 80 per cent satisfied customers, (b) at least 90 per cent satisfied customers or (c) at least 70 per cent satisfied customers? If we decide to use a target of at least 80 per cent satisfied customers, this is the outcome of a negotiation between superiors and the subordinates. They discuss and most likely the superior starts with 90 per cent; then the subordinate argues for a lower target, say 70 per cent; and they end up somewhere in between, in this example 80 per cent. But during the conference it was clear to me that our way of arriving at an appropriate target was highly criticized. Instead people talked about *continuous improvement* and *benchmarking* as two alternative ways of arriving at the appropriate target. I was interested. But before I make any changes I want to understand what these two types of target mean, and their advantages and disadvantages. Please help me.'

* This case was written by Professor Kalle Kraus, Stockholm School of Economics.

# Case 9.4

# Performance measurement in a cooperative: context issues and challenges*

**by Paul Thambar and Wen Shi He**

## Background to cooperative and mutual enterprises

The long history of Australian cooperatives and mutual enterprises (CMEs) can be dated back to as early as 1859, when the first registered consumer cooperative, Brisbane Co-operative Society, was formed. Over the past decades, CMEs in Australia have grown to diversify into different industries, including agriculture, housing, banking and financial services, and insurance. Today, there are more than 2,000 active CMEs nationwide and approximately 8 in 10 Australians are members of a CME.

CMEs are significantly different from investor-owned firms, in that they are owned and controlled by its members with an objective to redistribute any benefits and profits earned directly back into the business, its members and the local community. Rather than seeking to provide the greatest return to external capital investors through capital growth and profit distributions, these member-owned businesses are focused on delivering their mission and maximizing value for their members. Cooperatives around the world operate according to the same set of seven cooperative principles. These principles remain central to the operation of any cooperative:

1. Voluntary and open membership
2. Democratic member control
3. Member economic participation
4. Autonomy and independence
5. Education, training and information
6. Cooperation among cooperatives
7. Concern for community.

Despite their rich history, CMEs remain unrecognized and poorly understood by the Australian public. For many years now, CMEs have struggled to tell their story regarding the impact and unique value they create. The challenge of measuring and reporting on the total or 'mutual value' is due to the absence of a robust CME framework, as well as the lack of guidance provided by accounting standards and rules on how best to define and capture total social and economic value.

---

* This case is a part of the Mutual Value Measurement research study. The research team comprised Dr Paul Thambar, Dr Sarah Adams, Professor Matthew Hall, Dr Yolande McNicoll, Professor Yuval Millo and Ms Wen Shi He. Dr Thambar and Ms He have taken the lead in preparing this case.

## Case study

It was a quiet December Thursday afternoon at the office of Housing Union Victoria (HUV)[1] and the newly hired junior management accountant, Maia Cho, was one of the few people still in the office trying to finish off some last-minute tasks. As Christmas was fast approaching, many of her colleagues had taken leave and gone off on holiday to enjoy the festive season with their families and friends. Maia took a quick glance at the calendar sitting on the desk in front of her and mentally counted down the days until the HUV office closed for the Christmas and New Year period. There was still one week left before she would be free from work for two whole weeks!

Since the early morning, Maia had been diligently reviewing the organization's key performance measures. Before Levi Brown, the managing director of HUV, went on his holiday to Los Angeles, he had assigned Maia to explore possible solutions that could help solve HUV's current value reporting deficiency. Two weeks ago, when Levi was presenting the performance results for the final quarter of the 2019 fiscal year, Maia noticed an issue with the organization's use of performance measures. She was particularly concerned about how the measures used to monitor organizational performance were seemingly one-dimensional due to the strong focus on the financials. She discovered that the performance measures discussed during Levi's presentation were predominantly derived from the profit and loss statement (Appendix 1) and the balance sheet (Appendix 2).

Maia believes that conventional accounting measures such as sales revenue, finance costs and profit used as a means to monitor performance may not be adequate as they are derived from investor-owned firms with a commercial focus. As such, they tend to be focused on the short term, and they evaluate organizational performance through only one lens. As the largest not-for-profit housing organization in the state, which offers a unique housing programme, Maia is concerned that HUV's current performance measures do not recognize and holistically capture the unique value and impact that it generates to its members, employees, the broader community and the Australian economy.

At the moment, HUV works in partnership with 110 independent housing cooperatives to deliver an effective, sustainable cooperating housing programme across Victoria. The organization currently houses more than 4,000 individuals in 2,000-plus properties, and has the largest asset base of any community housing provider in Victoria. The housing programme seeks to provide secure, long-term tenancy at affordable rental prices, along with the ability for tenants to be actively involved in helping to plan for housing needs and the future of the programme. HUV's objectives are to advance cooperative value, to harness asset value and sustain growth, as well as to demonstrate proactive leadership in housing solutions. It also considers itself as an enabler and has a set of four core values, as described below:

1. **We work together:** 'We work together to achieve a positive impact in our community.'
2. **We are responsible:** 'We take pride in what we do, we are responsible for our actions.'
3. **We care for one another:** 'We treat everyone with care, and value their contribution.'
4. **We make a difference:** 'Our history informs our future, we learn and adapt.'

Maia believes that HUV is creating value in other areas beyond what is currently being captured financially. Having studied management accounting not too long ago, she wonders whether the organization could adopt one of the frameworks she has previously learnt to help capture and articulate its unique contributions. Thinking back to the many performance measurement tools she has come across in her studies, she suddenly remembers learning about the balanced scorecard – a performance measurement tool that can align organizational strategy to key performance measures, and can help organizations to think about how they are creating value in various areas. Maia believes that this just might be what HUV is looking for!

---

[1] This case is based on a social housing cooperative, CEHL, located in Melbourne, Australia (see https://www.cehl.com.au/). CEHL was a case firm in the Mutual Value Measurement research study. The case has been developed to focus on performance measurement, and details of participants referred to in the case are fictional.

### Measuring mutual value

For the past year, HUV has been working with a leading business school on a two-year research project, known as the Mutual Value Measurement (MVM) field study. The business school has been working collaboratively with 13 Australian CMEs from various industries to unravel the issues and implications relating to how mutual value is understood, created and measured by CMEs. Through extensive interviews, observations and review of archival documents, the MVM research team has developed a framework to address the value reporting deficiency in CMEs, and to provide a shared language and structure to measuring value.

The MVM framework uses six different, yet closely related dimensions – Commerciality, Shaping Markets, Member Relationships, Community Relationships, Ecosystem and Reciprocity, and the Mutual Mindset – to help measure and quantify the unique areas of value that CMEs generate (see Appendix 3). A list of common measures (Appendix 4) has also been provided for each dimension, and these can be used by a range of different CMEs when reporting on their economic and social contributions. Maia is thinking of expanding and integrating the balanced scorecard to include some of the six dimensions, along with some of the measures shown in the common measures list. She believes this could help HUV to further think about and understand the areas that it is creating value in.

### Tasks

1 Evaluate the six mutual value dimensions and advise Maia how they should be incorporated into the balanced scorecard.

2 Using the sample list of common measures in Appendix 4, identify which of the financial and non-financial measures HUV should use to monitor its organizational performance. Provide a brief justification for each chosen measure.

3 Explain how monitoring performance using a balanced scorecard is different to monitoring performance using a profit and loss statement.

## Appendices

### APPENDIX 1 Profit and loss statement

**STATEMENT OF SURPLUS OR DEFICIT AND OTHER COMPREHENSIVE INCOME[2] For the year ended 30 November 2019**

| | 2019 (AUS$) | 2018 (AUS$) |
|---|---|---|
| Sales revenue | 17,388,094 | 17,082,378 |
| Administrative expenses | (7,257,632) | (6,728,173) |
| Finance costs | (1,869,054) | (2,165,792) |
| Depreciation and amortization expense | (576,939) | (304,394) |
| Property expenses | (6,414,490) | (5,380,789) |
| **Gross surplus** | 1,269,979 | 2,503,230 |
| Gain on disposal assets | 64,326 | 1,818,867 |
| Fair value adjustment – investment property | 81,516,709 | 58,620,712 |
| Fair value adjustment – other financial assets | 61,198 | 4,142,744 |
| Grant amortization | 247,853 | 247,853 |
| **Surplus for the year** | 83,160,065 | 67,333,406 |
| **Other comprehensive income for the year** | – | – |
| **Total comprehensive income for the year** | 83,160,065 | 67,333,406 |

[2] This profit and loss statement has been adapted from a publicly available annual report. Available at: https://www.cehl.com.au/Attachment?Action=Download&Attachment_id=399 (accessed 5 November 2019).

## APPENDIX 2 Balance sheet

| STATEMENT OF FINANCIAL POSITION[3] As at 30 November 2019 | | |
|---|---|---|
| | **2019 (AUS$)** | **2018 (AUS$)** |
| ASSETS | | |
| **CURRENT ASSETS** | | |
| Cash and cash equivalents | 5,610,041 | 4,872,198 |
| Trade and other receivables | 2,097,875 | 1,892,678 |
| Other assets –prepayments | 113,605 | 138,866 |
| **TOTAL CURRENT ASSETS** | 7,821,521 | 6,903,742 |
| **NON-CURRENT ASSETS** | | |
| **Other financial assets** | **2,829,381** | **2,430,366** |
| Property, plant and equipment | 8,549,668 | 7,803,234 |
| Investment properties | 893,453,357 | 817,375,220 |
| **TOTAL NON-CURRENT ASSETS** | 904,832,406 | 827,608,820 |
| **TOTAL ASSETS** | 912,653,927 | 834,512,562 |
| | | |
| LIABILITIES | | |
| **CURRENT LIABILITIES** | | |
| Trade and other payables | 5,693,689 | 4,704,320 |
| Financial liabilities | 27,341,501 | 33,235,410 |
| Employee benefits | 668,154 | 527,348 |
| **TOTAL CURRENT LIABILITIES** | 33,703,344 | 38,467,078 |
| **NON-CURRENT LIABILITIES** | | |
| Financial liabilities | 36,470,739 | 36,718,592 |
| Employee benefits | 121,642 | 128,755 |
| **TOTAL NON-CURRENT LIABILITIES** | 36,592,381 | 36,847,347 |
| **TOTAL LIABILITIES** | 70,295,725 | 75,314,425 |
| **NET ASSETS** | 842,358,202 | 759,198,137 |
| | | |
| EQUITY | | |
| Issued capital | 123 | 123 |
| Reserves | 551,107,521 | 551,046,323 |
| Retained earnings | 291,250,558 | 208,151,659 |
| **TOTAL EQUITY** | 842,358,202 | 759,198,137 |

[3] This balance sheet has been adapted from a publicly available annual report. Available at: https://www.cehl.com.au/Attachment?Action=Download&Attachment_id=399 (accessed 5 November 2019).

## APPENDIX 3 Dimensions of mutual value[4]

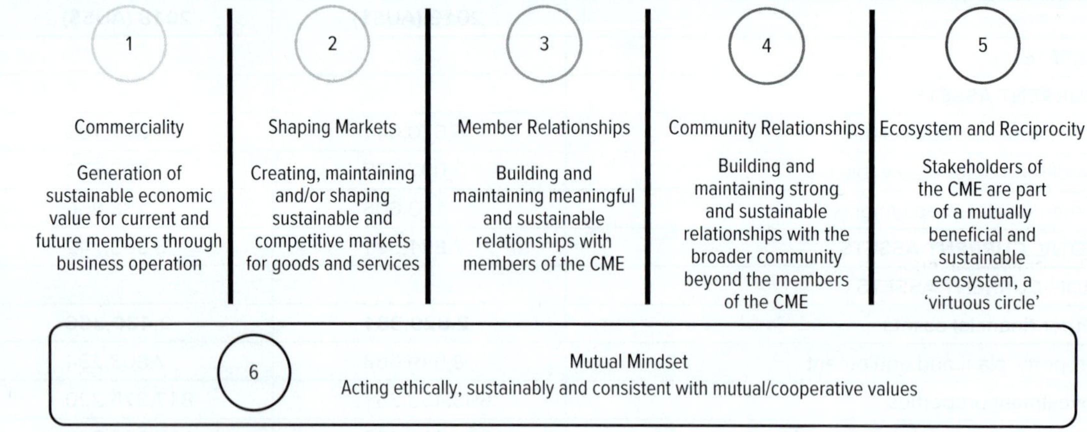


## APPENDIX 4 Sample list of common measures[5]

### 1 Commerciality

| Measure | Explanation/calculation |
|---|---|
| **Quantitative measures** | |
| Benefit per member | = Total dollar value of all benefits provided to members ÷ Total* number of members |
| | *Expressed in dollar per member* |
| Net asset growth | Percentage growth in net assets since preceding financial year |
| | *Expressed as a percentage* |
| Revenue growth | Percentage growth in revenue since preceding financial year |
| | *Expressed as a percentage* |
| **Qualitative measures** | |
| Provide a specific example of how your CME has delivered a product/service of higher quality. | |
| * Either average over period or at end of period | |

[4] This diagram has been sourced from the Mutual Value Measurement's phase one report.

[5] This sample list of common measures has been sourced from the Mutual Value Measurement's phase one report.

## 2 Shaping markets

| Measure | Explanation/calculation |
|---|---|
| **Quantitative measures** | |
| Price differential | Price of product/service to members compared to price for same/similar products from competitors* |
| | **Competitors would normally be considered as non-CMEs* |
| Product/service differentiation | = Dollar revenue from differentiated products/services§ ÷ Total dollar revenue or = Number of differentiated** products/services ÷ Total number of product lines |
| | *Expressed as a percentage* |
| **Qualitative measures** | |
| Provide a specific example of how your CME has delivered a product/service of higher quality. | |

* Competitors would normally be considered as non-CMEs

§ CME may choose to measure this using either revenue or products, selecting that which is more suitable for their business

** Differentiated means unique products/services that may otherwise not be available, or products/services with unique qualities not provided by others

## 3 Member relationships

| Measure | Explanation/calculation |
|---|---|
| **Quantitative measures** | |
| Total number of members | = Total number of members (or memberships) in your CME in the reporting period |
| | *Expressed as number of members* |
| Membership churn rate | = (Number of new members – Number of lapsed/exited members) ÷ Total* number of members |
| | *Expressed as a percentage* |
| Membership tenure distribution | Identify the longest-serving member (in years) (e.g., 30 years). Divide this number by 5 (e.g., 30/5 = 6 years) and then use it to create five 'buckets' corresponding to different lengths of membership tenure (e.g., 0–6 years, 6–12 years, 12–18 years, 18–24 years, 24–30 years). Then calculate the number of members in each tenure 'bucket' (e.g., how many members have a membership tenure of 0–6 years?) |
| | *Express the number of members in each bucket in a bar graph* |
| Member satisfaction (%) | Initially, report this figure using any single existing measure currently in use by the organization. If practicable, work towards a common measure of member satisfaction across CME sector |
| | *Expressed as average percentage satisfaction of all members surveyed* |
| Percentage of members engaging with AGM | = Number of members attending, voting, and/or watching the AGM online ÷ Total* number of members |
| | *Expressed as a percentage* |
| | |
| **Qualitative measures** | |
| Provide a specific example of how your CME has used member feedback in decision making. | |

* Either average over period or at end of period

## 4 Community relationships

| Measure | Explanation/calculation |
| --- | --- |
| **Quantitative measures** | |
| Community investment per member | = Combined dollar value of donations, sponsorships, advocacy activities ÷ Total* number of members |
| | *Expressed as a dollar per member* |
| Community investment scaled by revenue | = Combined dollar value of donations, sponsorships, advocacy activities ÷ Total revenue |
| | *Expressed as a percentage of revenue* |
| Number of FTE jobs in Australia | = Total number of full-time equivalent jobs provided by the CME in Australia |
| | *Expressed as a number of FTE jobs* |
| **Qualitative measures** | |
| Provide a specific example of how your CME has delivered benefits for the community. | |
| * Either average over period or at end of period | |

## 5 Ecosystem and reciprocity

| Measure | Explanation/calculation |
| --- | --- |
| **Quantitative measures** | |
| Local accounts payable to revenue ratio | = Total dollar accounts payable (to suppliers of products and services) ÷ Total revenue for period |
| | *Expressed as a percentage* |
| Percentage growth in revenue per member | = (Dollar revenue per member* in previous period – Dollar revenue per member* in current period) ÷ Total* number of members |
| | *Expressed as a dollar per member* |
| Percentage of expenses from trading with CMEs | = Expenses paid to other CMEs/Total expenses for the period |
| | *Expressed as a percentage* |
| **Qualitative measures** | |
| Provide a specific example of how your CME has benefited the business of your suppliers and/or members. | |
| * Either average over period or at end of period | |

## 6 Mutual mindset

| Measure | Explanation/calculation |
| --- | --- |
| **Quantitative measures** | |
| Member trust | Initially, report this figure using any existing measure currently in use by the organization; if practicable, work towards a common measure of trust across CME sector |
| | *Expressed as average percentage trust of all members surveyed* |

| Measure | Explanation/calculation |
|---|---|
| Executive tenure | Average tenure (years) of senior executives (in executive positions) |
| | *Expressed in years* |
| Board tenure | Average tenure (years) on board of all board members |
| | *Expressed in years* |
| Average CME experience | *Average years of experience working in a CME for all board and senior executives* |
| | *Expressed in years* |
| Regulatory breaches | = Total number of regulatory breaches (of any kind) |
| Complaints per 100 members | = Total number of complaints to CME ÷ Total* number of members x 100 |
| | *Expressed as a number per 100 members* |
| Employee satisfaction (%) | Initially, report this figure using any existing measure currently in use by the organization; if practicable, work towards a common measure of employee satisfaction across CME sector |
| | *Expressed as average percentage satisfaction of all employees surveyed* |
| Voluntary staff turnover ratio | = Number of voluntary staff leaving ÷ Average staff |
| | *Expressed as a percentage* |
| | |
| **Qualitative measures** | |
| Provide a specific example of how your CME has 'done the right thing' by members. | |

* Either average over period or at end of period

# Case 9.5

# Frescent: sustainability and the balanced scorecard*

## by Emilia Cederberg

Frescent was a manufacturer of beauty products, such as skincare, hygiene and haircare. The company was listed on the stock exchange. It had grown rapidly in the past decade and now employed 300 people, primarily in marketing and product development, but also in manufacturing.

Investors had increasingly been asking questions about sustainability. Kendall Spencer, the company CFO, had recently sat in a meeting where the sustainability analyst at one of its largest owners, an institutional investor, had questioned how the company's formal strategic vision, 'To give consumers a more

* This case was written by Dr Emilia Cederberg, Stockholm School of Economics.

enjoyable daily life by developing and selling safe, sustainable and high-quality beauty products', was reflected in KPIs and reward systems.

Frescent had published a sustainability report for some years, and had also employed Alex North, a sustainability specialist who had so far worked primarily with supplier control and the environmental impact of packaging. Moreover, Kendall's co-workers in the finance department had begun to suggest there was misalignment between the sustainability claims made externally and the internal management control system. One afternoon, one of Kendall's co-workers, a controller, came into Kendall's office.

*I just bumped into Alex by the coffee machine. We got to talking about integration, and the fact that none of our key metrics relates to sustainability. I am increasingly getting a sense we should do something about this.*

For years, a balanced scorecard (BSC) was the main management control tool that integrated Frescent's financial and non-financial performance, building on the strategic mission (see Exhibit 1). The dimensions and metrics had been carefully chosen and adapted over the course of a decade, and the tool was generally seen to function well.

As Frescent's products were in the mid-price range, pharmacies and department stores were the key retail outlet, and the BSC reflected this with a KPI on the average order size of key customers, like the major pharmacy chains. It had also become increasingly important to market products through influencers on social media platforms, and thus one metric in the 'customers' perspective was a compound metric of how many individuals were reached by, and interacted with, Frescent's influencer campaigns. The company manufactured some products internally, and others through contractors. As the products would be used directly on consumers' skin and hair, products that caused irritation or allergic reactions could have a disastrous impact on sales revenue. The company therefore included safety of products as part of the mission statement, and closely followed the number of consumer complaints filed. Top management was rewarded based on return on capital employed (ROCE).

**EXHIBIT 1** Frescent's balanced scorecard

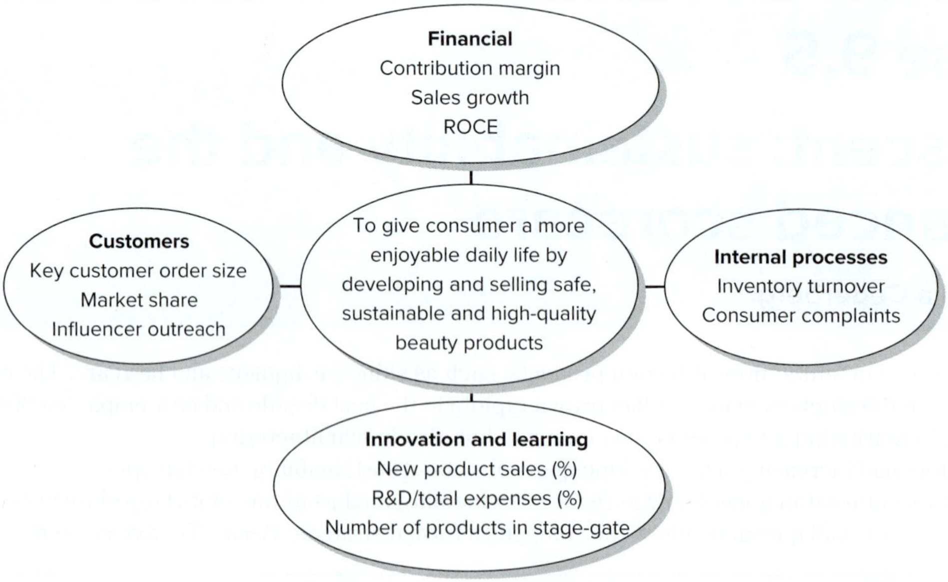

The focus of Alex North's work so far was the outcome of a mapping of key sustainability issues the firm had conducted with the help of external sustainability consultants a few years ago. The consultants had produced a materiality analysis, where issues were assessed based on their importance to the business. One finding was that consumers were increasingly concerned about the use of plastic in packaging, and many young women looked especially for products with organic ingredients. While Frescent had an eco range, the sales of which had grown to 7 per cent of total sales in only three years, these issues had not been of concern historically. In the country where Frescent had its largest portion of sales, there had been political proposals to introduce a mandatory declaration (on the product container) of its environmental footprint, including $CO_2$ emissions and water use, from the manufacture of each product. It currently looked like the proposal would get a narrow-margin majority in the parliament, and the consultants had recommended that Frescent address this somehow.

With the recent investor questions, and the internal pressures building up, Kendall concluded that the BSC needed to be revisited. He knew that any such process required bottom-up participation from different levels and departments. To start off the discussion, however, Kendall decided to sit down with the controller and Alex North, the sustainability specialist, and make a first suggestion that could be circulated beforehand. Your task is to help Kendall and colleagues with the first draft of the updated BSC.

## Questions

1 Which perspectives would be suitable for an update of Frescent's BSC?

2 Suggest a few appropriate KPIs in each such dimension. Make sure to argue for your choice, and how it relates to the overall strategy. You should also outline any potential challenges to implementing your suggested updated BSC.

3 Would you suggest any changes to the reward system?

# Chapter 10

# Monetary incentive systems and motivation

## Learning objectives

After reading this chapter, you should be able to:

1. Account for some roles that compensation in an organization may fulfil.
2. Describe different forms of incentives.
3. Explain the implications of agency theory for the design of incentive systems.
4. Explain the implications of self-determination theory for the design of incentive systems.
5. Discuss the critique against the two theories.
6. Discuss which theory (if any) you support the most and explain why.

### Real world vignette: Wikipedia and Encarta

An 11-year-old girl once asked her dad, 'Dad, what is an encyclopaedia?' Trying to explain, her dad asked her if she knew about Wikipedia. With a rather offended look she said, 'Of course I do, everybody knows about Wikipedia!' All of you who read this undoubtedly also know about Wikipedia. You probably use it frequently, perhaps even on a daily basis. But the question is, do you know about Microsoft Encarta? If the answer is no, you do not have to be ashamed to admit it. Because as the title of a *PC World* article[1] once read: 'What was Encarta? Look it up on Wikipedia!'

[1] Gralla, P. (2009) What was Encarta? Look it up on Wikipedia, *PC World*, 31 March. Available at: https://www.pcworld.com/article/162320/what_was_encarta_look_it_up_on_wikipedia.html (accessed 24 November 2019).

Microsoft Encarta, first released in 1993, was Microsoft's attempt at creating the leading digital multimedia encyclopaedia and atlas. Microsoft was at the time already a very successful company with the financial strength to back up the Encarta venture. It acquired three successful printed encyclopaedias that were incorporated into Encarta, and it also employed qualified managers and experts to produce, update and market the product. Encarta was successful for a number of years and its future looked very promising. It also looked like Encarta would be as successful as many of Microsoft's other software products and would continue to bring in revenue for Microsoft.

But we all know what happened. Wikipedia came along and Encarta was finally discontinued in October 2009. Wikipedia was first launched in January 2001 as an offshoot of the now abandoned Nupedia, whose founder donated server and bandwidth to the project. The success of Wikipedia is remarkable, with 500 million unique visitors per month and 40 million articles in 301 different languages.[2] But what is really interesting is that all this has been achieved with very little money. There was no money to buy existing encyclopaedias, very little money to invest in development and marketing and, perhaps more interestingly, no money to pay all the contributors, who work for free. This raises some very interesting questions; for example, how could this project with basically no financial resources so totally defeat the world's largest software producer? And what motivates all these people to put in, in some cases, so much time and effort into something that they do not even get paid for?[3]

## Introduction

Incentive systems is probably the part of the management control system that receives the most attention in the public debate, from the media and people in general. How much and in what way top managers and lower-level managers are being paid is a topic that seems to interest people a great deal. The main focus in the debate is often on the level of compensation, as well as on the scandals where top managers may have behaved in a questionable way in order to increase their bonus. It does not seem to be very hard to find examples where financial incentives have contributed to scandals, even if they appear to be more common in the USA than in Europe. Nor, as already mentioned in Chapter 3, is it very hard to find people who claim that financial incentives contributed to the major financial crises around 2008.

***Real World Example***: One reason for the severe financial crisis around 2008 was that US banks and credit institutions, in hindsight, took far too high risks when issuing loans to private real estate owners – that is, people who bought houses. One possible explanation for this might actually be the management control systems used by banks and credit institutions towards the mortgage brokers – that is, the people selling the loans to the house buyers. These mortgage brokers, who could be working for either the bank, a mortgage broker company or for themselves, were often paid according to a system where their pay corresponded to the future interest the bank expected to receive on the issued loan. This meant that the more interest the bank expected to receive on the loans sold by the broker, the more money the broker would make. This makes sense in the respect that the interest is the revenue the bank receives on the loans. The only problem was that high-risk customers had to pay a higher interest rate than low-risk customers, because the bank wanted compensation for the higher risk. And because the high-risk customers were charged a higher interest rate, the mortgage brokers made more money selling loans to them than to the low-risk customers.[4]

---

[2] https://en.wikipedia.org/wiki/Wikipedia (accessed 24 November 2019).

[3] The idea to compare Encarta with Wikipedia is attributed to Pink, D.H. (2010) *Drive: The Surprising Truth About What Motivates Us*. Edinburgh: Canongate.

[4] For a more thorough discussion about this see, for example, Murdock, C.W. (2014) How incentives drove the subprime crisis, *Loyola eCommons*, Loyola University Chicago. Available at: https://ecommons.luc.edu/cgi/viewcontent.cgi?article=1036&context=social_justice (accessed 1 December 2019).

The problem, though, is that while the critics of financial incentives see this as proof that financial incentives are a negative thing, the proponents of these incentives say that the negative effects are exaggerated and that the positive effects still outweigh the negative ones. The views of two CEOs from Deutsche Bank in 2015 and in 2019, which we displayed side by side in Chapter 3, offer a good illustration of how divided people are in this matter.

But it is not just in the public debate that incentives and motivation receive a great deal of attention. It is also very popular in research, and people from a number of fields such as psychology, sociology, economics and business administration have devoted attention to it. Therefore, it is hardly surprising that it is difficult to get an overview of the research, especially since the level of consensus appears to be very low. In fact, the camps seem as divided here as in other areas of society. The fundamental question is in regard to the role of monetary incentives in the motivation of employees in general, and managers in particular.

Over the last decades, many theories have been developed as to what motivates people and, even if we wanted to, we could not cover more than a small fraction of them here. Some of the older views still linger, as they are based on simplified models of humans. Some of the more modern theories have moved beyond those simple models and suggest that human motivation is, indeed, a very complex issue. Our discussion in Chapter 3 attested to this complexity. One old model of human motivation was expressed through a well-known dichotomy by Douglas McGregor.[5] McGregor presented *theory X* and *theory Y* as two different and opposing views on the motivation of human beings.

According to theory X, human beings have an instinctive aversion towards work and are in other words lazy. Therefore, they must be forced and governed in order to work. Human beings also want to escape responsibility and prefer to be led by others. According to theory Y, on the other hand, working comes as naturally to human beings as resting. Human beings can also lead their own work if it is done for important purposes and under the right circumstances human beings even desire responsibility. Inventiveness and the ability to work autonomously are common.

**Real World Examples:** In the 1990s, a research project was conducted that focused on the implementation of lean management, including decentralized responsibility and the forming of teams, in a number of manufacturing plants. One thing that always came up in the interviews was how the different plants succeeded in making their employees take on more responsibility, make more decisions and be more innovative than they had been before. In many of the plants, they said that their employees did not do this voluntarily, but had to be forced or tricked into doing it one way or another. In fact, several of the managers claimed that their employees were content with the repetitive jobs they used to have, where they did not have to think very much, suggest improvements or make decisions. The jobs may have been boring but they were uncomplicated, undemanding and made them feel safe, and this was how most of the employees wanted it. This view is very much in line with theory X.

However, in one particular plant the managers reasoned in a very different way. They said that many of their employees were involved in quite advanced activities in their free time, such as holding high positions in different types of organization such as sports clubs, unions or political organizations. Why is it, they said, that they can carry out these advanced activities in their spare time, while they can only manage the easiest tasks at work? The managers came to the conclusion that the problem did not lie with their employees, but with the organization that apparently suppressed their capabilities. So, they set out to change it and this plant was the one that, in fact, was the most successful in implementing lean management and ensuring that its employees contributed more. The managers' view is, of course, very much in line with theory Y.

In this chapter, we are going to take a closer look at the issues behind these two views on human motivation. We will do so by focusing in more detail on the role of motivation in agency theory and in self-determination theory. The main point is that these theories seem to propose a quite distinct view of humans, which has implications for the way we should design incentive systems. The main reason that we have chosen

[5] McGregor, D. (1960) *The Human Side of Enterprise.* New York: McGraw-Hill.

these theories is quite simply that they appear to be the ones with most impact on incentive system design and use in practice as well as in the debate on and critique against common practice. Another reason for focusing in detail on these two theories is that they are very different, with different implications for incentive systems, and therefore represent two of the major camps in the debate. Both theories have been mentioned earlier, in Chapter 3, and we will now link them specifically to the design of monetary incentive systems.

The first theory, *agency theory*, is based in economics and seems to relate in essence to theory X. It has had an enormous influence on the design of incentive systems, especially for top managers in stock listed companies. But it has also influenced our thinking about how to incentivize lower-level managers and employees across ranks and professions. Salespeople, for instance, are frequently exposed to incentive systems based on the agency theory logic. The fact that these types of system are so popular implies that the people who decide on the design of these systems, like top managers and board members, seem to believe in the the agency theory logic of motivation.

The second theory, *self-determination theory*, is rooted in psychology and can be seen as a further development of theory Y. It has not yet had the same impact on practice as agency theory. But, whenever agency theory, and incentive systems based on it, are criticized, the critique often uses arguments and terms from self-determination theory. If managers and board members tend to believe in agency theory, practically every consultant we meet seems to believe in self-determination theory. One possible explanation for this is the very popular book *Drive*,[6] which is based on self-determination theory. The theory is also starting to make some impact on practice.

In this chapter we focus mainly on the *effects* that compensation and other forms of incentives have, or do not have, on *motivation* and *performance*. But before we discuss the different theories, we are first going to discuss a number of different roles of compensation and different types of incentives. In our discussions, it should be noted that we intend to pit the two theories against each other to clearly illustrate their differences. As we have illustrated in Chapter 3, over the last decade we have seen more convergence in our thinking about incentives, by combining economics and psychology. In terms of McGregor's theory X and theory Y, we have come to understand that humans probably have elements of both.

## Compensation and incentives

### Different roles of compensation

The compensation in the form of money paid out to managers and employees in an organization may have many different roles: to fulfil the obligation to pay managers and employees working for the organization; to attract new managers and employees; and to motivate managers and employees to work harder. We are going to take a look at some of those possible roles.

#### *Pay*

Few organizations can get away with not paying their employees. It may be possible in some non-profit organizations such as charity organizations, sport clubs and so on, but even then probably only for employees that work for the organization in their spare time. Moreover, there are usually laws and union agreements that regulate to ensure employers pay their employees reasonably well.

#### *Attract managers and employees*

Most organizations, even public service and non-profit organizations, compete for personnel. Just like their competitors, every organization, whether it is a car dealer, hospital or football club, wants to employ the best people possible. One way to compete is to offer more money than their competitors because

[6] Pink, D.H. (2010) *Drive: The Surprising Truth About What Motivates Us*. Edinburgh: Canongate.

people are more likely to take a job the higher the pay is. However, most organizations can only offer high *fixed pay* to a certain extent, especially as competitors follow and offer equally high pay. Also, they do not want to have much higher costs than the same competitors. Another possibility, then, is to offer prospective employees the opportunity to earn much more than the fixed pay, but only under certain circumstances – for example, if the organization performs very well. It is, of course, quite likely that the organization's competitors do the same to attract the best possible employees for the work offered and in that case it might be very difficult for an organization not to offer bonuses or similar if they want to attract employees.

### Keep managers and employees

Organizations are fully aware that it is not only a question of getting the right employees in the first place; it is also a question of ensuring that managers and employees remain in their employment. In many organizations, however, this question seems to get less attention compared with attracting them in the first place. But if managers and employees that do a good job only stay for a short time, it may become extremely costly for the organization to continuously employ and train new personnel. It may, therefore, be a good idea in the long run to ensure that the compensation continues to be attractive enough to keep them. However, this is perhaps even more difficult than attracting them in the first place; it is not only a question of monetary compensation. It may be just as much about offering interesting work tasks and a pleasant working environment.

### Credit

The compensation is often also a way to give credit to a person for a job well done. From this perspective it is not only the actual money that matters, but perhaps even more the recognition of the person getting the money.

**Real World Example:** Once during a seminar when incentives were discussed, one master's student said that he thought that he, and many other students, would like to make more money than their fellow students. He thus saw it as a competition and he would like to win!

At another seminar, the CFO of a large and successful company said that compensation was mostly a sport, with the main purpose to give the papers something to write about. He was of course referring to media interest in comparing the remuneration of top managers in large companies.

The fact that CEO compensation tends to go up and not down when the figures are made public, supports this notion. The figures are usually made public to give owners the possibility to see that the CEO compensation is reasonable and not too high. But what also happens, and seems to have more effect, is that this makes it easier for the CEOs to compare their compensation with that of other CEOs.

### Effort

The role of compensation that we are going to discuss the most in this chapter is that of motivating employees, and one aspect of motivation is to encourage people to work hard. What exactly working hard means is, of course, highly subjective and may differ between organizations and different positions in the same organization. But according to agency theory, for instance, making managers put in more effort and hours is a very important role of the incentive system.

### Inspiration

But motivation is not necessarily only about working hard. It is also about being inspired, creative and smart. An inspired manager will make better decisions, think in new ways, have better ideas and probably also inspire other managers and employees in the organization. According to some people, this is just as important or perhaps even more important, than putting in many hours. In fact, there may even be a conflict between the two, because somebody who works under a lot of pressure and gets tired from working long hours may be less inspired and creative. Either way, it is potentially a positive effect for the organization if the incentives, in different forms, can make people more inspired.

### Goal congruence

It is usually not even enough to work hard and to be inspired; managers and employees also need to work in line with the mission, goals and strategies of the organization. This means that individuals, different levels of the organization, different departments and business units should all work towards common goals. This may be something that is extremely difficult to achieve, particularly in larger organizations. But the incentive system often plays an important role in this by sometimes aligning the goals of different individuals and departments. However, *goal congruence* can also be created by other means, related to input controls, such as shared values and a common culture.

### Flexible remuneration

Finally, one role of compensation may be to make the level of remuneration more flexible. Compensation that to a large extent is based on *variable pay* is also more flexible in the sense that the organization has to pay more money in some years and less money in others for basically the same managers or the same workforce. If the variable pay is linked to performance, which it usually is, this probably means that the organization has to pay more in good years and less in bad years. This means that the risk is shared between the owners and managers/employees who get variable pay. To have this flexibility without having to lay people off during bad years is often highly valued by top managers and owners. However, critiques argue that performance-related incentives often tend to increase rather than decrease the volatility in profitability and cash flow.

## Types of incentives and motivators

We now take a look at some of the aspects that are relevant when we discuss incentive systems. These include, among other things, fixed and variable pay, and stock options, but also more direct motivational factors such as *work satisfaction*.

### The basic salary

When we talk about incentives and motivation, we often tend to forget about the basic salary, but the salary is often very important. A reasonably good level of basic salary may make employees feel appreciated and valued, which may well contribute to their motivation. However, if the salary is not very good – we will get back to this later – this will have a negative effect on motivation. Moreover, the basic salary is normally only fixed for a certain period, usually a year, and then revised. This revision, how it is carried out and communicated, may also have both positive and negative effects on motivation. One major difference between fixed pay, even if it is fixed only for a certain period, and variable pay, is that once you have had a raise you are not likely to lose it no matter how you perform in subsequent years.

### Short-term variable financial incentives

What we usually think of when we discuss incentives is variable financial incentives. These can be divided into *short-* and *long-term incentives;* we are going to start with the short-term incentives, which can be designed in a number of different ways.

The simplest method is to make the bonus equal to a set percentage of the profits. Many companies do not like using this method because it means paying a bonus even when profitability is low. Many firms therefore use formulas that pay bonuses only after a specified return has been earned on, for instance, capital employed or equity. One method is to base the bonus on a percentage of earnings per share after a predetermined level of earnings per share has been attained. Other companies base bonuses on their profitability relative to that of their industry. But they may also be linked to strategic and other types of non-financial goals.

Although the amount of the bonus is calculated annually, payments to recipients may be spread out over a period of years, usually five. Under this system, executives receive only one-fifth of their bonus in the year in which it was earned. The remaining four-fifths are paid out equally over the next four years. Thus, after the manager has been working under the plan for five years, the bonus consists of one-fifth of the bonus for the current year plus one-fifth of each of the bonuses for the preceding four years.

The deferred time frame encourages decision makers to think long term. But, because bonus payments in a year are not related to performance in that year, they may act as less of an incentive. In some instances, a manager will not receive the deferred bonus if he or she leaves the company before it is paid. This may make managers less likely to leave the company. It should make managers less prone to make short-term fixes, cash in the bonus and then move on to another job. With this system, in order to get the bonus they have to stay long enough to see the more long-term effects of their decisions.

### *Stock options*

A basic premise of many long-term incentive plans is that growth in the value of the company's shares (or stocks) reflects the company's long-run performance. There are several types of such plans but the most common one is probably *stock options.*

A stock option is a right to buy a number of shares at, or after, a given date in the future (the exercise date), at a price agreed upon at the time the option is granted (usually the current market price or 95 per cent of the current market price). The major motivational benefit of stock option plans is that they direct managers' energies towards the long-, as well as the short-term, performance of the company.

The managers gain if they later sell the shares at a price that exceeds the price paid for them.

**Real World Example:** Historically, stock options have been a popular form of rewarding employees at both start-ups and established companies, particularly in the technology sector. Microsoft, Cisco, Amazon and eBay are just some of the companies that use stock options in their incentive systems. There are several reasons for this. First, stock options and their upside potential tend to attract highly talented employees to these companies, and technology companies depend on the high calibre of their human capital to succeed. Second, employees will volunteer innovative ideas only if they can profit from them. Third, companies can pay employees lower salaries and bonuses because of the stock option programme. Fourth, stock options are intended to encourage employees to focus on the long term.

### *Intrinsic incentives*

Intrinsic incentives include aspects that are often referred to as work or *employee satisfaction.* If the work tasks, environment and colleagues make the work satisfying, it will be rewarding and may very well contribute to motivation. Some researchers even claim that these types of incentive are more important than financial incentives for many types of work, something that we return to later in this chapter.

Let us now explore how work itself can be rewarding. One possibility is, of course, that managers or employees find their work tasks *interesting.* People often pay large amounts of money to be able to exercise their interests outside work. What if you can do something every day that is in line with your personal interest and even get paid for it? Another motivating aspect may be *challenge.* Once again people tend to do lots of things outside work in order to find challenges, not least in sports. Why not try to find challenges in your work? Succeeding may be just as satisfying as winning a marathon race!

*Meaning* may be another reward. Many people search for meaning in religion, politics, charity or their family, but it is also possible to find meaning in one's work. Most organizations produce products or services for private consumption or other organizations. These products or services should make life better for consumers or help organizations to make life better for other consumers. Moreover, many organizations are devoted to issues related to sustainability, which often appear meaningful to the employees. Some organizations are good at communicating this to their employees and it often raises their motivation. Linked to this is also the sense of *kinship* that people may find in organizations. Working together as a team towards common goals and with people you like may be very stimulating and rewarding.

## Agency theory and the design of incentive systems

***Real World Example:*** A Chinese story that was very popular when the leader Deng Xiaoping started to introduce market reforms in China, goes something like this. One day Deng Xiaoping decided to take one of his grandsons to visit Mao Tse-tung. 'Call me Granduncle,' Mao offered warmly. 'Oh, I certainly couldn't do that, Chairman Mao,' the awe-struck child replied. 'Why don't you give him an apple?' suggested Deng. No sooner had Mao done so that the boy took a healthy bite out of it, then happily chirped, 'Oh, thank you, Granduncle.' 'You see,' said Deng, 'what incentives can achieve.'

As described in Chapter 3, agency theory[7] explores how contracts and incentives can be written to motivate individuals to behave in a goal-congruent way. It attempts to describe the major factors that should be considered in designing incentive systems.

An agency relationship exists whenever one party (*the principal*) hires another party (*the agent*) to perform a service and, in so doing, delegates decision-making authority to the agent. In a corporation, shareholders are principals and the chief executive officer (CEO) is their agent. The shareholders hire the CEOs and expect that they will act in their interest. At a lower level, the CEO is the principal and the responsibility centre managers are the agents. The challenge becomes how to motivate agents so that they will be as productive as they would be if they were the owners of the organization.

One of the key elements of agency theory is that principals and agents have *divergent preferences* or objectives. Incentive systems can reduce these divergent preferences.

### Divergent objectives of principals and agents

Agency theory assumes that all individuals act in their own *self-interest.* Agents are assumed to receive satisfaction not only from financial compensation but also from the perquisites involved in an agency relationship, such as generous amounts of leisure time, attractive working conditions and flexible working hours. For example, some agents may prefer leisure to hard work or effort. Leisure is assumed to be the opposite of effort. Managers' efforts increase the value of the firm, while leisure does not. An agent's preference for leisure over effort is called *work aversion.* Deliberately withholding effort is called *shirking.* Principals (i.e., shareholders), on the other hand, are assumed to be interested only in the financial returns that accrue from their investment in the firm.

Agents and principals also diverge with regard to *risk preferences.* Agency theory assumes that managers prefer more wealth to less, but that marginal utility, or satisfaction, decreases as more wealth is accumulated. The first million is valued higher than the second. Agents typically have much of their wealth tied up in the fortunes of the firm. This wealth consists of both their financial wealth and their human capital. Their financial wealth is likely to increase with good performance since their

[7] See, for example, Jensen, M.C. and Meckling, W.H. (1976) Theory of the firm: managerial behavior, agency costs and ownership structure, *Journal of Financial Economics,* 3(4): 305–60.

compensation is likely to be higher. Human capital – the manager's value as perceived by the market – is also influenced by the firm's performance, since CEOs normally are more attractive to new employers if they can show a good track record. Because both financial wealth and human capital depend on the success of the company, agents are assumed to be *risk-averse*.

On the other hand, company stock is held by many owners, who reduce their risk by diversifying their wealth and owning shares in many companies. Therefore, owners are interested in the expected value of their investment and are *risk-neutral*. Managers cannot as easily diversify from this risk, which is why they are risk-averse.

## Non-observability of agents' actions

Divergent preferences associated with compensation and perquisites arise whenever the principal cannot easily monitor the agent's actions. Shareholders are not in a position to monitor the CEO's activities daily to ensure that they are working in their best interest. Likewise, the CEO is not in a position to monitor daily the activities of responsibility centre managers. Because the principal has inadequate information about the agent's effort, the principal can never be certain how the agent's effort contributed to actual company results. This situation is referred to as *information asymmetry*. These asymmetries can take on several forms. Without monitoring, only the agents know whether they work in a goal-congruent manner (that is, in the principal's best interest). Moreover, the agent may know more about the task than the principal. This additional information that an agent may have is called *private information*.

The divergence of preferences between the principal and agent, and the agent's private information, may lead the agent to misrepresent information to the principal. This misrepresentation is of such a general nature that the name *moral hazard* has been given to the situation in which an agent is motivated to misrepresent private information.

## Monitoring and incentives

Agency theorists state that there are two major ways of dealing with the problems of divergent objectives and information asymmetry: *monitoring* and *incentives*.

### *Monitoring*

The principal can design a system that monitors the agent's actions, limiting actions that increase the agent's welfare at the expense of the principal's interest. An example of a monitoring system is the audited financial statement. Financial reports are generated about company performance, audited by a third party and then sent to the owners. To the extent that the principal has access to internal and management control reports (as discussed in Chapters 8 and 9) these are also used in this monitoring.

Agency theory has attempted to explain why different agency relationships involve different levels of monitoring. For example, monitoring is more effective if the agent's task is well defined and the information, or 'signal', used in monitoring is accurate. If the task is not well defined or easily monitored, then incentive contracting becomes more appealing. Monitoring and incentives are not mutually exclusive alternatives. In most firms, the CEO has an incentive contract along with audited and other financial statements that act as a monitoring device.

### *Incentive contracting*

A principal may attempt to limit divergent preferences by establishing appropriate incentive contracts. The more an agent's reward depends on a performance measure, the more incentive there is for the agent to improve the measure. Therefore, the principals should define the performance measures so that they further their interests. The ability to accomplish this is referred to as goal congruence. When the contract given to the agent motivates the agent to work in the principal's best interest, the contract is considered goal congruent.

A compensation scheme that does not incorporate an incentive contract poses a serious agency problem. For example, if CEOs were paid only a basic salary, they might not be motivated to work as diligently as when compensation consisted of a salary plus bonus. The latter case motivates CEOs to work harder to increase profits, increase their compensation and, at the same time, benefit the principal. Therefore, contracts are written that align the interests between the two parties by incorporating an incentive feature – that is, the principal writes a contract permitting management to share in the wealth when firm value is increased.

Principals face the challenge of identifying signals that are correlated with both agent effort and firm value. The agent's effort, along with outside factors (e.g., the general economy or natural disasters), combine to determine performance. The more closely a certain performance measure reflects the manager's effort, the more valuable the measure is in an incentive contract. If the performance measure is not closely correlated with the agent's effort, there is little incentive for the agents to increase their effort.

Monitoring and incentives can never ensure complete goal congruence. This is because of the difference in risk preferences between the two parties, the asymmetry of information and the costs of monitoring. These differences cause additional costs. Even an efficient system of incentive alignments will still result in some divergence of preferences; this is called the residual loss. The addition of the incentive compensation costs, the monitoring costs and the residual loss are formally entitled *agency costs*.

## CEO compensation and stock ownership plans

A company that pays its CEO a bonus in the form of stock options offers an example of the agency costs inherent in incentive systems. One cost is the risk-preference differences between the owners and the CEO. The agents, already risk-averse, incur additional risks when their pay is based on stock price performance. To compensate the CEO for taking on this risk, the contract will have to increase the amount of expected pay. In addition, to minimize the possible downside potential, the agent may not take on high-risk/high-return projects that the principal may find desirable.

A second problem with a stock ownership bonus plan is the lack of direct causal relationship between the agent's effort and the change in stock price. Stock prices are affected by factors outside the agent's control (e.g., general economic conditions, government intervention). If these factors cause the stock price to rise, then the agent receives increased pay at the owners' expense without any increased effort. On the other hand, the stock price may decrease even if the agent works hard.

In spite of these two problems, the stock ownership incentive contract is preferred to a contract that does not have an incentive feature. As pointed out earlier, relying solely on a basic salary has larger agency costs associated with it.

## Responsibility centre managers and accounting-based incentives

The relationship between a responsibility centre manager's effort and the stock price is more remote than for the CEO. It is difficult to isolate the contributions that individual responsibility centres make to increases in the firm's stock price. For this reason, a company might base the responsibility centre manager's bonus on the centre's profit. However, this incentive contract still has agency costs similar to those discussed in the CEO stock ownership plan. For example, market demand for a product may fall because of a new substitute product, but the manager may still perform well within the new smaller market. If the bonus is based strictly on profit, however, the agent's compensation will decrease. In addition, the agent may inflate profit through accounting manipulations that do not affect firm value. One instance of this is the sale of fixed assets that have a market value in excess of book value. While a contract based on profit may have lower agency costs than a basic salary, these costs do not go to zero.

## The importance of agency theory

Agency theory is an old theory, its origins dating back to a famous American book, published in 1932, entitled *The Modern Corporation and Private Property.*[8] The background to the book was the emerging separation of ownership and management at the beginning of the previous century, and that is exactly the problem that agency theory is addressing; how can the owners ensure that managers act in the best interest of the owners?

Another influential agency theorist is Michael Jensen, who published an article in *Harvard Business Review* in 1990,[9] arguing that the monetary incentives for CEOs had not increased since the 1930s and that they did not give managers incentives to perform well. Jensen, together with his co-author, therefore made three suggestions:

1 CEOs should be substantial owners of stocks in the company.

2 CEOs' salaries, bonuses and stock options should be designed to provide big rewards for superior performance and big penalties for poor performance.

3 CEOs should be dismissed for bad performance more often.

If we look at the situation 30 years later, we may very well find that what they suggested back in 1990 is to a large extent the reality today, although to a varying degree in different countries. Agency theory has in this sense been extremely influential and many of the incentive systems we can find in larger companies are very much in line with it. This does not necessarily mean that managers or directors are familiar with the theory, but the systems they design or are exposed to are certainly often influenced by it.

## Critique against agency theory

### *The basic assumptions are wrong*

As stated, agency theory has had an enormous impact on both practice and research, but has not surprisingly also been the subject of massive critique. The main critique often deals with some of the basic assumptions in agency theory. Two of these assumptions are that humans are perfectly rational and always act out of self-interest. Would charity even exist in a world where everybody acts only in self-interest and how can we explain the success of Wikipedia with agency theory? There is also a lot of research which shows that people do not always make rational decisions; the best-known researchers in this field are probably the Nobel Prize winner, Daniel Kahneman, and his collaborator, Amos Tversky. The following Real World Example is based on one of their best-known experiments.

***Real World Example:*** One example of non-rational decision making is that people tend to make the decisions they do based on how the question and alternatives are formulated rather than on the alternatives as such. One famous experiment[10] illustrating this is when a number of students were faced with a choice concerning how to treat a disease. The students were informed that 600 persons would die of a disease if they did not get any treatment. They then had to choose between two alternatives:

A If programme A is adopted, 200 people will be saved.

B If programme B is adopted, there is 1/3 probability that 600 people will be saved, and 2/3 probability that no people will be saved.

---

[8] Berle, A.A. and Means, G.C. (1932) *The Modern Corporation and Private Property.* New York: Macmillan.

[9] Jensen, M.C. and K.J. Murphy (1990) CEO incentives – it's not how much you pay, but how, *Harvard Business Review,* 68(3): 138–49.

[10] Tversky, A. and D. Kahneman (1981) The framing of decisions and the psychology of choice, *Science,* 211 (4481): 453–58.

A total of 72 per cent of the students chose programme A and only 28 per cent programme B. However, another group of students chose between these alternatives instead:

C If programme C is adopted 400 people will die.
**D** If programme D is adopted there is 1/3 probability that nobody will die, and 2/3 probability that 600 people will die.

In this case 22 per cent chose programme C and 78 per cent chose programme D. The interesting thing here is, of course, that programmes A and C, in fact, have an identical outcome, and so do programmes B and D. But depending on how the outcome was formulated, we obtained very different choices from the students. Alternative A, which is formulated in terms of saving lives, is much more attractive than alternative C, which is formulated in terms of losing lives, although they are the same in essence.

The proponents of agency theory quite often admit these limitations of the theory, but claim that it can still be a useful approximation on which to base research.

### *It does not promote ethical behaviour*

It would be unfair to claim that agency theory is immoral. But it could be said to be amoral, since it does not really include much in the way of ethical considerations. This is at least true for the earliest theoretical models in the agency theoretic paradigm. The moral in those models focused on safeguarding the rights of the owners, but apart from that does not acknowledge that people, agents or principals actually may act out of moral standpoints. This was a direct consequence of the basic assumptions discussed above.

***Real World Example:*** The former London Business School professor, Sumantra Ghoshal, claims in his article 'Bad management theories are destroying good management practices',[11] that academic research based on, for example, agency theory, has had a significant negative influence on management practice and freed business students from 'any form of moral responsibility'. The reason, according to Ghoshal, for the increasing appearance of fraud in companies is thus not insufficient control mechanisms, but that we have removed ethics from the world of business. Interestingly, Ghoshal wrote his article well before the major financial crisis around 2008.

However, a proponent of agency theory would probably argue that the ambition to decrease moral hazard is a very moral standpoint in agency theory. But the question is whether the kind of incentives suggested by agency theory really hamper moral hazard, because there is actually quite a lot of research that indicates that financial incentives often increase rather than decrease moral hazard. This is not least so when it comes to manipulation of accounting data, so-called *earnings management*. One study on American data concludes that earnings management has increased at the same pace as equity-based compensation, such as stock options, since the 1980s.[12] Therefore, it might be interesting to look closer at the effects that stock options may have.

***Real World Example:*** A study finds that managers with high equity incentives (such as stock options) are more likely to report earnings just in line with or just above expectations, and less likely to report high unexpected earnings,[13] suggesting that managers with high equity incentives are more likely to indulge in *income smoothing*

[11] Ghoshal, S. (2005) Bad management theories are destroying good management practices, *Academy of Management Learning & Education,* 4(1): 75–91.

[12] Cohen, D.A., Dey, A. and Lys, T.Z. (2008) Real and accrual-based earnings management in the pre- and post-Sarbanes-Oxley Periods, *Accounting Review,* 83(3): 757–87.

[13] Cheng, Q. and Warfield, T.D. (2005) Equity incentives and earnings management, *Accounting Review,* 80(2): 441–76.

in order to avoid present and future disappointments. Also companies that manage earnings downwards are more likely to miss earnings targets if they are going to grant stock options.[14] Another study[15] shows that earnings management is used to increase the earnings in the period before the option exercises.

If we put these studies next to each other we get a pattern where managers tend to report below expectations before stock options are granted, which is likely to lower the strike price. They then report in line with or just above expectations when the options are running. Finally, they report well above expectations just before they are exercised, which is likely to increase the stock price. This way the managers can pay a lower price for a stock that is valued higher and thus optimize their personal profit.

This evidence supports the argument that incentives tend to increase rather than decrease moral hazard. Incentives based on original agency theory thus also seem to increase behaviour that can be regarded as immoral. Maybe this is not so surprising after all, because when might one be more inclined to manipulate figures: when one has a fixed salary regardless of the figures or if one has the opportunity to get a big bonus if the figures are good enough?

More recent approaches in agency theory find room to include the *prosocial incentives* that employees and managers may have. For example, studies show that lying and cheating provide a *disutility* to employees and managers. Agency models that pay attention to these factors, which are modelled as moral cost, are better at explaining behaviours in reality than models purely based on the classical examples.[16]

## Self-determination theory and incentives

***Real World Example:*** The 'not in my backyard' problem is a classic one that has received a lot of attention in both practice and research. One popular solution is that the people whose backyard it is we are talking about should be compensated for whatever it is that is being put there. This solution was tested in a Swiss context concerning the deposit of nuclear waste.[17] A survey was sent out to a number of people living in the area where it was proposed to deposit the waste, in order to see what people's attitude would be towards having waste deposited in their 'backyard'. In the survey it was also said that all the residents of the area should be offered substantial compensation should the waste be deposited in their area. What the researchers found was that 24.6 per cent accepted. However, the researchers did also send out another survey to other people in the same area asking exactly the same question, but not mentioning anything about any compensation. Interestingly, in this case the level of acceptance was twice as high (50.8 per cent).

It is not an easy task to explain these results with agency theory. In order to explain why twice as many people accepted the nuclear waste 'without compensation' compared to 'with compensation', we need a theory other than agency theory. Such a theory is *self-determination theory* (SDT).[18]

---

[14] McAnally, M.L., Srivastava, A. and Weaver, C.D. (2008) Executive stock options, missed earnings targets, and earnings management, *Accounting Review*, 83(1): 185–216.

[15] Bartov, E. and Mohanram, P. (2004) Private information, earnings manipulations, and executive stock-option exercises, *Accounting Review*, 79(4): 889–920.

[16] Charness, G., Blanco-Jimenez, C., Ezquerra, L. and Rodriguez-Lara, I. (2019) Cheating, incentives, and money manipulation, *Experimental Economics*, 22(1): 155–77.

[17] Frey, B.S. and Jegen, R. (2001) Motivation crowding theory, *Journal of Economic Surveys*, 15(5): 589–611.

[18] See, for example, Deci, E.L. and Ryan, R.M. (1985) *Intrinsic Motivation and Self-determination in Human Behavior*. New York: Plenum Publishers.

## Extrinsic motivation, intrinsic motivation and the crowding-out effect

In Chapter 3 we explained that self-determination theory (SDT) distinguishes between extrinsic and intrinsic motivation. *Extrinsic motivation* is related to everything a person gains from carrying out a certain task – for example, monetary reward. *Intrinsic motivation* concerns the satisfaction of carrying out a certain task and reaching the goal.

***Real World Example:*** For a tennis player playing at Wimbledon, extrinsic motivation would derive from the chance to win prize money and probably also from the chance to secure more favourable contracts with sponsors. If we look at the prize money at Wimbledon, we can see that the first prize for the singles in 2018 was £2,250,000. In 1984 the first prize for the men's singles was £100,000 and in 1968 £2,000, with the first prizes for the women's singles being even lower.[19] Does this mean that Wimbledon attracts better players today and/or that the players are more motivated today? Probably not, because Wimbledon has for as long as anyone can remember attracted the best players in the world and been the most desirable tournament to win. In fact, this has been the case although there have always been tournaments with higher prize money than Wimbledon, implying that not even players in one of the most money-driven sports are driven solely by extrinsic motivation. Intrinsic motivation for the same tennis player would derive from the inner satisfaction of playing with other very good tennis players and the chance to win the most prestigious tournament in the world.

In agency theory there is only extrinsic motivation. SDT, on the other hand, also brings in intrinsic motivation, as well as how these two types of motivation impact each other. More specifically, SDT claims that extrinsic motivation may also have an effect on intrinsic motivation. This means that if an extrinsic reward for doing a certain task is changed, not only is the extrinsic motivation likely to change, but the intrinsic motivation often changes too. If the extrinsic reward is increased, the extrinsic motivation is likely to increase, but if the extrinsic reward crowds out intrinsic motivation the intrinsic motivation will decrease. And if the intrinsic motivation decreases more than the extrinsic motivation increases, the total motivation will decrease.

***Real World Example:*** In the Swiss 'not in my backyard' example, some may have accepted the nuclear waste for intrinsic reasons. They may have seen the benefits of nuclear power and they may have understood the reasons why their particular area was well suited for depositing the waste, and may, therefore, have accepted it because they understood that accepting would be good for society. However, when they were offered compensation, they may have thought less about what would be good for society and more about the potential negative effects for themselves. Was somebody trying to trick them into something dangerous by offering them money? If that was the case the extrinsic reward clearly crowded out the intrinsic motivation of contributing to society.

This effect can be illustrated as in Figure 10.1. First, the person is motivated only intrinsically. An extrinsic reward is then added but this reward crowds out a part of the intrinsic motivation so that the total motivation is actually lower than before the addition of the extrinsic reward. This effect can also be found if we remove an extrinsic reward, as in Figure 10.2. Here we have an extrinsic reward to begin with but then remove it. What then happens is, of course, that the extrinsic motivation disappears, but also that the intrinsic motivation increases to such an extent that the total motivation actually increases.

[19] Wimbledon official website (2019) Prize money and finance. Available at: https://www.wimbledon.com/en_GB/aboutwimbledon/prize_money_and_finance.html (accessed 2 December 2019).

**FIGURE 10.1** Total motivation before and after adding an extrinsic reward

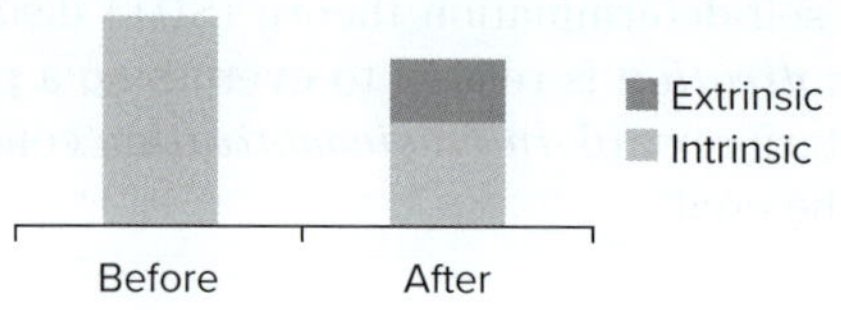


**FIGURE 10.2** Total motivation before and after the removal of an extrinsic reward

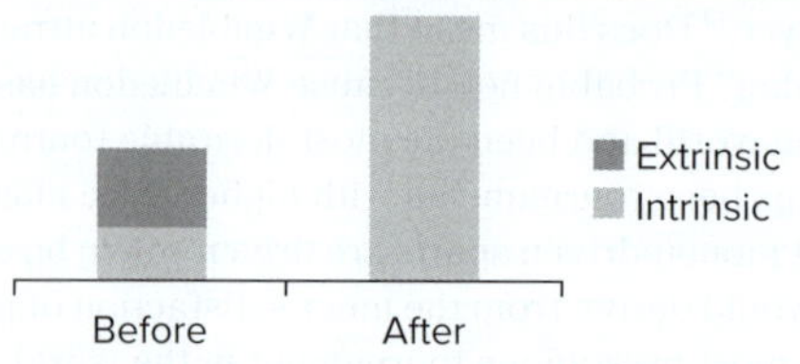


According to SDT research, these are two effects that may very well happen, and often do. This means that individuals *may* be less likely to accept nuclear waste in their backyard if they are offered compensation, that a tennis player *may* be less motivated to win if the prize money is really high, or that a manager or employee *may* be less motivated to do a really good job if offered a bonus. What the researchers back this up with are basically experiments, and they have conducted literally hundreds of experiments which support that the *crowding out effect* quite often does occur.

But extrinsic rewards do not always crowd out intrinsic motivation according to SDT. They may even crowd *in* intrinsic motivation and thus increase not only the extrinsic motivation but also the intrinsic motivation. Whether the extrinsic motivation crowds out or in intrinsic motivation basically depends on how the person in question perceives the intervention. If the intervention is perceived as *manipulating* the crowding-out effect will occur, but if it is perceived as *supportive* the crowding-in effect will occur. In the nuclear waste example, many seem to have perceived the offer of compensation as manipulating in the sense that they felt that somebody was trying to make them accept the offer and this probably made them more cautious and suspicious. A common example of an extrinsic intervention that often is perceived as supportive, on the other hand, is so-called management by walking around. This refers to when managers walk around and talk to their employees. They take an interest in the employees' situation, ask questions, offer advice, and encourage and praise them for doing a good job.

According to SDT, other situations when the crowding-out effect does not occur are if the extrinsic rewards are not expected or not directly linked to performance. An *unexpected reward* may appear if management in December announces that they think the company has performed so well that everybody is going to receive an extra bonus for Christmas. However, if this additional bonus is paid in December for several years, it will soon be taken for granted that the bonus will be paid every year. The same reward may also be said not to be directly linked to performance because it is linked to the performance of the whole company and not to the performances of individual managers and employees. A *collective reward* is, therefore, less likely to crowd out intrinsic motivation.

Another situation when the crowding-out effect does not occur, according to SDT is, of course, when there is no intrinsic motivation to begin with. If there is no intrinsic motivation, how can it be crowded out? This is often the case in simple, repetitive and boring jobs.

***Real World Example:*** Some people who worked at a peat bog, digging up peat, always described the job in terms of agony! If the sun was shining, it soon became very hot and dusty and they could hardly breathe! If it was raining they got soaking wet and the peat bog was soon transformed into mud! According to them, they were having a really hard time! But why then did they work there? The only answer was, of course, money; they were well paid and the harder they worked the more money they earned. Trying to motivate these people with intrinsic motivation in a job like that would probably have been an impossible task.

In fact, if there is no intrinsic motivation to begin with, there is no difference between SDT and agency theory. The only way to motivate people is through extrinsic rewards and there is no crowding-out effect. But this is, in fact, the only situation when the two theories agree!

## The importance of intrinsic motivation

According to SDT, intrinsic motivation is important not only because it can contribute to higher total motivation, but also because in intellectually demanding situations intrinsic motivation actually works better than extrinsic motivation.

***Real World Example:*** There is a classic experiment called the *candle problem* that was invented by the German psychologist, Karl Duncker, in the 1930s. The problem is to find out how to attach a candle on the wall over a table and light it without any wax dripping on the table. All you have is a candle, matches and a box of tacks, as you can see in Figure 10.3.[20]

Some time later the American, Sam Glucksberg, added another dimension to the experiment when he introduced extrinsic rewards for those who solved the problem the fastest. He divided the people participating in the experiment into two groups. He told the first group only that he was timing them in order to establish a norm for how long the task would take. The second group were told that they would gain some money if they were among the fastest 25 per cent and even more money if they were fastest of all. What happened was that the first group who had no chance of getting a reward were on average three-and-a-half-minutes faster than the second group!

**FIGURE 10.3** The candle problem

[20] There is a YouTube video of a version of this problem available at: https://www.youtube.com/watch?v=FRtQNS5dFO8 (accessed 6 June 2020).

**FIGURE 10.4** The solution to the candle problem

Have you solved the problem? If not, take a look at Figure 10.4.

As the experiment suggests, intrinsic motivation is especially important when creativity and thinking outside of the box is needed. According to SDT, when the task is unknown and complex, and when learning is required, intrinsic motivation gives better results. But for more simple tasks this is not the case. Glucksberg also conducted another experiment, where he first emptied the tacks on the table, leaving an empty box. This made it more obvious that the box could be part of the solution, and now the group with the possibility of winning a reward were faster than the other group.

## Reasons for the crowding-out effect

The reasons for the crowding-out effect are mainly two psychological processes. These two processes are *impaired self-determination* and *impaired self-esteem.*

Impaired self-determination refers to individuals who perceive that their *autonomy* has decreased due to an external intervention such as an order or the addition of an extrinsic reward. In the nuclear waste example people may feel that their autonomy has decreased by the offer of compensation. If they want the compensation they do not really have a choice, and not having a choice impairs their self-determination. A tennis player may want to skip the Australian Open one year and take some time off instead. However, this may be a difficult choice to justify, because the prize money in the Australian Open is so high. This means that the prize money impairs the tennis player's self-determination and may crowd out intrinsic motivation. A manager may want to make large investments in research and development (R&D) one year in order to develop better products for the future, but realizes that this will decrease this year's bonus. The bonus therefore impairs the manager's self-determination and may crowd out intrinsic motivation.

Impaired self-esteem is felt by individuals who feel that they are not trusted to do their best without incentives. Because if boards really trusted CEOs to do their best, why then would they offer them bonuses? Do not the bonuses express that the boards do *not* trust CEOs to do their best? So even if managers and others do want bonuses, they may still feel that there is an element of distrust in the fact that they have been given a bonus, and this feeling may crowd out intrinsic motivation.

## Motivation drivers

As we have already discussed, there is no difference between agency theory and SDT if the conditions are such that the likelihood of intrinsic motivation is low. Under such circumstances similar incentive system design, such as those suggested by agency theory, would also be relevant from an SDT perspective.

It seems, therefore, more interesting to discuss the type of drivers that, according to SDT, would be appropriate under circumstances where the likelihood of intrinsic rewards is high and/or when intrinsic rewards are particularly important. This would be a reasonably advanced and complicated task, rather than simple and repetitive work.

### *Financial compensation*

Even if financial compensation may be less important when intrinsic motivation is preferred, it does not mean that we can leave it out altogether because if the financial compensation is low, there is a high chance that people may feel that they are not being fairly treated and if they feel that way it may crowd out intrinsic motivation. So the minimum requirement on the financial compensation from an SDT perspective is a good basic salary.

A collective bonus is another form of financial incentive that may well be useful. From an SDT perspective, a collective bonus is less likely to crowd out intrinsic motivation, because its link to the individual's performance is weaker. Positive arguments for collective bonuses are that they often strengthen team spirit and the feeling of 'we-ness' in an organization, something that we return to shortly.

### *Interesting assignments*

Psychologists often claim that the most important factor driving motivation is *interest*. This means that people who are interested in their work tasks are much more motivated than those who are not; the work in itself is a reward if it is in line with the interest of the person performing it. This is not so hard to believe, but it does have some interesting implications. One implication is that people should be employed because they have a great interest in whatever it is they are going to work with, rather than because they have a great interest in the money they are going to make. Another implication is that it is in the organization's interest to make managers' and employees' work as interesting as possible, for example by designing broader and more varied work tasks.

### *Competence development*

One thing that drives people's motivation is the possibility to develop their *competence*. That is the reason why so many people spend endless hours playing instruments, sports or computer games in their spare time. The same driver is present in a work context and the good news is that competence development is not only good for the employee, but also for the organization. From this perspective it is actually quite sad that the time for competence development often is rather limited in many organizations.

### *Communication*

*Communication* is another issue that we have touched upon and that is very important for intrinsic motivation. Management by walking around, taking notice of subordinates, informing and listening to them are all activities that often tend to support both intrinsic end extrinsic motivation. Personal relations, as opposed to the impersonal character of a bonus and other systems, tend to be favourable to intrinsic motivation. People being not only informed but also listened to also relates to involvement, which is our next issue.

### *Involvement*

Orders and making decisions above people's heads may crowd out intrinsic motivation, but the opposite also seems to be true, meaning that *involving* people in decisions may increase their intrinsic motivation. By being listened to, being taken into consideration and having a chance to influence decisions, people often feel part of something bigger and more important than managing their daily tasks. This gives more *meaning* to their work and, therefore, makes it more rewarding.

### Autonomy

But it is not only involvement in larger decisions that drives intrinsic motivation. So does the *autonomy* to decide over how to perform one's own tasks. There is often nothing as demotivating as a manager interfering when there really is no need for it or, even worse, when that manager does not have the knowledge and understanding of the task that you have yourself. After all, you have done the task hundreds of times and your manager has not.

### Affiliation

Being part of something bigger does not only give meaning to work; it often also creates ties to other people in the organization, including colleagues, superiors and subordinates. Working, reaching goals and being successful together with others with whom one feels a strong bond may also be rewarding. A collective reward, as mentioned above, can often be used as a symbol to strengthen this feeling of working together towards common goals. *Affiliation* or kinship may be a strong motivator and is often present in successful organizations.

## The importance of self-determination theory

SDT evolved in the 1970s when researchers started to compare extrinsic and intrinsic motivation. Theoretically, SDT has mainly made an impression in psychology and to some extent in economics, but to a much lesser extent in business administration and management. However, the big break for these theories came when the American author, Daniel H. Pink, published his bestseller *Drive* in 2010. Pink can also be found on YouTube, where he talks about his book and as many as 17 million people have viewed one very interesting clip.[21] Not bad at all for a clip that relates to management control systems! As stated at the beginning of this chapter, SDT now seems to be *the* motivation theory among management consultants today. This is at least the case among the consultants that we meet, and we meet a lot of consultants. However, if and when SDT will have the same impact in practice as agency theory remains to be seen.

## Critique against self-determination theory

### Not in line with my experience

Many owners and top managers are aware of the critique against bonus systems resulting from research. However, many of them dismiss the critique with the argument that it is not in line with their experience. There is nothing strange about that, because most people tend to rely more on their personal experiences than on what they have read in a book. According to their experiences bonus systems are extremely powerful tools when it comes to creating commitment from managers, and their experiences seem more in line with agency theory than SDT.

There are several possible explanations as to why the views of practitioners and researchers often differ on this matter. One is, of course, that the practitioners are right and that the results found in research experiments are not the same as those found in real-life situations (we return to this below). Another possible explanation is that the present systems with bonuses attract a certain type of person, who is driven mainly by extrinsic rewards. But if this is the case, it could be argued that another type of person, who is driven more by intrinsic motivation, could have been even more motivated, more creative and more suited to the complex task it is, for instance, to be a manager.

---

[21] See RSA ANIMATE (2010) Drive: The surprising truth about what motivates us. Available at: https://www.youtube.com/watch?v=u6XAPnuFjJc (accessed 3 December 2019), or just search for 'Pink RSA' on YouTube.

***Real World Example:*** In an Australian survey[22] on the effect of incentive-based compensation on senior responsibility centre managers' performance, the researchers found that incentives do have a positive effect on performance, according to a self-rating survey carried out by the managers. However, this effect is present only among managers with a low organizational commitment and not among managers with a high organizational commitment. For the latter group – that is, managers who are committed to the organizations they work for – incentive-based compensation does not, according to them, have any effect on managerial performance.

A third possible explanation is that the positive outcomes of bonuses and extrinsic rewards are often more obvious than the negative ones. Let us say that the profit in a company has increased, but that this profit has resulted from fewer resources being put into R&D, marketing, HR, organizational development, and so on – savings that will have a negative impact on the company in the long run. The risk is, of course, that all the board of directors will remember is that profit increased because of the reward system and not the long-term negative effects it may have had.

### *The findings from experiments are not relevant in practice*

A problem with a lot of the experiments carried out in SDT research is that they are often performed with the help of American students, usually in psychology. One question is of course to what extent these results are generalizable for people in general. Would people from another culture, social group, age group or academic field behave the same way in the experiments as the psychology students?

Another critique against the relevance of the research experiments is that they all tend to involve rather small amounts of money, whereas top management compensation often involves quite significant sums of money. The critiques thus suggests that crowding-out effects appear only with rather limited amounts of money and not when it comes to top managers with substantial financial incentives.

This argument may actually to some extent be in line with SDT. Not in the sense that crowding-out effects do not appear, but if the extrinsic reward is big enough, total motivation may increase even if the intrinsic motivation is being crowded out. In this case the extrinsic motivation created by the substantial reward becomes so high that it is larger than the sum of the intrinsic and extrinsic motivation before the reward was introduced.

Still, some researchers set out to test the proposition that the crowding-out effect should not appear with more substantial rewards. As the Real World Example shows, they also tested the proposition on people that are very different to American psychology students.

***Real World Example:*** In order to test if the critique concerning experiments dealing with small amounts of money was justified, some American researchers went to Madurai in India.[23] The possibility to conduct experiments involving substantial amounts of money was, of course, limited in North America, but if they went to a rural part of India they could offer what were substantial amounts of money to the inhabitants living there. The experiments included a number of games that required skills, creativity and concentration. In group 1 the participants could earn about one day's pay, in group 2 they could earn about two weeks' pay and in group 3 they could earn almost five months' pay, if they reached the set-up targets. What the researchers found was that groups 1 and 2 performed about the same, while group 3 performed worst of all! In eight of nine tasks, higher rewards led to a worse performance. The results do not, of course, support the critique that the crowding-out effect and SDT are relevant only when using small rewards. Nor do they support the notion that they are relevant only to psychology students.

---

[22] Chong, V.K. and Eggleton, I.R.C. (2007) The impact of reliance on incentive-based compensation schemes, information asymmetry and organizational commitment on managerial performance, *Management Accounting Research,* 18: 312–42.

[23] Arieli, D. (2008) What's the value of a big bonus? *New York Times,* 19 November. Available at: http://www.nytimes.com/2008/11/20/opinion/20ariely.html?_r=0 (accessed 13 June 2013).

## Comparing the two theories

Looking at these two theories, it is striking how different they are and how different their implications for the design of incentive systems are. Whereas one strongly promotes the use of individual performance-related financial incentives, the other points to substantial risks with this type of incentive. It does seem like the two theories in most situations are so contradictory that they would be impossible to combine. Still, the question one inevitably faces is, of course, which one do you apply (or would like to apply) when designing incentive systems? As stated before, the answer depends on who you ask and research does not supply a definite answer. Some aspects to consider when trying to decide which theory to rely on are discussed below.

### What type of work task are we talking about?

Whether the work tasks that the incentive system is intended for are simple, repetitive and boring, or complex, changing and challenging is of great importance. In the first case, the two theories do not really differ and extrinsic rewards do seem like the way to go as far as the incentive system is concerned. But in the second case the theories are totally contradictory and the confusion remains.

However, even if the work tasks are simple, repetitive, boring and extrinsic rewards do seem like the only choice, this is not always the only alternative. In fact, what many organizations have done in the name of lean management and agility is to have made simple and boring work tasks more interesting. This may have been achieved by decentralizing more responsibility to the employees, broadening the work tasks, and implementing teamwork and job rotation. In many organizations this has led to significant increases in motivation among employees whose work traditionally has been regarded as simple and boring.

### What kind of people are we talking about?

In some professions financial incentives are considered as natural as basic salary and it may very well be unthinkable for most people in that profession to accept a job without some kind of performance-related incentive. It is, of course, very hard for an organization to compete for highly qualified people in such a profession if it does not offer incentives.

***Real World Example:*** The successful Swedish bank Handelsbanken does not apply individual and performance-based incentives for its top managers, because it does not believe in their motivating effects. In fact, this is something that is strongly rooted in the Handelsbanken management philosophy. However, despite this strong belief, it does apply this type of incentive for the financial analysts working in the bank. The reason for this is also very simple: it cannot attract the financial analysts it wants if it does not offer financial incentives.

This argument relates to one of the roles of compensation mentioned at the beginning of the chapter, namely that compensation is a way to give credit to people and that some people are very competitive when it comes to this credit. This type of person probably appreciates individual performance-based incentives much more than, for instance, a basic salary. However, this also highlights that it is important for the employer to think about what type of people the organization needs. Is it for instance very competitive people or people that cooperate well? The type of incentive system chosen may have a significant influence on the kind of people who want to work in the organization and how the culture develops.

### What do you believe in?

Do you believe economists or psychologists know best about human motivation? Do you believe more in the clearer agency theory that to a large extent is logically derived, or do you believe in the more complicated SDT that is based on experimental research? Or perhaps a third theory? Part of the success of agency theory is probably due to its rather simple and clear logic. This does not mean that SDT lacks logic, but its logic is definitely more complex and probably harder to understand. When it comes to empirical support for the theories, SDT has a solid foundation in experimental research. There is, of course, also a lot of research that supports agency theory, but it tends to support the notion that extrinsic rewards matter, rather than that *only* extrinsic rewards matter.

Another important question is: Which of the two sets of basic assumptions do you believe in? To what extent are these theories really different? Agency theory starts from assumptions that in Chapter 3 are referred to as 'the economic model of human behaviour'. According to this model, people are mostly rational, make the right decisions and base these decisions only on what will benefit themselves the most. SDT is more based on what in Chapter 3 is referred to as 'the psychological model of human behaviour'. According to this model, people have bounded rationality, which means that they to some extent are rational and to some extent also irrational. The psychological model of human behaviour, just like the economic model, recognizes the importance of material needs, but emphasizes also other needs, such as social and emotional needs. People may, among other things, want to be accepted, liked or even admired. They may also want to feel a sense of belonging with other people and to find a meaning in what they do. This is why our display of these two theories is very helpful to understand where the opposing views on the importance of monetary pay for motivation come from. However, the developments in behavioural economics that we sketched in Chapter 3 also suggest that there is room for convergence between these views.

## Summary

Incentives is the part of a management control system in which even people who otherwise have no interest in management control systems show great interest. The topic has also received significant attention in research, including researchers from several fields. However, the research offers contradictory knowledge on the effects of incentives on motivation and performance.

Compensation may have several roles, such as attracting and keeping employees, as well as motivating the same employees to do a good job. Compensation may be in the form of a basic salary, short-term variable pay and stock options. But incentives may also include non-financial aspects like interesting tasks, challenges, meaning and kinship.

The most influential theory on incentive system design and motivation is agency theory. Agency theory is based on the notion that principals (often owners) and agents (usually managers) have diverging interests and that they act out of self-interest. Therefore, the interest of the managers needs to be aligned with the interest of the owners. Since it is very difficult for the owners to monitor the managers fully, this alignment needs partly to be accomplished through the use of incentive systems. These incentives should be designed in a way that makes it in the self-interest of managers to work hard to fulfil the interests of the owners. This often includes bonuses based on the performance of the company or responsibility centre, as well as stock options.

Agency theory has been extremely influential, but has also received much criticism. It is often criticized for being based on a number of assumptions that are wrong, and some even claim that it has contributed to the abolishment of morals in business. Also, critiques claim that financial incentives tend to increase earnings management and immoral behaviour, rather than decrease them. Modern approaches to agency theory, which include *moral costs*, mitigate some of these accusations.

Self-determination theory (SDT) does not only bring in intrinsic motivation, but also focuses a great deal on how it relates to extrinsic rewards and motivation. One important notion in SDT is that extrinsic rewards tend to crowd out intrinsic motivation, often to the extent that total motivation actually falls when an extrinsic reward is introduced. The corresponding effect that total motivation increases when an extrinsic reward is removed is also often the case. However, an extrinsic intervention may also crowd in intrinsic motivation if it is perceived as supporting.

The crowding-out effect does not appear if the extrinsic reward is unexpected, not linked to performance or if there is no intrinsic motivation to start with. The crowding-out effect depends on two psychological processes: impaired self-determination and impaired self-esteem. An incentive system in line with SDT may, therefore, focus more on creating intrinsic motivation when possible. This may include working with aspects such as creating interesting assignments, competence development, employee involvement and autonomy, as well as affiliation.

SDT has been far less influential than agency theory, but has experienced quite a growing interest lately. It has also received criticism for not being in line with people's experience and for its notions being valid only when using small rewards.

The two theories are quite different and seem impossible to combine. Agency theory has its roots in economics and offers a rather straightforward and attractive logic. SDT is based in psychology and offers a much more complicated logic. Agency theory is based on the assumptions behind the 'economic model of human behaviour', which are that individuals are perfectly rational and only act out of self-interest. SDT is based on what we might call the 'psychological model of human behaviour', where individuals are only partly rational and driven not only by self-interest and material needs, but also by social and psychological needs such as being accepted and liked by other people.

## Suggested additional reading

Bareket-Bojmel, L., Hochman, G. and Ariely, D. (2017) It's (not) all about the Jacksons: testing different types of short-term bonuses in the field, *Journal of Management*, 43(2): 534–54.

Charness, G. and Grieco, D. (2019) Creativity and incentives, *Journal of the European Economic Association*, 17(2): 454–96.

Deci, E.L., Olafsen, A.H. and Ryan, R.M. (2017) Self-determination theory in work organizations: the state of a science, *Annual Review of Organizational Psychology and Organizational Behavior*, 4: 19–43.

Ghoshal, S. (2005) Bad management theories are destroying good management practices, *Academy of Management Learning & Education*, 4(1): 75–91.

Jensen, M.C. (2000) *A Theory of the Firm: Governance, Residual Claims, and Organizational Forms*. Cambridge, MA: Harvard University Press.

Matsumoto, Y., Yamagishi, T., Li, Y. and Kiyonari, T. (2016) Prosocial behavior increases with age across five economic games, *PLOS One*, 11(7): e0158671.

# Case 10.1

# Triathlon guy and golf girl*

**by Göran Nilsson**

Some of the best examples you hear as a teacher actually come from students and we are going to look at two of these examples here. Both come from the sports world and both illustrate how motivation actually can decrease when one might expect it to be higher than ever before.

The first example is from many years ago, when a student came up to me after a lecture on rewards and motivation. Actually, the lecture dealt with more or less the same things as this chapter does. First, the student said something along the lines of: 'It was interesting for once to hear about a theory that actually seems to correspond with reality!'

Then he explained that he was very into triathlon and trained very hard. For a long time he had done this without any kind of financial support and paid for everything out of his own pocket. However, recently he had managed to find a sponsor, which changed this situation. Now he had, among other things, been able to buy a new and expensive bike. But, to his surprise he did not find the training as much fun as it had been before he secured the sponsor. Previously, he never had any problem finding motivation to go out and exercise every day, since he enjoyed it so much. Now it was not as much fun as it used to be and he sometimes actually had to force himself to go out and practise.

The other example is more recent and comes from an essay on motivation by another student. This time it deals with a girl who loved to play golf. She started to play golf at a young age and she played a lot with her friends. She got better and better at it and eventually she got very good. Her real break came when she secured a scholarship that made it possible for her to go to an American school where she could combine golf with her studies. She was very encouraged by this scholarship because not only was it confirmation of how good she was, but it also made it possible for her to do what she loved most.

She enjoyed the time at the school and her playing improved to the extent that she eventually decided to go professional. Now her dream had really come true! However, she could no longer play golf just for the fun of it – now she had to play to put bread on the table. She had to play for prize money and sponsorship contracts. Unfortunately, she also soon realized that she did not enjoy the playing any more – the fun was gone. Her playing also started to deteriorate and eventually she quit her life as a golf pro.

## Questions

1. Have you ever experienced that your motivation has decreased when you would think that it would increase since things have become more important or the reward has increased?
2. Why do you think this happened in the examples above or in your own example(s)?
3. Do you think that we can prevent this from happening in these situations? How?

---

* This case was written by Dr Göran Nilsson, Uppsala University.

# Case 10.2

# Rome-Work*

**by George Kominis and Alvise Favotto**

From her window Carla Bedin watches the sunset over the Imperial Forums, on a muggy evening at the end of August. With a tired and troubled look, she has just finished a long meeting with Franco Monti, the chief controller of Rome-Work, where they discussed the financial performance of recruitment agencies in that wobbly third quarter of 2008.

Rome-Work had opened its doors as provider of commercial staffing in the early 2000s, in the aftermath of the liberalization of the Italian recruitment market. Since those days, the recruitment and staffing sector had grown steadily in Italy, and was structured around a few international players already established in other European countries and some local providers normally specialized by geographical area or industrial sector; Rome-Work is one of the latter. In just a few years, it had moved from opening a few offices in the city of Rome to having more than 70 recruitment agencies across central and southern Italy and the islands. Rome-Work offers a comprehensive line of temporary work solutions, including permanent, temporary and contract recruitment, as well as workforce selection, training and outsourcing.

Carla had joined the company five years earlier as chief financial officer, with almost a decade of experience in the retail sector; it was because of her that Rome-Work adopted the planning and budgeting systems currently in use. More recently, she had been one of the key advocates of the introduction of a performance-related reward scheme for branch managers. Indeed, branch managers – those in charge of local recruitment agencies – were offered a bonus tied to their agency's ability to meet or exceed budget targets in terms of gross margin. Under this scheme, managers who reach their semester gross margin objective receive a bonus payment calculated as a percentage of their base salary for that semester. A scale, depending upon branch performance in excess of the target, allows bonus payments up to 20 per cent of base annual salary. While performance assessment takes place on a semester basis, bonuses are given out in cash form at year end. The annual bonus represents a key feature of the reward package offered to branch managers and its generosity had certainly helped Rome-Work in attracting and retaining talented managers in an industry sector with a historically high employee turnover.

So far, senior management at Rome-Work has firmly held control over the setting of budget targets for branches, which are deliberated and revised on a semester basis. The rapid expansion of the business and relatively short tenure of most branch staff convinced Angela Bergamin, the managing director, of the need to maintain close oversight on the budgetary process. So far, the results had proved her right: the annual turnover had grown steadily by an average 11 per cent over the last four years, and even for 2008 and 2009 the estimates were positive although not as rosy as in the past. And that was exactly Carla's concern.

Earlier, in their meeting, the chief controller had reported that more than 60 per cent of the recruitment agencies were likely to miss their budget targets for the month of August. For some of them it was the fourth month such targets had been unmet. Branch managers, Franco continued, were on the warpath: they had long lamented that second-semester objectives were way too challenging and, on several occasions, they had called for a revision of performance targets to reflect the changed environment. The results of the employee opinion survey, showing a mounting dissatisfaction with the reward package early that year, were still fresh in Carla's mind.

---

* This case was written by Dr George Kominis and Dr Alvise Favotto, Adam Smith Business School, University of Glasgow.

Carla is going to discuss this issue with the managing director and the human resource director the next day, yet she can foresee Angela's position already: several times Angela had reiterated the need to stick to budgetary objectives even in tough times. As much as in the past, budgetary targets were deemed to be challenging yet achievable and, given the current economic contingency, the gross margin objectives were even more significant for recruitment agencies. Carla returns to her desk, glances over the spreadsheet on her screen and starts preparing for the meeting ahead.

## Questions

1 Critically evaluate Angela Bergamin's intention to stick to the budgetary objectives set at the beginning of the second semester of 2008.

2 What is your overall evaluation of Rome-Work's bonus system for branch managers? Looking ahead, what changes (if any) would you recommend Carla Bedin to propose?

# Case 10.3

# Eaglet Plc: the phone call*

**by George Kominis and Alvise Favotto**

What follows is an excerpt from a telephone conversion between Michael Shields, head of the Edinburgh division of Eaglet plc, and Frida Irvine, director of the sales department at the same division.

**Frida Irvine:** *Hi Michael, Frida speaking. Err . . . I would like to discuss the possibility to transfer back to Dundee. Moving forward, I see myself best in that branch.*

**Michael Shields :** *Oh Frida, that's surprising. My understanding was that you moved to Edinburgh for good. May I ask why? I thought you were getting on well with the team here and, to be honest, your performance has been excellent so far. This year you are on track to smash that bonus target again!*

**Frida:** *Don't get me wrong, I like the team and all here and I really appreciate your guidance especially on the customer side. And I love the city! It's just we are working very long hours and that isn't always easy . . .*

**Michael:** *I see, Frida. Yet, Dundee is unlikely to need a sales manager in the near future. Let me discuss this with Edwin and James.*

**Frida:** *That wouldn't be a problem. I guess I could just start again in the team and go from there.*

**Michael:** *Let me think about it, Frida. Perhaps we can have another chat about this next week?*

Frida had worked at Eaglet since its early days, initially as a junior sales assistant. When she joined, the business was expanding rapidly, transitioning from a local garage in Glasgow to the countrywide car dealer it would soon become. Frida remembered those times with fondness; there were plenty of chances for her to learn the craft of car dealership – from understanding the desires of clients to liaising with the service team and making sure sold cars were equipped effectively. Frida's commitment to the firm had been recognized a few years back when, in 2011, she became the director of sales of the Dundee division. At the time Eaglet had just established itself in Dundee, and Frida was tasked with designing and shaping

* This case was written by George Kominis and Alvise Favotto from the Adam Smith Business School, University of Glasgow.

the sales department from scratch. James Shields, the head of the Dundee division, gave Frida full autonomy to build the local sales team and identify policies that could meet the needs of such a challenging market. Frida personally selected and mentored a cohesive, mutually supportive group of salespeople. Based on her extensive experience in the motor trade, she identified ways to ensure the acquisition of high-quality used cars, and developed synergies with the service and repair department to make sure that sold cars were prepped to a high standard. Frida went on to establish guidelines for competitive pricing and discounting that soon granted Eaglet a solid 'value for money' reputation among local customers. Her hard work and dedication certainly paid off: in 2014, when she left to become head of sales in Edinburgh, Dundee's ROI stood out as the highest among the Eaglet divisions. Frida's capabilities and dedication were well known among the top management of Eaglet. For this reason, her request to move back to Dundee just two years after she had arrived in Edinburgh had taken Michael Shields by surprise.

## Eaglet's history

Eaglet plc has roots dating back to 1990, when Edwin Shields, a car engineer and a graduate of the School of Mechanical Engineering of the University of Glasgow, decided to open a local independent garage for the repair and service of automobiles in the West End of Glasgow. Up until the mid-1990s Eaglet was successfully managed by Edwin himself. In those early years, the company worked hard to establish itself in the local market, and by the end of the 1990s, Eaglet had come to be known for its provision of a quality service at reasonable prices. Strong links with the local community and a willingness to respond to the specific needs of the ever-demanding West End market contributed to the healthy financial position and steady organic growth of the company.

Competition in the mid-2000s, however, became more intense in the automobile repair and service sector, with major car manufacturing companies starting to offer, through their car dealers, services for the cars they produced and sold. These market-leading automobile manufacturers had all the latest technology to provide car service and repair to meet increasingly sophisticated customer preferences and demands. Such competitive forces in the industry encouraged Edwin Shields to diversify his business. In 2005 Eaglet decided to expand its operations to the sale of all makes of used cars, and the repair and service of new, used and external customers' cars. Initially Edwin attempted to manage the company centrally as before, but with the company essentially entering two related but distinct markets, he started to become overwhelmed with the coordination and management of transactions of increasing complexity and volume. Finally, in mid-2006, Edwin decided to bring in to the company his two brothers, Michael, who was also a graduate of the School of Mechanical Engineering of the University of Glasgow, and James, who had a background in marketing and a degree from Strathclyde University Business School. Immediately upon their arrival, Edwin decided to delegate some of his decision-making responsibilities: Michael and James had now distinct managerial roles and clearly defined responsibilities over the car service and car sales divisions, respectively, with Edwin overseeing both divisions as well as heading the finance, marketing and warehouse departments. In effect, Michael and James were expected to make the day-to-day operational decisions for their respective divisions, but report directly to Edwin, whose main responsibility lay in the overall strategic decision making, the coordination of the activities, and the setting and continuous reconciliation of the subgoals of the two divisions, so that the company as a whole could achieve its overall objectives.

In the late 2000s, the company continued to grow steadily. Eaglet presented an average annual 10 per cent increase in sales and profit between 2007 and 2008, and at the beginning of 2009 the Shields brothers decided to acquire another garage in Edinburgh and expand the company's operations. During that period, the company organization continued to reflect this emphasis on the distinction between car sales and car services, with Michael managing car service in both the Glasgow and the Edinburgh branches, and James looking over car sales in the two subsidiaries. Following the company's geographical expansion to Dundee through another acquisition in 2010, however, it started to become clear that the exposure of the company to an increasing number of product and geographical markets, and the increasing volume in the differentiated activities, necessitated new changes in Eaglet's organizational and decision-making structure. Both Michael and James had started complaining that they were finding it increasingly difficult to manage their respective divisions in Edinburgh and Dundee from Glasgow, mainly due to the critical distance they had from the branches, and the amount of information that needed to be collected, analysed and processed in a timely fashion for each of the firm's product/geographical markets. Edwin, although not openly admitting it, was also under pressure. The distance of the company's headquarters from the realities of the marketplaces in Edinburgh and Dundee was making the planning and coordination of the company's activities increasingly difficult. The number of hierarchical levels had increased, and as a result the number of people, communication channels and amount of information that needed to be managed for the coordination of internal transactions of increasing complexity and volume had also increased. Although the financial position and performance of Eaglet seemed to be still unaffected, the Shields brothers were concerned about the long-term implications of what was felt to be 'uncontrolled growth' for the company. Finally, in December 2011, they decided to discuss their concerns with a team of business consultants, and after the consultation exercise and two weeks of deliberations between them, they decided to transition to a multidivisional structure. The new multidivisional firm would be structured around three separate, fairly self-contained, independent operating organizational units (the Glasgow, Edinburgh and Dundee units), each of which would contain an appropriate set of functional departments that would enable it to respond, in a considerably independent manner, to the particular operational demands of the specific market in which it operated (see Exhibit 1).

**EXHIBIT 1** Eaglet divisional structure

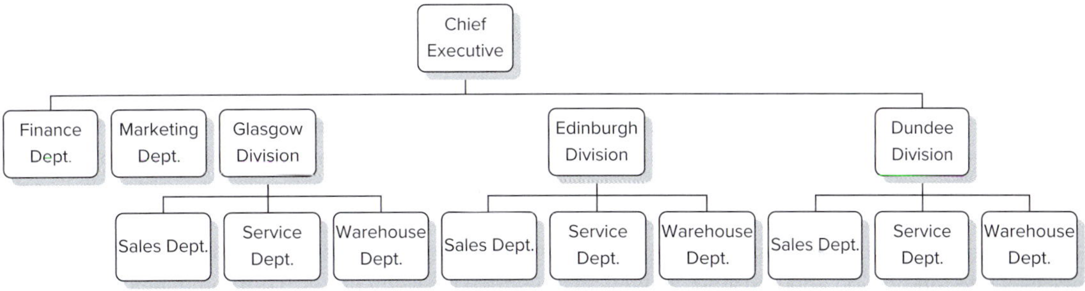


The predominant feature of this new multidivisional arrangement was that the organizational subunits would be now allowed a level of autonomy and independence to operate and determine their own strategies, subject to some loose accountability to the centre. Michael and James, who would be heading the Edinburgh and Dundee divisions, respectively, would now essentially run semi-autonomous profit centres, although the development of the strategic, long-term plans and the consequent allocation of resources among the divisions for the attainment of these plans would remain with the Glasgow division, which would be headed by Edwin. Each division would have a complete set of functions, with dedicated functional managers in charge of the division's sales, service and warehouse departments, and adequate level of decentralized authority so as to be responsive to the needs of its local market. The intention was for Michael and James, now closer to the internal and external environment of their respective units, to be able to make better and more timely decisions.

The main advantage of this new decentralized, multidivisional organizational form was that, while allowing Michael and James to deal with the short-term planning and coordination of the day-to-day operations of the Edinburgh and Dundee divisions, it was expected to allow Edwin to focus on the strategic planning and decision making for the company overall. Based at Eaglet's headquarters in Glasgow, Edwin would be able to concentrate mainly on the formulation of strategies that would assure the survival and future success of the company. At the same time, he was expected to manage all three divisions by exception, monitoring their progress in their respective markets through quarterly reports that he would receive from James and Michael.

## Eaglet's balanced scorecard

Soon after Edwin assumed his new executive role, he realized the need for a system that would enable him to monitor the performance of both the overall company and that of its divisions and divisional managers. Although he was determined to allow Michael and James the level of independence necessary to run their divisions autonomously, he still felt the need for a system that would provide him with periodic information about what was happening in Edinburgh and Dundee.

Almost by chance Edwin came across the idea of the balance scorecard (BSC) while attending an industry workshop. An information system like this, he thought, would provide information that would allow both himself at the centre, and James and Michael in their respective divisions, to keep an eye on those key success factors that were critical for the implementation of the firm's strategy and the achievement of its objectives. After discussing the issue, the Shields brothers decided to contract a major consultancy firm to design a BSC tailored to the needs of Eaglet. After three months of consultations with the Shields brothers, the company's functional managers running the sales, service and warehouse departments in the Glasgow, Edinburgh and Dundee divisions, and selected focus groups of engineers and sales representatives across the company, Eaglet's BSC was introduced to the company's top and middle managerial staff in May 2012 (see Exhibit 2).

## Key performance indicators

The BSC was to be conceived as an integrated framework of performance measurement based on a coherent set of key performance indicators (KPIs) that, together, would provide managers with a comprehensive view of the business from the four BSC perspectives. The process of translating Eaglet's vision and strategy into more specific strategic objectives, critical drivers and KPIs was coordinated by a team of consultants, and required input from Edwin, Michael and James, who were considered to have sufficient experience, knowledge of and familiarity with all the organization's functions and key processes.

The performance measures included in Eaglet's BSC were intended to incorporate an adequate balance between external measures relating to customers and internal measures relating to critical business processes and innovation and learning, as well as a balance between lagging outcome measures (reflecting results from past efforts) and leading indicators that would drive future performance. The financial perspective included four measures of importance to the shareholders. Divisional return-on-investment and divisional profit reflected an emphasis on short-term results, while disaggregated measures of revenue and costs for each function in each division signalled the need to keep track of the determinants of divisional profit. The customer perspective identified customer satisfaction as the main KPI, which was complemented by two lagging indicators, relating to the retention and further growth of Eaglet's customer base. The internal business perspective recognized the distinction between Eaglet's two main types of products and sources of income: car sales and car service. Measures were therefore formulated to reflect the key success factors for service (speed and reliability of service, quality of spare parts used) and sales (speed of delivery). Finally, innovation and learning at Eaglet were seen to be driven by good training and high motivation of staff, which were expected to create the right environment for the development of new ideas and the retention of car service and car sales staff; as well as by the perceived quality of management running the different divisions and functions of the company.

On the whole, there was agreement among those involved in the consultation process that the BSC reflected relatively accurately the key dimensions that were essential for Eaglet's success. A conscious attempt was also made to devise KPIs that were quantifiable and objective, so that both those controlling and those being monitored through the BSC could place a reasonably high level of confidence on the reliability of the system.

**EXHIBIT 2** BSC proposal as discussed by the Shields brothers

| | Strategic objectives | Performance indicators | Year 1 | Target Year 2 | Target Year 3 |
|---|---|---|---|---|---|
| Financial | Turnover increase | Sales (of cars) per period | | | |
| | Cost reduction | % reduction in operating expenses | | | |
| | Increase divisional profitability | Divisional ROI | | | |
| Customer | Customer base growth | No. of new customers | | | |
| | Customer base retention | No. of returning customers/total no. of customers | | | |
| | Customer satisfaction | Post-sale (service) customer satisfaction | | | |
| Internal processes | Availability of spare parts (cars) | Response time for parts (cars) in days | | | |
| | Quality of spare parts (cars) | % defect rate: no. of cars returned/ total no. of cars | | | |
| | Speed of service | Average time a car spends in the garage/no. of cars serviced per day | | | |
| | Quality and reliability of service | % of repeated jobs/total jobs on a yearly basis | | | |
| | Speed of car delivery | Average time to deliver a prepped car | | | |
| Learning and growth | Quality of management leadership | Top manager's report (per assessment rating) | | | |
| | Staff motivation and morale | Employee survey; overtime stats | | | |
| | Skilled workforce | Training budget; participation in training | | | |

## BSC implementation

Business consultants proposed an interactive approach to set specific and time-bound targets for each of the performance measures included in the BSC. In a series of yearly meetings involving relevant employees and functional managers, divisions were to be asked for realistic target estimates for all the KPIs in the BSC over a three-year period. These estimates were to be broken down on a yearly basis so as to ascertain progress towards long-term objectives. Targets would be subsequently submitted for authorization to Edwin, Michael and James, who would discuss them with supporting information and give their approval or propose changes.

This approach was deemed effective in light of the key role functional managers were to play in Eaglet's three divisions. As Edwin put it on many occasions:

> *No question about it, the dedication and professionalism of our functional managers is key to the success of the company. We know that our target clientele in the different cities we operate in have specific needs and demands, so we need good managers that will respond to these needs in a timely fashion. A good manager has knowledge of the market in which they operate and, if we are to be successful as a company, they should be allowed to make most of the day-to-day decisions about their area of responsibility.*

The BSC design proposed by the business consultancy was aimed at engaging divisional and functional managers in an open discussion around KPIs. Four years down the line, Edwin was still impressed by the ease with which staff had become accustomed to the BSC. Certainly, this was, at least in part, due to the clear links between BSC targets and incentive system they had strived to establish since the BSC idea came about. Nonetheless, at first, the authorization phase had been quite stressful and time-consuming for the Shields brothers, while over time the divisions had become more autonomous in undertaking the prep work, hence putting the final seal on the BSC targets was much simpler. 'Divisions have progressively developed their own outlook on the BSC,' Edwin observed in a recent board meeting. 'Take Edinburgh and Dundee; their approach is really quite different.' Indeed, in his attempt to establish Eaglet in Dundee, James found the BSC and its various KPIs could help managers organize their work by providing a 'vision' – that is, a sense of direction towards which one would want to strive. In addition, functional managers were actively encouraged to contribute to the continual improvement of the local BSC by proposing changes to the measurement of KPIs that could better reflect their understanding of the area of business. Michael in Edinburgh had a distinctly different approach. For him, KPIs were expressions of clear-cut business priorities and as such not really negotiable. He would work very hard with divisional managers to set future targets on the basis of past performance, especially for the key areas such as sales and customer retention. 'Both Edinburgh and Dundee have been quite successful financially,' Edwin reflected, 'hence both approaches must have their own merits.'

## Reward scheme

The issue of the incentivization of Eaglet's divisional and functional managers was debated between the consultancy team and the company's owners. There was discussion about whether the cost of designing a competitive reward system would outweigh the benefits it would have for the motivation and performance of managers and employees across Eaglet's organizational structure. In the end, the decision was made to delegate the decision regarding the need for incentives to Eaglet's divisional managers, who were in the best position to assess the necessity for the design of an incentive scheme and the costs associated with it. To support this process, the consultancy team put together a benchmarking report that provided details of the reward schemes typically found in companies of the same size and in the same industry as Eaglet.

Michael's decision to invest in the design of a performance-related reward system for the functional managers of the Edinburgh division surprised only a few in the company. In collaboration with the consultancy team, Edinburgh's management designed and implemented an incentive scheme that aimed to gain commitment to the wider organizational goals and the more specific targets set for the division within the BSC. Edinburgh's incentive scheme included a range of rewards, some allocated on the basis of a manager's individual performance, some dispersed on the basis of the company's overall performance, others simply deriving from the occupation of the managerial post. In detail, the scheme comprised the following components:

1 *An annual cash bonus award:* This is essentially a performance-related reward administered to functional managers in relation to their individual performance in two areas: customer retention (car service/car repair) for service managers, and car sales revenue (second-hand cars) for sales managers. The bonus is meant to be distributed at year end, on the basis of the managers' ability to meet their respective yearly targets in the aforementioned performance dimensions. It is typically given out in cash form, and its size is determined on the basis of the schedule shown in Exhibit 3.

**EXHIBIT 3** Cash bonus scheme

| | |
|---|---|
| Meeting the target | £3,000 |
| 10% in excess of target | £4,000 |
| 20% in excess of target | £5,000 |

2 *An executive stock options scheme:* Similar to the annual cash bonus, this is a performance-related reward scheme, which applies, however, only in cases of really outstanding individual performance. According to this scheme, functional managers who have demonstrated an exceptionally high performance throughout the year are given the option of an additional 1,000 company shares, which are provided at a reduced price. These executive stock options are awarded to functional managers only in exceptional cases and the decision for the award lies with each division's head in consultation with the others.

3 *A benefits scheme:* To ensure a competitive compensation package, Eaglet offers to all its functional managers a range of fringe benefits, which include:

- Private health cover
- A company car
- Subsidized holidays to predetermined destinations.

Some of these fringe benefits (such as the private health cover) are contributory – that is, they are provided at some cost to the manager; while for others (such as the company car) Eaglet assumes the full cost of the benefit.

At the time the reward system was designed, the consultancy team and Edinburgh's management had intense deliberations around the idea, to openly communicate information about attained performance and assigned rewards for each manager eligible for the scheme. Michael had certainly been the one who most vehemently supported a 'full transparency' approach. For him, transparent disclosure on performance and rewards within Eaglet would have maximized the motivational potential of the incentive scheme. As he said in one of meetings: 'This will hopefully develop trust in the system and reinforce the perception that what you get is what you deserve.'

Although one could see reason in Michael's position, Edwin and James thought that his approach could potentially backfire, particularly given the lack of clarity regarding the criteria on the basis of which some of the rewards were to be distributed. In the end, Michael's decision was that only information relating to the receipt of the cash bonus would be made available to all staff, while secrecy about all other rewards would be maintained until further notice.

## The email

Michael pondered on his phone conversation with Frida for a little while. He certainly did not want to lose one of his best members of staff just two years after she had moved to Edinburgh. He had been working hard with the various departments in his division to clearly communicate the objectives and priorities set in the BSC and, since Frida moved from Edinburgh, Michael had met her a few times to convey his customer expansion strategy.

This was totally out of the blue: as soon as Frida had moved to Edinburgh, they had what Michael considered a set of very constructive meetings, in which he had stressed the importance of the sales figures for the division and indeed for Frida's own compensation. He was sure that Frida had the skills to go at least 10 per cent beyond target and reach the target required for the bonus, and he advocated for her to put her best effort in. He decided to write a note to Edwin and James to touch base and let them know about the issue. Among other things, he wrote:

> *I spoke to Frida Irvine today. She enquired about moving back to Dundee, suggesting this has to do with her working time schedule. My impression is that this is a motivational issue. We all know Frida's commitment to Eaglet – her performance has been outstanding since day one. I am seriously considering putting her forward for the exec stock option scheme at the end of this year. What do you guys think?*

## Discussion questions

1 Assess the differences between the way in which the BSC is used by the Dundee and Edinburgh divisions.

2 Critically evaluate the design of the reward scheme Michael Shields has adopted to complement and reinforce the implementation of the BSC.

3 What is your evaluation of Michael Shields' proposal for bringing Frida Irvine back 'on board'? What changes (if any) would you recommend the Shields brothers to propose?

### APPENDIX 1 Extract from 2015 Annual Report of Eaglet plc

| | Glasgow | Edinburgh& | Dundee | Consolidated |
|---|---|---|---|---|
| Revenue (car sales) | £10,000,000 | £9,000,000 | £5,000,000 | £24,000,000 |
| Revenue (car service) | £2,000,000 | £1,450,000 | £800,000 | £4,250,000 |
| Total revenue | £12,000,000 | £10,450,000 | £5,800,000 | £28,250,000 |
| | | | | |
| Less variable expenses | | | | |
| Sales dept expenses | £2,800,000 | £2,000,000 | £1,900,000 | £6,700,000 |
| Service Dept. Expenses | £1,750,000 | £1,500,000 | £500,000 | £3,750,000 |
| Warehouse dept expenses | £900,000 | £600,000 | £300,000 | £1,800,000 |
| Total variable expenses | £5,450,000 | £4,100,000 | £2,700,000 | £12,250,000 |
| | | | | |
| Less corporate overheads | | | | |
| Accounting & finance | £100,000 | £100,000 | £80,000 | £280,000 |
| Marketing & advertising | £250,000 | £220,000 | £200,000 | £670,000 |
| Depreciation | £800,000 | £750,000 | £600,000 | £2,150,000 |
| Other administration expenses | £100,000 | £80,000 | £70,000 | £250,000 |
| Total corporate overheads | £1,250,000 | £1,150,000 | £950,000 | £3,350,000 |
| | | | | |
| Divisional profit before tax | £5,300,000 | £5,200,000 | £2,150,000 | £12,650,000 |
| | | | | |
| Capital employed | £70,000,000 | £45,000,000 | £15,000,000 | £130,000,000 |
| Corporate cost of capital | 10% | 10% | 10% | |

## APPENDIX 2 Rewards preference questionnaire

It is well accepted that employees can be found to enjoy a wide range of rewards provided by the companies in which they work for the services that they deliver. Different companies, however, provide different rewards for different positions, whereas, at the same time, employees themselves have varying preferences for the different rewards they are offered.

Please consider the rewards below and rate them on the basis of how important (desirable) each of them is to you. Circle on the rating scale provided the number that represents your own evaluation of how important (desirable) each job outcome–reward is. If you think that a reward is extremely desirable (important) to you, you would circle number 7. If you think that a reward is moderately important (desirable) to you, you would circle number 4, and so on.

For each job outcome, circle only one number.

| Form of Rewards | Rating Scale |
|---|---|
| a. Cash Bonus | 1 2 3 4 5 6 7<br>unimportant / moderately desirable / extremely desirable |
| b. Stock Options | 1 2 3 4 5 6 7<br>unimportant / moderately desirable / extremely desirable |
| c. Profit Sharing | 1 2 3 4 5 6 7<br>unimportant / moderately desirable |
| d. Private Health Care | 1 2 3 4 5 6 7<br>unimportant / moderately desirable / extremely desirable |
| e. Company Car | 1 2 3 4 5 6 7<br>unimportant / moderately desirable / extremely desirable |
| f. Subsidised Holidays | 1 2 3 4 5 6 7<br>unimportant / moderately desirable / extremely desirable |

## APPENDIX 3 Rewards preference questionnaire: summary findings

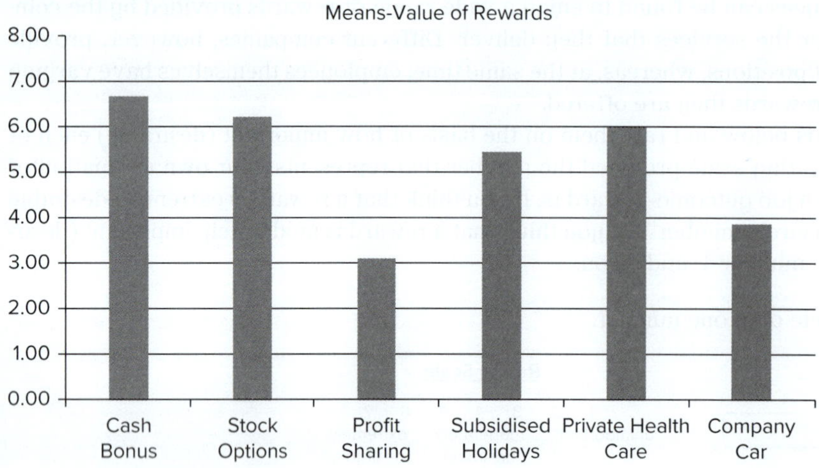


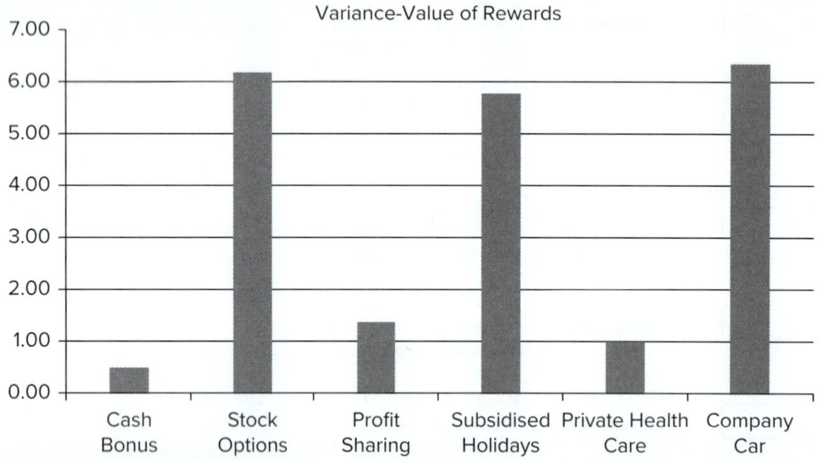


# Case 10.4 What is CEO talent worth?*

**by David F. Larcker**

## Introduction

The topic of executive compensation elicits strong emotions among corporate stakeholders, practitioners and observers. On the one hand are those who believe firmly that chief executive officers in the United States are overpaid. They cite as evidence the large and growing disparity between total pay

* Professor David F. Larcker, Usman Liaqat and Brian Tayan, Stanford University, prepared this material as the basis for discussion. 

granted to CEOs and the compensation of the average worker.[1] Their solution is the encouragement of more shareholder activism (primarily through proxy measures, such as say on pay) to communicate concerns to companies and induce a voluntary reduction in compensation levels or stricter performance-based features that more closely align compensation to financial and operating results. Some go so far as to suggest that CEO compensation be regulated at a fixed multiple of the average worker's pay.

On the other side of the issue are those who believe that chief executives are paid the going fair-market rate. They argue that if compensation levels are high among the largest US corporations, this is simply a reflection of the demands of a position that requires considerable time, skill and attention. They advocate continued disclosure on compensation size and structure so that market forces correct the mispricing of talent in situations where it arises.

Researchers have taken various approaches to evaluating whether CEO pay levels are appropriate. Gabaix and Landier[2] measured the relation between CEO compensation and company size. They found that although CEO pay increased sixfold between 1980 and 2003, the market value of the companies these CEOs managed also increased sixfold during this period. They concluded that 'the rise in CEO compensation is a simple mirror of the rise in the value of large US companies since the 1980s'. Similarly, Kaplan and Rauh[3] compare the growth rate of executive compensation to the growth rate of other highly paid professionals, such as hedge fund managers, private equity managers, venture capitalists, lawyers and professional athletes. They find that pay among these groups grew by roughly the same order of magnitude during the period 1994 to 2005. They conclude that CEO compensation has increased due to market forces that contribute to general wage inflation among highly paid professionals, and that extreme compensation growth has not been limited to the business world.

However, it is important to remember that demonstrating a correlation between executive compensation and firm size or performance does not mean that pay levels themselves are appropriate. It might still be the case that CEO pay itself is either too high or too low on average.[4] The only way to make a determination is to measure whether the total compensation received is commensurate with the value of services rendered. To do this, stakeholders need to understand (1) the value drivers of the organization, (2) the impact that the executive has on these value drivers, and (3) the percentage of value created that should be appropriately offered as compensation for performance. While this is simple in theory, it is exceptionally difficult in practice.

## Performance and compensation

The value drivers (or key performance indicators) of an organization include the financial and non-financial metrics that reflect the current and future performance of the company (see Exhibit 1). They might be generic in nature and applicable to most companies (such as revenue growth, profit margin and return on invested capital) or specific measures that are relevant to a particular industry or line of business (such as research and development pipeline productivity or on-time delivery rates).

---

1 Although precise figures vary depending on the sample and methodology employed, one recent estimate pegs this ratio at 343 among a sample of companies in the S&P 500. See AFL-CIO Executive Paywatch, available at: https://aflcio.org/paywatch/highest-paid-ceos (accessed 16 June 2020).

2 Gabaix, X. and Landier, A. (2008) Why has CEO pay increased so much? *Quarterly Journal of Economics*, 123(1): 49–100.

3 Kaplan, S.N. and Rauh, J. (2010) Wall Street and Main Street: what contributes to the rise in the highest incomes? *Review of Financial Studies*, 23(3): 1004–50.

4 Further complicating the matter is the fact that reported compensation figures in the proxy do not reflect what an executive has *earned* but instead combine cash compensation received plus a fair value estimate of the expected value of equity compensation granted. If performance does not meet expected results, the actual value of equity grants will be considerably lower than their original fair value. For a full discussion of this issue, see: Larcker, D.F., McCall, A. and Tayan, B. (2011) What does it mean for an executive to 'make' $1 million? CGRP-22, 14 December. Available at: https://www.gsb.stanford.edu/faculty-research/publications/what-does-it-mean-executive-make-million (accessed 9 July 2020).

**EXHIBIT 1** Measures to determine corporate performance (2008–2010)

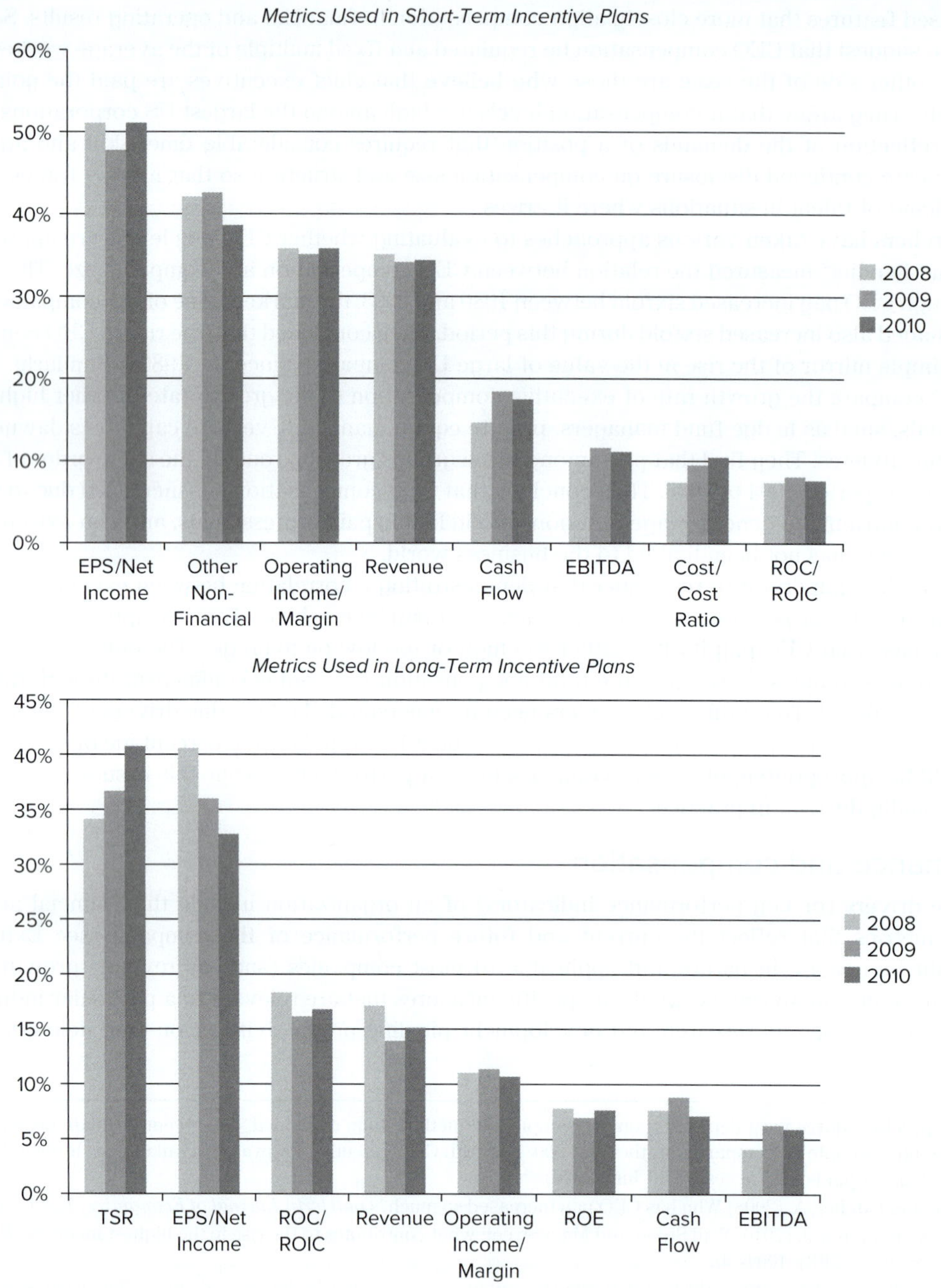


Sample includes the most prevalent metrics in short- and long-term incentive plans for CEOs at S&P 1500 companies. Note that non-financial performance metrics are not a common feature of long-term plans.

*Source:* CEO Performance Metrics. Equilar. June 2011.

Similarly, they might be readily quantifiable (such as product defect rates) or more qualitative in nature and therefore requiring proprietary methods of measurement (such as customer and employee satisfaction). It is the responsibility of management and the board of directors to identify the value drivers that are most critical to the success of the corporate strategy. This process is best accomplished through rigorous statistical testing that demonstrates a proven correlation between the relevant metric and changes in corporate value.[5] The valid performance indicators of the company then serve as the basis for measuring management performance and awarding compensation.

The challenge for the board is to determine what level of compensation to offer to chief executive officers for the achievement of specific performance objectives. This can be an extremely difficult task, not least because it is not always easy to determine how much corporate value creation should be attributable to the efforts of a single individual.[6] Although a considerable number of theorists and practitioners have argued that CEOs play a critical role in affecting firm performance, the empirical research on this issue is mixed. Thomas (1988) finds that CEOs are responsible for only 3.9 per cent of the variance in performance among companies, while Mackey (2005) finds that the impact is much greater: as high as 29.2 per cent.[7] The view that board members have on this issue will have a substantial impact on what they view as reasonable CEO compensation (see Exhibit 2).

**EXHIBIT 2** Compensation levels of the highest-paid CEOs (2010)

| Name | Company | Reported Pay | Disclosed performance metrics | 5 Yr TSR v. Peers |
|---|---|---|---|---|
| Phillipe Dauman | Viacom | $84,469,515 | Operating income, free cash flow, strategic initiatives, ratings,cost reduction, corporate goals, compliance, policy objectives | −3.5% v. −7.8% |
| Ray Irani | Occidental Petroleum | 76,107,010 | TSR, net income, EPS, governance, functional and operating accomplishments, health and safety, diversity, organizational development | 168% v. 56% |
| Lawrence Ellison | Oracle | 70,143,075 | Pre-tax profit growth | 78% v. 16% |
| Leslie Moonves | CBS | 56,859,166 | OIBDA, free cash flow, ad revenue growth, leverage, contract negotiations, Nielsen ratings, content, other strategic and operating metrics | −9% v. −8% |
| Richard Adkerson | Freeport McMoRan | 35,294,023 | Operating cash flow, return on investment, safety performance | 109% v. 26% |

[5] For a detailed review of this process, see: Larcker, D.F. and Tayan, B. (2011) Organizational strategy, business models, and risk management. In *Corporate Governance Matters: A Closer Look at Organizational Choices and their Consequences*. New York: FT Press, Chapter 6; and Ittner, C.D. and Larcker, D.F. (2003) Coming up short on nonfinancial performance measurement, *Harvard Business Review*, 81(11): 88–95.

[6] Sometimes it is even difficult to compute the value created by a firm. For example, does a one-year change in market capitalization validly reflect the change in value creation over the period?

[7] Thomas, A.B. (1998) Does leadership make a difference in organizational performance? *Administrative Science Quarterly*, 33: 388–400. Mackey, A. (2005) How much do CEOs influence firm performance – really? *SSRN*, 1 September: 42pp. Available at: http://ssrn.com/abstract=816065 (accessed 6 June 2020).

| Name | Company | Reported Pay | Disclosed performance metrics | 5 Yr TSR v. Peers |
|---|---|---|---|---|
| Michael White | DirecTV | 32,932,618 | Net subscriber growth, CFBIT, OPBDA, revenue, EPS, churn, ARPU, acquisition cost, market share, new products, customer loyalty, cost management, talent development | 196% v. −1% |
| John Lundgren | Stanley Black & Decker | 32,570,596 | EPS, cash flow multiple, TSR, return on capital | 49% v. 22% |
| Robert Iger | Walt Disney | 28,017,484 | Operating income, return on capital, cash flow, EPS, content quality and innovation, brand building, talent development, integration | 55% v. −5% |
| Brian Roberts | Comcast | 28,155,865 | Operating cash flow, free cash flow, revenue growth | 34% v. 36% |
| Alan Mulally | Ford Motor | 26,520,515 | Profit before taxes, cash flow, cost management, market share, product quality, functional and technical excellence, teamwork, modelling values | 112% v. 19% |

*Note:* Reported pay represents the fair value of compensation granted during fiscal year 2010, excluding change in pension value. Disclosed performance metrics include those discussed in the annual proxy. Five-year total shareholder return (TSR) as reported in the annual proxy or form 10-K, or calculated by the authors for those companies that did not disclose these figures. In some cases, the tenure of the current CEO is less than five years.

*Source:* Equilar, Securities and Exchange Commission, Yahoo! Finance.

Finally, the board must determine the percentage of value creation to award in compensation. Although there are no agreed-upon standards, observation of compensation practices among other talent pools might serve as a guide. For example, the CEOs that manage private equity owned companies receive on average 5.4 per cent of the equity upside (in the form of stock and options).[8] A-list actors in Hollywood receive $10 to $30 million per film, plus 10 to 20 per cent of gross profits.[9] Music artists receive 8 to 25 per cent of the suggested retail price of an album, a $0.08 performance royalty when a song is played live or broadcast, plus a percentage of the gross profit generated on tour (see Exhibit 3).[10] Similarly, in setting compensation for CEO talent, the board should target a payout in relation to performance or value creation. In this regard, the structure of the compensation contract will be as important as its overall size.

---

[8] Kaplan, S.N. and Strömberg, P. (2008) Leveraged buyouts and private equity, *Journal of Economic Perspectives*, 23(1): 121–46.

[9] Wikipedia (n.d.) Film budgeting. Available at: https://en.wikipedia.org/wiki/Film_budgeting#:~:text=Film%20budgeting%20refers%20to%20the,and%20production%20of%20the%20film (accessed 6 June 2020).

[10] Obringer, L.A. (n.d.) How music royalties work, *How Stuff Works*. Available at: http://entertainment.howstuffworks.com/music-royalties.htm (accessed 6 June 2020).

| Name | Company | Salary | Cash bonus | Stock | Options | Other | Total |
|---|---|---|---|---|---|---|---|
| Phillipe Dauman | Viacom | $2,625,000 | $11,250,000 | $41,833,309 | $28,620,000 | $141,206 | $84,469,515 |
| Ray Irani | Occidental Petroleum | 1,191,667 | 32,975,000 | 40,250,000 | 0 | 1,690,343 | 76,107,010 |
| Lawrence Ellison | Oracle | 250,001 | 6,453,254 | 0 | 61,946,500 | 1,493,320 | 70,143,075 |
| Leslie Moonves | CBS | 3,513,462 | 27,500,000 | 7,999,982 | 14,868,000 | 2,977,722 | 56,859,166 |
| Richard Adkerson | Freeport McMoRan | 2,500,000 | 10,000,000 | 5,818,492 | 15,420,000 | 1,555,531 | 35,294,023 |
| Michael White | DirecTV | 1,448,077 | 4,000,000 | 14,690,396 | 12,497,196 | 296,949 | 32,932,618 |
| John Lundgren | Stanley Black & Decker | 1,208,433 | 4,342,800 | 25,347,725 | 1,255,500 | 416,138 | 32,570,596 |
| Robert Iger | Walt Disney | 2,000,000 | 13,460,000 | 7,359,060 | 4,399,991 | 798,433 | 28,017,484 |
| Brian Roberts | Comcast | 2,800,761 | 10,922,968 | 5,308,989 | 5,917,380 | 3,205,767 | 28,155,865 |
| Alan Mulally | Ford Motor | 1,400,000 | 9,450,000 | 7,492,493 | 7,499,993 | 678,029 | 26,520,515 |
| Jeffrey Bewkes | Time Warner | 2,000,000 | 14,420,000 | 5,519,056 | 4,073,646 | 124,129 | 26,136,831 |
| Samuel Palmisano | IBM | 1,800,000 | 9,000,000 | 13,319,450 | 0 | 1,061,231 | 25,180,681 |
| Gregg Steinhafel | Target | 1,500,000 | 5,301,000 | 8,017,549 | 3,189,299 | 5,501,346 | 23,509,194 |
| David Farr | Emerson Electric | 1,187,500 | 2,200,000 | 19,081,600 | 0 | 474,865 | 22,943,965 |
| Wesley Bush | Northrop Grumman | 1,334,615 | 3,037,500 | 8,349,848 | 7,155,028 | 2,272,297 | 22,149,288 |
| Howard Schultz | Starbucks | 1,280,804 | 3,500,000 | 10,499,986 | 6,220,559 | 231,664 | 21,733,013 |
| William Weldon | Johnson & Johnson | 1,851,154 | 12,043,200 | 2,773,851 | 4,713,177 | 254,436 | 21,635,818 |
| Kevin Sharer | Amgen | 1,748,846 | 3,635,000 | 8,306,025 | 6,691,367 | 756,895 | 21,138,133 |
| Rex Tillerson | ExxonMobil | 2,207,000 | 3,360,000 | 15,465,375 | 0 | 443,921 | 21,476,296 |
| Michael Szymanczyk | Altria | 1,300,000 | 14,002,500 | 4,975,000 | 0 | 495,910 | 20,773,410 |

*Note:* Total compensation excludes changes in pension value and non-qualified deferred compensation.

*Source:* Equilar.

**EXHIBIT 3** Compensation levels among highly paid professionals (2010)

| *Highest-paid actors* | |
|---|---|
| **Name** | **Earnings** |
| Leonardo DiCaprio | $77 million |
| Johnny Depp | 50 million |
| Adam Sandler | 40 million |
| Will Smith | 36 million |
| Tom Hanks | 35 million |
| Ben Stiller | 34 million |
| Robert Downey Jr | 31 million |
| Mark Wahlberg | 28 million |
| Brad Pitt | 20 million |
| Robert Pattinson | 20 million |
| *Highest-paid actresses* | |
| **Name** | **Earnings** |
| Angelina Jolie | $30 million |
| Sarah Jessica Parker | 30 million |
| Jennifer Aniston | 28 million |
| Reese Witherspoon | 28 million |
| Julia Roberts | 20 million |
| Kristen Stewart | 20 million |
| Katherine Heigl | 19 million |
| Cameron Diaz | 18 million |
| Sandra Bullock | 15 million |
| Natalie Portman | 8 million |
| *Highest-paid musicians* | |
| **Name** | **Earnings** |
| U2 | $195 million |
| Bon Jovi | 125 million |
| Elton John | 100 million |
| Lady Gaga | 90 million |
| Paul McCartney | 67 million |
| Black Eyed Peas | 61 million |
| Justin Bieber | 53 million |
| Toby Keith | 50 million |
| Usher | 46 million |
| Taylor Swift | 45 million |

| Highest-paid athletes | |
|---|---|
| **Name** | **Earnings** |
| Tiger Woods | $75 million |
| Kobe Bryant | 53 million |
| LeBron James | 48 million |
| Roger Federer | 47 million |
| Phil Mickelson | 47 million |
| David Beckham | 40 million |
| Cristiano Ronaldo | 38 million |
| Alex Rodriguez | 35 million |
| Lionel Messi | 32 million |
| Tom Brady | 31 million |

*Source:* The world's most powerful celebrities, *Forbes* (2010). Available at: http://www.forbes.com/wealth/celebrities.

## Questions

1 Executive compensation is a topic that is filled with much rhetoric ('nobody is worth $20 million per year') but somewhat less critical analysis ('maybe some CEOs are worth $20 million per year while most others are not'). Why isn't more of the discussion focused on the actual observable impact that a CEO has on value creation and the percentage of value that should be offered for these efforts?

2 Why don't we commonly see *explicit* calculations of actual value creation by the CEO in proxy statements? Is it not possible for boards to perform this calculation? If not, how does the board make rational decisions regarding pay levels?

# Case 10.5

# The Pitfalls of achieving cost efficiency in the creative organization*

**by Jan Pfister**

## Background: AnimationCorp and commercial pressure

AnimationCorp is a medium-sized animation company with about 250 employees, operating in the animated feature film industry. Its business model builds on the development of commercially distributed sales of animation movies. The company produces its own films and also offers the production of specific movie sequences and features to external parties, which are often based on the use of its proprietary technology. The company has won several awards for its innovative productions. The success and

* This case was written by Dr Jan Pfister, University of Turku.

longevity of the company depends on nurturing an organizational environment that stimulates creativity, and is simultaneously aligned with meeting timely goals and achieving commercial success. The mission statement of AnimationCorp is 'to make a positive difference in people's lives by offering uplifting and humorous entertainment that inspires everyday life'. However, the mission is not simply to produce any commercially successful movie but to ingrain a message that supports suppressed minorities, elevates humanity or protects the planet. The company builds this mission on the values of diversity, tolerance, openness, risk-taking and ambition, but also responsibility and ethics.

Despite high returns at the box office in the past few years, the company has struggled to repeat its success with its last two major productions. This has raised concerns among the shareholders and the executive team about how the company should combine its creative culture with a stronger focus on cost-efficiency and profitability.

## A culture of creativity

AnimationCorp was well-known for its easy-going and trendy culture. Although long working hours and continuous pressure to meet production deadlines were the norm, working at AnimationCorp was prestigious, and for most employees the dream job. The culture was collaborative and empowering, where employees felt free in their artistic expression. Employees were encouraged and celebrated if they came up with new, sometimes even strange and bizarre, ideas. Although the company was not one of the big powerhouses of the industry, it was well-known for its unique culture that valued employees and their development.

Employees were attracted by the mission statement, which gave them purpose and a belief that they could contribute to changing the world for the better. Independent of whether their role was technical, artistic or administrative, most of the employees expressed such strong idealism. When they developed and produced a new storyline, they had endless debates on how to position specific elements of the story to raise awareness of critical humanitarian problems, or potentially change and influence the mindset of the audience to promote the corporate mission.

There was a strong team spirit and belongingness among employees. They were proud to be working for the company and were motivated to work together with a highly selected crowd of idealists, artists, technically versed nerds and out-of-the box thinkers. The working hierarchy was flat, and the executives (including the two founders) and senior managers were easily approachable.

The founders lived the values of the company and set an example. The tone at the top was to combine ambition with fun and creativity. They were aware of the commercial pressure to produce new movies that became box-office hits. Employees were encouraged to take risks and explore unconventional ways, even if those would sometimes not work out. The founders promoted learning, demanding from every employee and from the organization as an entity to continuously improve.

The building of AnimationCorp expressed its mission of being a place of creativity and inspiration. There were many co-working spaces and places to mingle, and it resembled a children's playground rather than a corporate office. There was colourful designer furniture and interior decoration. The faces of several famous artists had been sprayed on the wall by a graffiti artist, and many encouraging slogans aligned with the corporate mission were visible on the walls and doors. Food and beverages were provided free of charge. Every team had its own breakout areas and various recreational activities were available. Employees had flexibility in terms of their working times and dress code. It was also part of the culture to invite people from different fields – including celebrities, sportspeople, politicians and others – to inspire employees with new ideas. Employees were generally eager to help one another, and the workplace was a place of inspiration and creative mingling, despite high workloads and pressuring deadlines. New movies and achievements were celebrated, and some of the parties were even legendary.

Employees were paid better than industry standards but not as high as the big powerhouses of the industry. They typically received a flat salary, which was negotiated with the team leader. The team leader had some flexibility based on the skills, experience and expectations of the employee. However, compared with the high workloads, the salaries were still rather low. People worked in this industry because they had a passion for this type of creative work and were intrinsically motivated. Bonus payments were unusual but could be paid to the entire workforce of a commercially successful production, split among them depending on their role. But it was not a bonus culture. Those employees who repeatedly proposed key ideas for productions would be promoted. The executives were particularly careful in making sure that those who rose through the ranks were the ones who stimulated and fostered creativity. Ultimately, this was the life-blood of the creative industry.

## Hiring procedures

Due to its reputation in the industry and its well-known corporate culture, the company attracted a large pool of candidates for each open position. Based on the founders' values, new hires were expected to be not only talented but well versed in their technical ability and/or understanding of how to deliver a compelling storyline. The selection criteria depended on the particular position (i.e., creative director, technical director, production, administration), but typically candidates with a good reputation in the industry and highly educated in animation were selected. The company expected the candidates to be fully dedicated, even slightly perfectionistic, despite the commercial pressure to produce new movies to tight deadlines. Potential employees were expected to be motivated, self-driven by new ideas and the creative work. If they had to be told what to do, it was difficult for them to succeed at AnimationCorp. In recent years, the hiring process at AnimationCorp had become more professional, with several interviews and hurdles, but always based on the original values of the founders. The company offered development programmes and regular training, depending on the skills and duties of the employees.

## Financial turmoil, fierce market competition and the plans of the new CFO

However, AnimationCorp has made a few mistakes in the most recent past. Crucial for the company's success was to combine the experience of senior creative directors with the inspiration of young talents. For the creative process, it was particularly important that every employee had an equal say in the idea-generation process. In its endeavour to give young talents freedom and a chance to develop, executives decided to give them projects with only very limited involvement of experienced and previously successful movie directors. This had led to two recent productions that did not meet the financial expectations of the shareholders, with one of them ending up being a financial disaster. Coincidentally, there had also been a shift in the industry structure, with some new companies joining the industry, creating fierce market competition and increased commercial pressure in order to avoid a deeper financial turmoil.

Investors put pressure on the CEO to take action. As a result, AnimationCorp replaced two creative directors and its CFO. The new CFO had a background in a large consulting firm, and was focused on cost-efficiency and creating value by pursuing lean management practices. In one of his first strategic meetings with the CEO and the newly formed executive team, he presented his vision to cut down one-third of the operating cost within the next two years. This initiative entailed (1) learning more about the tasks of different roles in the organization, (2) focusing on the value-adding tasks and cutting down waste, and (3) ultimately defining rules of efficiency as guidance for employees in order to perform well and receive bonuses. The CEO and others ultimately supported this idea, even though they were at first reluctant and expressed some major concerns about undermining the organization's strength – its creativity. However, the new CFO was a persuasive person and promised that the reduction of the operating cost would give the company, at least for a short period of time, some room for manoeuvre that could be used to introduce new movies and regain traction. After some debate, he received the mandate to cut down the operating cost. Executives agreed that it would be kept a secret that some employees were likely to lose their jobs. The latter was to be presented as a project to achieve cost-efficient growth.

## Phase 1: Tracking work and designing new metrics for cost efficiency

Soon after he received the mandate, the CFO assembled a meeting with selected members of his staff. These people would form the performance measurement and management (PMM) team. This newly formed team started drafting a new dashboard that could be used to measure the productivity and output of the entire organization, and break down the data to the individual level. Their aim was, in the first instance, to track and measure individual tasks and identify different employee profiles. The PMM team wanted to find out how well people understood their tasks, what value different tasks would create for the company and how the tasks would add up to the team and company-level performance. The PMM team created an app, the aim of which was to make it relatively easy for employees to report their tasks and the amount of time they worked on them. They also planned to connect the time measurement to a watch that employees could carry and easily track their time per task. The PMM team was interested in how much time employees worked effectively, meaning performing tasks versus spending time on breaks and mingling, on social media or in more administrative meetings that did not directly correspond to their actual strategically important work. The PMM team would then get a better understanding of how the different tasks related to the strategic goals and how interventions into employee behaviour should be undertaken.

The new dashboard would provide a tool for senior executives to have a complete overview of the productivity of each employee. Over time, the tracking should entail all the data that an employee produces (i.e., email, correspondence, documents), projects that are signed off, revenue that is generated and time spent at the workplace.

The implementation phase started by introducing the new dashboard to the team leaders. The latter had to persuade their team members to keep track of their tasks during the first pilot phase of three months. The PMM team also explained to the team leaders that this tracking system was important to ensure time and money were spent optimally and ensured the survival of the company. The time-tracking app made it possible to save several core activities and would allow employees to immediately keep track of their tasks while carrying them out. At the end of each day, the new tool provided a diagram that showed the different tasks and how much time had been spent on them.

The CFO and the PMM team communicated to the employees that the art of finance and accounting is 'what you measure is what you get'. This, however, did not resonate well with the artistic people and their culture of freedom and expression: 'Do we really have to track what we are doing? This is big brother in reality!'

## Phase 2: Making entrepreneurs steer tasks and eliminate waste

The CFO and the PMM team argued that the new performance measurement system was misunderstood by the employees. From the perspective of the PMM team, performance tracking was supposed to empower employees. The goal was to create a culture where each employee felt like an entrepreneur who would sell their service to the company. In doing so, employees would naturally need to justify how specific tasks would contribute to the company's strategy, and why it was necessary to spend time on them. At the beginning of each week, the team leaders would receive from each team member an overview of all the tracked data from the previous week. The overview entailed the specific tasks and how much time was spent on strategically important versus less important tasks. The team leaders had to confirm the data and sign it off before it was accessible from the central database used by the executives and the PMM team for their analysis.

Based on the aggregated data, the PMM team learned about the different tasks in the organization and could rank them into strategic priorities. They realized that the employees had taken relatively long breaks and attended many meetings that were not directly relevant for their strategic work. The CFO, together with the PMM team, started to discuss strategies to reduce such wasted time. In turn, the employees struggled to note down when they gave creative input to neighbouring projects. The creative culture was built on cross-pollination (i.e., although employees would work in specifically formed team compositions for creative projects, they would still consult one another outside the current team structure). However, the CFO and the PMM team preferred that the employees would focus on their key performance indicators, which were related to their own projects. Although the PMM team was aware of the importance of mingling among employees as a way to stimulate creativity, they aimed to increase efficiency and create more order of how often this would happen. They defined the rule that each employee could claim strategic credit for helping other projects, but not more than two hours per month.

## Phase 3: Ranking the 'entrepreneurs' and weeding out low performers

After half a year of tracking data, and making interventions and adjustments in the behaviour of employees, the CFO and the PMM team were comfortable with the data. It could now be used to more actively reduce cost and focus on value creation. To do so, the PMM team introduced the 'value-creator tag' – the aggregated data and a newly introduced monthly assessment by each team leader (in addition to the weekly sign-off) was now used to rank employees into one of three value-creator categories: top, standard and low.

Team leaders were astonished about this new performance regime. They were essentially forced to rank their team members on a monthly basis. How should they do this? They were not assembly workers but creative thinkers! Many team leaders argued that they hired their team members because they were excellent workers with different skills who would complement the team and could not be ranked. They had different characteristics and made different contributions to the team, each valuable in their own way. However, the PMM team played the 'cost-cutting card' and insisted on the necessity of these performance evaluations to secure the survival of the company. Behind closed doors, the CFO and the PMM team discussed that the company should focus on and nurture the top performers, tolerate or improve the standard performers and let go of the low performers. While senior executives and the PMM team aimed to keep the purpose of those performance evaluations undisclosed, employees were quick to realize the real intentions.

## The escalation

Employees' resistance grew. They felt increasingly micromanaged and monitored. They also had a feeling that management was not honest about what they were doing. The executives and the PMM team seemed not to believe in their ability or willingness to work hard (but why on earth would one join an industry that was well-known for being low paid and creating high work pressure?!). Employees felt that they had to continuously spend time on justifying their existence, rather than being focused on creating valuable movies. It was as if the PMM team did not trust them, would not see that they were all hired as great performers. While in some teams conflicts between team members emerged about the measurements and the ranking, several teams started to systematically undermine the value-creator tag idea. They would do so by systematically alternating the low performers in the team so that all members would average in their performance over time. Frustration about the PMM team increased and the situation started to hamper employees' motivation.

Team leaders, creative directors and many others also increasingly complained about the conduct of the CFO. The situation escalated at a corporate event where the CFO got up on-stage to inform about the difficult financial situation and that further means were necessary to cut down cost. Employees started booing. While they understood the need for cost cutting, this performance regime undermined their creative culture, their motivation and the entire value why they chose to work in this industry. The CEO quickly understood the situation; he realized that he was about to destroy the creative culture of the company and would lose the trust of his people. He had to change the direction.

## Back to the roots, and the replacement of the CFO

The new CFO was dismissed after only 14 months. An interim CFO took control over the finances. As one of his first actions, he dissolved the PMM team. The interim CFO had worked for AnimationCorp in its early days and had its creative culture in his DNA. He took an entirely different approach to manage performance by combining the creative potential of the company with the situation of having limited resources. Instead of tracking employees' performance, he openly argued that each team should show how they could cut down their cost aligned with the company values. He argued that, while their culture would remain the same, one dimension had to be added to it: being creative with limited resources! Teams were challenged to find responsible solutions to produce movies with fewer resources. Letting people go had to be done in a responsible manner; if this was not possible, cost had to be saved elsewhere. Employees with the most creative solutions were praised at the monthly corporate events. Team leaders had to evaluate employees based on whether they brought up creative solutions to save cost while simultaneously contributing to creative projects.

## Regaining creativity and commercial success

The interim CFO turned around the atmosphere in the company. Although the company was still in a turmoil, employees took ownership of the situation, felt respected in their competence and could make the changes happen. When asked how they felt about the company, they expressed how much they loved to work for AnimationCorp. They believed in the mission and cared about its corporate culture despite being challenged with the financial situation, the need to work long hours and the constant pressure. But they would do so for the company, their workplace they were proud of, and to nurture their artistic expression. The company now also offered training in cost management so that different teams could take control of financial matters. Although it was difficult to make a creative crowd cost conscious, they were surprisingly inventive. For example, they created new open source platforms to integrate external people in the design and idea generation of movies. Doing so, they realized that working more with the outside stimulated the creative environment. They further stimulated such external co-creation through awards that were given to people if their idea went on to become a central part of a movie. Commercial success soon returned and the company thrived once again.

## Questions

1. Analyse the factors that facilitated intrinsic motivation of employees at AnimationCorp.
2. Analyse the factors that undermined, or even damaged, the intrinsic motivation of employees at Animation Corp.
3. Analyse the role and characteristics of different incentive systems (i.e., extrinsic motivators) in the case company. In your view, evaluate why some incentive systems worked better than others.
4. How did these incentive systems interrelate with other management controls in the company?
5. According to self-determination theory, employees need to feel supported in three basic psychological needs to be autonomously motivated. Which factors promoted competence, relatedness and autonomy at AnimationCorp?
6. Compare the case situation to another industry, such as banking, farming, technology or another industry you are familiar with. How important is intrinsic motivation in those industries?

# Chapter 11

# Risk management systems

## Learning objectives

After reading this chapter, you should be able to:

1. Explain the importance of risk management for organizations.
2. Discuss how risk management systems have become an important aspect of an organization's management control system.
3. Discuss and explain different theoretical and practical conceptions of risk.
4. Distinguish the logical steps in risk management and the concept of enterprise risk management.

## Real world vignette: Hudson's Bay

Management control systems aim to help organizations achieve their mission, goals and strategies. But what happens if, through some unforeseen event, things go completely differently than planned? The 2019–2020 pandemic caused by the COVID-19 virus is an example of an unforeseen event with a truly global scope, and consequences of a historic scale. Besides the many health and social effects on individuals and societies around the world, it has certainly had an enormous effect on the behaviour and performance of firms, governments and all types of organizations. Such an event is rightly labelled as an *act of nature* – that is, an event that cannot be categorized under the economic and competitive conditions that are a more regular source of risk. An example of the latter can be found in Wereldhave, a real estate investment company that was confronted by the rumour that one of its main tenants was about to abandon its operations in the Netherlands and terminate its lease with Wereldhave. Was the company well prepared?

*PRESS RELEASE (2 September 2019)*

**Wereldhave statement on media reports about Hudson's Bay**

Wereldhave has taken notice of recent media attention about the possible intention of Hudson's Bay Company (HBC) to close its operations in the Netherlands by the end of 2019. Hudson's Bay is a tenant at one of Wereldhave's properties, situated in the inner city of Tilburg. Hudson's Bay represents 1.2% of Wereldhave's gross rental income (as per 30 June 2019) and is the 10th largest tenant.

Wereldhave has not received any information from Hudson's Bay about potentially closing business at this location or terminating the rental contract. The rental contract with HBC Netherlands B.V. expires in 2037, with a Parent Company Guarantee provided by Canadian Hudson's Bay Company until 2027.

As Hudson's Bay earlier publicly announced to investigate a strategic move towards North America, Wereldhave has already been exploring several scenarios for the Tilburg property. It is situated on an A1-location in the sixth largest city of the Netherlands in terms of population, which provides a good perspective for multiple uses other than retail, such as offices, leisure, residential and student housing.

Wereldhave will inform the market in case there are material changes to the Hudson's Bay situation.

**About Wereldhave**

Wereldhave invests in dominant full-service centers for everyday life in larger provincial cities in northwest continental Europe. The area surrounding our centers will include at least 100,000 inhabitants within 10 minutes' travel time from the center.

We focus on shopping centers that strike a balance between convenience and shopping experience. With easy accessibility, products that cover all the daily shopping needs, a successful mix of international and local retail products and strong food anchor stores, our centers provide convenience shopping to accommodate a busy urban lifestyle as well as an ageing population.

We aim for an experience that goes beyond shopping, with restaurants, kids' playgrounds and high quality amenities in order to attract families - and keep them with us for longer visits.[1]

SHARE PRICE INFORMATION
WERELDHAVE

**Share Price**

| Symbol | Last | Change (%) | Bid | Ask | Volume | High | Low |
|---|---|---|---|---|---|---|---|
| WHA | 21.06 EUR | 0.00 (0.00%) | 21.04 | 21.06 | 60.512 | 21.12 | 20.52 |

| Open | Prev. Close | 52w High | 52w High date | 52w Low | 52w Low date | Updated |
|---|---|---|---|---|---|---|
| 20.66 | 21.06 | 31.54 | 04/11/2019 | 17.45 | 04/11/2019 | 04/11/2019 11:07 |

WERELDHAVE Comparision

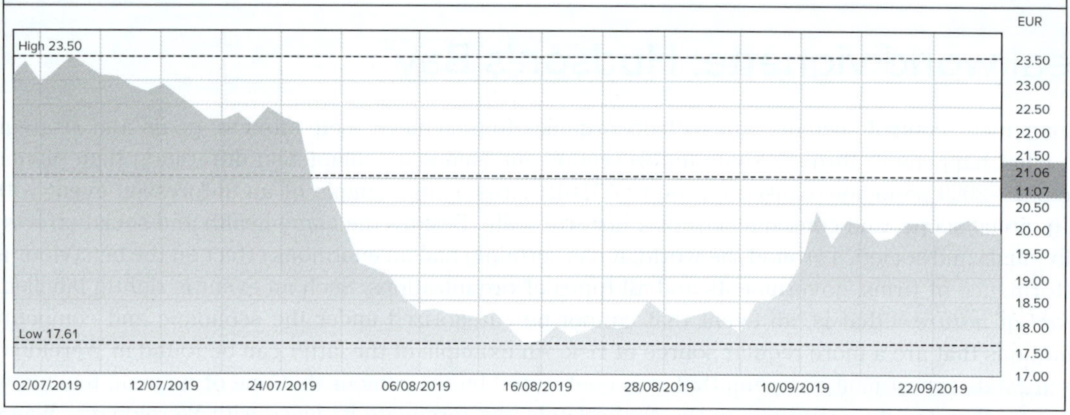


[1] Source: www.wereldhave.com (accessed 4 November 2019).

## Introduction

Management and entrepreneurship imply making a change in the world. Whether top management is considering new strategies or lower-level managers design new marketing policies and provide their employees with feedback, management means change. Entrepreneurship is the label that we like to give to an attitude that managers and employees, at all levels in the organization, may have to seize new opportunities in the organization's quest to achieve its mission, goals and strategies. Entering new geographical or product markets, investing in new subsidiaries and new plants, or taking over competitors – all involve innovations in the way the organization is run. These changes and innovations are mostly planned based on managerial expectations of the world. And as explained already in Chapter 1, management control systems have an important enabling role in this respect to support and strengthen an organization's innovative capabilities and work. But sometimes these managerial expectations are abruptly falsified by events that are either unexpected or have a larger negative effect on the organization than expected. These may threaten to throw the organization 'out of control'. To be able to counter such negative effects, organizations do well to pay attention to the risks of their operations. Risk management involves the continuous and constant awareness and attention of managers at all levels of the firm to the potential occurrence of developments that have a negative impact on the organization, and its chances to achieve its mission, goals and strategies. It also includes all the processes organizations implement to identify risks and mitigate their potential negative effects. Over time, various risk management practices have therefore firmly established themselves as an important aspect of a well-functioning management control system. They are increasingly seen as an ultimate way to stay 'in control'.

In a world that is uncertain, changing means taking risk. Risk and change are strongly connected. However, awareness of and attention to the risks of change and entrepreneurship have traditionally been coupled with change and entrepreneurship that are endogenous to the organizational strategies. When they are part of the execution of strategic, tactical and operational decisions taken by management, they are more likely to be taken into account in a more planned and controlled manner. Such executions develop over time, and allow management to apply the whole repertoire of management control practices to bring the change about. This was the case when the Canadian retailer Hudson's Bay Company decided to expand its investments in Europe by moving to the Netherlands in 2016, as featured in the Real World Example.

***Real World Example:*** 17 May 2016 at 2:00 am EDT

**Hudson's Bay Company advances strategy of organic growth with entry into the Netherlands**

- *Canada's premium department store banner Hudson's Bay and off-price banner Saks OFF 5TH expected to launch first stores in summer 2017 utilizing HBC's existing European platform.*
- *Plans to open up to 20 stores over the next 24 months.*
- *Expansion is expected to create approximately 2,500 store jobs and 2,500 construction jobs in key Dutch cities.*
- *Anticipates 300 million euros in capital investments, with majority to be funded by landlords.*

*TORONTO & COLOGNE, GERMANY & AMSTERDAM – (BUSINESS WIRE) – Hudson's Bay Company ('HBC' or the 'Company') (TSX:HBC) is pleased to announce that it is expanding its European presence with plans for up to 20 new stores in the Netherlands over the next 24 months. The Company has finalized and is in the process of finalizing long-term leases for select, sought-after locations. The first stores are expected to launch in the summer of 2017 and operate under the Hudson's Bay banner as well as the Saks OFF 5TH banner. The expansion into the Netherlands will build on HBC Europe's existing infrastructure and will utilize the same platforms, such as information technology, procurement and digital support.*

*Build-out of the stores will be funded primarily by the relevant landlords and HBC will invest in the operational aspects of the stores including merchandising and employees.*

*Source: Hudson's Bay Company Advances Strategy of Organic Growth with Entry into the Netherlands, 2020**

As a consequence of this impactful strategic change, Hudson's Bay entered into lease contracts with several real estate investment companies, among which was Wereldhave. Wereldhave leased one of its major locations in the Netherlands to Hudson's Bay. The decision to terminate the operations in this country hit the markets by surprise, as the Real World Vignette at the start of the chapter illustrates. For Wereldhave, this decision and the resulting changes clearly were exogenous to the company – that is, they formed an unfortunate event that Wereldhave could not control. The contract with Hudson's Bay was a source of risk for Wereldhave. In its Annual Report of 2018, Wereldhave showed awareness of this risk, as it understood the market pressures retail companies such as Hudson's Bay were facing (as highlighted in the Real World Example).

**Real World Example:** An extract from Wereldhave's Annual Report read as follows . . .

*Dear Shareholders – The rental markets show only modest prospect for rental growth at best, as retailers are facing increasing pressure to keep up their store performance. The real estate investment markets started to reflect this sentiment in 2018 with a low volume of property transactions.*

*Source:* Wereldhave Annual Report 2018, p. 81.

Risk management has attracted increased attention over recent decades. Whereas different operational definitions can be found across both the managerial literature and management practice, this attention underlines the perception of many that modern management control systems need to be designed and used to pay more and more explicit attention to risk. In particular, the risks stemming from outside the organization may be those that traditional management control systems consider out of scope. This is quickly changing and in today's world, many organizations view risk management as an important part of their management control systems.

In this chapter we address some of the principles of risk management. We do so by being agnostic about whether risk management is organized as an independent activity within firms, or whether risk management is seen as an integral part of the design and use of the organization's 'other' management control practices. Clearly, and as we will demonstrate, management control practices such as responsibility centres, budgeting and performance measurement share a lot of the underlying logic and process with risk management and could thus easily be integrated across the organization. Many organizations, however, choose to pay explicit and separate attention to the management of potential bad events, when their impact on performance can be large. The risk management process can then be considered as the part of a management control system that explicitly focuses on the occurrence of negative events.

The next section focuses on how managers evaluate risk, and why they may be unaware of risks or may have little incentive to focus on risks. The third section explores different types and sources of risk. The fourth section introduces some frameworks that organizations may apply to develop and instal firm-wide risk management systems. Throughout this chapter it should be noted that the distinction between other management control practices and risk management is a matter of focus, rather than principle. This means that organizations do well to realize that the design and use of management control systems include elaborate risk management work.

* https://www.businesswire.com/news/home/20160516006732/en/Hudson%E2%80%99s-Bay-Company-Advances-Strategy-Organic-Growth

# Behavioural aspects of risk management

## Risk

Even if, or maybe just because, the term 'risk' is used in everyday parlance in many matter-of-fact expressions, it is not easy to define it in terms that everybody agrees with. For many, the notion of 'risk' has mainly negative connotations. It is associated with unexpectedness, negative effects, loss of value or money and even fear. We are used to talking about risks as something that comes as a negative by-product of our choices and decisions. When we travel we might say that we fear the risk of being stuck in a traffic jam or missing our flight. Saying that we look forward to the risk of unhindered traffic or making it to the airport on time just does not make sense.

However, not in all quarters of mankind do we acknowledge the meaning of risk in such negative terms. For one thing, some people like to take risks. They enjoy the excitement of betting on sports, and seem to care little about the risk of losing money. These people seem to care less for predictable outcomes and take pleasure in exploring the unknown. Although such people may be in the minority, or although perhaps everybody does enjoy some risky excitement occasionally, it is important to know that in statistics and economics the notion of risk is in fact neutral.

## The statistical notion of risk

When we talk about risk in statistics we talk about it in the most neutral terms possible. In those terms, risk refers to the probability that a certain event or outcome will happen. Risk is, in other words, the chance of a certain outcome of importance, which can be positive or negative. We often talk about alternative terms, like chances or 'odds', which are often used to describe the probability that a certain, important, outcome or event will not occur. The statistical notion of risk is neutral and symmetric. It underlies the pure mathematical exercises to calculate the risks involved in a certain situation in which people face choices or decisions. For a variable of interest we can statistically describe its risk properties, for example by drawing a distribution of potential outcomes of this variable with associated probabilities. One could argue that the 'tails' of this distribution point to a deviation from being 'in control'. The best-known such distribution is the normal distribution (see Figure 11.1).

**FIGURE 11.1** The statistical representation of a risky variable

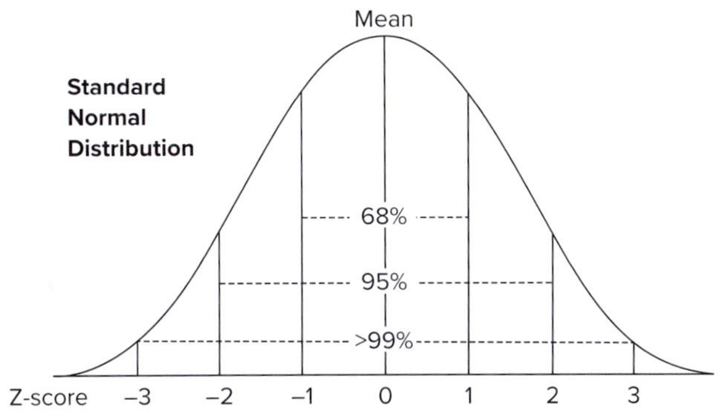

## The (behavioural) economic notion of risk

In economics, the use of statistical notions of risk has gained large acceptance. In particular, these notions have been used to describe and inform human choice and decision-making behaviour. Importantly, and as we have already discussed in Chapter 3, economists used the statistical notion of expected value to provide economic actors with a normative guideline. According to classical decision-making theory, actors should always try to take the option with highest expected value. Expected value, according to this guideline, can be calculated by multiplying the probability of various outcomes with the economic value of various outcomes. Actors were advised to take the option with the highest multiplied score.

However, as we saw at the start of this section, individuals often find it difficult to follow these guidelines. Rather than just focusing on expected value as the outcome of a mathematical calculation, which would mean they are indifferent about the probabilities, they can be meaningfully categorized as risk averse and risk seeking. Risk-averse individuals would settle for a less risky option with a lower expected value, whereas risk-seeking individuals would act in the opposite way. As discussed in Chapter 3, where we presented various models of managers, such risk preferences are an important factor not only for individuals, but they may also add up to becoming a norm of an organizational or national culture. Indeed, understanding how people interpret statistical risks in a non-neutral way has become an important undercurrent in economic thinking. In behavioural economics, these and other differences in human choice and decision making are attributed to whether people feel they are in a 'loss' situation or in a 'gain' situation. This is illustrated in Figure 11.2.

When people perceive themselves to be in a choice and decision situation in which they have options, they will weight those options in terms of the 'loss' the options are able to avoid. When they perceive themselves to be in a 'gain' situation, they will weight those options in terms of the 'gains' they can collect. Since perceptions can be influenced by irrelevant factors, this means that risk aversion and seeking, as well as other forms of strictly irrational behaviours, can be invoked by framing a decision as loss-avoiding

**FIGURE 11.2** Effect of 'gain' and 'loss' on risk taking

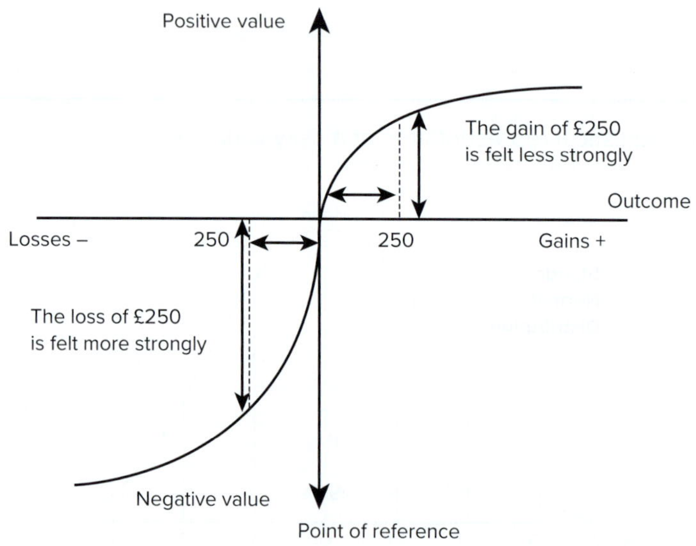

or gain-seeking. In addition to this behavioural asymmetry, many more behavioural tendencies seem irrational from a statistical-mathematical point of view. For example, people have a hard time applying even the very simple normal distribution curve. They neglect very small chances, but as the financial and corona crises suggest, events with a very small probability might have an enormous impact. Neglecting such 'tail risks' based on the low expectancy of their occurrence rather than on their huge potential economic impact *if* they happen is a standard error many people make.[2]

## The psychological notion of risk

The explanation of risk averse and risk-seeking behaviours of individuals in terms of such labels as irrationality and framing suggests that underlying such behaviours are rather fundamental psychological factors. Three such factors are worth mentioning.

First, people are capable of having all kinds of emotions that influence their behaviours, and also the way they perceive the world. Among such emotions, the emotion of *fear* is particularly strong. Fear is the feeling of danger that results from perceiving to be threatened by something or someone. Certainly, the most feared are threats that suggest a danger for survival. But the fear of negative evaluations, the fear of losing a job and the fear of losing status may also be strong drivers of behaviours that negate or overlook risk. Some of the findings from academic studies suggest that managers may have some of the following behavioural tendencies:[3]

- They focus on available information rather than complete or relevant information
- They focus on events that they recognize, from memory, rather than those that are new and relevant
- They focus on information that confirms their beliefs rather than challenge those beliefs
- They engage in automatic pre-filtering of information based on what comes first, rather than what is most relevant
- They may become subjected to positive and negative moods, that makes them overly optimistic or pessimistic, which stands in the way of neutral analyses.

## The managerial notion of risk

Finally, in addition to these analytical notions of risk, which form the basis of much academic analysis, of importance to the proper execution of risk management is the way managers talk about risks and deal with them. Notably, whereas many managers have some formal training in statistics, economics and perhaps psychology, the formal descriptions and definitions of risk in these disciplines is sometimes far removed from how managers experience risk. Some classical studies have shown that managers' position towards risk differs from the stated formal, academic, positions in at least three ways.[4]

First, managers use different definitions of risk. Most managers do not treat uncertainty about positive outcomes as an important aspect of risk. They do not see risk primarily as a probability concept, but rather as an event concept, in which the magnitude of the event is paramount. They also do not seek, as in statistics and economics, to have one overall quantitative risk figure.

Second, managers have various attitudes to risk, and more than just those of risk aversion and risk seeking in economic theory. They feel that risk taking is associated with job expectations and not so much driven by personality. Managers are very often aware of the emotional pleasures and pains of risk taking, which also provide a motivational effect.

---

[2] Taleb, N.N. (2007) *The Black Swan: The Impact of the Highly Improbable.* New York: Random House.

[3] Young, B.S., Arthur, W. and Finch, J. (2000) Predictors of managerial performance: more than cognitive ability, *Journal of Business and Psychology*, 15(1): 53–72.

[4] March, J.G. and Shapira, Z. (1987) Managerial perspectives on risk and risk taking, *Management Science*, 33(11), 1404–18.

Third, managers often deal with risk reactively. They are more inclined to react to negative events than prevent them, and often overestimate their ability to do so. This, sometimes inappropriate, feeling of control also leads them to simply reject unfavourable risk estimates.

### In sum

The diversity of ways in which academics and practitioners look at risk is helpful to illustrate the need for managers to have a good vocabulary to talk about risk and the tools to address risks. A main message is that there is an apparent discrepancy between our formal and theoretical understanding of risk in economics and the way managers define, relate to and address risk. By default, humans (and managers) are not good statisticians. They are rather poor in estimating chances, and show all kinds of biases depending on whether the 'risk' is positive or negative. Unexpected events may also give rise to emotions that aggravate these biases. These discrepancies, and the problems they may cause in having a full understanding of the riskiness of the organizational portfolio of activities, drive the development of formal risk management in firms. Risk management's main task may therefore be found in mitigating these behavioural and emotional tendencies, and replacing them with fact-driven and prepared responses. By addressing 'risk' in an explicit and more or less standardized way, it becomes one of the factors that managers can also handle in more or less similar ways. It becomes more visible and gets more attention. This is exactly the lesson that we should draw from disasters that hit companies that were formally unprepared. Risk management is therefore an important aspect of management control systems, given that such systems aim to help organizations achieve their missions, goals and strategies.

## Risk management

The risk management processes can be seen as consisting of four steps. These steps should, by and large, guarantee that risk management:

- Is beneficial in terms of costs and benefits
- Becomes a structured rather than haphazard and incident-driven exercise
- Is compatible with the design and use of the organization's other management control practices.

The four steps of the risk management process will be described in the text that follows. This description should not be understood in a full normative sense. That is, risk management – like other management control practices – is not the mechanical application of recipe-type prescriptions; rather, the four steps should be considered as the elements that the risk management process should entail. They thus point to important elements of risk management rather than portraying a formal, step-wise, exercise.

### Step 1: Assess the organization's risk appetite

In rather stark contrast with the formal descriptions of risk and risk-related behaviours of people, the notion of 'risk appetite' is a provoking but not yet very sharply defined term to stimulate organizations and their managers to think about risk in neutral terms. The question is not simply about what types and sources of risk can be identified (see below), but rather how much risk the organization believes it can carry. Table 11.1 invites organizations, and their managers, to enter into a dialogue about what kinds of risk-related behaviours are, or should be, typical to the organization, or some of its parts. One could argue that such an analysis provides some more depth to understanding when an organization feels 'in control' or rather 'out of control'.

**TABLE 11.1** Risk appetite scale

| Rating | Philosophy<br>Overall risk-taking philosophy | Tolerance for uncertainty<br>Willingness to accept uncertain outcomes or period-to-period variations | Choice<br>When faced with multiple options, willingness to select an option that puts objectives at risk | Trade-off<br>Willing to trade off against achievement of other objectives |
|---|---|---|---|---|
| **5. Open** | Will take justified risks | Fully anticipated | Will choose option with highest return; accept possibility of failure | Willing |
| **4. Flexible** | Will take strongly justified risks | Expect some | Will choose to put at risk, but will manage impact | Willing under right conditions |
| **3. Cautious** | Preference for safe delivery | Limited | Will accept if limited, and heavily outweighed by benefits | Prefer to avoid |
| **2. Minimalist** | Extremely conservative | Low | Will accept only if essential, and limited possibility/extent of failure | With extreme reluctance |
| **1. Averse** | 'Sacred' avoidance of risk is a core objective | Extremely low | Will select the lowest risk option, always | Never |

*Source:* Quail, R. (2012) Defining your taste for risk, *Corporate Risk Canada*, Spring: 24–30.

## Step 2: Define risk management responsibilities

Much like other management control practices, risk management is not typically embedded in an organizational structure that is independent from, or parallel to, the dominant hierarchical structure of the organization. Risk management should primarily be seen as an aspect of the job of all managers in the organization. However, also not unlike other management control practices that are facilitated by work done by an organization's controller department, many organizations decide to form a specific risk department to support the risk management process. This decision should be seen in the context of the more general discussion about the design and use of throughput controls, more specifically the organizational architecture as discussed, for instance, in Chapters 4 and 6. Typical job titles in such a risk department are risk manager and risk officer, which – much like operational or financial auditors – analyse processes and external (financial, operational and commercial) developments to assess the impact of risks on the organizations. But given the links between other management control practices and risk management systems, other organizations have chosen to bundle risk management in the portfolio of the CFO (chief financial officer) or COO (chief operational officer) as a function of the most dominant category of risks.

***Real World Examples:*** Here we take a look at examples from the United States, Europe and Singapore.

**United States**

***Risk analyst, ABC Financial Services***

ABC Financial Services is looking for an experienced risk analyst who will play a crucial role in mitigating risks for the company. The successful candidate will be evaluating risk from report monitoring, training personnel on risk issues, handling risk concerns, attending risk training, and forecasting risk for future mitigation tactics. The role is based in Sherwood, AR. [. . .]

***Market risk reporting analyst, UBS***

UBS has an exciting opportunity for a market risk report analyst to work in its market and treasury team. Main responsibilities include analysing risk sensitivities, monitoring risk measures then discussing with market risk officers about reasons for changes, producing daily market risk reports, and providing impact analysis to senior managers to help them in the decision-making process. The role is based in Weehawken, SJ. [. . .]

**Europe**

***Corporate Operational Risk Management Associate, JPMorgan Chase***

JPMorgan Chase is looking for a corporate operational risk management associate who will be a member of its corporate & investment bank operational risk management team. Key responsibilities include evaluating the implementation of the firm's operational risk management framework, identifying heightened areas of operational risk, and reviewing root cause analysis on internal operational risk events. The role is based in Bournemouth, UK. [. . .]

**Singapore**

***Risk analyst, OCBC Bank***

OCBC Bank is seeking a risk analyst who will uncover potential risk areas and initiate appropriate actions to ensure staff compliance, handle process redesign to support digital initiatives roll-out that will enhance customer experience, and participate in support initiatives. [. . .]

***Vice president for operational risk, Bluechip Platforms Asia***

Bluechip Platforms is looking for a vice president for operational risk who will represent the operational risk team in Asia-Pacific. Key responsibilities include developing risk management culture, maintaining an effective operational risk management framework that provides appropriate support for the business to make risk-based decisions, educating the business to effectively manage its risks, and ensuring appropriateness and transparency of risk information.

*Source:* Corporate Risk and Insurance (2019) This week's top risk jobs – September 26, 2019. Available at: https://www.insurancebusinessmag.com/us/risk-management/news/this-weeks-top-risk-jobs--september-26-2019-178880.aspx (accessed 7 June 2020).

## Step 3: Analyse the types and sources of risk

Obviously, the types and sources of risk that an organization faces vary widely with the type of organization, its major activities and processes, its markets, and also its strategies. To start with the latter, starting the risk management process with an appreciation of the 'risk appetite' may lead to strategies that bear a certain, and known, amount of risk. For example, when strategies involve moving a large retail chain into a country, and scaling up its activities, as Hudson's Bay did, at the same time they involve an acceptance of the risks involved, through a declining retail market, for the success of this strategy. This requires the constant monitoring of the risks that were accepted during the strategy formulation and execution stage.

For risks stemming from outside the company, there are, in principle, endless ways to classify and label them. One method of analysis focuses on categorizing risks by type. Besides strategic risks, risk could be associated with the organization's *operations, financial reporting* and *legal compliance.* Classifying risks in this way makes risk management an extension of internal control and financial reporting practices. Obviously, it is possible to detail these categories further. Other categorizations use more traditional classes like 'market risk', 'political risk', 'financial risk' or 'technological risk' to structure the analysis.

The description of risks typically follows this sequence:

- Specify the type and source of the risk
- Specify potential events in which the risk may manifest

- Specify the qualitative and quantitative (monetary) consequences
- Specify the likelihood, preferably in quantitative terms.

As a final note, recognition should be given to the significant developments of risk management in the banking sector, especially when it comes to output controls. For banks, the financial crisis in the first decade of this century has resulted in regulation that formally prescribes risk analyses in banks. The Basel Committee on Banking Supervision has been particularly active, issuing regulative statements known as Basel II (2005), Basel II.5 (2009) and Basel III (2016), which focus on 'market risk' and two essential metrics to measure market risk, namely Value at Risk (VaR) and Expected Shortfall (ES) (see the Real World Example).

***Real World Example:*** Below you find excerpts from the Basel Committee's view on risk management.

The Basel statements have become influential in our understanding of risk management in the financial sector. As important as risk management as a process is the clear understanding of the concepts in which the risk management policies are cast. This is why these statements rely on explicit definitions of its central risk-related concepts.

**What is market risk and why is its measurement being updated?**

Many banks have portfolios of traded instruments for short-term profits. These portfolios – referred to as trading books – are exposed to market risk, or the risk of losses resulting from changes in the prices of instruments such as bonds, shares and currencies. Banks are required to maintain a minimum amount of capital to account for this risk.

**FIGURE 11.3** The main drivers of market risk

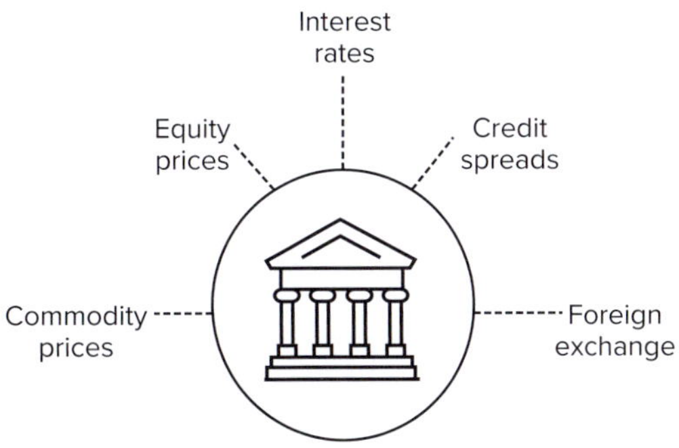


**Value at Risk (VaR)**

A measure of the worst expected loss on a portfolio of instruments resulting from market movements over a given time horizon and a pre-defined confidence level.

**Expected Shortfall (ES)**

A measure of the average of all potential losses exceeding the VaR at a given confidence level, which makes up for VaR's shortcomings in capturing the risk of extreme losses.

Many banks have engaged in so-classed 'stress tests' to see how different scenarios affecting the drivers of market risk would relate to the bank's survival chances. Based on these new regulations, minimal capital requirements have increased significantly for banks to be able to absorb and withstand the negative effects of market risk.

## Step 4: Communicate and report on risk

In terms of output control, reports on risks are typically free-formatted, and use a range of statistical and mathematical tools and concepts to describe the potential impact of the risks identified. Many of the risk reports make use of so-called risk assessment matrices, in which risk factors are identified and categorized as a function of their potential (financial) impact and probability. Figure 11.4 provides a simple example of such a matrix.

Reporting about risks can be done by combining such matrices with more accurate descriptions and by proposing a way to manage the risk. The format for this could be that of a 'risk event card'.[5] Figure 11.5 provides a simple example of such a card.

Typically such analysis and communication are performed by risk analysts, although the reporting can also be done in conjunction with the standard financial reporting channels. Ultimately, risk management is the responsibility of top management, and the reporting lines, not unlike financial reporting, will have to make sure that the risk analyses are communicated to those levels and managers who are accountable for their eventual consequences, and able and mandated to take action when needed.

Finally, it should be noted that the production of such risk and risk event cards is never a goal in itself, nor some end station after which the risk management process is considered to be completed. Rather, they are nothing but the simple ways of communication within the larger analysis and dialogue on risk. They serve to structure and support such an analysis and dialogue. This becomes quite clear when we attempt to plot the COVID-19 and Wereldhave risks in these maps. The latter can be regarded as a part of relatively normal *economic and competitive conditions*, which are likely to occur from time to time, and which may have a significant but not critical impact. However, it is quite a bit harder to

**FIGURE 11.4** Risk assessment matrix

**Risk Assessment Matrix**

| **Impact** \ **Probability** | 1 Extremely unlikely | 2 Likely | 3 Extremely likely |
|---|---|---|---|
| 1 Not critical | 1 | 2 | 3 |
| 1 Significant | 2 | 4 | 6 |
| 1 Fundamental to continuing operations | 3 | 6 | 9 |

Impact x Probability = **Risk score**

**Priority**
Low
Medium
High

*Source:* 5 Kaplan, R.S. and Mikes, A. (2012). Managing risks: a new framework, Harvard Business Review, 90(6): 48–60.

[5] Kaplan, R.S. and Mikes, A. (2012). Managing risks: a new framework, *Harvard Business Review,* 90(6): 48–60.

**FIGURE 11.5** A risk event card

| STRATEGIC OBJECTIVE | RISK EVENT | OUTCOMES | RISK INDICATORS | LIKELIHOOD/ CONSEQUENCES | MANAGEMENT CONTROLS | ACCOUNTABLE MANAGER |
|---|---|---|---|---|---|---|
| Guarantee reliable and competitive delivery of goods and services to customers. | Interruption of services due to an IT security breach. | Overtime<br><br>Late billing<br><br>Quality problems<br><br>Production losses | Inability to ship deliveries<br><br>Reduced systems availability<br><br>Incorrect shipments | 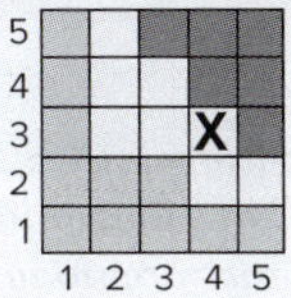 | Risk mitigation: Regularly updating security software on all computers.<br><br>Risk mitigation: Implement training for employees on best practices with regards to IT security.<br><br>Risk mitigation initiative: Upgrade suppliers' tooling<br><br>Risk mitigation intiative: Identify the key supply chain executive at each critical supplier | Mr. Samantha Edwards director of operations |

*Source:* 5 Kaplan, R.S. and Mikes, A. (2012). Managing risks: a new framework, Harvard Business Review, 90(6): 48–60.

assess the risk of the COVID-19 type. Certainly, epidemics and pandemics happen statistically with some regularity, but as the reactions to the this crisis suggest, the impact of such an *act of nature* seems extremely hard to estimate. In such cases, we speak of crisis management rather than risk management, which is hard to accommodate within our management control framework.

## Enterprise risk management frameworks

Based on the storyline in this chapter thus far, it seems both important and logical that organizations pay attention to the risks in their internal environment that may affect their critical human, and other, resources, their processes and operations and, ultimately their performance. In that sense, a management control system as discussed in this book provides an excellent structure to risk management efforts. Indeed, much if not all that we have dealt with thus far in this book also has an impact on risk management. Management control system design and risk management are heavily intertwined. The typical way to talk about systems, like the management control *system*, and the risk management *system*, may create an impression of disconnected, and stand-alone, applications, managed by different people, in different parts of the organization. We need to understand, however, the concept of *system* in terms of the logical connection between processes and procedures in order to achieve a certain goal or state. In this sense, an organization's risk management practices are an important part of the overall management control system. In line with our definition of risk at the start of this chapter, risk management systems traditionally focus on potential threats to the organization. Due to the negative connotations that many people perceive around the term 'risk', a limited – and by now out-of-date – conception of risk management would focus only on the factors that have a potential negative impact on organizations. This focus on negative factors can be understood by the fact that developments in risk management are often the response to crises in the financial reporting and financial management of firms. One of the most prominent 'think tanks' in risk management is the Committee of Sponsoring Organizations (COSO), which came into existence in reaction to concerns about fraudulent reporting due to lack of internal control (see the Real World Example).

**Real World Example:** The text below details the Committee of Sponsoring Organizations' (COSO's) mission, vision and history.

***Mission***

*The Committee of Sponsoring Organizations' (COSO) mission is to provide thought leadership through the development of comprehensive frameworks and guidance on enterprise risk management, internal control and fraud deterrence designed to improve organizational performance and governance and to reduce the extent of fraud in organizations.*

***Vision***

*COSO's vision is to be a recognized thought leader in the global marketplace on the development of guidance in the areas of risk and control which enable good organizational governance and reduction of fraud.*

***History***

*COSO was organized in 1985 to sponsor the National Commission on Fraudulent Financial Reporting, an independent private-sector initiative that studied the causal factors that can lead to fraudulent financial reporting. It also developed recommendations for public companies and their independent auditors, for the SEC and other regulators, and for educational institutions.*

*The National Commission was sponsored jointly by five major professional associations headquartered in the United States: the American Accounting Association (AAA), the American Institute of Certified Public Accountants (AICPA), Financial Executives International (FEI), The Institute of Internal Auditors (IIA), and the National Association of Accountants (now the Institute of Management Accountants [IMA]). Wholly independent of each of the sponsoring organizations, the Commission included representatives from industry, public accounting, investment firms, and the New York Stock Exchange.*

*Source:* COSO (n.d.) About us. Available at: https://www.coso.org/Pages/aboutus.aspx (accessed 3 November 2019).

COSO has become a very influential organization in today's debate on risk management. Over the decades, its focus has shifted and broadened from the link between internal control and external reporting to a comprehensive view on enterprise risk management, developed in influential conceptual frameworks to help organizations engage in organization-wide risk management. The need for such a comprehensive view rests on the developments of globalizing economies, increased competition, and the interconnections between trade and politics. Obviously, the impact of such developments is felt most by large, internationally operating companies. For such companies, COSO now often provides the framework for the design of risk management systems, and for them to report to their shareholders and stakeholders about the way these systems are designed and used. This is illustrated in the following Real World Example, which describes the definition of enterprise risk management, in which the focus lies not so much on reducing negative risks per se, but rather on managing risks in order to maximize shareholder value.

**Real World Example:** The COSO 2017 Statement on Enterprise Risk Management reads as follows:

*The underlying premise of enterprise risk management is that every entity exists to provide value for its stakeholders. All entities face uncertainty, and the challenge for management is to determine how much uncertainty to accept as it strives to grow stakeholder value. Uncertainty presents both risk and opportunity, with the potential to erode or enhance value. Enterprise risk management enables management to effectively deal with uncertainty and associated risk and opportunity, enhancing the capacity to build value.*

*Source:* COSO (2017) *Enterprise Risk Management – Integrated Framework.* Available at: https://www.coso.org/Documents/2017-COSO-ERM-Integrating-with-Strategy-and-Performance-Executive-Summary.pdf (accessed 3 November 2019).

The following Real World Example sketches the principles underlying the risk management standard developed by ISO, the International Organization for Standardization.

**Real World Example:** The ISO 31000 Standard on Risk Management (2018) is a document for use by people who create and protect value in organizations by managing risks, making decisions, setting and achieving objectives, and improving performance.

> *Organizations of all types and sizes face external and internal factors and influences that make it uncertain whether they will achieve their objectives.*
>
> *Managing risk is iterative and assists organizations in setting strategy, achieving objectives and making informed decisions.*
>
> *Managing risk is part of governance and leadership, and is fundamental to how the organization is managed at all levels. It contributes to the improvement of management systems.*
>
> *Managing risk is part of all activities associated with an organization and includes interaction with stakeholders.*
>
> *Managing risk considers the external and internal context of the organization, including human behaviour and cultural factors.*
>
> *Managing risk is based on the principles, framework and process outlined in this document [. . .]. These components might already exist in full or in part within the organization, however, they might need to be adapted or improved so that managing risk is efficient, effective and consistent.*

*Source:* ISO (2018) ISO 31000:2018(en) Risk Management – guidelines. Available at: https://www.iso.org/obp/ui/#iso:std:65694:en (accessed 3 November 2019).

It should be noted that these broad definitions may be confusing for those that would like to keep a clear distinction between the 'other' management control practices covered in Chapters 4–10 in this book. Indeed, if we understand entrepreneurship, innovation and growth as all positive contributors to an organization's prosperity, it is hard to understand how risk management, so broadly conceived, differs from other management control practices. To avoid such confusion, we want to stress that other management control practices and risk management have much in common in terms of goals and underlying processes, but still often are perceived by organizations to serve somewhat different purposes and audiences. Whereas the management control practices discussed in Chapters 4–10 aim to address the question of how top management can make good things happen, risk management systems address the question of how top management can make sure that the bad things happening have limited negative effects, or can even be turned around into challenges and opportunities. It is, in a way, the difference between the infamous glass of water being half full or half empty. In this sense, risk management can be seen as not a new set of control practices that complements the other control practices in an organization, but as an *ideology* to consider risk not just as the inevitably bad side of business, but as part of entrepreneurial life that can be put to good use. The Real World Example provides an illustration.

**Real World Example:** The sea around oil and gas platforms often brims with life, with room for endangered and exotic species. However, under current regulations, obsolete platforms are always completely dismantled without considering their positive ecological effects. Environmental experts are therefore arguing in favour of policy reform. This is evidenced by a survey of international environmental experts from universities, governments and industries, co-authored by researchers from Wageningen University & Research. In this survey, almost 95 per cent of the experts indicate that it is better to examine each platform independently to see whether or not it should be removed. In the coming decades, decisions will be taken on more than 7,500 obsolete oil and gas platforms worldwide.

*Source:* Wageningen University & Research (2018) Environmental experts: oil platforms present ecological opportunities. Available at: https://www.wur.nl/en/newsarticle/Environmental-experts-oil-platforms-present-ecological-opportunities.htm (accessed 3 November 2019).

In line with such sometimes unexpected benefits, current thinking on risk management spurs managers to develop a healthy attitude to risks, and develop a so-called, conscious 'risk appetite'. Organizations and their management should, in other words, not just take risks as simply bad, but consider that risks that are the other side of the coin called entrepreneurship should be understood, to be able to balance between their negative sides (threats) and positive sides (opportunities). This makes risk management not only an important part of management control systems, but also part of strategic management, and its various tools, which range from informal brainstorming sessions to formalized SWOT analyses, which identify 'Strengths', 'Weaknesses', 'Opportunities' and 'Threats' for the organization.

The Real World Example provides an example from the annual report of Huawei, in which it points to both COSO and ISO as sources of its risk management framework.

**Real World Example:** Huawei describes its risk management framework as follows.

*Based on the COSO framework, and referencing ISO 31000 risk management standards, Huawei has an Enterprise Risk Management (ERM) system that takes into account our unique organizational structure and operating model. In addition, we have a robust set of ERM policies and processes, and we continuously refine our ERM organizations and operating mechanisms to optimize risk management. Huawei's ERM system ensures the following:*

- *The Board of Directors approves solutions related to managing the company's major risks, crises, and unforeseen events.*
- *Business managers, as primary risk management owners in their respective business domains, proactively identify and manage risks to ensure they remain at an acceptable level.*

*At Huawei, risk management factors are incorporated into both strategic planning and business planning processes: Each business department and regional office systematically identifies and assesses risks during strategic planning, lists appropriate countermeasures in annual business plans, and monitors and reports on high-agenda risks during routine operations. Huawei ensures uninterrupted business operations by identifying major risk factors during strategic decision making and planning, coupled with taking necessary measures to control risks during business planning and execution.*

*Source:* Huawei Annual Report 2018, p. 127.

This focus on the external stakeholders is also evident in the annual report of Volkwagen. As shown in the Real World Example, Volkswagen relies on the COSO concept of risk management, yet signals a more conservative view on managing risks, as signalled by its use of the term 'defense'. Obviously, such differences in terminology may reflect different traditions and industries, rather than underlying material differences.

**Real World Example:** Volkswagen's annual report has this to say about its risk management framework:

*The organizational design of the Volkswagen Group's RMS/ICS is based on the internationally recognized COSO framework for enterprise risk management (COSO: Committee of Sponsoring Organizations of the Treadway Commission). Structuring the RMS/ICS in accordance with the COSO framework for enterprise risk management ensures that potential risk areas are covered in full. Uniform Group principles are used as the basis for managing risks in a standardized manner. Opportunities are not recorded.*

*Another key element of the RMS/ICS at Volkswagen is the three lines of defense model, a basic element required, among other bodies, by the European Confederation of Institutes of Internal Auditing (ECIIA). In line with this model the Volkswagen Group's RMS/ICS has three lines of defense that are designed to protect the Company from significant risks occurring.*

*Source:* Volkswagen Annual Report 2018. Available at: https://annualreport2018.volkswagenag.com/group-management-report/report-on-risks-and-opportunities/risk-management-and-control-system.html (accessed 3 November 2019).

In sum, the dual view on the positive and negative sides of risks – that is, of risks as opportunities and risks as threats – adds to the balance between optimistic and entrepreneurial forces in the organization and the realism of today's dynamics in a world of continuing globalization, increased competition and growing influence of information technology.

## Summary

This chapter on risk management is well placed near the end of this book. Traditionally, the design of management control systems has been defined in terms of realizing the organization's mission and strategies through the alignment of managerial behaviours. In this conceptualization, the management of risks could be considered to be captured by all the elements of the management control system. Developments in our thinking about risk management as a separate responsibility for the CEO and CFO have accelerated rapidly, however, over the last three decades. This was mostly in response to crises in the world's economic and financial systems, which also spurred legislation on more disclosure by organizations of the risks they faced, and the impact these could have on (financial) performance. In that sense, risk management can be seen as aiming towards the same objectives as management control, yet focusing on controlling the externally caused downsides of entrepreneurship rather than on the upsides associated with the realization of strategies. It is about some ultimate remedy to stay 'in control'. Risk management involves the continuous and constant awareness and attention of managers at all levels of the firm to the potential occurrence of developments that have a negative impact on the organization, and its chances of achieving its mission, goals and strategies. It also includes all the processes organizations implement to identify risks and mitigate their potential negative effects. Over time, various risk management practices have therefore firmly established themselves. They can now be seen as an important aspect of a well-functioning management control system, even if its terminology may suggest that 'enterprise risk management' requires a completely different and separate set of systems than those designed and used for management control purposes.

## Suggested additional reading

Arena, M., Arnaboldi, M. and Palermo, T. (2017) The dynamics of (dis)integrated risk management: a comparative field study, *Accounting, Organizations and Society*, 62: 65–81.

Bromiley, P., McShane, M., Nair, A. and Rustambekov, E. (2015) Enterprise risk management: review, critique, and research directions, *Long Range Planning*, 48(4): 26–76.

Falkner, E.M. and Hiebl, M.R. (2015) Risk management in SMEs: a systematic review of available evidence, *Journal of Risk Finance*, 16(2): 122–44.

Hoyt, R.E. and Liebenberg, A.P. (2011) The value of enterprise risk management, *Journal of Risk and Insurance*, 78(4): 795–822.

Kaplan, R.S. and Mikes, A. (2016) Risk management: the revealing hand, *Journal of Applied Corporate Finance*, 28(1): 8–18.

Krause, T.A. and Tse, Y. (2016) Risk management and firm value: recent theory and evidence, *International Journal of Accounting and Information Management*, 24(1): 56–81.

Steven Toms (2019) Financial scandals: a historical overview, *Accounting and Business Research*, 49( 5): 477–499.

Wong, J., Goh, Q. Y., Tan, Z., Lie, S. A., Tay, Y. C., Ng, S. Y., & Soh, C. R. (2020). Preparing for a COVID-19 pandemic: a review of operating room outbreak response measures in a large tertiary hospital in Singapore. *Canadian Journal of Anesthesia/Journal canadien d'anesthésie*, 1-14.

Wu, D.D. and Olson, D.L. (2015) Financial risk management. In *Enterprise Risk Management in Finance* (pp. 15–22). London: Palgrave Macmillan.

# Case 11.1 Future gains and future pains*

**by Ted Welten**

## Behavioural economics

Behavioural economics[1] studies the effects of psychological, cognitive, emotional, cultural and social factors on the economic decisions of individuals and institutions, and how those decisions vary from those implied by classical theory.

Behavioural economics is primarily concerned with the bounds of rationality of economic agents. Behavioural models typically integrate insights from psychology, neuroscience and microeconomic theory. The study of behavioural economics includes how market decisions are made and the mechanisms that drive public choice. The three prevalent themes in behavioural economics are:

1. *Heuristics:* Humans make 95 per cent of their decisions using mental shortcuts or rules of thumb.
2. *Framing*: The collection of anecdotes and stereotypes that make up the mental filters individuals rely on to understand and respond to events.
3. *Market inefficiencies:* These include mis-pricing and non-rational decision making.

## Mental accounting

Mental accounting[2] is the set of cognitive operations used by individuals and households to organize, evaluate and keep track of financial activities.

Mental accounting is a concept associated with the work of Richard Thaler.[3] According to Thaler, people think of value in relative rather than absolute terms. They derive pleasure not just from an object's value, but also the quality of the deal – its transaction utility.

One example from Thaler is as follows:

> *A friend of mine was once shopping for a quilted bedspread. She went to a department store and was pleased to find a model she liked on sale. The spreads came in three sizes: double, queen and king. The usual prices for these quilts were $200, $250 and $300 respectively, but during the sale they were all priced at only $150. My friend bought the king-size quilt and was quite pleased with her purchase, though the quilt did hang a bit over the sides of her double bed.*

In addition, humans often fail to fully consider opportunity costs (trade-offs) and are susceptible to the sunk cost fallacy.

---

* This case was written by Assistant Professor Ted Welten, Erasmus University Rotterdam.

[1] Wikipedia (n.d.) Behavioral economics. Available at: https://en.wikipedia.org/wiki/Behavioral_economics (accessed 8 June 2020).

[2] Behavioraleconomics.com (n.d.) Mental accounting. Available at: https://www.behavioraleconomics.com/resources/mini-encyclopedia-of-be/mental-accounting/ (accessed 8 June 2020).

[3] Thaler, R.H. (1999) Mental accounting matters, *Journal of Behavioral Decision Making*, 12(3): 183–206.

## The sunk cost fallacy

Individuals commit the sunk cost fallacy[4] when they continue a behaviour or endeavour as a result of previously invested resources (time, money or effort).[5] This fallacy, which is related to loss aversion and status quo bias, can also be viewed as bias resulting from an ongoing commitment.

The sunk cost effect is manifested in a greater tendency to continue an endeavour once an investment in money, effort or time has been made. Evidence shows that the psychological justification for this behaviour is predicated on the desire not to appear wasteful.

## The case of Kalkar

In the mid-1960s, agreements were made at government and industry level between Germany (70 per cent), Belgium (15 per cent) and the Netherlands (15 per cent) for the construction of a prototype breeding reactor,[6] and in 1972 it was decided to build it. The estimated total costs for the establishment of the Kalkar nuclear power plant amounted to approximately DM1.5 billion.

The construction work started in 1973. In the 1970s and 1980s the town of Kalkar was often in the news due to the many protest demonstrations held against the nuclear power plant. More than 1,000 contractors participated in this project. Due to changes in political commitments, permits and technical regulations, construction was delayed considerably. Due to this construction delay, inflation and interest, the costs rose from around 1.7 billion to 8 billion German marks.

From 1973, every consumer of electricity in the Netherlands paid a 3 per cent levy on their electricity bill. This so-called Kalkar levy was the start of a broad anti-nuclear energy movement in the Netherlands.

Political differences and the Chernobyl nuclear disaster in 1986 caused delays in the licensing process. The structure was ready for construction and was kept in operation from 1986 in its pre-nuclear state. The sodium coolant and the heat required to keep it liquid led to an annual cost of about 105 million German marks.

### Termination

Since 1985, the Land of North Rhine-Westphalia has refused to issue the last three sub-permits. This long-standing situation put the financing of the entire project at risk. This also took place in a context of ongoing protests focused on the safety of this type of reactor.

In March 1991, the German government announced the end of the project. Minister Heinz Riesenhuber announced the definitive shutdown on 21 March 1991.

The complex was sold in 1995 for 2.5 million euros to the Dutch entrepreneur Hennie van der Most, who demolished the unnecessary metal parts and established an amusement park in it. The leisure centre, with hotels and family park, was initially called Kernwasser Wunderland and was renamed Wunderland Kalkar in 2005.

### Tasks

1. Prior to the decision to stop the Kalkar project, a lot of different arguments, for and against, were discussed. One of the arguments was: 'Let's not stop this project, because we have already invested about 4 billion euros.' Comment on this argument. Explain how sunk costs can influence the decision.
2. Can you make an objective statement of cost and revenues for this project? Why? Why not?
3. Can you give another example in which non-rational arguments to come to a certain decision had top priority?

---

[4] Behavioraleconomics.com (n.d.) Sunk cost fallacy. Available at: https://www.behavioraleconomics.com/resources/mini-encyclopedia-of-be/sunk-cost-fallacy/ (accessed 8 June 2020).

[5] Arkes, H.R. and Blumer, C. (1985) The psychology of sunk costs, *Organizational Behavior and Human Decision Processes*, 35(1): 124–40.

[6] Wikipedia (n.d.) Kweekreactor Kalkar. Available at: https://nl.wikipedia.org/wiki/Kweekreactor_Kalkar (accessed 8 June 2020).

# Case 11.2
# Profit warning*

**by Ted Welten**

Let's have a look at three car manufacturers who released profit warnings during the last few years.

## Daimler

German carmaker Daimler warned on profits for the fourth time on 12 July 2019 after being forced to make further provisions to deal with a regulatory crackdown on alleged manipulations of diesel emissions.

Despite having already warned on profits on 23 June 2019, the Mercedes-Benz maker said it had uncovered new information that would make its earnings before interest and tax for the second quarter of the year even lower than it guided for the previous month and 'significantly below market expectations'.

While carmakers globally are facing a squeeze from falling sales in the USA and China, Daimler has been hit particularly hard by a number of factors. The company has been hobbled by the global trade war, because it ships vehicles from the USA to China, while also being hit by the decline in demand for diesel fuel across the UK and Europe.

Daimler said on Friday that it would report a €1.6 billion loss for the second quarter, down from earnings before interest and tax of €2.6 billion for the same period in 2018. Its Mercedes car division made a €700 million loss, compared with almost €2 billion of profit a year earlier, while its van division fell to a €2 billion loss, against a €200 million profit in the same quarter a year earlier.

Daimler also downgraded annual outlook, saying profits would be 'significantly lower' than last year, having previously said the results would be comparable. The company said that global car sales and availability of some of its vehicles because of difficulties in ramping up production would hurt it.

In addition, the carmaker said that, since 23 June, it had reassessed the financial risks from court proceedings and governmental measures relating to Mercedes diesel vehicles in multiple regions, which had 'led to an increase in expected expenses by around €1.6 billion'.

The issues stem from mandatory recalls and possible fines over allegations that its vehicles contain software that lower emissions in certain conditions found in laboratory tests.

The company previously said it continued to cooperate with regulators over the issue but would appeal against any recall decision because it considered the emissions control systems found in its vehicles legal.

Daimler had also found 'new information leading to a revised risk assessment' of an extended global recall of faulty car airbags made by Japan's Takata, adding another €1 billion of provisions. It also said profits were lowered by €500 million from the falling performance of the company's vans division.

## Ford

Ford Motor Company will have a lower profit in 2020 than last year. The American car concern announced this after the closing of Wall Street on Tuesday 4 February 2020.

The group assumes that earnings before interest and taxes (EBIT) this year amount to $5.6 billion to $6.6 billion, where analysts said $7.4 billion, according to Bloomberg news agency. For the whole of 2019, the EBIT result amounted to $6.4 billion, a decrease of 0.6 per cent compared to 2018. Turnover fell by 3 per cent last year, from $160 billion to $155 billion.

Jim Hackett, who became Ford's CEO in 2017, is cutting costs. At the same time, he is working on an investment programme worth $11 billion to make the group future-proof.

* This case was written by Assistant Professor Ted Welten, Erasmus University Rotterdam.

Like other car manufacturers, Ford is suffering from the advance of Tesla, the manufacturer of electric cars. Partly as a result, Ford saw its market share shrink from 6.3 per cent to 6 per cent in a year. Car sales fell by 10 per cent: in 2019, the group sold 5,386,000 cars, while in 2018, it had sold 5,982,000. Ford hopes to turn the tide with its electric Mustang Mach-E, launched in October 2019.

## BMW

Car manufacturer BMW issued a profit warning in September 2018 for the first time in 10 years. An impending trade war with the United States, and problems with a new measurement method for car consumption and emissions, had put sales and prices under pressure, the group management said. The warning came as a bit of a surprise, as BMW had still been expecting a consistent result in August.

BMW is struggling with, among other things, the European WLTP (Worldwide Harmonised Light Vehicle Test Procedure) method, which came into force in September 2019 to replace the old, unreliable measurement system. Because each version must be tested according to the new rules, test centres could not handle the influx and waiting lists were created. Various car manufacturers were forced to temporarily stop their production lines. Some versions were completely cancelled.

At the same time, many manufacturers had built up stocks of cars that were tested to the old standard and that could be sold until autumn 2019. This resulted in oversupply and manufacturers reducing prices to protect their market share.

Due to problems around the WLTP and trade turmoil, the profit margin has not achieved the target 8 to 10 per cent, but instead around 7 per cent, according to BMW.

Whether the diesel affair also plays a role is not clear. Now that a ban on relatively new diesels is imminent in a number of German cities, there is a growing chance that car manufacturers will have to convert older diesels or give owners the chance to exchange their old vehicle for a new one. Both outcomes will cost the industry billions.

## Questions

1. Obviously, there is a deviation between planning and realization in the car industry. This is known as the variance analysis within the planning and control cycle (management control process). Comment on the different causes of these variances in the examples above. Do they differ between the three car manufacturers? Why?
2. What can the companies do to minimize the difference between planning and realization? How can they improve the quality of the planning?
3. Apparently, the goals and strategy of the companies have to be adjusted in one way or another. What can be done about this from a MC perspective?

## References


de Volkskrant (2018) Winst BMW smelt door Trump emissiemeting. Available at: https://www.volkskrant.nl/economie/winst-bmw-smelt-door-trump-en-emissiemeting~b3fdeee2/ (accessed 8 June 2020).

fd.nl (2020) Ford komt met winstwaarschuwing. Available at: https://fd.nl/ondernemen/1333599/ford-komt-met-winstwaarschuwing (accessed 8 June 2020).

Rovnick, N. and Campbell, P. (2019) Daimler gloom deepens with profit warning, FT.com, 12 July. Available at: https://www.ft.com/content/79b677e4-a470-11e9-974c-ad1c6ab5efd1 (accessed 8 June 2020).

Winton, N. (2020) Another Daimler profit warning spooks investors, raising management shakeup, takeover fears, *Forbes*, 22 January. Available at: https://www.forbes.com/sites/neilwinton/2020/01/22/another-daimler-profit-warning-spooks-investors-raising-management-shakeup-takeover-fears/#2503b74c5fac (accessed 8 June 2020).

# Case 11.3
# Risk or challenges: Tiffany's and Quest Diagnostics*

**by Ted Welten**

## Theft by employees at Tiffany's and Quest Diagnostics

### The companies

Tiffany & Co., a luxury jeweller and speciality retailer based in in New York, sells jewellery a variety of high-end products including jewellery, crystal, china, sterling silver, fragrances, and watches. Tiffany goods are sold at Tiffany stores and through direct mail and corporate merchandising.

- Quest Diagnostics is an American clinical laboratory. This Fortune 500 company offers access to diagnostic testing services for cancer, cardiovascular disease, infectious diseases, neurological disorders, and employment and court-ordered drug testing.

### Theft at Tiffany's

A former Tiffany & Co. executive, the authorities said, stole about $1.2 million worth of jewellery from the store and effectively wrote it off the company's books.

As part of her job duties, prosecutors have said, she had access to jewellery that she could 'check out' to show, for example, to potential manufacturers for determining production costs.

Ms Lederhaas-Okun also had the authority to cancel the cost of jewellery that 'had been rendered unusable in some way', like being damaged in transit, the government said.

Normally such cancelled inventory is returned to Tiffany's and destroyed.

Instead, a criminal complaint said, Ms Lederhaas-Okun sold 'some if not all' of the merchandise to a leading jewellery buyer and reseller in Manhattan. Prosecutors have declined to identify the company.

'Okun gave false explanations for what happened to the missing jewellery', sometimes claiming that it had been lost or damaged, the complaint said.

### Theft at Quest Diagnostics

David Alan Smith, a 46-year-old resident of Wesley Chapel, Florida, pleaded guilty to three counts of wire fraud, three counts of mail fraud and two counts of aggravated identity theft.

According to the plea agreement, Smith was the facilities manager for Quest Diagnostics Incorporated's ('Quest Diagnostics') Tampa laboratory and laboratory annexe.

Starting in at least 2001, Smith began submitting with his expense reports fraudulent invoices from fake 'shell' companies that he claimed he had paid on behalf of Quest Diagnostics and for which he sought reimbursement. The fake 'shell' companies involved in the scheme were Smith's creations and were generally little more than a name, a fake address and fake invoices. For example, the address used by Smith for Environmental Tech was effectively the on ramp to Tampa Crosstown Expressway and TLSmith's address was a post office box opened by Smith. Approval of the fraudulent expense reports submitted by Smith to Quest required a countersignature by one of Smith's supervisors.

---

* This case was written by Assistant Professor Ted Welten, Erasmus University Rotterdam.

Smith simply forged the signatures of at least two of his supervisors on many of his expense reports. He used their means of identification – that is, their names – to cause wire transmissions (electronic funds transfers) and mailings (checks) to be made to him because, in forging their signatures, Quest Diagnostics approved his fraudulent requests for payments. Over the course of his scheme to defraud, Smith obtained $1,187,379 in payments from his employer Quest Diagnostics, by and through his false representations to Quest Diagnostics regarding the fake 'shell' companies. Quest Diagnostics also identified an additional $122,520 in fraudulent expenses for a total loss of $1,309,899.

## What are the consequences? What needs to be done?

### Internal control

Obviously, a company has to implement internal control measures to decrease unacceptable risks. This is discussed in this chapter against the background of the COSO framework. The major internal control measure is implementing an adequate Segregation of Duties (SOD) between Authorization, Custody, Recording, Checking and Execution. In these cases, there was a serious lack of SOD. These bottom-up internal control measures have to be implemented to avoid certain risks. But that's not all. A well-functioning internal control system cannot solve all problems.

### Management control

At the same time, from a management control perspective, which is a top-down approach, there are some serious issues in these companies that have to be addressed. In the book, these issues are centred around the MC system (Should we decentralize?), MC structure (How should we decentralize?) and MC process (is the planning and control cycle well executed?).

## Questions

1 If you analyse the two cases, what major problem do you recognize from a MC perspective? Relate this to the three central questions mentioned above.

2 What changes in the MC system, MC structure or MC process do you suggest be implemented parallel to the internal control measures?

3 Which contradictions and/or strengthening do you see between internal control and management control? Can one exist without the other?

4 Are the two fraud cases comparable from a MC perspective? Why? Why not?

## References


Law Admin (2008) Man Pleads Guilty to Theft Of Over One Million Dollars From Employer, Quest Diagnostics, *Law Fuel*. Available at: https://www.lawfuel.com/blog/man-pleads-guilty-to-theft-of-over-one-million-dollars-from-employer-quest-diagnostics-us-attorney/ (accessed 8 June 2020).

Weiser, B. (2013) Ex-Tiffany executive pleads guilty to stealing jewelry, *New York Times*, 26 July. Available at: https://www.nytimes.com/2013/07/27/nyregion/ex-tiffany-executive-pleads-guilty-to-stealing-jewelry.html (accessed 8 June 2020).

Wikipedia (n.d.) Quest Diagnostics. Available at: https://en.wikipedia.org/wiki/Quest_Diagnostics (accessed 8 June 2020).

Wikipedia (n.d.) Tiffany & Co. Available at: https://en.wikipedia.org/wiki/Tiffany_%26_Co (accessed 8 June 2020).

# Case 11.4

# Unilever and the risk of being taken over: a case on shareholder value creation . . . or lack thereof*

**by Frank G.H. Hartmann**

## Introduction

> *OUR BRANDS ARE AVAILABLE IN OVER 190 COUNTRIES. THIS GIVES US A UNIQUE OPPORTUNITY TO POSITIVELY IMPACT THE LIVES OF PEOPLE ALL OVER THE WORLD.*
>
> *Every day, 2.5 billion people use our products to feel good, look good and get more out of life. Our range of around 400 household brands includes Lipton, Knorr, Dove, Rexona, Hellmann's and Omo. We are one of the largest fast moving consumer goods (FMCG) companies globally. In 2018 we had 12 brands with turnover of over a billion euros or more. The strength of our global brands is reflected in Kantar's Brand Footprint report published in May 2018. It found that 13 of the world's top 50 FMCG brands – based on market penetration and consumer interactions – are owned by Unilever with these brands chosen 36 billion times each year. This is significantly more than any other FMCG company in the study.*[1]

Unilever is a multinational consumer goods company co-headquartered in Rotterdam, the Netherlands, and London, United Kingdom. The history of Unilever starts with a merger between the Dutch margarine producer Margarine Unie and the British soap maker Lever Brothers. The origins of Margarine Unie go back to the families of Jurgens and van den Bergh. These two merchants in butter were quick to see the potential of margarine as an affordable alternative to butter in the mid-1900s. In the UK, Lever & Co. started the production of Sunlight soap in 1886. During the second half of the twentieth century the company increased its scope in products and markets to become a truly worldwide player. Since 2009, and under the leadership of Paul Polman, the company started to focus on environmental and social performance next to financial performance. Unilever plc is listed on the London Stock Exchange, being part of the FTSE 100 Index. Unilever NV is listed on Euronext Amsterdam, being part of the AEX index. The company also adds to the the Euro Stoxx 50 stock market index.

This case describes some critical moments in the last years of Paul Polman's CEO-ship.

## Friday 17 February 2017: Kraft Heinz bids $143 billion for Unilever in global brand grab[2]

This was the headline of a Reuters news statement concerning the bid that US food company Kraft Heinz Co. put in to Unilever to take over Unilever plc. At the time of the bid, Kraft was controlled by US

* This case was written by Professor Frank G.H. Hartmann, Radboud University.

[1] Unilever (2018) Annual Report and Accounts. Available at: https://www.unilever.com/Images/unilever-annual-report-and-accounts-2018_tcm244-534881_en.pdf (accessed 8 June 2020).

[2] Geller, M. and Barbaglia, P. (2017) www.reuters.com, 17 February.

billionaire Warren Buffett and a private equity firm called 3G Capital. The offer was a surprise to Unilever and was immediately rejected. If successful, it would have been the third-biggest takeover in history and the largest concerning a UK-based company. The combination would have seen a massive company created, which would combine some of the world's best-known consumer brands in a product range from toothpaste to ice cream. Geographically too a strong combination would have emerged, with Kraft being powerful in the United States and Unilever in Europe and Asia. Kraft insisted that the deal should be discussed, but Unilever said it saw no financial or strategic benefit in pursuing it. Instead, Kraft seemed convinced that the combination would be more powerful in terms of innovation. It also appears to have promised that the three headquarters of the combination, in the United States, the UK and the Netherlands, would remain intact.

### How Unilever foiled Kraft Heinz's £115 billion takeover bid[3]

This was the headline of a *Guardian* newspaper commentary on the attempted takeover. The *Guardian* quoted so-called insiders who reported that Unilever would fiercely resist being taken over and that there was 'no appetite for any offer'. These signs should warn key investors like Warren Buffett not to push forward too much. Unilever reportedly said it would use every tool it could mobilize to make sure a deal would not be made.

As the *Guardian* reports, Kraft withdrew its offer 'amicably' on Sunday evening. This was just two days after expressing its interest in the takeover of Unilever. Unilever's stock price had increased by 13 per cent to a record high at the time it reported that it had declined the Kraft offer on Friday. The withdrawal of this offer by Kraft resulted in a decrease in share price by 8 per cent on the following Monday. A key role was played by Unilever's Dutch CEO Paul Polman, who was reported to have warned the takeover party that in his boardroom no one would support it and investors were unlikely to be appreciative of it either. Unilever shareholders consist of some 70 per cent term investors, holding shares for more than seven years, and were believed not to see many advantages in the takeover proposal.

## Thursday 6 April 2017: Further action announcements by Unilever[4]

In Fortune.com's CEO Daily, a commentary discussed Unilever's measures to please and pacify its investors. Surely, Unilever needed to respond to this takeover battle with Heinz Kraft, which some had baptized as 'a battle for the soul of capitalism'.

CEO Daily reminded us that Unilever CEO Paul Polman was very strong in setting up a business model for the company that would look beyond shareholders. This strategic vision had earned him a great deal of praise in society, but at the same time may have invited the bid he was fighting against. If shareholders would have believed that the Polman strategy was costing them shareholder value, a bid like this, from these well-known investors in particular, made sense. CEO Daily reported on the background of 3G, an equity firm from Brazil, known for its 'ruthless' practices of cutting costs and creating profits. So, while Paul Polman managed to counter the attack, now the time had come for Unilever to announce moves that would be in the interests of its shareholders. The announcement concerned the company selling its margarine activities and engaging in a share buy-back. Additionally, policies were announced to increase dividends, speed up cost cutting and increase profit margins. Finally, Unilever announced it would reconsider its expensive and inefficient legal structure, with legal positions in both the Netherlands (Rotterdam) and the UK (London).

---

3 www.theguardian.com, 20 February 2017.

4 Murray, A. and Smith, G. (2017) CEO Daily, www.fortune.com, 6 April.

## Thursday 29 November 2018: Paul Polman to retire; Alan Jope appointed as successor

This was the headline of a press release from Unilever's London and Rotterdam co-headquarters, announcing the retirement of CEO Paul Polman. The company confirmed that Alan Jope, then President, Beauty and Personal Care, would take the reins from Polman from 1 January 2019, though Polman would remain in a supporting role during the transition for the first half of the year. Polman was to officially leave the company in early July.

The release went on to explain that Paul Polman had acted as the CEO of Unilever for more than 10 years. The company had delivered consistent top- and bottom-line growth ahead of its markets during that time, with a focus on successfully establishing a new sustainable model of growth. This focus had served its many stakeholders well and had delivered a Total Shareholder Return of 290 per cent for its shareholders over this period.

The news release also shared some thoughts on the leadership changes from key stakeholders within Unilever, starting with the company's then Chairman, Marijn Dekkers, who praised Polman for being an 'exceptional business leader' who had transformed Unilever into one of the 'best-performing companies in its sector and one of the most admired businesses in the world'. Dekkers went on to acknowledge Polman as playing an integral role in defining 'a new era of responsible capitalism' exemplified by the Unilever Sustainable Living plan. Dekkers credited Polman as one of the shrewdest business leaders of his generation and noted he was leaving Unilever 'a more agile and resilient company . . . in a position to win in this dynamic industry'.

Polman himself warmly congratulated Alan Jope on his new role: 'I am highly confident that under his leadership, Unilever will prosper long into the future. His appointment demonstrates the strength of Unilever's succession planning and talent pipeline.'

Recognizing his decade at the helm of Unilever as an 'honour', Polman reflected on how he had been 'humbled by the commitment and hard work of [Unilever's] people, and their passion for creating a truly purpose-driven company'. He expressed his gratitude to them and Unilever's many other stakeholders for their support in building a 'long-term, sustainable business'. Of the future, Polman said: 'I look forward to engaging with many of these partners – in a different capacity – to help address the many environmental and social challenges facing the world.'

The original press release is available to read in full on Unilever's website.[5]

### Tasks

1 Explain the actions of the various actors (Kraft Heinz, Unilever, Polman) as they unfolded in time from the beginning of this story. In your explanation, analyse the effects of these actions on shareholder value creation (or destruction). In your analyses, you may use the information contained in the appendices that follow. They describe Unilever's management philosophy (Appendix 1), display some selected commentaries from the financial press, and contain press releases from the actors involved linked in Appendix 2 as well as some stock price information in Appendix 4.

2 Prepare a short presentation on these analyses and explanations, in which you highlight the challenges and risks faced by Unilever in combining its philosophy of long-term development with its day-to-day obligation to satisfy its owners. Try to point out some examples via which Unilever manages these challenges and risks, argue whether it is successful at this, and propose changes that you think are suitable.

---

[5] Unilever (2018) Unilever CEO announcement: Paul Polman to retire; Alan Jope appointed as successor, Unilever.com, 28 November. Available at: https://www.unilever.com/news/press-releases/2018/unilever-ceo-announcement.html (accessed 8 June 2020).

3 What are the pros and cons of having a dual-headquarters structure as Unilever did? What happened in reality to this structure?

## Appendix 1: Unilever CEO and his view on managing the firm[6]

### History

- *2016:* Polman is involved in global conversations about Sustainable Development Goals (SDGs) and addressing the effects of climate change. The UN Secretary-General asks Polman to become a member of the SDG Advocacy group to promote action on the 2030 Agenda. He receives France's Chevalier de la Legion d'Honneur, to recognize his efforts in strengthening business action on sustainability and his involvement in the 2015 UN Climate Change Conference (COP21) in Paris.
- *2015:* He serves on the High-Level Panel on the Post-2015 Development Agenda and makes recommendations on the SDGs on behalf of the business sector. He also becomes a member of the Business and Sustainable Development Commission.

  He joins the International Council of the Global Commission on the Economy and Climate where he works with the former Mexican President, Felipe Calderon, whose groundbreaking report, 'New Climate Economy', demonstrates that long-term economic growth is possible while reducing the risk of climate change.

  Polman receives the Oslo Business for Peace Award and the UN Environment Programme's Champion of the Earth Award.
- *2013/2014:* Polman receives many rewards for his part in developing responsible business:
  - The WWF's Duke of Edinburgh Gold Conservation Medal
  - The Centre for Global Development's Commitment to Development Ideas in Action Award
  - The Rainforest Alliance Lifetime Achievement Award
  - The UN Foundation's Champion for Global Change Award.
- *2009:* Becomes Unilever's Chief Executive Officer and member of the Unilever Leadership Executive, and sets out a vision to separate growth from an environmental footprint. As Chairman of the World Business Council for Sustainable Development he looks for collaboration with various companies to bring sustainable business strategies into play.
- *2008:* Executive director to the boards of Unilever plc and Unilever NV; the first time an external candidate had been chosen for the role.

  Nestlé SA Executive Vice President and Zone Director for the Americas.
- *2007:* Named by *Investor Magazine* as CFO of the Year.
- *2006:* Chief Financial Officer at Nestlé SA.
- *2001:* Group President Europe and Officer of the Procter & Gamble Company.
- *1979:* Joins Procter & Gamble.

## Appendix 2: The battle for the soul of capitalism explained in one hostile takeover bid[7]

An article by Bill George in 2017 reported that Kraft Heinz had recently abandoned its bid to take over Unilever, exploring how this brought the stark contrast between the different philosophies of capitalism into focus.

---

6 https://peoplepill.com/people/paul-polman/#:~:text=He%20is%20a%20former%20Procter,Dutch%20consumer%20goods%20company%20Unilever.

7 https://www.linkedin.com/pulse/cnbc-battle-soul-capitalism-explained-one-hostile-takeover-george/

Unilever was said to endorse sustainable growth in earnings to raise long-term shareholder value, while Kraft Heinz's Brazilian owner, 3G, endorsed maximized short-term earnings to increase near-term valuation.

What follows is a summary of the most pertinent points and arguments presented in this article.

### Long-term investors' perspective

Berkshire Hathaway, Disney and Johnson & Johnson are some examples of companies that have honed the ability to aim for sustainable growth in shareholder value, while still achieving short-term results. George outlined how CEOs of such companies must continue to invest in R&D, capital expenditures, people development and expansion to sustain growth, and use compound growth in revenues, earnings per share and return on capital investment as a measure of long-term performance. This does not, however, serve as protection against investors who want immediate returns.

### Traders' perspective

Traders want to show their investors above-market returns quickly, and thus seek immediate gains in stock values. CEOs grapple with the continuous compromise between using their cash flow for internal expansion and acquisition and increasing dividends and buybacks.

### Anglo-Dutch Unilever and Brazilian 3G

The proposed takeover of Unilever by Brazilian private equity firm, 3G, illustrates these clashing objectives.

Unilever was founded when Margarine Unie (founded in 1872) and Lever Brothers (founded in 1885) merged in 1930. This created the first modern company with roots in the UK and the Netherlands. Paul Polman was appointed CEO in 2009, declaring ambitious goals to double the company's size to €80 billion by 2020 and to achieve 70 per cent of revenues from emerging markets. Under his leadership, Unilever has become a growth-orientated global competitor that has penetrated emerging markets deeper than any other consumer products company.

In 2016, the company had made compelling progress towards these goals, with €53 billion revenues, which included 57 per cent coming from emerging markets. But many investors have expressed worry that Polman's commitment of the company's resources to sustainability has distracted from its financial performance. Unilever's financial results prove Polman's success during his eight years as CEO: revenues have grown by an average of 3.8 per cent in the past four years, the stock price has increased by 144 per cent and the total shareholder return is 214 per cent.

3G was founded by former investment banker, Jorge Paulo Lemann. Its strategy is to buy companies that are financially declining, cut its expenses by 30 to 40 per cent (which includes longer-term investments), replace the management team with young Brazilian managers, and then increase cash flow and earnings quickly. Through this aggressive strategy, 3G can use the cash it creates to repay debt and buy more companies. It has taken over many retail, beer and takeaway industries, like Kraft Heinz.

Kraft Heinz approached the takeover of Unilever by offering $50 per share, which was 18 per cent above the stock price. This offer was easily rejected, however, which surprised KHC executives.

As a consequence, KHC withdrew its offer only 50 hours after launching its takeover bid.[8]

Unilever realized that KHC's offer was a warning call regarding its vulnerability to another possible takeover bid. Polman announced that Unilever was to undergo an assessment of its balance sheet, cost structure and portfolio of products to enhance its near-term shareholder returns. Unilever is more likely to consider leveraging its balance sheet and announcing stock buybacks than allow an aggressor to buy the company using its own balance sheet. It will also consider splitting the business after a review of its product portfolio.[9]

---

8 https://www.unilever.com/news/press-releases/2017/Unilever-review-170222.html

9 https://www.unilever.com/news/press-releases/2017/Joint-statement-from-Unilever-The-Kraft-Heinz-Company.html

## Appendix 3: Unilever confirms sale of spreads business, which includes Flora and Stork butter[10]

This was the headline of newspaper article in the *Independent* about Unilever's announcement that it would be selling its spreads business, including Flora and Stork butter, after CEO Paul Polman declared that the 'faster pace of change' occurring in the market was challenging Unilever to raise the bar.

The article, published in April 2017, explores how Polman feels that the future of the spreads business lies outside of Unilever and that this change will hasten the company's transformation and the delivery of sustainable shareholder value over the long term. He said that the company strives towards a more focused and leaner business.

After Kraft Heinz dropped its takeover bid, which would have resulted in the biggest ever takeover in corporate history, analysts predicted that Unilever might shift its focus to adjust its range of products to changing consumer preferences – something that Kraft Heinz had already been forced to do. Mark Jones, a food and drink solicitor at Gordons law firm, said: 'The Kraft bid was motivated by the changing consumer market, and Unilever is now making its own moves to adjust. Packaged food growth has been slowing for some time, and while the margarine business remains very profitable, consumers are moving away from the spread in search of healthier alternatives.'

He added that, 'Unilever has never carried unprofitable brands. One of the reasons it is so successful is because it buys and sell brands at the right time and, in this case, parting ways with its margarine division, whilst the going is still good, will enable it to focus on markets which are likely to keep growing in the medium term.' Also on Thursday, Unilever announced it will launch a €5 billion share buy-back programme and raise its shareholder dividend by 12 per cent. The company said that this reflects 'increased confidence in the outlook for profit growth and cash generation'.

## Appendix 4: Unilever's stock price development in 2017[11]

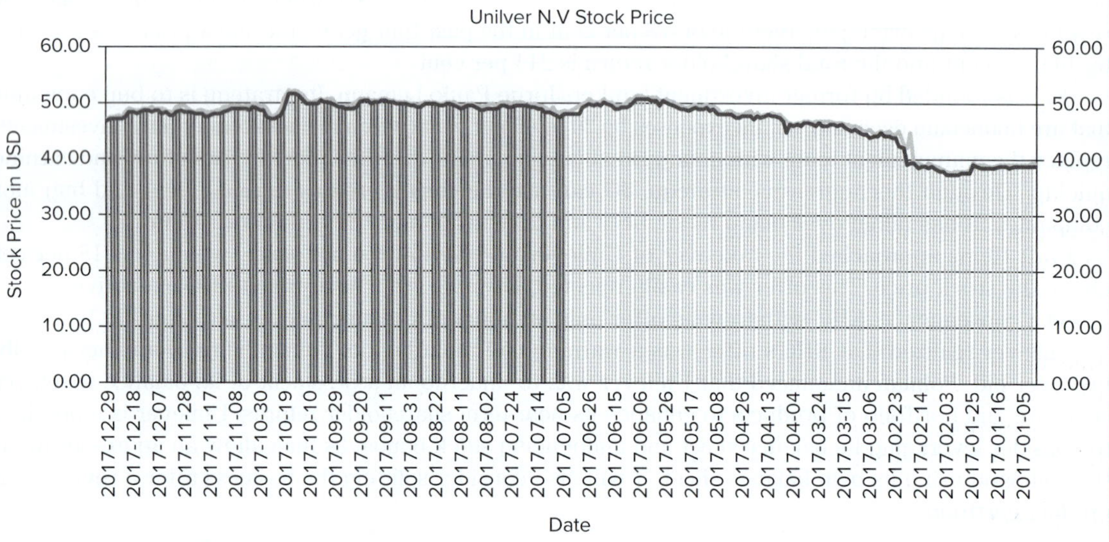


[10] Cox, J. (2017) www.independent.co.uk, 6 April.

[11] https://www.unilever.com/investor-relations/shareholder-centre/share-prices/index.html.

# Case 11.5

# Risks or challenges? Toshiba*

**by Ted Welten**

## Toshiba: background

In 1939 Tokyo Shibauri Denki K.K and Shibaura Seisaku-sho merged to form one company. This company became known as the Toshiba Corporation in 1978. The Toshiba Corporation is a multinational corporation with its headquarters in Tokyo, Japan. The group owns a variety of products and services that includes office equipment, home and electrical appliances, medical and office equipment and information technology and communication equipment. The company is organised into four business units: Digital Products, Electronic Devices, Home Appliances and Social Infrastructure.

Toshiba, the ninth largest semiconductor manufacturer in the world, is part of the Nikkei 225 and TOPIX indices on the Tokyo Stock Exchange.

## What happened?

In May 2015 Toshiba announced that it was investigating an accounting scandal that could result in a revision of profits for the three previous years. The news was shocking as up to this point Toshiba had been regarded as a figurehead for strong and virtuous corporate governance. When taking a closer look, it became clear that the Toshiba Corporation had been struggling to meet its financial targets since 2008 as a result of the global financial crisis, which had affected its profitability severely. This struggle finally caused Toshiba to commit a $1.22 billion accounting fraud and to present positive numbers that were up to three times their actual level. The use of inappropriate accounting techniques came to light, which varied between different business units. These included bringing forward future profits, sliding back losses and other similar techniques that resulted in overstated profits.

The issue was brought to light by a whistle-blower in early 2015 at the end of seven years of deception by senior management. Findings of an independent investigation into the company's finances confirmed this. According to this, unrealistic profit targets were set by top executives, which led systematically to accounting practices that contained a number of flaws. Because Toshiba has a basic principle that failures will not be accepted, heads of divisions saw that using irregular accounting techniques to hide data was the only way to achieve the goals.

## Dire consequences

Due to this accounting scandal, Toshiba CEO Hisao Tanaka resigned in July 2015 while quoting that this was 'the most damaging event for our brand in the company's 140-year history'. This was followed by the resignation of eight other senior officials, including two previous CEOs. Toshiba Corp. was removed from a stock index and in the months that followed, its stock price fell to its lowest point in two and a half years, which resulted in a net loss in the corresponding quarter, of $102 million. The company also performed poorly in the business units of televisions, home appliances and personal computers. The market value of Toshiba had dropped by about $8 billion by the end of 2015 and the loss over that year was approximately $4.6 billion.

---

* This case was written by Assistant Professor Ted Welten, Erasmus University Rotterdam.

## How did it happen?

A clear picture of how the accounting fraud was conducted is revealed by the investigation committee's report.

The basic underlying reason why this scandal could happen in the first place was the Toshiba 'principle' that the will of corporate management was considered more important than living up to the regular accounting standards.

Let's have a look at the way in which the book-keeping scandal was executed . . .

### 1. Violating the prudence principle

The prudence principle means that losses must be taken as soon as they are foreseeable and profits only if they have been realized.

Under the normal accounting standards, the prudence principle must be applied. To give an example, if a long-term power generation project becomes less profitable as a result of increasing costs and other negative factors, it is 'good' practice under the accrual-based accounting method to record the foreseen loss on the project in the results for the current fiscal period by making a reservation against future losses.

Within Toshiba, these write-offs needed approval from corporate management as well as the head of the business unit. Because booking those losses would reduce profit for the current year, there was a lot of pressure from top management on business units to come up with additional profits to make up for the amounts written off. The result was that employees bent the accounting rules and prudence principle by postponing losses to subsequent accounting periods to meet the high requirements from the top.

### 2. Carryovers

The television unit of Toshiba was using 'carryovers' to hide potential losses. This means that certain costs and benefits were carried forward to the next period or carried back to the current period to inflate profits. Reallocating costs and revenues between periods is a book-keeping transaction that distorts the actual turn of events.

This happened, for instance, by requesting vendors to carry forward issuing invoices for advertisement, distribution or other services until the next quarter, while carrying back projected discounts on parts to the current accounting period. In addition, it inflated profits by increasing prices of products sold to overseas business units. This topic is discussed extensively in Case 5.5, on international transfer pricing.

### 3. Masking prices

In its electronic devices business unit, Toshiba inflated revenues through transactions with companies that produce Toshiba brand computers under contract. The key parts for the computers are sold by Toshiba to the producing companies and then Toshiba buys the finished products back from them. In order to hide the actual prices of its parts from competitors, Toshiba sells them at an inflated 'masking price' to the manufacturing companies and then buys the finished computers from them at a price that incorporates the inflated masking price plus production and other costs.

The high masking price for the parts is passed on to a proportional inflated price for the finished product; the profits on these sales of parts are in fact not profits at all, but Toshiba treated them as if they were. To illustrate the seriousness of the problem, Toshiba raised its masking prices over the years until they were almost five times the actual cost of the parts. Additionally, it forced the manufacturing companies to buy more parts than they actually needed, resulting in a disclosed profit for the current accounting period that looked even bigger.

This example of artificially increasing revenue and profit was initiated by President Nishida Atsutoshi in January 2009 when he ordered the electronic devices unit to 'work desperately' to improve its results. He threatened to close down the unit if it failed to do so. This led to the overstating of revenues through the forced sales of parts to manufacturers. This is known as padding, which will be discussed next.

### 4. Padding

Sasaki Norio, Nishida's successor, promised to do better according to the investigation report, by cutting back on the padding of revenue figures. However, as early as September 2012 he broke his promise and forced the electronic devices unit and visual display business unit to meet a ē12 billion revenue enhancement goal in the last three days of the fiscal period. This led to the cooking of the books by employees because this challenge was not achievable.

Toshiba wanted to sweep this padding under the carpet because in September 2013 a meeting was held with Toshiba's chief financial officer, Tanaka, and the idea of using PC parts transactions as a means of improving the unit's performance was classified as a 'top secret discussion'.

The padding of accounts was also conducted by the semiconductor business by adjusting its inventory records.

However, these emergency means of temporarily boosting profits had to be accounted for in subsequent accounting periods. This was not possible of course, so Toshiba was 'forced' to continue padding its books.

## Corporate governance vs. corporate culture

The accounting scandal exposed how corporate culture, still prevalent in even globally operating Japanese businesses, may be in contrast with corporate governance and thus be damaging towards the interests of the shareholders.

This corporate culture manifests itself in Toshiba's top management, which 'pressured' employees to achieve ambitious profit targets and did not allow subordinates to oppose their bosses, which led to the dodgy book-keeping.

Another characteristic of Japanese culture is its extensive focus on producing numbers. The report stated that the firm's 'systematic' boosting of profits came to a total of ē151.8 billion over nearly seven years.

Toshiba had been seen as one of the leading companies in the area of corporate governance, so the scandal was a complete shock not only to its shareholders, but to all the stakeholders.

What can be concluded from this case? Toshiba gave the impression that it took the corporate governance system seriously, but the measures it embraced did not reflect this. Governance in any shape or form is ultimately ineffective if top management is not committed to implementing it. Tone at the top is essential. We will come back to this later on in this case. If directors and employees are subservient to those above them, nothing can check corporate criminal behaviour.

### Conservatism and diversity

The Toshiba book-keeping scandal happened at the same time as Japan's Prime Minister, Shinzo Abe, was stimulating more foreign investment. Japan had formulated a new corporate governance code, which stimulated companies to appoint multiple outside directors.

Toshiba's corporate culture is characterized by the presence of assertive shareholders who are focused on improving profitability, and the basic values are conformity in organizations and lifetime employment. To change this rigid corporate structure, the instruments of diversity would help bring new perspectives, enhance transparency and contribute to corporate growth over the long term.

Yamato Sato, Professor of Management at the Faculty of Business and Commerce of Keio University, formulates it as follows:

> *[Japan's] corporate culture encourages you to take the same action as others, and makes you believe that maintaining the status quo is the right thing to do. It's really hard to change. When people with different views come to an organization, they may face resistance at first. But accepting them will also allow the organization to find and fix what may be wrong with it.*

More Japanese companies realize that there is a need to promote diversity as they further grow globally, but this change is happening very slowly. It is not considered an investment in the long run that will generate corporate value.

During the last 20 years there has been an increasing debate in Japan about diversity, and this discussion focuses on hiring women for management positions and contracting more non-Japanese executives.

Because the Japanese population is ageing, Japanese companies are forced to look outside the country to allow the company to grow. This implies that new talent has to be found to deal with this global challenge.

One of the characteristics of globalization is increased cross-border mergers and acquisitions, but Japanese companies are very traditional when it comes to human resources management. They should switch to hiring more foreign nationals and implement diversity at different organizational levels.

This implies that the traditional rigid Japanese culture must be changed into a more flexible one, creating a work environment for diverse people, encouraging them to give their opinion, and striving for consensus rather than avoiding conflicts of opinions and just doing what top management wants them to do.

Japanese companies have been putting effort into strengthening corporate governance over the years, but the results of this are as yet unclear. One step in the right direction would be to have outside directors. This is already common for Japanese companies that operate on a global scale, but the question remains whether the right people are in the right jobs.

### Audit committee

The investigation committee concluded that the corporate audit division should be in charge of auditing the corporate divisions, the companies, branch companies and affiliated companies. But it seems that, actually, the corporate audit division mainly provided consultation services for the aforementioned companies and rarely conducted any auditing services to see whether or not an accounting treatment was appropriate.

The audit committee of Toshiba was incapable and not independent. Three external members of the audit committee were unfamiliar with finance and accounting. The CFO at the time of the accounting scandal was the only full-time member of the audit committee. As a consequence, the internal audit was not independent of the management. Earnings management had the tacit approval of top management.

A common definition of internal audit is providing assurance and consulting services. A balance has to be found between consultation service and assurance service. There is a problem when the internal auditor forgets that the internal audit is primarily an assurance function. The consultation service must be a by-product of the assurance service. The primary objective of an audit is to gain assurance that the internal control that is installed to achieve operation objectives is adequate and operating effectively. As a result of that operation, the organizational entity that has been audited asks advice from the internal auditor and looks for suggestions and consultancy. This is a logical consequence of a performed audit that shows some flaws in the auditing process. The consultation service cannot be excluded from the scope of the internal audit because that would result in suboptimal utilization of internal audit knowledge and experience.

Organization culture also determines the effectiveness of internal audit. One of the characteristics of the Toshiba corporate culture described earlier was the impossibility for employees to act contrary to the intent of their superiors. In such a culture it is impossible for an upright internal auditor to survive, particularly if he is not independent of management. One explanation for the (mal)functioning of the audit committee was that they choose the easier consultancy path instead of the more difficult road of reporting internal control weaknesses.

### The role of top management

As mentioned earlier in this case, the top management of Toshiba used to set targets that were unachievable, and there was excessive pressure from top management to lower-level management to realize these targets. This pressure was executed by using variable pay as a significant portion of total pay. The compensation of executive officers comprises two elements: first, a base compensation based on title; and, second, compensation based on work content and results. Some 40 to 45 per cent of the result compensation is based on performance of the overall company or business unit. This forms the basis for earnings management to meet the unachievable targets. Earnings management should have been the focus of an internal accounting audit, but clearly it was not.

This scandal at Toshiba was not an isolated incident caused by a single person or group, but a company-wide response of employees to the wishes of top management by carrying out dubious accounting practices. It is a deep-rooted problem. Therefore the conclusion is justified that this scandal goes beyond Toshiba and that this type of Japanese corporate culture has implications for other Japanese firms sharing a similar organizational character.

### Corporate culture

We have discussed corporate culture in relation to corporate governance. We saw that Toshiba's corporate culture, with obedience to superiors a core element, was an important enabler to the growth of fraudulent accounting practices. Toshiba's corporate governance was proven weak, with a poorly functioning system of internal control and the presence of internal control weaknesses at every level of the company. These weaknesses were spread across the whole company, including finance, auditing and risk management divisions. Identifying and stopping these inappropriate behaviours at an early stage became almost impossible.

The management of Toshiba and its board of directors have made significant efforts to improve internal controls and corporate governance programmes since the fraud came to light. Therefore, it is sad to mention that new issues were raised in late 2016 and early 2017. It seems similar to trying to control weeds – you think you have exterminated them, but after a while they come back.

## Toshiba Annual Report 2014

Let's have a look at the basic commitment of the Toshiba group, presented in the annual report 2014, one year before the accounting fraud saw the light of day:

***The Toshiba Commitment***

**BASIC COMMITMENT OF THE TOSHIBA GROUP**

We, the Toshiba Group companies, based on our total commitment to people and to the future, are determined to help create a higher quality of life for all people, and to do our part to help ensure that progress continues within the world community.

**COMMITMENT TO PEOPLE**

We endeavor to serve the needs of all people, especially our customers, shareholders, and employees, by implementing forward looking corporate strategies while carrying out responsible and responsive business activities. As good corporate citizens, we actively contribute to further the goals of society.

**COMMITMENT TO THE FUTURE**

By continually developing innovative technologies centering on the fields of Electronics and Energy, we strive to create products and services that enhance human life, and which lead to a thriving, healthy society. We constantly seek new approaches that help realize the goals of the world community, including ways to improve the global environment.

**Committed to People, Committed to the Future. TOSHIBA**

### Basic psychology

What happened at Toshiba can be brought back to basic human psychology: when a person says they are going to do something (see Toshiba's commitment above) but then does something completely different (see accounting scandal), you should always look at the action of the person instead of the words.

### A combination of internal control and management control

#### *Internal control*

From this and other book-keeping scandals it seems obvious that a company has to implement adequate internal control measures to decrease the unacceptable risks that the company faces. This is discussed in Chapter 11 of this book against the background of the COSO framework. The most important internal control measure is an adequate segregation of duties (SOD) between the five basic functions: authorization, custody, recording, checking and execution. In the Toshiba case, there was a serious lack of SOD, given the number and nature of the (illegal) accounting adjustments to meet the targets. These internal control measures are bottom-up initiated and start on a transaction level, and therefore have to be implemented to avoid certain risks. But that's not all. As we have seen in this case and as can be seen in other cases, there are underlying problems that a well-functioning internal control system cannot solve.

#### *Management control*

At the same time, from a management control perspective, which is a top-down approach, there are some serious issues at Toshiba that have to be addressed. In this book, these issues are centred around three basic questions:

1. MC system (Should we decentralize?)
2. MC structure (How should we decentralize?)
3. MC process (Is the planning and control cycle well executed?)

But there is more to it than organizing a well-thought-out decentralization. A number of issues remain:

- Does the company i.e. Toshiba really want to decentralize?
- Does this fit the Japanese culture?
- Can you solve the problems by implementing and extending the MC system?
- Can you really change the tone at the top?

## Discussion questions

1. If you analyse the case, what major problem or problems do you recognize from a MC perspective? Relate this to the three central questions mentioned above.
2. In the case, a number of possible explanations are given for the book-keeping scandal. Can you give additional reasons why things got out of hand at Toshiba?
3. What changes in the MC system, MC structure or MC process do you suggest to be implemented parallel to the internal control measures? Does Toshiba really want to decentralize? Do top management really want to give away some of their decision power?
4. Which contradictions and/or reinforcements do you see between internal control and management control? Can one exist without the other?
5. Discuss the role of the audit committee in Toshiba. Also discuss this against the background of the discussion within accounting firms concerning the separation of audit and advice (consulting).
6. Discuss the role of the whistle-blower. Do you think that his/her action was justified?

7 Discuss diversity policy within Toshiba and in Japanese firms in general. Is there room for foreign or female managers?

8 What MC measures do you suggest to change the underlying problems of conservatism, culture and corporate governance?

9 When you look at the passage from the Annual Report, what is your comment on the relationship between corporate governance and corporate social responsibility?

10 How can the aforementioned contradiction between actions (what people do) and words (what people say they will do) be solved from a MC point of view?

## References

Bhattacharyya, A.K. (2015) Toshiba – a case of internal audit failure, *Business Standard*, 9 August. Available at: https://www.business-standard.com/article/opinion/toshiba-a-case-of-internal-audit-failure-115080900760_1.html (accessed 8 June 2020).

Integrity-Indonesia.com (2017) Blog: Whistleblowing case: Toshiba's fraud scandal, 14 September. Available at: https://www.integrity-indonesia.com/blog/2017/09/14/whistleblowing-fraud-scandal-toshiba/ (accessed 8 June 2020).

Kazuo, M. (2015) Toshiba accounting scandal highlights issues in corporate governance, Nippon.com, 6 October. Available at: https://www.nippon.com/en/in-depth/a04802/toshiba-accounting-scandal-highlights-issues-in-corporate-governance.html (accessed 8 June 2020).

Suzuki, N. (2015) Toshiba scandal highlights need for diversity in corporate Japan, *Japan Times*, 14 August. Available at: https://www.japantimes.co.jp/news/2015/08/14/business/corporate-business/toshiba-scandal-highlights-need-diversity-corporate-japan/#.XlJ6_0NCfGI (accessed 8 June 2020).

Toshiba (2014) Annual Report 2014. Available at: https://www.toshiba.co.jp/about/ir/en/finance/ar/ar2014/tar2014e_or.pdf (accessed 8 June 2020).

Wikipedia (n.d.) Toshiba. Available at: https://en.wikipedia.org/wiki/Toshiba (accessed 8 June 2020).

Part 4

# Management control systems: summary and outlook

In this final part of the book we will sum up its main messages as well as devote attention to the roles of controllers, including some developments in the wider management literature that will affect these roles.

As we have emphasized in this book, a central question for all organizations is how to align managers' and employees' behaviour with the organization's mission, goals and strategies. Here *management control systems* play a key role, defined as comprising a combination of control practices designed and implemented by top managers to increase the probability that lower-level managers and employees will behave in ways consistent with the organization's mission, goals and strategies. These control practices can take many forms, such as responsibility centre structures (Chapter 4), transfer pricing, corporate service pricing and shared service centres (Chapter 5), general organizational structures such as a matrix structure, project types of organization, lean management and agile project management (Chapter 6), inter-organizational management control practices (Chapter 7), budgeting and forecasting (Chapter 8), performance measurement systems (Chapter 9), incentive systems (Chapter 10), and risk management systems (Chapter 11). In the book we have systematized the various control practices into three types: *input controls, throughput controls* and *output controls*. This follows an intuitive logic that lower-level managers and employees provide important cognitive abilities, skills and personal values to the organization (which top management can try to influence via input controls). These abilities, skills and values are transformed via the execution of effort – that is, the actual work and organization of lower-level managers and employees (which top management can try to influence via throughput controls) – into some sort of performance, or 'results' (which top management can try to influence via output controls). The actual combination of input, throughput and output controls will differ between organizations depending on the differences in their missions, goals and strategies, which are influenced by, for instance, the markets they serve and the nature of their value creation processes.

Our definition of management control systems expressed that we focused our attention on systematic processes in organizations that are deliberately designed to facilitate cooperation and goal achievement.

Thus, we have primarily been interested in the systematic and continuous, rather than ad hoc and incidental, control efforts. The distinction between input, throughput and output controls has proven to 'stand the test of time'. In the new era we live in, with digitalization/big data and climate change, the need for, and use of, information changes quickly, but the distinction between input, throughput and output controls remains relevant. The three types of control practices also highlight the important message of this book that the topic of management control systems is about so much more than performance measurement and incentives. We have worked hard to send a powerful message about the need to use a broad conception of what a management control system is. We provide a wider presentation of the organizational systems, structures and processes that enable managers and employees to take decisions, perform actions and influence the behaviour of other organizational members. It is this holistic and systematic view on creating organizational performance that distinguishes this book from others. It also helps us highlight that management control systems have an important 'enabling' role – that is, top managers need to design control practices that help maintain or enhance the skill set, job motivation and organizational commitment that lower-level managers and employees aim to contribute to the organization. They need to perceive control practices as something that supports them, that they can use to identify problems, prioritize issues and develop ideas for improvements. This supportive and empowering side of management control systems is very important to take into account when deciding on a management control system.

This also means that this book has a rather comprehensive view of what it means for an organization to be 'in control' or 'out of control'. These terms play an important role in many debates in practice about whether the organization is on the right track towards reaching its mission, goals and strategies. In those debates, it is easily argued that the organization is 'in control' or 'out of control'. It is clear by now that although these terms are fashionable statements, the actual design and use of management control systems is more dynamic than these terms suggest. Understanding this dynamic is probably the best way to create a feeling of being 'in control'.

Chapter 12 offers a summary, in which we would like to highlight that this enabling role of management control systems requires specialists who: (a) are able to advise on the design of these practices, (b) are able to help in visualizing how the various parts of the organization can create value together, and (c) have the professional accounting skills to help implement various control practices For more than 100 years now, we have referred to these advisers, specialists and accounting professionals using the common label of *controllers*. In a certain sense, therefore, this textbook can be seen as not only a top management's and lower-level managers' handbook but also as a controllers' handbook. We will therefore conclude this book by paying attention to the roles of controllers.

# Chapter 12

# Control and controllership: past, present, future

## Learning objectives

After reading this chapter, you should be able to:

1 Define the various roles of controllers.

2 Discuss the roles of controllers in the design and use of management control systems.

3 Discuss social and technical developments that affect these roles.

### Real world vignette: Controllers and controllership

It is hard to think about the design and use of management control systems without considering the roles of *controllers*. Controllers may be called management accountants, business analysts, data scientists or performance managers, but whatever their actual job title, the organizational function they perform is crucial for the operation and success of management control systems. In Chapter 1 of this book we defined these systems as comprising a combination of control practices designed and implemented by top managers to increase the probability that lower-level managers and employees will behave in ways consistent with the organization's mission, goals and strategies. We now define controllers broadly as the persons who are involved in the design and implementation of input controls, throughput controls (thoroughly discussed in Part 2 of this book) and output controls (thoroughly discussed in Part 3 of this book). Our basic message in this chapter is that the roles of controllers in organizations are broad, and subject to a large set of organizational dynamics. At the same time, the responsibilities of controllers can be described quite distinctly as: (a) helping top managers ensure that the management control system is designed and implemented as effectively and efficiently as possible (this includes issues related to visualization of control practices), (b) helping lower-level managers and employees to understand the logic and rationale of the various control practices in place, and (c) gathering feedback from lower-level managers and employees about how the management control system works, in order to improve it.

What does the controller job look like? Based on a study of controllers, Roy Barnard Kester, a prominent accounting academic, had the following suggestions in 1928, almost 100 years ago. Kester argued that the prime requisite is that the controller is a business-oriented person. The controller must of course also be a skilled accountant. But since the controller is expected to measure and report on performance to top managers as well as to lower-level managers, they should have sufficient knowledge of all functional activities of the business, like engineering, production, sales and marketing, and how the organization is operating. Because the controller works in close cooperation with the managers and employees in the organization, an understanding of human behaviour is also essential. The controller must know how to get along with them and be able to present an independent 'standpoint'. The controller thus needs to be thoroughly trained in business, combined with accounting knowledge as well as general knowledge about human behaviour. This, Kester concludes, will make the controller of great importance in any organization.

As we will see, these words are as valid today as when they were written nearly 100 years ago. In this chapter we will try to highlight some of the features of the modern controller role and how it has developed over the last decades. We will then highlight some developments in this role (including developments related to sustainability and digitalization/big data).

## Controllers

Like any other organizational system, the management control system is not an automaton – that is, an automatically running machine. It needs to be designed and operated by humans. Everything we have discussed about the various ways in which we can conceive human actors, see for instance Chapter 3, also applies to controllers. The controller is a psychological human being, and there are certainly personality traits that are believed to be more important to controllership than others. For example, controllers are considered to be 'conscientious' and 'emotionally stable' in terms of the big five personality categories we discussed in Chapter 3. Controllers, just like other organizational participants, are also economic creatures, which can be expected to respond to (monetary) incentives. Finally, controllers, in many countries, form a strong sociological group, and because of their professionalism have a strong and powerful organizational role. Below, however, our focus will be on the nature of the controller's formal job and role in the organization.

As a start, it should be noted that the term controller is more in use in some countries than others. Also, the term controller does not specify a level in the organizational hierarchy. By controller we here refer to the person responsible for helping managers with the design and use of management control systems. In many organizations, the most senior controller has the job title of chief financial officer (CFO). This job is positioned within the top management team of the firm. The controller function is taken on at various lower levels in the organization; some of the more precise job titles of such controllers are the generic term 'management' accountant', or the more precise term 'financial controller' (focusing more on the measuring and reporting side) or 'business controller' (focusing on helping line managers run their responsibility centres).

The CFO is usually responsible for:

- Guiding the top management team in their joint effort to design the appropriate mix of input, throughput and output controls
- Preparing financial statements and financial reports (including tax returns) for shareholders and other external parties

- Preparing and analysing performance reports, interpreting these reports for managers, analysing programme and budget proposals from various segments of the company, and consolidating these into an overall annual budget
- Supervising internal audit procedures to ensure the validity of information, establishing adequate safeguards against theft and fraud, and performing operational audits
- Developing personnel in the controller organization and participating in the education of management personnel in matters relating to management control systems.

Prior to the advent of computers, the CFO was usually also responsible for processing the information required by the management control system. Currently, with increased digital development and issues related to big data, companies typically have a chief information officer (CIO) who carries out this responsibility. In some companies, the CIO reports to the chief financial officer; in others, the CIO reports directly to the chief executive officer (CEO). The CIO's duties include managing the staff in the IT department, managing and optimizing the IT infrastructure, helping the other members of the top management team, as well as lower-level managers and employees, to understand the opportunities as well as risks with digitalization and big data.

## The controller's relationship to the rest of the organization

The controllership function is a staff function. Although the controller is usually responsible for the design and operation of the systems that collect and report information, the use of this information is the responsibility of managers in the rest of the organization. The controller may be responsible for designing and analysing performance measures and for recommending actions to these managers. Other possible responsibilities may include monitoring adherence to the spending limitations laid down by the CEO, controlling the integrity of the accounting system, and safeguarding company assets from theft and fraud.

As stated, however, the controller does not make or enforce management decisions. The responsibility for actually using the management control system runs from the CEO down through the rest of the organization. The controller may make some operational decisions; however these will be primarily those that implement policies decided on by other managers. For example, a member of the controller organization often decides on the propriety of expenses listed on a travel voucher since most managers prefer not to get involved in discussions about the cost of meals or why the traveller felt it necessary to fly first class rather than economy.

Controllers also play an important role in the preparation of long-term strategic plans and budgets. And they are often asked to scrutinize performance reports to ensure accuracy, and to call managers' attention to items deserving further inquiry.

## Responsibility centre controllers

Responsibility centre controllers, working, for instance, for a particular division or profit centre, inevitably have divided loyalties. On the one hand, they owe some allegiance to the CFO and the rest of the top management team, who are presumably responsible for the overall design and operation of the management control system. On the other hand, they also owe allegiance to the responsibility centre managers of their own units, for whom they provide support. This divided loyalty stems from the dual responsibilities that controllers typically have. These controllers contribute to the coercive role of a management control system by reporting about the activities and performance of their unit to the CFO, but also need to contribute to the enabling role of a management control system by supporting managers' and employees' strategic and operational decision making. While this dual responsibility has many advantages in terms of short lines of communication and increased expertise in financial management, it comes with some risk. For example, controllers' involvement in their own unit's decision making may reduce their independence from the responsibility centre manager, which could weaken the controller's 'corporate control' role. There could even be a conflict of interest when controllers are under local

**FIGURE 12.1** Solid line and dotted line reporting

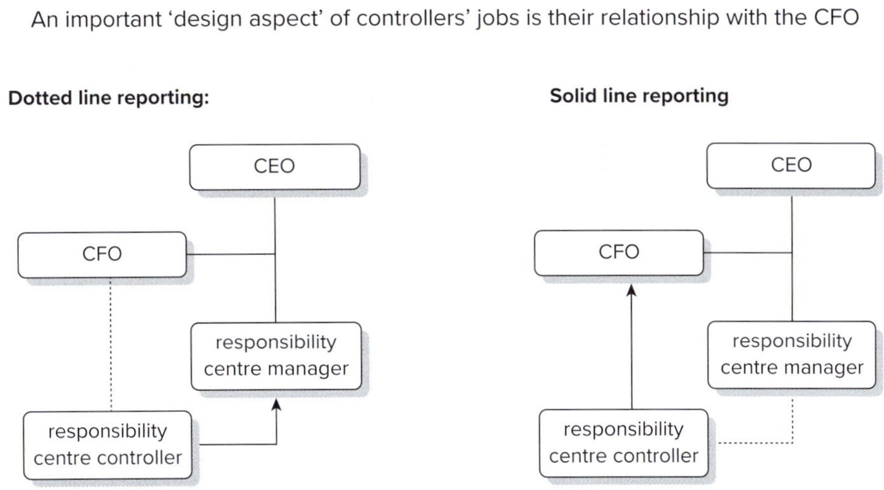


pressure to make life easy for their unit managers by allowing easy financial targets, which runs counter to the organization's overall goals. Academic studies show that the extent to which controllers are likely to withstand local pressures depends on their involvement in local decision making, the amount of social pressure they experience from their unit manager, and their personality. Regarding the latter, it appears that there are differences in the extent to which controllers consider ethical standards and norms, and are inclined to perform actions that benefit them personally, which is called *Machiavellianism*.

The extent to which this is a true risk for organizations may also depend on the way in which the controller's position is determined. In some companies, the responsibility centre controller reports to the responsibility centre manager, and has what is called *a dotted line relationship* with the CFO. Here, the responsibility centre manager is the controller's immediate boss, and has ultimate authority in the hiring, training, transferral, compensation, promotion and firing of controllers within that responsibility centre. These decisions are rarely made, however, without input from the CFO. In other companies, there is a *solid line relationship* with the CFO in that responsibility centre controllers report direct to the CFO – that is, the CFO is their boss. These two possible types of relationship are diagrammed in Figure 12.1.

There are advantages and disadvantages with each of these relationships, and the choice of a solid or dotted line depends on several factors. Solid-line reporting helps create a strong, cultural and professional, bond between controllers across the firm. This may benefit training, exchange of professional knowledge and norms, and opportunities for promotion and individual growth. Dotted-line reporting may benefit entrepreneurship of local controllers, and enhanced decentralized empowerment. If the responsibility centre controller works primarily for the responsibility centre manager, there is the possibility that they will not provide completely objective reports on responsibility centre budgets and performance to top managers. On the other hand, if the responsibility centre controller works primarily for the CFO, the responsibility centre manager may treat them as a 'spy' from the top management team rather than as a trusted aide.

***Real World Example:*** The story of Wirecard reads like a spy novel. Founded in Munich in 1999, Wirecard became listed in 2005 and became the darling of international investors and banks, such as ABN-Amro and ING. Wirecard rapidly became a dominant supplier of payment services, being licensed by VISA and Mastercard. Entering the Dax 30 in 2018, in 2019 the publication of annual figures was delayed several times, raising suspicion about the reality of its communicated economic position. In June 2020 the company was forced to disclose that an amount of €1.9bn of cash, supposedly held in the Philippines, was simply 'missing'. The affair resembles the famous cases of Enron, Ahold and Parmalat, in which fingers are typically pointed at audit firms wrongly approving annual statements, and CEO's accused of questionable practices.

Regardless of the design of the reporting relationships, it is of course expected that the controller will neither condone nor participate in the transmission of misleading information or in the concealment of unfavourable information. The overall ethical responsibilities inherent in the position do not countenance such practices. Cases such as presented in the example of Wirecard, thus, underline the importance of the fiduciary role of controllers. However, they at the same time also attest to the sometimes feeble bases of this role when these questionable reporting practices are actively endorsed by top-management.

## Roles and tasks of controllers

The jobs and career paths of controllers are subject to all the dynamic changes that organizations face. The impact of crises on controllers' jobs, ongoing internationalization coupled with digitalization and big data, as well as climate change, have made the job more dynamic and challenging. We will come back to these developments later in this chapter. At the same time, it is fair to say that the controller function as originally envisioned to cover all aspects of the management control system remains valid. Surely, the enhanced attention to risk management, and the complexity and pervasiveness of information technology, lead many firms to refocus on the core competencies and responsibilities of the controller.

Yet the core roles and responsibilities of controllers that were documented as early as 1928 have been confirmed by several authors over the last decades, with slight updates in terminology, as the overview in the Real World Example shows.

***Real World Example:*** For more than 100 years there have been various attempts to classify the roles and duties of controllers in organizations. Although the labels and number of categories differ, the dual role of supporting actual business and reporting about business results can be clearly demarcated in our overview below of developments in the roles and tasks of controllers.

**Kester (1928) Tasks of the controller**
Measure the efficiency of the operating executives
Report findings
Suggest policies or remedies

**Anderson (1947) Tasks of controllership**
Protection of business assets
Compliance with rules and regulations
Assistance to decision makers

**Simon et al. (1954) Roles**
Scorecard keeping
Attention direction
Problem solving

**Sathe (1982) Fields of responsibility**
Support management team in business decision-making process (management service responsibility)
Ensure accuracy of financial information and integrity of internal control practices (fiduciary responsibility)

*Sources:* Anderson, D.R. (1947) *Practical Controllership.* Chicago: Richard D. Irwin. Kester, R.B. (1928) The importance of the controller, *Accounting Review,* 3(3): 237–51.Sathe, V. (1982) *Controller Involvement in Management.* Englewood Cliffs: Prentice-Hall. Simon, H.A., Guetzkow, H., Kozmetsky, G. and Tyndall, G. (1954) *Centralization versus Decentralization in Organizing the Controller's Department.* New York: Controllership Foundation.

We have already discussed the inventory that Kester made in 1928, suggesting that controllers work in close alignment with responsibility centre managers. Their specific tasks were to measure the performance of the organization and its responsibility centres. They should make management reports, and present these to responsibility centre managers. Moreover, based on their understanding of the various operational processes, controllers would also be able to make suggestions to managers about potential performance improvements and efficiency gains. Anderson is known for a threefold categorization of the controller function. Next to the internal role in supporting decision makers, which was emphasized by Kestler, Anderson points to a larger set of stakeholders who benefit from the controller's expertise. Controllers make sure that the organization's assets are not used in vain, thus protecting the interests of shareholders. They should also make sure that the organization behaves in line with (legal) rules, which benefits all external stakeholders of the firm. With Sathe, the focus of controllers' responsibilities had become twofold. On the one hand, controllers should support the business. They would help managers in making the 'best' business decisions, and ideally the controller would be part of the management team. This management-serving responsibility is sometimes expressed as the controller becoming a 'consultant'. On the other hand, controllers would have a fiduciary obligation to make sure that managers adhere to rules and regulations, as endorsed and enforced by top management. This fiduciary obligation is sometimes expressed as the controller becoming like a 'police officer'.

Sathe's discussion of the role of the controller has become quite influential over recent decades. This especially goes for his plea to create 'strong controllers'. Controllers are 'strong' if they are able to both safeguard the company's assets, assure the integrity and guarantee the quality of performance reporting, and support responsibility centre managers. Strong controllers would know how to combine these roles and be able to develop the necessary competence. Switching between roles is demanding, as that comes not only with different obligations and goals, but also with a different way of acting. Kester had already noted this in 1928. Firms who have the size and resources to commit to investments in controllership may prefer the model in which 'financial controllers' focus on the aspect of asset security and reporting integrity, and 'business controllers' focus on the informational and analytic needs of responsibility centre managers. In fact, such firms apply a 'split controller' philosophy. The other two quadrants in Sathe's analysis are named 'involved controller' and 'independent controller'. These types of controller have a relatively large focus on providing management services and on providing fiduciary quality, respectively. This focus is sometimes displayed in job titles too, with the former labelled 'business controller' and the latter 'financial controller' (see Figure 12.2).

**FIGURE 12.2** Types of controllership

| | Business support HIGH | Business support LOW |
|---|---|---|
| Corporate control LOW | *Involved controller*<br>High priority for business support, low priority for reporting and internal control<br>Decision support 'business partner'<br>Risk of faulty reporting<br>Typical label: 'business controller' | This is a situation that companies should avoid |
| Corporate control HIGH | *Strong controller*<br>High priority for business support, and for reporting and internal control<br>Flexibility<br>Risk of conflict of interests | *Independent controller*<br>Low priority for business support, high priority for reporting and internal control<br>Organizational 'conscience'<br>Risk of limited added value<br>Typical label: 'financial controller' |

When combined this is labelled 'split controllership'

## Developments in controllership and management control systems

Controlling and management control systems are often said to change slowly compared to other parts of organizations. The still very relevant tasks of the controller described by Kester almost 100 years ago offer a good illustration of this, even if he was way ahead of his time. There are probably several reasons for this. One is the rather conservative guardian role as the controller has to protect the organization from individual wrongdoings; another may be the personality of the controllers. A third reason may be that many CEOs prioritize the business part of the organization rather than administrative staff, such as the controlling department, when it comes to organizational development.

But even if this is to some extent the case, we live in a changing world, and in most organizations this means that all parts of the organization have to follow this development, at least to some extent. Therefore we have not just described the traditional roles of the controller and management control systems in this book. We have also described many more modern features that we argue have changed the nature of controlling and management control systems, and will continue to do so in the future.

One such change is that we introduced the stakeholder perspective as an alternative to the more one-sided shareholder perspective (see the discussions in, for instance, Chapters 2 and 9). Traditionally, management control systems have been mostly concerned with the owners. But in a world with increased competition and greater need for highly competent employees, this is changing. The stakeholder perspective also has ethical aspects, including the organization's influence on not only employees and customers, but also on society. In line with this, we have also discussed sustainability and CSR as important dimensions to take into account when designing a management control system.

We have also introduced alternative perspectives on human behaviour in Chapter 3. Traditionally, the economic model of human behaviour has dominated the design of management control systems. However, with an increased focus on employees, more sophisticated models, like the sociological and psychological models, are called for. Human behaviour is often more complicated than we may think at a first glimpse and that is something we have stressed throughout this book, the section on motivation and self-determination theory (SDT) in Chapter 10 being one obvious example.

Traditionally, management control systems have also had a rather vertical perspective where goals and authority are broken down in a logical chain of command and where different organizations are seen as totally separate entities. This implies a view on organizations where the different responsibility centres are coordinated from above and where different organizations are coordinated by market mechanisms. However, we believe that this coordination to an increasing extent is achieved by creating relations and bringing different responsibility centres, as well as whole organizations, closer to one another. This is discussed in the form of cross-functional integration in Chapter 6 and inter-organizational relationships in Chapter 7, which both represent a more horizontal perspective on organizations.

The vertical view on organizations mentioned above also implies a rather top-down and centralized view. However, we believe that a more decentralized approach is gaining interest, for at least two reasons. The first is that employees are better educated and more competent than before and a centralized management control system often does not utilize this competence to the fullest. The other reason is that a too-centralized management control system tends to make organizations more rigid and slower. We have stressed the need for finding a balance between more centralized aspects of management control systems and more decentralized systems and features. This is represented by more general discussions of the enabling role of management control systems (in Chapter 1) and organic systems (in Chapter 2), as well as more specific discussions of control practices such as beyond budgeting (in Chapter 8) and the balanced scorecard as an enabling performance measurement system (in Chapter 9).

There are of course many other topics and features that are discussed as possible routes of development in controlling but perhaps are still less prevalent in practice. Some of these are related to what we discussed above, some are not. We are going to take a look at some of these in the following section, which finalizes this chapter.

## Predicted paths for development

First, as a response to the various crises in the financial world, and the issue of climate change, the call for more ethical and sustainability-oriented controllership is heard across the globe. Controllers should not simply 'follow' the organization's mission, goals and strategies and implement a management control system already more or less designed by top management, but should instead be more independent thinkers, who are able to evaluate the longer-term and wider ethical implications of such goals and strategies. This could be labelled as 'financial ethics and sustainability competence', which goes beyond business and accounting skills and requires the development of other competencies. The demands for such competencies are well understood by the many professional organizations that educate and certify professional controllers, such as the Institute of Management Accountants (IMA) and the Certified Institute of Management Accountants (CIMA) (see Real World Example).

***Real World Example:*** Some ethical resources for controllers are described below.

**IMA code of conduct**

The US-originating organization of Certified Management Accountants (Institute of Management Accountants - IMA) states that:

> *IMA has been committed to advocating the highest standards of ethical business practices – both for its members and the profession at large – since the organization was founded in 1919. In the early 1980s, IMA took a bold leadership role in the area of ethics by developing its first written code of ethics: Standards of Ethical Conduct of Management Accountants. In 2005, in the wake of global financial scandals and an increasing need for more direct ethical guidelines, IMA issued new guidance to better reflect the ethical climate of the time. The result was the IMA Statement of Ethical Professional Practice, which required each IMA member to be committed to the highest ethical behavior. [. . .] More concise and simpler to understand and apply, this updated version more fully reflects the global scope of management accounting. It also requires IMA members to contribute to a positive ethical culture in their organization and to place integrity of the profession above personal interests. These requirements recognize the need for members to take an active role in ensuring their organization has a strong, open, and positive ethical culture.*

*Source:* IMA Statement of Ethical Professional Practice, 2017.

**CIMA**

The UK-originating, internationally present Chartered Global Management Accountant body (CGMA), together with the American Institute of Certified Public Accountants (AICPA), state that:

> *In an ever-changing global environment, ethics continues to be a growing priority to corporations around the world. A broad range of powerful trends, including rapid economic development in emerging markets, differing rates of economic recovery in mature markets, complex political and environmental issues and challenging regulatory regimes impacts the work of Chartered Global Management Accountant (CGMA) designation holders. It calls for a unified set of ethical guidance for CGMA designation holders around the world.*
>
> *To address this need, the AICPA and CIMA worked together to align the sections of our respective ethical codes for CGMA designation holders in business and industry. The Code of Ethics for CGMA designation holders is non-authoritative guidance that provides a robust and uniform standard of behaviour applicable to all CGMA designation holders.*
>
> *The aligned code recognises that CGMA designation holders are committed to upholding high standards of professionalism and to acting ethically. As such, they play a key role in supporting leadership and other colleagues in setting, communicating and embedding an ethical performance culture.*

*Source:* CIMA Code of Ethics, 2015.

Second, since controllers are involved in information verification and processing, their jobs are faced with an enormous increase in complexity due to recent developments in digital technologies and big data. Over recent decades, most larger companies have automated, centralized and outsourced their financial administration. The advent, and continuous evolution, of big data and integrated information systems supplied by SAP, Oracle and other developers of such enterprise resource planning (ERP) systems, have drastically changed the controller's job. It has moved from hands-on understanding of administrative procedures, carefully decided on by the financial department, to a fully hands-off handling of information. Financial processes happen in physically dislocated areas, or are captured in computer algorithms. This development challenges controllers to remain cognisant of the underlying accounting principles, move themselves up to a higher level of services that they provide to their organizations, and stay in touch with computer technology. This means that controllers face a greater challenge of aligning the technological possibilities of reporting with the ethical principles of sound reporting. Controllers are thus expected to move towards becoming 'information engineers' or 'data scientists', or at least to be aware of the information-technological developments in this field, and to communicate with information managers and IT managers across the organization.

Third, controllers are under more scrutiny to prove their added value to organizations and, indeed, societies. Combining traditional insights in accounting, safeguarding the integrity of financial reporting and acting as the rational 'conscience' of organizations, remain the foundations of the controller's role. Besides the technological challenges, controllers are also expected to keep up with current business complexities. Organizations used to develop long-term strategies, on which the management control system design should be based. Management control systems would basically cut the longer-term strategy into yearly cycles – for instance, through the annual budgeting procedure. Control in such a setting is based on a rigid organizational and procedural setting. But those days seem gone for ever.

Increased international competition from globalizing companies, coupled with increased pressure for short-term financial performance by the globalizing financial industry, urge companies into shorter cycles. Controllers are invited to change from the reactive managers of stability into the proactive directors of change. Obviously, as previously mentioned, they still have as one of their prime responsibilities to support responsibility centre managers. However, controllers are more and more pressed to become *decision architects*. They do not take business decisions, but can provide managers with the right frame in which such decisions can be taken. This does not only include the task of organizing data discussed above, but also adds another aspect to the long list of competencies that modern controllers should have, namely a good understanding of how managers behave and take decisions. Our attention to this aspect, and controllers' ability to use the *management control model of human behaviour* (as discussed in Chapter 3), has moved from the nice-to-know into the need-to-know category in controllers' education and training.

Fourth, linked to the previous discussion, there are several ways that controlling can contribute to more flexible and agile organizations. In a world that was often referred to as VUCA even before the coronavirus crisis, this is becoming more and more important for an increasing number of organizations. VUCA stands for Volatile, Uncertain, Complex and Ambiguous, and implies a growing need for flexibility and agility. In a study of companies in Silicon Valley,[1] researchers even claimed that there are no MBAs in Silicon Valley, since MBAs are trained for traditional, hierarchic and bureaucratic companies, rather than modern, agile and fast-moving ones. Other companies even experiment with organizational structures where all hierarchies and managers have been abolished,[2] in order to become more agile.

---

1 Steiber, A. and Alänge, S. (2016) *The Silicon Valley Model: Management for Entrepreneurship.* Cham: Springer.

2 One example can be found here: Hamel, G. (2011) First, let's fire all the managers, *Harvard Business Review,* 89(12): 48–60.

The majority of organizations of course do not go that far to become more agile, but according to many voices in the current debate it does require a major shift in most organizations' management control systems. The idea is to empower lower-level managers and employees so that they can take immediate action when a problem occurs or a customer poses a demand, instead of processing everything through a slow hierarchy. One such framework[3] suggests that the following shifts are required:

- From owner focus to customer focus
- From extrinsic rewards to intrinsic motivation
- From monitoring to trust
- From planning to adaptability.

According to this framework you have to move in all four aspects to really become agile and it is, for instance, not recommended to combine trust with extrinsic rewards. Most of these aspects have to some extent been discussed in this book. Trust is frequently discussed in academia and practice, and the idea is that too much monitoring tends to decrease the motivation and creativity of managers and employees, as well as increase short-termism and data manipulation. Trust, on the other hand, often increases confidence and motivation, as well as creating loyalty to the organization. An agile and trust-based control approach implies a more coaching and supportive role for both managers and controllers.

The Real World Example summarizes these developments, which can be seen as an extension of the development in controllers' roles in the first 100 years of controllership that the earlier Real World Example summarized.

***Real World Example:*** The following list sums up the likely development of controllership beyond 2020.

- *Guardians:* of financial ethics and of sustainability-oriented thinking.
- *Information engineers:* data integrity, privacy protection, big data analysis.
- *Decision architects:* understanding decision-making processes, providing accurate decision-making frames; develop decision-making models.
- *Agile coaches:* Increasing flexibility by supporting empowerment, motivation, creativity and loyalty with the organization and its customers.

## Summary

This chapter closes the text on the design and use of management control systems. Understanding of such systems is incomplete without first understanding the key roles that controllers play in making these systems work. We have highlighted the responsibilities of controllers and described some developments in controllers' roles, providing both opportunities and challenges for the controllers in our organizations. The chapter closes by pointing out some of the developments in controllership, which are all highly determined by developments in information technology on the one hand and the organizational and societal demands for efficiency and transparency. Although it is hard to predict how management control and controllership will exactly develop and in what pace, all the developments point to an increase in importance of management control systems and one of its key players, the controller.

[3] Francke, L. and Nilsson, G. (2017) *Det agila företaget: fiskstim eller supertankers i en dynamisk värld?* Malmö: Roos & Tegnér.

## Suggested additional reading

Anderson, D.R. (1944) The function of industrial controllership, *Accounting Review*, 19(1): 55–65.

Bogt, H.T., van Helden, J. and van der Kolk, B. (2016) New development: public sector controllership – reinventing the financial specialist as a countervailing power, *Public Money & Management*, 36(5): 379–84.

Roehl-Anderson, J.M. and Bragg, S.M. (2007) *Controllership: The Work of the Managerial Accountant, 2008 Cumulative Supplement*. New York: John Wiley & Sons.

Shim, J.K., Siegel, J.G. and Dauber, N. (2019) *Corporate Controller's Handbook of Financial Management 2019–2020*. Chicago: CCH Inc.

Weber, J. (2011) The development of controller tasks: explaining the nature of controllership and its changes, *Journal of Management Control*, 22(1): 25–46.

# Case 12.1 Controller involvement*

## by Frank G.H. Hartmann

LimoDrinks Ltd is a company producing various foods and beverages. It employs about 4,000 people, who work across five business units in several European countries. LimoDrinks' home and headquarters are in the United Kingdom. The company is not listed on a stock exchange. The structure of the way in which controllers operate at LimoDrinks is roughly as follows. Every business unit (BU) employs a BU controller, who is responsible for leading a set of junior and senior controllers in the BU. The BU controller is a member of the BU's management team. Apart from these two, the BU management teams also comprise a production and logistics manager and a marketing and sales manager.

The BU controllers all report to both their BU's general manager and to the CFO of LimoDrinks' headquarters. All BUs are run as 'investment centres'. LimoDrinks applies a rather classical budgetary control system, in which BU and corporate managers together decide yearly about an annual budget for the BU. As the BU is an investment centre, the main financial target for each BU is formulated in terms of return on capital employed (ROCE). It is calculated as the BU's earnings (earnings before interest and taxes, or EBIT) divided by the BU's capital employed (which is total assets minus current liabilities).

BU managers receive an annual bonus that is based on the ROCE achieved by their BU. If the BU meets the target level ROCE, BU managers obtain a bonus payment that is equal to 12.5 per cent of their fixed salary. The maximum bonus BU managers can earn is 25 per cent of their annual fixed salary, which depends in a linear way on the actual ROCE achieved. To avoid BU controllers possibly having an incentive to 'cook the books', all controllers are excluded from this ROCE-based bonus system. Instead, they are eligible for a bonus based on other, more subjective, performance criteria.

Flush BV is the smallest of the five BUs of LimoDrinks and has about 500 employees. Flush mainly produces ice cream for consumers and the leisure industry. George van Oosten has been the general manager of Flush for three years. Samantha van Kesteren has been Flush's BU controller for the past five years. During this period, Flush has divested some of its activities that were unrelated to the production and sales of ice cream. This change of focus also brought about a change from mainly focusing on the customer market towards the professional market of restaurant chains and some other companies in the food and beverages industry. In October 2019 it becomes evident to the BU management team that the results of this strategic change are somewhat disappointing, and the chance that Flush will be able to reach its 2019 ROCE target is getting quite small (see Exhibit 1).

**EXHIBIT 1** Flush ROCE targets and realization over the years 2015–2019

| Year | ROCE targets (%) | ROCE realized (%) |
|---|---|---|
| | | |
| 2015 | 10 | 9 |
| 2016 | 12 | 12.2 |
| 2017 | 12.5 | 13.0 |
| 2018 | 13 | 13.6 |
| 2019 | 14.0 | 13.3 (expected) |

* This case was written by Professor Frank G.H. Hartmann, Radboud University.

In October 2019, the Flush management team meets to decide on the 2020 budget proposal they have to submit to the LimoDrinks CFO. George van Oosten suggests basing the proposal on conservative estimates. Both he and Samantha van Kesteren believe Flush should be able to realize a ROCE of 13.5 per cent in 2020. However, George asks Samantha if she can come up with a proposal of a ROCE target of 11 per cent instead. George explains that he feels it would be bad for his BU to miss its ROCE target in both 2019 and 2020, and he wants to avoid any risk. He also mentions that it would be unfair if Flush's managers miss their bonus again next year. Samantha realizes that the only way to explain a ROCE proposal for 2020 of 11 per cent would be to use very low sales estimates and very high cost estimates, which would both have to be unrealistic. She also knows that George does not have the formal authority to order her to make such unrealistic estimates. Samantha thus needs to decide for herself what to to. Based on her experience with corporate headquarters in the past, she is aware of the fact that they are very unlikely to find out that the ROCE proposal of 11 per cent is unrealistic.

## Questions

1. How likely do you think it is that Samantha will choose to proceed with developing a budget proposal that is based on a ROCE estimate of 11 per cent?
2. Imagine you are in the same situation as Samantha. How likely would it be that you will proceed with developing a budget proposal that is based on a ROCE estimate of 11 per cent?
3. How would your answer to questions 1 and 2 change if you knew the following facts? BU controller Samantha van Kesteren has always been very actively involved in the BU's strategic and operational management. She has contributed substantially to the initiation, development and implementation of Flush's new strategy.
4. How would your answer to questions 1 and 2 change if you knew the following fact? George van Oosten and the other two members of the BU management team put severe pressure on BU controller Samantha van Kesteren to agree to a ROCE proposal of 11 per cent.

*Source:* Based on Hartmann, F.G. and Maas, V.S. (2010) Why business unit controllers create budget slack: involvement in management, social pressure, and Machiavellianism, *Behavioral Research in Accounting,* 22(2): 27–49.

# Case 12.2 Crisis management: strategic or tactical responses?*

**by Frank G.H. Hartmann**

## The COVID-19 crisis

As the 'corona' crisis evolved during the first part of the new '20 decade into a global pandemic, many attempts were made to estimate its impact on the world economy in both the short and the long run. Below you will find three (extended) quotes from press releases of three firms, commenting on the nature and impact of the corona crisis. These quotes all aim to describe the situation at the end of the first quarter of 2020, and predict the consequences for the years to come.

* This case was written by Professor Frank G.H. Hartmann, Radboud University.

*[Shenzhen, China, April 8, 2020] Recently, HUAWEI CLOUD announced that they launched a global action plan to help customers around the world to fight COVID-19 with cloud and AI services. As part of this international action plan against the coronavirus, HUAWEI CLOUD will be providing free AI and cloud services and will be recruiting partners around the world to help fight this pandemic together.*

*Source:* Huawei.com (2020) HUAWEI CLOUD: fighting COVID-19 with technology, 7 April. Available at: https://www.huawei.com/en/press-events/news/2020/4/fighting-covid-19-with-technology (accessed 9 June 2020).

*[Roissy, France, 9 April 2020] Air France-KLM Group, Air France and KLM are holding in-depth discussions with their respective governments and financial institutions. The Group has implemented strong measures since the beginning of the crisis which include, amongst others:*

*– Negotiation with governments of payment deferral for taxes (civil aviation, solidarity . . .), social contribution and various charges;*

*– Negotiation with lessors and airports of payment deferral;*

*– Cost reduction measures, estimated at this stage at €500 million in 2020, an increase of €300 million compared to previous announcements;*

*– The possibility of early retirement of certain sub-fleets of aircraft;*

*– Implementation by Air France of partial activity measures and application by KLM for the 'Temporary Emergency Bridging Measure for Sustained Employment' (NOW), with an impact estimated at this stage at around €1.1 billion for 2020;*

*– Review of the investment plan to reduce the capital expenditure plan by €700 million in 2020, an increase of €350 million compared to previous announcements, to which will be added the impact of the decline in own and third-party activity on the amount of maintenance investments.*

*Source:* airfranceklm.com (2020) Air France-KLM Group, Air France and KLM are holding in-depth discussions with their respective governments and financial institutions, 9 April. Available at: https://www.airfranceklm.com/en/air-france-klm-group-air-france-and-klm-are-holding-depth-discussions-their-respective-governments (accessed 9 June 2020).

*[Irving, Texas, April 7, 2020] ExxonMobil reduces 2020 capex by 30%, cash opex by 15%; maintains long-term outlook*

*[. . .] Capital investments for 2020 are now expected to be about $23 billion, down from the previously announced $33 billion. The 15 percent decrease in cash operating expenses is driven by deliberate actions to increase efficiencies and reduce costs, and includes expected lower energy costs.*

*'After a thorough evaluation of the impacts of the pandemic and market conditions, we have worked closely with business partners to plan and execute capital adjustments that preserve long-term value, maximize cost efficiency, and put us in the strongest position when market conditions improve,' said Darren Woods, chairman and chief executive officer of Exxon Mobil Corporation.*

*'The long-term fundamentals that underpin the company's business plans have not changed – population and energy demand will grow, and the economy will rebound. Our capital allocation priorities also remain unchanged. Our objective is to continue investing in industry-advantaged projects to create value, preserve cash for the dividend and make appropriate and prudent use of our balance sheet.'*

*[. . .] 'While COVID-19 has had a significant impact on the global economy, we are confident that trade, transportation and manufacturing will recover,' said Woods. 'ExxonMobil continues to invest in the projects that will position us to support economic recovery and capture value for our shareholders.'*

*Source:* ExxonMobil (2020) ExxonMobil reduces 2020 capex by 30%, cash opex by 15%; maintains long-term outlook, Newsroom, 7 April. Available at: https://corporate.exxonmobil.com/News/Newsroom/News-releases/2020/0407_ExxonMobil-reduces-2020-capex-by-30-percent-cash-opex-by-15-percent (accessed 9 June 2020).

## Questions

1 To what extent are the policies and policy changes suggested by these companies of a strategic nature?

2 To what extent are the policies and policy changes suggested by these companies the result of the use of management control systems?

3 To what extent are the policies and policy changes suggested by these companies the result of the use of risk management systems?

# Case 12.3

# Ethical dilemmas in a controller job*

**by Frank G.H. Hartmann**

Reflecting on his career, having been 30 years in the financial profession, Robert Johnson decided that things could have been better, but things could also have been a lot worse. As a young graduate from a renowned business school in the south-eastern part of England, Robert had for some time entertained the thought of entering one of the big merchant banks in the City. Certainly, some of his close friends had done so, and apparently had made big money, besides a big ego. However, he had always considered himself to be interested in broader things than just making money. Especially after taking a minor (a short specialization track) in auditing he decided that an audit career might be the way forward.

He started working at one of the big five auditing firms, Arthur Andersen, as a rookie. He followed the typical career path, starting in a junior position in 1991, moving to a team leader position in 1993, and manager in 1996. Over the years he enjoyed the role of auditor, moving from client to client, and becoming more responsible for larger clients. In 1998 he faced the first serious choice in his career. Stay in auditing or move out and enter business? One of his major clients during his last year in auditing showed a keen interest in hiring him. The CFO of that company, Jacqueline Simmons, admired his technical skill, but above all praised him for his trustworthy and transparent style of working.

'My company is in need of people like you, Robert. We need the skills that you have acquired in your job as auditor. What I need to do is convince you to make the step into business control. I hope I can tempt you to become one of our senior business unit controllers. Everybody is talking about strong controllership these days, but to be honest, I believe that controllers add value to the firm only if they know how to support their business unit managers.'

Obviously, Robert was attracted to the idea of changing his focus from checking the numbers towards preparing them. He also became intrigued by the role that controllers seemed to play in managing firm value. It was the time, he recalls vividly, of great dotcom firms, like Amazon, Enron and Worldcom, which dominated the pages of the financial press. These companies, somehow, managed to create value, whereas their accounting figures were not that impressive. There was talk about 'new economy' companies that were guided by shareholder value consideration rather than 'old economy' bottom-line profits. The relationship between share price and accounting profits had always both intrigued and puzzled him. Now was the time to help create value.

* This case was written by Professor Frank G.H. Hartmann, Radboud University.

So he decided to accept the offer, and considered himself lucky when soon after he joined his new firm, the world came down on Enron and his old employer. His career went smoothly, and he was quick to respond when Jacqueline asked him to become mentor for some of the junior staff at Integrity Systems Ltd. The idea was to provide junior controllers with a sounding board in case they met with dilemmas in their work. Soon, Robert was facing a couple of tough cases presented to him. Fortunately, Jacqueline seemed fully trustworthy, and gave Robert enormous support and confidence. She also asked him to share his experiences with her, in all anonymity, so that he could advise her on company policy regarding the training of controllers, or the redesign of their role in the firm. During the first year of their cooperation, the following cases were discussed between them (names and facts were anonymized).

Jim is BU manager and direct supervisor of BU controller Carl. For most of the current year, the BU's performance has been quite good. In large part this is due to Jim's excellent management skills. However, a major production problem in December threatens the BU to face a loss this year. This would cost Jim his full bonus for the year. He was counting on the bonus, so this prospect seriously distresses him, as his family situation is problematic. Jim proposes to release part of an existing provision to improve the BU's bottom line. The provision is in a grey area, so that accounting rules allow interpretation both ways.

Victor is BU manager and direct supervisor of BU controller, Bob. The BU has shown three years of solid performance. Victor has been working very hard in this period and has turned the BU into a successful business. However, this year the BU is about to end below the sales target. This would strongly decrease Victor's chances of getting the promotion he was hoping for. Victor is very excited about a possible step up the hierarchy in the company, and very keen on making the target. Victor asks Bob to authorize a sharp price discount for a sales promotion in December, which would ensure the BU will meet its target, even though sales early next year would suffer.

Ben is BU manager and direct supervisor of BU controller, Claire. Their company is starting the budget rounds for the coming year. As BU manager, Ben is responsible for meeting the target, which the BU will fail to meet this year due to unforeseen market circumstances. Ben fears the risk that the BU will miss its target again next year. This could cost him his job as BU manager. Ben tells Claire that he is very afraid of losing his job, which would put him in serious personal trouble. He therefore wants to include a safety margin in next year's budget proposal by submitting a lower sales budget than the best estimate. HQ does not have sufficient market insight to detect this.

Mark is BU manager and direct supervisor of BU controller, Helen. Mark is planning to hire a consultancy for a project next year, which is dependent on having sufficient budget. Mark has shown enormous enthusiasm and passion for the project. This year's consulting budget has not been used, due to a delay in one of the other projects. HQ might therefore cut next year's budget, in which case the project would have to be cancelled. Mark is very motivated to do everything he can to save it. He proposes to Helen to pay a substantial part of the fee from the current year's budget, even though the real work won't start until next year.

David is BU manager and direct supervisor of BU controller, Henry. Henry is preparing the innovation budget for next year, using best estimates of costs. David describes several of the innovation projects with great enthusiasm and belief. However, it is likely that HQ will make budget cuts across all BUs. This would render it impossible to carry out some of the projects in the BU's pipeline. David shows real passion to make the projects happen. He therefore proposes to increase the cost estimations somewhat. David says that in order to end up with fair amounts, Henry needs to submit overestimated numbers, in spite of the corporate policy to use best estimates.

George is BU manager and direct supervisor of BU controller, James. The BU is considering a small acquisition, which George strongly supports. James is required by HQ to use the standard 25 per cent discount rate. HQ does not allow deviations from the standard discount rate. This yields a slightly negative NPV, leaving the target undervalued; the company has a solid, proven track record, and a 15 per cent rate would be more appropriate. George is absolutely furious about the standard rate of 25 per cent.

He proposes to increase projected sales growth beyond Year 3 in order to get a realistic NPV with a reasonable chance of approval by HQ. This sales growth prediction would most likely not be met.

## Questions

1 What are the similarities and differences in desired competencies between auditors and controllers?

2 Discuss each of the above cases, taking into account the following questions.

  a What is the essential problem?

  b Are the suggested behaviours legally or ethically inadmissible?

  c What trade-offs exist in the potential reaction of the controller?

  d What advice would you have for the controllers in each of the cases?

3 Is the sounding board a good idea? What other solutions exist to alleviate potential role conflicts in controllers?

*Source:* Eskenazi, P.I., Hartmann, F.G. and Rietdijk, W.J. (2016) Why controllers compromise on their fiduciary duties: EEG evidence on the role of the human mirror neuron system, *Accounting, Organizations and Society*, 50: 41–50.

# Case 12.4

# Nucor corporation*

**by Vijay Govindarajan**

*We are a cyclical business. . . . Basically when we are at the peak of the cycle – times are good, interest rates are low, people are building – our margins increase. When we go through the trough, of course, the margins are squeezed. But over the last 25 years Nucor has never had a losing quarter. Not only a losing quarter, we have never had a losing month or a losing week.*[1]

**John D. Correnti, President and CEO, Nucor**

In 1998 Nucor was a Fortune 500 company with 6,900 employees and sales of $4.3 billion in steel and steel-related products. Its chairman, F. Kenneth Iverson, had headed the company for more than 30 years. During his tenure, the steel industry faced a number of problems, including foreign competition, strained labour relations and slowed demand for steel (related in part to the substitution of alternative materials). Despite these industry challenges, Nucor's sales during Iverson's tenure grew at an annual compound rate of about 17 per cent per annum. Selected comparative financial data are shown in Exhibit 1. In different years, both Iverson and Nucor CEO John Correnti were named Steelmaker of the Year by *New Steel* magazine.

---

* This case was prepared by Professor Vijay Govindarajan. The cooperation and help provided by F. Kenneth Iverson, Chairman, Nucor Corporation, in preparing this case study is greatly appreciated. © Dartmouth College.

[1] Franklin, R. (1996) An Interview with John D. Correnti, President and CEO, Nucor Corporation, *Wall Street Corporate Reporter*, 9–15 September, pp. 19–20.

**EXHIBIT 1** Selected financial data 1993–1997

| | Sales 1997 ($ billions) | Return on equity (5-year average) % 1993–1997 | Debt/capital % 1997 | 5-year sales growth % 1993–1997 | Profit margin % 1997 |
|---|---|---|---|---|---|
| Nucor | $4.1 | 18% | 7% | 23% | 8% |
| Texas Industries* (parent of Chaparral Steel) | 1.0 | 12 | 22 | 12 | 8 |
| National Steel† | 3.1 | 7 | 27 | 6 | 7 |
| USX-US Steel† | 6.8 | 10 | 21 | 7 | 6 |
| Bethlehem Steel† | 4.7 | Deficit | 28 | 3 | Deficit |
| LTV† | 4.3 | 11 | 18 | 3 | 1 |
| Northwestern Steel* | 0.6 | 2 | 71 | 7 | Deficit |
| Industry median | $1.9 | 10% | 30% | 8% | 3% |

* Mini-mill.
† Integrated steel producer.

*Source: Forbes*, 12 January 1998, pp. 196–97.

## History

Nucor traced its origins to auto manufacturer Ransom E. Olds, who founded Oldsmobile and, later, Reo Motor Cars. Through a series of transactions, the company Olds founded eventually became the Nuclear Corporation of America, a company involved in the nuclear instrument and electronics business in the 1950s and early 1960s.

The firm suffered several money-losing years and in 1965, facing bankruptcy, installed 39-year-old Ken Iverson as president.

Iverson had a bachelor's degree in aeronautical engineering from Cornell and a master's degree in mechanical engineering from Purdue. He began his professional career as a research physicist, and held several technical and management positions in the metals industry. He joined Nuclear Corporation of America as a vice president in 1962 and was appointed president three years later.

Iverson focused the failing company on two businesses: making steel from recycled scrap metal and fabricating steel joists for use in non-residential construction. In 1972 the firm changed its name to Nucor Corporation. By 1998 it had become America's second-largest steel maker.

## Operations

Nucor located its diverse facilities in rural areas across the United States, establishing strong ties to its local communities and its workforce. As a leading employer with the ability to pay top wages, it attracted hard-working, dedicated employees. These factors also allowed Nucor to select from among competing locales, siting its operations in states with tax structures that encouraged business growth and regulatory policies that favoured the company's commitment to remaining union-free. By 1998 Nucor and its subsidiaries consisted of nine businesses, with 25 plants. These businesses included the following:

### *Nucor Steel*

- Products: steel sheet, bars, angles, light structural carbon and alloy steels
- Plants: Darlington, SC; Norfolk, Nebr.; Jewett, Tex.; Plymouth, Utah; Crawfordsville, Ind.; Hickman, Ark.; Mt Pleasant, SC

*Nucor-Yamato Steel Company*

- Products: wide-flange steel beams, pilings, heavy structural steel products
- Plant: Blytheville, Ark.

*Vulcraft*

- Products: steel joists, joist girders and steel deck for building construction
- Plants: Florence, SC; Norfolk, Nebr.; Fort Payne, Ala.; Grapeland, Tex.; Saint Joe, Ind.; Brigham City, Utah

*Nucor Cold Finish*

- Products: cold-finished steel products for shafting, precision machined parts
- Plants: Norfolk, Nebr.; Darlington, SC; Brigham City, Utah

*Nucor Fastener*

- Products: standard steel hexhead cap screws, hex bolts, socket head cap screws
- Plants: Saint Joe, Ind.; Conway, Ark.

*Nucor Bearing Products, Inc.*

- Products: unground and semi-ground automotive steel bearings, machined steel parts
- Plant: Wilson, NC

*Nucor Building Systems*

- Products: metal buildings, metal building components
- Plants: Waterloo, Ind.; Swansea, SC

*Nucor Grinding Balls*

- Products: steel grinding balls used by the mining industry to process ores
- Plant: Brigham City, Utah

*Nucor Wire*

- Products: stainless steel wire
- Plant: Lancaster, SC

## Strategy

Nucor's strategy focused on two major competencies: building steel manufacturing facilities economically and operating them productively. The company's hallmarks were continuous innovation, modern equipment, individualized customer service, and a commitment to producing high-quality steel and steel products at competitive prices. Nucor was the first in its industry to adopt a number of new products and innovative processes, including thin-slab cast steel, iron carbide and the direct casting of stainless wire.

In 1998 Nucor produced a greater variety of steel products than did any other steel company in the United States – both low-end (non-flat) steel, such as reinforcing bar, and high-end (flat) steel, including motor lamination steel used in dishwashers, washers and dryers, as well as stainless steel used in automotive catalytic converters and exhaust systems.

Nucor's major customer segments were the construction industry (60 per cent), the automotive and appliance industries (15 per cent), and the oil and gas industries (15 per cent), with the remaining 10 per cent divided among miscellaneous users. All the company's low-end steel products (50 per cent of its total output) were distributed through steel service centres. Its high-end products (the other 50 per cent) were sold direct to original equipment manufacturers (OEMs), fabricators or end-use customers.

Nucor's ratio of debt to total capital was not allowed to exceed 30 per cent. In 1997 that ratio was 7 per cent. The company did not believe in acquisitions or mergers, choosing instead to commit to internally generated growth. It had no plans to diversify beyond steel and steel-related products.

## Organization structure

Compared to the typical Fortune 500 company, with 10 or more management layers, Nucor's structure was decentralized, with only the four management layers, illustrated below:

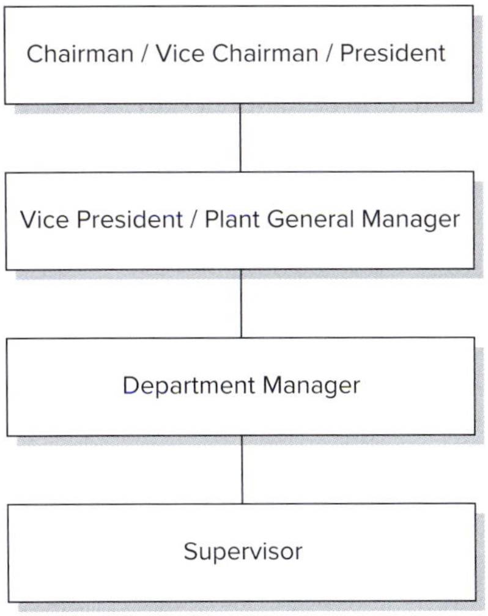


'We have a very flat organization structure,' said president and CEO John Correnti. 'The standard joke in the company is if you are a janitor and you get five promotions, you have Correnti's job. If you take a typical organization chart, it is the typical pyramid. You take our company, you turn the pyramid upside down; 6,800 people do not work for me, I work for 6,800 people.'[2]

In 1998 Nucor's board of directors had only six members: the current chairman, president and chief financial officer, and three retired Nucor executives. Only 22 employees (including clerical staff) worked at the corporate head office, which was located in an unassuming office building across the street from a shopping mall. All other employees worked in one of the company's 25 plants, each of which employed, on average, between 250 and 300 people.

The general manager at each plant was granted considerable autonomy, essentially operating the facility as an independent business. Each plant could source its inputs either from another Nucor plant or from the outside market. With the day-to-day decisions being made on site and the lines of communication to employees kept open and informal, problems could be solved quickly without having to wait for decisions from headquarters. 'We are honest-to-God autonomous,' said the general manager of one plant. 'That means that we duplicate efforts made in other parts of Nucor. The company might develop the same computer program six times. But the advantages of local autonomy are so great, we think it is worth it.'[3] One such advantage, noted Iverson, was greater operating efficiency. 'None of our divisions are in the same town as our Charlotte, North Carolina, headquarters,' he said. 'If any of them were, us headquarters types would always be over there making suggestions and wasting their time with our opinions. A general manager running a division in Charlotte would feel like he was living with his mother-in-law.'[4]

Other remarks by Iverson provided insight into the company's tolerance for experimentation and willingness to take risks: 'We try to impress on our employees that we are not King Solomon. We use an expression that I really like: "Good managers make bad decisions." We believe that if you take an

---

[2] Franklin, R. (1996) An Interview with John D. Correnti, President and CEO, Nucor Corporation, *Wall Street Corporate Reporter*, 9–15 September, pp. 19–20 (p. 20).

[3] Iverson, K. (1998) *Plain Talk*. New York: John Wiley & Sons, p. 27.

[4] Iverson, K. (1998) *Plain Talk*. New York: John Wiley & Sons, p. 37.

average person and put him in a management position, he'll make 50 per cent good decisions and 50 per cent bad decisions. A good manager makes 60 per cent good decisions. That means 40 per cent of those decisions could have been better. We continually tell our employees that it is their responsibility to the company to let the managers know when they make those 40 per cent decisions that could have been better. . . . The only other point I'd like to make about decision making is, don't keep making the same bad decisions.'[5]

In a 1998 interview, Iverson said that 'management can't be effective without taking some amount of risk. A group of us were just recently thinking about the pluses and minuses of sinking millions of dollars into a new process for pickling steel, removing all the rust before finishing it. Right now, that's done by using acid. But maybe it can be done better, faster, cheaper electrolytically. . . . I can't stand it when there are not strange ideas (like this one) floating around the company.'[6]

## Human resource policies

Nucor was very selective in recruiting employees and was able to choose from a large applicant pool. Noted Iverson, 'Darlington [SC] needed eight people, and we put a little ad in the county weekly newspaper that said, "Nucor Steel will take some applications on Saturday morning at 8:30 for new employees." When we went out there for the interviewing, there were 1,200 people lined up in that plant. We couldn't even get into the plant to get to the personnel department. . . . Finally, we called the state police and said, "You've got to do something. We've got a traffic jam out here." And the cop on duty said, "We can't do it, because we've got three people out there applying for jobs ourselves!"'[7]

Employee relations at Nucor were based on four principles:

1. Management is obligated to manage Nucor in such a way that employees will have the opportunity to earn according to their productivity.
2. Employees should feel confident that if they do their jobs properly, they will have a job tomorrow.
3. Employees have the right to be treated fairly.
4. Employees must have an avenue of appeal when they believe they are being treated unfairly.

As part of its commitment to fairness, Nucor had a grievance procedure that allowed any employee to ask for a review of a grievance if he or she felt the supervisor had not provided a fair hearing. The grievance could move up to general manager level and, if the employee was still not satisfied, could be submitted to headquarters management for final appeal.

General managers were required to hold annual dinners with every employee, meeting with groups of 25 to 100 at a time. These meetings gave employees a chance to discuss problems relating to scheduling, equipment, organization and production. The ground rules were simple: All comments were to be business related and not involve personalities, and all criticism was to be taken under advisement by management for decisive action. Like traditional New England town meetings, the format was free and open. Topics varied widely from year to year, and sometimes the sessions lasted well beyond midnight.

Another key aspect of Nucor's relationship with its workers was its commitment not to lay off or furlough employees in periods when business was down. Instead of reducing the workforce during recessionary periods (as was the usual industry practice), Nucor would reduce the work week. A former employee of an integrated steel company said, 'At Nucor, the cold-mill manager says that almost all of the

[5] Iverson, F.K. (1991) Effective leadership: the key is simplicity, in Y.K. Shetty and V.M. Buchler (eds) *The Quest for Competitiveness*. New York: Quorum Books, p. 287. Quoted in Ghemawat, P. and Stander, H.J. (1984) Nucor at crossroads, *Harvard Business School Case*, pp. 8–9.

[6] Interview with Ken Iverson (1998) The art of keeping management simple, *Harvard Management Update*, May, p. 7.

[7] Interview with Ken Iverson (1998) The art of keeping management simple, *Harvard Management Update*, May, p. 42.

improvements have come from operators and operating supervisors. At my former plant, operators are reluctant to suggest improvements for fear of reducing or eliminating another worker's job.'[8]

Nucor's labour force was not unionized. An employee at Nucor Steel in Hickman, Arkansas, presented the majority view: 'Why is Nucor non-union? I see two main reasons. First, it's just not needed. Nucor takes very good care of its employees. Its pay and benefits package is top-notch. No one has been capriciously fired. There are no layoffs. Nucor listens to its employees through monthly crew meetings, annual dinners and employee surveys. We just don't need union mediators. . . . The second reason is that we all work together. We don't need divisiveness. We don't need adversaries. We can talk among ourselves and work out our own problems.'[9] Iverson noted the effectiveness of this approach: 'People like to work here. For example, the last time we had a union organizer in Darlington, we had to send management out to protect the union guy passing out the pamphlets.'[10]

## Compensation

Nucor provided employees with a performance-related compensation system. All employees were covered under one of four compensation plans, each featuring incentives for meeting specific goals and targets.

### *1. Production incentive plan*

This covered most Nucor workers. Under this plan, employees directly involved in manufacturing were paid weekly bonuses based on actual output in relation to anticipated production tonnages produced. The bonuses were paid only for work that met quality standards and were pegged to work group, rather than individual output. (Each work group contained 25 to 40 workers.) Once the standard output was determined, it was not revised unless there was a significant change in the way a production process was performed due to a source other than the workers in the bonus group. Bonuses were tied to attendance and tardiness standards. If one worker's tardiness or attendance problems caused the group to miss its weekly output target, every member of the group was denied a bonus for that week. 'This bonus system is very tough,' said Iverson. 'If you are late, even only five minutes, you lose your bonus for the day. If you are thirty minutes late or you are absent for sickness or anything else, you lose your bonus for the week. Now, we have four forgiveness days per year when you might need to close on a house or your wife is having a baby, but only four.'[11]

Maintenance personnel were assigned to each shift, and they participated in the bonus along with the other members operating on that shift; no bonus was paid if equipment was not operating. Production supervisors were also a part of the bonus group and received the same bonus as the employees they supervised. The weekly output by, and bonus for, each work group were displayed at the front entrance to the factory. While there were no upper caps, the production incentive bonus, in general, averaged 80 to 150 per cent of the base wage.

Iverson gave an example of how this plan worked: 'In the steel mills, there are nine bonus groups: three in melting and casting, three in rolling, and three in finishing and shipping. Take melting and casting, for example. We start with a base of 12 tons of good billets per hour: Above that, the people in the group get a 4 per cent bonus for every ton per hour. So if they have a week in which they run, say, 32 tons per hour – and that would be low – that's an 80 per cent bonus. Take the regular pay, the overtime pay, everything, multiply it by an additional 80 per cent – and we give them that check along with their regular check the next week.'[12]

---

8 Edwards, A. (1996) How efficient are our work practices?, *New Steel,* July, p. 31.

9 Riggin, C. (1996) Freedom and a hell of a lot more at Nucor (Newsfront column), *New Steel,* July.

10 Steel man Ken Iverson, *Inc,* April 1986, pp. 41–42.

11 Steel man Ken Iverson, *Inc,* April 1986, pp. 44–45.

12 Steel man Ken Iverson, *Inc,* April 1986, pp. 44–45.

*2. Department manager incentive plan*

Nucor's department managers oversaw the production supervisors and, in turn, reported directly to the general manager of their plant. They earned an annual incentive bonus based on the performance of the entire plant to which they belonged. The targeted performance criterion here was return on assets. Every plant operated as a stand-alone business unit. All the plants had the same performance target: a return of 25 per cent or better on the assets employed within that plant. In recent years, bonuses averaged 82 per cent of base salary.

*3. Non-production and non-department manager incentive plan*

All employees not on the Production Incentive Plan or the Department Manager Incentive Plan – including accountants, engineers, secretaries, clerks and receptionists – received a bonus based primarily on each plant's return on assets. It could total over 25 per cent of an employee's base salary. Every month each plant received a chart showing its return on assets on a year-to-date basis. This chart was posted in the employee cafeteria or break area together with another chart that showed the bonus payout; this kept employees appraised of their expected bonus levels throughout the year.

*4. Senior Officers Incentive Plan*

The designation 'senior officers' included all corporate executives and plant general managers. Nucor senior officers did not have employment contracts, nor did they participate in any profit sharing, pension, or retirement plans. Their base salaries were lower than those received by executives in comparable companies. Senior officers had only one incentive compensation system, based on Nucor's return on stockholders' equity above certain minimum earnings. A portion of pretax earnings was placed into a pool that was divided among the officers. If Nucor did well, the officers' bonuses, in the form of stock (about 60 per cent) and cash (about 40 per cent), could amount to several times their base salaries. If Nucor did poorly, an officer's compensation was only base salary and, therefore, significantly below the average pay for this level of responsibility.

During a slack period in the 1980s, Iverson was named the Fortune 500 CEO with the lowest compensation. He saw this as an honour. 'When I walked through a plant during that period of time when we had to cut back to a four-day work week, or even three-and-a-half days, I never heard an employee who complained,' he said. 'His pay may have been cut 25 per cent, but he knew that his department head was cut even more and that the officers were cut, percentage-wise, even more than that. I call it our "share-the-pain" program. . . . I think in 1980 I earned $430,000. In 1982, I earned $108,000. Management should take the biggest drop in pay because they have the most responsibility.'[13]

## Information systems

Every week each plant sent data to headquarters on the following six operations-related variables: bids, orders, production, backlog, inventory and shipments. Taken together, these numbers provided a snapshot of the plant's basic operations. The figures for all 25 plants were pulled together onto one 8.5″ × 11″ sheet of paper. Each plant also submitted a second weekly report comparing the numbers on the six variables for the current week with those for the previous week, and the numbers for the most recent 13-week period with those for the corresponding period in the previous year. This second group of data from all 25 plants was compiled in a four-page report. Thus, all weekly data for the 25 plants were pulled together onto just five sheets of paper for corporate review.

Each plant also submitted a monthly report comparing actual to budgeted figures for sales revenue, costs, contribution and return on assets employed.

Iverson made the following observations regarding the design of Nucor's information systems: 'We don't look over the shoulders of our general managers and we don't ask them to submit voluminous reports explaining their actions. But that doesn't mean we are not paying attention. Delegation without

[13] Steel man Ken Iverson, *Inc*, April 1986, p. 44.

information is suicide. . . . In short, while we work hard to get the information we need, we've worked just as hard to keep our reports streamlined and ourselves free of "information overload". A lot of managers seem to miss the link between information overload and their compulsion to overcontrol their operations. But the connection is really obvious. Too much information puts you in the same position as too little information – you don't know what's going on. And when you don't know what's going on, it is hard to stay out of your people's hair. It's hard to tell them "trust your instincts", and really mean it.'[14]

All the plant general managers met as a group with headquarters management three times a year (in February, May and November) to review each plant's performance, and to plan for the months and years ahead. In addition, detailed performance data on each plant were distributed to all plant managers on a regular basis. Plant general managers and machine operators also commonly visited one another's mills.

## Benefits

Nucor took an egalitarian approach towards employee benefits. Senior executives did not enjoy such traditional perquisites as company cars, corporate jets, executive dining rooms, or executive parking places. 'Our corporate dining room is the deli across the street,' remarked Iverson.[15] All employees travelled in economy class, including Ken Iverson. Certain benefits, such as Nucor's profit-sharing and scholarship programmes, its employee stock purchase plan and its service awards, were not available to Nucor's officers. All employees had the same holidays, vacation schedules and insurance programmes, and all, including the CEO, wore the same green hard hats. (In a typical manufacturing company, people wore different-coloured hats in accordance with status or seniority, and the CEO's often was gold-plated!) Every Nucor annual report contained the names of every employee listed alphabetically on the front cover.

The company maintained a profit-sharing plan for employees below the officer level, contributing a minimum of 10 per cent of Nucor's pretax earnings each year. Of this amount, approximately 15 to 20 per cent was paid out to employees in March of the following year as cash profit sharing. The remainder was placed in trust and allocated to employees based on their earnings as a percentage of the total earnings paid throughout Nucor. The employees themselves made no contributions to this plan. They became fully vested after seven full years of service, and received payment when they retired or terminated employment with Nucor. In the 1990s, several employees had more than $300,000 in the trust.

Nucor had a monthly stock purchase plan featuring a 10 per cent Nucor matching contribution, and a 401(k) retirement savings plan that included a matching contribution of 5 to 25 per cent of the employee's contribution based on Nucor's return on shareholders' equity. Additionally, employees received five shares of Nucor common stock for each five years of continuous service as well as standard medical, dental, disability and life insurance coverage, and standard vacation and holiday packages.

Nucor's benefit programme also attested to the company's commitment to education. On-the-job training was a matter of policy, with employees being taught to perform multiple functions. The Nucor Scholarship Fund provided awards of up to $2,200 a year for up to four years to employees' children who pursued higher education or vocational training past high school. In 1996 the plan covered more than 600 students attending some 200 different learning institutions. According to Correnti, these scholarships cost Nucor about $1.3 million a year but created a priceless reservoir of goodwill. 'This gets Nucor around the dinner table at night,' he said. 'It creates loyalty among our employees. . . . Our turnover is so minuscule we do not even measure it.'[16]

Nucor encouraged employees to recruit their friends and relatives to work for the company. As an industry observer remarked, 'In fact, for existing employees, Nucor often means *N*ephews, *U*ncles, *C*ousins, and *O*ther *R*elatives.'[17]

---

[14] Iverson, *Plain Talk*, pp. 37–39.

[15] Iverson, *Plain Talk*, p. 59.

[16] Franklin, An interview with John D. Correnti, p. 19.

[17] Maciariello, J.A. (2000) *Lasting Value*. New York: John Wiley & Sons, pp. 140–41.

## Technology

Nucor did not have a formal R&D department, a corporate engineering group or a chief technology officer. Instead, it relied on equipment suppliers and other companies to do the R&D, and adopted the technological advancements they developed – whether in steel or iron making, or in fabrication. Teams composed of managers, engineers and machine operators decided what technology to adopt.

Integrated steel companies produced steel from iron ore using blast furnaces. Nucor successfully adopted the 'mini-mill' concept – first developed in Europe and Japan – in the plant it built in Darlington, South Carolina, in 1969. Unlike integrated steel companies, mini-mills did not start with iron ore; instead, they converted scrap steel into finished steel using small-scale electric furnaces. Nucor purchased its scrap requirements from third-party agents at open market prices. For the non-flat, commodity segment of the steel industry (reinforcing bar for construction and rods for pipe, rail and screws), mini-mills had a cost advantage over integrated steel producers, eventually driving the latter out of the low end of the steel industry.

Until the mid-1980s, however, mini-mills could not produce the flat steel products required by automotive and appliance customers, and this high-end market was monopolized by the integrated steel producers. Then, in 1987, Nucor made history by building the first mini-mill that could make flat steel (in Crawfordsville, Indiana), thus gaining entry into the premium segment of the steel industry.

At its Crawfordsville facility, Nucor gambled on the thin-slab casting technology developed by SMS Schloemann-Siemag, a West German company. Staff engineers from more than 100 steel companies visited SMS to explore this technology, which had been demonstrated in a small pilot but not yet proven commercially. But Nucor adopted the process first, obtaining the rights from SMS by signing a non-exclusive contract with an additional technology flowback clause. Nucor's investment in the Crawfordsville plant represented approximately five times the company's 1987 net earnings and virtually equalled the stockholders' total equity in the company that year!

By 1997 Nucor had built two more mini-mills (in Hickman, Arkansas, and Charleston, South Carolina), both using the thin-slab casting process to produce flat-rolled sheet steel. The first competitive facility to make thin-slab-cast flat-rolled steel did not appear until 1995 – eight years after Nucor's pioneering effort.

In 1987 Nucor's pursuit of technical excellence had led to the establishment of Nucor-Yamato Steel Company, a facility jointly owned by Nucor and Yamato Kogyo of Japan, which operated a structural steel mill in the United States that used its own continuous-casting technology.

Several years later, Nucor became concerned that mini-mill start-ups by several other companies would significantly increase the price of scrap steel or even cause scrap to become wholly unavailable. To guard against that possibility, the company established a plant in Trinidad, West Indies, in 1994. This plant successfully adopted a commercially unproven technology to make iron carbide, a substitute for scrap steel, which it supplied to the flat-rolled plant in Crawfordsville. However, in 1998 Nucor concluded that the iron carbide supplied by the Trinidad facility was uneconomical, and closed the facility.

In addition to developing new plants, Nucor was committed to continuously modernizing its existing ones. Its philosophy was to build or rebuild at least one mill every year, in the latter case rebuilding entirely rather than just 'put[ting] new pipes in parts of the old mill'. In building new plants or rebuilding existing plants, the company did not rely on outside contractors, but instead handed the responsibility for design and construction management to a small group of engineers selected from existing Nucor facilities. For example, when it decided to add a second rolling mill at Nucor-Yamato in Blytheville, Arkansas, it assigned the meltshop supervisor in the first mill to coordinate the design and construction of the meltshop in the second mill. As Greg Mathis, this meltshop supervisor, observed, 'They put it all on my shoulders – the planning, the engineering, the contracting, the budgets. . . . I mean, we are talking about an investment of millions of dollars and I was accountable for all of it. It worked out fine . . . because my team and I knew what not to do from our experience running the meltshop on the first line.'[18]

[18] Maciariello, J.A. (2000) *Lasting Value*. New York: John Wiley & Sons, pp. 89–90.

Further, the actual construction of the plant was done by workers from the local area, who were aware that they would subsequently be recruited to operate the mills as well.

Iverson explained the rationale behind this approach to technology management: 'We accept that roughly half of our investments in new ideas and new technologies will yield no usable results. . . . Every Nucor plant has its little storehouse of equipment that was bought, tried, and discarded. The knowledge we gather from our so-called "failures" may lead us to spectacular success. . . . We let employees invest in technology. People in the mills identify and select most of the technology. Technology is advancing too quickly on too many fronts. No small group of executives can possibly keep fully informed.'[19]

In 1991 President Bush awarded Iverson the National Medal of Technology, America's highest award for technological achievement and innovation.

## Future

For Iverson, the national medal was not a culmination but a signpost along the way. 'Our biggest challenge [in the future] is to continue to grow the company at 15–20 per cent per year, and to keep earnings parallel with this growth,' he said. 'Business is like a flower: You either grow or die.'[20]

## Questions

1 Why has Nucor performed so well?

- a Is Nucor's industry the answer?
- b Is it the 'mini-mill' effect?
- c Is it market power (scale economies)?
- d Is it a distribution channel advantage?
- e Is it a raw material advantage?
- f Is it a technology advantage?
- g Is it a location advantage?
- h Is it the result of an entrenched brand name?
- i Is it Nucor's choice of a unique strategy?
- j Is it Nucor's ability to execute its strategy?

2 What are the most important aspects of Nucor's overall approach to management control systems that help explain why this company is so successful? How well do Nucor's organization and control practices fit the company's strategic requirements?

3 A crucial element of Nucor's success is its ability to mobilize two types of knowledge: plant construction and start-up know-how; and manufacturing process know-how. What practices does Nucor employ to manage knowledge effectively?

- a What practices help the company accumulate these two types of knowledge in individual plants?
- b What practices exist within the company to facilitate sharing this knowledge among its 25 plants?
- c How does Nucor transfer knowledge to a greenfield, start-up operation?

---

[19] Maciariello, J.A. (2000) *Lasting Value*. New York: John Wiley & Sons, pp. 5, 96, 150.

[20] Interview with Ken Iverson: The art of keeping management simple.

4 Nucor has repeatedly demonstrated the ability to be a successful first mover in the adoption of new technology. How does the company's approach to management control systems contribute to this first-mover advantage?
5 Would you like to work for Nucor?
6 Why have competitors not been able to imitate Nucor's performance so far?

# Case 12.5

# Aluminum container corporation*

**by Anil R. Chitkara, Vijay Govindarajan and Robert N. Anthony**

In 2016, Aluminum Container Corporation was the largest manufacturer of aluminum beverage cans in the United States. Exhibit 1 shows the company's organizational chart. Reporting to the CEO were two line managers: one vice president (VP) in charge of manufacturing and another in charge of marketing. These vice presidents headed all of the company's activities in their respective functional areas.

The company had plants scattered throughout the United States. Each plant produced several different sizes of cans for a range of customers that included both large and small breweries and soft drink bottlers. The company had the highest market share among metal container producers.

## Industry background

The packaging industry offered a number of options: aluminium, steel, glass, fibre foil (paper and metal composite), paper carton and plastic.

The metal container industry consisted of the 100-plus firms that produced aluminium and tin-plated steel cans. Aluminium cans were used for packaging beverages (beer and soft drinks), while tin-plated steel cans were used primarily for food packaging, paints and aerosols. In 1980, steel cans accounted for 90 per cent of the metal can production, but over time aluminium came to dominate the industry. By 2016, aluminium cans accounted for more than 90 per cent of metal can production. The soft drink bottlers who purchased the containers were primarily small, independent franchisees of Coca-Cola and PepsiCo. However, the parent companies (Coca-Cola and PepsiCo) represented their independent bottlers in negotiating terms with container producers.

The minimum efficient scale for a container plant was five lines and it cost $25 million in equipment per line. Raw materials typically accounted for 64 per cent of the production cost. The remaining costs included labour (15 per cent), marketing and general administration (9 per cent), transportation (8 per cent), depreciation (2 per cent), and research and development (2 per cent).

For beverage processors, the cost of the can usually exceeded the cost of the contents, with the container accounting for approximately 40 per cent of the total manufacturing cost. Rush orders were common in this industry. Most beverage processors maintained two or more suppliers and spread purchases among them. If the container manufacturer failed to meet the customer's cost and quality specifications, or its standards for delivery and customer service, the customer would turn to another supplier.

* This case was titled Vershire Company and included in the 10th Edition of Management Control Systems. Sources on which this case is based are contained in the Vershire Company Case.

**EXHIBIT 1**

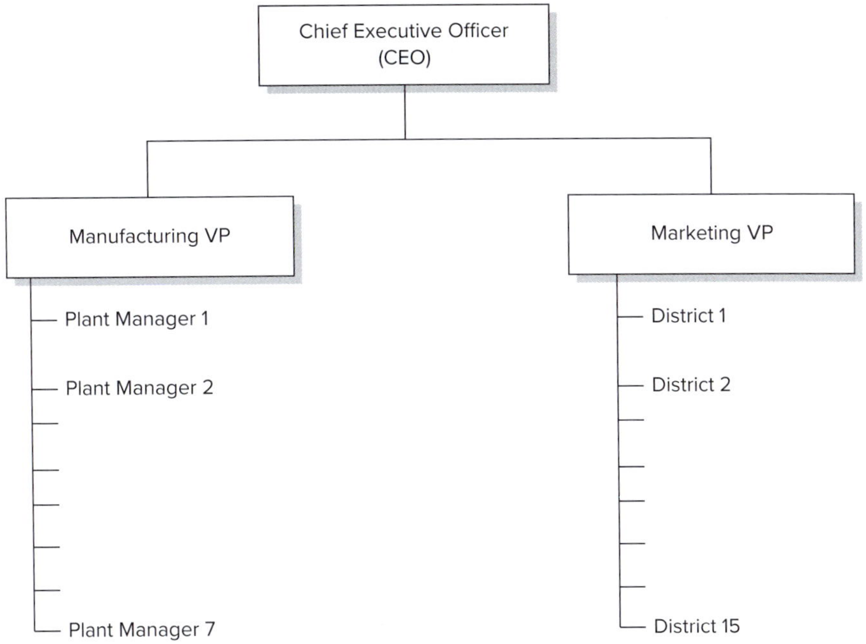


Some beverage companies integrated backwards, manufacturing cans themselves. One large beverage company produced one-third of its own container requirements and was ranked as one of the top five beverage container producers in the industry.

Prior to 1980, cans were produced by rolling a sheet of steel, soldering and cutting it to size, and attaching both the top and the bottom. In 1982, the industry was revolutionized when aluminium producers perfected a two-piece process in which a flat sheet of metal was pushed into a deep cup and a top was attached. All aluminium can producers employed essentially the same technology.

In addition to production efficiency, aluminium had other advantages over steel. It was easier to shape, it was less likely to affect the contents' flavouring, it permitted more attractive packaging because it was easier to lithograph, and it reduced transportation costs because of its lighter weight.

Additionally, aluminium was a more attractive recycling material because a ton of scrap aluminium had almost three times the value of a ton of scrap steel.

Four global companies supplied aluminium to can producers: Alcoa, Alcan, Reynolds and Kaiser Aluminium. Three of these companies – Alcan, Alcoa and Reynolds – also manufactured aluminium containers.

## Sales budget

The budgeting process for Aluminum Container Corporation started with the preparation of the sales budget. The sales forecasts were generated from the bottom up. Each district sales manager estimated sales for the coming budget year. The district managers could request help from the head office but, in the end, assumed full responsibility for the forecasts they submitted.

All district sales forecasts were consolidated for review by the marketing VP, but no changes were made in a district's forecast unless the district manager agreed. When all the responsible parties were satisfied with the sales budget, the figures became fixed objectives, with each district held responsible for its own portion.

## Manufacturing budget

After final approval at the corporate level, the overall sales budget was translated into a sales budget for each plant, broken down according to the plants from which the finished goods would be shipped. At the plant level, the sales budget was then categorized according to price, volume and end use.

Once the sales numbers were estimated, each plant budgeted gross profit, fixed expenses and pretax income. Profit was calculated as the sales budget less budgeted variable costs (including direct materials, direct labour and variable manufacturing overhead, each valued at a standard rate) and the fixed overhead budget. The plant manager was held responsible for this budgeted profit number even if actual sales fell below the projected level.

Cost standards and cost reduction targets were developed by the plant's industrial engineering department, which also determined budget performance standards for each department, operation and cost centre within the plant, including such items as budgeted cost restrictions, allowances for unfavourable variances from standards, and fixed costs, such as maintenance labour.

On or before 1 September each year, plant budgets were submitted, consolidated, and presented to the manufacturing VP for review. If the budgets were not quite in line with management's expectations, plant managers were asked to look for additional savings. When the manufacturing VP was satisfied with the budget, it was sent to the CEO, who either approved it or asked for certain modifications. The final consolidated budget was submitted for approval at the board of directors meeting in December.

Any problems that arose between sales and production at a given plant were expected to be solved by the people in the field. If a customer called with a rush order, it typically disrupted production and increased set-up costs. Manufacturing and sales were expected to negotiate the best course of action. The customer was always the primary concern.

## Performance measurement and evaluation

On the second business day after the close of each month, every plant emailed certain critical operating variances, which were combined into a 'variance analysis sheet'. A compilation of all variance sheets was distributed the following morning to interested management. Plant managers were not supposed to rely on these monthly statements to identify unfavourable variances; rather, they were expected to be aware of them (and to take corrective action) on a daily basis.

Four business days after the close of every month, each plant submitted a report showing budgeted and actual results. Once these reports were received, corporate management reviewed the variances for those items where figures exceeded budgetary amounts, thus requiring plant managers to explain only the areas in which budgeted targets had not been met. The focus was on net sales, including price and mix changes, gross margin and standard manufacturing costs.

The budgeted and actual information submitted is summarized in Exhibit 2. Supplemental information was provided by supporting documents (see Exhibit 3).

The fixed costs were examined to see if the plants had carried out their various programmes, if the programmes had met budgeted costs, and if the results were in line with expectations.

## Management incentives

The sales department had sole responsibility for the price, sales mix and delivery schedules. The plant manager had responsibility for plant profits.

Plant managers were motivated to meet their profit goals in a number of ways. First, only capable managers were promoted, with profit performance being a main factor in determining capability. Second, plant managers' compensation packages were tied to achieving profit budgets.

**EXHIBIT 2**

| Items | Month | | Year-to-date variances $ |
|---|---|---|---|
| | Actual $ | Variance $ | |
| Total Sales Variances Due to | | | |
| Sales Price Sales Mix Sales Volume | | | |
| Total Variable Cost of Sales Variances Due to | | | |
| Materials Labour | | | |
| Variable Overhead Total Fixed Cost | | | |
| Variances in Fixed Costs | | | |
| Net Profit | | | |

**EXHIBIT 3** Supplemental reports

| Individual plant-level reports | |
|---|---|
| **Report** | **Content** |
| Sales by customer groups | • Detailed analysis of sales volume, sales dollars, profit dollars and profit margin by end-use customers (e.g., beer companies, soft drink companies) |
| Analysis of sales | • More detailed back-up analysis to Exhibit 2 regarding variances due to sales price, sales mix and sales volume |
| Analysis of costs | • More detailed back-up analysis to Exhibit 2 regarding variances due to variable costs and fixed costs of manufacturing |

## Questions

1 Outline the strengths and weaknesses of Aluminum Container Company's management control system.

2 Trace the profit budgeting process at Aluminum Container Corporation, starting in May and ending with the board of directors' meeting in December. Be prepared to describe the activities that took place at each step of the process and present the rationale for each.

3 Should the plant managers be held responsible for profits? Why? Why not?

4 How do you assess the performance evaluation system contained in Exhibits 2 and 3?

5 On balance, would you redesign the management control system at Aluminum Container Corporation? If so, how and why?

6 Should the plant managers be held responsible for profits? Why? Why not? Evaluate the answer to this question in the context of the strategy of Aluminum Container Corporation.

# Case A1
# Quality metal service center*

**by Vijay Govindarajan**

In early March 1992, Edward Brown, president and chief executive officer of Quality Metal Service Center (Quality), made the following observation:

> *Though I am satisfied with our past performance, I believe that we are capable of achieving even higher levels of sales and profits. Considering the market expansion and the state of competition, I feel we might have missed out on some growth opportunities. I don't know if our controls have inhibited managers from pursuing our goals of aggressive growth and above-average return on assets, as compared to the industry, but you might keep that in mind while evaluating our systems.*

## The metal distribution industry

Service centres bought metals from many of the mills including USX, Bethlehem, Alcoa, Reynolds, and such smaller firms as Crucible, Northwestern and Youngstown. These suppliers sold their products in large lots, thereby optimizing the efficiencies associated with large production runs. Service centres sold their products to metal users in smaller lots and on a short lead-time basis.

The metal distribution industry was generally regarded as a mature, highly competitive, and fragmented industry. However, there were a number of key trends in the metal industry that were enhancing service centres' growth potential.

### Steel mills' retrenchment

In their efforts to become more competitive through increased productivity, most of the major domestic metals producers had been scaling back product lines by dropping low-volume speciality products. Further, they had cut back on service to customers by reducing sales force size and technical support. Full-line service centres, recognizing that many customers preferred to deal with only a few primary suppliers, had profited from this trend by maintaining wide product lines and increasing customer service.

### Just-in-time inventory management

Given the high cost of ownership and maintenance of inventory, most metal users attempted to reduce their costs by lowering their levels of raw materials inventories ('just-in-time' inventory management). This resulted in smaller order quantities and more frequent deliveries. Metal service centres had a natural advantage over the mills here because inventory was the service centre's stock-in-trade.

While the service centre's price was always higher than buying from the mills, customers were increasingly willing to pay the extra charge. They recognized that the savings they generated from lower inventories and handling costs, plus reduced scrap and risk of obsolescence, would lower the total cost of getting the metal into their production system.

### Productivity improvement and quality enhancement

Quality and productivity had become overriding issues with metal users. They had implemented major quality and productivity improvement programmes aimed at increasing both the reputation of their

---

* This case was prepared by Vijay Govindarajan, with the assistance of Rony Levinson (T'05). © Dartmouth College.

products and the overall profitability of operations. In their attempt to focus on quality, end users were reducing the number of suppliers with whom they did business and were concentrating their purchases with those that were best able to meet their specific quality, availability, and service requirements. End users found that closer relationships with fewer suppliers resulted in better quality conformance and stronger ties between supplier and customer as each sought to maximize the long-term benefits of the relationship.

## Quality metal's strategy

Quality Metal had been established a century ago as a local metals distributor. Since then, it had grown into a firm with national distribution, and its sales in 1991 were well over $750 million. Quality's business strategy provided the framework for the development of specific goals and objectives. According to Mr Brown, three fundamental objectives guided Quality.

### Objective 1: To focus sales efforts on targeted markets of speciality metal users

Quality recognized that it could compete much more effectively in specialty product lines of its own selection than in the broader commodity carbon steel markets where price was the primary determining factor. Consequently, Quality decided to diminish its participation in commodity product lines and redeploy those resources into higher-technology metals, such as carbon alloy bars, stainless steel, aluminium, nickel alloys, titanium, copper and brass, which offered higher returns and had less-effective competition. More than 60 per cent of its revenues were derived from higher-technology metals in 1992, compared with 29 per cent in 1982.

Quality had made a long-term commitment to high-technology metal users. The company's introduction of titanium, a natural adjunct to the existing product line, was indicative of the company's strategy of bringing new products to the market to meet the needs of existing customers. Previously, titanium was not readily available on the distributor market. Quality planned to continue to diversify into complementary higher-technology products as new customer requirements arose.

### Objective 2: To identify those industries and geographic markets where these metals were consumed

To identify more accurately the major industries and geographies for these products, Quality developed the industry's first metal usage database. Mr Brown believed that this database, which was continually refined and updated, was the most accurate in the country. Its use enabled Quality to profile product consumption by industry and by geography. It also enabled the company to analyse total market demand on a nationwide basis and to project potential sales on a market-by-market basis. As a result, Quality had a competitive edge in determining where customers were located and what products they were buying. It used this information in selecting locations for opening new service centres.

### Objective 3: To develop techniques and marketing programmes that would increase market share

To build market share, Quality offered programmes that assisted its customers in implementing just-in-time inventory management systems coordinated with their materials requirement planning programmes. The company worked with customer representatives in purchasing, manufacturing, and quality assurance to determine their precise requirements for product specifications, quantities and delivery schedules.

Similarly, Quality emphasized value-added business by offering a wide range of processing services for its customers, such as saw cutting to specific sizes, flame cutting into both pattern and non-pattern shapes, flattening, surface grinding, shearing, bending, edge conditioning, polishing and thermal treatment. Because of Quality's volume, the sophisticated equipment required for these production steps was operated at a lower cost per unit than most customer-owned equipment.

## Organizational structure

Since the Great Depression, Quality had experienced rapid sales growth and geographical expansion. In 1992, Quality operated in more than 20 locations, situated in markets representing about 75 per cent of metal consumption in the United States. Consistent with this growth was the necessity to decentralize line functions. The firm currently had four regions, each of which had about six districts for a total of 23 districts. There were staff departments in finance, marketing, operations and human resources. A partial organizational structure is given in Exhibit 1.

Typically, a district manager had a warehouse superintendent, a sales manager, a credit manager, a purchasing manager and an administration manager (Exhibit 1) working under them. The decision-making authorities of these managers are described below:

*The warehouse superintendent oversees transportation, loading and unloading, storage, and preproduction processing.*

*The sales manager coordinates a staff that includes 'inside' salespersons who establish contacts and take orders over the phone, and an 'outside' team who make direct customer contacts and*

**EXHIBIT 1** Partial organizational chart

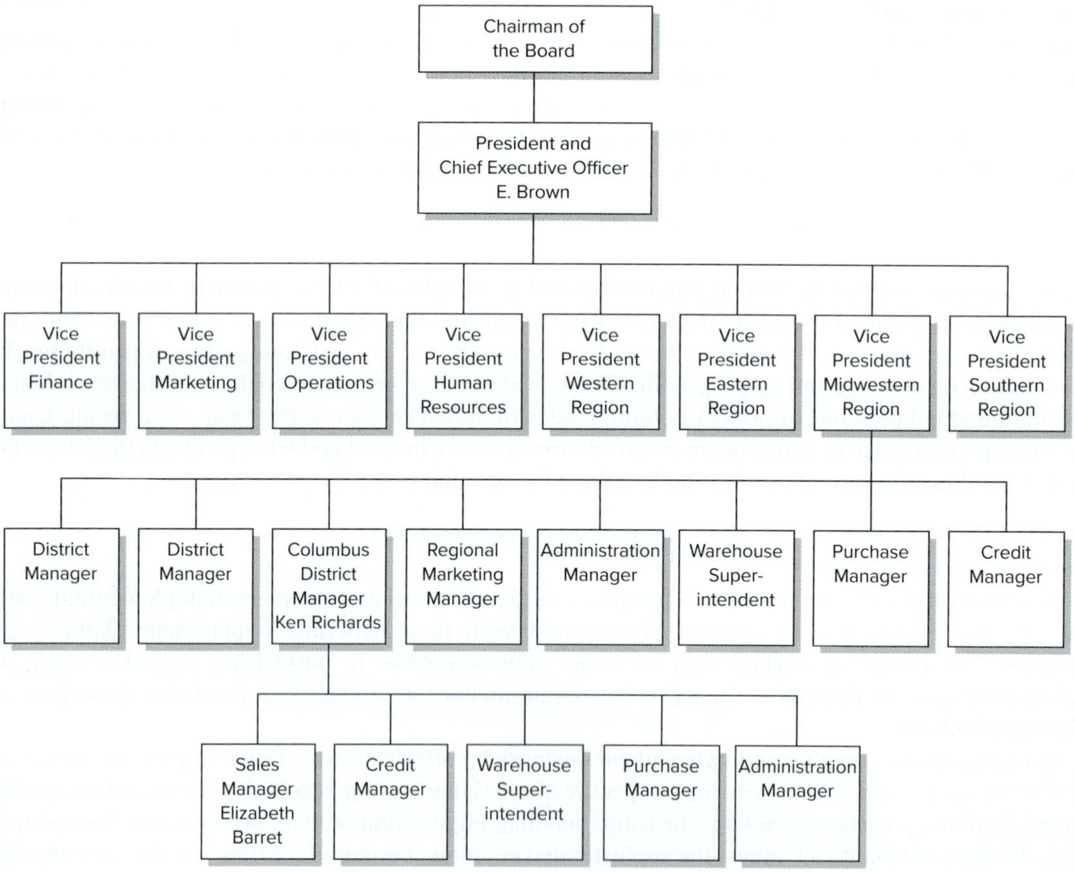

*close large deals. Sales price and discount terms are generally established by the district manager; freight adjustments are also made at the district level.*

*The credit manager assesses the risk of new customer accounts, approves customer credit periods within a range established by corporate headquarters, and enforces customer collections.*

*The purchasing manager acquires inventory from the regional warehouse, other districts and outside companies. Districts have freedom to purchase from outside suppliers. However, senior management has established economic order quantity guidelines for the purchase of inventory, and metals are stocked in a district warehouse only if local demand is sufficient to justify it. Within this overall constraint, the purchasing manager has authority to choose suppliers and negotiate credit terms, although payments to suppliers are handled centrally at the home office.*

*Capital expenditures in excess of $10,000 and all capital leasing decisions require corporate approval.*

## Responsibility allocation and performance measurement

District managers were responsible for attaining predetermined return on asset (ROA) levels, which were agreed to at the beginning of the year. The following items were included in the asset base for ROA calculations.

1. Land, warehouse buildings and equipment were included in the asset base at gross book value.
2. Leased buildings and equipment (except for leased trucks) were included in the asset base at the capitalized lease value. (Leased trucks were not capitalized; rather, lease expenses on trucks were reported as an operating expense.)
3. Average inventory, in units, was calculated. The replacement costs, based on current mill price schedules, were determined for these units and included in the asset base.
4. Average accounts receivable balance for the period was included in the asset base. (Cash was excluded from district's assets; the amounts were trivial.)
5. As a general rule, accounts payable was not deducted from the asset base. However, an adjustment was made if the negotiated credit period was greater than the company standard of 30 days. If this occurred, 'deferred inventory', a contra-asset account, was deducted from the amount of the inventory value for the period in excess of the 30-day standard. This was equivalent to a reduction of inventory asset corresponding to the excess credit period. For example, if a district negotiated a credit period of 50 days, then the inventory expenditure was removed from the asset base for 20 days. However, a penalty was not assessed if the negotiated credit period was less than the 30-day company standard.

Income before taxes, for each district, was calculated in accordance with generally accepted accounting principles, except for cost of sales, which was calculated based on current inventory replacement values. Expenses were separated into controllable and non-controllable categories. Controllable expenses included such items as warehouse labour and sales commissions; non-controllable expenses included rent, utilities and property taxes.

No corporate overhead expenses were allocated to the districts. A few years earlier, the company had considered a proposal to allocate corporate overheads to the districts. However, the proposal had been rejected on the grounds that the 'allocation bases' were arbitrary and that such expenses could not be controlled at the district level.

## Performance evaluation and incentives

The incentive bonus for district managers was based on a formula that tied the bonus to meeting and exceeding 90 per cent of their ROA targets. Exhibit 2 contains the detailed procedure used to calculate the incentive bonus. The calculations determine an applicable payout rate, which was then multiplied by the district manager's base salary to yield the amount of the bonus award. Thus, the size of the bonus depended on (1) the amount of the manager's base salary and (2) how far 90 per cent of the ROA target was exceeded; there was a maximum bonus amount.

The bonus of a district manager was also affected by his or her region's performance. In 1992, 75 per cent of a district manager's bonus was based on district performance, and 25 per cent was based on his or her region's performance. The bonus of the district manager's staff was based solely on the performance of that district.

**EXHIBIT 2** Incentive calculation procedure

| | |
|---|---|
| Step 1: | Measure actual asset base and compare it with targeted asset base. If actual assets exceed targeted assets, multiply excess by the targeted ROA for the district and charge this amount to profits.<br>**Assets overemployed × District ROA target = Charge to profits**<br>If actual assets are less than targeted assets, multiply difference by the district's ROA target and credit this to profits.<br>**Assets underemployed × District ROA target = Credit to profits** |
| Step 2 | Adjusted profits are compared with 90 per cent of the original profit objective.<br>**Adjusted profits − (90 per cent of objective) = Incentive profits** |
| Step 3 | Incentive profit ÷ 90 per cent of objective = Payout rate |
| Step 4 | Payout rate × Manager's base salary = Bonus payable |
| Step 5 | Bonuses are awarded on the basis of incentive profits. If incentive profits are less than zero, no bonus is awarded. The bonus increases in proportion to incentive profit, with a maximum bonus of 75 per cent of manager's base salary. |

## Meeting with the columbus district manager

A few days after speaking with Mr Brown, the case writer visited Ken Richards, the district manager for the Columbus Service Center. Mr Brown recommended him as one of the company's brightest and most successful district managers. The district had been highly successful in recent years, consistently earning well above 30 per cent ROA (pretax).

For 1992, Ken Richards's targeted figure for operating profit was $3.8 million; targeted assets were set at $10 million. He felt that an ROA of 38 per cent was reachable, considering historical performance and market opportunities.

As of March 1992, Ken was reviewing a capital investment proposal (for the purchase of new processing equipment), which he had received from his sales manager (Exhibits 3 and 4). Before submitting the proposal to corporate headquarters for approval, Ken wanted to make sure that the new investment would have a favourable effect on his incentive bonus for 1992. Using 1992 profit and asset targets as the benchmark, he compared his incentive bonus for 1992 with and without the new investment. These calculations are shown in Exhibit 5.

## EXHIBIT 3 Memorandum

To: Kenneth Richards, District Manager

From: Elizabeth Barret, Sales Manager

Subject: Purchase of Processing Equipment

This district, at present, sells no inventory that has been altered through preproduction processing. Such alterations can be made at other districts with processing capabilities, but many customers in this area complain that because of transportation time, the lead times are too great to satisfy their needs in acquiring such inventory.

Market research has established that a reasonable demand for processed inventory exists within this district. Therefore, our district should consider obtaining the processing equipment necessary to satisfy this demand.

The economics of this project are summarized in the attached sheet [Exhibit 4]. Let me provide some information as background for these calculations.

We can acquire the equipment for $600,000. Since its expected life is 10 years (negligible salvage value), Quality would benefit from a 10 per cent Investment Tax Credit, making the net investment equal to $540,000.

Sales projections were made by the district's sales department, and costs were based upon the experiences of districts with processing capabilities. Growth in sales and costs include a 7 per cent inflation factor and projected increases in production.

Annual cash flows are calculated by adjusting earnings after taxes to account for depreciation, which is expensed by the sum-of-the-years'-digits method, and growth in working capital investment, which is calculated using our standard 20 per cent of sales on incremental growth. The resultant end-of-year cash flows, discounted at the cost of capital of 15 per cent (which is the rate head office requires on projects in similar risk classes), yield a positive net present value of $286,000. The payback period for this project is 4.5 years, which is well within the company's criterion of 10 years.

This investment is worth your careful consideration, Ken. This district has the opportunity to expand into a new market and to benefit from favourable earnings and positive sales growth.

I hope you will submit this proposal to the home office for consideration. Please let me know if you have any questions.

Sd/-

Elizabeth Barret

## EXHIBIT 4 Columbus district processing equipment proposal

| | 1992 | 1993 | 1994 | 1995 | 1996 | 1997 | 1998 | 1999 | 2000 | 2001 |
|---|---|---|---|---|---|---|---|---|---|---|
| **I. Cash flows (000s)** | | | | | | | | | | |
| Sales (1) | $600 | 1,375 | 1,510 | 1,665 | 1,830 | 2,010 | 2,215 | 2,435 | 2,680 | 2,945 |
| Cost of sales | $(560) | (1,145) | (1,236) | (1,355) | (1,490) | (1,660) | (1,845) | (2,051) | (2,290) | (2,545) |
| Earnings before taxes | 40 | 230 | 274 | 310 | 340 | 350 | 370 | 384 | 390 | 400 |
| Tax at 50% | $(20) | (115) | (137) | (155) | (170) | (175) | (185) | (192) | (195) | (200) |
| Earnings after taxes | 20 | 115 | 137 | 155 | 170 | 175 | 185 | 192 | 195 | 200 |
| Depreciation | 110 | 100 | 85 | 75 | 65 | 55 | 45 | 35 | 20 | 10 |
| Working capital investment (2) | $(120) | (155) | (25) | (35) | (30) | (35) | (45) | (40) | (50) | 535 |
| Cash flow | $10 | 60 | 197 | 195 | 205 | 195 | 185 | 187 | 165 | 745 |

*(1)* Revenue for 1992 reflects 3-month start-up period

*(2)* Working capital investment

| | 1992 | 1993 | 1994 | 1995 | 1996 | 1997 | 1998 | 1999 | 2000 | 2001 |
|---|---|---|---|---|---|---|---|---|---|---|
| 20% of sales | $120 | 275 | 300 | 335 | 365 | 400 | 445 | 485 | 535 | 590 |
| Old level | 0 | 120 | 275 | 300 | 335 | 365 | 400 | 445 | 485 | 535 |
| Increase in working capital | $(120) | (155) | (25) | (35) | (30) | (35) | (45) | (40) | (50) | (55) |
| Recovery of working capital | | | | | | | | | | 590 |
| Net incremental investment in working capital | $(120) | (155) | (25) | (35) | (30) | (35) | (45) | (40) | (50) | 535 |

**II. Project evaluation**

A. Payback period: 4.5 years

B. Internal rate of return: 21.8%

C. Net present value (at 15% cost of capital): $286,000

**EXHIBIT 5** Incentive bonus for Columbus district manager for 1992

**A. Incentive bonus for 1992 without the new project**

| | Target for 1992 | Projected actual for 1992* |
|---|---|---|
| Profit | $3,800,000 | $3,800,000 |
| Asset | $10,000,000 | $10,000,000 |

$$\text{Incentive profit} = \text{Actual profit} - (90\% \text{ of targeted profit})$$
$$= \$3{,}800{,}000 - \$3{,}420{,}000 = \$380{,}000$$

$$\text{Payout rate} = \frac{\text{Incentive profit}}{90\% \text{ of targeted profit}}$$
$$\$380{,}000/\$3{,}420{,}000 = 11.1\%$$

*Therefore, incentive bonus without the new project = 11.1% of base salary.*

**B. Incentive bonus for 1992 with the new project**

| | Target for 1992 | Projected actual for 1992† |
|---|---|---|
| Profit | $3,800,000 | $3,840,000 |
| Asset | $10,000,000 | $10,720,000 |

*Step 1:*

$$\textbf{Actual assets} - \textbf{Target assets} = \textbf{Asset overemployed}$$
$$\mathbf{\$10{,}720{,}000 - \$10{,}000{,}000 = \$720{,}000}$$

*Step 2:*

$$\textbf{Asset overemployed * District ROA target} = \textbf{Change to profits}$$
$$\mathbf{\$720{,}000 * 0.38 = \$273{,}600}$$
$$\textbf{Actual profits} - \textbf{Charge to profits} = \textbf{Adjusted profits}$$
$$\mathbf{\$3{,}840{,}000 - \$273{,}600 = \$3{,}566{,}400}$$

| | |
|---|---|
| *Step 3:* | **Adjusted profits − 90% of targeted profit = Incentive profit** |
| | **\$3,566,400 − \$3,420,000 = \$146,400** |
| *Step 4:* | $\dfrac{\textbf{Incentive profit}}{\textbf{90\% of targeted profit}} = \textbf{Payout rate}$ |
| | $\dfrac{\$146,400}{\$3,420,000} = 4.28\%$ |
| *Therefore, incentive bonus with the new project = 4.28% of base salary.* | |

*Notes:*
* Assumes that actual results exactly meet the targets in 1992.
† Reflects marginal effects of project implementation *only* – that is, an addition of earnings before taxes of \$40,000 and an addition to assets of \$720,000 (equipment \$600,000 plus working capital \$120,000). Otherwise, assumes that other district operations meet targets exactly in 1992.

## Questions

1. Is the capital investment proposal described in Exhibit 3 an attractive one for Quality Metal Service Center?
2. Should Ken Richards send that proposal to home office for approval?
3. Comment on the general usefulness of ROA as the basis of evaluating district managers' performance. Could this performance measure be made more effective?
4. In deciding the investment base for evaluating managers of investment centres, the general question is: What practices will motivate the district managers to use their assets most efficiently, and to acquire the proper amount and kind of new assets? Presumably, when his return on assets is being measured, the district manager will try to increase his ROA, and we desire that the actions he takes towards this end be those that are in the best interests of the whole corporation. Given this general line of reasoning, evaluate the way Quality computes the 'investment base' for its districts. For each asset category, discuss whether the basis of measurement used by the company is the best for the purpose of measuring districts' return on assets. What are the likely motivational problems that could arise in such a system? What can you recommend to overcome such dysfunctional effects?
5. While computing district profits for performance evaluation purposes, should there be a charge for income taxes? Should corporate overheads be allocated to districts? Should profits be computed on the basis of historical costs or on the basis of replacement costs? Evaluate these issues from the standpoint of their motivational impact on the district managers.
6. Evaluate Quality's incentive compensation system. Does the present system motivate district managers to make decisions that are consistent with the strategy of the firm? If not, make specific recommendations to improve the system.

# Case A2
# Pirelli*

**by Professor Paolo Perego**

Pirelli, a publicly listed firm based in Milan, is the fifth largest tyre manufacturer in the world focused on the consumer business (tyres for cars, motorcycles and bicycles). The company is structured in 19 manufacturing sites located in 13 countries, with 37,000 employees and a network of more than 14,000 distributors and retailers. Pirelli is a leader in sustainability management in the auto components industry, as recognized by the Dow Jones Sustainability World and Europe indices. The Pirelli Sustainability Model is inspired by the UN Global Compact (of which Pirelli has been an active member since 2004) and by the Stakeholder Engagement Principles set out in international standards on corporate social responsibility (i.e., ISO 26000 guidelines).

Pirelli's Sustainability Model integrates financial and non-financial dimensions of performance into the company's strategy and cascades them down to the whole organization. Every operating unit integrates economic, social and environmental responsibility in its decisions, while cooperating constantly with the other units and implementing the Group's strategic guidelines. Marco Tronchetti Provera (CEO) stated: 'Sustainability is a fundamental choice for Pirelli. It is fully integrated into the Group's Vision and Strategies for growth, in all business areas and in all management decisions, everywhere in the world.'

Pirelli draws upon the Porter's Five Forces model of value creation. The underlying philosophy is to instil awareness of the indivisibility of economic, social and environmental dimensions that permeate the company's activities. Such a proactive, integrated and coherent strategy is considered essential to preserve Pirelli's assets with a long-term orientation, especially for a listed company active in the global economy. Exhibit 1 illustrates how the Sustainability Model creates value for Pirelli's shareholders and stakeholders.

The Sustainability Model incorporates the three dimensions of performance by putting each management area in constant dialogue with other functions and with stakeholders. The strategic guidelines of the Group clearly define responsibilities in each area of the business. The internal performance measurement system defines, collects and reports internally selected indicators that gauge the accomplishments of planned targets on several economic, social and environmental dimensions. For instance, the company's sustainability plan for 2020 sets a reduction target of energy consumption of 19 per cent compared to the reference base year of 2009 (normalized on tons of tyres produced). Another area of

**EXHIBIT 1** How the Sustainability Model creates value for Pirelli's shareholders and stakeholders

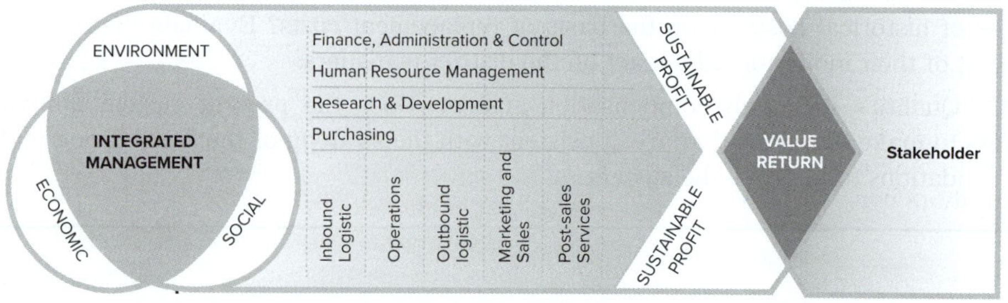


* This case was written by Professor Paolo Perego, Associate Professor, Free University of Bolzano-Bozen.

improvement refers to $CO_2$ emissions, with a plan focused on increased productivity of Pirelli's operations combined with enhanced use of renewables and electricity vehicles.

Pirelli discloses annually this complex set of metrics and related targets in an Integrated Report. Unlike other multinationals, Pirelli has embraced the philosophy of producing a corporate report that merges in one document both financial and non-financial performance. This is an emergent approach that should help investors and stakeholders to overcome the potential disconnect in processing different types of information from a variety of disclosures. The Integrated Report fulfils the guidelines developed by main international sustainability reporting frameworks like the Global Reporting Initiative. An external auditing firm certifies the quality of the information disclosed.

Pirelli reinforces its formal management control system with an organizational culture that makes sustainability a core belief among all employees. Elements that permeate this culture refer to the company's attitude towards innovation or the inside and outside dialogue with stakeholders. In fact, Pirelli's sustainability management extends beyond the physical boundaries of manufacturing sites through the entire value chain. For example, it relies on a network of suppliers of natural rubbers for its tyre production, mostly located in South East Asia. The Group developed a natural rubber sustainability policy aimed at ensuring enhanced levels of transparency in a supply chain upstream that is replete of potential social and environmental risks (e.g., deforestation, child labour and so forth). This voluntary policy has the objective to protect labour rights, prevent conflicts related to land ownership and promote the development of local communities. Pirelli currently plans to implement innovative digital tools like Blockchain to ensure traceability of the natural rubber production and distribution, along with risk evaluation activities through local engagement.

## Questions

1 Evaluate the Sustainability Model implemented by Pirelli. What are the main features of such a model? What is the rationale behind considering both shareholders and stakeholders in the goal of pursuing long-term value creation?

2 Pirelli identifies several indicators that gauge its performance on economic, social and environmental dimensions. What are the challenges in measuring social and environmental indicators compared to more traditional economic indicators? List and discuss critical differences vis-à-vis the measurement of such rather different dimensions of performance.

3 The management control system of Pirelli relies on an internal set of targets on the economic, social and environmental dimensions of performance. Managers are responsible for achieving these targets, and undergo an annual evaluation that compares planned and actual data. For example, each manufacturing site and its managers are accountable towards a specific reduction of $CO_2$ emissions per year. How would you create the right incentives to align management's decisions towards the accomplishment of social and environmental targets? Would you involve the management in setting the target? Would you attach, and how, a monetary compensation or another type of incentive for target accomplishment? How many targets would you evaluate per manager?

4 Pirelli has established a natural rubber sustainability policy aimed at ensuring enhanced levels of transparency in the supply chain. What are the expected benefits of this policy? How would you ensure that the policy is implemented effectively? Consider the challenges of measuring the impact of corporate policies on local communities and elaborate your thoughts on effective solutions to tackle this issue.

5 What are the advantages and drawbacks of producing an Integrated Report in comparison with stand-alone financial and sustainability reports? In developing your arguments, take the position of an investor, a consumer and a representative of a local community. Provide your opinion by emphasizing the type and quality of information demanded by each of these potential users.

# Case A3
# Johansen's: the new scorecard system*

by Luann Lynch, Almand R. Coleman

Jill Landon's palms were starting to sweat. It was the morning of Johansen's annual performance summit and she was still unsure about what overall performance rating to give Jared Clark. It was clear from the data that he deserved the highest rating on the financial, strategy and leadership initiatives on the new scorecard. But his performance this year in customer service had fallen far short of the level required by the guidelines in the new scorecard system. Based on the data, she did not think she could justify more than a 'meets expectations' rating of 3 for Clark's customer service rating. As a result, she knew that Clark would be ineligible for the best overall performance rating of 5 and, subsequently, would not receive the maximum bonus possible. In fact, based on the new system, he would receive a lower bonus than he did last year if given a 4 overall this year (Exhibit 1).

**EXHIBIT 1** Southwest regional manager Jared Clark's historical and projected annual compensation

| | 2012 | | 2013 | |
|---|---|---|---|---|
| Jared Clark's salary: | $85,000 | | $91,000 | |
| + bonus | | | | |
| Overall rating = 3 | 10% | $ 8,500 | 10% | $ 9,180 |
| Overall rating = 4 | 25% | $21,250 | 25% | $22,950 |
| Overall rating = 5 | 40% | $34,000 | 40% | $36,720 |

Landon knew the importance of the company's new scorecard system. Although Clark's scorecard suggested that he should receive an overall rating of 4, the thought of giving him anything less than a 5 overall was difficult to stomach. Landon was Johansen's Southwest regional manager and Clark had been her best store manager for a number of years. She had never seen another store manager who could deliver the financial performance that he could year after year. Landon's own annual performance evaluation was based primarily on the sales and financial performance of the Southwest region, performance that was affected greatly by what happened in Store 51; she was grateful for a manager like Clark, since her own future promotion and compensation prospects depended on continuing to turn in top results.

Landon recalled a conversation she had had with Clark the previous November. When Clark informed her that one of Johansen's largest national competitors was planning on opening a store in the same mall as Store 51, her immediate thought was, 'This is our highest-performing store in the region. How will this affect sales?' Clark then proceeded to tell her that he had been approached by the competitor to be the store manager for this new store. Clark also detailed the generous increase in salary he had been offered, as well as the opportunity for larger annual bonuses. Despite the appealing offer, he shared that he loved

* This fictional case was prepared by Luann Lynch, Almand R. Coleman Professor of Business Administration; Jennifer Forman (MBA '14); and Graham Gillam (MBA '14). It was written as a basis for class discussion rather than to illustrate effective or ineffective handling of an administrative situation. 

Store 51 and Johansen's because of the corporate culture, and the positive encouragement and interest in his success as a store manager that he had received over the years. The potential for higher pay was understandably attractive, however. He also remarked that he hoped Landon would bear this in mind when evaluating his performance and when the company considered which store managers to promote within the company. Landon was concerned about the competitive threat, but relieved that Clark was forthcoming about it and seemed open to working things out so that he could remain at Johansen's.

## Background

Johansen's, a large high-end department store, first opened its doors in New York City in 1950. Founded on the principle of superior customer service, Johansen's quickly found success and expanded its stores across the country. It built its reputation and brand on putting the customer first and offering an unparalleled level of customer service. This core value was integral to maintaining its position as the premier high-end retailer for decades.

As of 2014, Johansen's had 121 stores across 32 states. Due to its growth over the years, Johansen's was divided into five regions: Northeast, Southeast, Midwest, Southwest and Northwest (Exhibit 2). Each region had a regional manager who oversaw all the store managers in that region. Generally, Johansen's promoted from within, and it was not uncommon for an associate at one store to be promoted to manager of another. At the store manager level, it was more typical for a promotion to regional manager to occur within the same region, but there were instances in which a store manager from one region was promoted to regional manager of another region.

In 2006, Johansen's was facing financial difficulties. As a result, most of the senior executives were replaced. The new leadership team was eager to drive across-the-board improvements in financial

**EXHIBIT 2** Johansen's regional breakdown*

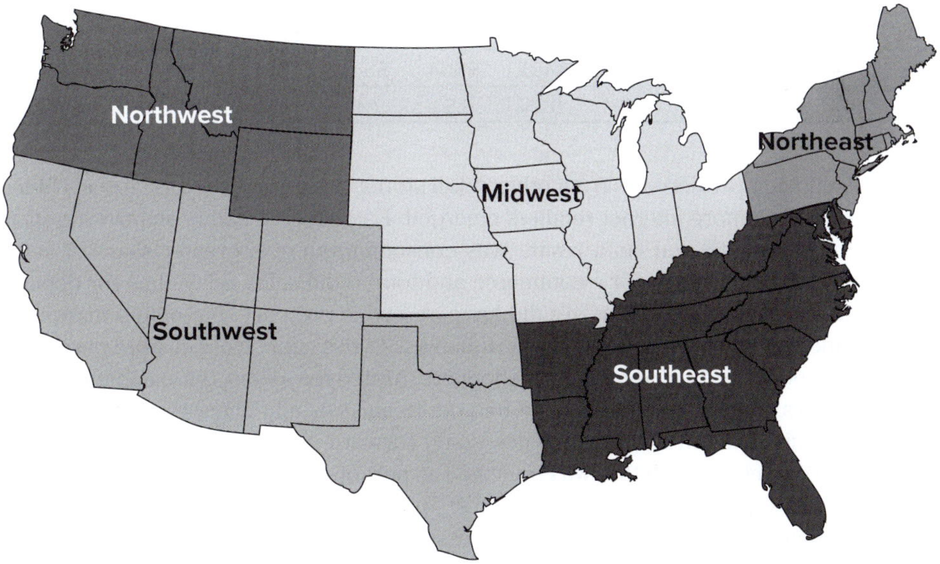


Source: Author adaptation of 'Blank USA, w territories.svg', posted to public domain under Creative Commons (CC BY-SA 3.0) by Lokal_Profil, 12 February 2007, https://commons.wikimedia.org/wiki/File:Blank_USA,_w_territories.svg (accessed May 13, 2014).

performance. To this end, a financially based incentive system was implemented. Johansen's store managers were the 'boots-on-the-ground' employees, and were critical to driving sales; Johansen's believed in empowering its employees, and store managers had a great deal of autonomy and control over their stores. They had little to no influence over store location – and consequently customer demographics – and other major store investments. But they had the ability to influence sales levels, and they affected the in-store customer experience, determined individual store marketing and sales promotions, handled individual store merchandising, and were responsible for training and developing employees. As a result, the leadership team considered the stores to be profit centres and decided that store managers would be rated and compensated based on three key financial metrics for their stores: same-store sales growth, gross margin and net income.

Although Johansen's saw a modest improvement in its financial performance early on, by 2012, the company's financial performance had stagnated again (Exhibit 3). Management commissioned a study to figure out why Johansen's was facing financial difficulties once more. The study provided three key insights. First, it became clear that Johansen's industry-leading position was far from assured. It used to be that Johansen's main competition was from other retail stores. Now, however, Johansen's faced additional competition as more and more internet retailers emerged. E-commerce had been growing faster than any other retail sector since 2008 and, as a result, was consuming an ever-greater share of retail spending. Exhibit 4 shows the growth trends for e-commerce and total retail sales, as well as for department stores and apparel. Like most retailers, Johansen's did have an online presence, but only a marginal percentage of its revenue came from online sales. Nearly all Johansen's sales came from in-store purchases due to the robust customer experience that appealed to shoppers. Moreover, given the e-commerce retailers' cost structures, Johansen's knew it was unlikely to be able to successfully engage in a price war, placing an even greater emphasis on its in-store experience going forward. Second – and to make matters worse – recently published market research that was reviewed as part of the study indicated that a rival company's customer service was superior to that of Johansen's. This news seriously jolted upper management. Certainly, improving financial performance had been essential to this new leadership team, and to varying degrees the team had succeeded in this regard. Delighting customers had always been Johansen's key value proposition, however, and the prospect of losing this important differentiator caused great angst among senior managers. Finally, an analysis of detailed financial and employee data suggested that cost-cutting efforts that led to greater profitability may also have fuelled customer service-related compromises.

**EXHIBIT 3** Johansen's financial overview

| | 2013 | 2012 | 2011 | 2010 | 2009 | 2008 | 2007 | 2006 | 2005 |
|---|---|---|---|---|---|---|---|---|---|
| Net sales | $8,300 | $7,790 | $7,800 | $7,600 | $6,610 | $6,600 | $7,000 | $6,725 | $6,612 |
| Cost of goods sold (COGS) | $5,400 | $5,140 | $5,130 | $4,950 | $4,350 | $4,390 | $4,500 | $4,350 | $4,166 |
| COGS *as % of net sales* | 65.1% | 66.0% | 65.8% | 65.1% | 65.8% | 66.5% | 64.3% | 64.7% | 63.0% |
| Gross profit | $2,900 | $2,650 | $2,670 | $2,650 | $2,260 | $2,210 | $2,500 | $2,375 | $2,446 |
| *Gross profit as % of net sales* | 34.9% | 34.0% | 34.2% | 34.9% | 34.2% | 33.5% | 35.7% | 35.3% | 37.0% |
| SG&A expenses | $1,950 | $1,830 | $1,830 | $1,750 | $1,650 | $1,650 | $1,675 | $1,650 | $1,621 |
| *SG&A expenses as % of net sales* | 23.5% | 23.5% | 23.5% | 23.0% | 25.0% | 25.0% | 23.9% | 24.5% | 24.5% |
| EBT | $950 | $820 | $840 | $900 | $610 | $560 | $825 | $725 | $825 |
| *Taxes (40%)* | $380 | $328 | $336 | $360 | $244 | $224 | $330 | $290 | $330 |
| Net income | $570 | $492 | $504 | $540 | $366 | $336 | $495 | $435 | $495 |
| *Net income as % of net sales* | 6.9% | 6.3% | 6.5% | 7.1% | 5.5% | 5.1% | 7.1% | 6.5% | 7.5% |

**EXHIBIT 4** Historical retail industry trends

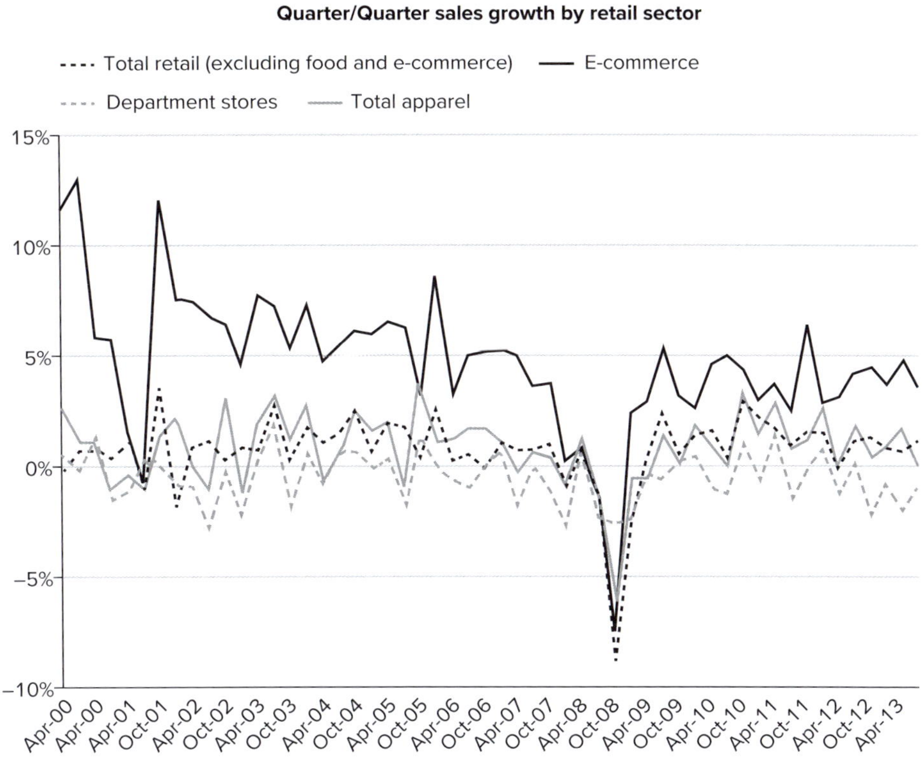


Source: Federal reserve (FRED)

When the leadership team implemented the incentive program focused on financial metrics in 2006, it had assumed managers knew that customer service was at the heart of the company's identity. Now, the leadership team was convinced that an overemphasis and focus on financial performance had eroded performance around its key success factor, customer service.

The leadership team was determined to make any necessary changes to restore Johansen's position as the premier customer service provider in the industry, while also continuing its trend of improved financial performance. Superior customer service had always been associated with the company's name, and it was an even more important success factor considering the growth in e-commerce. To ensure a customer experience that pulled patrons away from the internet and into Johansen's retail locations, it was imperative that the company refocus its efforts along this dimension. The leadership team agreed that incentives drive behaviour, and it became clear that the financially driven incentive system needed to be overhauled.

## The new performance measurement and incentive compensation system

After much discussion and analysis, the leadership team agreed that a new performance measurement and incentive system was needed. The leadership team reflected on the role of the company's store managers and decided to implement a new assessment tool that it called the 'scorecard system'. Under the new system, store managers would be assessed across four categories: financial, customer service, leadership and strategy. The store managers would receive a rating for each of these individual categories on a 1-to-5 numerical scale: 1 conferred a 'below expectations' rating, 3 a 'meets expectations' rating, and 5 an 'exceeds expectations' rating.

1 *Financial:* The regional manager worked with the corporate finance department to establish year-over-year (YoY) sales-growth and profitability targets for the individual stores.[1] These targets included a baseline target that stores had to hit in order to achieve the 'meets expectations' rating. These baseline targets appropriately accounted for each store's unique demographics; as such, stores that had more favourable demographics could be expected to have more aggressive baseline goals. In addition, a stretch target was issued by the corporate finance department that, although achievable, would require an impressive performance to meet. If met, however, it would qualify stores and managers for the maximum rating of 'exceeds expectations' in this category.

2 *Customer service:* The company had always measured customer service through customer surveys. The surveys were developed, administered and analysed by a third party to preserve the integrity of the questions and the results. Every customer had the opportunity to take the survey – instructions were featured on the bottom of the receipts printed at checkout. Sales associates often circled the instructions with a highlighter to draw the customer's attention to them. Customers who took the survey would be eligible for a monthly drawing to win a $500 gift card redeemable at any Johansen's store. Until 2005, customers who wished to take the survey called a toll-free number and provided numerical answers to a sequence of questions using the telephone keypad. In 2005, this changed, and the receipts instead directed customers to a website so that they could take the survey online. The survey had 10 questions about the customer's in-store experience. Each of the questions allowed the customer to answer on a scale from 1 to 5, with 5 being the best score. The scores for the 10 questions were averaged to get an overall survey score. All the overall survey scores for an individual store were then averaged to get a customer satisfaction score at the store level. In addition, customers had an opportunity to provide qualitative feedback at the end of each survey. Company-wide, the response rate of the survey in 2012 was 18.5 per cent and the average customer satisfaction score was 3.6.

   In this category of the scorecard, store managers were evaluated quantitatively and qualitatively. First, the regional manager considered the store's survey response rate. Managers whose stores achieved less than a 12 per cent response rate could earn a maximum of a 'meets expectations' rating in the customer service category, even if the feedback was positive. This constraint was part of the system because in cases of particularly low response rates, the sample size was considered too small for the data to be meaningful. Second, the regional manager considered the average customer satisfaction score for the store. To get a 5 rating in customer service, store managers needed to get an average customer satisfaction score of 4.4 or higher. Third, the regional manager made a subjective assessment of the qualitative customer feedback that the store received.

3 *Leadership:* Johansen's believed in 360-degree feedback, which the human resources (HR) department administered annually. HR forwarded the results of the exercise to regional managers so they could factor those results into a store manager's leadership rating. HR also communicated turnover and employee complaint information to the regional managers so that this too could be factored into the leadership rating. The regional manager weighed all the information received from HR to determine what rating to give the store manager in this category.

4 *Strategy:* The purpose of this element of the scorecard was to achieve cohesiveness and alignment throughout the company. Store managers were subjectively evaluated by the regional manager on

[1] Johansen's had company-wide sales, profitability and same-store sales growth targets. Company sales goals could be met in one of two ways: same-store sales growth or adding new stores. At the individual store level, however, sales growth and same-store sales growth would be redundant metrics.

promotion of the Johansen's brand and branded merchandise, and also the implementation of corporate initiatives such as inventory management, training, merchandising mix and initiatives from corporate (e.g., inventory management and employee training). After assigning a rating for each of the four dimensions, the regional manager gave the store manager an overall rating, also on a 1-to-5 scale. Ultimately, the overall rating determined a store manager's bonus (Exhibit 5). Additionally, when regional manager positions became available, store managers who had the highest performance ratings were the first ones considered for promotion.

But the overall rating was not a simple average of the ratings in the four categories of the scorecard. Rather, it was a subjective rating by the regional manager that was supported by the underlying individual ratings in each category and the following corporate guidelines. In order for a store manager to receive an overall rating of a 5, he or she needed to be rated at least a 3 in all four categories, achieve a 5 in three of the four categories, and achieve a 4 or higher in the customer service category. Requiring a store manager to get at least a 4 in the area of customer service emphasized Johansen's renewed focus on this key success factor.

The new system was rolled out company-wide and implemented beginning 1 January 2013. It initially received mixed responses from the regional managers. Those who had been with the company for several years were relieved to see that corporate management was working to restore Johansen's original culture and character. But some regional managers resisted the new system and were quite reluctant to buy in. The sceptics, having always exceeded their financial goals, were concerned that their performance evaluation under this new system would be adversely affected by non-financial, 'soft' metrics. Moreover, many of these managers had been promoted or hired during the period when improving financial performance was the company's number-one goal, and they now felt vulnerable to a system that didn't fully appreciate their unique skill sets, which were more geared toward running highly efficient, financially savvy stores.

**EXHIBIT 5** Store manager compensation and bonus structure

| | 2012 | 2013 |
|---|---|---|
| Average store manager salary: | $73,000 | $76,650 |
| Bonus as a % of salary | | |
| Overall rating = 3 | 10% | 10% |
| Overall rating = 4 | 25% | 25% |
| Overall rating = 5 | 40% | 40% |

## The new scorecard system: early success

The time had come for Johansen's first annual performance review under the new scorecard system. Despite the lack of buy-in from some of the regional managers, the leadership team believed that the new system had proved successful so far. During the first three quarters, most regions showed both increased profitability – as a result of growth in revenue – and increased customer satisfaction scores. It appeared that Johansen's was on its way back to the top!

## The store 51 dilemma

Store 51, located in the Southwest region, generated annual revenue of $150 million in 2013, the highest in the region and the sixth highest in the United States (see Exhibit 6 for a financial summary of Store 51 compared with the average Johansen's store). Store 51 typically led the region in sales due to its advantageous location in Orange County, California. The store was located in a shopping centre that had numerous upscale shops and restaurants but no direct competitors to Johansen's. Store 51 was also a flagship store, resulting in a number of advantages for it. First, given its status and history in the area, it had a very loyal customer base. This helped drive the second advantage: extensive, detailed historical customer data. This data provided Store 51 with a heightened understanding of and insight into its customers and, consequently, provided great merchandising advantages. Additionally, the surrounding neighbourhoods were very affluent; this resulted in people who entered Store 51 generating higher-than-average revenue per transaction than those in most other Johansen's stores.

**EXHIBIT 6** Johansen's store financials ($ millions)

| 2013 | Johansen's | Average store | Store 51 |
|---|---|---|---|
| Sales | $8,300 | $68.60 | $150.00 |
| Gross profit | $2,900 | $23.97 | $60.00 |
| Gross profit % | 34.94% | 34.94% | 40.00% |
| YoY sales growth* | 6.41% | 4.49% | 5.50% |

*Note:*
*YoY sales growth for the company as a whole came from two sources: same-store growth and new stores.

Despite its continued success, Store 51 was in an interesting predicament. The store manager, Jared Clark, was known as one of the best store managers in the country. Under the old performance system, he exceeded every financial metric and received the highest store manager bonus possible every year; his record was pristine. Under the new scorecard system, Clark still exceeded the financial targets. The new system, however, revealed several issues regarding Clark's performance as a manager that had previously gone undetected by Landon as the Southwest regional manager. In the first and second quarters under the scorecard system, Landon noted particularly high employee turnover (45 per cent) and relatively low customer satisfaction scores of 3.2 and 3.4, respectively, at Store 51. She approached Clark to discuss these shortcomings, and was relieved to find that he was receptive to the feedback.

Clark was able to modestly improve his customer satisfaction score in the third quarter, and the latest results for the fourth quarter indicated further improvement. Per usual, Store 51's financial performance was well above that of the other stores in the region. But Clark's performance in customer service remained below the company average, even with his improvement throughout the year. Another complicating element that needed to be considered was the relatively low customer survey response rate (the highest it had been in 2013 for Store 51 was 7 per cent in the fourth quarter). It was not particularly surprising that Store 51's response rate was less than the average, since the older, wealthier demographic of Orange County was less likely to go online and fill out a survey (Exhibit 7). Landon could not help but wonder, however, whether the low survey participation rate for Store 51 was the root of Clark's low customer service scores. Perhaps if the sample size was larger, Clark would be able to achieve a higher rating in the customer service category, making him eligible for the overall rating of 5. Or was the fundamental customer base inherently disadvantageous to Store 51's customer service score? Based on the feedback through the survey, the majority of survey participants only took the survey when upset.

Landon was faced with a dilemma: How should Clark be rated this year? (See Exhibit 8 for Clark's scorecard.) At Johansen's annual performance summit, regional managers and the managers of several corporate functions (finance, customer service and HR) discussed overall regional performance and store manager ratings (see Exhibit 9 for information about these managers). Landon knew that regardless of the rating she gave Clark, she would have to justify it to all these managers at the performance summit, as well as to Clark afterwards.

**EXHIBIT 7** Johansen's customer demographics

| | Johansen's | Store 51 |
|---|---|---|
| Average customer age range | 24–55 | 32–64 |
| Average customer annual household income | $100,000 | $135,000 |
| Average sales/square foot | $408 | $772 |
| Average store size | 160,000 sq. ft | 195,000 sq. ft |

**EXHIBIT 8** Johansen's scorecard for Store 51's manager

**Store manager:** Jared Clark

**Evaluation period:** 1 January–31 December 2013

**Store number:** 51

**Region:** Southwest

**Regional manager:** Southwest regional manager

**Rating summary:**

| | Financial | Customer service | Leadership | Strategy | Overall |
|---|---|---|---|---|---|
| Rating | 5 | 3 | 5 | 5 | 5 |

**Rating explanation and justification**

*Category 1: Financial (quantitative)*

Store managers must meet the 'baseline target' to achieve a rating of 3.

Store managers must exceed 'stretch target' to achieve a rating of 5.

| | Q1'13 | Q2'13 | Q3'13 | Q4'13 |
|---|---|---|---|---|
| Profit: | Y | Y | Y | Y |
| – Baseline target met? | Y | Y | Y | Y |
| – Stretch target exceeded? | | | | |
| YoY sales growth: | Y | Y | Y | Y |
| – Baseline target met? | Y | Y | Y | Y |
| – Stretch target exceeded? | | | | |

Additional note:

This year, aggressive financial stretch targets were set for Clark's store. Clark exceeded the stretch targets and achieved figures well beyond expectations.

*Additional note:*

This year, aggressive financial stretch targets were set for Clark's store. Clark exceeded the stretch targets and achieved figures well beyond expectations.

**Financial rating:** 5

*Category 2: Customer service (quantitative and qualitative)*

Store manager must achieve a survey response rate of 12 per cent to receive a rating of 4 or 5.

| | Q1'13 | Q2'13 | Q3'13 | Q4'13 |
|---|---|---|---|---|
| Response rate | 3.5% | 3.7% | 5.5% | 7.0% |

Store manager must achieve a store customer satisfaction score of 4.4 to receive a rating of 5.

| | Q1'13 | Q2'13 | Q3'13 | Q4'13 |
|---|---|---|---|---|
| Customer satisfaction score | 3.2 | 3.4 | 3.7 | 4.1 |

**Qualitative assessment:** Although Clark did not achieve the 12 per cent minimum customer service survey response rate, his customer service performance improved throughout the year. In the first quarter, the feedback was generally negative; customers were able to find the merchandise they demanded, but were very unsatisfied with the customer service. In Q2, I spoke to Clark about the importance of customer service. He was receptive to the feedback, and saw an increase in survey response rate (from 3.7 per cent in Q2 to 5.5 per cent in Q3). Additionally, the feedback from customers was not overwhelmingly positive, but certainly was not as negative as it had been in the first half of the year. In Q4, Clark's performance increased again. The survey response increased to 7 per cent, and customers had positive things to say about Store 51.

**Customer service rating:** 3

*Category 3: Leadership (qualitative)*

**Questions to consider when rating store manager:** Were there many employee complaints? What was the nature of the complaints? Isolated incidents or ongoing issues? Was there an increase in turnover throughout the time period being assessed? What was the nature of the 360-degree feedback? Was store manager interested in developing leadership skills?

**Qualitative assessment:** Clark's turnover was notably high at 45 per cent during the first half of the year. In Q3 and Q4, however, turnover was reduced to 33 per cent, a turnover figure better than the corporate average of 35 per cent. There were 23 employee complaints throughout the year. 17 of them were from the same two employees, however. This does not necessarily imply that Clark's leadership was poor; the high volume of complaints from two individuals could simply indicate a mismatch in personalities. Those two employees voluntarily left Johansen's in November. Clark's 360-degree review was highly positive for the most part.

**Leadership rating:** 5

*Category 4: Strategy (qualitative)*

**Questions to consider when rating store manager:** Did store manager actively promote the Johansen's brand? Was branded merchandise in high-visibility areas throughout the store? Were corporate initiatives implemented? Was store manager proactive in seeking corporate guidance and initiatives?

**Qualitative assessment:** Clark exceeded my expectations in this area. He regularly asked me about new corporate initiatives and how he could best implement them in Store 51. Clark also worked hard to enhance the Johansen's brand. He engaged members of his team and store managers across the Southwest region to brainstorm ways to promote Johansen's as a whole and also Johansen's branded merchandise. Clark is the strongest Johansen's corporate ambassador in the Southwest region.

**Strategy rating:** 5

**OVERALL RATING:** ____________

### EXHIBIT 9 Managers attending the performance summit

Last year, Harold was ready to leave Johansen's. After six years, his job had become monotonous, the company was struggling and morale was low. He was just starting to look at opportunities elsewhere when senior management announced an overhaul of the existing performance measurement system. The company had been too focused on financial performance and had lost sight of its strong customer service value proposition. The new scorecard system was an effort to bring the company back to its core values. Harold was offered a promotion within human resources to develop and implement the scorecard system. This was exactly the type of opportunity that he was looking for, so he eagerly accepted the promotion and stopped looking for other positions.

As much as the change in responsibilities was refreshing, it was challenging to develop the new system. While crafting it, Harold had his own performance assessment in mind. He would be evaluated and compensated based on the successful implementation of the new system, buy-in from employees and changes made after system implementation. He wasn't sure exactly how those factors would be measured, but he did know that his boss would do the evaluation after seeking input from other constituents to get their assessment about the implementation process and general support of the system design, as well as reflecting on the extent of changes needed after the first year under the system. Harold was eligible for a one-time bonus of up to 30 per cent of his salary based on the outcome of that review. He worked hard to come up with the best system possible and he thought it was truly a stellar system.

**Corporate customer experience manager Mitch Dougan**

After several years at Johansen's, Dougan was given the opportunity to become the company's first customer experience manager. This position was created alongside the development of the new scorecard system and was considered instrumental to Johansen's return to its core value of premier customer service.

In this role, Dougan's main objective was to improve customer service across the company. He would be evaluated and would be eligible for a bonus based on the increase in customer service survey response rates, and also the customer satisfaction scores and qualitative feedback received through the surveys. He hoped that the new scorecard system would help boost the scores. He was very enthusiastic about the company's renewed focus on customer service, as well as his new opportunity to shine in this role.

**Corporate finance manager Marjorie Thompson**

This year, Thompson was celebrating her 15th anniversary with Johansen's. She started as a finance intern when she was in college and had moved up the finance ranks over the years. During her tenure with the company, she saw several years of stellar financial performance. In 2005, however, she watched the company's financials, as well as her bonus, start to stagnate. Johansen's began to recover after implementing a financially based incentive system, but that recovery was short-lived. Then the company implemented the new scorecard system, and Thompson was worried about what would happen as a result. She just wanted to see the company return to an exceptional financial standing.

Although Thompson was in finance, she was quite in tune with the stores in the different regions, and she had strong relationships with the regional and store managers. She recently caught wind of a rumour that a Johansen's competitor tried to recruit Store 51's manager, Jared Clark. Given that Clark's financial performance exceeded that of any other store manager's performance in the region, she was deeply concerned about the possibility that Johansen's could lose Clark to a competitor. Thompson saw Clark as a real star and few store managers had been able to turn in the stellar financial performance that he had over time. Thompson believed that the company needed managers like him, particularly since her performance evaluation depended on the company's financial performance.

**Other regional managers (Northeast, Midwest, Southeast, Northwest)**

The annual performance evaluation of the regional managers was based in large part on the sales and financial performance of each region, and these regional managers considered themselves fortunate to have these top performers managing stores in their regions. They knew that these star performers were counting on the new scorecard system to rate them fairly.

The top-performing store manager in each of these regions excelled in all areas of the scorecard, including customer service. Depending on the region, the top store manager achieved a customer service survey response rate from 18 to 19 per cent, had an average customer satisfaction score from 4.4 to 4.6, and received positive qualitative feedback from those responses. Each of them truly deserved an overall rating of 5.

# Appendix

## Variance analysis

In Chapters 8 and 9 we discussed budgeting and performance measurement systems. By comparing the outcome of the chosen performance measures against appropriate targets (of which the budget is one type of target for financial measures), top managers can assess the performance of the organization. In this appendix, we provide details about how the outcome of financial performance measures should be analysed. Such analysis is called *variance analysis* and is often discussed extensively in basic textbooks on management accounting. By using variance analysis – that is, comparing the outcome of the financial performance measures against appropriate targets – top managers can analyse in detail the financial performance of responsibility centres.

We discuss how variances between actual and budgeted data are calculated for profit centres. Because expense and revenue budgets are part of the budgets for profit centres, the discussion can be extended to cover expense and revenue centres as well. We then describe how reports of these variances are used by top managers to evaluate responsibility centre performance.

Many companies make a monthly or quarterly analysis of the differences between actual and budgeted revenues and expenses for each business unit and for the whole organization. Some companies merely report the amount of these variances, as in Exhibit A1. This *performance report* shows that the actual profit was £52,000 higher than budget, and that the principal reason for this was that revenues were higher than budget. It does not illustrate why the revenues were higher or whether there were significant offsetting differences in the variances of the expense items that were netted out in the overall numbers.

**EXHIBIT A1** Performance report, January (£000s)

| | Actual | Budget | Actual better (worse) than budget |
|---|---|---|---|
| Sales | £875 | £600 | £275 |
| Variable costs of sales | 583 | 370 | (213) |
| Contribution | 292 | 230 | 62 |
| Fixed overhead | 75 | 75 | – |
| Gross profit | 217 | 155 | 62 |
| Selling expense | 55 | 50 | (5) |
| Administration expense | 30 | 25 | (5) |
| Profit before taxes | £132 | £ 80 | £ 52 |

A more thorough analysis identifies the causes of the variances and the organizational unit responsible. Effective systems identify variances down to the lowest level of management. Variances are hierarchical. As shown in Exhibit A2, they begin with the total business unit performance, which is divided into revenue and expense variances. Revenue variances are further divided into volume and price variances for the total business unit and for each marketing responsibility centre within the unit. They can be further divided by sales area and sales district. Expense variances can be divided between manufacturing expenses and other expenses. Manufacturing expenses can be further subdivided by factories, and departments within factories. Therefore, it is possible to identify each variance with the individual manager who is responsible for it. This type of analysis is a powerful tool, without which the efficacy of profit budgets would be limited.

**EXHIBIT A2** The hierarchy of variances

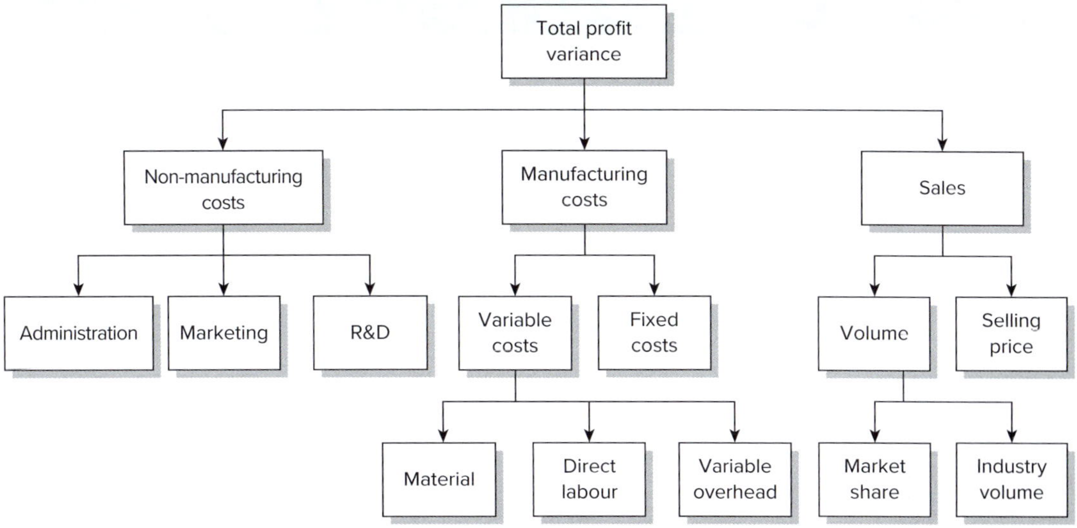


The profit budget has embedded in it certain expectations about the state of the total industry and the company's market share, its selling prices and its cost structure. Results from variance computations are more 'actionable' if changes in actual results are analysed against each of these expectations.

The analytical framework we use to conduct variance analysis incorporates the following ideas:

- Identify the key causal factors that affect profits.
- Break down the overall profit variances by these key causal factors.
- Focus on the profit impact of variation in each causal factor.
- Try to calculate the specific, separable impact of each causal factor by varying only that factor while holding all other factors constant ('spinning only one dial at a time').
- Add complexity sequentially, one layer at a time, beginning at a very basic 'common-sense' level ('peel the onion').
- Stop the process when the added complexity at a newly created level is not justified by added useful insights into the causal factors underlying the overall profit variance.

Exhibit A3 provides details of the budget of the business unit whose performance is reported in Exhibit A1.

### Revenue variances

In this section, we describe how to calculate selling price, volume and mix variances. The calculation is made for each product line, and the product line results are then aggregated to calculate the total variance. A positive variance is favourable, because it indicates that actual profit exceeded budgeted profit, and a negative variance is unfavourable.

#### *Selling price variance*

The selling price variance is calculated by multiplying the difference between the actual price and the standard price by the actual volume. The calculation is shown in Exhibit A4. It shows that the price variance is £75,000 unfavourable.

**EXHIBIT A3** Budget for January (£000s)

| | Product A 100* | | Product B 100* | | Product C 100* | | |
|---|---|---|---|---|---|---|---|
| | Unit | Total | Unit | Total | Unit | Total | Total budget |
| Sales | £1.00 | £100 | £2.00 | £200 | £3.00 | £300 | £600 |
| Standard variable cost: | | | | | | | |
| Material | 0.50 | 50 | 0.70 | 70 | 1.50 | 150 | 270 |
| Labour | 0.10 | 10 | 0.15 | 15 | 0.10 | 10 | 35 |
| Variable overhead | 0.20 | 20 | 0.25 | 25 | 0.20 | 20 | 65 |
| Total variable cost | 0.80 | 80 | 1.10 | 110 | 1.80 | 180 | 370 |
| Contribution | £0.20 | 20 | £0.90 | 90 | £1.20 | 120 | 230 |
| Fixed costs: | | | | | | | |
| Fixed overhead | | 25 | | 25 | | 25 | 75 |
| Selling expense | | 17 | | 17 | | 17 | 50 |
| Administrative expense | | 8 | | 8 | | 8 | 25 |
| Total fixed costs | | 50 | | 50 | | 50 | 150 |
| Profit before taxes | | £(30) | | £ 40 | | £ 70 | £ 80 |

*Note:*
*Standard volume (units)

**EXHIBIT A4** Selling price variances, January (£000s)

| | Product | | | |
|---|---|---|---|---|
| | A | B | C | Total |
| Actual volume (units) | 100 | 200 | 150 | |
| Actual price per unit | £0.90 | £2.05 | £2.50 | |
| Budget price per unit | 1.00 | 2.00 | 3.00 | |
| Actual over/(under) budget per unit | (0.10) | 0.05 | (0.50) | |
| Favourable/(unfavourable) price variance | (10) | 10 | (75) | (75) |

### *Mix and volume variance*

Often the mix and volume variances are not separated. The equation for the combined mix and volume variance is:

**Mix and volume variance = (Actual volume – Budgeted volume) × Budgeted unit contribution**

The calculation of mix and volume variance is shown in Exhibit A5; it is £150,000 favourable.

The volume variance results from selling more units than budgeted. The mix variance results from selling a different proportion of products from that assumed in the budget. Because products earn different *contributions* per unit, the sale of different proportions of products from those budgeted will result in a variance. If the business unit has a 'richer' mix (i.e., a higher proportion of products with a high contribution margin), the actual profit will be higher than budgeted; and if it has a 'leaner' mix, the

**EXHIBIT A5** Sales mix and volume variance, January (£000s)

| (1) Product | (2) Actual volume | (3) Budgeted volume | (4) Difference (2) − (3) | (5) Unit contribution | (6) Variance (4) × (5) |
|---|---|---|---|---|---|
| A | 100 | 100 | – | – | – |
| B | 200 | 100 | 100 | £0.90 | £ 90 |
| C | 150 | 100 | 50 | 1.20 | 60 |
| Total | 450 | 300 | | | £150 |

profit will be lower. The volume and mix variances are joint, so techniques for separating them are somewhat arbitrary. One such technique is described next.

### *Mix variance*

The mix variance for each product is found from the following equation:

**Mix variance = [(Actual volume of sales) − (Total actual volume of sales × Budgeted proportion)] × Budgeted unit contribution**

The calculation of the mix variance is shown in Exhibit A6. It shows that a higher proportion of product B and a lower proportion of product A were sold.

**EXHIBIT A6** Mix variance, January (£000s)

| (1) Product | (2) Budgeted proportion | (3) Budgeted mix at actual volume | (4) Actual sales | (5) Difference (4) − (3) | (6) Unit contribution | (7) Variance (5) × (6) |
|---|---|---|---|---|---|---|
| A | ⅓ | 150† | 100 | (50) | £0.20 | £ (10) |
| B | ⅓ | 150 | 200 | 50 | £0.90 | 45 |
| C | ⅓ | 150 | 150 | – | – | – |
| Total | | 450 | 450 | | | £ 35 |

*Note:*
†1/3 × 450 = 150

As product B has a higher unit contribution than product A, the mix variance is favourable by £35,000.

### *Volume variance*

The volume variance can be calculated by subtracting the mix variance from the combined mix and volume variance. This is £150,000 minus £35,000, or £115,000. It can also be calculated for each product as follows:

**Volume variance = [(Total actual volume of sales) × (Budgeted proportion) − (Budgeted sales)] × (Budgeted unit contribution)**

The calculation of the volume variance is shown in Exhibit A7.

**EXHIBIT A7** Sales volume variance, January (£000s)

| (1) Product | (2) Budgeted mix at actual volume | (3) Budgeted volume | (4) Difference (2) − (3) | (5) Unit contribution | (6) Volume variance |
|---|---|---|---|---|---|
| A | 150 | 100 | 50 | £0.20 | £ 10 |
| B | 150 | 100 | 50 | 0.90 | 45 |
| C | 150 | 100 | 50 | 1.20 | 60 |
| Total | 450 | 300 | 150 | | £ 115 |

*Other revenue analyses*

Revenue variances may be further subdivided. In our example, Exhibits A4, A5, A6 and A7 provide the information needed to classify them by product. Such a classification is shown in Exhibit A8.

**EXHIBIT A8** Revenue variances by product, January (£000s)

| | Product | | | |
|---|---|---|---|---|
| | A | B | C | Total |
| Price variance | £(10) | £ 10 | £(75) | £(75) |
| Mix variance | (10) | 45 | – | 35 |
| Volume variance | 10 | 45 | 60 | 115 |
| Total | £(10) | £100 | £(15) | £75 |

## Market penetration and industry volume

One extension of revenue analysis is to separate the mix and volume variance into the amount caused by differences in market share and the amount caused by differences in industry volume. The principle is that the business unit managers are responsible for market share, but they are not responsible for the industry volume because that is largely influenced by the state of the economy.

To make this calculation, industry sales data must be available. This calculation is given in Exhibit A9.

Section A of Exhibit A9 provides the assumptions that were made in the original budget shown in Exhibit A3, and Section B provides details on actual industry volume and market share for the month of January.

The following equation is used to separate the effect of market penetration from industry volume on the mix and volume variance:

**Market share variance = [Actual sales − (Actual industry volume × Budgeted market share)] × Budgeted unit contribution**

The market share variance is found for each product separately, and the total variance is the algebraic sum. The calculation is shown in Section C. It shows that £104,000 of the favourable mix and volume variance of £150,000 resulted from the fact that market penetration was better than budget. The remaining £46,000 resulted from the fact that actual industry pound volume was higher than the amount assumed in the budget.

**EXHIBIT A9** Industry volume and market share variances, January (£000s)

| A. Budgeted sales volume | Product | | | |
|---|---|---|---|---|
| | A | B | C | Total |
| Estimated industry volume (units) | 833 | 500 | 1,667 | 3,000 |
| Budgeted market share | 12% | 20% | 6% | 10% |
| Budgeted volume (units) | 100 | 100 | 100 | 300 |
| **B. Actual market share** | **Product** | | | |
| | A | B | C | Total |
| Actual industry volume, units | 1,000 | 1,000 | 1,000 | 3,000 |
| Actual sales (units) | 100 | 200 | 150 | 450 |
| Actual market share | 10% | 20% | 15% | 15% |
| **C. Variance due to market share** | **Product** | | | |
| | A | B | C | Total |
| (1) Actual sales (units) | 100 | 200 | 150 | 450 |
| (2) Budgeted shares at actual industry volume | 120 | 200 | 60 | 380 |
| (3) Difference (1 – 2) | (20) | – | 90 | 70 |
| (4) Budgeted unit contribution | £0.20 | £0.90 | £1.20 | |
| (5) Variance due to market share (3 × 4) | (4.00) | – | 108 | £104 |
| **D. Variance due to industry volume** | **Product** | | | |
| | A | B | C | Total |
| (1) Actual industry volume | 1,000 | 1,000 | 1,000 | 3,000 |
| (2) Budgeted industry volume | 833 | 500 | 1,667 | 3,000 |
| (3) Difference (1 – 2) | 167 | 500 | (667) | – |
| (4) Budgeted market share | 12% | 20% | 6% | |
| (5) (3 × 4) | 20 | 100 | (40) | |
| (6) Unit contribution (budget) | £0.20 | £0.90 | £1.20 | |
| (7) Total (5 × 6) | 4.00 | 90.00 | (48.00) | £46 |

The £46,000 industry volume variance can also be calculated for each product as follows:

**Industry volume variance** = **(Actual industry volume – Budgeted industry volume) × Budgeted market share × Budgeted unit contribution**

This calculation of variance due to industry volume is shown in Section D.

## Expense variances

### *Fixed costs*

Variances between actual and budgeted fixed costs are obtained simply by subtraction, because these costs are not affected by either the volume of sales or the volume of production. This is shown in Exhibit A10.

**EXHIBIT A10** Fixed-cost variances, January (£000s)

| | Actual | Budget | Favourable or unfavourable variances |
|---|---|---|---|
| Fixed overhead | £ 75 | £ 75 | £ – |
| Selling expense | 55 | 50 | (5) |
| Administrative expense | 30 | 25 | (5) |
| Total | £160 | £150 | £(10) |

### *Variable costs*

Variable costs are costs that vary directly and proportionately with volume. The budgeted variable manufacturing costs must be adjusted to the actual volume of production. Assume that the January production was as follows: product A, 150,000 units; product B, 120,000 units; and product C, 200,000 units. Assume also that the variable manufacturing costs incurred in January were as follows: material, £470,000; labour, £65,000; variable manufacturing overhead, £90,000. Exhibit A3 shows the standard unit variable costs.

The budgeted manufacturing expense is adjusted to the amount that should have been spent at the actual level of production by multiplying each element of standard cost for each product by the volume of production for that product. This calculation is shown in Exhibit A11.

**EXHIBIT A11** Variable manufacturing expense variances, January (£000s)

| | Product | | | | | |
|---|---|---|---|---|---|---|
| | A | B | C | Total | Actual | Favourable (unfavourable) Variances |
| Material | £ 75 | £ 84 | £300 | £459 | £470 | £(11) |
| Labour | 15 | 18 | 20 | 53 | 65 | (12) |
| Overhead (variable) | 30 | 30 | 40 | 100 | 90 | 10 |
| Total | £120 | £132 | £360 | £612 | £625 | £(13) |

Exhibit A11 shows that there was an unfavourable variance of £13,000 in January. This is called a *spending* variance because it results from spending £13,000 in excess of the adjusted budget. It consists of unfavourable material and labour variances of £11,000 and £12,000, respectively. These are partially offset by a favourable overhead spending variance of £10,000.[3]

The volume that is used to adjust the budgeted variable manufacturing expenses is the *manufacturing* volume, not the *sales* volume, which was used in finding the revenue variances. In the simple example given here, we assumed that the two volumes were the same; namely, that the quantity of each product manufactured in January was the same as the quantity sold in January. If production volume differed from sales volume, the cost difference would show up in changes in inventory. Depending on the company's inventory costing method, this might or might not result in a production volume variance.

In this example, we assumed that all the non-manufacturing expenses were fixed. If some of them had variable components, the variances should be calculated in the same way as was used for the calculation of manufacturing cost variances.

---

[3] It is also possible to split variable cost variances into volume variances and price variances.

### Summary of variances

There are several ways in which the variances can be summarized in a report for management. One possibility is shown in Exhibit A12. It is used primarily because the amounts can be traced easily to the earlier exhibits. Another form of presentation is to show the actual amounts, as well as the variances. This gives an indication of the relative importance of each variance as a fraction of the total revenue or expense item to which it relates.

**EXHIBIT A12** Summary performance report, January (£000s)

| | |
|---|---|
| Actual profit (Exhibit A1) | £ 132 |
| Budgeted profit (Exhibit A1) | 80 |
| Variance | £ 52 |
| **Analysis of variance – favourable (unfavourable)** | |
| Revenue variances: | |
| Price (Exhibit A4) | £ (75) |
| Mix (Exhibit A6) | 35 |
| Volume (Exhibit A7) | 115 |
| Net revenue variances | £ 75 |
| Variable-cost variances (Exhibit A11): | |
| Material | £ (11) |
| Labour | (12) |
| Variable overhead | 10 |
| Net variable-cost variances | £ (13) |
| Fixed-cost variances (Exhibit A10): | |
| Selling expense | £ (5) |
| Administrative expense | (5) |
| Net fixed-cost variances | £ (10) |
| Variance | £ (52) |

## Additional considerations and limitations of variance analysis

There are some additional considerations for managers when using variance analysis.

### Limitations of targets

A variance between actual and standard performance is meaningful only if it is derived from a *valid target*. Although it is convenient to refer to *favourable* and *unfavourable* variances, these words imply that the target is a reliable measure of what the performance should have been. Even a standard cost may not be an accurate estimate of what costs should have been under the circumstances. This situation can arise for either or both of two reasons: (1) the target was not set properly, or (2) although it was set properly in light of conditions existing at the time, changed conditions have made the target obsolete. When calculating variances so far in this Appendix we have used a *predetermined target* in the form of budgets. As discussed in Chapter 8, if the majority of organizations use budgets, this type of standard has a number of problems. When budget numbers are collected in a haphazard manner, they will obviously not provide a reliable target to be used in variance analysis. Then continuous improvement or benchmarking (discussed in Chapter 9) might be more appropriate ways of arriving at targets to be used in variance analysis. Managers tend to forget that an essential first step in the analysis of a variance is an *examination of the validity of the target.*

### Full-cost systems

If the company has a full-cost system, both variable and fixed overhead costs are included in the inventory at the standard cost per unit. If the ending inventory is higher than the beginning inventory, some of the fixed overhead costs incurred in the period remain in the inventory rather than flowing through to cost of sales. Conversely, if the inventory balance decreased during the period, more fixed overhead costs were released to cost of sales than the amount actually incurred in the period. Our example assumed that the inventory level did not change. Thus, the problem of treating the variance associated with fixed overhead costs did not arise.

If inventory levels change, and if actual production volume is different from budgeted sales volume, part of the production volume variance is included in the inventory. Nevertheless, the full amount of the production volume variance should be calculated and reported. This variance is the difference between budgeted fixed production costs at the actual volume and standard fixed production costs at that volume.

If the company has a variable-cost system, fixed production costs are not included in the inventory, so there is no production volume variance. The fixed production expense variance is simply the difference between the budgeted amount and the actual amount.

The important point is that production variances should be associated with *production* volume, not sales volume.

### Amount of detail

In this Appendix, we have analysed revenue variances at several levels: first, in total; then by volume, mix and price; then by analysing the volume and mix variance by industry volume and market share. At each of these levels, we analysed the variances by individual products. The process of going from one level to another is often referred to as 'peeling the onion' – that is, successive layers are peeled off, and the process continues as long as the additional detail is judged to be worthwhile. It is possible, and in some cases worthwhile, to develop additional sales and marketing variances, such as the following: by sales territories, and even by an individual sales person; by sales to individual countries or regions; by sales to key customers, principal types of customer, or customers in certain industries; by sales originating from direct mail, from customer calls or other sources. Additional detail for manufacturing costs can be developed by calculating variances for lower-level responsibility centres, and by identifying variances with specific input factors such as wage rates and material prices.

These layers correspond to the hierarchy of responsibility centres. Taking action based on the reported variances is not possible unless they can be associated with the managers responsible for them. With modern information technology, more or less any level of detail can be supplied quickly and at reasonable cost. The problem is to decide how much is worthwhile. In part, the answer depends on the information requested by individual managers – some are numbers oriented, others are not. In the ideal situation, the basic data exist to make any conceivable type of analysis, but only a small fraction of these data are reported routinely.

### Engineered and discretionary costs

As we pointed out in Chapter 4, variances in engineered costs are viewed in a fundamentally different way from variances in discretionary costs.

A 'favourable' variance in engineered costs is usually an indication of good performance – that is, the lower the cost, the better the performance. This is subject to the qualification that quality and on-time delivery are judged to be satisfactory.

By contrast, the performance of a discretionary expense centre is usually judged to be satisfactory if actual expenses are about equal to the budgeted amount, neither higher nor lower. This is because a favourable variance may indicate that the responsibility centre did not perform adequately the functions that it had agreed to perform. Because some elements in a discretionary expense centre are, in fact, engineered (e.g., the book-keeping functions in the controller organization), a favourable variance is usually truly favourable for these elements.

### Management action

There is one cardinal principle in analysing formal financial reports: *the monthly profit report should contain no major surprises.* Significant information should be communicated quickly as soon as it becomes known. The formal report confirms the general impression that the top managers have learned from these sources. Based on this information, they may have acted prior to the receipt of the formal report.

The formal report is nevertheless important. *One of the most important benefits of formal reporting is that it provides the desirable pressure on lower-level managers to take corrective actions on their own initiative.* In addition, the information from informal sources may be incomplete or misunderstood; the numbers in the formal report provide more accurate information, and the report may confirm or cast doubts on the information received from informal sources. The formal report also provides a basis for analysis because information from the informal sources is often general and imprecise.

Usually, there is a discussion between the business unit manager and the top managers, in which the business unit manager explains the reasons for significant variances, the action being taken to correct unfavourable situations, and the expected timing of each corrective action. These explanations are necessarily subjective, and they may be biased. Operating managers, like most people, do not like to admit that unfavourable variances were caused by their errors. Top managers need to take this into account when they judge the report.

Profit reports are worthless unless they lead to action. The action may consist of praise for a job well done, suggestions for doing things differently, 'chewing out' or more drastic personnel actions. However, these actions are by no means taken for every business unit every month. As long as business is going well, praise is the most that may be necessary, and most people do not even expect praise routinely.

### Limitations of variance analysis

Although variance analysis is a powerful tool, it does have limitations. The most important limitation is that although it identifies where a variance occurs, it does not tell us *why* the variance occurred or what is being done about it. For example, the report may show that there was a significant unfavourable variance in marketing expenses, and it may identify this variance with high sales promotion expenses. It does not, however, explain why the sales promotion expenses were high and what, if any, actions were being taken. In other words, analysing variances without reference to mission, goals and strategies can often be uninformative or misleading. Therefore, many scholars argue that the traditional variance analysis discussed so far in this appendix needs to be more firmly connected to the company's and the respective business unit's mission and strategies. This is called *strategic variance analysis* and aims to determine the extent to which deviations between actual and budgeted performance are, or are not, consistent with the firm's and the business unit's mission and strategies. In this way, strategic variance analysis will help to identify dimensions of performance that need improvement. Strategic variance analysis includes a quantitative aspect where emphasis is put on decomposing the measures of budgeted versus actual income into sub-variances which managers can relate logically to the firm's or business unit's mission and strategy. Examples are deviations between actual and budgeted sales volumes and mixes, market sizes and shares, and manufacturing costs. Strategic variance analysis also includes a qualitative aspect, where a narrative explanation of the variances related to the mission and strategy accompanies the (otherwise quantitatively oriented) performance report.

A second problem in variance analysis is to decide whether a variance is significant. Conceptually, a variance should be investigated only when the benefit expected from correcting the problem exceeds the cost of the investigation, but a model based on this premise has so many uncertainties that it is of only academic interest. Managers, therefore, rely on judgement in deciding which variances are significant. Moreover, if a variance is significant but is uncontrollable (such as unexpected inflation), there may be no point in investigating it.

A third limitation of variance analysis is that as the performance reports become more highly aggregated, offsetting variances might mislead the reader. For example, a manager looking at business unit manufacturing cost performance may notice that it was on budget. However, this might have resulted from good performance at one plant being offset by poor performance at another. Similarly, when different product lines at different stages of development are combined, the combination may obscure the actual results of each product line.

In addition, as variances become more highly aggregated, managers become more dependent on the accompanying explanations and forecasts. Plant managers know what is happening in their plant and can easily explain causes of variance. Business unit managers and everyone above them, however, must usually depend on the explanations that accompany the variance report of the plant.

Finally, variance analysis is performed on the income statement and its components. This has two major weaknesses. First, there may be too little focus on the capital invested to generate the profit. As discussed in Chapter 9, the investments in non-currents assets, such as machinery and equipment, and in working capital, such as accounts receivables, are also important to take into account when calculating profitability. This means that financial measures such as ROI, RI and EVA® are superior to profit measures for evaluation of profitability because these measures take profit as well as invested capital into account. Second, variance analysis may lead to too much focus on the financial performance of the company – that is, what has happened. It does not show the future effects of actions that the manager has taken. For example, reducing the amount spent for employee training increases current profitability, but may have adverse consequences in the future. Also, the report shows only those events that are recorded in the financial accounts, and many important events are not reflected in current accounting transactions.

# Case

# Variance analysis problems*

by John Dearden.

I. In this case you are asked to analyse the February and March financial performance of the Temple Division of the ABC Company as compared with its budget, which is shown in Exhibit A3 (the same as the January budget).

### Part A: February

Below is the data describing the actual financial results of the Temple Division for the month of February:

| | | | | | |
|---|---|---|---|---|---|
| Sales | | | | | £781 |
| Variable cost of sales | | | | | 552 |
| Contribution | | | | | 229 |
| Fixed manufacturing costs | | | | | 80 |
| Gross profit | | | | | 149 |
| Selling expense | | | | | 57 |
| Administrative expense | | | | | 33 |
| Net profit | | | | | £ 59 |
| **Sales product** | | **Unit sales** | **Price** | | **Pound sales** |
| A | | 120 | £0.95 | | £114 |
| B | | 130 | 1.90 | | 247 |
| C | | 150 | 2.80 | | 420 |
| Total | | 400 | | | 781 |
| | **Manufacturing cost** | | | | |
| **Production product** | **Units produced** | **Material** | **Labour** | **Variable overhead** | **Total** |
| A | 150 | £ 80 | £20 | £40 | £140 |
| B | 130 | 91 | 21 | 35 | 147 |
| C | 120 | 190 | 15 | 30 | 235 |
| Total | 400 | 361 | 56 | 105 | 522 |

## Questions (Part A)

1 Prepare an analysis of variance from profit budget assuming that the Temple Division employed a variable standard cost accounting system.

2 Prepare an analysis of variance from profit budget assuming that the Temple Division used a full standard cost accounting system. Under this assumption, the actual cost of sales amount would be £632,000. (Can you derive this figure?)

3 Industry volume figures are presented in the table below. Separate the mix and volume variance into the variance resulting from differences in market penetration and variance resulting from differences in industry volume. Make the calculation for the variable cost system only.

Industry volume, February

| | Units (000) |
|---|---|
| Product A | 600 |
| Product B | 650 |
| Product C | 1,500 |

## Part B: March

Below are the data describing the actual financial results for the Temple Division for the month of March.

| Income statement | | | | | |
|---|---|---|---|---|---|
| Sales | | | | | £498 |
| Variable cost of sales | | | | | 278 |
| Contribution | | | | | 220 |
| Fixed manufacturing costs | | | | | 70 |
| Gross profit | | | | | 150 |
| Selling expense | | | | | 45 |
| Administrative expense | | | | | 20 |
| Net profit | | | | | £ 85 |
| **Sales product** | | **Unit sales** | **Price** | | **Pound sales** |
| A | | 90 | £1.10 | | £99 |
| B | | 70 | 2.10 | | 147 |
| C | | 80 | 3.15 | | 252 |
| Total | | 240 | | | 498 |
| | **Manufacturing cost** | | | | |
| **Production product** | **Units produced** | **Material** | **Labour** | **Variable overhead** | **Total** |
| A | 90 | £40 | £8 | £17 | £65 |
| B | 80 | 55 | 10 | 18 | 83 |
| C | 100 | 150 | 8 | 19 | 177 |
| Total | 270 | 245 | 26 | 54 | 325 |

## Questions (Part B)

1 Answer the same questions posed at the end of Part A. The actual cost of sales using full standard costing would be £340,500 in March.

Industry volume, March

| | Units (000) |
|---|---|
| Product A | 500 |
| Product B | 600 |
| Product C | 1,000 |

The profit budget for the Crocker Company for January was as follows:

| | | ($000) |
|---|---|---|
| Sales | | $2,500 |
| Standard cost of sales | | 1,620 |
| Gross profit | | 880 |
| Selling expense | $250 | |
| Research and development expense | 300 | |
| Administrative expense | 120 | |
| Total expense | | 670 |
| Net profit before taxes | | $ 210 |

The product information used in developing the budget was as follows:

| | E | F | G | H |
|---|---|---|---|---|
| Sales – units (000) | 1,000 | 2,000 | 3,000 | 4,000 |
| Price per unit | $0.15 | $0.20 | $0.25 | $0.30 |
| Standard cost per unit: | | | | |
| Material | 0.04 | 0.05 | 0.06 | 0.08 |
| Direct labour | 0.02 | 0.02 | 0.03 | 0.04 |
| Variable overhead | 0.02 | 0.03 | 0.03 | 0.05 |
| Total variable cost | 0.08 | 0.10 | 0.12 | 0.17 |
| Fixed overhead ($000) | 20 | 60 | 60 | 160 |
| Total standard cost per unit | 0.10 | 0.13 | 0.14 | 0.21 |

The actual revenues and costs for January were as follows:

| | | ($000) |
|---|---|---|
| Sales | | $2,160 |
| Standard cost of sales | | 1,420 |
| Net standard cost of variances | | 160 |
| Actual cost of sales | | 1,580 |
| Gross profit | | 580 |
| Selling expense | $290 | |
| Research and development expense | 250 | |
| Administrative expense | 110 | |
| Total expense | | 650 |
| Net loss | | $ (70) |

Operating statistics for January were as follows:

| | | E | F | G | H |
|---|---|---|---|---|---|
| Sales (units) | | 1,000 | 1,000 | 4,000 | 3,000 |
| Sales price | | $0.13 | $0.22 | $0.22 | $0.31 |
| Production | | 1,000 | 1,000 | 2,000 | 2,000 |
| Actual manufacturing costs (000): | | | | | |
| Material | $360 | | | | |
| Labour | 200 | | | | |
| Overhead | 530 | | | | |

2 Prepare an analysis of variance between actual profits and budgeted profits for January.

# Company Index

# Subject Index

## S



## T